ALSO BY MARTIN TORGOFF

*American Fool:*
*The Roots and Improbable Rise of John Cougar Mellencamp*

*The Complete Elvis* (editor)

*Elvis: We Love You Tender*

# CAN'T FIND MY WAY HOME

America in the Great Stoned Age, 1945–2000

Martin Torgoff

Simon & Schuster

New York London Toronto Sydney

SIMON & SCHUSTER
Rockefeller Center
1230 Avenue of the Americas
New York, NY 10020

For information about special discounts for bulk purchases,
please contact Simon & Schuster Special Sales: 1-800-456-6798 or
business@simonandschuster.com

Book design by Ellen R. Sasahara

Manufactured in the United States of America

10   9   8   7   6   5   4   3   2   1

Library of Congress Cataloging-in-Publication Data
Torgoff, Martin.
    Can't find my way home : America in the great stoned age, 1945–2000 / Martin Torgoff.
        p.            cm.
    Includes bibliographical references and index.
    1. Drug abuse—United States—History—20th century.   2. Drug abuse—
United States—Case studies.   3. Subculture—United States.   4. Popular culture—
United States.   I. Title.
HV5825.T68   2004
306'.1—dc22                                                    2004042904

ISBN 0-7432-3010-8

For my mother, Bess Torgoff,
and in loving memory of my father, Irving Torgoff:

In the end and always, the Greatest Generation.

# CONTENTS

The more prohibitions you have
The less virtuous people will be.

Try to make people moral,
And you lay the groundwork for vice.

—Lao-tzu, *Tao Te Ching*

# CAN'T FIND MY WAY HOME

# PREFACE

THIS BOOK is not a formal history but rather a journey through the experience and culture of illicit drugs in this country during the second half of the twentieth century, from roughly 1945 to the present. I conceived of this book as a collection of scenes from the world of illicit drugs, scenes that have had a significant impact on the American experience. In essence, this is the story of how the American Century turned into the Great Stoned Age, how the use of illicit drugs moved from the criminal underground and the avant garde fringe to mainstream America. Roughly one in four Americans has used illegal drugs, and this is the story of what has happened to their lives and to the world around us.

*Can't Find My Way Home* traces the impact on American society of numerous substances currently classified as schedule one drugs: narcotics, amphetamines, cocaine, psychedelics, MDMA (ecstasy), and marijuana. The story is told by people who have used those substances in various cultural settings, from the Beat Generation and the bebop jazz musicians of the 1940s and 1950s to the psychedelic counterculture of the 1960s, the amphetamine and pop-art underground of New York during the 1960s, the war in Vietnam, the gay sexual culture of the 1970s that used amyl nitrate, the cocaine culture of the 1970s and 1980s, crack and the inner cities of America during the 1980s, and the rave cyberculture of the 1990s.

This book will not make everybody happy, nor is it intended to. The political and religious right will not appreciate any book about drugs that is not dogmatically antidrug, that shows any permissiveness about drug use. The last thing that proponents of a "drug-free America" want to hear is that drugs have become as American as apple pie, which they arguably have. On the other hand, those who use drugs may find the parts of the book about addiction and recovery anathema to their notions of acceptable "personal" or "recreational" use. Those people often believe that they can use drugs safely and responsibly, that their use of drugs should be nobody's business but their own as long as they do no harm to others, and that the very notion of addiction has little or nothing to do with them. Finally, for those individuals in the recovery community who have experienced the lash of addiction and have crawled back to new lives as clean and sober members of society, the parts of the book that have to do with "ecstatic" drug experiences and "consciousness expansion" may seem wrongheaded or a form of denial—certainly the wrong message for young people, an inevitable percentage of whom are headed for drug-abuse problems.

"This is the sort of book I'd be very interested in reading but not something I really want to talk about," responded Judy Collins when I asked her for an interview—neither a surprising nor an uncommon reaction in this time of drug-sniffing dogs at airports and drug-tip hotlines. The writer Ishmael Reed was eager to talk about drug issues as they related to the African American community but refused to discuss his own use of drugs—"I have nothing to gain from talking about that." Such is the toxic and paranoid atmosphere that surrounds this subject. In order to allow people to feel safe sharing their experiences, I provided pseudonyms for some of those who are not public figures, sometimes changing certain details while preserving the substance of their experiences. In some cases, this was done in order to protect the anonymity of individuals I encountered in 12-step recovery fellowships. But aside from the changing of names and certain personal details, there is no experience about drugs in the book that did not actually occur in the set and setting it is rendered in, and nothing about the drug culture that has been invented. My intention has always been to write a true-life chronicle of the use of illicit drugs in America without sensationalizing, apologizing, moralizing, or demonizing—simply to tell the truth and let readers draw their own conclusions. To the hundreds of people, then, both well known and pseudonymous, who have shared their lives so intimately with me over the many years it has taken to write this book, I am humbly grateful.

In January of 1993, I found myself standing on a street corner in Compton, California, immersed in the story of rock cocaine and the Crips and the Bloods. Seeing a strange white guy hanging out in their neighborhood, various gang members were certain that I had to be a television reporter or an undercover cop. When I told one of them that I was neither but a writer gathering material for a book on drugs in America, he looked at me like I was crazy and exclaimed, "You got you a long book!"

How right he was. It's been twelve years since I started this book, thirty-five since I began living it. The book became my life and my life became the book; the journey of it has been long and at times hard, but while it has often felt as though it would never end, I've found my way home.

I learned in writing this book that as a society we face enormously difficult and complex problems concerning the use of illicit drugs. But in addition, we have to grapple with cultural amnesia and distortions that are the products of the ideological agendas that have so long shaped the debates and policies regarding illegal drugs. I have come to believe that only through the most rigorously honest appraisal of this subject will we ever be able to make sense of the past and begin to find solutions to the problems that currently confront us regarding drugs. As Ram Dass observed at the end of an interview, "If your book is going to have the richness it deserves, it needs to raise as many questions as it tries to answer." I hope this book does exactly that. My most heartfelt wish has always been that it might serve to promote an honest and open discourse on this subject—a dialogue through which we can begin, perhaps, to find our way home as a nation.

**Martin Torgoff**
*New York, July 2003*

# 1

# Fearless, Immune, and Ready for All

**❝ The higher you fly the deeper you go. ❞**

> —John Lennon and Paul McCartney, "Everybody's Got
> Something to Hide Except for Me and My Monkey,"
> the White Album, 1969

**❝ Marijuana is a halfway house to something else. ❞**

> —President Richard M. Nixon, 1969

## I. A Real Pack of Idiots

OUR STONED BROTHERHOOD came together in the season after Woodstock, the moonwalk, and the Manson murders. The world seemed forever altered by those events, as if anything, from the transcendentally high to the most unspeakably malevolent, were entirely possible.

Everything about that time seemed so compressed: Nixon, the invasion of Cambodia, the shootings at Kent State and Jackson State, the Vietnam moratorium, the strike at our high school and the threatened suspensions for it, the public hearings and bitter shouting matches. The combination of what was going on in the world, what was happening in our lives, and the fact that we were always stoned and getting more intensely into psychedelic drugs created the feeling that events and people and feelings and images were all part of a chain reaction. More and more kids became interested in getting high and quietly approached us. A small but significant portion of our graduating high-school class got stoned for the first time thanks to our secret ministrations of the hashish that was around that season.

There were four of us in the stoned brotherhood that year. First there was Charles Robert Manian—Little Manny—scion of a well-to-do East Island family who drove a 1969 gold GTO convertible, white top, gold leather upholstery, mag wheels with whitewall tires, and a fuel-injected 400-cubic-inch V8 engine with custom Thrush pipes that made it sound like a powerful speedboat when it revved. The second member of the club was David Benjamin, who had taken to sitting in his room in the lotus position, smoking joint after joint and running his television with no sound as he practiced the same Alvin Lee guitar riff over and over again. And finally there was Innie, or Larry Insdorf, with his stoned blue eyes that seemed to open wide and say, "Oh, *wow*, man," at everything he looked at.

Every afternoon after school we'd be together at the Manians' plush beach house on East Island, righteously stoned, careening through the sonic dimensions of Cream's *Disraeli Gears,* Dylan's *Highway 61 Revisited,* the Moody Blues' *Days of Future Passed,* the Beatles' White Album. Staring out the big picture window in the living room, mesmerized by the patterns of wind-tossed whitecaps on Long Island Sound, we'd play air guitar to Hendrix's *Electric Ladyland,* frolicking as if those afternoons would last forever. We were young and thought we could solve the ancient and infinitely complex mysteries of man and his place in the universe simply by lighting up a joint and listening to the Beatles. As compelled as we were over the years to try to recapture the sweet, giddy rush of that first year of highs, it would turn out to be as irretrievable as one's own virginity.

As pot entered my life, my relationship with my father became a running exercise in teenage guerrilla warfare. My mother disapproved of marijuana just as much, of course, but whereas she was even tempered, with a sunny, optimistic disposition, my father was moody, intense, uncompromising. He asserted his love for his children in the only way he knew how, trying to control and protect us in the classic old-world manner of his immigrant parents. Having just watched his eldest daughter become a hippie, he wasn't about to stand idly by and watch the same thing happen to his only son. Our relationship had been tumultuous to begin with, but as his suspicions that I was smoking marijuana began to grow, the stage was set for serious conflict. It began in earnest on the night I came home very high from a night out with my friends. I slapped on the headphones and put Led Zeppelin's "Dazed and Confused" on the turntable, jacking up the volume as high as I could take it.

The headphones were brand-new, a miraculous invention that allowed me to play music as loud as I wanted, blowing my mind while my parents slept obliviously in the next room. Closing my eyes, I plunged as deeply as I could into the music and whirled about like some delirious Sufi in the center of the room until my sixth sense made me aware that something was dreadfully wrong and I opened my eyes to see my father standing in the doorway in his underwear. In my stoned trance, I had apparently forgotten to turn off the speakers. It was two o'clock in the morning, and not only our house but the whole block was vibrating to Jimmy Page's caterwauling guitar and Robert Plant's unholy shrieking. My father had a look of complete horror on his face. It was after this episode that the anti-marijuana tirades began.

My father's fears about drugs went back to his boyhood. The world that he had grown up in, the concrete labyrinth that ran along Livonia and Saratoga Avenues in the Brownsville section of Brooklyn, was the world of school yards, alleyways, tenement buildings, and corner candy stores that had produced not only the great Giants third baseman Sid Gordon but also the likes of Bugsy Siegel, Abe Reles, Pittsburgh Phil Strauss, and other killers of Murder Inc., who would park their gleaming black Cadillacs in a neat row right underneath the el. As a boy, he had been largely unaware of the hysteria about "reefer madness" and "Marijuana: Assassin of Youth" that was generated by Harry Anslinger of the Federal Bureau of Narcotics and promoted in the Hearst newspapers. But he did know a small group of kids who smoked pot furtively in the alleyways and hung out on the street corner across from the school yard where he put in the long hours practicing basketball that would make him a two-time all-American at Long Island University and, later, a notable player in the NBA.

What alarmed my father about those kids was their slack-jawed lassitude. Most of the second-generation immigrant kids of his neighborhood had been desperate to grab hold of their piece of the American Dream during those hardscrabble years of the Great Depression—as desperate to go to college and become lawyers, doctors, businessmen, and leave the teeming city for the suburbs, as their parents had been to leave behind the shtetls of Russia—but here was a group of kids who seemed perfectly content to slouch against a chain-link fence and just stare off into space. A few of them went on to become junkies. My father once observed one of them shooting up in the balcony of the Ambassador Theatre, the grand old Art Deco movie palace on Livonia Avenue, where he had seen Al Jolson in *The Jazz Singer* in 1927. It was a sight he would never forget: the spoon, the spike, the expression of blissful stupefaction on this kid's face in the flickering lights of the projectionist's booth. Long before sociologists and politicians and law-enforcement officials would provide the words, my father became convinced that the two main criticism of marijuana use, which would frame the debate over it in the United States for the next fifty years, were absolutely true: that people who smoked it would become aimless and lackadaisical (the "amotivational syndrome") and that it would lead to harder drugs (the "stepping-stone," or "gateway," theory). He believed that there would be a heavy price to pay for what I was doing and that this entire business of marijuana smoking would lead to nothing but stunted lives and diminished possibilities. "You mark my words," he would say portentously, his hazel eyes glistening with worry. "One day you'll see I was right. I just hope it's not too late."

By that point, I had long since tuned him out. Getting high wasn't just about having fun; it was about rebellion and bohemia and utopia and mysticism and so many other things that were being embroidered into the experience by the counterculture at that moment. It was about being young and strong and carefree and unafraid of anything, refusing to accept or even acknowledge limits of any kind. It was about ecstasy, rapture, the ethos of the party being exalted above all else—the kind of soaring, mind-bending, heart-bursting romanticism you can know only when you are eighteen and stoned and naked with a girl in a creek on a summer night, making love in the mud amid the frogs and bulrushes under an umbrella of shining stars.

As surely as that winter of 1970 turned to spring, lysergic acid diethylamide made its grand entrance into my life. I was lying naked in my room with a girl named Lucy on a sun-drenched Saturday morning when it all happened. Clearly not about to be daunted by the LSD media horror stories of the time, I accepted as my destiny that I would simultaneously lose my virginity and take LSD for the first time together. Approaching the experience with as much of a positive outlook as possible, I recalled the words that Tom Wolfe had used to describe Gretchen Fetchin the Slime Queen in the recently published *Electric Kool-Aid Acid Test* as the mantra for my virgin psychedelic voyage. Gretchen Fetchin was an Oregon girl named Paula Sundsen who had hopped on board with Ken Kesey and the Merry Pranksters at the age of eighteen and had taken acid for the first time when the psychedelically painted bus called *Furthur* had stopped in Wikieup, Arizona. As Lucy handed me the orange sunshine, I repeated Wolfe's words—"fearless, immune, and ready for all"—popping the little orange tablet into my mouth as casually as if I'd eaten a Pez candy.

Shortly thereafter, the street in front of my parents' house metamorphosed into water, my sister's '63 Chevy turned into some kind of otherdimensional vaporetto—and that was only the beginning. As we drove down to East Island, the road swelled underneath us like a roiling sea, and the trees began dancing as if animated by some deranged Walt Disney cartoonist. On the beach, a seashell came alive in the very palm of my hand, containing within its ridged textures a diorama of aquatic life that included prehistoric fish and sea horses, images of Greek gods, and whole underwater civilizations. Thoughts reverberated in my head like feedback in a never-ending loop, pushing me toward questions whether I liked it or not: *Who Are You? Do You Like Who You Are? What Is God? What Is Death? What Is Your Purpose Here on Earth?* And so it went for hours, a relentless Technicolor wraparound movie of existence generated by the brain, nervous system, and soul. When it was over, despite searing moments of the most inexpressible existential loneliness, I couldn't wait to trip again. I felt open, completely free, invincible, as if I would live forever. I was never more certain that all would be well in my pursuit of drug experience as long as I remained fearless, immune, and ready for all.

As the summer came to an end, Little Manny took a giant hit of mescaline for his army physical, figuring that it might help raise his blood pressure; he got out of the draft all right but barely made it back alive from Fort Hamilton on the Long Island Expressway. Heroin appeared on the streets of our town for the first time, and Innie watched helplessly as his sixteen-year-old brother began taking the train to Harlem to cop smack. As unsettling as any of these events might have been, they had no impact on the way we used drugs, especially as we clutched desperately at an innocence we felt slipping away in those last days before we left for college.

Several days before our departure, the four of us gathered at David Benjamin's house. His mother and her husband were away, and it seemed like the perfect time to take the yellow mescaline we had procured. It was going to be the first time that we did a psychedelic drug together. Around midnight, we dutifully swallowed our little yellow pills and within the hour began stepping into another realm of consciousness. Suddenly everything began to breathe and billow in the book-lined living room, including Little Manny's face, which was lighted up like a hundred-watt bulb. Manny had grown a bristling handlebar mustache, and as we began getting off on the drug, he began to look more and more like a cross between Salvador Dali and a youthful Latin American dictator.

The proceedings got under way as the four of us fixated on a ceramic sculpture that David's younger sister had done, a blue figurine of a woman—

"*Wow,* man, look at *that!*"

"Fan-*tas*-tic, man . . ."

"Oh, wow, far *out,* your sister did *that?*"

"That's *so* heavy!"—

studying the thing as if it held the answers to the deepest questions about the causes of creation itself, but as we settled in, the trip began to take on its own very specific emotional context. As much as we might have fancied ourselves intrepid psychedelic travelers, we were, after all, only four suburban boys about to leave our hometown and go off to college, and as this startling and inescapable reality loomed before us, it set the tone for the whole night. Try as we might to evade the fact, we were pervaded by the knowledge that were now facing a life in which our mothers would no longer be there to do our laundry for us and that a nice home-cooked meal would no longer be waiting each night on the table at suppertime. The mescaline amplified this feeling, and as the night wore on toward morning, we became lost little puppies. Walking a thin line between laughter and tears, we wandered outside and made our way up the street to watch the sunrise.

The four of us sneaked into a backyard that offered a high vantage point, took off our shirts, and lay on our backs in the dewy grass as the first pink slivers of dawn appeared in the sky. Within minutes, the horizon became a flaming vista of magenta bursting with the promise of a new day, streaked by orange and blue rainbow sherbet. We lay there in complete silence, shattered by the beauty of it. By the time we made our way back down the hill to sit on the wooden fence in front of the Benjamins' house, it seemed as if we had arrived at an acceptance, a new willingness to submit ourselves to college and the process of life. Sitting there on the fence, I reveled in the silence of the morning, feeling more alive in that moment than ever before in my life. I was feeling absolutely certain that I was finally experiencing those "myriad pricklings of heavenly radiation" that Jack Kerouac had written about in *On the Road* when we saw a silver 1969 Pontiac Bonneville turn onto the road and drive toward us.

"Hey, isn't that your *old man's* car?"

No, it couldn't be, I thought. But it was. Watching the car approach made me suddenly aware of how high I still was. My father's Bonneville was cutting its way toward us like an icebreaker moving through my whole state of consciousness. I had no idea what he was going to say or do, just that he was going to be hopping mad.

My father bore a startling resemblance to Burt Lancaster, and as the car came to a halt before us and the electric window came down and he surveyed the four of us, bare chested on that fence, he looked like Lancaster in his first film, *The Killers*. Barely awake, unshaven, his hair mussed down on his forehead, he had probably gotten up to go to the bathroom, noticed that I hadn't come home, and gone off in search of me. I saw a whole progression of emotions come flashing across his face: confusion, sadness, anger . . .

"My God, you're a real pack of *idiots*" was all he chose to say at that moment, but with contempt so complete and pure that it took my breath away. *"A real pack of idiots!"*

The window slid back up as if to punctuate his pronouncement, and he drove off, leaving us there to digest it.

Twenty-three years later, I was sitting with my parents on a redwood deck in the Poconos, still trying to digest it. By that time, I had become interested in writing a book that would somehow journey across the continuum of the American experience of illicit drugs in the postwar era, and I was curious about my father's impressions of that time when drugs had first come to our hometown, changing our lives within the course of a single year. My father was then in his midseventies, fourteen years past a heart bypass operation; with his full head of white hair, he now looked like the Burt Lancaster of *Rocket Gibraltar.* The conflicts of those bitter adversarial years had long since been put behind us, and we had become the best of friends.

My friends and I were really typical products of that overheated decade, I tried to explain to him. What he was seeing may have seemed like a pack of idiots but was really nothing more than four eighteen-year-old boys having some form of an ecstatic experience on a psychedelic substance. We were America's first psychedelic children, swept up in the most dramatic statistical explosion of drug users in American history. What had happened to me on my journey through the self-expansion and self-deception of drug use represented only one transit in tens of millions, but the more I talked about it, the more he couldn't seem to hear what I was saying.

"You raise a child and they grow up, but there's something about them that always remains a child to you," he told me on that day. "You remember when they were a defenseless baby, and you try to protect them and teach them how to live. I'd see how the look in your eyes changed after you did that stuff. I never knew what you were on, but I always knew when you were on it because I could see it in your eyes, and that's what scared me, how the look in your eyes changed from the child I had known. No, I didn't understand any of it . . ."

"Here we were, a country that was at the height of its power and wealth and influence. Who was it, Henry Luce or Walter Lippman, I think, who called it the American Century? And here were four young boys going off to college, the most important time in your lives, with the whole world in front of you, the most educated and affluent generation in history, given every possible advantage—and whacked out of your minds on some drug! Like you were on another planet or something.

That was the worst part of it to me, the hardest part to understand and accept about drugs, because I really felt like you were all hurting yourselves, and there didn't seem to be anything we could do."

The more we talked, the more I could see that even after all that time, both of us carried scars from those years. Like so many of his generation who had lived through the Depression and the Second World War to build the American Century, he would remain the concerned parent, utterly bewildered by the children who grew up to reject the very values upon which he had built his whole world.

"Go ahead," he said, issuing the challenge that would inspire this book, "you try and tell me how it all happened and what it all meant. Go ahead, because I don't understand any of it, and I don't think I ever will. Go ahead and tell me—what did *any* of it really mean?"

## II. One of the Great Myths of the Age

ONE NIGHT IN 1976, I found the perfect blend of marijuana, methaqualone, cocaine, and alcohol for my particular nervous system. I was at the Ocean Club in downtown Manhattan with my friends, dancing to Marvin Gaye's "Got to Give It Up," when it went resounding through me in waves of the most visceral pleasure—the consummate high, the ideal psychopharmacological cocktail.

Drugs would take me to many scenes and places as I chased that high well into the 1980s—the East Village, Miami, the Dam in Amsterdam, the back room of Max's Kansas City, CBGB, the Mudd Club, the basement and balcony of Studio 54, the hot tubs of California—and they would take me to encounters with many people, from tycoons like Huntington Hartford to street kids in South Central Los Angeles. The only time I ever turned down a drug was when I didn't understand the question. Every new drug hit my life and the lives of my friends like a succession of tidal waves crashing over us. I watched as drugs permeated the industries of music, film, television, publishing, art, advertising, and finance, making and breaking lives and fortunes, saturating every socioeconomic level of the society, intersecting with virtually every aspect and dimension of the American experience. I watched as drugs defined identities and relationships, set people sexually free and rendered them sexually dysfunctional, initiated a search for spirituality only to be perverted into a kind of God. I watched my entire generation have the time of its life on drugs and then have to deal with the consequences. Some of those who crashed and burned were fortunate enough to recover, but others never made it back.

By the time Katrina and I were together in the early 1980s, she wanted to do cocaine and I wanted to save her from it. Katrina was a beautiful spirit in flight, an ex-ballerina who had exiled herself from dancing and was searching for something else. She had not been down the same long and winding road with drugs that I had, and when she found cocaine, I was instantly alarmed because I recognized in her attraction to the drug the same kind of hell-bent longing that lures someone inevitably toward the very thing that poses the greatest danger. So I tried to intercede, convinced that if I shared with her my vast experience and knowledge about drugs, then surely I could dissuade her, somehow insulate her from their dangers by surrounding her with the walls of a deep and unconditional love. Of course I found myself in exactly the same situation with Katrina and her cocaine as my father had once been in with me. The results were painfully similar. Katrina would completely ignore me or lie; and then, after much browbeating, she would agree to stay away from the drug. Initially she would comply, only to end up doing the stuff with her friends when I wasn't around, after which I would howl and condemn her and she would call me a bold-faced hypocrite and I would end up doing the drug with her at home.

My convoluted logic for taking a drug I was coming to loathe was the realization that she was going to do it anyway and better she should be at home with me, where she would at least be safe, than out at clubs and bars with God knows what kinds of sleazeballs. What the hell, I was in love with her. I couldn't let her get high by herself, could I? By that time, I was experiencing severe depressions on the drug. A single night of doing it could plunge me into a black pit for days. During those long and horrible teeth-clenching, gum-numbed hours of desiccated nasal passages and psychotic anxiety, I would try to lobby her for some sense of control and moderation and she would only want more. As I would do it with her, I felt small parts of my soul dying inside me with each line.

Two years later, New Year's of 1985, I found myself standing at the bar of Cafe Central in New York. It was about six in the morning, and the door was locked as the bartender continued to pour drinks for the stalwarts from the night before. There I was, still knocking back vodka with a furious vengeance. At the four parties I had been to over the course of that night, I had smoked pot and hash oil and a quantity of opium; I had hooked down a handful of Quaaludes and mixed them with an endless flow of champagne and vodka, and I had snorted cocaine almost continuously, with a mad devil's hunger. At the last party, whose denizens had appeared like black-clad hordes out of some cocaine-induced Hieronymous Bosch vision of hell, there was a guy dressed up as the Pied Piper of Hamelin, dispensing the stuff out of a large business envelope, with a gleaming switchblade, to groups of men and women in tuxedos and evening gowns following him around all night. And none of it was working, not even a buzz. There was nothing I could do to get myself off, short of sticking a needle in my arm—the one thing I had promised myself I would never do—and it was the most horrible, maddening feeling in the world, to be struck dumb with the realization that none of it was working anymore. I had succeeded at nothing more than making myself numb, but not numb enough to kill the pain that was gnawing inside my gut.

With the bright morning sun streaming in through the windows on Columbus Avenue, I was aware of a few things. I was aware of how badly my eyes hurt, how brittle they felt against the harshness of the light, and I longed for a pair of sunglasses as much as I longed for peace. I was aware that my journey with drugs was coming to an end, that my days of playing fast and loose were over. What I was most aware of at that precise moment, what swept through my soul like a cold black gust of wind, was the most compelling urge I had ever experienced to place a gun to my temple and blow my brains all over the bar top.

I was aware of the role that drugs had played in bringing me to this place. And I was aware that there was nothing I could have done even had I been there when Katrina got out of bed one morning six months after we broke up and noticed that one of the cats had crawled onto the ledge. She must have had very little sleep, and she went out onto the fire escape, as she had done so many times before, to scoop up the cat and place it back inside. I was aware that some drastically impaired sense of depth perception must have caused her to miss the railing as she stepped back.

Beyond that point, my awareness ended. I simply could not fathom what she felt as she fell five stories or what she looked like there on the street, her beautiful ballerina's legs shattered like matchsticks, her life's blood running out on the pavement. Nor could I fathom how she survived except to discern the hand of God in her survival—the same God who had brought me to understand, as I perched on the fragile precipice above that yawning abyss, that suicide would have been a permanent solution to a temporary problem. The boy who had first picked up a hookah at sixteen and the little barrel-shaped orange pill of LSD not long after had been very wrong about being "fearless, immune, and ready for all." Fearless, yes; ready for all, certainly; but at least in my case, there had been no immunity. As far as drugs were concerned, that aphorism had turned out to be one of the great myths of the age.

In the years since my father's death, his words of that summer day have come back to me again and again as I've attempted to answer his question of how it had come to pass that the American Century had turned into the Great Stoned Age. I've heard them as I've traveled thousands of miles, scoured the shelves of libraries, immersed myself in the lives of hundreds of people, and searched for his face in the night skies.

In the end, what did any of it really mean?

# 2

# Bop Apocalypse

> **“**Music is your own experience, your thoughts, your wisdom. If you don't live it, it won't come out of your horn. They teach you there's a boundary line to music. But, man, there's no boundary line to art.**”**
>
> —Charlie Parker, 1948

> **“**Ask him if we can get any tea. Hey kid, you got ma-ree-wa-na?**”** The kid nodded gravely. **“**Sho, onnytime, mon. Come with me.**”** **“**Hee! Whee! Hoo!**”** yelled Dean.
>
> —Jack Kerouac, *On the Road*, 1957

## I. Ready to Introduce New Worlds with a Shrug

“I'M GONNA LIGHT A JOINT,” said the man who gave William Burroughs his first shot of narcotics—a shot that would be heard around the world. “Would you like a blast?” Herbert Huncke leaned his frail frame back against the wall and took a deep hit. That single word, *blast,* was enough to put one right there: Times Square circa 1945–46, Ginsberg at nineteen with cigarette holder, belted raincoat, and horn-rimmed glasses, Kerouac in his seaman's coat, Burroughs in overcoat and homburg. During that first season of their drugs, Huncke was procuring interview subjects for Alfred Kinsey's groundbreaking sexual research at the same time he was scoring tea and Benzedrine inhalers at the Angler Bar. He was seated on the bed in his subterranean apartment on the Lower East Side, the man who became Elmo Hassel in Jack Kerouac's *On the Road,* Herman in Burroughs's *Junkie,* the original "angelheaded hipster" in Allen Ginsberg's *Howl*—hustler, petty thief, jailbird raconteur, lifelong drug addict, the man who first put the word *beat* in what became known as the Beat Generation.

"People have moralized about my using drugs my whole life," Huncke reflected. "Man, I started to use drugs back in the Thirties, that's when I started. There were very few kids at the time that messed with them—it was quite unheard of, especially for white kids. There were a lot of taxi drivers around Chicago and guys in the sporting life, so to speak, boxing joints, pool halls, that's where you'd find junk. Get a cap of dynamite horse for sixty-five cents. You got ten Benzedrine tablets from Smith and Kline for eighty-nine cents. Once you started, it was so easy, everything fell right into place. Of course, those were also the early days of Harry Anslinger and the beginning of the Federal Bureau of Narcotics. *Awful* man, Anslinger, must have been bred in some stool pot in hell somewhere, caused more misery in the name of saving so-called civilization than anybody since Hitler."

Huncke was "a little late for the hard-core old junkies of New York that just prior to my hitting the streets had already become established," as he related it. "In *Naked Lunch,* the material about Sailor—that was Phil White, and he was a part of that scene. Burroughs constantly refers to 103rd Street. Those were the old-time schmeckers who hung around there. A lot of Irish, people like that who hung around the cafeterias. The Jewish guys were all hooked up to the mobs, and they lived on the Lower East Side. That's how it got started, really—the Jewish guys hanging around the bars on East Broadway, Henry Street, Madison Street, all that below Canal and east of Chinatown. You would hear about some of the old guys way back there in the Twenties, guys like Louie the Lip and Crazy Ozzie, guys who remembered what it was like when you could buy heroin right across the counter in a cold-cream jar. Imagine that! The Italians got into it later, and when they did, the scene got bigger, heavier, and they started cutting the dope more and more, which changed everything. Eventually, it all moved up to Harlem and 110th Street . . . "

Huncke frowned and put his feet up on the bed. Somehow the whole journey of illicit drugs through the culture and consciousness of midcentury America seemed to begin with those very feet. What long, hard mileage they logged, what wear and tear as he searched so relentlessly for the junk that he pumped into his veins over the course of a lifetime, haunting the parks, squares, bars, cafeterias, coffee shops, the endless pacing of jail cells, cheap hotel rooms, methadone clinics.

Born in Greenfield, Massachusetts, in 1915, the son of an anti-Semitic German Jew who later joined the pro-Nazi German American Bund, from the beginning Herbert Huncke felt trapped by everything in his life: school, family, and gender. It was during his Chicago boyhood, after being introduced to marijuana by a cabbie, that he became captivated by a book called *The Little White Hag*, about "smugglers and Chinese junks and opium dens in Shanghai, posh layouts with cushions on the floor and naked or half-naked men and women laying about," as he recalled it. "It was called 'lying on the hip,' and that's where the word *hip* comes from, of course. You sat in a big circle, and there was a gigantic bowl of fruit; velvet and satin curtains, soft light and soft music, dancing girls, the works. I don't know where I got this book from, and I know I wasn't supposed to be reading it, but it fascinated me. Of course, it ended up that everybody went to hell, but so be it. It sounded like a pretty interesting way to go to hell to me."

Huncke would always gravitate to others who were interested in going to hell in interesting ways. At the age of fourteen, Elsie John came into his life. A six-foot five-inch man who passed himself off as a hermaphrodite and worked on West Madison in a freak show, Elsie John had "hennaed hair a fire engine red and gigantic deep blue eyes, the most expressive eyes I've ever seen." Holing up in her room in an old vaudeville hotel on North State Street, she would stretch out in her huge brass bed, surrounded by five Pekinese dogs, fussing and combing and petting them as they yipped and yapped. Elsie John was the forerunner of the pill-popping drag queen, the prototype of many characters to come: the Georgette of Hubert Selby Jr.'s *Last Exit to Brooklyn*, the Miss Destiny of John Rechy's *City of Night*, the Holly Woodlawn of Lou Reed's "Walk on the Wild Side." Dressing like a diva, cursing like a sailor, and selling joints out of her room, seven for a quarter, Elsie John mesmerized Huncke. The "piddling amounts" of heroin she let him taste were enough to ignite his lifelong obsession with the drug. "They used to sell it in decks in those days; instead of glassine bags they'd fold a piece of paper into a little pack-age called a deck." Huncke used to love to watch Elsie John get off in her room, her eyes glistening like "a pair of headlights."

One day when they were sitting around getting high, the police came bursting into Elsie John's room and screamed, " 'Get a load of this degen-erate bastard—we hit the jackpot this time!' " After they found the heroin, the police dragged Elsie John, Huncke, and his friend Johnny down to the city jail on South State Street. Huncke would always re-member his last glimpse of Elsie John locked up in the bull pen, "cower-ing in a corner, surrounded by a group of young West Side hoods that had been picked up the same night we were, exposing themselves to her and yelling all sorts of obscenities." He would tell Elsie John's story many times in the years to come, regaling the young Allen Ginsberg with her exploits until Ginsberg's eyes would go wide with astonishment. "At that time in my life, I could scarcely have imagined that such a person could really exist," the poet related.

Within a year, Herbert Huncke was a full-fledged heroin addict—Huncke the Junkie became his moniker for the rest of his days. When he told his mother about it after she saw him junk sick for the first time, she tried to help him; his father told him to get lost and never come back. After his friend Johnny was shot dead by a Treasury agent while making a delivery of heroin, Huncke disappeared from Chicago, never to return. For the next six years, from 1934 to 1940, he rode the rails and traveled the highways, a teenage heroin addict on the bum in Depression-era America. Huncke carried everything he owned in a little cigar-box toilet kit, working as a bellhop, scouring every city he landed in for dope—Galveston, El Paso, New Orleans, Reno, Needles, California—develop-ing the uncanny instinct for locating illicit drugs that Burroughs would later compare to a dowser's wand. By the time he hit New York in 1940, he had learned the rudiments of survival through petty criminality. Huncke had absolutely no interest in a conventional career or steady oc-cupation but lived purely by his wits. Though at times he would consort with hardened criminals, he was anything but a hard-core criminal him-self. He belonged, rather, to what Nelson Algren would describe, in *The Man with the Golden Arm,* as the "world of petty cheats, phony braggarts, double clockers, elbow sneaks, small-time chiselers, touts and stooges and glad-hand shakers." Yes, he was most certainly a thief, a grifter, a parasite, a hustler never afraid to use his body to get what he needed, but for the most part he was harmless. His greatest crime was that he was an unreconstructed, unredeemed drug addict who made no apologies for his behavior, who had learned from hard experience that those who used drugs in America were not simply downtrodden but truly among the damned. Next to blacks and poor immigrants, they were the most despised and persecuted outcasts of the society, without rights, beneath dignity, beyond the pale of compassion. The word that Huncke coined for such a condition was *beat*. In *Desolation Angels,* Kerouac would use the word for the first time in his work, describing Huncke as "somnolent and alert, sad-sweet, dark, beat, just out of jail, martyred, tortured by sidewalks, starved for sex and companionship, open to anything, ready to introduce new worlds with a shrug."

"I'm sort of a legend here, down on the Lower East Side," Huncke explained. "A *strange* legend, to be sure. People meet me and are in awe of my survival. As am I! Nobody could have convinced me at your age that I would live to be seventy-eight—never in my wildest imaginings. When I was twenty-one, I was perfectly satisfied with the idea of packing it in at thirty; forty was out of the question. I wanted to live fast, see and do as much as I could, cram it all into a speedy exit. See, I've never *stopped* using drugs. I'll even use some H still when I want to."

For the first time, I noticed the telltale little Band-Aid over the vein on the back of Huncke's seventy-eight-year-old hand, and despite everything I knew about him, I found myself chilled by it.

"Shows weakness, doesn't it?" he said, his face a mask of irony. "After all the pain and discomfort of my life, you'd think a man wouldn't want to subject himself to it anymore. Well, what do *you* think?"

"I guess what I think is that you can't get between a man and his lover" was all I could say.

"Yes, man, that's right," he said quietly. "Once known, never forgotten. One does what one does."

"Tell me, Huncke," I asked, "those days in New York there at the end of the war, what was it all really like?"

"What was it *like?* Oh, man, like hearing Charlie Parker playing 'Lover Man,' " he rejoined, "wailing on his sax, breaking down from being junk sick. Oh, man, the *pathos*—how does one even *speak* of it? You can literally hear him breaking down—the tone, he blows so piercingly on that song—it's like he's crying! Oh, my, my—*yes,* man, you can hear his agony, one junkie to another. The people I was with felt the same way about it."

Huncke closed his eyes as if to savor the sound of some far-off jazz musician blowing, and he took another hit of his joint.

"Do you remember when you first met them all?"

"Oh, sure. It's all right there in *Junkie,* exactly the way it happened. I met them all around 1945, right after the first of the year. I'd just returned from a sort of wild trip to the Caribbean with Phil White. It was a crazy time, that last year of the war. We thought we'd ship out and kick our habits at sea, but we ended up getting as much morphine as we could possibly use out of the ship's pharmacy, and by the time we got back, our habits were worse than ever before."

Huncke closed his eyes again and gently rocked back and forth on his bed.

"We were living in this apartment on Henry Street under the bridge, and there was this guy we heard about from up around Columbia. We heard he had this sawed-off shotgun to sell and these morphine syrettes—and one day Burroughs just strolled in, dressed like the president of a bank. I thought he might have been a cop; imagine my surprise when he wanted to shoot up with us, so I obliged him and gave him his very first pop. Oh, yes. I'll never forget what he said, 'Well, now, that's very *interesting,*' like some scientist doing research or something. It didn't take long for him to come back for more, and that was how I came to meet them all—Kerouac, Allen Ginsberg—just kids, really, looking to get high. Who could have ever imagined they'd become so famous and have the impact they did?"

Huncke took another hit and laughed softly. Kerouac and Cassady died back in the Sixties, and soon Ginsberg and Burroughs would be gone as well. Huncke would live out his last days in a room in the Chelsea Hotel paid for by the Grateful Dead through the Rex Foundation. He was the last living connection to a part of our past that we had always sought to disavow and bury in jails—the time of the old schmeckers like Louie the Lip and Crazy Ozzie, Harry Anslinger and reefer madness.

Despite his talent as a writer, he might very well have remained another faceless junkie and petty thief, ended up another unmarked grave in potter's field, had his orbit not intersected with that of a group whose lives and literature would change as a result of meeting this lifelong drug addict "ready to introduce new worlds with a shrug."

"Oh, it's quite a story, dope in America! Oh, yes, indeed!" He took yet another hit. "Sure you don't want a blast?"

## II. Lover Man and the Ultimate Truth

PERHAPS IT WAS FITTING that when Charlie "Bird" Parker arrived at J. P. McGregor Studio in Hollywood on Monday, July 29, 1946, to record his version of "Lover Man"—the song that would make such an impression on a young junkie named Herbert Huncke—he was so strung out he was barely able to stand.

Written by Roger "Ram" Ramirez, the song had first been recorded by Billie Holiday in October 1944 and had become a hit for her in May 1945. Bird had already done a version of it with Dizzy Gillespie for Savoy. Like Bird, Billie Holiday had developed an enormous capacity for handfuls of pills and alcohol and marijuana, but what had begun with opium in her coffee had graduated to full-blown heroin addiction by the time of the release of her version of the song. When Bird recorded his own cover of the song for Dial, Lady Day's habit had been roaring for several years. She was never without her dope, which she carried in a bag rolled up at the top of her stocking, along with a needle and a razor blade, tying off with a stocking around in her arm in her dressing room before every show. If "Lover Man" personified how Billie Holiday would become every bit as famous for her problems as for her talent, Bird's version of the song would now encompass a similar destiny.

The name Bird, for Yardbird, came from a couple of dead chickens Parker found in the road on his way to a date with the Jay McShann Orchestra. Parker had scooped up the dead birds and asked the lady at the boardinghouse if she would be so kind as to cook them. The nickname would follow him for the rest of his days. What would also follow him was a reputation for consuming prodigious amounts of drugs and alcohol and for having the kind of passion for life and music that would devour him like a steadily raging brushfire. Even as a young man, Parker was known to have sat Buddha-like in a room over the course of a day, devouring an immense bucket of chicken, a reefer dangling from his lips as he swallowed handfuls of Benzedrine and drained a fifth of whiskey and a woman knelt between his legs fellating him, a spike sticking in his arm as he jacked heroin into a vein—and then he would get up on a stage and, by some process of wizardry and genius, all of it would metabolize and take pure and transcendental flight into music of such brilliance and originality that it would leave his fellow musicians openmouthed with wonder.

As surely as reefer had come to be associated with swing, heroin would mark the transition from swing to bop. Bird would make the drug as much a part of the genesis of the music as the flatted fifth of the diatonic scale or Thelonious Monk's black beret and crazy windowpane glasses and strange little shuffle. Heroin was with him on that very night in 1939 when he jumped a train in the Kansas City freight yard heading north to Chicago, carrying little else but the habit he had acquired as a sixteen-year-old alto player during that first spreading of the drug from the East Coast to the cities of the Midwest. It was there with him during those visionary mornings with Dizzy and Monk and Kenny Clarke in the basement of Minton's Playhouse as bebop was being invented in jam sessions with the excitable unpredictability and propulsion of neurons firing across some uncharted musical synapse. It was with him in the twilight unreality of 52nd Street at its wartime peak, when Bird and Dizzy moved down to the Three Deuces to showcase the music for the first time and perform tunes like "Salt Peanuts," "Groovin' High," and "Dizzy Atmosphere." When Diz struck a deal to bring his sextet out to Billy Berg's in Los Angeles, Bird's habit followed him out to the West Coast, where for the first time he had to deal with his unsparing appetite for the drug in a place where he didn't know the ropes.

By that time, Parker had been an addict for a solid decade, and his habit would brook no interruption in his use of the drug. The cost of heroin in Los Angeles was high and the drug scarce. Bird managed to hook up with a dealer named Emry Byrd, known colorfully along Central Avenue as Moose the Mooche. A paraplegic in a wheelchair, Moose would appear at designated times in alleys outside the clubs, and as soon as Bird found him, his entire existence began to revolve around their assignations, much to Dizzy Gillespie's continuing dismay. After Gillespie had to drop Parker from the band in April 1945, and Moose the Mooche was busted and dispatched to San Quentin, wheelchair and all, the panic was on. Not only was Bird broke, but he was also strung out in a way he had never experienced before. He was soon living in the garage of trumpet player Howard McGhee.

"He was always up," McGhee remembered. "I went there five o'clock in the morning, he was up. I went there twelve o'clock during the day, he was up. I'd go eight o'clock in the morning, he was up. Every time I went over there he was up. I said, 'Damn, when this guy sleep?' He was taking Benzedrine and all that stuff. . . . Oh man he could take some—he really could. I seen him take a handful of Benzedrine like that. I don't know how his system stood it. Look like it would stop his heart. Any other man, it would. I know a lot of cats tried to act like him, and they found them lyin' on the side of the road somewhere, fuckin' with shit like Bird was."

In this condition, all Bird could do was lie on his back, listening to Bartók and Stravinsky. He became so desperate that McGhee finally went to Ross Russell of Dial on Bird's behalf and begged him for a recording date. "That's why I went to Ross and said, 'We'd better do something, 'cause this cat is uptight.' . . . He said, 'Okay.' So we set up the date. But Bird couldn't find nobody with no shit, and he was trying to make it off alcohol."

To stave off the horrible symptoms of heroin withdrawal, Bird consumed large quantities of whiskey, but what made his condition even worse on the day of his recording date was that somebody had given him a handful of Benzedrine tablets. Thinking the pills were goofballs, he swallowed them like candy, but instead of bringing relief, the drugs had just booted up his already overstretched nervous system to the breaking point. What emerged on record was the ragged document of a man's pain, the raw agony of his soul. Charlie Parker played with everything he had left in him, and you can hear him foundering, drowning, and breaking inside.

After one final attempt at a fast song, "The Gypsy," all Bird could do was crumple into a chair. With the advance from the session, Howard

McGhee got him a room at the Cecil Hotel. That night he came stumbling through the lobby twice without his pants on and later fell asleep in his room while smoking a cigarette. In the ensuing chaos of the smoke and flames from the burning mattress, members of the LAPD showed up, and when Bird protested their presence, he was blackjacked, handcuffed, and dragged away. "That night, after he got a shot of dope at the hospital, he was cool," McGhee recollected.

When the producer Ross Russell finally found him five days later, Bird was handcuffed to an iron cot in the psychiatric ward of the L.A. County Jail. McGhee and Ross persuaded a sympathetic judge to have him committed to Camarillo State Hospital, but when he came out after six months, nothing about his behavior had changed. His return to New York marked the beginning of his grace period, 1947–48, when he would appear at the Royal Roost and record with the famous quintet of Miles Davis on trumpet, Duke Jordan on piano, Tommy Potter on bass, and Max Roach on drums. It was during this time that the legend of Charlie Parker began to coalesce.

Bird would become many things to many people: the large man with the stentorian voice and the gold-toothed smile lumbering down the streets at dawn in a perpetually rumpled brown pinstriped suit, who always carried his mouthpiece in his pocket along with a pistol, flush with a roll of cash one minute, bumming money the next, loving his family but having sex with three or four different women a day, falling asleep in someone's armchair or riding subways all night because he had no place to go, loving life with total passion and doing everything possible to destroy himself. Parker would lock himself in a bathroom with his works and emerge to break through the sound barrier, playing sets that left people wondering how a human being could conjure such sublime music, and then he'd walk around the corner to a bar only to be called a lowlife nigger by some bartender. Composers like Ravel and Prokofiev wrote him the most gushing letters of praise, yet he could barely make a living from his own recordings.

As Parker defined the aesthetic of jazz that would become known as bebop, his name would come to mean much more: the Bird who soared, the Bird of unpredictable migratory patterns, the Bird of fierce beauty, the Bird who was free. The true power of his metaphor was about freedom, musical and otherwise. Poets, painters, dancers, writers, actors, filmmakers, and philosophers began to cite him as their inspiration, as the catalyst for their own breakthroughs. The cultural philosophy that he would come to exemplify during the period of his great comeback was designated as *hip,* a word that presented as many meanings in the underground culture as *cool.* Many writers of the time would seek to define the hipster, but all could agree that Charlie Parker seemed the ultimate living expression of hip.

The hipster "is to the Second World War what the Dadaist was to the First," wrote the jazz impresario Robert Reisner. "He is amoral, anarchistic, gentle, and over-civilized to the point of decadence. . . . He knows the hypocrisy of bureaucracy, the hatred implicit in religions—so what values are left for him?—except to go through life avoiding pain, keep his emotions in check, and after that, 'be cool' and look for kicks. He is looking for something that transcends all this bullshit and finds it in jazz."

The use of heroin would spread in direct proportion to the cult of Charlie Parker, and by 1948 Bird was at his most dazzling. "Music is your own experience, your thoughts, your wisdom," he declared. "If you don't live it, it won't come out of your horn. They teach you there's a boundary line to music. But, man, there's no boundary line to art."

If musicians became willing to indulge in his vices because they thought it might make them *play* like Bird, many would now also pursue them because they thought it might make them *feel* like Bird. Ross Russell had released "Lover Man," and though Bird would never forgive him for releasing music that he felt was far from his best, perhaps nothing did more to weave the mighty legend of Charlie Parker. The record became the testimonial of a man who had not only looked deep into the abyss but had crawled inside it to play his horn with all the naked truth his soul could muster. "Lover Man" seemed stunning proof that Bird had lived the pain and dissolution of his way of life and had wrested from it the triumph of great art. In fact, it seemed as if Charlie Parker could keep doing whatever he wanted to do, as if he could keep coming back and playing more brilliantly no matter how savagely he abused himself. The myth of "Lover Man" would therefore always entail at its core the image of a righteous dope fiend and the romantic notion that somehow heroin and all the pain and melancholy and self-obliteration it involved might fuel and authenticate and ensure the creative growth of the music called bebop. It was a peculiar and compelling myth that would provide heroin with a dark glamour, along with an irresistible mystique of creativity and freedom. Many would become inflamed and infected by its appeal. For the piano player Hampton Hawes, it started before Bird had even left Los Angeles, where the musicians would whistle the first three notes of "Parker's Mood" as their secret signal to let each other know that they wanted to cop.

"When I came early one night he motioned me to follow him up to his room," Hawes recalled. "I waded through piles of sandwich papers, beer cans and liquor bottles. I watched him line up and take down eleven shots of whiskey, pop a handful of bennies, then tie up, smoking a joint at the same time. He sweated like a horse for five minutes, got up, put on his suit and a half hour later was on the bandstand playing strong and beautiful. . . . Those of us who were affected the strongest felt we'd be willing to do anything to warm ourselves by that fire, get some of that grease pumping through our veins. He fucked up all our minds. It was where the ultimate truth was."

### III. The Eye Altering Alters All

WILLIAM BURROUGHS eventually took Herbert Huncke up to the rambling six-room apartment at 419 West 115th Street, where the whole group seemed to live and congregate. Huncke had never seen a group of people like that before, always carrying on, arguing, rushing into the apartment and declaiming lines from books and poems, addressing one another by literary references. Everything was like a scene from a play, everything a "Dostoyevskian confrontation," or a "Kafkaesque situation or horror." Huncke began to view them as "Oscar Wilde types, witty, acerbic—vitriolic in their sarcasm. I didn't understand a lot of what they were talking about."

What Huncke understood perfectly well, however, was their interest in drugs. Though uncomfortable, he was flattered by their interest in him. He had always used his mouth and wits to get by and now found himself in with a group of people who placed a premium on those very skills. Astonished to find himself accepted by these people, Huncke willingly told them the story of his life, and when he had exhausted that, he began to *show* them the story of his life. Huncke was a born storyteller, and the world of his stories was the world of illicit drugs. And so they started to follow him down to Times Square, to the buckets of blood along Eighth Avenue and the infamous Angler Bar, where a small underground population of drug users mixed with criminals and people of every conceivable sexual persuasion, and they all became the same.

To Allen Ginsberg, the sharp-witted, jug-eared, bespectacled nineteen-year-old student who was caught in the throes of deep and thorny questions about his sexual identity and what he wanted to do with his life, Huncke appeared like some Virgilian guide to a new underworld, the connection to an entire subterranean population of outlaws, rebels, nihilists, outsiders, eccentrics, bohemians, romantics, artists, dreamers, adventurers, cultural experimenters, self-explorers, hedonists, spiritual seekers, thrill merchants, and black marketeers. Ginsberg's fascination with these people and the mind-altering substances they used became increasingly fervent. "There was really no place to even go to get any reliable information on drugs and their effects at the time," noted the poet. "The only place to look was in the foreign literature, in literary terms. But in terms of popular information? In America, there was nothing. It was really quite amazing. I had heard about marijuana, for example, but I could never seem to come across any."

Before long, Ginsberg found some Puerto Rican seamen who sold him some pot. The first time he got really high—"a red letter day in my life"—he felt himself floating in a boundless universe of automobiles going up and down the streets very slowly and traffic jams and people walking between the cars and cops with whistles and people walking dogs and restaurants in the middle of what had transmuted into some vast robot megalopolis that seemed inside a great universe of brilliant blinking lights. Unable to tell the difference between north and south, he was frightened at first as he tried to make sense of what seemed like radical changes in his perception of time and space. Just parking the car was a monumental challenge, and when he and Walter Adams finally got it squared away, they walked into an ice-cream parlor at a corner of Broadway, sat down at a round table, and ordered a black-and-white sundae.

"This great plate of white ice cream just appeared—huge, round, beautiful, creamy—this great mound of snow-like ice cream but absolutely sweet and pure and clean and bright," he remembered. "It had some thick, great-tasting, hot, steaming chocolate syrup on top of it, which, when touching the cold ice cream, formed a kind of hard, chewy candy. And I'll never forget putting a spoon into it and putting it into my mouth. What an amazing taste it had! I don't think I ever truly appreciated what an outstanding invention a black and white ice cream sundae was—and how cheap it was, too!"

Halfway through the sundae, Ginsberg experienced the whole place swaying back and forth. The lights were dazzling, the sky seemed infinite, the plate-glass windows of the restaurant showed people walking back and forth with their dogs, smiling, chattering away, one of them weeping. "It all just seemed so perfectly joyful and gay and what came upon me at that moment in time was . . . the only way to describe it was that it was all like one great shattering moment of synchronicity!"

Ginsberg's experience of that single black-and-white sundae had been every bit as powerful as Burroughs's first shot of dope or Kerouac's first taste of benny, but his visit to the Metropolitan Museum shortly thereafter to view an exhibition of the paintings of Paul Cézanne would be just as significant. "I was studying art at the time, and made sure to take along a couple of sticks of grass and smoked some before going in, and there they were, the Cézannes. I kept staring at them, and somehow, just looking at them in that state of consciousness I was able to discern his use of space, really understand his use of hot colors advancing and cold colors receding—'eyeball kicks,' I later called it in *Howl*—optical consciousness. I would later come to understand it in Buddhist terms as *maya,* maya sensory space. Cézanne was very conscious of that optical space, and marijuana had sensitized me to that precise awareness or mindfulness, and so I'll always thank it for leading me to the paintings, into modern optics—the same eyeball experiments that led into cubism, or through Paul Klee into the magic squares. For me it was only the beginning of the exploration of the senses, the first scratchings of the Buddhist meditation exercises I would learn—the actual observation of how the senses operate, and the exploration of the wall of the senses of sight, smell, sound, taste, touch and mind."

Smoking marijuana may have created sensory openings that Allen Ginsberg would always identify as "educational" in his life, but the experience would also foster a paranoia that would become equally important in framing his attitudes about the substance. In the years ahead, he would experience the awesome "fear and trembling" that came simply from being in that state of mind and sensing the enormity of the universe, as well as the attendant paranoia connected to exploring the illegal unknown. "Remember, there was always the association of what society was laying on you, the notion of the 'dope fiend.' If you altered consciousness, there was something wrong with you, and I would often find myself pondering the official terminologies and implications of just what it meant to be a 'fiend,' which is a very strange, horrific, almost science fiction distortion of reality, wicked and diabolically cruel. If you smoked marijuana back there in the 1940s, you couldn't help but be affected by this giant official government propaganda machine called the Federal Bureau of Narcotics because you found it in the media everywhere you looked."

And so that was the ambiance in which it began for them, Ginsberg, Burroughs, Kerouac, and soon Neal Cassady, when he showed up. "Oh, we knew the trouble we could get into, but the curiosity and what it had to offer far outweighed the dangers, it seemed. So we began smoking marijuana when we could find it, and putting Benzedrine in our chewing gum, and going down to Times Square."

The Times Square night seemed endlessly vast to them as they stood, righteously stoned, under the great neon Pokerino sign and the huge billboards of the man blowing smoke rings and the black washerwoman bending over the tub with the suds flowing out. The pulsing red neon would cast a surreal apocalyptic glow over the multitudes of people and cars until the sense of a dying postnuclear world, of "the storm just begun" and "the Great Molecular Comedown," became chillingly palpable. As a result of those altered states, Ginsberg and Kerouac began to develop the "panoramic awareness" that would become such a philosophical and artistic touchstone for both of them: the holiness of the street and the sacredness of all the people walking it, no matter how lowly, the idea that Times Square was one giant room "hanging in space," the perpetual awareness of the infinite universe surrounding them. It was at this point that they began referring to themselves as ghosts—"Hello, drunken ghost" or "What have you got to say tonight, old phantom?"

Others had fought in the battles, but it would become the peculiar lot of Burroughs, Ginsberg, Kerouac, and Cassady to perceive and digest the meaning and magnitude of the Second World War, the Holocaust, the dropping of the atomic bomb, and the bitter, uneasy peace that followed, as they experimented with drug-induced altered states of consciousness. From the outset, there had been strong intellectual and artistic motivations behind their pursuit of drugs—what Ginsberg would later call "the ancient heavenly connection" in *Howl*. All of those forces moving them toward drugs had been swirling around them since 1945, during the initial conjunction of the group around Columbia University.

To begin with, there was "the New Vision," which the group had so passionately discussed in the heavy oak booths of the West End Gate or hunched over coffee in the cafeterias of Times Square. As formulated by Lucien Carr, another Columbia student, from his reading of revolutionary poets like Rimbaud and Baudelaire, the New Vision put forth the notion that "self-expression" was the highest form of art and that the writer would, in essence, create literature out of his individual mind and experience. Rather than be limited by strictures of language or morality or any styles of established literature or beholden to any notion that art should serve some higher purpose like the welfare of society or some moral good, the writer would, as Rimbaud had suggested, experience a supreme reality through *le dérèglement de tous les sens*—"a derangement of the senses"—thereby allowing him to define such things as beauty and horror directly through his own experience. From Rimbaud, the group also derived the concept of the seasons, during which they would all go through similar phases of development, and from Baudelaire, this maxim: *Plonger au fond du gouffre, Enfer ou Ciel, qu'importe?*—"To plunge to the bottom of the gulf, Hell or Heaven, what does it matter?"

From William Blake had come still another crucial phrase in their developing sensibility about the use of drugs—"the eye altering alters all"—the notion that change in consciousness was not only a means to an end but an end unto itself. From Jean Cocteau and others, they adopted the scientific, personal approach to drugs and their effects, which would involve extensive note taking and discussion and the acceptance of drug taking as a legitimate avenue of self-expression. From French Romantic writers and poets like Théophile Gautier, Gérard de Nerval, Victor Hugo, Balzac, and others in the Paris of the 1840s came the idea of a society, the famous Club des Haschischins, revolving around the ingestion of substances like hashish to enhance their creative sensibilities.

But no book was more influential than Oswald Spengler's *Decline of the West.* Implicit in the Spenglerian view of the ineluctable decay and demise of Western civilization in the grand cycle of history is the seed of an antiestablishment perspective that would color virtually everything the group did as they came to experience altered states of consciousness and consider the corruption and darkness of the postwar world.

As the members of the group took these disparate influences and synthesized them into their own experience, they evolved them into *kicks*— another of those words, like *cool* and *hip,* that had direct origins in jazz and the underground use of drugs and would eventually become a staple of the pop vernacular. Kicks could seem like mindless excursions in the pursuit of pure sensation and pleasure, but there would always be method in the madness. In the existential emptiness of the Spenglerian world as they perceived it, kicks would always seem a valid substitute for the rubble of past philosophies, moralities, and aesthetics; drug kicks, especially, seemed a proven shortcut, a potent method of cleansing the palate so that the world could be experienced anew. Therefore, exactly as the French Romantics had evolved the manifesto of art for art's sake, so would this little group of aspiring writers naturally expand this aesthetic philosophy to include drugs for art's sake.

"From the beginning, it wasn't a party drug scene," Ginsberg elaborated. "It was aesthetic, more of a curiosity as to the nature, the texture, of consciousness itself. So from 1945 on, we began experimenting—myself, Burroughs, Kerouac, Herbert Huncke—with Benzedrine inhalers. Those were pretty interesting, but from the beginning I was leery of amphetamines because after the sixth, seventh hour, there would be complete mental chaos. I quickly found out that I could hardly write under them because your mind got so tangled, but Kerouac would find that he could write *whole novels* on them."

Kerouac began taking more and more Benzedrine, staying up for days at a time, wandering around the city, furiously taking notes for his first novel, a tapestry that would contrast this life he had come to know in the city with the life of his boyhood in Lowell, Massachusetts. "Benny has made me see a lot," he wrote Ginsberg in November of 1945. "The process of intensifying awareness naturally leads to an overflow of old notions, and voilà, new material wells up like water following its proper level, and makes itself evident at the brim of consciousness. Brand new water!"

By the end of 1946, Burroughs had taken his first bust for narcotics, and Kerouac had fallen ill with thrombophlebitis from excessive Benzedrine use and drinking. Within the year, Kerouac would complete his first novel, *The Town and the City.* Burroughs emerges in the book as Dennison, "with his baby son in one hand and a hypo in another, a marvelous sight"; Ginsberg, as the mad young poet Levinsky, "one of the strangest and most curiously exalted youngsters" one could ever know, who stands in Times Square and predicts, " 'You'll see the great tycoons of industry suddenly falling apart and going mad, you'll see preachers in the pulpit suddenly exploding—there'll be marijuana fumes seeping out of the Stock Exchange!' "

It was a vision of America that seemed wildly far-fetched, with the mushroom clouds of the Second World War barely settled and the soldiers returning to resume building the great American Century. But within that first season of drugs, Allen Ginsberg, Jack Kerouac, and William Burroughs had all encountered the consciousness-altering substances that over the next ten years of alienation and gestation and wandering would become central vehicles in the creation of a body of work that would make the image of marijuana fumes seeping out of the Stock Exchange seem not only plausible but prophetic.

## IV.  Looking for Bird

AS SOON AS DIZZY GILLESPIE announced the event to celebrate the return of Charlie Parker to New York, Jackie McLean begged his stepfather to let him go. McLean was pressed tightly in the crowd on that February night in 1947 with his stepfather and Jelly, his best friend from up the street. Dressed in his sharpest clothes, McLean grew more and more restless as the hours passed. He knew he had to be in school the next day, and if Bird was too late, his stepfather was going to send him home. Bird was coming home from California, home from Camarillo, home to stay, and Jackie McLean, sixteen years old and the owner of a brand-new alto saxophone, was not about to miss it.

Like many young men of his neighborhood and generation, McLean had been looking for Bird since 1946. He had gown up in Sugar Hill, in a neighborhood that was steeped in jazz like a delicious roast simmering in rich gravy. His father, a guitar player, had died when McLean was six, and his stepfather owned a popular record shop at 141st and Eighth Avenue that carried all the latest sides. As a boy, he had been used to seeing the likes of Nat King Cole, Duke Ellington, Arnett Cobb, and had even thrown snowballs at Don Redman. White kids might have had heroes like Zorro, but he had Max and Dizzy and Prez, and from the first time he ever heard Charlie Parker play, he had been looking for Bird. By the age of fifteen, he knew that he would play an alto saxophone and play it for the rest of his life.

"So many people say the same thing," observed McLean, today a professor of music at the University of Hartford and one of the true elder statesmen of jazz. "They heard Charlie Parker, and it just drew them from one place to another, mentally, in so many ways. That's exactly how it was with me. Walter Bishop says the same thing. He was walking down the street when he was in the army, and he passed a bar and he heard this music playing and he stopped and looked in at the jukebox to see who it was, and it was Bird, 'Shaw 'Nuff' or one of those early things he did with Dizzy, and he put another coin in and hit that song, and from that day on he was looking for Bird."

The place to look for Bird at the time was down on 52nd Street, and McLean had gone down there to look for him in exactly the same way that Bird had looked for Lester Young back in 1936 in Kansas City. The search went beyond music. McLean was looking for Bird culturally, emotionally, spiritually, metaphorically, looking for his meaning as well as his music—"I'd run down there just to hear him warm up, just to hear him hit *one note*."

The year before, 1946, on a trip to Los Angeles, McLean had gone looking for Bird and had almost found him. "I went out there with my friend Jelly. We went for a walk far away from the house after lunch so we could have a smoke. We were walking along, and all of sudden I could hear Bird playing. The music was coming from an apartment somewhere, and we followed it and just stood there and heard him practicing, coming out of a window. 'Wow, he must *live* here!' It was like the most coincidental thing that could have ever happened to me. 'Man, let's remember the street and come back here tonight and ring the bell!'

"That night after dinner we went back, and we heard the record *Jazz at the Philharmonic* coming from the apartment this time, and we rang the bell, and Howard McGhee, the trumpet player, opened the door. I said, 'Oh, man, are you *Howard McGhee*?' 'Yeah, who are you?' 'I'm Jackie and this is Jelly. We thought we heard Charlie Parker practicing here before.' 'Yeah, he stays here sometime. What do you want?' 'Well, I play alto, and we know that record *Jazz at the Philharmonic*.' He was surprised because we were just kids. 'Come in,' he said. And when we walked in, we saw these three guys on the couch. They were slumped over, nodding. There was another guy in the bathroom, looking in the mirror. His eyes were like two pinpoints, man. The lights were way down low, and everybody was really out of it. We stayed and listened to the record for a little while—and then I got scared. It was a very strange feeling. I had never seen anything like that before in my life."

And so it was that Jackie McLean came to find himself in the audience at Small's Paradise. By 11:00 p.m., he was beginning to despair because his stepfather was just about to tell him to leave when there was commotion at the door and Bird strode in with his wife, Doris. The place erupted in screams and cheers as Bird headed for the stage.

"Bird, you don't have a horn with you," McLean heard the announcer say. "No, I don't," Bird replied, and before Jackie heard him say another word, he saw the alto sax come sliding across the small dance floor. He couldn't see who had flung the horn like that, but it looked as if it had come out of nowhere, like some beautiful celestial trophy gleaming in the stage lights—and in one graceful motion, Bird scooped up it and started blowing "Cool Blues."

McLean was ready to leave after that one song. He had seen exactly what he had come to see and walked home knowing he would remember the moment for the rest of his life.

It was right around the time of Bird's return that Jackie McLean also remembered first becoming aware of heroin in the neighborhood. "I would go to a party, and I would see some of my friends nodding. I had one friend. Someone said to me, 'He's *bangin'.*' I said, 'What do you mean?' 'Well, you know, man, that was what was wrong with Bird when he made the record 'Lover Man.' And all of a sudden it began to register. That's when I first started seeing it in my neighborhood. And from the very beginning, in the neighborhood and in my own mind, it was associated with Bird. Then Sonny Rollins and a bunch of the guys that were just a year or two older than me—there were rumors that they were doing this new thing. And then up on 164th Street, there were things happening, people who knew about it, talking about it. It was suddenly just there, the first big influx of it, beginning to pour into Harlem, and it seemed to come out of *nowhere.*"

McLean's long transit through drugs began at the age of sixteen with a one-and-one snort while playing at a Sunday-afternoon cocktail sip at a bar on 145th Street during that time when young men in his neighborhood began reaching for dope the way Bird had snatched up that glowing alto sax at Small's Paradise. It was the same story for all of them: snorting led to a snorting habit, which led to shooting—taking skin, as they called it—which led to a shooting habit, which led to that dreadful and decisive moment when the monkey of addiction was fully recognized. McLean's first big recording session was a Prestige date on October 5, 1951. Considered something of a musical prodigy from a young age, he was taken under the wing of Bud Powell. After Powell introduced him to Miles Davis, Miles asked him to record with Sonny Rollins, Walter Bishop Jr., Tommy Potter, and Art Blakey. The session was notable because it was one of the first to use the new microgroove technology, which would free musicians from the strictures imposed by the three-minute limit of 78 r.p.m. records and allow them to record compositions at whatever length they chose. But if microgoove technology represented new freedom, the heroin that by that time had overtaken the lives of each musician there meant something else. McLean had written a song called "Dig" that was going to be recorded that day, a song that if nothing else illustrated the pervasive influence of his idol, Charlie Parker. He was excited and nervous enough as it was, but what made it worse was that he couldn't get any heroin that day, had arrived at the studio in a junk panic, and was completely unnerved to see Parker himself seated in the control room to observe the session.

"I ran down there, and by the time I arrived, I was sick, and everybody else like Sonny Rollins was high. It made it so hard. The drugs got you straight so you could do something, anything. It was strange; it felt like it had all come full circle in a way. At the beginning, Bird recorded 'Lover Man' when he was so sick, and here I was at nineteen come to record for the first time in a big session, and I was sick, too—and there was Bird, sitting right there! I'd had a shot four, five that morning, but by that afternoon it was starting to get bad, and right after the session was over, I ran and cashed the check and scored. I was already into pawning my horn, pawning everything I could get my hands on. That's how I became a junkie, and that was only the beginning of it."

McLean was now part of a hip brotherhood, all from different family backgrounds, playing different instruments, with different personalities and tastes: Max Roach, Miles Davis, John Coltrane, Philly Joe Jones, Dexter Gordon, Art Blakey. It mattered how you looked in this group. Mephistophelian goatees were in. Dark wraparound shades. The kind of berets worn by Left Bank artists and intellectuals. Dark suits with white-on-white shirts. Silk ties. Marcelled hair with double-dip pompadours . . . Of course, there were plenty of white boys, too: J. R. Montrose, Gerry Mulligan, Red Rodney, Zoot Sims, Al Cohn, a whole other crew out on the West Coast that included Art Pepper, Chet Baker, Stan Getz, Anita O'Day. The list goes on and on: Tadd Dameron, Sonny Stitt, Gene Ammons, James Moody, J. J. Johnson. They represented the best and brightest young modern jazz artists that their generation had to offer, and by 1950, only three years after Bird had returned from California, they were all stone hard-core junkies themselves.

Dope was a whole way of life, like living inside a walled city with those of your own kind, where you could make up your own language and create your own set of rules. "That's right, and you didn't have to be a musician to be in that club, either," McLean pointed out. "I had plenty of buddies who followed the music, and they ended up getting strung out, too. It was us against the world, and it had no racial lines."

"That was our badge," Red Rodney explained to Ira Gitler. "It was the thing that made us different from the rest of the world. It was the thing that said, 'We know, you don't know.' It was the thing that gave us membership in a unique club, and for this membership, we gave up everything else in the world. Every ambition. Every desire. Everything. It ruined most of the people. It turned out that the drugs had to be done away with and if it had to kill many of us, it was a lesson."

The lesson would be a hard one to learn, and for many a long time coming. Life with heroin would change everyone as surely as Chet Baker's beautiful young face would become ravaged, transfigured by his life of addiction, like a hipster-junkie version of *The Picture of Dorian Gray*. The craving necessity of a constant supply alone would drive many to crime and humiliation and self-destruction. Sonny Stitt would steal and pawn every musician's horn he could get his hands on; Red Rodney would invent elaborate criminal scams that involved check machines and faked deaths; Stan Getz would walk brazenly into a Seattle pharmacy and try to hold up the place. Some, like Miles and Jackie and Dexter Gordon, would somehow manage to look clean and togged out in their suits no matter how strung out they were; others, like Sonny Rollins, would appear unkempt, hollow eyed.

But as different as they looked, there were certain experiences that all would come to know intimately. Smooth dealers like Pensicola and Collar. The going prices for wristwatches and rings and instruments in pawnshops across the United States. How to fix anywhere at a moment's breathless opportunity like the piano player Joe Albany, who could duck out between sets at the Three Deuces, race up to 110th Street, cop, cook up in a bent spoon, tie up and shoot up in the back of a cab hurtling down Fifth Avenue, and be back in time to play the next set without missing a beat. The heat of narco persecution with constant spot checks by police for needle marks and strip searches at bus and railway stations and in alleys outside clubs. What it was like to be thrown junk sick into kick tanks and prison cells and to have their cabaret licenses revoked so that they would be deprived of income at the worst possible moments of addiction. Salt shots and ice cubes on testicles after near-fatal overdoses. Hospital beds and rooftop nods. Dope-sick dawns and the desperation of dope panics. In their hip secret society, they would gaze at the square world with heavy-lidded eyes of irony and disdain and play their music as if nothing else in the world mattered. As surely as jazz is a deeply personal art form peopled by great artists who at their best are reaching deep into themselves to access and let forth the heart cry of their deepest emotions, they would create a classic American music that dripped with the profound isolation and pathos of the life around heroin and smoldered with all of its dark romanticism and melancholy: the onset of the cravings, the desolate loneliness of the search, the blissful relief of the shot, the anguish of withdrawal. Some, like Miles and Coltrane and Sonny Rollins, would kick, freeing themselves from the fetters of dope in what seemed like mythic modern-jazz versions of Booker T. Washington's *Up from Slavery,* experiencing quantum creative leaps and changing the direction of the music in the process. Others would perish and in death become even more legendary.

As for Harlem itself, within only a few years the whole place changed. Nobody would recognize the difference more than Charlie Parker. The heroin that Parker had copped in Los Angeles from Moose the Mooche back in 1945 was a crude Mexican product that had dribbled over the border in piddling amounts. Now when Parker needed to cop, he was flabbergasted by how much dope there was on the street and how easy it was to get it. "Man, why do you think we've got two bars on every street?" he once wondered aloud to Max Roach. "Why is it we can cop drugs anytime we want to? You can buy *drugs* and *whiskey* before you can buy *milk*!"

Had he been privy to the details, the answer to Parker's question of how heroin had come to flood the neighborhoods of Harlem and created what many would call the first drug epidemic in modern American history would have seemed like a fiendish plot devised to victimize a generation of unsuspecting African American teenagers that involved foreign nations, the cold war, the intelligence agencies of France and the United States, the mafia's organization of the global heroin trade, the history of the prohibition of narcotics in America, evolving public attitudes and policies regarding the treatment of drug addiction, and corrupt New York City narcotics police.

In fact, what Parker observed was only the most visible element in a drama that began on the plains of Turkey and in the mountains of Asia, where opium poppies were harvested and turned into opium base, which was moved into Lebanon, where it came under the supervision of wealthy and powerful men who bribed public officials so that it could be shipped in boats that would be met by fishing trawlers from Palermo, then smuggled into the fishing villages along the rugged coastline of Sicily, and finally moved to Marseilles, which, by the early 1950s, had become the world's busiest processing center of heroin under the protection of the Corsican syndicates.

Had Parker been able to trace even one of the packages from its source to the streets of Harlem, he would have been astounded to discover a vast distribution maze though Europe involving thousands of people as the heroin was concealed in fruits, vegetables, candy, furniture, and crates of wax oranges that were shipped to Canada or prerevolutionary Cuba, where Meyer Lansky had ingratiated himself with the dictator Fulgencio Batista, and then to Florida, where Santos Trafficante provided distribution and muscle as the dope made its way up to New York. There it would arrive in shipments of twenty to one hundred kilos and come into the hands of the five big crime families—Bonanno, Colombo, Genovese, Gambino, Lucchese—who were responsible for selling 95 percent of the heroin that came into the United States. The families would divide the heroin into wholesale lots and control it all the way down through three levels of distribution, until it reached the street, where its value would have increased tenfold. Whatever wasn't sold in New York would be moved out to St. Louis, Chicago, and Kansas City in false-bottomed trucks, cans of sardines, barrels of olive oil, wheels of caciocavallo cheese. The man who controlled it all, Charles "Lucky" Luciano, would never lay eyes on the dope, only the colossal amounts of money that Meyer Lansky would move through an intricate system of transfers back to Swiss bank accounts, where it was well beyond the reach of the IRS, the FBI, and everyone else.

Of course, why the Men of Honor had chosen Harlem as the marketplace for their product was simple enough. In one memorable scene of *The Godfather*, the heads of the families are sitting around the table making their peace after a mob war, debating the pros and cons of the new business of heroin. "So what if they lose their souls," says one crime boss about putting the drugs in the black neighborhoods. "They're animals anyway."

## V.  The Season of Wild Form

"SOMEDAY I'M GOING to write a huge Dostoyevskyan novel about all of us," Jack Kerouac proclaimed in a letter to John Holmes during his sojourn in Mexico City in 1952. "If I could only stick to novels long enough to tell a few good big stories, what I am beginning to discover now is something beyond the novel and beyond the arbitrary confines of the story . . . into the realms of revealed Picture . . . revealed whatever . . . revelated prose . . . wild form, man, wild form . . . Wild Form's the only form that holds what I have to say—my mind is exploding to say something about every image and every memory in it . . . at this time in my life I'm making myself sick to find the wild form that can grow with my wild heart."

Kerouac's hunger for "wild form" arose from his deep desire to create a new kind of writing that could somehow encompass the possibility of the pure emotional "cry" of jazz, as well as his belief as a writer that the truth existed in the movement "from moment to moment, incomprehensible, ungraspable, but terribly clear," and that its rush across the brain would force him "to catch the fresh dream, the fresh thought," as though he were "a fisherman of the deep with old, partially useful nets."

It was a style that began to evolve almost from the very first appearance of Neal Cassady, who showed up in New York at the beginning of 1947, twenty years old and standing buck naked in a doorway when Kerouac first saw him—"a young Gene Autry—trim, thin-hipped, blue eyed with a real Oklahoma accent—a sideburned hero of the snowy West."

Allen Ginsberg had met Cassady in the West End. Cassady didn't make much of an impression on that occasion, but the second time was very different indeed. Ginsberg was there on January 10, 1947, when Kerouac brought Cassady over to an apartment in Spanish Harlem to smoke pot for the first time. It was a night that would change the course of their lives—the first of hundreds of all-night nonstop mind-bending marijuana rap sessions.

After a single night of smoking tea with Kerouac and Ginsberg, Neal Cassady knew that he had found the great and ecstatic stimulation of minds that he craved. He had come to town hungry, exactly like a jazz musician looking to jam, desperately wanting to blow, only what Cassady

had to blow were words, experiences, modes of being. He was like Charlie Parker in that regard—an improvisational genius but an artist whose
instrument was not pen, horn, or brush but his very life. Narcotics, however, would never be his drug of choice. Neal Cassady would become one
of the great potheads and speed freaks of the age.

To the conventional middle-class American, Neal Cassady would
have appeared mad, a psychopath who used people in the manic pursuit
of pleasure, but to Jack Kerouac, the Catholic mill-town boy from Lowell
who wanted to be a great writer, the figure standing naked in the doorway
was nothing less than the embodiment of the Rimbaudian adventurer of
the New Vision, a beautiful lost wandering Dionysian spirit, a hip noble
savage. Kerouac was essentially an observer, a man who stood apart and
watched; Cassady, on the other hand, was a pure force of nature. He lived
his entire life with a preternatural squint for danger, sensation, and mind-
altering experiences of any kind, as if his nervous system and brain operated at a much higher octane than those of a normal human being.

The story that everybody likes to relate about Cassady's youth is how,
when he went to live with his mother after he started school, his sadistic
bully of a half brother would make him lie on a Murphy bed and then
close it, entombing him for hours in complete silence and darkness. Cassady had apparently liked it, or at least had learned to cultivate the sensation experientially. He would experience an acceleration of image and
thought and time, all of it rushing at him with alarming speed—"an
awareness that time, in my head, had gradually apexed to about triple its
ordinary speed of passage," as he described it in *The First Third*, "and
while this thing was happening I thought of it as just a circular flying object twirling through my mind, for lack of a better way to think about this
spinning sensation."

Cassady was the living essence of kicks. To Kerouac, he would become "that wow-mad Cody" in *Visions of Cody*—someone able to live
completely, un-self-consciously in the moment, where he seemed to burn
radiantly with the pure ecstasy of life. Kerouac was known during his
youth as Memory Babe, the Great Rememberer, but Allen Ginsberg
would call Cassady "the great experiencer and driver and talker." The avocation he cultivated to the level of spoken improvisational art form was
rapid-fire conversation on a dozen different levels, each digression beget-

ting another one, which would inevitably split off in several new directions.

As Kerouac and Ginsberg made plans to head west for their own reasons—Ginsberg in pursuit of his romantic love for Neal, Kerouac in search of "America"—it was already well established that what was going to happen between them was an unraveling of the mind, a journey across the landscape of the soul, and that they would get mightily high along the way. They would even bring forth a new phrase for it—*to elitch*—derived from the Elitch Gardens in Denver, where the local hipsters would congregate to blast. In what they perceived as a loveless age where the greatest disease afflicting man was the barrenness of the heart, the group opted out of conventional life, but in doing so, its members would have to opt in to something else: a vision of life in which everything was holy. In order to more fully dig "all the details" of their journey, to be able to love "all things, all ways," they would cultivate what Gerald Nicosia, in *Memory Babe,* his biography of Kerouac, would call "the sacralization of the mundane." Perhaps no better phrase exists to describe the role that marijuana (and, later, psychedelic substances) would play, not only in what followed on the road, but in the whole evolution of the Beat Generation and the counterculture that subsequently derived from it. In the case of Kerouac and Ginsberg, it was a sacralization that each had been searching for since childhood, but one that would now be graced and accentuated by their use of the weed. For the next four years, as they poured out the details of their souls to one another, Cassady, Kerouac, and Ginsberg would elitch together as often as possible, and when they ran out, they would search incessantly until they could elitch once more. "I'm sorry, but we gotta get a renewal of the supply of the material which makes it possible for us to *be* this way," the Neal Cassady character remarks in *Visions of Cody.*

And so their story had started to pulse like an accelerating heartbeat: the loves, the road, the mad kicks of sex and drugs and spirit, and the writing that would pour forth to chronicle all of it—Ginsberg desperately in love with Cassady; Cassady in love with Carolyn Robinson and hundreds of other girls of the moment; Burroughs in love with dope and Ginsberg, living first in New Orleans with his wife and then in New Waverly, Texas, becoming an exile in Mexico City after still another narcotics bust, where he would shoot his wife in a bizarre drunken William Tell act before landing in Tangiers and developing the worst oil burner of a narcotics habit he had ever experienced, all before writing *Naked Lunch;* and Kerouac taking it all down in his little five-cent notebooks.

As the new decade dawned over the first ten days of January 1951, Jack Kerouac wrote a series of letters to Neal Cassady in which he attempted to "proceed to the truth" of his life, letters that would form the foundation of all of his subsequent books. Whenever possible, he would smoke marijuana and dredge his subconscious for the same kind of intimate "excruciating details" about his earliest years in Lowell that Neal Cassady had related about his own life in letters to Kerouac, expressing a sense that what they had both experienced on the road might be used to somehow break out of their quotidian lives and unlock what they might now achieve as writers.

Cassady, in his letters, explained to Kerouac that he could now utilize this mode of panoramic consciousness and heightened perception anytime in his daily life just by recalling the state of mind and applying it to what he was regarding at the moment, in effect composing reality "as one looks into a picture." Kerouac began referring to this state of mind as being "wrapped in wild observation of everything."

Kerouac was then in the middle of his short-lived second marriage to Joan Haverty, and it was she who posed the question, "What did you and Neal *really* do on the road?" Kerouac decided to simply sit down and write a book in response to her question. He wanted to be able to tell the whole story as though spinning the yarn in a single sitting, barely pausing for breath. As he could type one hundred words a minute, he now improvised a writing method that would allow him to take full advantage of his skill. Taping together twenty-foot strips of Japanese paper to make a roll that could be fed continuously into his typewriter, he sat down in Lucien Carr's loft and began pouring forth the story. He took Benzedrine constantly, sleeping and eating very little, existing only on pea soup and coffee and cigarettes, sweating so much that he soaked through T-shirt after T-shirt, getting up to change the shirts and hang them out to dry as he changed the music he listened to.

The music was bebop—Max Roach records and a particular piece called "The Hunt," which he and Cassady loved—the B side of a Savoy release that featured Dexter Gordon and Wardell Gray blowing in a wild bout of dueling tenor saxophones recorded live in Los Angeles on July 6, 1948. It was music that was described by an unknown writer in the original Savoy liner notes as a "wild, rompin', stompin', jumpin', wailin', roaring balling session," and few pieces of jazz committed to wax have ever managed to live up to those words more completely. The cut featured a raucous audience of overheated hipsters shouting, *"Go! Go!"* throughout, and as Gordon blew on his tenor and Roach pounded the skins, Kerouac wailed on his typewriter exactly as he and Cassady had gone blazing across the country, down into Mexico.

The book that emerged would become mythic for many reasons, having to do with characters and story and style and cultural impact, but as time went on, those mythic qualities would become inseparable from the creation of the work itself. Kerouac wrote about Neal (Dean Moriarty) and himself (Sal Paradise) and Ginsberg (Carlo Marx) and Burroughs (Old Bull Lee) and Herbert Huncke (Elmo Hassel). He wrote about neon nights, cheap hotels, hitchhiking, floods, rivers, towns, the plains, hobos, freight trains, black music and the "dawn of Jazz America," the brotherhood of man and the spiritual decline of America as the dark, chilling cloud of McCarthyism was just beginning to gather over the country and money and consumerism were becoming deities in the pantheon of modern American culture. And he wrote about drugs—Benzedrine, morphine, but mostly marijuana—in the authentic language of those who used them as a way of life, making the drug content of the book inseparable from its consciousness and sensibility, rendering it in ways that presaged the entire relationship between drug use and the counterculture of the 1960s and beyond.

The work contained writing about drugs on two levels: explicit descriptions of drugs and the people who used them and aspects of drug consciousness implicit in the entire inner journey of the book, in the "whole mad swirl" of everything that was to come as Sal Paradise goes shambling after Carlo Marx and Dean Moriarty because "the only people for me are the mad ones, the ones who are mad to live, mad to talk, mad to be saved, desirous of everything at the same time, the ones who never yawn or say a commonplace thing, but burn, burn, burn, like fabulous yellow roman candles exploding like spiders across the stars and in the middle you see the centerlight pop and everybody goes 'Awww!' "

In that single passage, which would become one of the most quoted of twentieth-century American literature, Kerouac was writing specifically about Ginsberg and Cassady (high on marijuana for the first time), but he was also invoking the spirits of Huncke and Burroughs, offering a powerful metaphor for the whole way of life embroidered into the hip subculture of jazz as personified by people like Charlie Parker and Billie Holiday. That paragraph and many others like it would resonate as loudly with the feeling of drugs as the other parts of the book where characters actually take them. In a single image, Kerouac had not only presciently encompassed the destinies of himself and Cassady but had augured an entire era of brilliant human supernovas and flameouts when the "fabulous yellow roman candles" would have names like Jimi Hendrix and Jim Morrison and Janis Joplin.

Although marijuana is a predominant presence in the final part of the story, when Sal and Dean travel to Mexico, the consciousness of it is everywhere. By implicitly linking the use of the weed with a powerful ethos of freedom, Kerouac presents it as a metaphor for the untamed human spirit, a philosophy of life, a spiritual antidote and mystical medicine. As a result, the book would infuse the idea of marijuana with a new kind of numinous romanticism, linking it to spiritual searching, Eastern religion and philosophies, and great sensory exploration, placing it within a worldview that would have powerful political and cultural implications.

Kerouac's romantic association of the "fellaheen" culture of Mexico with marijuana consciousness was revolutionary in itself. Since the 1930s, the signature images of the marijuana smoker in America as purveyed by Harry Anslinger and the Federal Bureau of Narcotics had been those of a knife-wielding Mexican laborer, a wild-eyed ax murderer—fiend, or a salacious Negro jazz musician seeking to corrupt innocent white youth. Kerouac had taken the entire raison d'être of marijuana prohibition and turned it upside down, transforming Anslinger's nightmare of marijuana—the "killer weed" and "assassin of youth"—into something not only desirable but morally good. He had taken the dirty Mexicans and their dirty, evil weed and presented them as nothing less than great teachers for a philistine, spiritually bankrupt, and crassly materialistic American culture.

For Kerouac and his friends, marijuana was no stepping-stone to hard drugs or human degradation but a light-bringing weed of healing. It was the gateway to the "magic mothswarm of heaven," poetic instrumentality for an ecstatic "moan for man," the cosmic facilitator of "the moment where you know everything and all is decided forever."

Jack Kerouac had committed the ultimate subversion. He had written his *Huckleberry Finn* but had sent Huck and Jim down the river with a great big burrito of *Cannabis sativa*.

Although Kerouac was certain that he had broken through to a new form of writing, everything unique about the style of the book would only work against it. When he walked into the office of his editor, Robert Giroux, and proudly unrolled the 120-foot-long work on the carpet, Giroux was less than enthusiastic. Giroux had edited Kerouac's first book and now grumbled about how difficult it would be to edit this new work in its present form, with no paragraphs. Kerouac called him a "crass idiot" and stormed out, certain that he didn't need the likes of Giroux or his firm, Harcourt, Brace.

It was a decisive moment in Kerouac's life. The book that he would re-type on regular bond paper and name *Road* and *The Daybreak Boys* and finally *On the Road* would meet with similar responses everywhere else it was submitted, regardless of revisions or title. Kerouac was crushed. He resolved to write on without compromising his principles, but the rejection of the book would consign him to penury for the next five years. He would journey further down the path of the new writing, but in the process he would become "the loneliest writer in America." Over the next five years, his life would come to taste of poverty and bitterness and the shame and guilt of living off his mother. He would come to know fear and parsimony and the sadness of failed marriages and misbegotten affairs. As this profound melancholy entered his soul, the rejection of the book served to guarantee that of all the substances in the panoply of his use, alcohol would ascend in importance, and that was perhaps the most fateful consequence of all.

All the while, though, writing would become the anchor, the one constant of his life. Even as his career stood still, the story of his life and the lives of the others would go on as if the roll of Japanese paper had never stopped its continuous feed into his typewriter, moving in a stream of consciousness perfectly synchronous with real-life events, love affairs, writing, and the experience of mind-altering substances, which would fracture and deconstruct it, collapse it with memory and render it as synesthesia and synchronicity and heartbeat itself. He would work everywhere he could during those five years—at his neat roll-top desk at his mother's houses, along roadsides, in skid-row hotels in San Francisco, on freight trains, ships, in the stick huts and on the adobe rooftops of Mexico. His life would become his work exactly as Sal Paradise had become one with the environment on top of the car in the jungle outside Limón, and the substances he used would become ever more a part of the process.

By the time he came to write *Mexico City Blues,* in the summer of 1955, Kerouac had become exactly like a "Perfect Musician" himself—"a jazz poet blowing a long blues in an afternoon jam session on Sunday. I take 242 choruses; my ideas vary and sometimes roll from chorus to chorus or from halfway through a chorus to halfway into the next"— achieving with words what Charlie Parker and Bud Powell and Miles Davis were doing musically. Like Bird, Jack Kerouac had become a pioneer of the New Reality Jam Session. The season of wild form was now truly upon them.

## VI. An Awareness of His Most Human Pain

IF CHARLIE PARKER'S life were a Shakespearean tragedy, the final act would be the saddest spectacle of all: the loss of his most prized asset, his mythic ability to play great music. When club owners became reluctant to book him for more than a single night or set, Bird found himself reduced to playing in dives and storefronts. Suffering terribly from his ulcers, he only drank more, and then came the terrible rasping cough, which sounded like something had torn loose deep inside him. More and more, he would be seen wandering around the city at dawn, shabby and broke, sleepless, alone, piteously lost.

"The last time I saw him was at the Beehive in Chicago," Frank

Sanderford remembered. "The owner had asked me to get Charlie to go on. He was in a little room where they stored beer. I went back there; Charlie met me at the door and threw his arms around me as if I were the only person in the world. He couldn't go on the stand, he said; he was in no condition. He looked bad. The house was jammed. I asked him to take a look and see how many people had come just to hear him play, and I opened the door a little. He glared out. 'They just came to see the world's most famous junky,' he growled. . . . He made a few awful, bleating sounds. He couldn't play."

In years to come, as many tried to digest the meaning of Bird's transit, those withering moments and images would become as much a part of his mythology as the expression of his genius. "In attempting to escape the role, at once sub- and super-human, in which he found himself, he sought to outrage his public into an awareness of his most human pain," wrote Ralph Ellison in *Shadow and Act*. "Instead, he made himself notorious and in the end became unsure whether his fans came to enjoy his art or to be entertained by 'the world's greatest junky,' the 'supreme hipster.' "

The community of musicians who had become accustomed to the relentless brilliance and unsurpassed vitality of Bird's music and the seeming indestructibility of his constitution found his downfall particularly hard to abide or even acknowledge. His colleagues and admirers could only stare and pray that it wasn't happening, that it wasn't as bad as it looked. They could only hope that Bird might pull himself out of it as he had so many times before. One night at Birdland in 1955, he reached out desperately to Dizzy Gillespie, like a drowning man going down for the last time . . .

"Diz," he stammered, "why don't you save me?"

"What could I do?" Dizzy wanted to know.

"I dunno but just save me, save me, man!"

Gillespie was horrified to realize at that moment that he was as powerless to help Bird in 1955 as he had been ten years earlier in Los Angeles. Bird's closest friends and associates had become nothing more than helpless spectators, overwhelmed by the final scenes of some tragic real-life opera.

Bird had long since become Jackie McLean's champion, sitting out in the audience at Birdland and loudly applauding McLean's solos to get the people to take notice of him, rushing over and giving the young saxophonist a kiss on the neck after his set was over. Because McLean was such an obvious and unabashed prodigy of everything Charlie Parker represented musically, the years of Bird's decline were particularly difficult for him. Not only was their relationship emotionally charged by this strong mentor-prodigy bond, but they were also fellow addicts at a time when Bird was slipping away and McLean's own addiction was hardening. McLean was now in his early twenties, nationally recognized but four years into the life of a heroin addict.

"He knew I loved him so much that he could do anything to me," McLean reflected. "He'd see me when I was getting ready to work with Miles, backstage at Birdland, watch me come in and rush into the bathroom and take ten dollars out of my pocket. 'Bird, *please.*' 'Don't worry, you gonna get it back,' he'd say. Maybe, a month later. He used to borrow my horn, and then pawn it."

At a party in the Bronx in 1954, McLean had met the woman he would marry. Clarise Simmons, known as Dollie, was a warm and exquisitely beautiful girl from a West Indian family. "She didn't know anything about drugs or their implications," explained McLean. "Her family came from Antigua, and they were different from American blacks in that they were much more sheltered. We fell in love as soon as we met, and I wasn't about to tell her anything about my habit. But after we got married, being so close, it finally came to pass, of course, that she found out. She used every method she could to help me, walking the streets with me from doctor's office to doctor's office. Back in the fifties, nobody could help you, not Bellevue, not any hospital you could think of. And finally, she would tell me I could sign myself into Rikers Island. I said, 'But, Dollie, that's *jail.* I'll be signing myself into a *penitentiary.*' She said, 'Anything beats this.' "

After Dollie became pregnant with their first child, MacLean's struggle to get off heroin became all the more urgent and grievous. Nothing worked for him—locking himself away in rooms, entrusting his money to others on tour, combinations of drugs, signing himself into the U.S. Public Health Services Hospital, affiliated with the federal prison, at Lexington. After his first arrest, in 1957, he was dragged into the maw of the

criminal-justice system in New York and deprived of his cabaret card—
the most common punishment for any musician with a narcotics conviction because it forced him to look for gigs out of town or in Europe. For
someone like McClean, a New York musician with a family, it was particularly cruel, tantamount to exile.

As Bird began to fade, McLean's mounting tribulations became all the
more distressing for him to witness. "He always wanted me not to use,"
McLean recognized. "He loved Dollie and my family." Everyone who
knew Bird well would have some story of him at the end, all of them
heartbreaking experiences of his deterioration and helplessness. For
McLean, it came one night when he and Dollie were hanging out with
Bird at the Open Door. Bird wanted to jam, but nobody seemed to care
who he was. Stone broke, savagely depressed, he was trying to cadge some
money for drinks. When they went to Arthur's, off Seventh Avenue,
where they had to talk the owner into letting Bird play, it all seemed to hit
him at once, how low he had sunk. It was one of those soul-shattering
moments when the veil was ripped away and all Charlie Parker could do
was stare into the abyss of what had happened to him and what was going
to happen. He was completely overwhelmed not only by what had happened to him but also by what had happened to Jackie, a whole generation of musicians, and a whole community in their wake.

"Man, I feel so sorry for this whole thing you're doing," Bird told him.
"You should be like Horace Silver or one of those cats. You got your wife
and she's pregnant, man, and here you are strung out. I feel like it's my
fault. I want you to kick me right in the ass."

When Bird bent over to receive the kick, McLean was mortified.
There they were, right out in front of the club. Charlie Parker had been a
god in the Village, and there he was bending over to be kicked like a
mangy cur by someone who had idolized him from the age of sixteen.

"Man, I can't do that," McLean told him.

"Here I am, begging pennies for drinks, *begging* people to buy drinks
for me, and putting myself down. And here I am begging people to let me
play! I am *Charlie Parker*, and I have to beg people to let me *play*! Kick
me, Jackie, and don't you ever allow this to happen to you."

McLean still wasn't about to comply, but Bird was insistent. "He had
a very deep voice, and he was saying very loud, 'Kick me in my ass.' Like

he spoke very proper, he said, 'Jackie McLean, I want you to kick me in my ass . . . I want you to kick me in the ass for allowing myself to get into this position.' So I stepped back and just playfully brought my foot up, you know. I didn't kick him. Nobody could kick Bird."

But McLean was capable of becoming furious at him. When McLean was playing the Montmartre and got sick and Ahmed Basheer offered to take him home, Bird told McLean that he would mind his alto, and he promptly hocked it. This wasn't the first time it had happened, but McLean was incensed. Even though Bird had the instrument back to him in time for his next gig at the Open Door, McLean wouldn't talk to him. At the end of the night, Bird approached him.

"Going uptown? I'll get a cab for us."

"I'll get my own, Bird," McLean said and turned angrily away.

On March 9, 1955, on an uptown bus, McLean read about the death of Charlie Parker. The article in the *New York Post* paid more attention to Bird's drug use and the fact that he had died in the apartment of a wealthy white woman than to the passing of one of the greatest artists of the twentieth century.

McLean got off the bus at the next stop and wandered down the street, weeping so uncontrollably that he didn't know where he was. If only I had known, McLean kept thinking. If only I had known it would be the last time I would ever see him, I would have shared that cab with Charlie Parker to the ends of the earth.

Bird was supposed have gone to Boston to play Storyville but had fallen desperately ill. Instead, he had gone to the suite of the Baroness Pannonica de Koenigswarter at the Stanhope Hotel, looking for refuge and solace. Nica, the legendary jazz baroness, was a great patroness of the musicians, especially Monk and Bird. Alarmed by his appearance, Nica had asked if she should call a doctor, but Bird had asked for a drink instead. He was settled in an armchair, watching jugglers on a TV variety show, and she was in another room. Nica would always claim that she heard a loud crack of thunder at the moment he died.

The body arrived at Bellevue more than five hours after his death, marked John Parker, age fifty-three. Bird, only thirty-four years old, was so physically ruined that he looked twenty years older. Death was attributed to lumbar pneumonia, but everybody knew that the real cause was a profound exhaustion that had consumed him, body and soul. The two women in his life, Doris and Chan, began fighting bitterly over his body. Charlie Parker was buried in Kansas City despite his stating that he never wanted to return there, his tombstone displaying the wrong date of his death. There are those who say that they observed a golden nimbus around his head as he lay in his coffin before burial.

Almost immediately, the legend began appearing on the walls of buildings and subways: BIRD LIVES. Jackie McLean could never figure out who was doing it; in fact, the poet Ted Joans was responsible. Joans lived above the San Remo bar in the Village and had set out with three of his friends in four different directions after Parker's death, like disciples spreading the gospel after the crucifixion. That first weekend of his death, others seized on the slogan and began writing it all over the city—BIRD LIVES—the graffiti of a growing alternative cultural identity. Suddenly it seemed to be everywhere, on subways and buses, in the johns of subterranean bars from the Village to Harlem, spreading quickly to all the boroughs, and thence out across the country like some proclamation from the underground heralding the coming of a new age—

BIRD LIVES!

However one chose to regard the demise of Charlie Parker, whether he'd destroyed himself or was victimized by the society he lived in, it hardly mattered in the end. Parker had become an epochal symbol of enduring truth, love, freedom, and the incandescent creative life of pure genius. The facts of his life may have involved drugs, but all of it would now be woven together into a myth of terrible beauty and incorporated into the tapestry of his music, which would live on forever.

The myth of Bird had always been complex, but at the center of it was Icarus, who had had insisted on flying too high, too close to the burning radiance of the sun, and had plummeted to his death, the wax on his wings melted by the heat. But the myth went much deeper, for underneath everything else was the sense of a shaman's journey, the notion that Bird's flight through the night skies of America had been undertaken as a form of ritual self-sacrifice on behalf of many others, who would now be healed and lifted by it. The voyage of his life was over, but his journey into the American imagination was just beginning.

In the wake of Bird's death, the journey of musicians into and out of heroin would continue to shape jazz, and people would be drawn to the music like moths seeking the brilliance of a lone bulb burning in a darkened room. All through the 1950s, bebop was the touchstone of those who walked the jagged improvisational edge through a shadowy human geography of the night.

Jackie McLean would continue recording fine jazz for Prestige and Blue Note and would become one of the prime forces of the hard bop school in the 1950s, but would remain unable to stay off heroin for any length of time. In fact, his plight would turn out to be the subject of Jack Gelbar's groundbreaking 1959 play at the Living Theatre, *The Connection,* in which McLean would perform brilliantly as one of the heroin-addicted musicians—a play that mirrored the predicament of his life so closely that there would be virtually no transition as he stepped from street to stage. He would tour Europe with the production, but with two arrests for possession, he lost an appeal of his three-year-old narcotics conviction after his return and came to experience all of the horrors and inhumanities of prison.

Everyone who knew Jackie McLean during those years would remark that he was an enormously intelligent, likable, talented man, a man with a good heart and a fine wife and beautiful kids but a man who suffered from a seemingly unconquerable problem called heroin addiction. In the early 1960s, he met a bold and progressive doctor named Marie Nyswander, who was developing an experimental program for addicts based on the use of methadone. McLean would be among her first patients to use the substance successfully as a bridge back to a life of normalcy. Eventually he would work in the burgeoning methadone program as a counselor and wean himself from everything, but it would be twenty-five torturous years from the time of his first snort of heroin before he became completely drug free. After becoming a professor of music at the University of Hartford, McLean would reclaim more than his life. When he and Dollie opened the Artists Collective at Albany Avenue and Woodland Street, in one of the worst neighborhoods of the city, he would rescue a significant sector of Hartford's African American community as well. On the day McLean arrived to check out the abandoned school building that they would renovate for the collective, he couldn't help but notice the name Parker on the door lock; as he emerged into the urine-soaked, littered hallway, he felt the unmistakable spirit of Bird there with him. In place of litter, crime, crack, and broken bottles, the Artists Collective would offer music, theater, dance, and education. "It all comes from bebop," McLean said. "It's not just music; it's a movement."

## VI. Angel in Moloch

THE SEASON OF WILD form began for Allen Ginsberg in San Francisco in early August of 1955 with a snippet from his notebook on a sunshine-filled afternoon: "I saw the best mind angel headed hipster damned."

Seated in front of his secondhand typewriter at the desk by the window facing Montgomery Street, only blocks from the two-year-old City Lights bookstore, which would figure so prominently in the history of what he was about to write, Ginsberg decided to try something very different from anything he had ever written. He reached for the new form, discarding the short line in favor of the long "saxophone line" favored by Kerouac—the style inspired by Charlie Parker, among others.

*I saw the best minds of my generation*
*generation destroyed by madness*
*starving, mystical, naked*

Ginsberg later deleted *mystical* in favor of *hysterical,* which would change the whole tone of the poem. It was an apt change, considering the life he had led for the past ten years. Since adolescence, in fact, Ginsberg had been lacerated by the confrontation with his own confused self-image and identity. At the age of nineteen, he had fancied himself a Times Square Rimbaud of the New Vision. By the time he came to write *Howl,* in the summer of 1955, he had been the product of a long and Kafkaesque alienation, but he had also become a young man capable of brutal self-honesty and expression. Ten years had passed since he and Kerouac had stood in Times Square, sublimely stoned on marijuana and Benzedrine, perceiving "the Great Molecular Comedown." Now, at the age of twenty-nine, the whole of his difficult life would become substance for the poem he was writing.

"That first line of 'Howl' could never have been written without having encountered Carl Solomon, in his bathrobe, bloated from insulin shock treatments, on my first day at the Columbia Presbyterian Psychiatric Institute," Ginsberg acknowledged. "That was 1949, when I was being admitted to the nuthouse in lieu of an actual jail sentence after being implicated in the larcenies of Herbert Huncke and a band of his fellow junkie burglars then congregating at my apartment and using the place to stash their loot. Huncke was sentenced to spend the rest of the decade in jail, but it was really Solomon who became a metaphor at that moment for what seemed to me the relativity of any definition of so-called madness in what appeared to be a completely insane mechanistic society that crushed the human spirit."

The first line of *Howl* was certainly embroidered with this experience and with virtually everything else that had ever happened to Ginsberg since—"the scene I had been a part of at the apartment on West 115th Street," the poet elucidated, "the sound of an iron jail-cell door slamming behind me and the harsh slap of a detective interrogating me about my homosexuality after my arrest. It could never have been written without having known people like Solomon and Burroughs's wife, Joan, these brilliant but dislocated minds on a collision course with disaster. It couldn't have been written without them any more than it could have been written without having had a mother like the one I had."

In a single line, Ginsberg had drawn upon all of those thoughts and feelings and applied them to all of the broken, thwarted, isolated, and alienated spirits he had known over the last ten years, extrapolated from them in a way that encompassed what he perceived as a spiritual holocaust affecting his entire generation. But if the first line of *Howl* was autobiography that would also serve as generational metaphor, the second—

*dragging themselves through the negro streets at dawn*
*looking for an angry fix*

—presented a juxtaposition of generational destruction and drug use that would become epochal.

When it was over, Allen Ginsberg had composed his "lament for the Lamb in America," and within the poem's Whitmanesque cataloguing he had also definitively rendered the small subculture of drug users he had known so intimately for the past decade, calling them "angelheaded hipsters." Like Kerouac, Ginsberg had incorporated the consciousness of marijuana into the writing itself, into what he later called "the mechanisms of surrealist or ideogrammatic method, the juxtaposition of disparate images to create a gap of understanding which the mind fills in with a flash of recognition of the unstated relationship (as in 'hydrogen jukebox')." He was writing poetry exactly like the "eyeball kicks" he had first observed in Cézanne's use of hot and cold colors when he had smoked marijuana and gone to the museum to study his paintings as a Columbia student. The aesthetics of *Howl* were therefore only part of the reason why Allen Ginsberg would always claim that for a certain kind of person, marijuana could offer the possibility of an "educational experience." Moreover, as one substance had helped fashion the whole style of the first part of the poem, another would crack open the central metaphor of the second.

The image that would define the countercultural perception of American society more than any other appeared to Ginsberg as a peyote vision in the night sky of San Francisco several weeks after beginning the poem. It was not the first time Ginsberg had ingested the little, round dark-green pincushion-like cactus called *Lophophora williamsii,* which grows wild in the Rio Grande Valley. The Aztecs had worshipped the cactus as *peyotl,* "flesh of the gods," and their Spanish conquerors had demonized it as *raiz diabolica,* "diabolical root." Ginsberg had taken peyote not long after arriving in San Francisco. Staring out the window of his Nob Hill apartment, the Sir Francis Drake Hotel began to transmogrify into what seemed a giant Cyclops rising malevolently out of the "timeless city gloom." The more he stared at the hotel in that state of consciousness, the more it looked like the skull face of a robot—impassive, inhuman, antenna-like.

Now, in the middle of composing an epic poem about a monolithic social system, Ginsberg was also in the company of Peter Orlovsky, the "eternal boy" he had met after moving to San Francisco who had become his lover—"the fulfillment of all my desires ever since I was nine." Ginsberg and Orlovsky had eaten the cactus buttons together, and as the peyote began to overtake them and they hopped on a clanging trolley descending Powell Street, there came a wrenching moment when Ginsberg was horrified to perceive nothing but vacancy and emptiness in his lover—"two phantom ghosts with empty eyes, laughing fiendishly." Perhaps it was all of those feelings of alienation and emptiness combining with the dislocating transport of the peyote itself that began to amplify Ginsberg's perception of the Sir Francis Drake Hotel looming before them as dark tower in the night, a smoking death head in the red glare of the city.

"*Moloch! Moloch!*" Ginsberg began muttering, overwhelmed by the image of the ancient Cannanite fire god and parents burning their children in ritual sacrifice to the horned beast. He and Peter wandered down Powell Street like lost children and went into a cafeteria at the foot of the hotel, "deep in the hellish vale," where he began scribbling furiously, a biblical prophet thundering against the soul-murdering iniquity of a social system that consumed its own children.

It would always seem fitting to Ginsberg that the central metaphor of a poem marking the first shot in a cultural war that would permeate and polarize American life for the next half century had been catalyzed by a powerful psychoactive cactus that had been embraced as a religious sacrament by the Plains Indians at the exact time that the buffalo were disappearing and the once-great tribes were being herded onto reservations, their cultures decimated.

"What I had heard about peyote was that it was a medicine which could sustain an otherwise troubled people by making every one of its users a shaman who could find salvation through the natural elements of a God-given world," Ginsberg recounted. "Peyote was regarded by Native Americans as the vegetable incarnation of a deity, as the means of ascending toward God, a panacea in medicine, a key which could open to them all the glories of another world."

From the turn of the century, when more than fifty Native American tribes had adopted its use, Christian missionaries and public officials had tried to stamp out the peyote cults, despite evidence that the use of the substance was not corrupting the participants. The practice of the peyote ritual had not only survived but flourished, with a number of whites even observing that the use of peyote seemed to help Native Americans lead better lives and forsake alcohol, which had plagued their cultures ever since it had been introduced by the Europeans.

Saturday-night tribal peyote meetings were held inside a tepee around a fire in front of a crescent-moon altar to "father peyote," and would last until sometime after sunrise. The ritual would be presided over by the roadman or road chief, who represented the Great Spirit and showed "the peyote road." Those who took part would prepare themselves with fasting and prayer. The fleshy slices of the cactus, called mescal buttons, would be dried in the sun; then the wrinkled little brown disks were crushed and boiled in water or eaten raw. Given the nauseating taste of the substance, purgative vomiting and the spitting up of bile were integral parts of the experience, along with singing and chanting, meditation and prayer. The fire chief would guard the door, tend the stick, and stoke the ever-burning fire; the cedar chief, representative of the Holy Ghost, would bring disoriented participants back by waving cedar incense; the drum chief would keep up the ever-present beat. As the night wore on, the drum would start to sound as though it were coming from inside the soul. Voices would begin to speak out of the rattle. Thoughts would escape out of the head like a stampeding herd, and visions would begin dancing in the fire . . .

"The legend of peyote was that its very use was a prayer," Ginsberg elaborated. "It was said that it contained the whole universe, that it could show you everything there was to see—all the people in the world, all the different animals, everything that was in the sky, everything under the earth. Peyote could turn your eyes into X-rays so that you could see the insides of things; it was like telepathy, like electricity, and those who took it believed they could send their thoughts to loved ones twenty miles away."

In 1936, Antonin Artaud had traveled to northern Mexico to experience the peyote rite of the Tarahumara Indians. While the true secrets of the peyote dance had been denied him, Artaud had taken the substance and had heard "human body, Spleen, Liver, Lungs, Brain, thundering at the four corners of the Divine Infinite." The experience had been a psychic ordeal as well as a spiritual revelation, and the images he brought back with him—the signs and crosses, the movements of the peyote dance, the ritual slaughter of the bull and the drinking of its blood—would haunt him for the rest of his life. *The Peyote Dance,* the book documenting his struggle to integrate what had been an overwhelming mystical experience into his religious and mental being, would not be translated until the early 1970s, but it had already become the stuff of legend in bohemian circles during the mid-1950s, when peyote became available via COD shipments from Smith's Cactus Ranch in East Texas for eight dollars for one hundred buttons and from a store on East Second Street in New York. Suddenly the vision-vaulting substance of the Yaqui and the Kickapoo was available to the subterraneans of the San Remo bar, where, as the writer Terry Southern would recall, "people started chopping them up and eating them like figs." Ginsberg had ingested the buttons for the first time in April 1952 on a beautiful Sunday in his father's backyard in Paterson, New Jersey, gagging down a second chunk before opening his journal to describe his experiences. But that first time had been mild compared with the time when Moloch appeared to him in the San Francisco night like a vision escaping from his soul, turning him into the shaman poet of a new generation.

## VIII. A Conspiracy to Overthrow Civilization

ALLEN GINSBERG had never read a poem aloud in public before his reading of *Howl* at the Six Gallery on Thursday, October 13, 1955. The reading would become legendary, an important chapter in the history of the American counterculture, the story of how five poets—Philip Lamantia, Gary Snyder, Philip Whalen, Michael McClure, and Ginsberg—would come together for an evening to read from their works in an experimental bohemian gallery in a converted automobile-repair shop on Union and Fillmore in a city that by that time had become a remarkable amalgamation of every conceivable alternative lifestyle in America.

By the mid-1950s, the North Beach bohemia that had risen amid the old Italian community had become a hothouse of the arts, populated by Abstract Expressionist painters, performance artists, poets, jazz musicians, experimental theater artists, underground filmmakers, modern dancers, and painters' models who looked like coffeehouse Madonnas in their black leotards. With its thriving community of Zen students, spiritual seekers, and cultural and political radicals of every conceivable stripe, including gays, lesbians, pacifists, anarchists, Wobblies, Communists, protofeminists, vegetarians, and sexual libertarians, the city had become a rich oasis of radicalism and free-thinking eccentricity in the parched and repressed cultural desert of Joseph McCarthy's America. It had also become a magnet for every conceivable type of drug user: benny eaters and poppers of barbiturate goofballs, tea heads and junkies, the peyotized and the bemushroomed. *Lophophora williamsii* was the talk of North Beach that season, when "there was a mystery about drugs," as the poet Michael McClure remembered it, "and they were taken for joy, for consciousness, for spiritual elevation, or what the Romantic poet Keats had called 'Soul-making.' "

The gathering was organized by Ginsberg himself and publicized with handbills that he passed out at a number of North Beach bars: "Six poets at the Six Gallery, Kenneth Rexroth, MC. Remarkable collection of angels all gathered at once in the same spot. Wine, music, dancing girls, serious poetry, free satori. Small collection for wine and postcards. Charming event."

The "charming event" would be chronicled by Jack Kerouac in *The Dharma Bums:* "It was a mad night. And I was the one who got things jumping by going around collecting dimes and quarters from the rather stiff audience standing around in the gallery and coming back with three huge gallon jugs of California burgundy."

The evening featured an unusual group of charismatic young poets, all reading from works that were redolent of Eastern religion and philosophy, pacifism, ecological awareness, back-to-nature rusticity, human rights, and visionary transcendentalism—all strains that would characterize the flowering of the counterculture during the next decade. Dressed in a gray suit and tie, the evening's main event, Allen Ginsberg, was described by Kerouac as a "hornrimmed intellectual hepcat with wild black hair." Nipping liberally from one of the large jugs of wine, he was inebriated by the time it was his turn to read.

Ginsberg began reading in a "small and intensely lucid voice," and as he got going, his voice began to rise, and he started to come alive. Kerouac was banging on the wine jug after each line and shouting *"Go!"* and soon the 150 people packed into the little gallery were hanging on every line and yelling, *"Go! Go!"* By the time it was over, Ginsberg was utterly spent, in tears, and the audience was stunned.

Like many others present that night, Michael McClure instinctively realized that the mere reading of the poem had left the audience "standing in wonder, or cheering and wondering, but knowing at the deepest level that a barrier had been broken, that a human voice and body had been hurled against the harsh wall of America and its supporting armies and navies and academies and institutions and ownership systems and power-support bases." As McClure saw it, that night marked Ginsberg's "metamorphosis from a quiet brilliant burning Bohemian scholar, trapped by his flames and repressions, to epic vocal bard. Shelley had made the same transformation."

So began the San Francisco Poetry Renaissance. That night, Lawrence Ferlinghetti, the poet, publisher, and proprietor of the City Lights bookstore, sat down at his desk and typed out a telegram to Ginsberg that echoed Ralph Waldo Emerson's salute to Walt Whitman on his poem *Leaves of Grass*—"I greet you at the beginning of a great career. When do I get the manuscript?" Within the year, the San Francisco Poetry Renaissance would succeed in revitalizing poetry as an oral form in America.

*Howl and Other Poems* was published in October 1956 as Number 4 of Ferlinghetti's small, square-format City Lights Pocket Poets Series. The publication of the book in the new paperback format, with its stark black-and-white cover, assured that it would be affordable, but its notoriety was all but guaranteed by what followed. The arbiters of public morality—the censors of the U.S. Customs office in San Francisco—may have been disturbed by the poem's focus on drugs, but they were far more outraged by its explicit sexual content. As Ginsberg acknowledged, "I may have conjured the pleasure of a 'teahead joyride,' but what really summoned down the fury of Moloch was writing about the 'cocks of the grandfathers of Kansas.' "

On March 25, 1957, the San Francisco office of U.S. Customs, under the direction of Chester McPhee, declared the book obscene and seized

520 copies of the second, three-thousand-copy shipment of the book, which had arrived from its British printer. The American Civil Liberties Union then challenged the legality of the seizure in court.

In the trial that followed, Lawrence Ferlinghetti argued passionately that *Howl* was the most important poem published in America since the Second World War, possibly since T. S. Eliot's *Waste Land.* Ginsberg wasn't obscene, claimed Ferlinghetti; he was merely an artist expressing a point of view contrary to the prevailing philosophy of the times: "It is not the poet but what he observes which is revealed as obscene," he wrote in the *San Francisco Chronicle.* "The great obscene wastes of *Howl* are the sad wastes of the mechanized world, lost among atom bombs and insane nationalisms."

On May 21, after the U.S. Customs Bureau in Washington had advised the San Francisco office not to take further action, the confiscated copies of the book were released. Then, in the first week of June, Captain William Hanrahan of the Juvenile Department of the San Francisco Police Department arrested Ferlinghetti and his bookstore manager, Shigeyoshi Murao, on the grounds that the books were not fit for children to read. Both were taken to the Hall of Justice and fingerprinted.

During the celebrated trial that continued over the summer, outrage over the poem and over its suppression steadily mounted, generating passion on both sides. By the time the trial was over and Judge Clayton W. Horn had released his twelve-point opinion ("12. In considering material claimed to be obscene it is well to remember the motto: *Honi soit qui mal y pense.* [Shame to him who thinks evil thoughts]"), ten thousand copies of the book were in print.

By seeking to protect the public from reading about people "who let themselves be fucked in the ass by saintly motorcyclists, and screamed with joy," the conservative advocates of censorship succeeded in doing more than anyone else to spread the news of the poem about a "teahead joyride" and the "peyote solidities of halls."

*Howl* contained no fewer than twelve explicit references to the use of illicit drugs, in effect proclaiming them holy. Ginsberg had sat on a San Francisco bus, weeping as he wrote what would become the "Footnote," the coda and final movement of the poem, the spiritual counterpoint to the fiery indignation of the Moloch section. Before the poem was over, he had proclaimed everything holy: friends, lovers, jazz bands, instruments, every private part of the body, every conceivable sex act, the middle class, cities, visions, time, eternity, the soul, his mother in the insane asylum, his father's cock, the heavens, the cafeterias, the rivers, the pavement, the sea, the desert, the very shit in the toilet, the typewriter, poetry, the voice, heaven, ecstasy, "the Angel in Moloch," Everyman was holy, Everything was holy, holy in "the bop apocalypse."

"Virtually from that moment on, I knew that the fundamental issues of drug use in America in our time were going to become inextricable from issues of free speech and First Amendment rights and obscenity laws," Ginsberg asserted. "The scenario would soon enough repeat itself with Burroughs and *Naked Lunch* . . . In the end, I knew you couldn't have it both ways. You couldn't have a society that allowed free and unfettered creative expression, which also might incorporate material about the use of consciousness-altering substances, without a significant segment of the population becoming interested in their use as well. The use of drugs was going to be a cutting-edge issue—one of the fundamental ways we would define ourselves as a people in the second half of the twentieth century."

*Howl* was only the beginning. In the rapid metamorphosis of the work from poem to cultural event, history would confer upon Allen Ginsberg the role of ambassador of an entirely new cultural sensibility, particularly after Jack Kerouac's *On the Road* was finally published in September of 1957 by Viking Press, and word about the almost completely unknown author and his book about a new generation of rootless young people driving across America and looking for kicks started spreading like wildfire. *On the Road* was a book that the age seemed to demand, with an audience of high-school and college students who seemed to know exactly what it was about even before opening its cover.

Almost as soon as the Beat Generation began emerging as a cultural movement that transcended its literature, the media spin became vitriolic. The common thread of attack began with the viewpoint that the Beats were nothing but a bunch of juvenile delinquents and drugged eccentrics who refused to grow up and take responsibility for themselves, producing an irrelevant and misguided literature. Their criminal activities and use of drugs made them a menace to society; their moral decadence undermined not only law and order but national security. They were deviants, dropouts, homosexuals, drunkards, pill takers, junkies, and convicts. Liberals decried their apolitical stance; conservatives viewed them as a threat to middle-class morality and ethics. An article by Norman Podhoretz in the spring 1958 issue of the the *Partisan Review,* "The Know-Nothing Bohemians," typified the accusations. Podhoretz, later to become one of the nation's leading neoconservatives, claimed that the motto of Kerouac and his colleagues was as follows: "Kill the intellectuals who can talk coherently, kill the people who can sit still for five minutes at a time, kill those incomprehensible characters who are capable of getting seriously involved with a woman, a job, a cause." What the Beat Generation really represented, Podhoretz claimed in *Esquire,* was nothing less than "a conspiracy to overthrow civilization."

The ferocity of the attacks, as well as their sanctimonious bombast, only drew more young readers to investigate the literature. Poetry readings were soon booming in North Beach at places like the Co-Existence Bagel Shop, the hungry i, the Gas Haven, and the Place, attracting to the city larger groups of kids who had read *Howl* and *On the Road* and had gone on the road themselves to search hungrily for some part of the experience that they had perceived in the writing. When Herb Caen of the *San Francisco Chronicle* derisively labeled them beatniks in his column (because, like the Soviet Sputnik then orbiting the earth, they were so absolutely "out there"), he also observed that "the smell of marijuana is becoming stronger than the smell of garlic" in the North Beach area. The police began increasing their presence, and by the "beatnik summer" of 1958 a crackdown was in full swing, drawing a line that would merely succeed in charging the scene with more energy and excitement. What had begun with the publication of the novel had quickly turned into a media storm that would launch *On the Road,* its author, and a whole way of life to the level of a national industry.

The advent of the Beat Generation brought nothing but grief for Jack Kerouac, however. As he was writing *The Dharma Bums,* Grove Press released *The Subterraneans,* which was immediately savaged by the press. The reviews plunged Kerouac into a black despair. Worse than the outright attacks were the parodies, an endless barrage of articles and commentaries and shows that trivialized and ridiculed him. Kerouac responded by going on six-day drinking binges, lurching from bar to bar, making pathetic spectacles of himself. For the next three years, he would watch, helplessly drunk, bitter, and bewildered, suffering a kind of nervous breakdown as the media fed the public their stereotypical images of the beatnik: a dirty, goateed, black-clad, pacifist pot smoker wearing sandals, playing bongos, snapping his fingers, obsessed with jazz and poetry, drinking espresso, and uttering phrases like "Cool, daddy!" Before long, the Beat Generation was being turned into cliché television fare such as the character of Maynard G. Krebs in *The Many Loves of Dobie Gillis*. The more his audience seemed to become interested in marijuana as a result of reading his books, the more Kerouac sought to disassociate himself from what Gilbert Millstein had called the "readily recognizable stigmata" of drug use in his rave review of the book in *The New York Times*. And considering the events in California and the fate of Neal Cassady—busted for possession and sale of three joints and sentenced to two terms of five years to life to run concurrently in San Quentin—Kerouac's was a well-founded apprehension.

Ginsberg and Kerouac reacted differently to Cassady's arrest and incarceration. Though he felt partly responsible due to the publicity unleashed by his novel, Kerouac distanced himself almost immediately; Ginsberg, on the other hand, was galvanized into action.

"To me, Neal's arrest was graphic proof of how the whole phenomenon of the Beat Generation could be stigmatized because of the use of these substances. It was becoming clear to me that the only way people like Neal and myself who smoked marijuana as part of a way of life would ever be safe was when the laws were changed."

# 3

# Psychedelic Spring

**"** In the beginning was the Turn On. The flash, the illumination. The electric trip. The sudden bolt of energy that starts the new system. **"**

—Timothy Leary, *High Priest*, 1968

## I. The Buzz Begins

"WHAT WAS IT LIKE IN THE BEGINNING? Where to even *begin,* what to *read,* what to *do*!"

Seated at the round glass table on his patio, Timothy Leary waxed with the enthusiasm of a little boy as he recounted the early days of the Harvard Psilocybin Project.

"Remember, here I was, a guy who never had even considered anything like smoking marijuana. In many ways, I was a very straight, conventional scientist. We just started taking off. The idea was, just go! Those first few weeks we just went to each other's houses and took it. In front of fires. Candles. Music. We were like the Wright brothers, you know—*'Hey, watch that tree!'*—soaring off beyond normal consciousness; then we'd get lost somewhere and come back for a landing and talk about it. Wow! Did that happen to *you?* There were no maps or guides in Western psychological literature to describe these states. We were completely on our own. Oh, it was exciting, wonderful, those days. Such brave explorers we were!"

It was during the summer of 1960 that Leary first ingested *Psilocybe mexicana,* the mysterious magic mushrooms of Mexico, on the sloping lawn of the Casa los Moros, the rambling white stucco villa that he and his colleagues had rented for four consecutive summers in Cuernavaca. During the experience, his mind had completely deliquesced, opening to the most enthralling visions: "Nile palaces, Hindu temples, Babylonian boudoirs, Bedouin pleasure tents, gem flashery, woven silk growns breathing color, mosaics flaming with Muzo emeralds, Burma rubies, Ceylon sapphires." He continued to liquefy with the passing moments, slipping further and further back down the "recapitulation tube," so far back that he became the first living thing . . .

The whole voyage had lasted a little over four hours. "Like almost everyone who has had the veil drawn, I came back a changed man." But what changes, what lessons!—the implications of it all were staggering. For Leary, the experience had been like a personalized guided tour through the Technicolor wonders of the brain and nervous system and into consciousness itself. "I learned that normal consciousness is one drop in an ocean of intelligence. That consciousness and intelligence can be systematically expanded. That the brain can be reprogrammed."

The next lesson was that you needed a day or two just to sit with it, absorb what had happened, let it settle a little. The first place he went was nearby Tepztlán, to see David McClelland, who had no idea what Leary was talking about when he showed up and started ranting about how everything had come "alive," how he had actually "become" a musical instrument. McClelland, a scholarly and progressive Quaker psychologist, couldn't fathom what these Aztec mushrooms might have to do with the transactional psychology he had hired Leary to teach at Harvard the year before, but Leary kept insisting that he had experienced the most vitalizing "transaction" of his life and that the mushrooms could "revolutionize" psychology.

"It's axiomatic in psychology that true insight and self-awareness is the key to any real behavior change," Leary argued passionately, "and here is the possibility of *instantaneous self-insight*! And if you don't believe me, David, well, just come along and eat some for yourself!"

McClelland agreed to return with Leary to the villa in Cuernavaca, only to find that a maid had destroyed the remaining supply of mushrooms. As head of the Center for Personality Research and Leary's faculty adviser, he was wary of potential administrative and political problems when Leary began proposing "systematic" experiments involving the mushrooms at Harvard, but hadn't William James experienced peyote and written about it in *The Varieties of Religious Experience*? He felt that Leary deserved at least to test his proposition and gave the initial approval for the research to go ahead. And that was how it had all started in the fall after Leary returned from Mexico—drug experiments at Harvard, the apotheosis of American civilization and higher learning, the cradle of the liberal technocracy, where the elite managers of the American Century were cultivated and intellectually groomed like Thoroughbred horses.

The problem of the mushroom supply was solved straight away when Leary learned from a graduate student named George Litwin that a chemist at the Sandoz Corporation, Dr. Albert Hofmann, had recently synthesized the psychoactive molecule of the mushroom, calling it psilocybin. Leary quickly dispatched a letter on Harvard stationery to the New Jersey branch office of Sandoz. Just before Thanksgiving of 1960, the much-anticipated package arrived at Leary's office, containing four brown bottles filled with little pink tablets. "I shook out a few of the pills, which glistened like pink pearls in my hand," Leary later wrote. "We stared at them, thinking solemn thoughts. The lives of all of us would be transformed by these pills."

Truer words were never written. The great time of metamorphosis had arrived. Before long, the look of Dr. Timothy Leary's small office on the first floor of the Center for Personality Research, at 5 Divinity Avenue, began to change. Passersby noticed the Moroccan motif. Thick carpets, white pillows on the floor. No furniture. Candles. Brass trays. The buzz began in the department; something very unusual was going on in there . . .

"First I read my William James, then somebody suggested Huxley, *The Doors of Perception,* and there it all was, the man had taken mescaline and shucked off the mind and awakened to a vision of eternity, and from reading him, I learned what it was to relate the chaotic events of an activated brain to the perennial issues of ontology."

Ever the magniloquent lecturer, Leary gesticulated against the panoramic view of Benedict Canyon as he spoke.

"Then I found out Huxley was actually in town, as a visiting lecturer at MIT. Synchronicity! I wrote him a letter, and suddenly there he was, long legs and brilliant mind and all, but starting to get frail from his throat cancer, just finishing *Island* at that time. We had lunch, and soon he was sitting in on meetings, and then there we were, taking the drug together in my house in front of my fireplace, talking about what we were going to do with this 'incredible philosopher's stone,' as he called it."

It was Huxley who first cautioned Leary, telling him that there were people in the society who would do anything to stop this kind of research. The celebrated British author of *The Doors of Perception* understood very well that the first drug prohibition went all the way back to the Bible, to the forbidden fruit of the Tree of Knowledge. Huxley gave Leary one simple message: Go slow. Be a cheerleader for slow, scholarly evolution. Work privately, within the institution. First, quietly initiate the intelligent rich, the scholars, and the artists; that was how everything of value had been passed on anyway. Later, when Leary began to explore the erotic component of the psychedelic experience, how it could open up the channels of sensuality and turn sex into "mythic mating" and the "cellular and neurological merging of archetypes," Huxley would beseech him not to let the "sexual cat out of the bag."

"That first year, there was a group of some thirty-five of us," Leary continued, "professors, instructors, graduate students, organizing in what became the Harvard Psychedelic Research Project. We were sharing high-dosage psychedelic experiences conducted in an atmosphere of aesthetic inquiry, inner search, philosophical inquiry, courage, openness, and always with a lot of humor."

Leary gazed off at the hills, squinting at the neighboring houses' pools glinting in the smoggy Los Angeles sunshine. He was white-haired and near the end of his life but sharp as a tack. There were still a few good years left before cancer would begin wasting him so horribly.

"What was the whole ballgame about? From the very beginning, we wanted to take the power to change and treat and diagnose minds away from the doctor, and make it available to individuals. We wanted to take the power to self-medicate away from all these responsible and respectable people and make it available to the average adult individual."

Leary paused for a moment and laughed ruefully. "Of course, what actually happened was a lot more complicated, and something that's taken a lifetime to digest and analyze."

## II. I've Come Down to Preach Love to the World!

THE ACTION CENTERED on the old, stately three-story colonial house on Grant Avenue that Leary was renting with his children and his colleague, Frank Barron, in the suburb of Newton Center, Massachusetts, right next to a Little League baseball diamond. "I remember lots of people coming all the time and turning on," Leary's daughter Susan would recall. There was the poet Charlie Olson, who looked like "a gigantic mountain of teddy bear"; Alan Watts, running a session on Easter Sunday, "very Christian"; and of course Huxley, "tall and thin and sort of stoopy," who reminded her of Gandalf in Tolkien's *Fellowship of the Ring*. Susan could usually tell when her father was high because his face would be "glowing and radiating." There would be other interesting characters with glowing and radiating faces in days to come: William Burroughs; Arthur Koestler; the great Canadian jazz trumpet player Maynard Ferguson and his wife, Flora Lu "Flo" Ferguson, blond and chic and savvy, who would open up social avenues for Leary and turn the place into a glamorous salon, making a "psilocybin weekend" in Newton the trendy thing to do for New York cultural sophisticates. But none of that would have happened without the visit of the poet with the black horn-rimmed glasses and the beard—the one who went ranting through the house naked with his boyfriend and changed everything.

By November of 1960, the Harvard Psilocybin Project was reaching a critical moment. By that time, Leary had become well aware of the small international network of researchers doing work with psychedelic drugs, as well as the intellectuals pondering them. "We couldn't see ourselves as part of a secret priestly class following models that belonged to the Old World. We realized we were approaching a crossroads. From the beginning the all-important question was going to be, *Who gets to go? Who gets to select this experience for themselves?*"

There are many points in this story where Leary's background and character become paramount, but none more significant than in the contemplation of this central issue. "I was a rootless city-dweller" was how Leary described himself before that first day of his mushrooming in Mexico. "An anonymous institutional employee who drove to work each morning in a long line of commuter cars, and drove home each night and drank martinis and thought like and acted like several million middle-class liberal intellectual robots."

It was not just a statement about the malaise of a life, but a portrait of what Leary had come to view as the state of a whole society. As good as he was at playing the Harvard game, he loathed the Waspy snobbishness of the place and delighted in pointing out its pretentiousness and pomposity, wearing red socks and tennis shoes to class. There was always something more than a bit reckless about this game of social and cultural iconoclasm that he'd had been playing since his boyhood in Springfield, Massachusetts. In 1934, his dashing and handsome and totally unreliable father, Tote Leary, who had practiced dentistry "sporadically, as a gentlemanly hobby," had disappeared after learning that the family inheritance had been woefully depleted. Leary would always maintain a sense of "warmth and respect" for this distant figure in his life who "never stunted me with expectations," romanticizing his disappearance in profound ways that shaped his own character and worldview. "Tote dropped out, followed the ancient Hibernian practice of getting in the wind, escaping the priest-run village, heading for the far-off land, like one of the Wild Geese of Irish legend."

Leary himself had become a "disdainer of the conventional way" at a young age: the deeply estranged Irish Catholic in a world of Wasps, the creative, fun-loving young rebel in a world of staid businesspeople. He seemed to be the kind of natural-born outsider who was drawn toward confrontation, and this aspect of his character was never more evident than when he arrived as a plebe at the U.S. Military Academy at West Point. When Leary was hauled before the Honors Committee and asked to resign after being accused of lying about bringing back a couple of bottles of alcohol from the 1940 Army-Navy game in Philadelphia, he refused, causing the committee to impose coventry, or strict silencing. Coventry was a watershed experience for Tim Leary—nine months of torment and silence and never-ending harassment—a classic confrontation of one young man armed with nothing but the courage of his convictions standing against the full power and authority of the U.S. military establishment. In the end, Leary agreed to resign, but only after getting the Honors Committee to agree to vindicate him publicly by announcing the terms of the agreement and his honorable discharge. An experience that could have ended in complete capitulation, humiliation, and dishonor had left him with powerful lessons about optimism, human nature, power, control, and the struggle of the individual confronting the system.

Just as Leary was grappling with the essential question of the future role of psychedelic drugs in American society, a hand-scrawled message arrived from Allen Ginsberg, the "secretary general of the world's poets, beatniks, anarchists, socialists, free-sex/love cultists," expressing Ginsberg's interest in the Harvard project. Leary wasted no time responding. What happened on November 26, 1960, when Ginsberg and Peter Orlovsky came to visit and Leary took them upstairs to a bedroom on the third floor and dispensed a large dose of eighteen pills—thirty-six milligrams of psilocybin—has become a cornerstone event in the history of the psychedelic counterculture in the United States.

Making sure they were comfortable, the professor told them he would be back to check on them every fifteen minutes and shut the door quietly behind him. As Wagner's *Gotterdämmerung* thundered and crashed on the record player, an image of the star of Bethlehem ignited Ginsberg— an image as soul-stirring as the image of Moloch he had seen in the San Francisco night in 1955. His whole being was pervaded by an awareness that all of human consciousness was waiting. For *action.* For *revolution.* For someone to take on the "responsibility of being the creative God and seize power over the universe." Well, I might just as well be the one, Ginsberg reckoned, and he rose from the bed, a naked messiah ready to pronounce his nakedness as the first act of revolution against the destroyers of the human image . . .

Leary was in his daughter's room, telling her not to read in such poor light. He turned at the sound of bare footsteps padding down the hall, just in time to see Peter Orlovsky's naked body descending the stairs. What on earth was happening? He walked into the study, and there was Ginsberg, naked except for his glasses with their one cracked lens, waving his finger in the air at Frank Barron.

"I'm the Messiah!" the poet proclaimed. "I've come down to preach love to the world! We're going to walk through the streets and teach people to stop hating!"

Ginsberg saw the whole thing vividly in his mind: a universal cosmic network of switched-on interconnected minds and exultant souls all spreading peace and love . . . a Coming Union of all consciousness.

To Leary, Ginsberg and Orlovsky looked like "apostles, martyrs, prophets" who had just stepped out of a fifteenth-century canvas. Then, as Ginsberg began talking about all the people he wanted to help—the junkies and the lost and the homeless—and how the drug could be used to bring all kinds of people together, Leary heard the poet give voice to all the messianic passions about the potential of the psychedelic experience that had been stirring in his own soul. They were two very different men, yet the character of each was woven through with the thread of the seeker, the utopian visionary, and the rebel. The more they talked about the social potential of the experience—about world peace, nuclear disarmament, the end to ignorance, conformity, unhappiness—the more impassioned they became.

"It seemed to us that wars, class conflicts, racial tensions, economic exploitation, religious strife, ignorance and prejudice were all caused by narrow social conditioning," Leary theorized. "Political problems were manifestations of psychological problems, which at bottom seemed to be neurological-chemical-hormonal. If we could help people plug into the empathy circuits of their brain, then positive social change could occur."

Everything seemed possible as they threw in their lots together, planning what Leary called "the neurological revolution, moving beyond scientific detachment to social activism." Ginsberg's zealotry was tempered by what he had already experienced with the use of mind-altering substances in the land of Moloch; more than anything, he didn't want to see the unhappy fate of marijuana befall psilocybin and other psychedelic substances.

"The idea was to give it to respectable and notable people first, who could really articulate the experience," Ginsberg explained, "all the while keeping it under the august auspices of Harvard. I would act as the go-between, keeping as much of a low profile as possible considering my visibility as America's most conspicuous beatnik. Really, it was a perfect role for me to play: Ambassador of Psilocybin."

Ginsberg's mind began brimming over with a *Who's Who* of the American avant-garde underground. He would give the pills to Thelonious Monk and Dizzy Gillespie first, to painters like Willem de Kooning and

Franz Kline, to Barney Rossett of Grove Press. As he explained to Neal Cassady in a Christmas letter, "We're starting a plot to get everyone in Power in America high."

But the far-reaching strategy of this plot was to educate the public, create massive research programs, licensing procedures, training centers in the intelligent use of psychedelic drugs, and ultimately make it available to any adult who chose the experience. It was nothing less than a "blueprint to turn on the world," as Leary later called it. "It was at this moment that we rejected Huxley's elitist approach and adopted the American egalitarian open-to-the public approach. And thereby hangs the tale."

Thereby, indeed.


## III.  All Started in California

WHEN BOB STONE saw the jagged waves of frost issuing forth from John Coltrane's horn, he suspected that he had taken too much peyote. That afternoon, back at Perry Lane, Stone had taken twelve pharmaceutical gel capsules stuffed with the dried cactus before driving into the city to see Coltrane at the Jazz Gallery in North Beach.

It didn't matter that Stone was an experienced peyote user from his days in New York when his wife, Janice, was a waitress at the Seven Arts. At the time, there was an espresso house on East Sixth Street with a dollar sign hanging out in front, run by an Ayn Rand follower named Barron who sold peyote from Smith's Cactus Ranch in East Texas. They would put the stuff in the blender and mix it with tomato juice and get these strange charges from it. Stone had once gone so far as to cover a wrestling match at Madison Square Garden for the *Daily News* after taking it, but as surreal and transporting as that experience might have been, it was mild compared to this.

Stone had known some strange and disorienting experiences in his life to be sure, like being on the road with his schizophrenic mother during his youth and ending up in Salvation Army shelters in Chicago and homeless on rooftops in New York. When he was in the navy in 1956, he witnessed the French attack on Port Said, Egypt. Peering through binoculars, he watched the donkeys and people flying through the air all chewed up by the 7.62s and rockets. All of that might have somehow conditioned him to accept different states of consciousness, but what he was seeing now seemed no less phenomenal.

Stone didn't know the word for what he was experiencing as he sat in the crowded club anymore than did his friend Ken Kesey: *synesthesia*—being actually able to *see* the sounds and *hear* the colors and feel them all in the mind and body in a completely new way. All he knew was that the frost kept coming out of Coltrane's soprano saxophone in these big jagged waves and that he was actually seeing Jimmy Garrison's bass lines and the percussion of Elvin Jones forming and gathering in the air above the stage and coming at him at the instant the music was being played, as if the notes themselves had danced up off the pages of some invisible musical score and were coming to life in front of his eyes. He and his friends were supposed to go on to another club and see Lenny Bruce perform, but it was all too much. As much as Bob Stone loved Coltrane, as much as he wanted to see Lenny Bruce, he had to get out. He and Janice got up from the table and walked outside, and then it hit him even harder—

Chinatown!—electromagnetic wavelengths and glowing concentric halos of whirling lights and buildings shimmying and the people looking like strange little mythological beings in some numinous Oriental dream as they flew past, their voices pounding in his ears. They started walking toward Confucius Square, all of it getting even more overwhelming and bewildering at the same time that it was utterly fantastic. He knew that he probably should have been taking more advantage of his Stegner Fellowship, writing at home instead of wandering around San Francisco out of his mind like this, but the feeling kept growing that the Fifties were finally ending and that something very different was about to happen.

They would always say it, how the Sixties began early in California, how the great Day-Glo adventure was jump-started there, hot-wired from those little weather-beaten two-bedroom shotgun bungalows on Perry Lane, that rutted tree-lined street overgrown with honeysuckle vines and alive with dragonflies in the days when northern California was a sylvan paradise and the hills around Stanford were covered with live oaks and tuli grass, when Silicon Valley didn't exist and America was rich and limitless and rent was sixty dollars a month and there was no heat yet from the cops or the crazies and everything was free and open under the redwood trees and their kids were just babies and they were all crazy in love with each other and looked as if they were participating in some kind of strange fraternity party as they lay there on the golf course staring up at the blue sky, experiencing "death and transfiguration and rebirth" on LSD . . .

"It all started in California," Kesey would later write, "went haywire in California, and now spreads out from California like a crazy tumor under the hide of the continent," kaleidoscopic sparks of color discharging in every direction like psychedelic fireworks on some new-sprung Fourth of July before it all turned into something else.

## IV. Here We Go, Dick

"YOU HAVE TO REMEMBER, Tim was way ahead of me" explained Ram Dass, seated on the couch in a friend's apartment on the Upper East Side of Manhattan. "I don't just mean that he was ten years older. He had to bring me along. His mind was beautiful. At that time, his creative ability to envision things was incredible. He was a real explorer, a very interesting scholar, extremely well read about everything he went into, and I was this square jerk. I mean, I was very straight, and still very much trying to keep my Harvard scene together. At the beginning, I was cautious about everything. Tim was always like, *'Here we go, Dick!'* And I was always like, *'Tim, wait a minute!'* So I became a straight man for him, the person that tried to ground it all the time. I raised the money, took care of his kids, cooked the food, made sure the bills were paid, and the more I did it, the farther out Tim would fly."

Somewhere during the 1960s, the psychedelic wave turned to the East, and nobody would embody the journey more remarkably than Baba Ram Dass, the former Dr. Richard Alpert, author of *Be Here Now,* cofounder of the Seva Foundation, and spiritual mentor to countless thousands. As Richard Alpert, he had taken psilocybin for the first time in Leary's house during a raging blizzard in November of 1961. The son of an immigrant junk dealer in Boston's West End who had risen to become wealthy from real estate and railroad speculation, Alpert had been very busy building an empire at Harvard, and his interest in researching "achievement anxiety" was more than an academic reflection of what W. H. Auden had called the Age of Anxiety. Dick Alpert had grown up anxious and compulsive in a family where achievement meant everything—anxious about his weight, his looks, his athletic ability, his Jewishness, his grades, his bisexuality. He had dieted and exercised and cultivated himself mercilessly, honing an awkward, flabby teenager into a trim, cultured scholar who knew all about art and wines and antiques and scuba diving and played beautiful classical music on his cello and became increasingly less shy about his bisexuality. Within three short years, Alpert had succeeded in garnering appointments in four different departments. Though rapid and unrelenting, his progress was built on shaky emotional and psychological foundations, however. Everywhere he looked in his life, he saw the external validation of his material and professional accomplishments, which only seemed to make the growing emptiness he felt inside more searing. Perhaps his greatest fear was that he would squander the rest of his life as a department chairman, prominent on government committees, leading a life of endless grants and plenty of travel and the great prestige of Harvard but with "that horrible awareness" that he would never discover the one thing that would make it all fall together and have meaning.

Alpert's first psilocybin experience had been a perfect manifestation of this set of dynamics: he had watched as his various identities completely dissolved like some rear-projected kinescope cartoon of his unconscious and he began disappearing limb by limb until nothing remained but a disembodied essence of consciousness and soul. It was then that he heard a voice say cryptically, *"But who's minding the store?"*— and at that moment, he met his true spiritual self for the first time in his life and knew in his innermost being that he would be all right. The experience had been so intense, so joyous, so liberating that he had rushed out into a great snowstorm and found himself rolling down the hill in total ecstasy. "The next morning when I showed up to teach at Harvard, the whole thing seemed like a joke. In a way, that single experience foreshadowed everything that was going to happen to me."

In those early years of the Psilocybin Project, Leary and Alpert were the Tim and Dick show—"a Sundance–Butch Cassidy alliance of psychological outlaws working to market and merchandise expanded consciousness," as Leary described them, setting up lectures, workshops, seminars, running sessions for confidants of Nehru, J. B. Rhine researchers, psychologists. They would sweep through fashionable cocktail parties in New York and Cambridge, these two sparkling Harvard professors always full of cheer and optimism as they worked the well-heeled crowd. As Alpert continued to take the drug, he found himself powerfully drawn to the spiritual and transcendental aspects of the psychedelic experience, particularly after the group discovered the Tibetan Book of the Dead through people like Huxley and Alan Watts.

"Suddenly, all of the mystical literature—Eastern, Christian, the kaballah—I looked at it, and it turned real," he elaborated. "Before, I had seen all of it as an anthropologist, as a kind of projection of the human mind to avoid fear of death—a reductionist view from the intellectual and analytical side of things . . . It was as if I now had the key that opened the door, and I could read this stuff instead of putting it all down cynically. These were the maps, and the key map was the Book of the Dead, which I first encountered after I'd had about five or six sessions. I'd open it up, and there was a description of the very experience I'd had the previous Saturday night! One of our cardinal observations had been that this experience was ineffable, and suddenly here was this description that was two thousand five hundred years old, which described it exactly. I mean, certain adjectives were exact—it would just blow me away."

Nothing accelerated the growing perception that the Psilocybin Project was some strange cult growing within the Social Relations Department than the injection of this mystical Eastern literature. It was bad enough that the group ate lunch off by themselves every day, not to mention the rumors of the strange goings-on at Leary's house; now there was all this weird talk about "bardos," "the clinging of mind," "the realization of Voidness." At the same time, members of the group began to feel more and more emotionally bonded by the experience and increasingly alienated by the growing antagonism of the behaviorists, who were becoming more critical of Leary's research methods.

"Here we were exploring this inner realm of consciousness we had been theorizing about, and suddenly we were traveling right through it and right around it," Ram Dass continued. "It was as though the bunch of us had been off traveling in Tibet somewhere, and back there in the lunchroom whom do you hang out with? Well, the guy you'd gone to Tibet with, of course. Harvard was a temple to the intellect, and these professors were like high priests, and here we were off by ourselves, and basically what we were saying was, Oh, the *intellect*? No big deal, guys; it's really just this interesting *subsystem*. It was like walking into the Catholic Church and proclaiming that the Eucharist was full of shit!"

The more Timothy Leary delved into those bottles of little pink pills, the further away he seemed to get from the traditional methodologies of clinical research, and the wider the gulf between the bemushroomed and the outsiders would grow. With his brass candles and Indian raga music, the colloquialism that would soon come into vogue to describe Leary's style was, simply, *far out*. In photos of the time, his expressions illustrate someone flying very high indeed—the rapt preoccupation of a man involved in the deepest contemplation, acutely aware that his mammalian cortex was being extravagantly bombarded with millions of psilocybin-released signals from every quadrant of his nervous system.

## V. Harvard Eats the Holy Mushroom

JUST HOW FAR OUT Dr. Timothy Leary intended to fly became evident in August of 1961, when he and Dick Alpert journeyed to Copenhagen to deliver a manifesto to the International Congress of Applied Psychology in the form of a signature paper entitled "How to Change Behavior." By that time, Leary was firmly convinced that the lecture he was about to deliver was even more revolutionary than the papers of Sigmund Freud.

Western man had turned his back on consciousness, Leary explained to the auditorium of solemn-faced psychologists. Studying behavior had become part of the zeitgeist of Western psychology, "very much in tune with the experimental bent of Western science," but now it was all going to change. All of human behavior was most accurately understood as a culturally determined "game" that consisted of learned behavior, he asserted, evoking the game of baseball as infinitely superior to the games of psychology or psychiatry precisely because at least it was recognized as such—a game—and could therefore change the behavior of its players through that recognition, as well as activities like coaching. Leary then identified culture as the reason for man's basic inability to change behavior:

"Cultural stability is maintained by keeping the members of any cultural group from seeing that the roles, rules, goals, rituals, language and values are game structures. The family game is treated by most cultures as far more than a game, with its implicit contacts, limited in time and space. The nationality game. It is treason not to play. The racial game. The religious game. And that most tragic and treacherous game of all, the game of individuality. The ego game. The Timothy Leary game. Ridiculous how we confuse this game, overplay it."

The answer was simple, direct, and profound: the visionary experience. The new term for it was going to be *consciousness expansion* . . .

"The most efficient way to cut through the game structure of Western life is the use of drugs. Drug-induced satori. In three hours, under the right circumstances, the cortex can be cleared." Leary then laid out the right circumstances for such "drug-induced satori": eleven egalitarian principles that respected human equality and dignity, that destroyed the traditional doctor-patient relationship in psychology, that provided all information about the chemicals available and completely removed the atmosphere of secrecy, that gave participants complete control over dosage and allowed the drugs to be taken in the comfortable surroundings of one's home. And there it was, all neatly laid out: the new Timothy Leary game, the psychedelic game he and Alpert would play, the very theoretical seeds of the Psychedelic Sixties.

"The psychedelic experience was going to shape and change all our lives; there was no doubt about it," Ram Dass averred. "We had found something that was going to change the culture and the whole way people played social games. We were very grandiose in our expectations, not only about the impact it would have on the culture, but how fast it was going to happen. Why? Because we saw how fast it was happening to *us*."

The story of how Leary and Alpert eventually got kicked out of Harvard was a classic drama of high cultural conflict and academic alienation that unfolded over the next two years. The problems began with their very first clinical experiment, when they tested the potential of psilocybin for social reengineering by administering the drugs to the hardened cons of Concord State Prison. The changes in the bemushroomed inmates were dramatic: friction and tension were lowered, and there was talk in the sessions about "love" and "God" and "sharing." Leary attributed the success of the experiment to what Konrad Lorenz, the German ethologist, and Nico Tinbergen, the Dutch ethnologist, had observed in other species as imprinting and began to assert that the psychedelic experience, by suspending "previous imprints of reality," could be used as a means of "re-imprinting" new belief systems and attitudes that could not only remake inmates into noncriminals, but remake society. Psychedelic reimprinting would rank with DNA deciphering as "one of the most significant discoveries of the century," claimed Leary as he lobbied to introduce psilocybin into the entire federal penitentiary system.

Convicts on miracle mind drugs from Mexican Indians? Psychedelic "re-imprinting"? The other members of the Social Relations Department would have found such grandiose notions laughable if Leary and Alpert were not becoming so popular. Here they were, team teaching the seminar in Introductory Clinical Psychology, confidently claiming to every potential doctoral candidate at Harvard that the future of the field belonged to "brain change" drugs. It was more than just sloppy science, their critics claimed. It was getting downright dangerous. Dark storm clouds quickly gathered over the project. In a bitter debate within the Social Relations Department, Herb Kelman and other professors demanded that the project be terminated. Before it was over, all parties had agreed to the establishment of a committee to continue to evaluate the issues at hand. Leary hoped that his critics had been calmed for the time being, but the *Crimson*'s front-page coverage of the meeting— PSYCHOLOGISTS DISAGREE ON PSILOCYBIN RESEARCH—spread for the first time to the local Boston papers and the national wire services. The media was about to discover an irresistible story—HARVARD EATS THE HOLY MUSHROOM—professors and students taking wild mind-altering drugs together at the alma mater of President John F. Kennedy.

In the aftermath of the debate, the game began moving inexorably away from science, toward politics, prophetic philosophy, the sweeps of a social movement, the ranges of religion. Leary's desk was soon piled high with books on tantric Buddhism. He was visiting ashrams, pondering the relationship between psychedelic experience and religious mysticism. If psychedelic experience could initiate mystical and religious experience, as people like Huxley had long claimed, could it ever be scientifically proved, quantified, documented? It was a proposition Leary intended to put to the test. A Harvard doctoral candidate in the philosophy of religion, Walter Pahnke, wanted to determine whether the so-called transcendent component of psychedelic experience truly was the equal of those reported by the saints and mystics. Supported by Professor Walter Houston Clark, he gathered twenty divinity students from the Andover Newton Seminary and selected and divided them into five groups of four, each group with two "guides" with considerable psychedelic experience. The experiment was to take place in Marsh Chapel of Boston University.

"Harvard would provide neither setting nor drugs by that time," related Ram Dass. "We had to find another source for their psilocybin, so we had to get street drugs to use. Walter Pahnke was very good, a very sophisticated researcher. He had never taken psilocybin himself and didn't want to take it until after the study was done. The young theologians were to be given a nine-point rating scale after it was over, using criteria put forth by the Bible for a genuine religious revelatory experience."

About one hour before noon on the appointed day, Good Friday 1962, the dean of the chapel, Howard Thurman, conducted a three-hour devotional service; then the experiment commenced. Ten subjects from each group were to be given thirty milligrams of psilocybin; the remaining ten subjects, a placebo containing nicotinic acid, which would produce only hot and cold skin flashes. It was a triple-blind study with subjects, guides, and experimenters not knowing beforehand who received what. After a short prayer, the envelopes were opened, the pills ingested, and the young seminarians settled expectantly into the pews. Before long, one particular student walked to the window and looked raptly out. "God is *everywhere*," he then cried, his face flushed and glowing. "Oh, the glory!"

After thirty minutes, it was very apparent who had taken the psychedelic and who had not. The ten who had ingested the nicotinic acid were simply sitting there facing the altar; the others were lying on the floors and pews, wandering around in rapt wonderment, murmuring prayers as one of them played "weird, exciting chords" on the church's pipe organ.

Another started tearing the buttons off his shirt and needed to be subdued, but not before he had thrown his dental plate at the altar. Still another clambered across the pews and stood facing the crucifix, transfixed, arms outstretched as if somehow trying to identify physically with Christ and his suffering on the cross.

Over the following weeks, Pahnke and his group of psychologists tape-recorded interviews and handed out their questionnaires. To Leary and the group, the results and interpretations seemed clear-cut: "Our administration of the sacred mushrooms in a religious setting to people who were religiously motivated provided a scientific demonstration that spiritual ecstasy, religious revelation, and union with God were now directly accessible."

As soon as *Time* magazine published its detailed account of the experiment, calling it "The Miracle of Marsh Chapel," the firestorm erupted. Trustees of the Harvard Divinity School came down on Walter Clark, pressuring him to distance himself from the experiment; Pahnke was awarded his Ph.D. but follow-up studies were canceled. A medical administrator from the FDA then commented that any such conclusions about the psychological benefits based on these drugs were, by their very nature, "pure bunk."

Leary had expected priests and rabbis and ministers and God-seeking masses of people to come flocking to this good news. The implications of the ferocious attacks were disturbingly clear: "Of course they had to organize against the results of the experiment because it was very threatening to the organized religious structures," Ram Dass commented. "Why? The experiment seemed to say that everybody could have a direct experience with the Christ head; you didn't need the Christian church for it. It was an extremely profound experiment. I still don't think we've ever dealt with it adequately."

Timothy Leary was coming to apprehend that the "bureaucrats of Christian America" would never accept his research, no matter how objective or scientifically valid. The Miracle of Marsh Chapel represented another in a continuing line of decisive moments. Leary was struck by how right indeed Aldous Huxley had been when he'd warned him that the biblical original sin had really been about the ingestion of forbidden brain-change "fruit" and that his most implacable foes would be among the nation's clergy, threatened by the potency and implications of the psychedelic experience.

As Leary and his colleagues were coming to acknowledge, the clerical counterreaction to their research was in fact an old story, deeply embedded in the history of man. Mind-altering drugs had always been employed as sacraments in different cultures at different times, but so too had they been brutally suppressed. It had always come and gone in waves: the soma of the ancient Vedic religion, the mysterious *kykeon* used for over two thousand years in the Eleusinian mysteries of Greece, followed by the rise of Christianity, the banishing of the mysteries, and the suppression of pagan drug use by the church. A psychedelic underground had been crushed by the Holy Inquisition as witchcraft. Spanish conquerors had tried to stamp out the indigenous use of peyote and coca by the natives as soon as they arrived in the New World; the British had been equally careful to outlaw the use of kava in Tahiti. And so it had gone, the efforts over the centuries by church and government to keep the genie of psychedelic experience firmly locked in the bottle, strictly circumscribing the use of the substances and always stigmatizing them as forms of madness and degeneracy and demonic possession.

What nobody could have imagined was that this drama would now play out on an unprecedented scale in the American society that only thirty years earlier had outlawed cannabis in a wave of public hysteria. If nothing else, the response to the Miracle of Marsh Chapel foreshadowed the coming of a backlash that would not only succeed in outlawing the use of LSD but also quash the whole scientific investigation of it. Interest in the Harvard Psilocybin Project was soaring, but the university continued to back away. For Tim Leary, the answer was beginning to become clear: A whole new political game. A new social-movement game. A new religion game. In short, the alternative-society game.

## VI.  Breaking Free and Running for Open Country

"INNOCENCE IS A FUNNY THING," Bob Stone observed in the backyard of the summer home he was renting on Block Island. "California seemed a garden virtually without snakes. It made me feel like I had found a special worthy place. I never relaxed so much in my life, and I had been so full of New York attitudes, had considerably more embittered sensibilities than the kids I met out there, who were mainly people who had grown up in upper-middle-class circumstances and lived in a world that was extremely benign. Some people used to say about San Francisco in those days that living there was like getting stuck in an elevator in Lincoln Center, because it was all so middle class and educated. That statement would be meaningless now . . . Life seemed nice and easy then; the United States could afford to have us in graduate school, so there I was. One minute it seemed I was on the streets of New York, the next minute in the baths at the place that later became Esalen, naked with these people, smoking marijuana and watching the fog roll in off the ocean, and these hard feelings and attitudes started just melting away."

By the time Bob and Janice Stone stepped off the train in California, Ken Kesey had become the focal point of the energy, the resident literary celebrity on Perry Lane. There was talk of a Broadway play based on *One Flew Over the Cuckoo's Nest,* Kirk Douglas was interested in playing the role of Randle P. McMurphy, and money was beginning to appear in Kesey's life. Bob and Janice moved in a couple of blocks away from where Ken and Faye lived on Perry Lane and were introduced to the group by Ed McClanahan, another writer in the Stanford program. Kesey would always remember their first meeting, Stone's face "lit by whiskey and anarchism" when he first showed up: "And he said, 'I hear you're the bull goose looney writer in this neck of the woods.' I took it as a challenge. What impressed me about Bob was his ability to riff."

As they became close friends, Kesey recognized more than an ability to riff in Bob Stone. There were elements of profound loneliness and isolation in him, as well as the moral courageousness of a fellow warrior; he was the sort of guy who would "get high, stand in the broken glass, and shout."

Stone's childhood had been solitary and filled with uncertainty. Born in Brooklyn in 1937, raised on the streets of Manhattan, Stone was an infant when his parents separated. His father had worked for the New Haven Railroad but had never been a presence in his life; his mother, a schoolteacher, was schizophrenic, in and out of hospitals. Stone had never had the conventional underpinnings of stability in his life that other kids seemed to enjoy. His youth couldn't have been more different from Kesey's. Kesey had grown up in Springfield, Oregon, boxing and fishing and hunting in the Willamette Valley, plunging down the rapids of the McKenzie and Willamette Rivers on inner tubes, the very model of a blue-eyed blond-haired Fifties teenager; an intelligent, literate jock; a potent, charismatic blend of gentleness, intelligence, physical strength, sensitivity, and self-confidence; the boy voted most likely to succeed.

Kesey may have represented everything the civilization held up as the right stuff, but he had the soul of an outsider. Something inside him identified with the strange offbeat pimply-faced loners who were so alienated during the Fifties: "the weird kid interested in stuff nobody else is interested in—doing tricks, studying the stars, reading science fiction, boiling strange things." After marrying his high-school sweetheart, Faye Haxby, and graduating from the University of Oregon, Kesey was awarded a Woodrow Wilson Fellowship and entered the creative writing program at Stanford in the fall of 1958.

Stone had arrived at Stanford with a novel he would eventually call *A Hall of Mirrors,* the first chapters of which had gotten him his Stegner Fellowship. It was a work seething with the sights and sounds and characters of New Orleans, brimming with sophisticated dialogue, ambitious themes about religion, politics, American culture, and the nature of evil. Stone had no idea the book would take him the next six years to write, or what he would find in California, or how what he would find there would condition and shape the writing of his book. He fell in with these people—Ken and Faye Kesey, Vic Lovell, Jane Burton—and one day he took some LSD on a sugar cube, and the next thing he knew he was marching around with a bucket on his head and a broom handle in his hand as a Teutonic knight, he and Kesey shouting at each other in mock Polish.

"It was like we had found a bunch of people that we had always been looking for. We spent all our time talking, and when you have people that close, you wanted a sacrament to share . . . There wasn't a great awareness of psychedelics at first, but it didn't take much to get me to experiment. Some of us had read Huxley; there were some psychologists hanging around, like Vic Lovell and Irving Kupfermann, all interested in being able to study schizophrenia; there was a mixture of motives in using them, some transcendental, religious in nature. Some people, like us, smoked marijuana, but not many; we were arrogant and snobbish about our dope smoking at the time, quite pleased with ourselves about it. The world was just beginning to be separated into the hip and the square, and we were firmly ensconced in the notion of being hip. Perry Lane was becoming a kind of wandering scene, a movable feast. Everybody's house seemed to adjoin, and the parties we had filled the whole street."

As good LSD was always hard to come by, the group also took morning-glory seeds. "We kept them in stock a surfeit. You could take three hundred seeds, and you would get violently ill but very, very high. They had names like Pearly Gates and Heavenly Blue, and such transcendental names easily convinced us that the people who put them out must have known exactly what we were doing, and we were young and dumb enough so that it didn't matter if we got violently ill in order to get high like that."

If LSD was available, they would get together during the afternoon for the great adventure. "This is around the time we first started calling it acid. I remember lying flat on our backs for hours. We'd listen to Ravi Shankar and Missa Louba, from Zaire, which is the mass, partly in Latin, done entirely with drums and African chanting. That was one of our favorites, along with the late quartets of Beethoven. It was always so incredible to listen to those quartets when we were tripping, going all through them, but it always felt like you were hearing them for the first time. I still feel that way whenever I hear one—like a flashback." When they were high on acid, the thing they loved to do the most was go out and play shadow tag at night. "We'd be marching across the Stanford Golf Course, the whole bunch of us at one o'clock in the morning, chanting these African chants. The cops were constantly coming to the golf course, and then we would escape into the darkness. There were days we would roll around in these huge piles of seed husks, just roll around in them for hours, watching those California sunsets."

The whole psychedelic scene at Stanford was really the fault of a thin bohemian graduate student in clinical psychology named Vic Lovell, a Perry Lane neighbor who worked as a psychiatric intern and loved to talk about Freud and schizophrenia. It was Lovell who had told Kesey all about Dr. Leo Hollister and the government-sponsored program at the

Veterans Hospital at Menlo Park, where you could make twenty dollars a session trying these experimental "psychotommimetic" drugs if you were willing to sit there in a white-tiled room while they drew blood from you and asked you questions about your mother.

Just what was it that might have opened Kesey to the possibility of such an unusual experiment in consciousness alteration in the first place? His Wilson Fellowship had been petering out, and he was interested in a little extra money, but Kesey had a curious mind and very little fear. Moreover, there were no connotations of illegality or depravity whatsoever surrounding these chemicals at this time, especially as the government was administering them. Kesey was nothing if not a responsible U.S. citizen, so when he looked up on the day he first took the psilocybin and saw the ceiling start coming to life and looked into the face of the doctor and could actually see the tremor in his lower lip happening as this great cellular drama pulling the fibers of flesh and firing off and twitching along the nerve endings, the fact that the whole experience was countenanced by Uncle Sam made it all seem on the up-and-up. Kesey would later refer to it as "going to the nuthouse to take dope under official auspices" and compared the experience to being allowed to go inside a "magic box" . . .

"They gave me mine, paid me and quite a few other rats both black and white $20 a session in fact to test it for them, started it so to speak; then, when they caught a glimpse of what was coming down in that room full of guinea pigs, they swatched the guinea pigs out, slammed the door, locked it, barred it, dug a ditch around it, set two guards in front of it, and gave the hapless pigs a good talking to and warned them—on threat of worse than death—to never go in that door again."

Why Kesey wouldn't stay out of the box, of course, why he kept coming back through the door for the LSD and the psilocybin, the ditran, and the IT-290 and the mescaline, and why he eventually decided to take the pills home was a whole other story, far more significant than why he was interested in going in the first place.

Six weeks after his first "session," Kesey bought his first ounce of grass; six months later, he had a job in the hospital as a psychiatric aide. He settled into the midnight-to-eight shifts, mopping and buffing floors, pecking away on the typewriter they allowed him to bring in. Of course, his employers never knew about the "chemical alternatives" that he kept down in the locker, which the young writer was using to "blow his mind" right there on the ward. Kesey accomplished this task with such purloined experimental substances as the "double-aught capsule of pure mescaline (more than I ever again or would even consider taking now) and I managed the night by mopping fervently whenever the nurse arrived so she couldn't see my twelve gauge pupils, and the rest of the time argued so heatedly with the big knotty pine door across the office from me that I actually chalked a broad yellow line across the floor between us and told the door, 'You stay on your side, you goggle-eyed son of a bitch, and I'll stay on mine!' "

Arguing with pine doors was only the half of it. The chemicals were opening Kesey to another world—"not just shock not just invention but something that arrives on your familiar wavelength and overloads all your skinny little lines of reason and forces admission of vistas beyond all those horizons you were certain were absolutely permanent." There were instantaneous insights to be gleaned from these chemicals, powers to be derived that both unleashed and humbled the user, and some of them were arduous, challenging, downright painful . . .

"When we first took those drugs in the hospital, it was like the books God keeps," Kesey observed. "You had heard about the Bible and the Akashic records, but suddenly you had a glimpse of them. These were the real books. These weren't kept in the school library, these were the real books. . . . So we wanted to see these books and took more and more drugs, until finally, at one point, God said, 'You want to see the books? I'll show you the fucking books,' and it was like this big hand grabbed us by the back of the neck and held us there for twelve hours. We were in absolute hell because we saw ourselves; we saw all the stuff we had done, mistakes we had made, our indulgences, our cruelties. That was hell."

Along with the raw truths of such self-revelation, Kesey found himself peering deeply into the faces of the patients. Being on the ward under the effects of LSD and mescaline had the effect of a veil being pulled back to reveal a darkness in the American soul. Were the people in the ward really insane, or was it the society that had put them there that was somehow to blame? And why did so much of human behavior seem to move in concert with some unnamed evil?

"I saw the looks on these people's faces . . . and realized that Freud was full of shit. Something really dug deep in these people's minds, and it wasn't the way they were treated when they were toilet trained; it wasn't the way they were rejected when they were thirteen. It was something to do with the American Dream. How the American Dream gave us our daily energy and yet the dream was perverted and not allowed to develop fully."

The book that Kesey wanted to write would be set in the mental ward, but it would be "about America, about how the sickness in America is in the consciousness of the people." It was there in the hospital that Kesey began truly perceiving the snake in the grass of the all-controlling socioeconomic entity he would call the Combine. One night he took peyote on the ward, "choking down eight peyote plants," and it all started coming to him, the face and voice of Chief Bromden, the Choctaw Indian who would narrate the story . . .

> They're out there.
> Black boys in white suits before me to commit sex acts in the hall and get it mopped up before I can catch them.

The voice of the Chief was the masterstroke that seemed to unleash it all, everything tumbling into place after those first three pages. Who better to tell this story about the sickness in the head of America than a broom-pushing schizophrenic Vanishing American feigning muteness? Into the world of the mental ward, Kesey introduced his hero and alter ego, Randle P. McMurphy, the swaggering redheaded roustabout who finagles his way into the hospital in order to get away from the hard labor of the work farm. McMurphy is basically a fun-loving, good-hearted shit kicker, but one easily victimized by his own pride and passion—exactly the sort of hard-drinking, sexed-up motorcycle-racing rebel who would have been stigmatized as a "delinquent" by the conservative society of the 1950s. Nurse Ratched has seen the type before, of course, and knows that McMurphy is no psychopath or sociopath or schizophrenic or manic-depressive; he represents something far more dangerous. She quickly pegs him as a "manipulator": "And sometimes a manipulator's own ends are simply the actual disruption of the ward for the sake of disruption. There are such people in our society." Behind that prim smile, the Big Nurse is ruthless, a tightly wrapped villain capable of raising the hairs on the back of the neck. What Nurse Ratched really wants, the Chief tells us, is for the patients to become "adjusted to surroundings" in exactly the way they were unable to adjust in the outside world—and if they don't comply, well then she'll simply stupefy them with drugs, have them dispatched to the Shock Shop, or worse, lobotomized.

While Kesey had experimented by writing more on different chemicals, he could easily see that the drug-induced passages that were most useful to his narrative were those rendering the Chief's schizophrenic haze, and he was therefore able to write the Chief in a way that allowed the character to see directly into the evil workings of the Combine everywhere, exactly as Kesey had seen into the ward under the influence of a psychedelic substance, its very "beams and frequencies coming from all directions."

Kesey presents McMurphy as exactly the kind of freethinking nonconformist rabble-rousing American who can really foul things up by putting spirit and fight back into the hearts of the other inmates. When McMurphy bets the other patients that he can "put a betsy bug up that nurse's butt within a week," an epic confrontation ensues. But while McMurphy certainly succeeds in putting a burr in the Big Nurse's bloomers, he pays the supreme price in the end. When the Chief discovers McMurphy after the lobotomy, he suffocates him with a pillow out of respect for him. In the process the Chief finds his own pride and will to fight, breaking free and running for open country.

That Kesey had written a novel with profound political implications was indisputable. "I mean, here's a writer who is looking at American society as a loony bin," commented the writer Gurney Norman, another member of the Stanford program at the time. "And the hero is someone who is messing with the system, and the narrator—the consciousness and soul of the book—is a Native American whose final act is to rip out the controls of the system and use it to smash a hole in the wall of the hospital, which creates an image of a force that smashes though the barriers of American thinking. The novel has to be read that way."

And it would be. Published by Viking Press in February of 1962, *One Flew Over the Cuckoo's Nest* quickly became an important marker for the passing of the Eisenhower era. It seemed as right, as culturally perfect,

when it appeared as Jack Kerouac's *On the Road* had been five years earlier, its vision of the Combine every bit as resounding as the Moloch of
Allen Ginsberg's *Howl*. The twenty-seven-year-old author became famous virtually overnight and began planning another book. Kesey was
also emboldened to liberate more of those amazing experimental chemicals that had been so important to the writing and take them back to
Perry Lane. He was now more convinced than ever that the true potential
of those drugs would unleash itself outside the sterile environment of
the hospital, away from the rigid minds of the government researchers.
Before long, Kesey would become emboldened enough to take on the
Combine himself. The novel had created a powerful paradigm that
would self-actualize in the author's life as he set out to put the "betsy bug"
of LSD of in the bloomers of American society, initiating a time when
more and more people, like his Chief Bromden, would break free and
head for open country.

"Ken was far from your average fellow to begin with," Bob Stone
averred. "He was aware of his force but not exactly sure what he was trying to do with it, and he was starting to see the effect he was having on
other people and I think recognizing the lack of confidence on the part of
many institutions. At that moment, the early Sixties, these august institutions seemed to be losing self-confidence—the universities, the corporations, the very fabric of the state—everything seemed like it would fall
over if you pushed it, like it was up for grabs. And there was Kesey, who
was really a born shaman, a great adventurer. It was like he was playing
with this great fire, this great mystery he was going to control and use, for
purposes of art and insight and adventure and so many things. He was
amazed at his own power and the power of the drugs, but the other thing
about Kesey was that he was always basically a very decent guy, and he
had a certain generosity, and he was courageous, very imaginative. What
he wanted to do he intended as a very positive thing."

## VII. The Beginning of the Great Happening

THINGS JUST STARTED EVOLVING around Kesey, materializing and hooking up—the word they would soon use for it was one they

borrowed from Carl Jung, *synchronicity*—like how Neal Cassady appeared in his driveway on Perry Lane just as Kesey was pulling in from doing research up in Oregon for his big logging novel. There he was, Kerouac's Holy Goof, the famous Dean Moriarty from *On the Road,* fresh out of San Quentin, where he had picked up a copy of *Cuckoo's Nest* and knew in his soul that he was Randle P. McMurphy.

When Cassady appeared, it seemed a powerful omen, as if he had walked right out of the pages of one era and stepped into the pages of another, the one that Kesey would write. Ed McClanahan remembered his showing up at a reading on Alpine Road in January of 1963, shirtless and sinewy and moving incessantly and rapping a mile a minute and calling Kesey the Chief.

Kesey was instantly smitten by this man he would call Sir Speed Limit and Fastestmanalive, who could carry on three or four conversations at once while constantly flipping a small hammer, this T-shirted maniac "with his bony Irish face dancing continuously and simultaneously through a dozen expressions, his sky-blue eyes flirting up from under long lashes, and his reputation and his unstoppable rap." While many in the circle saw Cassady as a quaint throwback to a 1950s hot-rodder, to be tolerated because he liked to get high and was so celebrated in the great literary canon of Kerouac, Kesey saw something profound and spiritual. The phrase they were using around Perry Lane to describe the new openness and caring in their adventure in living and consciousness was *out front*—one of those hip, acid-tinged colloquialisms originating in California at the time that would soon invade the popular usage, like *too much*—and nobody was more out front than Neal Cassady. Kesey saw him as the Totally Present Man, like a Zen master, the archetype of where the whole scene was going.

When Kesey finished his logging novel, *Sometimes a Great Notion,* he felt utterly spent. By the end of it, he had come to feel that writing would somehow become obsolete in this new age. "When we got into acid as a group of people, we felt like we were dealing with the end of time," he explained. "It was a different consciousness than writing. I could not do the same kind of writing I had been doing. We got into what I would call Rosicrucian art. Tim Leary, Bobby Dylan, John Lennon, Bill Burroughs—we were all reaching in to wrench the language apart. It was as if the syntax were anchoring us to something older—something ancient, something staid—and we were trying to tear it out. The slate was ours. We wrote on it what we wanted. We felt like the consciousness revolution was going to take us off physically—like *Childhood's End.*"

"A lot of it changed when Cassady showed up," Bob Stone recognized. "Everything kind of ended around Perry Lane, and Kesey moved up to La Honda, which was the beginning of a whole new phase."

Perry Lane had been a bohemian literary salon, but La Honda, fifteen miles east over the hill from Palo Alto, was the beginning of the great happening, the psychedelic theater of life.

The spread consisted of six acres dense with redwood trees that stretched far up the side of a hill. The log cabin had six paneled rooms, exposed beams, a large, rustic fireplace in the main room, and french doors. You drove onto the place over a small wooden bridge that spanned a scenic little stream. The young novelist had sunk his money into the land but had also acquired a lot of equipment—hi-fi, tape recorders, microphones, speakers that he placed on top of the roof and in the trees, motion-picture cameras and projectors—anything to encourage the spontaneous expression of the group. The nearest neighbor was a mile away. Soon there was freakish vocal gibberish and avant-garde jazz and rock and roll and folk music coming through the relay system, echoing through the woods. Before long, strange items and sculptures began to appear—tin horses and wild paintings. Soon Kesey got his hands on this new paint called Day-Glo that allowed him to turn the woods themselves into a psychedelic stage setting, upon which each new day would unfold, the sun showering colors and glittery particles and neon dust down on them through the foliage as if they were children playing in a dream.

The days were perfect down there in the great domed enclosure of the forest, and the people who gathered at La Honda came to use LSD in a spirit that was vastly different from the approach being pursued by Leary at Harvard or by the researchers at the hospitals. They were all somehow connected to Kesey, for one thing, bonded to his energy and mind. Through the next phases of the experience, their real names disappeared, and the new ones they gave one another playfully reflected qualities and roles and transfigurations just as the forest had been transformed into something else: Swashbuckler, Sir Speed Limit, Intrepid Traveler, Mal Function, Hardly Visible, Gretchen Fetchin, Mary Microgram, Mountain Girl, Generally Famished—the Merry Pranksters forming.

The core group was about ten, but a fringe group numbered about forty. It included people like Stewart Brand, the future organizer of the Trips Festival and publisher of the *Whole Earth Catalog*, another Stanford graduate and ex-serviceman, who met Kesey after he read *Cuckoo's Nest* and sent him his photographs of Native Americans. To Brand, the scene around Kesey was the most interesting thing happening in the Bay Area.

"At the time, there was the structured session of the research approach, and Leary and Alpert and Metzner were coming up with set and setting, and then the approach of Eastern mysticism, which a lot of us felt was very sanctimonious," Brand recalled on his houseboat in Sausalito. "What made the Pranksters so different was that they were pursuing the recreational sports approach . . . To be a Prankster was adventurous and dangerous and to be involved in real cultural electricity. It was also sloppy and slow and lazy, cheerily revolutionary and fiercely apolitical, some of the same revolutionary kind of art and attitude that I later encountered among the computer hackers of the Eighties and Nineties. I think the fact that there were a fair number of ex-military guys in the Pranksters was very important because it would make us less sloppy than the average hippie group that developed in that we had had responsibilities and had done actual things at a young age. We wouldn't just sit around imagining how great something would be—we'd just do it!"

As Brand described it, the Pranksters were really like a work of fiction that Kesey was telling—exactly like unleashing a set of characters and watching them evolve in an ongoing narrative. "The attraction of being part of it was enormous because Kesey is a very, very good storyteller. People would routinely do dramatic things and then competitively outdo each other. It was fun—and surprisingly few casualties, considering. Lots of chances were taken."

Dosages were one of the chances taken by the group. How much was enough, how much was too much, and was too much ever a bad thing?—these were questions they played with. Bob Stone remembered a particular day when Denise Kaufmann, the captivating Berkeley student known as Mary Microgram, became convinced that they hadn't been taking "nearly enough," and that it might be "smoother" if they took a lot more, so they all dutifully swallowed whopping doses.

"I remember going for cigarettes at the convenience store in La Honda and trying to make it out of there and back before everything just came down on me. It could be terrifying . . . and I got back and saw everybody laying on their backs in the yard, and the next thing I knew, I was down there too. Nobody could move. Totally paralyzed."

Stone approached the happenings at La Honda with some degree of enthusiastic caution. "It was becoming a full-time job for some, rather than recreational. I was still taking classes and trying to write a novel. We were still living in Palo Alto, so we had to go up there by driving all through the mountains. It was a commitment. We'd take our kids up there, and it became a whole production to go, and we did it, but not all of the time because it was so exhausting. It was a lot of work. It's a young man's game. I remember waking up and trying to figure out why my jaw hurt so much. It was because I had been smiling for ten hours the night before!"

One day out at La Honda, Stone saw it while walking the woods, the hallucination he would always remember. He had taken something called IT-290, this psychedelic superamphetamine that Kesey had taken back at the hospital and had then appropriated for the group, and during the trip Stone saw this amazingly detailed green locomotive with gold trim come rolling right through the redwoods. Such experiences were bound to have a powerful impact on the writing he was doing at the time. "The chemicals made my first book much less realistic," he recognized. "They helped me get free of the realist way, and the writing became much more freewheeling, much more fast and loose with reality. The trouble I began to find with writing and acid was that it tempts you toward superlatives, and superlatives cancel themselves out and they're rendered less effective by overuse."

"Stone writes like a bird, like an angel, like a circus barker, like a con man, like someone so high on pot that he is scraping his shoes on the stars," Wallace Stegner would remark about Stone's work, and for good reason. Indeed, the use of drugs would be present in every one of Stone's books—all critically acclaimed in the years to come: *Dog Soldiers, A Flag for Sunrise, Children of Light, Outerbridge Reach, Damascus Gate.*

"In many ways, those early days with Kesey informed much of what I would write about in years to come. The language, sensibility, the humor in my books, the way people relate to each other, not to mention actual settings and characters—I would use it in all my stuff. It was a time I was learning a lot. It was something I wouldn't have missed for anything even though there was always a downside . . . From the beginning, deep down, I never felt that drugs were a good thing, but they were something that was wild and open and free—and at that moment, these things were very important to us. When I look back on it and what followed, I was really not in favor of masses of people doing the stuff; I never really wanted to do it except in that small bunch of people I knew so well. Nothing is free, and perhaps the biggest mistake we made was thinking that these experiences could be. Acid could be as scary and overwhelming as anything, war included, and I think the downside had to surface eventually because human nature was involved, and when you stir up all that stuff from such a deep level, eventually there was going to be trouble. We never imagined back there in the early Sixties that there would be this whole youth culture with so many people getting involved with it."

By 1963, Stone was planning to head back east with his wife and two kids. He had shared a moment with Kesey that had changed their lives and would certainly begin to transform the culture, but while he and Kesey would remain lifelong friends, Stone would move out of the immediate orbit of the Pranksters during the next phase—the bus and the acid tests. "Everyone went their separate ways. I went back to New York and worked on my book and lived on St. Mark's Place, and Ken was going to go on with a different cast of characters and do this for years."

As Stone observed the unfolding of the counterculture, it seemed to have sprung full-grown from them like Athena from the mind of Zeus.

"I would always wonder how it was that this party I had gone to in 1963 had somehow followed us out the door and down the street and was filling the world with Day-Glo colors and all manner of motion. I would wonder how we could get back to that party, back to the garden. Even now I do."

VIII. Our Assignment Was to Topple This Prudish, Judgmental Civilization

IT WAS ONLY a matter of time before Harvard lost all patience with Dr. Timothy Leary and his strange clan.

In the fall of 1962, after the group returned from Zihuatanejo, Mexico, where they had conducted six sublime weeks of psychedelic summer camp in an atmosphere of absolute freedom and adapted the Evans-Wentz translation of the Tibetan Book of the Dead into *The Psychedelic Experience,* Leary prepared to enunciate his goals at Harvard with the same kind of clarity and "great vigor" that John F. Kennedy had used to present the objectives of his New Frontier. But what Timothy Leary had in mind was a New Frontier of Expanded Consciousness. In a widely covered speech to the Harvard Humanists, he announced the formation of the International Foundation for Internal Freedom. The politics of the nervous system would be every bit as complicated as external politics, he maintained; the fifth freedom would be defined as "freedom from the learned, cultural mind." If America was to be prevented from becoming "an anthill civilization," the fifth freedom would become absolutely essential. It should become the most basic freedom of human existence, directly guaranteed by the U.S. Constitution: *Congress shall make no law abridging the individual's right to seek an expanded consciousness.*

"That was the year the shit really hit the fan," Ram Dass recognized. "The project was just too powerful, too charismatic, and too chaotic. First, our neighbors in Newton brought a lawsuit against us for too many people living in a house in a single-family zoning community. Word about us had spread so fast that by 1963 twelve out of fifteen grad students only wanted to work with us. And Tim just wouldn't stop."

Leary was becoming less and less interested in Harvard. More convinced than ever that he was precisely on the cutting edge of a phenomenon that would transform the nation, from Hollywood to the pinnacles of American government, he was committed to "architecturing" a future of hope, turning the tide of history away from "the generals and arms merchants and power brokers and their obsession with planning for the Third World War," as he expressed it, seizing the reins of social control from the whole crowd that he had long come to abhor as those "stern-eyed business-suited WASPS who shuttle from home to office in limousines—the information brokers, editors, board members, executive branch members, youngish men with oldish eyes (faces you used to see around Harvard Square or in the Yale quad) . . . manipulators of secret documents, facts, rumors, estimates, arms inventories, stock margins, voting blocs, industrial secrets, gossip about the sexual and drug preferences of every member of Congress, trained to grab and maintain what they can, all loyal to the Protestant belief that the Planet Earth sucks."

It's doubtful that Leary would have stayed beyond his contract, but as it turned out, his hand was forced, and what decided the matter was again the central and defining issue of who would be allowed to go on the trip.

"Truth be known, we had been told that we could have gone on with the research at Harvard if Dana Farnsworth of the Health Service controlled the drugs we used for any project and if we agreed not to use any undergraduates, and we had agreed to those terms," Ram Dass explained. "We were trying to control it, but at the same time we saw that it wasn't to be controlled—and that there was hypocrisy in it. The predicament was this: there was an undergraduate living in our house who had taken many drugs, and there were other undergraduates who had taken them and started to hang around with us, and it was becoming harder in this social situation to say, 'No, you can't; you're in the wrong category.' They were incredibly eager, and the pressure was intense. So we didn't turn on any undergraduates actually involved in our research proper—it was in our private life. And we didn't turn on anybody who hadn't taken it before. Of course, what happened was really my fault. Partly it was because I was gay, and these were guys I was attracted to. There was a lot of complex motivation."

The university was just licking its chops, waiting for an excuse to pounce. While Leary was off setting up business for the IFIF in Mexico, readying Zihuatanejo for the next psychedelic hegira, Harvard officials received the information they needed, and on May 23, Dick Alpert was called in to Dean Munro's office. He was asked simply, "Did you give drugs to an undergraduate?"

Even though he had planned to stay on and teach for just one more year, Richard Alpert certainly never expected to become the first professor fired in the history of the university. "I remember looking at them all that day, the press and the professors and the administrators, and thinking, They think I'm the very definition of pathology, that I'm really psychotic at this point. They think I'm one way, but I'm really another. But I also felt clear and greatly relieved—great release, like all controls were now off, and I could really do what I wanted to do with the research. In a way, that was the problem with the drugs: they gave me a sense of validity in my being that was so much more valid than anything my intellectual world had created."

With time, both Tim Leary and Dick Alpert came to view the events of Harvard as inevitable. "The university was right to fire me," Ram Dass maintained. "I would have done the same thing." "As Kuhn pointed out in the *Structure of Scientific Revolutions*," Leary noted, "almost all intellectual breakthroughs have been produced by mavericks pushed out of and operating independently of established knowledge systems." However predictable or justifiable, what happened at Harvard would remain a powerful metaphor for how the America of the 1960s would never officially embrace its psychedelic child.

What followed was a brief period of foreign exile. Leary had gathered together a sum of money in contributions to the IFIF, something like twenty thousand dollars; the money didn't last long, and neither did Zihuatanejo. Eden would not be without its serpents. Itinerant young Americans started showing up at the compound, early bands of sandal-wearing longhairs, an occurrence that did little to please the authorities. Worse, an irate Mexican psychiatrist complained to the government about their work, with the result that a couple of *federales* appeared at the idyllic compound disguised as journalists. The whole group was unceremoniously deported like a bunch of dangerous anarchists. What awaited the neurological adventurers of the IFIF, cast adrift on the high seas of psychedelic uncertainty, would turn out to be a series of "inglorious routs."

"We went to the isle of Dominica and got thrown out of Dominica," Ram Dass recalled; "we went to Antigua and got thrown out of Antigua—all within a matter of weeks. We became like this wandering band without a place to call our own . . . I got very depressed and returned to Newton. We didn't know what we were going to do, and then Peggy

Hitchcock said, 'My brothers just bought this place up in Millbrook, a cattle ranch. I think there's an old house on it.' And I said, 'Let's go, Peggy,' and we drove there that night, and as soon as I saw it, all boarded up, I knew it was the place. If we wanted to get it, all I had to do was turn on her two brothers, Billy and Tommy, young, wealthy stockbrokers, heirs to the Mellon fortune."

The first time Leary saw the baroque sixty-four room, four-story mansion, with its two turrets and steep gables, it was suffused in the pastel colors of the September sunset. Surrounded by exquisite lawns, stables, and a two-story chalet that held a bowling alley, it looked like some slightly ruined vision or dream that they could now restore. The whole place seemed to suggest myths that had not yet been created, let alone integrated into their personalities, a dimension of consciousness as much as a place, where space and time could be suspended so that medieval kings could materialize to mix with ancient prophets and space-age philosophers and mad scientists and renaissance revelers and beautiful maidens of the new psychedelic spring.

Built around the turn of the century by William Dietrich, a German-born glass-lamp magnate who had first brought the electric light to many American cities, the Big House featured a baronial fireplace and ornate woodwork that had been carved by the master craftsmen of Europe. The walls were covered with rich, faded tapestries, the ceilings inlaid with gleaming wood panels. There was a huge kitchen with a walk-in refrigerator, a spacious library, and long, dark corridors with plush red carpets. At the top of the mansion was the "tower room" with its own cheery little fireplace. From this vantage point—only one of many extraordinary places to trip—you could look out through the surrounding windows at night and see the lights of the little town of Millbrook twinkling over the masses of pine.

It was here, on this bucolic twenty-five-hundred-acre estate in Dutchess County, two hours' drive up the Hudson River from Manhattan on the Taconic Parkway, secluded behind imposing jagged stone walls, that they now established the Castalia Foundation, funded and protected by the wealth of the Hitchcocks, one of America's richest families.

For Richard Alpert, it was the beginning of a truly incredible year.

"Millbrook was like a ship on the high seas of the most adventurous thing you could imagine. The place quickly started filling up, Maynard and Flo Ferguson in the gatehouse with their family, Charlie Mingus in the grove, Paul Desmond . . . Soon the whole cultural and intellectual world began coming through, all the great poets, writers, artists—everybody—forty people to dinner every night. The Hitchcock boys had this whole other scene going, all the gorgeous models and the beautiful people from New York, screwing away in their marble bungalow, and these two different scenes could interact and still stay separate, everyone taking LSD in this incredible experiment."

History would soon overtake them in the form of growing numbers of college students using LSD, the psychedelic rumblings of San Francisco, the growing media hysteria, and the government moving to declare LSD illegal, which would force them toward the game of politics and salesmanship and the search for social support. As it all unfolded and the Tibetan Book of the Dead gave way to the Grateful Dead, some of the lines written by Dr. Timothy Leary in the turrets of Millbrook would become the slogans for the psychedelic revolution, captions for the overheated images as they flashed—

> The paradox may be stated as follows: it becomes necessary for us to go out of our minds in order to use our heads. . . . The game is about to change, ladies and gentlemen. . . . Drugs are the religion of the twenty-first century. . . . Turn on. Tune in. Drop Out.

"Everything we did in the 1960s was designed to fission, to weaken faith and conformity to the 1950s social order," Leary declared, looking back on his motives during much of what was about to happen. "Our precise surgical target was the Judeo-Christian power monolith, which had imposed a guilty, inhibited, grim, anti-body, antilife repression on Western civilization. Our assignment was to topple this prudish, judgmental civilization."

# 4

# Everybody Must Get Stoned

**"Anybody who knows he is God go up on the stage."**

—Message flashed on the projector by Ken Kesey at the Trips
Festival, January 22, 1966

## I. Vikings in Your Oatmeal

"WE WERE CRAZED with this strange sense of release
we thought was granted to us by the civilization. LSD
was years away for us but already we were driven
specks of foment. We were like walking ergot."

Still sporting the Zapata-style mustache he wore when he was
fronting the Fugs, Ed Sanders quoted one of his own stories from *Tales of
Beatnik Glory* to set the mood of the Lower East Side during the early
1960s. Sanders was ensconced in the small shack he used as a combination office and studio next to his small rustic home in Woodstock, New
York, reflecting on the time of "Total Assault on the Culture," when he
converted an old kosher butcher shop at 383 East Tenth Street, into the
"vegetarian literary zone" he called the Peace Eye Bookstore. It was a
heady time to be a young artist on the Lower East Side. Underground
film and performance art were blossoming; backroom mimeo presses
seemed to be everywhere. Within those grubby run-down blocks stretching from Cooper Union to Tompkins Square Park steeped in immigrant
life, Sanders began taking the pulse of the simmering process of unrest
and undoing that he would liken to the creation of a "free zone" of culture, consciousness, behavior, and political expression.

"The timidity of 1950s American culture was swept aside as it dawned on an entire generation that there was oodles of freedom guaranteed by the United States Constitution that was not being used," Sanders would later write. "It seemed that the essence of the moil and toil of my generation was contained in those archetypal streets. Everything that was good and bad about America in the 60s seemed distilled and boldly drawn to the Lower East Side."

What made James Edward Sanders's background in Missouri different from the typical all-American midwestern upbringing of Boy Scouts and baseball and Sunday school at the First Christian Church was the powerful message of left-wing American individualism he received from his parents. His father, Lyle David Sanders, was a traveling salesman who used to chant folk songs and poetry; his mother, Mollie Cravens, was the daughter of a railroad construction engineer and a descendent of Sam Houston. It was his mother who sparked Sanders's lifelong interest in political philosophy and dissent, telling him, "Don't take anything from anybody. If you think something is right, then do it; if you don't like something, don't cooperate. Act out your life as you see what is right."

Sanders bought a seventy-five-cent copy of *Howl* at the state university bookshop in 1957, the effect of which he later likened to a force that ripped through his mind "like the tornado that had uprooted the cherry tree in his backyard when [he] was a child." This single experience had pivoted him decisively toward New York, NYU, and the life of a poet. The cultural landscape that he found in the East Village would become the basis for *Tales of Beatnik Glory,* his vivid collection of stories about a poet from the hinterlands named Sam Thomas and friends like Johnny the Foote and Avram Maniac as they went careening from scene to incredible East Village scene of weirdos, pill heads, schizoids, Washington Square philosophes, cultural deviationists, and political insurrectionists. The stories of *Tales* would become Sanders's paean to the wonder and innocence and pain and lunacy and sheer exuberance of the era, but they also made up the definitive sociological portrait of the hip underground culture of the Lower East Side (the LES) at the time when everyone hung out in Tompkins Square Park and drank at Stanley's at 12th and Avenue B and ate at the Metro Coffee Shop, and poetry readings and hootenannies and peace walks were flaring up along with the sexual experimentation of "skin-clings" like those of the "Siobhan McKenna Group Grope." The right image to project in this scene was one of "controlled wildness—exposing just the 'correct' amount of nuttiness, drug-abuse, alcoholism, and feigned flip-out." The philosophy of the era was governed by "the Dickens Principle": "it was the best of times, it was the worst of times, but it was our times, and we owned them with our youth, our energy, our good will, our edginess. So let's party. Under the Dickens Principle everything was a party." It was also the era of "rebel pharmaceuticals," when the "oodles of freedom" that Sanders had perceived would produce one of the first freewheeling experimental drug scenes of the nascent counterculture.

"There was already plenty of pot around, which had come directly out of jazz and out of Mexico, hitting the folk scene around '59 and '60 in New York City, filtering in through the civil rights movement in '61, '62, to some extent," Sanders recounted. "At NYU, where I had gone to college, it had been around in the Greenwich Village literary crowd, but it wasn't being done openly, and it was done with a lot of fear—*great gobs of fear,* in fact, always looking over your shoulder. Fear was a subtheme, the ritual of the experience itself; the very ceremony included fear and the anticipation of being arrested, which was very different from the later Sixties, when it was done brazenly, with a complete sense of abandon."

The pot trade of the time that Sanders remembered was "a mom-and-pop operation. I saw it as something fairly benevolent, with grass-roots origins, young enthusiasts and adventurers; the media would have referred to them as beatniks, of course. You started seeing them, these guys with Mexican sandals wandering on the Lower East Side; they had a certain air, and there were these manila grocery bags full of the stuff. It was sold in all kinds of ways—joints and five-dollar bags. You knew it came from somewhere but didn't analyze it. I didn't bother to find out why; I viewed it as a market phenomenon."

Sanders pointed to the ever-increasing references to marijuana in the culture of the underground, along with a definitive set of values being formed about its use. "There was the paradigm from *Howl* of course, of hipsters 'who got busted in their pubic beards returning through Laredo with a belt of marijuana for New York,' and doing the forbidden also had its paradigm in another Ginsberg line: 'Now it's time for prophecy without death as a result,' which had its correlative in 'Now it's time for a lifestyle without death as a result.' The feeling among us was that certain substances, like pot, mescaline, and peyote, didn't create death—they were nonthanatotic lifestyles, not about death tripping, as we later called it. Smoking pot was doing the forbidden without having to put your feet in the flames, so it was very attractive, and the feeling was that it didn't lead to any kind of addiction, that you could take it or leave it."

Unlike others who smoked whenever possible, Sanders would quickly learn that he couldn't really work well under the influence of the substance. "This was also confirmed by people like Julian Beck at the Living Theatre, who also said he couldn't work under it—others felt differently, of course. You learned how it affected your time-motor coordination or your linguistic skills. It became like anything else—like being streetwise, learning what streets to walk down, applying this growing street knowledge to these substances and figuring out why and how they should be taken."

As references to the substance expanded and information was gathered, so did the meanings and contexts of its use. "The gestalt provided the high, too," Sanders emphasized. "Just by being immersed in this culture, you were *high,* you were *groovy,* you wore *sandals,* you went to *poetry readings.* It was there in the politics. We got stoned on the peace march—it was very verboten, and I was careful not to carry anything. You had the new issue of *Evergreen Review.* You took *peyote.* You were *chosen,* man!"

As soon as Ishmael Reed arrived in New York from Buffalo, in 1962, he became aware of two separate cultures. "On the Lower East Side, it was grass all over the place; in the West Village, it was liquor, the scene left over from the Cedar Tavern," Reed remarked in his attic office in Oakland, reflecting on the time when he was a regular at Stanley's and writing for *The East Village Other.* "A whole philosophy was evolving out of marijuana. There was a connection—political, cultural, and otherwise—with the feeling that people were becoming less uptight and that marijuana could bring more peace, could somehow relax what was essentially a violent and racist culture. Most of the people I knew weren't doing things like coke or heroin—it was just grass—and I think a lot of people thought that the laws were just stupid and that grass would eventually become legalized, which was the whole point of the smoke-ins later in the

Sixties. At the time, all the problems of the world were attributed to whiskey drinkers. The political and cultural leadership of the United States drank alcohol; the establishment culture, whose drug of choice had always been alcohol, was evil; the emerging hip culture thought that love and liberation were embodied in marijuana."

"You had to be *extremely* careful about smoking pot," Wavy Gravy concurred. At the time, he was still Hugh Romney, living right above the Gaslight Café in Greenwich Village, in an apartment that would become a central meeting place for the poets and folk artists of the day (Bob Dylan would write "A Hard Rain's A-Gonna Fall" there on Romney's typewriter). "Marijuana was something that was done in closets with towels under the door with cans of Glade on hand to squirt after the act. It was dangerous, and it stayed dangerous, and when they came in to bust you, they would turn off the water first so that you would only have one flush of the toilet as they came breaking through the door!"

For Hugh Romney, the use of marijuana in the beginning was about learning "that food tasted better, that music could be amazing, that every breath was absolutely incredible . . . It was about being hip and knowing what was going on—not yet about that what was happening all contained the Godhead, no. It was about knowing tunes and not being a slave to a nine-to-five job; you were 'following your bliss,' as Joe Campbell would later call it. It was about attitude, soul, but more about awareness of this new lifestyle, and the music was the soundtrack to that lifestyle."

Back in those days of hanging out at the Gaslight, the end of the evening was when all the musicians playing around the Village would congregate and get high. "It was a period that only lasted in its pure state for maybe two or three years. There was no money involved, and everybody was young, and the feeling in the air was that this is as good as it gets. You'd be there after hours and hear Dylan's new song or Tom Paxton's latest thing, everybody showing each other their work before they laid it on the public, and we'd hang out together and get high, but you had to be so careful. Joints were really thin; stashes were extremely intricate."

Like many others, Wavy Gravy would remain astounded by the potency and impact of the weed he smoked at the time. "Oh, yes, there was

Mexican shit back there in the early Sixties that was so strong, what used to come from somewhere down there in these wax-paper-covered bricks, that would put Vikings in your oatmeal and jewels shining in the wall if you smoked it! I've often wondered, Was the stuff really that strong, or was it just that our straight, young, virgin middle-class Eisenhower-era minds were so susceptible, so ready to be blown by it? I don't know, but the big question that arises was an obvious one: Was America ready for Vikings in its oatmeal?"

Given the ever-greater availability of marijuana, it was a good question. By 1965, there seemed to be more potential pot smokers on American campuses than ever before. It was easy enough to spot them: rebels, die-hard nonconformists, egghead intellectuals, abstract painters, campus romanticists, dream-eyed poets, blue-jeaned folk musicians, fanatical jazz disciples, firebrand civil rights activists, leotarded modern dancers, visionary philosophers, offbeat loners, passionate vegetarians, flagrant sexual libertarians, and the simply weird. Some were looking to cast off the fetters and inhibitions that had come from religious backgrounds; others were emotionally aggrieved spirits in desperate flight from some aspect of American family life that had somehow metastasized like an episode of *Father Knows Best* gone dreadfully haywire. Whoever they were and wherever they came from, most of them seemed as fundamentally alienated from the conventional American society of the mid-1960s as the Paris Communards had been from the French bourgeoisie of their time. What this youthful amalgamation had in common as it groped its way into the new decade was one basic demographic trait: they were the advance guard of the Baby Boom generation, the true sons and daughters of the American Century; the best-educated, most physically robust and affluent generation in the history of the United States, newly vaccinated against polio, weaned on hot dogs and milk shakes, raised on television, rock and roll, baseball, Chevrolets, hula hoops, and the great American crusade against communism.

They also shared a search for definition and meaning that seemed to grow ever more restless and acute. It began as a mood more than anything else, an undefined yearning that was palpable in the ambience of social and political ferment steadily gathering over the land from Cambridge to

Berkeley. Forming cabals that were hidden from view for the time being, they read their Ginsberg and Kerouac and Burroughs, their Gregory Corso and Ferlinghetti and Snyder, their Eliot and Pound and the French poets, passing around William Burroughs's *Soft Machine* and their copies of *Evergreen Review* the way Soviet dissidents passed around their samizdat. They listened to Monk and Coltrane, Sonny Terry and Brownie McGhee, Big Bill Broonzy and Woody Guthrie, Joan Baez and Bob Dylan, and it was here among these college-age Americans, on wine-stained mattresses in candlelit dormitory rooms, in the dark alleys around the corner from bars and coffeehouses, and around campfires, where the smell of marijuana first began to emanate most conspicuously and where talk began about the experiments at Harvard and the peyote cactus and the Native American cultures who used it and places like the Newers Orchid Farm and Smith's Cactus Ranch, where they could get it. In that critical season, the single most important issue in the lives of those young people, what defined consciousness and attitude and stirred the soul, was the burgeoning civil rights movement.

"It had an extraordinary impact on everything we did," declared Peter Coyote, then still Peter Cohon, looking back at that transitional moment in American history. "By and large, white people felt completely trumped by black people at the time, who went out and set this incredibly courageous moral example by putting their lives on the line. And I think that those of us who were not actively involved with freedom marches in the South were pressed to come up with an identity and self-image of equal integrity or at the very least didn't want to participate in a culture which produced that kind of racism . . . You just can't talk about anything that happened during the Sixties without talking about black people as moral thinkers and artists because the whole thing was started by a little woman named Rosa Parks who got tired of it all and turned the whole economic and social and political superstructure of the South on its ass. I think everybody was influenced by that, and there was this growing desire to create this other realm, imagine yourself into it and act it out—and one of the tools that would soon materialize to pry yourself out of that box was psychedelics."

In the summer of 1965, the relationship between drug use and the new alternative culture took a decisively political turn as Ed Sanders became involved in a series of events that would signal the formal beginning of the movement to legalize marijuana in the United States.

"I had dropped out of graduate school and organized my bookstore," he remembered. "Allen Ginsberg lived just down the street, and I'd hang out with him. Allen was an example of a guy I almost worshipped. I knew all his poetry, *Howl* and *Kaddish*, by heart. That spring, there was a guy arrested named Jack Martin, and the Feds wanted him to set up Ginsberg, William Burroughs, and maybe Herbert Huncke. When Allen found out about it, he was absolutely enraged. There had been that earlier incident in California where Neal Cassady had been arrested and was asked to inform on his friends, so Allen was very aware of the kind of bravery involved in not becoming an informant. It was one of the first tastes I had about what kind of trouble you could get into."

On the Lower East Side of Manhattan, it was the season of the Fugs and the advent of blatant dope-law defiance—the summer that Dylan went electric at Newport and the Beatles were moving toward *Rubber Soul.* The word *hippie* was still several years away; phrases like *far out* had yet to enter the popular culture. On August 22, 1965, when Sanders sat at the typewriter in his bookstore, it wasn't the composition of verse that he had in mind. Instead, he began banging out the following press release: "*Federal Narcotics Agent to Force Defendant to Set Up Entrapment of Internationally Famous Poet Allen Ginsberg.*" The release, routed on a mimeographed letterhead that read "LEMAR, the New York Committee to Legalize Marijuana," stated that the federal agent had also indicated that LEMAR itself had become a target for such entrapment.

"Around the first of that year, we had gone down to Centre Street and to the Women's House of Dentention on the West Side and demonstrated. I used to go there with a group from *The Catholic Worker* to sing Christmas carols outside the windows for the convicts. That was when Ginsberg had his picture taken in the snow by Fred McDarrah of *The Village Voice* with a sign that said, "POT IS FUN." A lot of people were paranoid about it—'Oh, they'll never get away with it!'—but we felt that it was a legitimate political position. It made quite a splash at the time because it quickly became a worldwide image—this bearded poet with a gleam in his eye, carrying this sign in the snow. In a sense, that single image became like a shot heard around the world."

## II. A Gang of Innocents Playing with Fire

THE FIRST TIME Carolyn Adams saw the painted bus called *Furthur*, she couldn't believe her eyes. In the first light of dawn, it looked enchanting under the great redwoods. Soon she found herself crawling all over it, caressing the bus as if it were some kind of cherished object from her childhood that had always remained lost to her until that moment.

The Pranksters would call her Mountain Girl because when one of them asked her where she lived, she told him matter-of-factly, "On a mountain," and indeed that was where she was living at the time, in a one-room shack on top of a mountain, with no electricity and a rifle to shoot at all the squirrels and rats. Almost twenty-five years later, Carolyn "Mountain Girl" Adams Garcia was still living on top of a mountain— outside Bolinas, in a much nicer house—but she still had a rifle. "So there I was, just sitting in a coffee shop in St. Michael's Alley, in Palo Alto, when Neal Cassady suddenly appeared and sat down as if we were old friends. 'Hey, you wanna go for a ride and smoke a joint?' "

Of course it was a pickup line, but Carolyn Adams was eighteen and fearless. To get stoned and hear Neal Cassady rapping for the first time was in itself an unforgettable experience, but he was talking a blue streak about Ken Kesey and his bus called *Furthur* and this group of people called the Merry Pranksters that had assembled around him and this strange and wondrous journey they had just returned from taking across the country.

"About a week later they had a party, and I went. The party was called the Debriefing, and I took acid for the first time. There was a big bonfire, and I was just giggling and rolling around in the ferns and bouncing up and down the hill. I remember looking down at my feet and seeing all these little redwood needles rearranging themselves into these incredible patterns. '*Look, they're marching! They're making little armies!*' Within three months, I was living there."

Carolyn Adams had grown up in an upper-middle-class family in Poughkeepsie, New York. As Tom Wolfe described her, she was "big, about five-foot-nine, . . . and loud and sloppy," but "she had beautiful teeth and a smile that lit up one's gizzard." Mountain Girl was "one big loud charge of vitality" with big brown eyes that "exploded like sunspots in front of your face," and from that first night it was clear to her that she fit right into the Prankster program.

"The forest was turned on! I had the most fun painting stumps and roots and dipping redwood cones into orange fluorescent paint and rear-ranging them back into the environment—it really upset the hikers, though. I just loved that whole attitude, that life was such a gift and that given the proper attitude, you could turn the whole thing into a play or movie or a way of describing yourself to other people that would intrigue them and draw them into your drama. It was life as a movie."

What made the movie even more fascinating, of course, was Kesey himself. "He was the center that it all moved around; he was pulling all the strings and manipulating it and getting people to do what he wanted. Of course, usually what he had in mind was so damn interesting and so outside of anything people would normally think of that you wanted to go along with the phenomenon. Ken put a telephone up there in the woods that wasn't hooked to anything. People would slip into the tree and 'make a call.' He loved to play like that—it was so much fun to trip around him." Over the next year, Mountain Girl would become "a sol-derer and taper of wires, a mender of microphones," as she put it. "I im-mediately took on a responsibility act, somebody who looks out for other people and tries to keep the whole thing going. It's kind of funny; I still do that." She would also fall in love with Kesey and have a child with him, a girl named Sunshine.

It was clear from the Debriefing that the Pranksters were having a hard time letting go of the trip they'd made to New York the previous summer in the specially modified bus. Kesey needed to be in New York for the publication of his second novel, *Sometimes a Great Notion,* but the other and more important purpose of the trip had been to make a movie in which the fourteen passengers were all going to be ensemble players and the LSD they were carrying in an orange-juice container in their lit-tle refrigerator would become the main prop of the production. The bus was driven by none other than Neal Cassady, Fastestmanalive himself, a man with a rather extensive and celebrated cross-country driving résumé, and in Kesey's vision the bus and the Pranksters would become the movie, and the movie would become the bus and the Pranksters, and the totality of the experience, along with the LSD, would evolve into the "trip" itself.

What happened to the Merry Band on its trip during the summer of 1964 ranged from the cosmically sublime to the ridiculous, from peak ecstasy to full-tilt satori. To say that they were merely high would do a disservice to how stoned they really were, and when they were all high and playing music and everything was happening at once—the countryside rolling past, with everybody plugged into the sound equipment with the headsets and the tape loops reverberating and Cassady talking a mile a minute behind the wheel, rapping away in his unique stream of consciousness with the words foaming out of his mouth and the eyes bulging out of his head like bright beaming headlights—it seemed like the whole bus became one consciousness flying off the road through space and light and time. It was hard to find the words to describe this thing they called Group Mind when everything seemed to fuse: word and image, intention and synchronicity, rapture and wonder and innocence, heat and flesh and light, sky and spirit and wind, water and mountains and motion and mind.

By the time they arrived back at La Honda, there were thirty hours of footage, but it was jumbled and amateurish. *The Merry Pranksters Search for the Cool Place,* as they called the movie, would remain a work in progress for the next thirty years and would never become the fully realized work that Kesey had always wanted it to be. "To me, the real significance of Kesey's bus trip in the summer of 1964 was as a cultural signal that happened just as the nation was on the precipice of enormous awakening and change," Allen Ginsberg observed. "It was like a very colorful flag going up a flagpole, signaling the news that something was about to happen, something was about to shake."

When they took LSD at La Honda, the Pranksters liked to play with concepts, experiment with different games. Kesey would usually initiate the process with a theme or anecdote or perception, and the others would leap in, toying whimsically with it, fleshing it out, making it spin and dance, turning it on its head and shaking it to see what would come out until the Group Mind clicked in. Then the whole thing would take on its true form, and they would all ride it into some kind of inexpressible transcendence where new kinds of power and energy and thought seemed possible. To the Pranksters, what happened when you took acid was anything but a fairy tale; real power was unleashed. In fact, they even played a game called Power, in which a chosen person was allowed unlimited power over the others for half an hour. The acid they used was liquid Sandoz—"incredible, really pure," as Mountain Girl remembered it. "I never got to see it, only consume it."

The events of the next months would only raise the stakes of the game: Kesey and Mountain Girl were arrested and charged with possession of marijuana by officers of the San Mateo Sheriff's Department. From that moment on, Kesey would find himself in an epic confrontation with the law, locked in the classic struggle of a man horrified by the prospect of incarceration yet not about to back down from his pursuit of freedom and choice. Over the course of the year, Kesey would become a kind of psychedelic superhero in the Bay Area. "I'd rather be a lightning rod than a seismograph," he would often say. If trying to attract lightning was what Kesey was doing, where he looked for it next would only enrage the local authorities even more: he invited the Hells Angels down to La Honda for a three-day bash.

The seeds of this storied encounter were planted on the day Kesey appeared on a local public-television station with a Louisville-born freelance journalist named Hunter S. Thompson, who was gathering material for the first book about "the rottenest motorcycle gang in the history of Christendom." In the public mind, the Hells Angels had come to represent the 1950s American nightmare of juvenile delinquency not only made flesh but magnified a hundredfold and updated to the Great Society. If Kesey's dauntless invitation had set in motion a process that would bring characters like Buzzard, Gut, Tiny, Freewheelin Frank, and Terry the Tramp into the mix of a nascent psychedelic counterculture, the man who was determined to play the role of Margaret Mead to this "strange and terrible" phenomenon and tell their story was now also about to become a player in the scene. Though Hunter Thompson hardly looked like a gang member, with his loud Hawaiian shirts, madras jackets, short hair, and aviator glasses, few journalists were ever better matched with their subjects. Having grown up lower middle class in a southern society that vaunted wealth, conformity, gentility, and privilege, Thompson, the son of an alcoholic, was sentenced by a local judge to sixty days in jail after a rampage of uncontrolled drunken vandalism at the age of seventeen. He had missed his high-school graduation—a watershed event in his story. He later received an honorable discharge from the air force, but only after a kindly master sergeant who had encouraged his writing for the base newspaper interceded on his behalf. Following a path that led him from Greenwich Village to Big Sur in 1960, where he worked as a caretaker for the Murphy family on the estate that would eventually be turned into Esalen, he traveled to South America, wrote some of the finest articles of that time for *The National Observer,* and returned to San Francisco, settling on Parnassus Street with his first wife and newborn son just as the Haight Ashbury was budding into a psychedelic community. First and foremost, Hunter Thompson was a ferocious natural-born hellion drawn to the edge of extreme experience, and from the outset his literary acumen would match his unbridled hell-raising spirit.

Kesey was instantly intrigued by the freedom of these benighted outlaws called Hells Angels. After all, was he not well on the path to becoming an outlaw himself? "We're in the same business," he told them. "You break people's *bones,* I break people's *heads.*" What would happen, he wondered, if the Angels took acid? When Thompson realized that Kesey was serious about finding out, he was horrified. "When we left the Angel hangout I told Kesey, 'You motherfucking, crazy bastard, you'll pay for this from Maine to here,' " he recalled. "I thought they would take the Pranksters apart like cooked chicken. I had been to La Honda and knew they were a gang of innocents playing with fire."

Thompson's concern was ignored, and on Saturday, August 25, 1965, the redwood hills around Route 84 echoed with the thunder of the San Francisco chapter of the most fearsome motorcycle gang in the United States. To Mountain Girl, "they were a cross between the lost boys and the pirates. There was a fairy-tale aspect to it." It was culture shock for the Angels, too, what with all the children, educated middle-class students, artists, lawyers, psychologists, and intellectuals roaming about and so many young beautiful girls with long, fragrant hair and scarlet tights.

Richard Alpert was in attendance; Allen Ginsberg danced around with finger cymbals, chanting; Kesey presided over the scene like some New Age druid priest in a white hooded robe. The Pranksters had laid in enough beer to keep a battalion of thirsty marines happy for a week, and the Angels wasted no time tearing into it, smoking reefer and popping pills prodigiously until Kesey began doling out the LSD. The Angels apparently thought they were taking some kind of powerful amphetamine that would keep them up; within the hour, they were turning into what looked like a bunch of docile, awestruck little boys. The party wailed on for the next seventy-two hours, ebbing and flowing in waves of ecstatic dancing and dope smoking and sex, with Dylan and the Rolling Stones blaring and the red lights from police cruisers parked across the road flashing through the leaves.

For Kesey and the Pranksters, the great bash with the Angels only confirmed that they were on the right path. They had watched some of the Angels arrive with mistrust and bloodlust in their eyes and leave with flowers in their beards; in effect, they had "absorbed" the gang, easily drawing them into their Movie. This mix of people in an atmosphere of complete freedom and spontaneity would become the prototype for the next phase: a multimedia psychedelic experience that would move out from La Honda into garages and small halls up and down the Bay Area, all of it summed up by six cryptic words on a little handbill: CAN YOU PASS THE ACID TEST?

## III. Enough Acid to Blow the World Apart

THE ACID TESTS WERE "one of those outrages, one of those *scandals,* that create a new style or a new world-view," wrote Tom Wolfe, "the *epoch* of the psychedelic style and practically everything that has gone into it."

Besides the people and LSD, the primary elements of the experience were the whirling sounds of the Grateful Dead, the Pranksters playing their own brand of avant-garde music, the extemporaneous hipalogues of people like Kesey, Ken Babbs, Neal Cassady, and Hugh Romney at the microphones, the application of newly available strobe lights, and footage of the Pranksters from the bus trip projected on the screens. Perhaps nobody would ever describe this first "mass acid experience" better than Tom Wolfe. The book that he would write about it, *The Electric Kool-Aid Acid Test,* is a tribute to his unique literary acumen in that he never attended a single acid test and certainly never took acid himself: "Everybody's eyes turn on like headlights, fuses blow, blackness—wowww!—the things that shake and vibrate and funnel and freak out in this blackness—and then somebody slaps new fuses in and the old hulk of a house shudders back, the wiring writhing and fragmenting like molten snakes, the organs vibro-massage the belly again, fuses blow, minds scream, heads explode."

What would emerge from this protracted pandemonium was a kind of alter reality, a new-fashioned medium that encouraged the expression of life as art through the senses. It was thrilling, but it could also be scary and dangerous, with more freak-outs as the events grew in size. "The room is a spaceship and the captain has *lost his mind,*" was one of Kesey's intonations that perfectly summed up the proceedings. Richard Alpert became increasingly alarmed as the acid tests attracted more attention. "They were attempts to engage people in their senses so totally as to make it a transformational experience through sensory overload. It was an attempt to overload one dimension so much that it forced people into another dimension. In many ways it was an attempt to find a collective unconscious in a Jungian sense." As the government moved closer to making LSD illegal that year, Alpert was certain that Kesey's acid tests would bring the full heat of the law down on the burgeoning psychedelic movement and stop it in its tracks.

But the anarchy of larger groups of "freshly psychedelicized" people was precisely what made the tests so exhilarating for the Grateful Dead lead guitarist Jerry Garcia, who described them as "thousands of people, all helplessly stoned, finding themselves in a room full of other people, none of whom any of them were afraid of. It was magic—far out, beautiful magic." The Grateful Dead, the house band of the acid tests, were, as Garcia characterized them, a "social configuration" before they were a band. They played bluegrass and folk music in pizza joints and clubs around Palo Alto and Stanford as Mother McCree's Uptown Jug Champions before they evolved into the Warlocks and got their hands on some of the pure pharmaceutical LSD going around and realized that playing "short, fast stuff" in bars wasn't going to allow them the "vision of a truly fantastic thing" offered by Kesey and the acid tests. From their inception, they were a vital cog in the unfolding of the psychedelic story in the Bay Area. The Dead were aware of being involved in something that had never happened before, and the kind of music they would create would evolve naturally out of the unique situation of playing music on LSD in the midst of people in the same state of mind. "If the Acid Tests hadn't happened, we might have been just another band," Garcia declared. "But you can also say that without the Grateful Dead, the Acid Tests wouldn't have happened in the same way. . . . We had an opportunity to visit highly experimental places under the influence of highly experimental chemicals, before a highly experimental audience. It was ideal!"

Sometimes they were too stoned to play; other times they played music that was like an electrifying roller-coaster ride with ecstatically extended improvisational jams that sprawled out on as many different levels as a Neal Cassady rap before coming back together. For that first year, they played what Hank Harrison referred to in his social history of the band as "dragon music"—"esoteric, asymmetrical music that could only be intellectualized by a few, and then most inaccurately. It was truly cliché-free, uncontrived music, even beyond the free form jazz structures of Miles and Coltrane."

And it was loud, thanks to the sound system developed and paid for by the group's patron, Augustus Owsley Stanley III—Owsley, as he was known all over the world during the Psychedelic Sixties; Bear, as he was called by friends and associates.

The acid tests would never have been possible without Owsley, and it's doubtful whether the Haight Ashbury or psychedelic rock would have happened in quite the same way without his presence on the scene. He was one of those characters who would never have existed at any other time or place. The disaffected grandson of a Kentucky senator, he was a brilliant but eccentric college dropout who had split with his family at the age of eighteen, before becoming a radar technician and electronics whiz in the air force. By the time he showed up in Berkeley, late in 1964, he had moved on to the art and science of illicit chemistry.

Owsley happened to hear the Grateful Dead play at the Fillmore Au-

ditorium for the first time in December of 1965; he thought Garcia's guitar sounded "scary, like the claws of a tiger," and that the band could be
bigger than the Beatles. The next night, he followed the band out to the
Muir Beach Acid Test, where he ingested his first LSD and found himself
regressing to eighteenth-century Paris, fragmenting into pixilated molecules, and disappearing into the intergalactic ooze—but not before driving his sports car into a tree. A few days later, he informed Kesey that
what he was doing with the Pranksters was like "messing around with ancient wisdom but without any of the maps" and that he needed to be very
careful. The acid tests, he recognized, were like being shot out of a cannon—"sort of like a crash course in how to become a jet pilot when you
never had seen a jet before. The way they did it was they dropped you in
there, took you up, and said, *'The controls are yours!' Whoa! Barrel rolls!
Immelmanns! Tailspins!*"

After his first experience, Owsley recognized that some of these first-
time "jet pilots" at the tests were bound to crash right into the ground,
but whatever hesitation he initially felt about traveling in the psychedelic
realms ultimately encouraged rather than allayed his ambition to make
the purest and cheapest acid in the history of the world. He would always
attribute this aspiration to a simple desire not to poison himself—"All I
knew was that it was better to take a known substance in a known quantity than an unknown mixture of who-knows-what at god-knows-what
quantity"—but if he could make some money, well, that would be fine,
too. At first, his Berkeley roommates didn't believe he could do it. One of
them was Charlie Perry, later to become one of the first managing editors
of *Rolling Stone.* "But Owsley could surprise the hell out of you," as Perry
put it. When his methedrine lab was busted in February of 1965, for example, Owsley hired the deputy mayor of Berkeley as his attorney. He got
off on a technicality—police had found the equipment but not the substance on the premises—and then he had the audacity to sue the police to
get his equipment back. After moving to Los Angeles and setting up another lab, he formed a company called Bear Research Group and made
the last legal purchases of lysergic monohydrate, the essential ingredient
in LSD synthesis, accumulating eight hundred grams from Cyelo Chemical and International Chemical and Nuclear Corporation and paying
twenty thousand dollars in cash, all in hundred-dollar bills. By May, he

had returned to Berkeley with his first batch of blue barrels, acid that Perry remembered as being "devastatingly strong."

It was only the beginning of his legend. Owsley became a wizard alchemist with a messianic philosophy of how divine forces had placed the sacrament of LSD on the planet at the same time as nuclear fission, thereby providing mankind with both the means of salvation and the seeds of destruction. He was obsessed with making LSD even purer than Sandoz, producing it first in powder form in gelatin capsules as well as light-blue liquid ("Mother's Milk") that was easily recognizable when titrated onto sugar cubes. At Millbrook during an East Coast trip, he met Billy Hitchcock, who became his financier, and then acquired the services of Tim Scully, an associate chemist who would become equally renowned in the psychedelic world. They set up a lab in suburban Point Richmond and began working in twenty-four-hour shifts, making another great leap in the operation when they acquired a tabbing machine that allowed them to control dosage. Soon Owsley was dyeing each new shipment of perfect, hard little double-domed pills a different color. He believed that the psychic energies in the lab at the precise moment the ingredients came together in the process of making LSD were a critical factor in the kinds of trips people would have, and with each new batch, word would spread like wildfire among his ever-growing clientele that one color was more mellow and another more visual and still another speedier. It was always assumed that he cut his acid with a little amphetamine to enhance the psychedelic effects, but whatever the chemical components, his pills of 245–400 milligrams were guaranteed to provide the vital components of a great acid trip: blast off, rapid ascent, towering peak, plenty of ego dissolution, and the full whirlwind of sensory effects.

From 1966 to 1968, Owsley and his associates produced four major brands: first, the barrel-shaped pills he called Blue Cheer, which became the name of another San Francisco rock group he was backing; then, White Lightning, which marked the first use of the tabbing machine; next, Purple Haze, from which Jimi Hendrix would take the title of a song; and finally, Orange Sunshine, perhaps the most widely disseminated of them all. Nobody knows how much LSD he made before the Bureau of Narcotics and Dangerous Drugs finally took him down in 1969, when Billy Hitchcock testified against him in return for a slap on the wrist and Owsley was sent away to Lompoc Prison for several years. Estimates range in the millions of doses, but as much money as he made, he would never raise the price of a hit above two dollars because he believed that acid for the masses would be the engine that would save the world. But while his output would be impossible to determine, its effects were everywhere: in the ballrooms, on the streets of the Haight, at every outdoor concert and major event that would make San Francisco the psychedelic capital of the world. *Newsweek* would compare Owsley to Henry Ford; Timothy Leary called him "God's secret agent"; in Britain, John Lennon wanted to procure a lifetime supply of his product. In 1967, the new federal penalties for the manufacture of LSD would be popularly known as the Owsley laws.

"When he started making acid in bigger quantities, dirt cheap and stronger than you'd ever been able to get it, and drenching the Bay Area with it, it was like somebody had opened a munitions factory for getting high," acknowledged Perry. "The competition couldn't catch up, and neither could the cops. He was like a Pied Piper in that he was leading people, but he was also an ideal in that here was the model of a guy being completely outrageous and getting away with it big-time. It was like a sign that we could all do the same."

It wasn't easy working with him, however. "Bear came with a price," Mountain Girl explained. "We tried not to let him into our scene too much because he was such an overpowering personality, but the Grateful Dead scooped him right up. He wanted to be in the band, so he bought them all that fabulous equipment and rented houses for them and supported them for the first couple of years. But Owsley always knew better than everybody, and after a while you found yourself trying to find ways to get around him."

Owsley was every bit as passionate about rock as he was about the quality of his product and wanted a sound system for the Grateful Dead that was worthy of the space age. The group would not only have some of the best equipment in San Francisco; in Garcia's words, they would also have access to "enough acid to blow the world apart."

IV.  How I Passed the Acid Test

AS OWLSEY CRANKED out the Blue Cheer, the Pranksters continued their operations up and down the coast. From Ken Kesey's perspective, they were becoming "like a really crack terrorist group. We could hit a place, get in there, mess it up, and be gone before people knew what happened."

Everything came together with the Trips Festival of January 21–23, 1966, organized by Stewart Brand at the San Francisco Longshoreman's Hall as a showcase of all the arts and crafts and forms of expression of the new psychedelic wave. The event would include the Open Theater, Tape Music Center activities, rock bands, and light shows, with the acid test as the main attraction, and was billed as a simulation of an LSD trip but "without the LSD," a notion that was utterly laughable from the outset, of course, because everyone involved and all the acid heads in San Francisco knew that free-flowing acid was precisely the point. The event took place against the backdrop of Kesey's second arrest for marijuana, which had occurred only four days after he pleaded no contest to the first one. With this second offense, the 3.4 grams of marijuana retrieved by the police carried an automatic five-year sentence with no possibility of parole. It was obvious that the judges "wanted to make an example of him," as Mountain Girl saw it. "They were really going to sock it to him and try and strip him of everything. It was scary."

Kesey's second arrest was front-page news. "If ever I wanted to draw a crowd" he recognized, "all I ever had to do was get busted"—the three-day Trips Festival was engulfed by six thousand people. The festival was a "huge wild carnival," as Wolfe reported, the first great public convocation of the tribes: "For the acid heads themselves, the Trips Festival was like the first national convention of an underground movement that had existed on a hush-hush cell-by-cell basis. The heads were amazed at how big their ranks had become—and euphoric over the fact that they could come out in the open, high as baboons, and the sky, and the law, wouldn't fall down on them."

At least not yet.

The other notable development of the Trips Festival was the emergence of the man hired to be its coordinator. As the rising psychedelic wave already had its avatars and gurus, its poets and philosophers, its ringmasters and evangelist chemists and electric minstrels, it was now about to find its greatest impresario. Bill Graham, born Wolfgang Grajonca in Berlin, had escaped the Nazis by crossing Europe on foot as an eleven-year-old refugee. He had grown up playing stickball and delivering groceries on the streets of the Bronx, won a Bronze Star for valor in Korea, drove cabs, hustled tips in the Catskills, and dreamed of becoming an actor before coming out to San Francisco and serving as the manager of the San Francisco Mime Troupe just as the group was igniting and catalyzing the new cultural underground. Graham had been around commedia dell'arte productions like *Il Candelaio* where a little weed might have been smoked, but the Trips Festival was something else entirely. Great big tubs of LSD-laced Kool-Aid were set out downstairs and up in the balcony; practically everybody was tripping but him. It was the first time Graham had ever seen "the acid thing in full force," and he was duly shocked. "They might as well have been offering hand grenades to people. When LSD exploded inside a body, how did they know how much damage the shrapnel could cause? They had ices spiked with acid, available to all, children as well."

Bands like Big Brother and the Grateful Dead were playing a big event for the first time; the Pranksters had their Thunder Machine and a huge tower that Ken Babbs had built in the center of the hall. Graham was running around frantically with a clipboard under his arm, doing his best to keep something organized that was designed to go completely out of control. There were five movie projectors going at once, throngs of acidheads in serapes and mandala beads and Indian headbands, exploding strobes, black lights and Day-Glo paint everywhere. When it was all over, there was no doubt in Graham's mind that the free use of LSD would present serious challenges for any such future events. "There were a lot of people who were having serious problems with where this drug was taking them. . . . I was worried about people getting hurt after they left." Nonetheless, within the pandemonium, Graham had also recognized his destiny. "I realized what I wanted to do. Living theater. Taking music and the newborn visual arts and making all of that available in a comfortable surrounding so that it would be conducive to open expression. What I saw was that when all this truly worked, it was *magic*."

And lucrative. The fact that the festival had grossed $12,500 in three days had not gone unnoticed. Within weeks, Graham was presenting his first shows. If the era of the Haight Ashbury was kicked off that very weekend, it was also the beginning of one of the most remarkable careers in the history of rock. Once fully unleashed, Bill Graham became a raging typhoon of energy, ambition, tenacity, and sheer chutzpah. As San Francisco became the world capital of psychedelia, Graham would provide the emporium of its sound and in the process build an empire.

The acid test was snowballing fast. There was talk of moving it to Madison Square Garden, and *Look, Newsweek, Time,* and *Life* were now covering the psychedelic story. But even as the Pranksters recognized that they had a hit on their hands, they worried that for Kesey, at least, the show was about to close. But the Chief was not about to go gently off to prison. "If society wants me to be an outlaw, then I'll be an outlaw, and a damned good one," Kesey declared. He fled to Mexico, but not before faking his own suicide. He got his cousin Dale to dress up like him, drive his truck up the coast, park it at the edge of a cliff, and throw Kesey's trademark blue cowboy boots over the side. The police were supposed to think that Kesey had taken acid before taking the leap. They found a suicide note on the front seat that was the equal of any fiction Kesey had ever published—"So I Ken Kesey being of (ahem) sound mind and body do hereby leave the whole scene to Faye, corporation, cash, the works. And Babbs to run it." The cops didn't believe it for a second.

With all the busts and the frenetic activity of the acid tests, things were crazy enough, but by this time Mountain Girl was several months pregnant with Kesey's child. "Everyone had been through so much together; that was the inevitability of living the way we were living. Ken is the kind of person who doesn't say no, and I didn't know how to say no. I was so young and impressionable and very smitten—happy to be pregnant—but I was too naive to know what I was getting into, so lighthearted about life that I didn't take any of it seriously. I tried not to let it slow me down and only took acid in microdoses." Kesey had always maintained a powerful sense of family. He insisted on everyone staying together, which made it difficult for everyone when he left—Faye, their kids, and Mountain Girl.

The Pranksters and the Grateful Dead organized a series of events in

Los Angeles, culminating in the Watts Acid Test, held in a large warehouse on the outskirts of the black community only six months after the rioting. Kesey's flight was big news, and the photographer Larry Schiller was arranging to shoot all the Pranksters for the cover of *Life* after the event. Ken Babbs, an ex-marine helicopter pilot, was now running the show—a man of fierce energy and commitment who lacked Kesey's stature and easygoing charm. Watts would turn out to be the final bash before LSD was criminalized. The event was conspicuous for the large contingent of military personnel who were on the scene but had no idea what to expect and for the fact that the Kool-Aid was overdosed. "We used these little six-ounce cups, and it was about double what it should have been, way too strong," remembered Mountain Girl. "Two or three cups and you were gone—blazing!"

There were freak-outs everywhere. At the peak of the madhouse festivities, a woman became seriously unhinged on the chemical in one of the anterooms. "RAAAAY! *WHO CARES!*" she began shrieking hysterically, and when Babbs held a microphone up to her mouth, the woman's ragged existential despair was instantaneously hot-wired into the collective nervous system of the entire event. "RAAAAY! *WHO CARES!*"

Hugh Romney was deep into one of his tongue dances when he realized the woman's brittle state of being, and what he did next—or "how I passed the acid test," as he puts it—involved nothing less than a full-blown epiphany. Romney had come to look more and more like a leprechaun since his early days in the Village as a beatnik poet and comedian; his teeth had long since departed, for one thing, victims of a constant diet of Snickers bars and Hoffman's black-cherry soda. After marrying a beautiful French woman in a ceremony at the Gaslight nightclub performed by a blind Harlem singer and musician called the Reverend Gary Davis, Romney had moved out to California in 1962, where he joined the Committee, the seminal improvisational San Francisco theater company. He was living the good life—his own condo, plenty of bookings, a Packard Caribbean convertible, a baby daughter named Sabrina—when one day a sugar cube containing lysergic acid diethylamide-25 came across his transom. GOD IS FUN, he scrawled across the garage sometime during the experience. It seems that Romney received "information" during the experience about a coming global cataclysm and left for northern Arizona to join up with the Hopi Indians because it was written in the Book of the Hopi that "in a condition of planetary emergency the people of all races would gather together on the main mesa and await instructions from the spirit world." Some of the tribesmen had gently informed him that he was "a bit early for the apocalypse" and recognized that their visitor needed to hang around for a while to "regroup" his head.

Romney eventually returned to L.A., but things were never quite the same. He divorced his wife and gave away everything he had to float aimlessly on "the Ocean of Sacred Coincidence." He was calling himself Al Dente for a while as he hung around with characters like Del Close and Tiny Tim and supported himself by selling decorator Baggies of marijuana to Hollywood stars that contained tiny multicolored sparkly toys like Cracker Jack surprises. Then he walked into a restaurant where he encountered a beautiful Minnesota-born-and-bred actress and ex–Playboy bunny behind the counter named Bonnie Jean Beecher and fell in love with her the moment he realized she had put peanuts in his hamburger. Hugh and Bonnie Jean married and were living on Lemon Grove Street near Western Avenue just as forty-two of the Pranksters arrived and moved into Hugh and Bonnie Jean's one-room apartment and asked them to help organize the Watts Acid Test. And that was how Romney came to find himself there that night, microphone in hand, hurtling through the cosmic ether and wondering what on earth to do about this poor woman screaming, "*WHO CARES!*" over and over—and how to prevent the whole event from turning into a hospital for the insane.

"At that moment some deep instinct took over, and I rushed over to her and found myself trying to organize a circle of loving and caring strangers to help her," he recalled. "Then, as the group of us surrounded and took care of her, I felt the love we were generating as an actual current of warm, glowing energy which kept building and building until it was like we all seemed to slip our earthly bonds and fused into a shimmering radiance of jewels and light. I experienced it as a pure healing power, an awe-inspiring benevolent force for good, and what it taught me in that instant was that when you get to the bottom of the human soul, . . . somehow you manage to reach down and help someone who is sinking worse than you are, . . . and that's when you get really high and you don't need any LSD."

It was a lesson about compassion and service that Romney would carry in his heart for the rest of his days and one that would establish him as one of the most enduring folk figures of the American counterculture. From that moment on, wherever he went, he would be working for "the Management," as he puts it. The psychedelic wave had just washed up its first hippie saint—the man B. B. King would call Wavy Gravy.

By morning, it was all over. The people arrested that night and the extensive media coverage would further establish the link in the public mind between LSD and a rock-and-roll delirium of complete anarchy, but as far as the Pranksters were concerned, the major ramification of the Watts Acid Test was the bus prank. As everyone was setting up for Schiller's group portrait, Babbs excused himself to go to the bathroom, then climbed on the bus along with Mountain Girl and a few others, and headed to Mexico to join Kesey, leaving the rest of them stranded in Los Angeles. As the saying went, "Never trust a Prankster."

Sunshine was born in a little hospital in Manzanillo—"with no *anaesthetico*," as Mountain Girl related, "under very primitive conditions"— and the group stuck it out for six months, until they could no longer stand the heat and dirt and loneliness and paranoia. Kesey came back over the border disguised as a singing cowboy on a horse. As soon as they got back to the Bay Area, he did a live broadcast from San Francisco State College and announced that he intended to remain at large and "rub salt in J. Edgar Hoover's wounds." Call it hubris or fate, but the next day he was spotted by the FBI driving to San Jose and was taken into custody after a wild chase.

Kesey was let out of jail to hold the Acid Test Graduation after promising the judge that he would use the event to tell everyone that it was time to "move beyond" acid and to live the "healthy life." Tom Wolfe arrived in the middle of everything, charming everyone in his white suit and polka-dot tie as he took notes with a bemused expression on his face, gathering material for *The Electric Kool-Aid Acid Test*, a book that would become a classic of the New Journalism and enshrine the psychedelic story in the pantheon of American pop culture. But the event itself was melancholic because it formalized what everyone already knew: Kesey was going to jail, and there was nothing anyone could do about it; the only question was how long the sentence would be.

In the interim, however, things had changed in San Francisco and were changing all over the country. Kesey may have advocated going "beyond acid," but quite the opposite was happening. In fact, the Pranksters had become the focal point for a psychedelic community that would extend in its various forms into the next millennium. When Mountain Girl returned, everyone was buzzing about an event that had happened, called the Human Be-In, with Allen Ginsberg and Timothy Leary. It seemed as though all of San Francisco had been turned on by it.

"Guys would be walking down the street in handmade doeskin bell-bottoms, strings of beautiful tinkling bells sewn down the sides. People were walking around playing flutes. It was like everyone had completely let down their boundaries. It was the ultimate sweetness."

In the Haight Ashbury, every day was the Trips Festival.

## V. This Was Not "My Boy Lollipop"

PAUL ROTHCHILD KNEW how to set a mood in the recording studio, and for this particular song he lighted a single candle where the band was set up in its magic circle. Other than the lights from the console in the control room, where Rothchild sat with the engineer Bruce Botnick, the flame from the candle was the only illumination in the studio. When Jim Morrison stepped out of the dimness and approached the microphone, the whole thing looked like some acid-age version of a Carravaggio painting. Rothchild listened intently; the beginning of the song was impeccable.

*This is the end, Beautiful friend . . .*

The day before, Morrison had tried to record the song on acid, and it hadn't worked at all; the twenty-two-year-old singer had broken down completely. *"Does anybody understand me?!"* Morrison had screamed through his tears, and Rothchild was forced to scrub the session. But now it all seemed to be working perfectly. By the second verse, the whole band was falling into the trance.

There was nobody better equipped to produce the Doors than the smallish, blond-haired thirty-year-old man sitting in the control booth of Sunset Sound at 6650 West Sunset Boulevard in Los Angeles. Paul A. Rothchild was a veteran of successful and progressive albums by the Paul Butterfield Blues Band and Love. His most significant goal for the first Doors album was that each song should carry the audience off to another place of sound and feeling and meaning entirely. Six minutes into the take, he knew they were succeeding beyond his wildest dreams because he felt as if he were out of his own body, traveling on the same journey as the band. Rothchild looked over and saw that Botnick was lost in the hypnotic state as well, his head down on the console. "Do you understand what's happening here?" he asked the engineer in a hushed voice, scarcely believing the magic of it himself. "This is one of the most important moments in recorded rock and roll."

Producer and engineer then watched the band explode into the orgasmic delirium of the instrumental break, falling into an eerie silence before the final verse, and when the music picked back up, it was soft, gentle, Morrison's voice aching with fragility, loss, death, peace.

*This is the . . . end.*

" 'The End' was the most intelligent piece of music I'd ever heard," the producer reflected in the kitchen of his Laurel Canyon home. "This was not 'My Boy Lollipop' or the Beach Boys, but young, savvy artists of a new avant-garde. This was music that not only experimented lyrically but used forms that had never been touched before in popular music."

"The End" was the crown jewel in a repertoire that had been germinating since the summer of 1965, after Morrison graduated from the UCLA film school and was living on the roof of an abandoned warehouse in the beachfront community of Venice. Morrison had spent that whole summer in a corner of the roof near the chimney, with nothing but a sleeping bag, his books, a coffee can, and his notebooks, gobbling Owsley's White Lightning "like candy." He would later remember it as the summer of his metamorphosis from the shy, pudgy, admiral's son to the poet and shaman of pop legend, when he embraced his destiny to "break on through to the other side," and the words had just rushed out of him, and most of the song-poems that would form the first two albums of the Doors were born.

Rothchild understood the myriad elements at play very well. The song was a dark psychosexual drama about myth and patricide and Oedipal love, but there was so much more going on in it than simply a recycling of Sophocles or even Freud. He recognized in the music all the influences that Morrison had been imbibing during and since that Venice summer: blues, rock, Blake, Rimbaud, Poe, Joyce, Brecht, Weill, Artaud, Nietzsche, notions of shamanism, the Dionysian vision . . . Only here it was being filtered through a new LSD-enhanced state of reality—or non-reality, however you looked at it. So many of the images of the song—"ride the snake," "the blue bus is callin' us"—could be interpreted as allegories of mystical psychedelic experience. The lyric about killing the father, as Rothchild interpreted it, was never meant to be taken literally; rather, it meant kill all the things that are instilled in you by society or parents that are not "of yourself"; and the whole idea of fucking the mother meant get back to the natural essence, to the primordial reality, and thereby to the real true self. The whole song, in fact, could be seen as an allegory for something called the psychedelic revolution, which was a part of Rothchild's own résumé and certainly another reason why he was such a good match as a producer for the Doors.

"From the very first joint I ever smoked on 52nd Street back in the mid-1950s, it was like my whole life was an odyssey leading me to that very moment," he remarked. "I was only seventeen at the time, and the higher I got, the more I felt like I was living inside one of the novels I grew up on—you know, like I'd passed through some door and entered the world of D'Artagnan." The jazz musicians in the clubs that night had appeared to him as magnificent musketeers dueling not with guarded foils but with true pointed foils—"and that was when it started, when I began to get it, what was really going on in the jam sessions. These were the greatest jazz musicians in the world, trying their best to use the Darwinian principles of survival to advance their art: survival of the fittest, survival of the freakiest, survival of the fastest. It was like witnessing the miracle of evolution from instant to instant right before my eyes." Before the evening was over, Rothchild had met John Coltrane and had even watched Charlie Parker shoot up in the back of his hand, a sight that had both intrigued and terrified him.

Rothchild had grown up in Teaneck, New Jersey, in a suburban world of milk shakes and split-level houses. His mother sang opera and had studied conducting, and his father wanted him to be an insurance executive, but all it took was that single night of smoking pot to know in the deepest part of his being that he was not going to live the life of his parents and that his whole life was going to center on music. As soon as he moved to the Village, he learned how to go up to Harlem and buy little five-dollar matchboxes of marijuana. He got a job running the classical and jazz record shop on Bleecker Street—"the hippest in the city"—and every night brought another musical adventure, the scintillation of some new heightened experience: the wild bebop at Birdland, the coffeehouses on Bleecker, poetry and jazz performed together, truly the first multimedia performance.

"The marijuana seemed to catalyze and enhance everything that was happening as people with different artistic bents tried to find common ground," he elaborated, likening the relationship of mind-altering substances and the creative nexus of the Village during that time to the era of Mozart and Freemasonry. "The Masons were a secret society that espoused a higher ethic and understanding, which would be promulgated through the arts, and it seemed like that was what was happening right there in the Village: the coalescing of this great little underground society of people who knew better, who understood a more pure, a more daring way of life. The possibility of any harm we might have been doing to ourselves seemed a rather minor point, especially after events like the Second World War and Korea; it was about exploration—and to be cool, of course, which was another massive underlying platform."

The kind of cool that Rothchild was talking about derived from the hallowed school of hipness handed down through a whole generation of jazz musicians, only now it was being incorporated into the lives of white middle-class exiles seeking new identities. It was a complete role reversal as Rothchild and his colleagues tried to take on the speech, dress, attributes, and mores of the black musical culture of the time.

"We became groupies to this jazz and blues revolution. See, the blacks had tried to integrate into white society, and now this small group of whites was trying to integrate into black society and was finding out how hard it really was to exist in it, but we were learning new ways of walking, talking, thinking, being. We became the diametric opposite of the beer-drinking fraternity types who formed the majority of the youth culture of America. Instead of being loud, we were quiet; instead of being anti-art, we were pro-art; and instead of being drunks, we were drug users. We began dressing funny: black chinos, work shirts, berets, army coats, cheap stuff, and we rarely ventured north of 14th Street."

Rothchild would remain fascinated by the changes he went through as he began to travel through the landscape of drugs and by how his use of them would later shape his creativity as a producer. Marijuana, he believed, had allowed him to crawl deeply inside the music of Bach, for example, and understand the composer's love of Christ—"an experience I might have never have allowed myself as a Jew unless I had gotten high and opened my synapses enough to truly experience the gestalt of the music." He was also certain that without marijuana he would never have had the "balls" to break those tribal rules of society that enabled him to reach for a life of no security and be an artist, "because at that time you were a pariah if you were an artist—a weirdo, a faggot, a Commie, a leech on society, deviant, not to be trusted."

And then came peyote. They learned how to make milk shakes with the substance, and suddenly it all began to change to discussions about "the oneness of mankind." One morning, Rothchild found himself at the Central Park Zoo, higher than he had ever been in his life. It was dawn, and he was walking around as the animals were just waking up, and he was standing in front of the bear cage when a giant grizzly started to stir. Rothchild stood riveted as the creature slowly rose to its full height and stretched its arms as high as it could, and there it was, the most beautiful, monumental animal he had ever seen, its coat of brown fur glistening in the early-morning light, making him feel Lilliputian. Just at that moment, the bear locked eyes with him and seemed to be looking into his very soul, and in a snap he got it, "that we were brothers on the planet; that one was no better than the other as we were both creatures of God." In that instant of humility, the creature let out a roar that pierced the silence of that early morning with such power that it seemed to shake the ground underneath his feet.

"From that moment on, I believed it was possible to find your way to God through psychedelics! After that, I set about very consciously to turn as many people on as possible—just to see them expand and explode and become new and larger people, but also to have them as allies. At that time, getting high was never just about getting high. It was about our willingness to accept change and visualize another world—what later became known as 'grokking' it, to quote Robert Heinlein in *Stranger in a Strange Land.* To deepen understanding. To expose the beast and the angel within. To shatter the crusty shell around our minds. To find other explorers roaming free in the streets and connect with them."

From 1959 to 1965, Rothchild cut his teeth as a producer on the folk-music scene, experiencing the world from the Kettle of Fish Bar and the Gaslight Café in Greenwich Village. Then acid began trickling in, and Rothchild witnessed its immediate impact on music when he and Victor Maimudes returned to Albert Grossman's Woodstock home one night with Bob Dylan after his tour of New England colleges they opened the refrigerator to find the sugar cubes with the little gold dot on them, wrapped in aluminum foil.

"Let's get Bob and take it!"

"It was a magical night of camaraderie and conversation, with Dylan strumming his guitar, but from that moment on his music changed," Rothchild remembered, "from simple but powerful songs of social observation and protest and moral conscience to those elusive compositions of no single message or ultimate meaning." It was the beginning of Dylan's period of intense self-examination, the protracted exploration of his "inner cosmos" with LSD and other drugs, all of which produced an immediate and drastic change in his aesthetic, evident in his next album, *Bringing It All Back Home.* The experience of drugs seemed to splinter Dylan's mind into brilliant kaleidoscopic flashes of poetry; the result was strange, mystical, beautiful compositions like "Mr. Tambourine Man." "I never have and never will write a drug song," Dylan declared in 1966, when "Rainy Day Women #12 & 35" was banned by American and British radio stations after a feverish controversy over the lyrics. By that time, there were kids on college campuses all across America beginning to smoke marijuana, trying to decipher the meaning of his lyrics, quite certain that they understood the droll message of the song very well: "Everybody must get stoned." Of course, it was cleverly couched in the playfulness of the raucous ensemble singing and the fun of the New Orleans slide trombone and marching-band drums and set up in a way only Dylan could do it (the song implied that you could get stoned on virtually anything if you were of a mind to and left open the distinct possibility that Bob was also talking about being stoned with metaphorical rocks by his angry audience after he had gone electric at the Newport Folk Festival), but it was all there: the giggling and laughter, the shouting and giddy abandon of the high. For millions of American youth just beginning to experience altered states of mind, it seemed as if Bob Dylan were inside their very heads. The impact of Dylan's music on his fellow musicians and audience had only confirmed the power of marijuana and psychedelics for Paul Rothchild.

"Bebop had featured a small community of musicians using drugs in a secret underground society of hipsters," he noted, "and the Beats had an impact that initially extended only as far as their literature, but this represented something else entirely: artists avidly using drugs, creating music shaped by the use of drugs—writing songs about the explicit use of drugs—for an ever-growing audience using the same drugs in an age of mass media. The effect of it could be instantaneous, and the potential of it—artistic, spiritual, cultural, and political—seemed nothing short of revolutionary."

The unprecedented role that pop music would come to play in proliferating the use of drugs in America can be appreciated only by taking into account the impact of that phenomenal period of fertility from 1965 to 1967—the great psychedelic moment of transition in the story of so many important artists and bands of the era, during which pop music would provide unity, identity, and synthesis for a generation. Quantum leaps in musical freedom and technological sophistication occurred with the speed of flowers blooming in rapid time-lapse sequence; icons were born; songs were written that would become actual anthems and manifestos of drug use.

The summer after recording their first album, the Doors had the number-one single in the country with "Light My Fire," and like every hot pop group was invited to appear on America's favorite television variety hour, *The Ed Sullivan Show*. Morrison's stage image was off-putting enough, but it wasn't his skin-tight black leather pants and writhing that the CBS censor had a problem with—of course, it was the word *higher*. When Bob Precht, the show's director and Sullivan's son-in-law, visited the group, they agreed to come up with another line. "It was all a ruse," Rothchild admitted. "They really had no intention of acquiescing—it was a conspiracy from the get-go. The plan was to sing another line in rehearsal but sing the original one during the live broadcast, when there would be nothing the censors could do about it."

Although what followed would become part of the band's legend, Rothchild's role in the affair would be largely overlooked. "I went to the control room for the broadcast, where I was going to help supervise the mixing of the sound for the band, and when the moment arrived, to make sure there could be no interference whatsoever, I literally threw my body across the console to prevent the censor from hitting the button. It was guerrilla warfare."

The Doors would never play *The Ed Sullivan Show* again, but the Sunday-night family audience of ten million Americans heard Morrison sing the original line. In a show that included the likes of Steve Lawrence and Eydie Gormé, the message came through clearly enough. A flood tide was altering the musical and cultural landscape of the nation.

## VI.  A Snide Piece of Writing If Ever There Was One

ALONG WITH KEEPING her ex-husband's name, Grace Slick emerged from her marriage to Jerry Slick and their group, the Great Society, with "White Rabbit," a strange bolero-like number that would sound the clarion call of the new psychedelic spring when it was recorded and released by the Jefferson Airplane on their second album, *Surrealistic Pillow*, establishing Slick as the archetypal Bitch Goddess Acid Queen, the Elizabeth Taylor of the Haight Ashbury, the Euterpe of the San Francisco sound.

"It was a snide piece of writing if ever there was one," Slick acknowledged in the living room of her Mill Valley home. "What I'd intended was to remind our parents, who were sipping on highballs while they badgered us about the new drugs, that *they* were the ones who read all those fun-with-chemicals children's books to us when we were small."

The style of "White Rabbit" had come, aptly enough, from an acid trip during which Slick had realized her great affinity for all things Spanish, from music to architecture, but the lyrics were right out of Lewis Carroll's *Alice's Adventures in Wonderland,* one of the stories she had grown up on as the daughter of a prosperous Republican investment banker in Palo Alto. Peter Pan and Tinker Bell's white dust, Dorothy and her companions getting off on poppies in the *Wizard of Oz*—she saw the evidence of it everywhere, but nowhere was it as transparent as Alice taking a nice bite out of the Caterpillar's "magic" mushroom and pulling a toke on the hookah. As Slick saw it, Alice was "thoroughly ripped all the way through the book." In her song, "logic and proportion have fallen sloppy dead," the White Knight talks backward and the Red Queen's 'off with her head.' " But it was what the dormouse said that would by far turn out to be the most provocative line.

"When I said, 'Feed your head,' everybody knew I wasn't talking about alcohol," she allowed. "But the message was also 'read a book!' Nobody believes that, because they figure it was all about drugs—and yes, it *did* mean take psychedelics—but it also meant look around, ask questions; what you've been given so far may not be the whole picture."

In the spring of 1967, the Airplane was using the song as the finale of its sets in San Francisco, and its rousing crescendo of *"Feed your head!"* was being screamed back at Slick by thousands of tripped-out kids packed into the ballrooms, a performance rendered more dramatic by Slick's magnetic stage presence and delivery. "Grace had such attitude, wow," Charlie Perry observed. "She was so arresting, I could see why she had been a fashion model. It was like she was going to make the world stop just by the power of her appearance and voice. Janis Joplin was emotionally moving, but Grace was *fierce.* I once described her voice as being like she was circling around something she was going to *kill.*"

As Mountain Girl remembered her, Slick was a "tremendously outspoken person who was so sharp and intense—one smart cookie—and when she looked at you with those incredible blue eyes, you were caught, pinned in the headlights." Sassy, self-confident, and well read, Slick had a razor-sharp wit, and far more than simply outspoken, she could be down-right caustic. "She would take the offensive in any conversation and go right for the throat, stab you in the heart—and then laugh! The whole music scene in San Francisco was like this boys' club, and there was Grace, this female star. She had to cut quite a swath to keep up with those guys—and, believe me, she did. She dressed the part, too."

Slick's favorite outfit at the time was "a crocheted top, with the holes in it so wide that you could see right though it," as she recalled. "There were two pockets right where the boobs were. I didn't wear a bra—I didn't wear *anything*. I was shocking, and I loved to do it for the hell of it. Some days I'd wear an LAPD uniform with handcuffs; another day it would be a fourteenth-century buccaneer's outfit with thigh-high boots. I looked the same onstage as off, and so did everybody else. Pigpen looked like an outlaw from the California of the 1880s; Paul Kantner wore Prince Charming clothes from the 1700s; Janis Joplin looked like a wild, funky madam in a Texas whorehouse. The only style was what you felt like wearing when you got up that morning."

Slick had fallen in love with the freedom of the new hippie scene of San Francisco as soon as she returned from posh Finch College in New York. "You could hang out, come and go as you pleased. Some people were married; some were not and chose to just boink whoever they wanted to. Whatever you decided to do was okay except to hurt people—violence was unacceptable. You did whatever occurred to you at that moment. It was *right now*, man, rather than planning for the future or thinking about the past. As for the rules, it wasn't that you consciously had to disregard them—they were just *irrelevant*. The motto was 'Try it. If it works, fine; if not, don't do it.' "

One thing that worked for Grace Slick was consciousness-altering substances. She enjoyed playing and listening to music on marijuana, but "it didn't do for me what it did for a lot of other people, but peyote, *whoa!* I was a city kid, and with peyote I fell in love with the sky, the grass." And then came acid, in doses as large as nine hundred mikes (micrograms), which she did "whenever it felt appropriate. It could be five days in a row, then nothing for two weeks."

Marijuana may have enhanced and distorted experiences, and you could get loose or aggressive on alcohol, "but walls didn't breathe and change color!—and you wouldn't see cloud formations over time as some kind of crazy cosmic time-lapse cartoon!—and you certainly didn't see through your skin! The most important thing that the psychedelics did was give you a take that things are not and do not have to be the way they seem around you. When you sat there and saw these things happen, you realized that the reality of the world isn't as *fixed* as you thought; therefore, why does *anything* need to be that fixed? Boy, that gives you a wide range of things to think about—emotionally, culturally, politically, musically. Before this, I'm sure that if you'd said, 'Let's put a plate crashing in the middle of this song,' people would have said, 'Oh, don't be silly.' Acid meant freedom from all constraints, but mostly it had to do with electricity. The instruments, the ability to manipulate the sound of drums, voices, anything—you could modulate *everything,* play around in ways you couldn't before. Acid encouraged that kind of electronic as well as lyrical freedom. Pop songs didn't have to be three and a half minutes anymore; performing could be more free-form, like jazz even though it was rock."

The endless, sloppy, often inspired freewheeling jams, the ear-splitting squelching feedback—it was the kind of music that could have been created only by acidhead musicians for their acidhead audience, all together in the acidhead community of the Haight Ashbury and soon to be available for the turntables of Acidhead America courtesy of RCA and other major record companies. Of course, playing when you were loaded presented its own set of challenges, not the least of which were the most basic effects of the drug. "Time would be so different!" Slick exclaimed. "Three minutes could seem like an hour on acid, or half an hour could seem like a few seconds. It was largely impossible to play a cohesive set on a full dose of three hundred to five hundred mikes—you'd get some strange-sounding shit. If you talk to the Dead, they didn't really play that much on acid. But you could snort a little. Break off little bits with your fingernail and snort it, and you got high rather than so blazing that you couldn't play. That's how people like the Dead would do it, but not full-bore. But we would end up doing it because we got dosed a lot, or we would dose each other or make a mistake and take the wrong stuff."

The road manager of the band kept the group's supply of drugs in a special box, all organized and categorized neatly for each need and occasion—one slot for speed, one for downers, one for acid, one for cocaine—and one night at a concert, backstage in some very dim light, they thought they were snorting a little cocaine. "Fifteen minutes into the performance we all looked at each other . . . *Uh, oh,* guys. It was acid. I was supposed to be playing piano, and Jack Casady was doing something absolutely fascinating on bass, and I just had to stop playing. I turned around and watched him with my mouth open—you know, as if I was just another member of the audience. That's what could happen when you snorted out of the wrong slot!"

For Slick, the ramifications of acid went far beyond the music. "It wasn't a goal-oriented process; it was a feeling of hope that we had stumbled upon a means of realizing an evolutionary process. . . . I felt that within the next ten to fifty years we were going to undergo a swing from the idolization of the material intellect and manifest form to what cannot be possessed or collected. I felt that we were headed for a move to the intuitive where we would put our feelings foremost and follow lives of trust and the simple word, Love."

## VII. A Darkened Dance Floor Full of Astonished, Conspiratorial Glee

THE POSTER ADVERTISED it as a dance, but the title of the event alone, A Tribute to Doctor Strange, was ample evidence that it was going to be anything but a traditional sock hop.

Dr. Strange was a well-known Marvel Comics character, Master of the Mystic Arts, who fought evil by casting spells depicted by colored rays of energy that shot out of his palms. It was a vision that acidheads like Charlie Perry could readily appreciate. Perry would become a regular attendee at such events, and for this inaugural gala he arrived seriously loaded on some of Owsley's finest.

"Who knew how many people were taking psychedelics? You really had no idea, and when you realized that all these people were just openly doing it and getting completely weird and not giving a shit, it was inspiring. It validated what I was doing. I didn't tell my date—who was this rather conventional little Japanese girl—I was loaded. We were standing up on the stage overlooking this whole room of weirdos, and she said, 'I have to think these people are just going through a phase.' And I said, 'Well, *life* is just a phase'—real impressed with myself for coming up with that one."

The guitarist John Cippolina, soon to form Quicksilver Messenger Service, also climbed up on the stage to survey the scene; so kaleidoscopic and brilliant was the tableau before him, so elated were the vibes with everybody tripping away, that "it hurt my eyes." Longtime *Chronicle* jazz critic Ralph J. Gleason thought it looked "like everyone was going to a costume party. Longhaired girls in trailing dresses skipped along the street. Tall men with mustaches, long hair à la Bonnie Prince Charlie, or, sometimes, Buffalo Bill Cody, wearing high boots and Stetson hats, accompanied them. There were box-backed coats and exotic costumes that would have delighted the wildest party giver." And how they danced! "Some of the people danced all night long, as if the mere opportunity for such expression was god-given and might never be repeated. It was orgiastic and spontaneous and completely freeform." When the night was over, Gleason watched approvingly as everyone picked up the trash, put it in garbage cans, and went home peacefully.

Gleason began chronicling and promoting the local music scene from that night on. Allen Ginsberg had been there and was completely captivated by the peculiar beauty of the event. Also present was Chet Helms, a genial hippie from Texas with hair down to his waist and a long, flowing beard, whose appearance suggested Jesus Christ with wire-rimmed glasses. An early marijuana-rights activist, Helms was putting together a band in the basement of a rooming house on Page Street that he was going to manage, called Big Brother and the Holding Company (*holding* in the slang sense of holding drugs, of course). Affiliating himself with a collective of artists called the Family Dog, Helms was soon putting on his own dances, and when the Trips Festival amped up the phenomenon of local rock music, he began alternating shows on weekends with Bill Graham at the Fillmore Auditorium, an old beige-brick building at the corner of Fillmore and Geary in the black neighborhood—really nothing more than a large dance floor with a balcony. After Graham acquired the lease for the Fillmore and began producing shows nightly, Helms took over the Avalon Ballroom, an old swing venue upstairs at the Puckett

Academy of Dance, on the corner of Sutter and Van Ness—a gorgeous bauble constructed in 1911 that was smaller than the Fillmore but filled with gilded booths and mirrors. By the end of April 1966, the psychedelic ballroom scene that would drive the San Francisco sound was in full swing, and the bands were taking home a thousand dollars a night, turning the city into the most significant pop-music scene since the Liverpool of the British Invasion. On any given weekend, the venues would offer a bill that presented the very best of the new San Francisco bands, combined with artists ranging from Muddy Waters to the Young Rascals.

The dances were advertised by the nouvelle vague of poster artists, each trying to outdo the other in attracting attention and suggesting the psychedelic experience. Between the Fillmore and the Avalon and places like the Straight Theater and California Hall, anywhere from four to eight new posters were coming out every weekend, which kept the cream of the San Francisco poster artists—Rick Griffin, Victor Moscoso, Wes Wilson, George Hunter, and Stanley "Mouse" Miller—very busy. The artists borrowed from one another as well as the aesthetics of the musicians in a continual attempt to push the envelope and pioneer a new graphic style. For Victor Moscoso, certainly one of the most original of the crowd, it meant using "as many vibrating colors as you could. You'd make every edge a vibrating edge. After all, musicians were turning their amps all the way up so that you'd be deaf for a week, and it was cool. I would just turn the color up as high as I could so I would blind you." The posters were so dazzling that people took them down to collect as soon as they were put up, prompting the ever-enterprising Bill Graham to begin giving them away to everyone who came to the Fillmore, as a promotion. Before long, the psychedelic style of the San Francisco poster artists would make its way across the country, until it reached the mainstream of Madison Avenue commercial design.

The ballrooms developed a kind of yin-yang relationship. The Fillmore embodied Graham's energetic and combative New York personality from top to bottom. The spotlight was always on the performer; everything was tightly organized. The Avalon was a much cooler and looser venue, with Chet ambling around in his hippie finery, loaded and enjoying the scene as much as anyone else. The stage at the Avalon was dark, so that the whole place became about the light show; puppeteers in the balconies made life-size marionettes dance along the floor with the crowd, and people liked to bring odd little things to hand out just to blow one another's minds. Perhaps the differences in sensibility were most exemplified by the catch phrases posted at the venues. At the Filmore there was Graham's sign, ONCE INSIDE NO OUTSY-INSY; at the Avalon, there was Helm's motto, MAY THE BABY JESUS SHUT YOUR MOUTH AND OPEN YOUR MIND. Nuances of style aside, the ultimate effect of being under the influence was the same at either place. "You walked onto a darkened dance floor full of astonished, conspiratorial glee," Perry related. "Sometimes the Fillmore or the Avalon felt like a pulsing, organic spaceship that might escape the world of war and racial conflict outside by the collective energy of hundreds of people celebrating life as they tried to solve the riddle of LSD."

The audience and the musicians were on a common vision quest, searching for answers about the powerful wonders of LSD and what it might reveal. As Perry explained, "LSD raised questions about the nature of reality and tantalizingly half-suggested answers. It seemed that a radiant solution to every problem, personal and philosophical, was just around the corner. By singing about the situation, the musicians proclaimed themselves brothers in the quest. People even imagined that the musicians might have part of the answers." And if you wanted, you could go right up to them on the streets and ask them—"these were not remote, adored celebrities with auras. They were just part of the crowd—comrades, really—and that was part of their appeal."

The bands were a varied and volatile pastiche of personalities and egos, visually, musically, and otherwise, all of them passionate acid-magnified hippie insurrectionists. The members of the Jefferson Airplane were the aristocrats of the scene, prosperous and showy compared with the other scuffling bands. It was *Surrealistic Pillow* that had brought the San Francisco sound to national distinction. With their slogan THE JEFFERSON AIRPLANE LOVES YOU, the group became the very voice and image of the Haight Ashbury and the Love Generation.

The national success of the Airplane stood in stark contrast to the obscurity of the Grateful Dead. For a period after the acid tests, the Dead were living with Owsley down in Los Angeles, in a pink house off Western Avenue, where he was then tabbing up his product, existing on a diet of milk and acid and Kentucky Fried Chicken. They spent the summer of 1966 at Rancho Olompali, Novato, in the rolling hills of northern Marin County, in a ranch house with a swimming pool and barn that had been a summer home for mentally retarded children, turning the place into a summer home for seriously tripping musicians playing for days on end with people romping naked in the sunshine. From there, the scene shifted to the old Victorian rooming house at 710 Ashbury Street, "a twenty-four-hour combination flop house and feed palace," as Mountain Girl described it. "We never locked the door until two in the morning, and people came in and out all the time. There were two kitchens, and I cooked a lot. They were making fifty dollars a week, and I'd go around and collect money from everybody for food." The Dead had gone from being the house band of the acid tests to being the house band of the Haight and were developing into true tribal anarchists as they played often and for free on flatbed trucks in the Panhandle. "The thing about the Dead, they created community wherever they played, and it wasn't even an intentional thing at that time," explained Mountain Girl. "Back then, Garcia was an early riser, and he'd get up and practice for six hours. Pigpen would drink all night and sing the blues. They rehearsed, wrote songs, and tried to act like a band, but it was like trying to write tunes in an inferno because there were so many things going on in San Francisco." That winter of 1966–67, Warner Brothers executive Joe Smith signed the band to the label. Managers Rock Scully and Danny Rifkin had wanted Smith to drop some righteous acid before they signed—how else could he truly understand the band? Smith refused, the Dead signed anyway, and they made their first album in a three-day onslaught of Dexamyl.

The scene just went on from there. Up in Marin, there was Quicksilver Messenger Service, the "drugstore-cowboy band" rich with the fierce ringing guitars of John Cippolina and Gary Duncan and the vocals of Dino Valenti. Over in Berkeley, Country Joe and the Fish, the infectious psychedelic jug band, mixed political awareness and sardonic slapstick humor with rock, the first group to unite the worlds of Berkeley political protest with the hippies of the Haight, recognized for dope songs like "Flying High" and "Bass Strings" and "Feel-Like-I'm-Fixin'-to-Die Rag," their demented mock celebration of death in Vietnam set to the tune of an old rag, complete with football-style "fuck" cheer. Other bands appeared like hallucinations out of the fog of the Panhandle—Blue Cheer, Moby Grape, It's a Beautiful Day—and captured the spotlight before disbanding. Steve Miller soon showed up from Texas and methodically set about the business of becoming a star, bringing Boz Scaggs to public attention in the process. By the end of the decade, Sly and the Family Stone, Creedence Clearwater Revival, and Santana would emerge from the Bay Area to become staples in the pantheon of rock music.

One of the foremost groups to exemplify acid rock was fronted by a singer who abhorred LSD. "EEEECK!" was Janis Joplin's horrified response to finding out that she had been dosed. "Blow my mind to see a bunch of wiggly lines," she'd screech, "*Not this girl!*"—and then she'd run straight into the bathroom to try and vomit out the acid before it launched her out of her head. Although all of the members of Big Brother and the Holding Company had tripped out at one time or another, alcohol and speed were really the group's staples—they were "alkydelic," as Janis liked to call them.

By 1966, the legend of the wallflower who emerged from the swamps of an oil-refinery town near the Texas-Louisiana border to wail the blues as no white person ever had was already flourishing. Reams of prose would attempt to describe Janis as a singer—*Cashbox* would call her "a mixture of Leadbelly, a steam engine, Calamity Jane, Bessie Smith, an oil derrick and rotgut bourbon funneled into the 20th Century somewhere between El Paso and San Francisco"—but few writers would fully capture her. Janis Joplin had to be seen and heard. Perhaps the most salient points about her were that she was a real blues singer who revered the music— someone who *had* to sing rather than someone who simply *wanted* to—and that she was insecure every time she stepped onto a stage. Consequently, nothing was ever held back. "Janis Joplin's talent was that you believed she was singing her guts out every night," Bill Graham observed. "In that sense, she was like Piaf. You were watching a candle burn, with no wax to replace what had already been used up."

All throughout 1966 and into 1967, as surely as a butterfly breaks out of a cocoon, Joplin was transforming herself in San Francisco, leaving behind the homely beatnik with the acne-pitted face from Port Arthur, Texas, and turning into the hippie-floozy rock-blues queen who would eventually be known as Pearl. Janis had a personality that inspired cascades of adjectives: smart, funny, sad, insecure, vulnerable, emotionally needy, funky, free-spirited, wildly rebellious, trashy, loud, vulgar, fun loving, hard partying, generous, warmhearted, lusty, garrulous, self-pitying, gregarious, down-to-earth, reckless, ballsy, soulful, driven . . . She hurtled from one relationship to the next, from Pigpen to Country Joe, to liaisons with band members and fans and female lovers. The statement that she would make so famous—"Onstage I make love to twenty-five thousand people, then I go home alone"—exemplified her life and music; the bottle of Southern Comfort she carried was ample proof of her love for alcohol and her admiration for hard-drinking blues singers like Bessie Smith, but her bible was *Lady Sings the Blues,* the autobiography of Billie Holiday, and the same drug that had so bedeviled the life of Lady Day, heroin, was already a presence in her life. Janis could provoke, charm, and delight you all in the same breath—and break your heart like no one else. "Do It If It Feels Good" was her motto, as was "Get It While You Can."

In November of 1966, Janis went to see Big Mama Thornton perform at the Both/And on Divisadero Street. As soon as the show was over, she and guitarist James Gurley hurried backstage and begged her for permission to use a song called "(Love Is Like a) Ball and Chain," and Big Mama was happy to write down the lyrics. Before long, Janis was electrifying the ballrooms with a version of the song that was slowed down by Gurley and filtered through the psychedelic peak distortion of Sam Andrew's guitar. By the time she brought the song to Monterey in the spring of 1967, she was filling in the lyrics about being enslaved by the love of a cruel man with the most primal expression of her being. The music business was about to find out what had become common knowledge in San Francisco, and very shortly the whole world would watch her flame out like that candle Bill Graham had described as having "no wax to replace what had already been used up."

## VIII. Acid Angel

DAWN REYNOLDS was an eighteen-year-old alabaster beauty with cobalt eyes and the figure of a ripe voluptuary. People who saw her at parties up and down the hills and canyons of Los Angeles called her an acid angel—and as she walked through the crowds at the Monterey International Pop Festival, wearing a sheer white peasant shirt that billowed out of a brightly embroidered vest, her long auburn hair garlanded with mountain flowers, she could see that she was among other acid angels, but she still turned plenty of heads in her purple velvet bell-bottoms. Except for the sunburst of girlish freckles over her button nose, she looked sophisticated way beyond her years and exuded a bold open sensuality.

Some people she barely knew had given her a ride up from Los Angeles, and Dawn had lost them in the throng, but it didn't matter any more than it mattered that her parents in Encino didn't know where she was, any more than it mattered that she had no idea where she was going to sleep that night. Dawn was one of those girls they seemed to be writing songs about: "She's got everything she needs, she's an artist, she don't look back" . . . "Young girls are coming to the canyon" . . . "She's a twentieth century fox." Even the Beatles had written about her on their new album: "She's leaving home bye bye" . . .

Dawn was happy to be leaving home, even though it was definitely a case of "with no direction home, . . . like a rolling stone." She was just getting out of high school, and as concerned as her parents had been with her lately, they did not yet know that she was pregnant. Worse, she didn't know who the father was . . . Well, that's not entirely true; it had to be one of the two guys at the party that night up in Topanga Canyon. The three of them had found themselves down around Zuma Beach after taking the little blue barrels, and one thing had led to another, and she knew she was going to find out if what Timothy Leary had said about sex and LSD in *Playboy* was true.

In the controversial interview, Leary had called LSD "the most powerful aphrodisiac ever discovered by man and talked about "cellular communion" and "complete merging," making love with eyeballs and breath, every touch an orgasm. "In a carefully prepared, loving LSD session, a woman can have several hundred orgasms," he claimed, and while Dawn wasn't aware of several hundred orgasms during the experience of making love to two men at the same time, it had been just as boundless.

Every step in the mud was ecstasy, every grain of sand beaming with the miracle of creation. They pulled off one another's clothes and frolicked in the water for hours, where they became fish, seals, coral reefs, embryos floating in the womb, and they made love in the sand with the stars overhead and the surf crashing around them. Every taboo came down as they tried every conceivable flavor and sensation and combination possible with the particular sex organs of two males and a female; it was orgiastic but religious, there were no words for it because it was all touch, sound, liquid, images, and energy. She was making love to God, and their bodies became a configuration of light, and they seemed to meld into one another electromagnetically until she experienced the Great Oneness that all life came from. There were reincarnation flashes in which she became Mary Magdalene, the archetypal Mother Mary, and she knew she had been with Jesus and could feel the crucifixion inside her, but it always came back to the Oneness. It reached a level of such intensity that their cries of ecstasy became like one long ululating howl that resounded above the sound of the thundering waves and ascended into the night sky. When it was over, her heart had swelled with breathtaking waves of love. All people were brothers and sisters. God was All.

In the weeks afterward, tears came to her eyes whenever she thought of that night and how beautiful it was, but the truth was that she hardly knew those two guys and didn't particularly want either of them as the father of her child. No, Dawn was going to be the pioneering single mother of the New Age, and every step that she took toward the festival seemed only to confirm the wisdom of this decision. She was the kind of girl for whom things had always materialized just as she needed them. All around her, everyone was sharing, lighting joss sticks, and she could feel the openness in everyone's gesture. It was better than Mardi Gras, like the preparation for a saint's feast day. She would pick the man that she wanted as the father of her child, maybe even find him here at Monterey, and if she recognized him, all an acid angel had to do was smile.

## IX. Monterey Purple

AS HE STROLLED around the Monterey Pop Festival grounds on the first day, with the flowers glowing in the sunshine and the silver fog rolling in off the ocean, Paul Rothchild's overriding feeling was victory.

It was June 16, 1967, and people were still filing in, seventy-five hundred in all, but there were fifty thousand more clogging the roads and sprawling out over the fairgrounds. A bluish cloud of cannabis hovered over the scene, but everyone wanted to get psychedelic, and the doyen of LSD himself was there to oblige, striding about in a grape-colored suede jacket with his baggy pockets filled to overflowing with tabs of Monterey Purple. Augustus Owsley Stanley III liked to concoct special batches of acid for particular events. He had cut Monterey Purple with a generous pinch of speed in order to keep everyone going full tilt for the three days of the festival. LSD was now illegal, but Owsley was nonetheless handing the stuff out by the fistful. "The entire place was getting off," Rothchild related; "you could feel it, and the cops were letting it happen!—cops with flowers in their pistols, tucked into their lapels, and hanging from the antennae of their cruisers."

Just as Owsley had anticipated the special pharmacological requirements of the event, so for the first time the festival organizers had planned for the possibilities of bad trips. The bummer, or freak-out tent, as it would hereinafter be called, was staffed by people from the Haight who knew how to talk people down, how to soothe them with music and help them get their heads together. It was an example of the new culture learning how to care for its own, and as Rothchild surveyed its colorful terrain, holding one of the little purple pills in his hand, he marveled at all of it. "All of a sudden the nation—no, the *world!*—is ours, I was thinking. The spore was only going to spread. Monterey was only a microcosm of what was about to happen."

The entire music industry had converged to bear witness to this first global music festival of the Love Generation. Over one thousand journalists had gathered to spread the news, and a documentary crew under D. A. Pennebaker was on hand to capture it. Thirty-one acts from every niche of the pop-music world were going to play. The new L.A. pop aristocrats like the Byrds and the Mamas and the Papas. New York folkies like Simon and Garfunkel. A handful of soul singers like Lou Rawls and Otis Redding. British Invasion bands like the Who. Top-forty hit makers like the Association. But the real buzz was about the San Francisco groups: Big Brother, the Jefferson Airplane, Country Joe and the Fish, the Grateful Dead, Quicksilver Messenger Service, Steve Miller. In the six months since the Human Be-In, the Haight Ashbury had moved more and more into the national consciousness, powered by a new sound coming out of places like the Fillmore and the Avalon Ballroom, but many of those bands would now get to play in front of people like Clive Davis, the new head of Columbia Records.

Everyone was there but Bob Dylan, but he was well represented by his heavyweight manager, Albert Grossman. The Stones were not there either, because Mick Jagger and Keith Richards had recently been busted in what was the beginning of a police campaign in Britain to go after pop musicians who were using drugs, but Brian Jones was walking around backstage, caparisoned in satin robes, flowing scarves, and fur, looking like a dissipated medieval dauphin, popping pills with abandon and slurring his words, with his impossibly stoned blue eyes and the stunning Nico on his arm. Jones had flown in to introduce the Jimi Hendrix Experience, scheduled to play Sunday night. Little was known about Hendrix. A few industry insiders and musicians remembered him as a backup guitar player for artists like Little Richard and the Isley Brothers or from his time scuffling around the Village when he was trying to play the clubs. He'd had to go to London to make his first record, which had just been released in the United States.

Something seemed to give way in those first few weeks of June 1967 that changed the world, and the Beatles personified it. *Sgt Pepper's Lonely Hearts Club Band,* released just two weeks earlier, was everywhere, and it was this album more than anything else that validated the new culture. The long-awaited album was light-years beyond what anyone could have imagined. From the first listening, it was universally regarded as the masterpiece of the psychedelic age, a dazzling pageant of overdubs and rich orchestral sounds that set a benchmark for studio inventiveness and confirmed that the Beatles had incorporated the sensibility of consciousness-altering substances into every aspect of its creation. The album's towering finale tells the whole story. "A Day in the Life" begins with Lennon's sad, sweeping theme, culled from the *Daily Mail,* of a death evocative of drugs ("He blew his mind out in a car"), followed by McCartney's breathless bridge ("Found my way upstairs and had a smoke"), returning to Lennon's theme with the definitive phrase ("I'd love to turn you on"). Then the music steadily mounts, like a dynamo revving out of control, the sound of a full orchestra freaking out, going from lowest to highest note in fifteen bars before it reaches a vertiginous climax in the final explosion of an E major chord, played by George Martin and all four Beatles hitting the chord simultaneously on three pianos as hard as possible. At the moment of impact, the engineer had pushed the volume-input faders way down, then slowly pushed them back up to the top as the noise gradually diminished. On the album, it takes a full forty-five seconds for that final chord to resound, decay, and dissolve into thin air. If the Beatles had designed those forty-five seconds to blow minds all over the world, in only a matter of weeks they were succeeding beyond their wildest dreams. *Sgt Pepper's Lonely Hearts Club Band* made it seem as if the Beatles were ushering in from the tips of their fingers on the knobs and faders of the Abbey Road studio the new era of Music, Love, and Flowers that was materializing that weekend at the Monterey Pop Festival. As John Phillips of the Mamas and the Papas would remark, "Now there was an album that proved to the masses what musicians had believed for years: that music and drugs work wonders together. The nation-wide hunt for rock-enhancing psychedelics had begun."

Everyone would have his or her own peak moments at Monterey. For some, it was Ravi Shankar on Saturday afternoon, playing in a soft incense-redolent rain, with thousands of lavender orchids being thrown from the top of the stage as he smiled and blessed the audience. For Paul Rothchild, it was Janis Joplin's wrenching performance of "Ball and Chain" on Saturday. "It just galvanized me. I knew who she was and wanted to record her before that, but after that performance it became a compulsion with me—I had to work with her!" Many others would claim that the high point was Otis Redding closing the Saturday-night show with his sweaty blistering rendition of "Shake." Stars were born, deals were closed, legends were made; and in the wake of the festival, the alternative-music media made its debut when Jann Wenner and Ralph Gleason founded *Rolling Stone* magazine. Everyone uniformly agreed that if this festival was prototypical, it was also the best. As Grace Slick walked around the grounds, the light slanting down through the cypress and pine trees made the fairgrounds look like a Disney version of Sherwood Forest. "Even the stalls selling food and concert items were quaint and uninfected by corporate logos and pitchmen," she marveled. "I'd never seen anything like it, and I felt lucky to be there, observing one of the great examples of human celebration."

For Dawn Reynolds, the high point came on Sunday, the final night of the festival. Moderation was in order because of the pregnancy; she had decided to take acid only once and had kept the little pill in her pocket all weekend long. While she had so far failed to recognize the man she might select as the father of her baby, she knew the moment to take acid had arrived just as the sun was going down. The sky seemed huge and timeless, and there was something about the primeval, untamed smell of trees, ocean, rock, stream, and earth. She placed the pill on the tip of her tongue, where it rested like a little purple pearl, and swallowed.

The Who were playing their final song, "My Generation," when the acid really started coming on. The drumsticks that Keith Moon was twirling and throwing up into the air suddenly turned into rainbow pin-wheels in the stage lights; when the smoke bomb went off and the micro-phone came flying out of Roger Daltrey's hand to break the bass drum, she saw the whole thing in time-lapse traces across her field of vision that repeated like a loop of visual feedback. When Pete Townshend turned from the audience and rammed his guitar violently into his amp, she felt the sound of it go off in her spine, shoot up into her head, and then rocket back down her body in a bombshell of orange that made her knees shake. Smoke was belching from the destroyed amplifiers, and Moon then kicked his drums all over the stage in an act of lunatic slaughter that frightened her. Townshend picked up his shattered guitar and began smashing it furiously down on the stage, and then when there was noth-ing left to destroy, they all just walked off.

After so much music, love, and flowers, she felt benumbed, thunder-struck by this psychedelic *Gotterdämmerung*. It was like some surreal feat of annihilation. Her heart was up in her throat, as if someone had pulled the rug out from underneath her and she was free-falling through the air. The people around her were reeling, too. This guy next to her was grin-ning crazily, muttering, *"Too much, too much."* When he turned and handed her the second pill, his face was sprouting little tufts of brown fur; as she swallowed it, he was morphing into what looked like a cunning little fox.

Waiting backstage to play the most important set of his life, Jimi

Hendrix had also swallowed two hits of Monterey Purple. The moment he appeared, the mere sight of him stunned Dawn Reynolds. The way he was dressed—red velvet pants, Mongol vest, ostrich boa, white silk ruffled shirt, Spanish boots, pounds of jewelry—would have been more than enough to enthrall her, but it was his physicality that blew her mind: the broad shoulders, long legs and arms, narrow waist, protruding behind, big, angular head, and the wild frizzed-out hair that was pushed straight up off his forehead by the headband. She couldn't help it; she found herself almost immediately imagining his penis, and from that moment on, the guitar became an extension of it, and every single thing about his performance was submerged in the most torrid eroticism.

Through eight songs—"Killing Floor," "Foxy Lady," "Like a Rolling Stone," "Rock Me Baby," "Hey Joe," "Can You See Me," "The Wind Cries Mary," "Purple Haze"—she watched him play his guitar behind his back, play a solo with his mouth and perform cunnilingus on the strings, play it between his legs, do a backward roll and stand back up without missing a lick, and hump his amplifier until it came in a wailing orgasm of feedback, all the while calmly chewing gum. There were moments when she would have sworn that she heard three or four guitars at once and instruments of some hidden other dimension. Whatever it was, it was all coming out of his amplifiers in concentric crimson waves that seemed to flow from his fingertips directly into her womb, where it enveloped the fetus in some electric current that seemed to allow him to communicate with it telepathically. By the time he came to the end of his last song, "Wild Thing," she was certain that it was not some projected visualization but was really happening to her—he was inside her! commingling with the embryo itself!—and when he dropped to his knees at the end and squirted the lighter fluid on the guitar, she could only watch in spellbound wonder. Tossing a match, he coaxed the flames higher and higher like some voodoo medicine man, and then he picked up his guitar and swung it like an ax, smashing it until it was nothing but shattered kindling.

Tears were running down her cheeks at the strange beauty of it. She had felt somehow violated by the demolition of the Who, but Hendrix, it seemed, had made love to her and had then torched the thing most dear to him, the very instrument of his love, and in a flash the knowledge came to her: they were living in a time when things would be sacrificed to the fire in order for something else to be born. Shiva would do his dance, and what would emerge would be a new golden age. By the time he left the stage, a generation may have claimed Jimi Hendrix as the Perfect Artist of that age, but Dawn Reynolds had claimed him as the spiritual father of her child.

The Mamas and the Papas closed out the festival, but it was as if they weren't even there. Dawn was thinking about where to go next, and the answer was as obvious as a song on the radio. John Phillips had penned and produced the song for Scott McKenzie about all the kids who were going to Monterey, called "San Francisco (Be Sure to Wear Flowers in Your Hair)," that was being played around the clock. Like two hundred thousand other kids, she would follow its call and head for the Haight Ashbury.

The psychedelic spring was over. The Summer of Love was about to begin.

# 5

## White Light, White Heat

**❝Speed and sex, wow! Like, oh, God. A twenty-four-hour climax that can go on for days. And there's no way to explain it unless you've been through it . . . ❞**

—Edie Sedgwick, *Ciao! Manhattan*, 1972

### I. Babylon in Flames

WHEN IT WAS GOING FULL BLAST, with the Velvets thrashing away on their instruments at an earsplitting decibel level, it was an extraordinary spectacle. COME BLOW YOUR MIND, read the advertisement in *The Village Voice*, "The Silver Dream Factory Presents The Exploding Plastic Inevitable with Andy Warhol/The Velvet Underground/and Nico," and for that whole month of April 1966, blown minds were a nightly occurrence at the Polski Dom Narodowy on St. Mark's Place.

The band was always dressed in black, except for the blond German model-chanteuse Nico, who would just stand in her white pantsuit as everything raged around her, trancelike in a lone spotlight. Mary Woronov and Gerard Malanga danced ferociously in front of the band, Malanga shaking like a wet dog, with his peroxided hair, whirling flashlights, and whip, Waronov slinking across the stage in her shiny black spike-heeled boots. The white walls of the large hall were awash in movies projected three at a time, enveloping the performers in images from *Couch, Banana, Sleep, Empire, Blow Job, Vinyl,* and other Warhol films. The effect was like casting the performers in movies of themselves before an audience that became part of the same movie. Phosphorescent nuggets of light swirled off the old mirrored ball hanging above the stage, which turned the ceiling into a glittery psychedelic firmament; colored spots washed onto the stage from the balcony, where Warhol himself hovered in black leather, a pale, detached figure wearing dark sunglasses and a glow-in-the-dark crucifix around his neck, calmly inserting colored gels into the projectors. The strobe lights firing off everywhere at once, the scene looked like flickering snapshots of some unsheltered new reality, the very "Babylon in flames" that Lou Reed referred to in an essay he wrote at the time, aptly titled "Concerning the Rumor That Red China Has Cornered the Methedrine Market and Is Busy Adding Paranoia Drops to Upset the Mental Balance of the United States."

The scene was rife with heavy amphetamine, which was like pouring gasoline on a fire. The "A men" were given free reign of the place, and Brigid Berlin, known as the Duchess in the New York underground, glided about, openly brandishing her needle on the dance floor, giving free pokes to people in the crowd (hence her otter moniker, Brigid Polk) "You could do any drug you wanted, but things like pot and acid seemed ridiculous on methedrine," declared the artist Ronnie Cutrone, only sixteen years old at the time of the Exploding Plastic Inevitable and soon to dance with the Velvets as well. "You didn't need anything else!—and it was totally uncool to take anything else while you were on it."

The Velvet Underground and the stage dancers enhanced the overwhelming drugginess of the atmosphere. The music they played was loud, cacophonous, but at the same time uniquely crafted; the songs themselves were dark and sinister, with spare, Poe-like lyrics describing the same provocative subjects that Warhol treated in his films. The tense, emaciated Lou Reed sang the songs in a detached and nasal monotone, with an attitude that seemed to reek of methamphetamine hydrochloride. There was a song with an S&M theme, called "Venus in Furs," and a song that Reed had written during his unbridled senior year at Syracuse University, about copping heroin in the dingy hallways of Harlem. With the music rising from the softness of the verses in a throbbing crescendo and then back, the song "Heroin" itself had become like a shot of dope being jacked into the bloodstream. As the Velvets played it, Gerard Malanga would act out the ritual of injection, crouching down and tying off and shooting up in a pantomime that looked so authentic people barely noticed that he wasn't really using a spike. "People thought it was a needle, but it was only a pen or pencil," Malanga related. "I had never been through the ritual myself, and I never even saw anybody ever shoot up in the Factory. I was just mimicking it from the movies I'd seen, like *Man with the Golden Arm*."

"Oh, it was all very prodrug, the whole presentation," Mary Woronov acknowledged. "When the Velvets played 'Heroin,' people would shoot up right there on the dance floor, and we'd spotlight them."

Warhol was unquestionably reaching a new level of fame and influence. Words like *revolutionary* would be commonly used to describe the Exploding Plastic Inevitable, along with notions of "religious fervor" and provocative phrases like "the beauty in evil, the evil in beauty." Parallels would be drawn to the degenerate Berlin of the 1930s. "The flowers of evil are in bloom. Someone has to stamp them out before they spread" was one oft-quoted line from the ensuing media reaction. The EPI represented nothing less than the multimedia expression of a new cultural sensibility, the enshrining of the latest New York underground aesthetic; its underlying message of nihilism, hard-drug use, and sadomasochism was completely at odds with American mainstream culture during the mid-1960s, but equally anathema to the new counterculture efflorescing on the West Coast. When Warhol accepted the invitation of Bill Graham to play the Fillmore Auditorium in San Francisco at the end of May and the EPI brought its whips, needles, and black leather into the land of peace, love, and flowers, it was a clash of evolving drug cultures in the truest sense—the difference in a song about heroin or speed written by Lou Reed and performed at the Dom by the Velvets and a song inspired by LSD and psychedelic transcendentalism performed at the Fillmore by the Grateful Dead.

"We spoke two completely different languages because we were on amphetamine and they were on acid," Mary Woronov pointed out. "They were so slow to speak, with these wide eyes—'Oh, *wow!*'—so into their vibrations; we spoke in rapid-machine-gun fire about books and paintings and movies. They were into free and the American Indian and going back to the land and trying to be some kind of true, authentic person; we could not have cared less about that. They were homophobic; we were homosexual. Their women—they were these big, round-titted girls; you would say hello to them, and they would just flop on the bed and fuck you; we liked sexual tension, S&M, *not* fucking. They were barefoot; we had platform boots. They were eating bread they had baked themselves—and we never ate at all!"

The New York underground was a classic example of what sociologists would later call a total amphetamine subculture. Everyone took speed in every conceivable form, from the mother's little helpers that were stocked in medicine cabinets of middle-class housewives across America to the purest pharmaceutical methamphetamine sulfate. When injected, meth produces a rush that feels like an instantaneous white-hot blast going down from your hair follicles to the tips of your toes, a speed flash that Lou Reed would describe in a song called "White Light/White Heat"—

*Lord have mercy white light have it goodness knows*

That summer of 1966, Andy Warhol seemed ubiquitous in New York, as did amphetamine. He produced an epic called *The Chelsea Girls* and brought the cinema of the underground to a mainstream audience for the first time. Max's Kansas City opened for business off Union Square and the back room became not just the mecca of the underground but also the nexus of a new kind of celebrity that Warhol exemplified. The whole world seemed silver that season: the silver tinfoil of the Factory walls, the silver-rinsed hair of Warhol and Edie Sedgwick; Warhol's silver helium pillows drifting willy-nilly along the ceiling of the Castelli Gallery; the silver hypodermic needle that the Duchess brandished as casually as a toothbrush and poked into the creamy derriere of Ingrid Superstar in reel 3 of *The Chelsea Girls.* "Who wants to buy some amphetamine?" asks the Duchess. "It's like snow in the middle of January on the windowpane. It's the *end*!"

## II. The Perfect Time to Think Silver

IT ALL MOVED in concert from the very beginning: amphetamine, the new underground aesthetic, the films, the superstars, the Velvets, fifteen minutes of fame. No sooner had Warhol encountered the "amphetamine rapture group" at Billy Linich's down on the Lower East Side in 1963 than the style and sensibility began to come together. The entire place was silver—mirrors, tinfoil, and paint—uniformly, overwhelmingly silver. The artist, newly celebrated for his Campbell's soup cans and "Death and Disaster" silkscreen series, took one look at the apartment and saw a vision of the future: "It must have been the amphetamine—everything always went back to that," Warhol recounted. "But it was great, the perfect time to think silver. . . . Silver was the future, it was spacey—the astronauts . . . and silver was also the past—the silver screen. . . . And maybe more than anything else, silver was narcissism—mirrors were backed with silver."

The history of amphetamine in the United States reflects such widespread usage that it can arguably be viewed as the most quintessentially American of the modern psychoactive drugs. "Amphetamines were unique," observed Lester Grinspoon and Peter Hedblom in *The Speed Culture: Amphetamine Use and Abuse in America*. "Never before had so powerful a drug been introduced in such quantities and in so short a time, and never before had a drug with such a high addictive potential and capability of causing irreversible physical or psychological damage been so enthusiastically embraced by the medical profession as a panacea or so extravagantly promoted by the drug industry."

The availability of the drug would only expand as huge amounts were siphoned off from legal production to a growing black market along a distribution network that ran from basic suppliers to dosage manufacturers to wholesale distributors to retail pharmacists to physicians. When combined with the increasing amounts of "home-cooked" methedrine manufactured in growing numbers of clandestine laboratories by a new breed of underground chemist, the accessibility of amphetamines, both licit and illicit, would come to represent something wholly unprecedented even within the vast pharmacological smorgasbord of the era. Sociologists studying the use of the drug would also observe that it had great appeal to various "deviant" subcultures of the time, whether prison populations or outlaw biker gangs like the Hells Angels; cultural historians would trace the impact of the drug across a wide spectrum of popular culture, from the Mods of Britain to the new anorectic chic of the fashion world as exemplified by models like Twiggy. But it was here, among the gathering cognoscenti of the New York underground—a "deviant" subculture if ever there was one—that the drug would find its unique and far-reaching aesthetic.

The Amphetamine Rapture Group, or A men, as they soon became known, was a flaming gang of gossiping speed queens. The personalities in this crowd were dazzling and original, like William Burroughs or Jean Genet characters brought to life: Billy Linich, Ondine, Silver George, Rotten Rita, Mr. Clean, Birmingham Birdie, Stanley the Turtle, the Sugar Plum Fairy. Called Mole People because they lived nocturnally, and in this era before gay liberation they would remain underground (and then, during the early 1970s, emerge like moles), most of them were good-looking, brimming with creativity, flamboyantly gay, and seething with an unabashed promiscuity (whereas Warhol was shy and insecure about his sexuality). Moreover, there was a certain high-camp theatricality about them, a sense that every minute of their lives was the premiere of some great opera or Hollywood movie in which they were the glorious stars.

Warhol asked Billy Linich (soon to be known as Billy Name) to come uptown to his studio, not far from Grand Central Terminal, and replicate the environment of his apartment. It took about four months for Linich to completely paint and tinfoil the low-ceilinged one-hundred-by-fifty-foot space with its crumbling brick walls and four columns. He accomplished the task with thousands of minute bits of broken mirror, meticulously pasting them everywhere. Visitors entered the gunmetal gray lobby of the industrial building and took the open freight elevator to the sixth floor, stepping out into a completely silverized dimension in which every surface was a reflection of something else. "This was all amphetamine busy work," Warhol related, "but the interesting thing was that Billy could communicate the atmosphere to people who weren't taking drugs: usually people on speed created things that only looked good to them. But what Billy did went past the drugs."

From the outset, the Factory was a cultural epicenter that represented something unique in the social history of New York—"a Pop temple," as art critic David Bourdon characterized it in his study of Warhol—"a new kind of underground atelier, a free zone where all conventional morality stopped dead at the doorway." The place was usually teeming with people of every conceivable social background, as long as they were good-looking or interesting or rich—artists, photographers, writers, editors, models, dancers, filmmakers, cultural arbiters, movie stars, rock stars, scions of industry—the beautiful people, as they came to be known during the Silver Sixties, all of them coolly eyeballing one another, many of them vying competitively for Warhol's attention. Everything swirled casually together at the Factory, show business and fashion, media and the art world, Park Avenue society and the downtown demimonde of sexual deviance and drug use.

"It represented the true cracking of the 1950s in New York," observed Mary Woronov. "It was the place where the rich and famous were excited because they could meet these 'things' from the other side. They'd come to the Factory and meet someone who previously was thought to have been exactly the sort of person who should have been put away for the benefit of society, and here they couldn't seem to get enough of it. It made things very interesting."

Of course, Warhol would profess ignorance of the drug use. The truth was that there was an unspoken etiquette about the use of drugs at the Factory. For one thing, nobody would ever snort or shoot up in front of Andy. "He didn't know that people were shooting up because they were very discreet," Billy Linich recognized. "And anyway, once he had his Obetrol he would be joyously in tune with everything they were doing."

"What did I love about amphetamine so much? The power, the energy," Mary Woronov explained. "Oh, you were like God, so thrilled with yourself that you could spend twenty-four hours hearing yourself talk. Of course, someone not on amphetamine might find everything coming out of your mouth extremely stupid, but who the fuck cared? You could think more, and the rush was like sexual orgasm. It was about being bigger, better, stronger, smarter, and quicker. It was the perfect ego drug of the 1960s."

Mainstream moviegoing audiences might remember Mary Woronov conking victims over the head with a frying pan before she and Paul Bartel prepared them as gourmet fare in *Eating Raoul,* the sleeper hit of 1982. Underground audiences first saw her in *Hedy* in 1966, the year she left Cornell to come to the Factory and join Gerard Malanga as a dancer for

the Velvet Underground and become one of the notable underground ac-
tresses of the time.

"I think I suffered from insecurity, and amphetamine is perfect for
that," Woronov reflected. "I wasn't an injector, I was an ingestor, and I ingested a lot. Being afraid of needles might have kept me out of harm's
way—but, oh, yes, I found it all immensely attractive. Oddly enough, I
enjoyed coming down, too, which is really strange. This was not a problem for me even though you grinded your teeth horribly, and it felt like
the end of the world. Even the crash rang some kind of a bell for me
somehow. I loved the *endurance* of it, like being on this giant bus ride and
you arrive at your destination just as the dawn is coming up. You can't go
up without coming down—that was my philosophy."

Daybreak was the trickiest time of all when you were crashing. They
called it the Dawn Patrol, when they would find themselves caught out-
doors and the morning sun would send them scurrying for cover, pasty
faced and cowering in doorways down on the Lower East Side. It was
hideous being hit by the sun after you had been up for so long. After the
marathon amphetamine high, the central nervous system would be
singed, stretched to its absolute limits, the synapses shorting out like critically overheating fuses. In a hair-trigger instant, everything could pivot
to its exact opposite: boundless exuberance to dry-mouthed despair, om-
nipotent self-confidence to jaw-grinding paranoia, superhuman energy
to ragged exhaustion. The verbal acrobatics and comic bitchiness that always seemed to animate conversation could suddenly erupt into the most
searing cruelties. With the clubs closed and the parties long over, this vicious, amphetamine-fueled abuse of each other was a strange but compelling form of entertainment for them when there was really no place
else to go, when there was nothing left to do but seek refuge in an early-
morning coffee shop as far away as possible from the rush-hour throngs
on their way to work, whose very existence seemed a brutal assault to
their senses.

For the hard-core Mole People, dawn was usually time for more amphetamine—a handful of Obetrols, Eskatrols; a snort, skin poke, or
mainline shot of meth if they had it, anything just to keep on going somehow because who ever wanted to go to sleep? You might miss something,
and there was always a lot to miss. It was even harder to let go of the ride

if you had been going for seven or eight days because then you'd sleep for thirty hours straight, and when you woke up, that was the worst time of all: the Twilight Zone. The Great Darkness. Extreme isolation. Double vision and pounding temples. The whole world seemed to tilt and stretch, and objects and thoughts whirled madly out of control, and you went stumbling around rooms and lurching into the corners of buildings. That was when you really wanted to die.

During those years of their "everlasting publicity," from 1965–68, the Dawn Patrol became an underground movie that featured an ongoing cast of debutantes and drag queens, actors and musicians, painters and poets, hustlers and hangers-on, bit players and superstars. They came from backgrounds that ranged from the backstreets of Miami to the alleyways of the Bronx, from suburban Long Island to the most capacious Fifth Avenue apartments, but for the most part they were young, talented, creatively driven, emotionally alienated, psychologically unstable, desperate for attention, wildly exhibitionist, hysterically high-strung or coldly detached to the point of undiminished passivity. They exuded an exotic, unpredictable sexuality that could go firing off in any direction like some polymorphous high-tension power line that had suddenly snapped loose. Most were homosexual, but their ranks were sprinkled with virtually every flavor of the sexual rainbow. Above all else, they were absolute narcissists preening in the romantic universe of their own fantasies and imagination, devoted worshippers in the great vaulted cathedrals of themselves.

"It was so much fun, nobody ever went to sleep," Woronov went on. "I used to go back to my house in Brooklyn and drop into my childhood head and go to sleep for a little while and go right back. Some of the A men did not sleep at all—they would die, they would go crazy. But it was unbelievable, the energy. Every time it started to flag, Ondine just *dove* for it—he just never, *ever* stopped! He was this very special person with an enormous generosity and talent but also clearly trying to destroy himself. It was like the A men were intentionally trying to burn themselves out. Nobody wanted to see old age—we thought it was stupid. And there was a great humor. That was another thing: these people were very funny! We were accustomed to being bored, and a major part of our existence was standing around some street corner, trying to figure out where to go, very high on amphetamines, and a lot of the humor would come out of those situations."

"Paranoia was really our drug of choice, and we made jokes about it, even though it could be a scary, weird thing," related Ronnie Cutrone in his art studio in downtown Manhattan. "It was that New York black T-shirt kind of existence of constantly being paranoid of your best friends, of Andy, of who was trying to do what behind your back in that cutthroat competition of who was going to get in the next movie. That was the whole methedrine experience for us. You remember Stevie Wonder's song 'Uptight (Everything's Alright)'? It went, 'Ev'rything is all right, uptight, *out of sight*'—meaning that it was *good,* so even the word *uptight* had positive connotations. If you were uptight, you were cranked out of your skull, you jaw was locked, and you were paranoid. We loved that nasty amphetamine edge."

Cutrone displayed his arms matter-of-factly as he continued painting. "See that bump? And that other bump and vein? That's nine years of shooting up . . . Methedrine—you shot it two or three times a day, and you were always flying. Once I started to shoot up, I never wanted to come down."

As Warhol recognized, "Amphetamine doesn't give you peace of mind, but it makes not having it very amusing." The people who used the drug as a way of life "believed in throwing themselves into every extreme—sing until you choke, dance until you drop, brush your hair till you sprain your arm."

It was precisely that quality that would make Warhol's entourage a perfect subject for his films.

### III. Our Godless Civilization Approaching the Zero Point

ALMOST FROM THE MOMENT Warhol began making his own films, the camera became a central, defining presence in the life of the Factory. If the artist's paintings, silk screens, and sculptures were predicated on an aesthetic of duplication, which created complicity between the artist and viewer as consumers of popular culture, the films would not only continue this aesthetic but create new ones.

A perfect example was *Empire,* the eight-hour filming of the Empire State Building as seen from the forty-fourth floor of the Time-Life Building from the night of June 24 to the morning of June 25, 1964. In all of Warhol's early films, the camera never once moved, and the sense of time was displaced and slowed down even more by the techniques of loop printing, frozen frames, and retarded projection speeds. The effect was to take something completely static to begin with and render it trancelike, otherworldly, in a state of suspended animation—a style that David Bourdon would call "cataleptic cinema."

To what degree might the amphetamine sensibility have inspired a work such as *Empire*? Although Warhol himself would liken the building to a "giant hard-on," others who later watched the film began to see something else as the hours passed. "It was dull, dreary, boring, weird, and above all long," remarked Cutrone, "but it looked like this giant hypodermic needle rising into the skies of Manhattan, experiencing sunset and sunrise."

"I don't think any of those films we made during that time would have been possible without drugs," Gerard Malanga allowed. "The thing that was synonymous with Andy's films and amphetamine was the sense of repetition and the constant stretching of time, which was very amphetamine-like."

The next critical element in the underground was the emergence of the "superstar." With her long, "eloquent" legs and huge, teacup-saucer eyes the color of anthracite, Edith Minturn Sedgwick, with her chauffeured Mercedes, Park Avenue address, and unimpeachable social pedigree that included Cabots, Lodges, and Lowells, was the personification of everything that Andy Warhol seemed to crave. Edie dressed in dark leotards and tights with loose shirttails, along with mod dresses, Pucci slacks, huge false eyelashes, dangling hoop earrings, and gold glitter on her cheeks. When Warhol discovered that he loved the way Edie looked on-screen after she made a brief appearance in *Kitchen,* he set out to make her the queen of underground movies—the Greta Garbo, the Marlene Dietrich of the avant-garde. Edie had screen persona in the purest sense of the word, but it wasn't simply her aloof, androgynous beauty. With her hair cut short and rinsed tinfoil silver to look like his own, it seemed as if she could create Warhol's alter ego in a film just by being in it. Her face would become a perfectly beautiful blank slate upon which all the madness of the era would seem to write itself.

The year 1965 was the beginning of very heady times at the Factory, when many around Warhol began to feel as if they were living out a twentieth-century version of the French Romantics. "People took us seriously, and it built up our self-confidence and self-esteem because it made you feel that whatever you were doing had relevance," Malanga explained, "whether it was taking photographs or writing poetry or being in a movie. Andy gave you the opportunity, and you'd be in a movie, and all of a sudden it was playing at the Cinematheque."

Of course, by that time there were already casualties of the scene. The most spectacular was Freddie Herko, a young dancer at the Judson Theater who had become a colossal speed freak. Everyone knew that Freddie was taking too much amphetamine, especially when he would retreat for long periods into the walk-in closet of an apartment where he was staying down on St. Mark's Place. Showing up at the poet Diane di Prima's apartment, he invited everyone to a "special performance" he was going to give—he was going to leap off the top of his downtown building, he announced—and then went to Johnny Dodd's apartment on Cornelia Street to take a bath. LSD had hit the scene by this time, and Freddie had taken some—a large amount, no doubt, as all of the doses tended to be in those days of pure liquid Sandoz and sugar cubes. People would later wonder what on earth he might have been hallucinating as he made everyone leave, saying that he had a "new ballet" to do. Alone and naked, he put Mozart's *Coronation* Mass on the hi-fi and began to dance. Right at the arrival of the Sanctus, he raced down the full length of the hallway in the railroad flat and took a flying leap out the open fifth-floor window. It must have been quite a leap because it carried him a good way down the block, where he landed on a car, his broken, bleeding body splayed out grotesquely on the hood.

The death gave rise to many interpretations. Freddie was depressed, lonely, and sad because his career was going nowhere. The fact that he was on LSD contributed to the growing notion at the time that the drug might induce other deaths by defenestration in the cases of emotionally unstable personalities. Ondine maintained that the death was really the "completion" of someone who had chosen to make art of his own demise—almost as if the death itself had presented some new aesthetic. Freddie had gone out in a blaze of glory, like Nijinsky in *Spectre de la rose,* and the dark mythos of the death would only be compounded by Warhol's reaction.

"Why didn't he tell me he was going to do it?" the artist was heard to exclaim when he heard the news. "We could have gone down there and filmed it!" It was this comment that began shaping Warhol's reputation as some sort of pop-art archangel of death feeding ghoulishly on the twisted lives of those who gathered around him.

Herko's death did nothing to restrain Edie Sedgwick, who soon developed fantasies of stardom on a much grander scale than the cult of underground films in downtown Manhattan would allow. By the time of *Lupe,* her swan song as a Warhol superstar, she was already moving away from the scene at the Factory. "Edie wasn't happy with the way her career was progressing with Andy," Billy Linich recognized, "but of course, she had gotten into amphetamine—crystal stuff, with me and Ondine and Brigid Polk, and that really devastated any possible career, because, you know, you would have to stay in your place and get ready for six hours."

Consumed by her affairs and disappointments, Edie began to unravel, plunging precipitously into drugs. Just how far would become painfully evident in *Ciao! Manhattan*—"The Story of Edie Sedgwick, Superstar of New York's Silver Sixties"—an independent film by John Palmer and David Weisman that was started in 1967 but not completed until 1972 because of Edie's repeated breakdowns.

"You want to hear something I wrote about the horror of speed?" Edie says, reflecting on the amphetamine scene in New York at the time in her life when she was just beginning to sell her furs and Chanels and Balenciagas for drugs. "Well, maybe you don't, but the nearly incommunicable torrents of speed, buzzerama, that acrylic high, horrendous, yodeling, repetitious echoes of an infinity so brutally harrowing that words cannot capture the devastation nor the tone of such a vicious nightmare."

Edie wanted to "turn on the whole world just for one moment," she declares. Hers was a compelling kind of lust, a preternatural greediness for the feeling of amphetamine that she craved for herself and her friends—"to keep that superlative high, just on the cusp of each day . . . so that I'd radiate sunshine."

Even in the months after she left the Factory, it was becoming apparent that Edie Sedgwick was going to take the same proverbial leap out the window as Freddie Herko. Perhaps it was going to take her a few years longer, but this time everyone who wanted to would get to watch.

New versions of the Girl of the Year would appear—Ingrid von Scheven, Christa Pafgen, Isabelle Collin Dufresne, Susan Bottomly, and Susan Hoffman—soon to be enshrined in the new galaxy of superstars as Ingrid Superstar, Nico, Ultra Violet, International Velvet, and Viva, respectively.

All through that climactic summer of 1966, in reel after reel of sixteen-millimeter film shot at the Factory and the Chelsea Hotel and apartments around New York, the "flowers of evil" bloomed in front of Andy Warhol's camera as he shot his underground magnum opus, *The Chelsea Girls*. The idea was to present a voyeuristic gaze into the lives taking place in eight different rooms of the Chelsea Hotel; what emerged was an epic document of what the world around Andy Warhol had become by that time. Paranoia and competition motivated the cast to indulge in the most aberrant behavior possible—in effect, to out-blaspheme one another. Fantasy and real life blurred together; fictional characters became inseparable from actual identities. As Warhol put it, "Their lives became part of my movies, and of course, the movies became part of their lives; they'd get so into them that pretty soon you couldn't really separate the two. You couldn't tell the difference—and sometimes neither could they." And whatever moral restraint might have gotten in the way was completely dissolved by drugs.

"The whole Catholic Church is *gone,* and Greenwich Village is in its place," Pope Ondine pronounced in his memorable papal bull. "My flock consists of homosexuals, perverts of any kind, thieves, criminals of any sort—the rejected by society, that's who I'm Pope for." Then, running out of things to say, he matter-of-factly shot up amphetamine into the back of his hand, right on camera. The real act of shooting up had rarely been observed in the cinema, underground or otherwise, and the effect of this improvised injection would have been raw and kinky enough, but it was rendered all the more shocking by the explosion of real-life violent rage that followed.

"You dumb *bitch!*" Ondine screamed at Rona Page after striking her hard across the face, rushing out of the frame after her. "How dare you come onto the set and tell me I'm a phony? You miserable phony, you miserable *whore*! I'll hit you with my hand, you dumb bitch! I want to *smash your face*!"

Malanga remembered how nervous but fascinated Warhol looked at that moment. Others might have stopped the camera, but this was reality, and Warhol was going to get it on film.

*The Chelsea Girls* created an instant buzz when it opened at the two-hundred-seat Filmmakers Cinematheque. The reaction to the film was strong, with champions every bit as impassioned as detractors. Independent film doyen Jonas Mekas fanned great interest among the cognoscenti by famously claiming that the work conjured Victor Hugo and *The Birth of a Nation*: "The terror and desperation of *Chelsea Girls* is a holy terror . . . it's our godless civilization approaching the zero point. It's not homosexuality, it's not lesbianism, it's not heterosexuality: the terror and hardness we see in *Chelsea Girls* is the same terror and hardness that is burning Vietnam and it's the essence and blood of our culture, of our ways of living: this is the Great Society." *The New York Times* called the film "a travelogue of hell—a grotesque menagerie of lost souls whimpering in a psychedelic moonscape of neon red and fluorescent blue." When Jack Kroll penned a long review in *Newsweek* that proclaimed the film a "fascinating and significant movie event," he all but guaranteed the film a solid run in local theaters. When it was booked in art houses in Los Angeles, Dallas, Washington, San Diego, and Kansas City, *Chelsea Girls* became the first work of the New York underground cinema ever to be distributed commercially across the country.

In the year that followed, the Factory continued to churn out more films and attract still more hopeful superstars and hangers-on. The film made Warhol more money than any other of his ventures ever had, empowering the artist and those around him even more, but it also created a backlash that put the Factory under siege from police and the media. The atmosphere around the artist became supercharged with even more drugs, sex, jealousies, paranoia, and manipulation. Warhol fully understood that the drugs had become inseparable from the behavior of the people around him, with all of it made even more complex by the new vogues of free love and bisexuality. In *Chelsea Girls,* he had peered through a dark keyhole to conjure the reverse image of the peace and love ethos of the 1960s—the exact film negative of the Age of Aquarius—and what he revealed was a world of malignant, pill-popping, syringe-jabbing speed freaks.

THE SHOOTING OF ANDY WARHOL by Valerie Solanis on June 3, 1968, marked more than simply the end of the A men at the Factory. It was the passing of an era. The song by Lou Reed that would stand as the musical document of their underground intravenous speed scene was released on the second Velvet Underground album the same year. Warhol recalled Reed coming to the Factory to play an advance pressing of "White Light/White Heat" and talking about how he was trying to curtail his use of the drug even as Ondine had come over to his loft with several ounces and was making it very difficult for him.

Not surprisingly, after Warhol recovered from the nearly fatal shooting, he turned increasingly paranoid. The sound of the elevator now made him tremble with fright; the Factory quickly became a place of locked doors and surveillance cameras. In this new atmosphere, the amphetamine crazies who had fed the artist's creativity since 1964 found themselves less and less welcome. As it turned out, many were flaming out anyway. The sheer physical wear and tear of living at such a level over several years was simply too much to take, making the great crash inevitable for many and turning the New York underground of the mid- to late 1960s into a story filled with epitaphs as well as epilogues.

Mary Woronov went "deeper into the drug culture and really joined Mole People, like Ondine and Rotten Rita. But finally," she said, "I fucked up, I took too much speed. I knew how I felt before I started taking drugs, and I knew I wasn't that same person. I was starting to mumble, and I'd seen people in that situation, and I knew what was happening to me, and Gerard even told me, 'You've gone over the edge.' " Woronov began a period of "hibernation," staying home for a full year. "I thought I got fat, but I was probably just eating regularly! I didn't do much, just painted a little. That's what it took. I knew I'd come around, and I did."

Ronnie Cutrone spent the entire summer of 1967 "locked in my apartment with my girlfriend, shooting methedrine nonstop, having no visitors and making art and listening to *Sgt Peppers Lonely Hearts Club Band* over and over. One day, I was down on all fours like a dog, with blood on my forehead, and my girlfriend said, 'Ronnie, you have to stop.' I looked in the mirror and said, 'You're right.' " For the next ninety days, Cutrone did nothing but lie on his back. "That was all I could do. On the ninety-second day, I got up and said, 'I guess it's time to live my life,' and I haven't used methedrine since. But the transition wasn't easy. It was hard to sleep at night, and there were moments of terror."

Gerard Malanga left the Factory after a falling-out with Warhol over the sale of a painting. He would remain in good health even though by 1966 he had been experiencing what his dentist referred to as "unusual enamel erosion." "I think it was partly due to amphetamine and alcohol and maybe a low calcium count, but I stopped doing it. Amphetamine never left me with a good feeling in the end. Drugs for me were not the lifestyle that they might have been for other people in the group, and I never shot it. When I did it, I always tried to bring it back to creativity, writing poetry about the things going on around me, staying up for twenty-four hours and watching the sun come up over the city. I romanticized it but fortunately never got caught up in a habit-forming situation. But quite frankly, I really thought I was involved in a very important social phenomenon at the time."

Leaving amphetamine behind did not necessarily mean leaving drugs behind, of course. In 1965, the people around Warhol had sat motionless, gazing into his sixteen-millimeter Auricon camera for the portraits of *Screen Test,* a film that was also published as a book. As Gerard Malanga flipped through its pages thirty years later, his comments on the fate of those individuals provided vivid testimony to the attrition suffered by many. "Debbie Dropout, she's about sixteen here," he remarked, displaying the images of a beautiful young girl with dissipated long-lashed eyes staring out from underneath long, Jean Shrimpton–like bangs. "She got intensely involved in the whole amphetamine scene, just swallowed up. Later she went on to heroin. I don't know what happened to her . . . Harry Fainlight, he was a gigantic A head, lived in a down-and-dirty apartment in Chinatown. He's dead now."

"The drugs were fuel and inspiration," Mary Woronov concluded. "Countless paintings, books, films, songs, came out of that experience of a whole group going through that altered state of mind, that heightened state."

After moving to Los Angeles and playing in a series of low-budget films, Woronov had gone careening headlong once again into another drug underground, this time the L.A. punk-rock scene. She attained a kind of cult status in several Roger Corman movies before turning her attention to painting and writing.

"Do I miss those years? Yes, in a strange way I do, but it was never comfortable going through it. Of course, people died. Freddie Herko danced right out the window. Eric Emerson, this beautiful young god who could literally fly through the air, got on his bicycle and never came back—a pitiful junkie when he died. Nico became a junkie and died the same way, hit by a car while she was on a bicycle—another pitiful junkie . . . On the other hand, so many of us also survived—Lou, Gerard, Ronnie, I survived okay, Brigid survived okay, even Billy survived. He went to San Francisco and went on this monumental acid trip and got amnesia for five years or something and lived in a hotel and later he got fat and woodsy looking with a beard. Of course, Ondine didn't survive; his body just eventually gave out on him. But then he never had any intention of surviving, did he?"

# 6

## Next Stop Is Vietnam

"Let smiles cease," Converse said. "Let laughter flee. This is the place where everybody finds out who they are."

—Robert Stone, *Dog Soldiers*, 1974

"I knew one 4th Division Lurp who took pills by the fistful, downs from the left pocket of his tiger suit and ups from the right, one to cut the trail for him and the other to send him down it."

—Michael Herr, *Dispatches*, 1977

### I. The Worm Has Definitely Turned for You, Man

IT DIDN'T TAKE LONG for Oliver Stone to realize that the war he had volunteered for was about survival and not victory and that it was being fought largely by those elements of American society not privileged enough to go to college: minorities and poor and working-class whites.

Already, by the fall of 1967, units of the Twenty-fifth Infantry were seriously demoralized by the senselessness, the ambiguities, and the utter hopelessness of the conflict. The South Vietnamese peasants in the countryside, for whom they were presumably fighting, seemed indifferent at best, and you could never tell whether they might be the enemy. The so-called Vietnamese allies of the ARVN were cowardly and notoriously corrupt. The American command was involved in its own follies, delusions, and deceptions, lying about VC body counts and the number of

American casualties from friendly fire. Back at the PXs, the REMFs (rear-echelon motherfuckers)—the support troops involved in transportation, supply, and administration, who outnumbered the combat troops in Vietnam nearly six to one—were indulging in black-market schemes and pleasures while Stone and his buddies out humping the boonies did the fighting, putting their lives on the line. The officers in the field were oftentimes distrusted, if not actually despised, by the very men they were leading into battle. Fraggings—the intentional killings of officers by their own troops—were already occurring. It was in this environment, and with these deeply disturbing realizations, that Oliver Stone smoked his first marijuana.

"In the Twenty-fifth Infantry, there were a few smokers, but I didn't smoke when I first came to Vietnam because I was scared of it," Stone acknowledged. "I'd been exposed to marijuana back in New York, but I'd never done it. But my view of things had changed pretty radically; it was a life-or-death situation over there, and everything was topsy-turvy. I was wounded twice, and some of the support systems had been eradicated . . . And when I went to the First Cavalry unit up north, there were some real heads up there, funny guys—black, white trash—with sort of a prison mentality about everything. The first time I smoked pot over there, I just remember a tremendous sense of release and surrender—a uniting, a sense of harmony with the external world."

As one of four hundred thousand American servicemen and women serving in Vietnam, Oliver Stone was a true believer in the cause of anti-Communism, but his enlistment in the U.S. Army had also been the rash act of a young man in disarray, in flight from his privileged background. The watershed event of his life had occurred in February of 1962, during his sophomore year at the exclusive Hill School in Pottstown, Pennsylvania, on the day he learned that his parents were divorcing. His father, a stockbroker, had lost his money and closed up their Manhattan townhouse and moved to a hotel; his mother had left New York for her native France without even telling him. The family life he had known had disintegrated in a single afternoon. By the time he dropped out of Yale, Stone was suicidal. "They were great parents but not always consistent. They betrayed me, lied to me about a lot of things . . . Yes, I was scared and felt persecuted, running from one institution to another—boys schools to churches to the merchant marine to army life." He joined the army seeking both the anonymity of the ranks and the opportunity to prove his manhood. "I wanted to see what I was made of. Would I be a coward? How would I react? I really wanted to kill myself, but instead decided I'd just go into combat. I asked for Vietnam and the infantry—and they gave it to me."

Stone was about to take part in the first psychedelic war in history. Resolute in his determination to show that America would win in Vietnam, President Lyndon Johnson had authorized one of the fastest and largest military expansions in the history of warfare. By doing so, he also unwittingly sent the men and women of the armed forces of the United States into a country where the most powerful opium, the purest heroin, and some of the most potent, resinous marijuana on earth would be readily available, turning the troops into potential drug users. Neither LBJ nor his commanders could have ever imagined or calculated the impact of drug use on the war—how it would change the lives of a generation of soldiers, how it would affect the conduct and perception of the war itself, or how the blowback effect of the policies of the U.S. government and the returning veterans on the drug scene at home.

In the screenplay that he would write about Vietnam in the summer of 1976, which would become *Platoon,* Stone attempted to portray his in-country initiation rite of marijuana as accurately as possible. Chris Taylor, the character Stone based on himself, played by Charlie Sheen, is taken down into a "specially constructed cellar-like hutch dug deep into the ground on an isolated edge of the battalion perimeter." Taylor has entered "another world. Chris looking around amazed. It's like a private cabaret for the heads who are there cooling out," decked out in their "Saturday night rage" of headbands, medallions, "anything distinctive and individualistic," with the Jefferson Airplane's "White Rabbit" setting the mood as it plays from a tape deck. Chris begins smoking and isn't sure he's getting high until the benevolent Sgt. Elias (Willem Dafoe) takes him under his wing: "Elias pulls out a Remington 870 shotgun, jacks it to the rear, points it at Chris . . . takes a hit and blows it down the bore—'shotgunning' it into Chris' lungs." As Chris falls back in a fit of coughing, everybody cracks up.

*ELIAS  First time?*

*CHRIS  Yeah.*

*ELIAS  Then the worm has definitely turned for you, man.*

For Oliver Stone, the turning of the worm meant many things, foremost among them being membership in the fraternity he depicts at the end of the scene. The hutch now looks like a "Turkish bath," and the heads have their arms around one another, passing the pipe and snapping their fingers as they sing Smokey Robinson's "Tracks of My Tears" into the night. It is a display of precisely the kind of brotherhood that seems so sorely missing from the platoon as it becomes increasingly polarized into two separate camps that reflect the same bitter cultural and political divisions emerging in American society in the 1960s. In Stone's experience, this division would become tantamount to "civil war"—"on the one hand, the lifers, the juicers, the moron white element (part Southern, part rural) against, on the other hand, the hippie, dope smoking, black, and progressive white element (although there were exceptions in all categories, and some lifers did more dope than I ever dreamed). Right versus Left."

The demarcation of Right versus Left, hawk versus dove, Jack Daniel's versus Cambodian Red, and the growing conflict in the ranks it produced were most dramatically embodied in two sergeants, Barnes and Elias. Barnes (played in the movie with ferocious intensity by Tom Berenger) was "Achilles," "a warrior king" with a "cold, quiet stare" that could wither you completely—"you'd feel it right down to your balls." Sgt. Juan Angel Elias—"dashingly handsome, with thick black hair, a flashing white smile, and Apache blood"—was every bit the soldier that Barnes was, but unlike Barnes his men loved rather than feared him. In a place like Vietnam, his compassion and sense of morality seemed nothing less than saintly, an oasis of sanity and spirituality amid the madness and carnage, but he pissed off the lifers because he smoked dope and spoke the truth about the war. The character of each soldier would become powerful metaphors for Stone because they represented a conflict that was happening in every unit.

The turning of the worm also meant immersion in the new music, which Stone experienced as nothing short of salvation. "I had never heard Motown before then. Or Jefferson Airplane . . . I'll never forget being on the helicopters and singing the Airplane song, 'Comin' Back to Me.' I was in love with Gracie Slick. . . . It was all part of the Zeitgeist. I was a Yale boy who heard soul music and smoked dope for the first time in his life." Stone firmly believed that he was able to emerge from Vietnam with his soul "intact" because of the blacks and potheads who turned him on. "The times in the field deadened me, but hanging out with them in the bunkers, doing dope and listening to that kind of music, restored me."

The turning of the worm also meant secrecy, hiding out underground from the lifers always eager to bust them. Stone started to change, talking the black argot, wearing Buddhist bracelets and long hair "as long as I could get it, and I was into 'hey, man,' and being cool."

The first thing a head had to learn in Vietnam was that you had to be extremely judicious about when and where you smoked. "The grass over there was whacko, mucho powerful," he explained. "It really hit you hard, so I tried to smoke in the rear. I didn't do it much on patrol at all—though some guys did. It was dangerous because we'd be out at night and the smell was very strong. Not only would our own officers pick it up, but also it was a dead giveaway if the enemy picked it up. We didn't do it out in the bush unless we were in a very low security situation, like a forward base camp or something. I would never do it in a foxhole or out on a perimeter. You had to really stay alert to everything. Smoking dope in those situations was a risky thing because you were also putting people whose lives depended on you at risk."

When two full regiments of Vietcong attacked Firebase Burt on January 1, 1968, Stone found himself part of a desperate counterattack to restore the perimeter of a company that had completely collapsed. "What made it worse was that we were somewhat stoned from getting high the night before," he admitted. "Sometimes you'd be wound so tight that the stuff would hit you even harder because it enabled you to really relax for a change. It was New Year's Eve and there was a cease-fire so we figured, what the hell, nobody would hit us then."

The pitched battle that lasted until daylight was a nightmare of explosions from mortars and RPGs, with vicious hand-to-hand combat and red tracer bullets whizzing from every direction, wounded men screaming, and dying and dead men everywhere. When they were over-run, an air strike was called in, and the planes laid bombs right on their positions. By the time it was over, Stone had been blown thirty feet through the air by a beehive round as he was running across a field, knocked out by the concussion of the blast. When he came to, he stag-gered back to his lines to witness the grim results of the battle: 25 dead Americans in body bags and 175 wounded, 500 Vietcong corpses being bulldozed into a mass grave.

And then Stone started hearing about this thing called acid. "There was this feeling in the air about it. The black guys I was doing dope with were definitely not into it—it was a white man's thing. And then when the Doors' album came over, I just thought, My God, who *are* these guys? If they're making that kind of music, this is a breakthrough—what are they on? The guys said, 'Acid.' We just knew it was this thing you could get on the streets of Australia. I felt that if it was producing this kind of music, it would be good for me, too."

Sure enough, when Stone went on his five-day R&R in Australia, he got his hands on some LSD. "I was with a wonderful girl and a bunch of guys from Vietnam, and it was a crazy night on the beaches," he related. "Australia was so hedonistic; there were a lot of GIs there spending lots of money. We were like pirates. It was an awesome experience but not a deeply spiritual one that first time. It was more about *wow!*—and *hey!*—and this is *different!*—and, my God, the dawn is *pink!*" Back in Vietnam, Stone would drop acid only once; by then, he had gotten busted a couple of times, and the lifer sergeants made him nervous. "I felt very threatened and paranoid because the lifers—they were always out to get you—so that was the only time . . . But I have to tell you that the night battles in Vietnam were hallucinogenic to me. To this day, I feel like I was on drugs during them, even though I know I wasn't."

Stone continued to smoke marijuana avidly for the rest of his tour. The paradox was that while smoking grass was sensitizing him and en-hancing his experiences, he was becoming a battle-hardened veteran, numbed and increasingly inured to killing. He became sharply attuned to the environment, his senses so finely honed that he became like part of the jungle itself, so stealthy, in fact, and so skilled at walking point that he was once able to walk right up to a deer without its knowing that he was there. It was all part of Stone's journey from a "cerebral product of the East Coast," as he put it, to a purely instinctual soldier whose entire universe became "the six inches in front of my face."

"How did marijuana change me or my view of what we were doing there? It's a good question. I tried to make the point in *Platoon,* where the character reevaluates himself and begins to find his own values as opposed to the values of the machine. If anything, marijuana pushed me in the direction of individualizing experience and putting more worth on my individual responsibility."

In Stone's experience, these differences between the individual and the machine, as personified by the heads versus the juicers, became most apparent during the pillaging and burning of hamlets. "A lot of people who were smoking were much more respectful of life and seemed less inclined to take life," he claimed. "The heads may have had a sense that the villagers might have been NVA or VC sympathizers, but we tended to respect them more and mistreat them less than the drinkers. It was a tremendous point of demarcation between the behavior of those who smoked and those who didn't."

By the time his tour was over, Stone had served in four units, sustained two wounds, and won a Bronze Star for bravery during a three-day battle at South China Beach in August 1968; he had also clashed repeatedly with the lifer sergeants and was busted several times. Just before returning to "the world," he learned that Elias had been killed in the A Shau Valley by an American grenade. Stone would always suspect that Elias had been fragged but would never learn the truth; the only certain thing about the death of Elias was that it broke his heart. When he boarded a boat for Fort Lewis, Washington, Stone carried these painful memories home along with a supply of "mucho whacko" Vietnamese pot.

Reentry into the world was a descent into disorientation. As soon as he was discharged, Stone copped acid and drifted down the coast of California—San Francisco, Santa Cruz, Los Angeles, all the way down to Tijuana—drifting in a psychedelic miasma. "I took major acid in the Santa Cruz area and just wandered around, lost on the planet, completely out of it. I was so numbed out by Vietnam and what had happened. You didn't want to mention that you were back from there—it really bummed people out. It was such a strange experience."

Attempting to cross the border back into the United States, Stone was searched and arrested when the marijuana was found. He was thrown into the San Diego County Jail—a fate like that which awaited many of his brother Vietnam vets who would return home, twisted and broken by the war, not knowing what to do or having any outlet for what they were feeling, only to run afoul of the drug laws. "I was back and a criminal in chains in ten days! The jail was a shit house, a processing plant packed full of black kids and hippies that had a capacity of two or three thousand with, like, ten thousand guys. Nobody knew who you were, and nobody gave a shit. The Legal Aid guys never showed. Some guy said, 'I've been here for five months, man!' I was told I'd be there for a long time. There were two judges. If I got the judge there on Tuesday or Thursday, I'd get a suspended sentence because I was a Vietnam vet. But if I got the judge on Monday or Friday, I'd probably get five years and be out in three. I was really sweatin' it!"

Stone was allowed one call and rang his father. "The good news is I'm back," he said. "The bad news is, well, I'm jail . . ." After Lou Stone engineered his son's release, Oliver returned to New York to find an America that had been dramatically transformed from the one he left. His father was a conservative, an old, hidebound cold warrior. "He thought that we were doing the right thing over there—that it was just a 'police action'—I had just been through it and felt that a serious compromise of something American was going on, but I couldn't verbalize it. It was emotional, internal. I was brooding, and I wanted to really shock him." He accomplished that easily enough by slipping acid into his father's Scotch one night. "I gave him a heavy dose, too, and he really tripped out. He went to a party and he was hanging from a tree, eating Oreos." Stone still laughs at the memory. "His universe had turned insane . . . He was in Africa somewhere with black women and drums and drugs and shit. He was scared, but he was having a ball and suspected I had done it. He talked about it until the day he died."

Stone eventually moved to the Village—"my first time on my own as a civilian. I was doing acid once a week, playing with a lot of things, a lot of fire." With his penchant for "stimulating contrasts," he liked to drop acid and ride the subways. "I always found acid to be extremely volatile. I would have all these separate moods I couldn't control. It was insane; sometimes I'd get very scared on it. I was very alone, with no one in my life, other than my parents, who meant anything in any deep way."

Oliver Stone floated around without direction until he landed in the NYU film school. As time went on, he knew that to tell his story, he would have to go back and find that "solitary and wide-eyed youth standing under those raggedy Asiatic clouds." When he did—"in the summer of the two-hundredth birthday of the United States, broke and going nowhere at thirty"—he would find that the marijuana he smoked had dislocated his memory, but he would also find that it had provided other benefits.

"Conventional memory and narrative, connective logic receded. But I would remember other things. The shadows as opposed to the images, the textures, the moods, are forever lodged in me. That's why I was able to recreate it in *Platoon,* because I remembered it from smoking marijuana."

## II.  A Soldier's Best Friend

FOR TERRY CARISI, the war began on a day he was eating a tuna-fish sandwich, sitting in his father's living room in southern California, when the military police showed up because he hadn't responded to his draft notice.

"I was fucking freaked," Carisi related in the small art studio in his New York apartment. "I felt completely trapped—they were gonna put me in jail! I kept thinking, How did I let this happen? How can I get out of it? This was late '67, so the shit was at its peak. I'd already had friends who'd come back, and they were real bitter, very fucked up, and I was this longhair musician. I was really ignorant, didn't give a fuck about why America was there. So I said something stupid to them about the war, and they beat the shit out of me and dragged me down to the induction center."

It was one of the sergeants administering the battery of written tests who first picked up on Carisi's potential to become a member of the elite

Long Range Reconnaissance Patrols (LURPs). "Don't act stupid," the sergeant told him, "you're much too smart for that," and pulled him out. They were on the lookout for certain qualities in the recruits that would earmark them for LURPs, and this sergeant had seen it almost as soon as he had looked at him. Yes, he looked like a typical nineteen-year-old hippie, with his long hair and dissipated air, but there was furtiveness about him, a kind of steely emotional detachment. Being a LURP in 'Nam was serious business. You had to be someone who could deal with being inserted far into enemy territory for long, nerve-racking periods of time. The perfect ones were loners who displayed strong psychological self-sufficiency, who could be trained to become experts at field craft and survival.

Before he knew it, Carisi was on his way to jump school at Fort Bragg. The first time he refused to jump out of the plane they told him they'd shoot him if he didn't go. He jumped, and that single incident foreshadowed his entire experience in the military—every time he would reach a precipice and refuse to proceed, they would threaten him, and he would jump. After Fort Bragg, it was off to the special school in the Philippines for intensive jungle training.

"I was in incredible shape when I finished, this six-foot length of nerve and muscle," he recalled. "I was trained to survive at any cost and to kill in a thousand ways. I became a demolition expert—I know how to blow up this whole city block. But mostly I was trained to be superaware of everything that was going on. To be completely invisible. My job wasn't to kill people—it was to search and find. There were two other guys with me, *their* job was to kill. And in some ways, it was the most natural thing for me to do—perfect, actually—because of my background. I was always the kind of guy who could stand next to you and you wouldn't know I was standing next to you, so they just took that aspect of me and trained it for Vietnam."

The sergeant who selected Terry Carisi for the LURPs had been right about one thing: he was a loner, but had become one by circumstance rather than choice. From his earliest memories, he had felt isolated, never comfortable in his own skin; he had spent his whole life running, hiding inside himself, afraid but learning to hold his fear inside, one of those kids who always seem to have a problem talking to other people and live in a world of silence and subterfuge. "When I was a little boy, I was fearful of everything. Fearful of shadows, noises. But I could never express it, the way I was brought up. I'd been to a zillion psychologists by the time I was twelve."

Carisi's father, a barber, could be abusive, sometimes violent; his mother was a housewife who sometimes worked as a waitress in nightclubs. He had grown up in the three-block radius at the center of the valley among the Mexicans—the only working-class section of a town filled with upper-middle-class and wealthy people. His memories of school were crawling with shameful and alienated feelings about being dyslexic and knowing something was wrong and not knowing what it was, but he was not without talent. He displayed great athletic ability in baseball and football but gravitated toward music and characteristically chose the drums so that he could be by himself, behind everybody else. He fell into the surf culture of southern California right when the Beach Boys were making the sport a national craze. Surfing the coast from Ventura County down into Mexico, he loved the exhilaration and freedom of riding the waves, but as with many things in his life, he felt inadequate while doing it even though he was one of the better surfers in his crowd. And then came drugs. At the age of ten, he had been playing baseball at the school yard on a Saturday when he had walked into the bathroom and froze at the sight of a Mexican kid shooting up. "I watched him go through the whole process, and something inside of me instinctively was attracted and felt it was not a bad thing. And then when I started hearing about the beatniks and jazz guys, it was like I couldn't wait to get my hands on it."

Carisi first entered the world of narcotics at the age of sixteen, in a cavern underneath the local Salvation Army, where Willie and Mack, two old black jazz musicians, would shoot up and hide away from the world. He recalled his first shot as if it had happened the day before—the rush coming up his esophagus and then spreading out through his body in waves of chilling pleasure like coolant through an overheated engine— "like a blanket going over you, like your mother hugging you, like you're completely safe and never have to be afraid of anything ever again. It was like armor against life. I wasn't the only guy in that group who went from surfing to heroin." He had found his true avocation.

In 1966, Carisi dropped out of school and wandered Sunset Strip, transfixed by the music scene at Bido Lido's, Grizarri's, the Trip, Ciro's, and the Whiskey. The Strip was incandescent, swarming with hordes of hippies, but while Carisi had grown his hair and was playing in a band himself, he could never be a true hippie. For a while, he hung around the Mystic Arts Bookstore in Laguna Beach and the Brotherhood of Eternal Love, the nexus of the burgeoning psychedelic scene of Los Angeles (later to become one of the largest LSD networks in the country) and took acid up in the canyons, but melting walls were just not his thing. He loved speed because you never went to sleep and barbs because they were easy to get, but the experience of his first habit had already taught him that he was most comfortable in the netherworld of the junkie. Heroin was his drug of choice. He had been able to kick but was still chipping and popping pills on the day he was picked up by the military police. Yes, the sergeant who had plucked Terry Carisi out of thousands of raw draftees and directed him into one of the most elite corps serving in Vietnam had recognized a bona fide loner, a classic outsider and observer. But he had no idea that the young man in front of him had already received advanced survival training in one of the most clandestine subcultures of American society.

"Three months after the day I was hauled in, I was on my way to Vietnam," Carisi continued. "There were ten of us flying over. The flight was real sketchy—my mind was going crazy—but then there I was, in Saigon. It was like a weird fantasy, this bizarre movie going on, the beginning of this dream world for me. You know those strange little sparkly things you see going around when you do too much speed? Being in Vietnam felt a lot like that—this spooky, sparkly feeling."

Carisi was now part of the teams working out of Project Gamma, Detachment B-57, Saigon. He had joined that mysterious hidden culture of covert American warriors quartered in hotels all over that city—"Lurps, seals, recondos. Green-Beret bushmasters, redundant mutilators, heavy rapers, eye-shooters, widow-makers, nametakers, classic essential American types," as the journalist Michael Herr would describe them in *Dispatches,* "point men, *isolatos,* and outriders like they were programmed in their genes to do it, the first taste made them crazy for it, just like they knew it would."

The Communists in Vietnam had adopted a strategy of infiltration, subversion, and terrorism. In the key areas of confrontation—the northern provinces, the central highlands, and the approaches to Saigon from the Cambodian border—they would absorb the U.S. attacks, inflicting casualties as part of their own war of attrition and then retreating as soon as the pressure became too great. In the areas around Saigon, the Vietcong and elements of the NVA were badly mauled in operations like Junction City and had pulled back to sanctuaries in Cambodia, which made the covert cross-border intelligence operations conducted by the Military Assistance Command Vietnam–Studies and Observation Group (MACV-SOG)—the joint-service high command unconventional warfare task force responsible for organizing the Greek-alphabet projects like Gamma—as imperative as they were illegal under U.S. regulations.

As Terry Carisi moved noiselessly through the Cambodian jungles, these grand dynamics of strategy were the furthest thing from his mind. The army had discovered that Carisi had talents even beyond surreptitious movement and survival. His job was to be the unit's camera, its top-secret documentarian of infiltration and supply routes, bridges, bunker complexes, troop concentrations, and command centers. But what most concerned him was how to breathe normally, in a way that would allow him to focus his mind on the task at hand and somehow control the pounding palpitations that made his heart feel as if it would explode clear through his chest. He knew that his greatest challenge would be to contain the fear so that he could function. The most terrible time for him seemed to come at the very end of the mission, when they would be waiting at the pick-up point, in those moments before the chopper would appear over the horizon. His mind would race, and he would become that little boy who'd been afraid of the shadows and noises, and he couldn't seem to stop it, the horrifying thoughts of capture and torture and imprisonment and death. His fears would circle closer and closer until he would feel like a man treading helplessly in the shark-infested waters of his own dark imagination. And then he found opium.

"I hadn't gotten high since induction. It took me a little while after arriving in Saigon, but I sniffed it out. I met the right guy and had the right conversation. This guy told me, 'Don't shoot dope over here, because it's so strong, and in your position if you get ever get too loaded or checked, you'll end up in the stockade forever—or dead.' I believed him because I literally saw some guy snort some heroin one time in this crazy bar—I'll never forget it—and he keeled right over onto the bar top. He was just lying there with his face on the bar top, dead, and no one even knew it—the dope was that strong and pure . . . So I snorted some in my hotel room but I just felt more alone than I'd ever felt in my life. And then I found out where I could get opium. It was cleaner, and I could hide it easier."

The next step was figuring out how to use it out on operations. Carisi certainly couldn't smoke it out in the bush because it involved a whole ritual of heating and inhaling the vapors—chasing the dragon, it was called. Moreover, he was loathe to smoke it before leaving on an operation; he couldn't be drifting in and out of some opium dream or going on the nod somewhere deep inside Cambodia. The logical thing was to eat the stuff—not exactly an innovation because the first means of ingesting opiates in the West had been taking it in medicinal tinctures like laudanum. But even eating opium was dangerous because if someone saw him pop a chunk into his mouth, he'd be on his way to the military stockade at Long Binh. Then he remembered a story one of the old junkies in that sub-basement under the Salvation Army had told him about another method of administering the substance.

"I'd cut off a little slice of O and roll it in a little cigarette paper and stick it up my ass. It was even better than eating it because it bypasses the stomach and only takes three or four minutes to hit you. And it would hang in there, last all day like that. I could get a whole Tootsie Roll of it for five dollars, and it would last a long time. You only had to sliver off a tiny bit a couple of times a day. I would take speed, too, and the speed would calm and focus me, and the opium would push everything away and give me the armor. It worked perfectly!"

Carisi was never without his stash of raw opium in the jungle again. Just to know that he carried several Tootsie Rolls of the brownish, gooey, bitter-tasting substance in his pocket made the chopper rides into Cambodia infinitely more tranquil—meditative, in fact. During his twenty missions, the substance was lodged in his rectum like some holy suppository as it dissolved and coursed through his blood vessels, working its tranquilizing magic. Carisi not only made peace with the jungle; he was also now able to take in its natural wonders, to feel that it was his home. The jungle colors seemed to seep into his brain until his very consciousness was saturated with soft, pulsing green. Best of all, he felt completely invisible. "Everything was blunted, and I felt totally within myself. To the same degree that I was armoring myself, I was sensitizing myself. You saw things out there you just knew you'd never see again in your life: unbelievable trees and light and sky and colors and animals. It was like some enchanted kingdom."

Carisi had never seen an opium field before but knew what it was as soon as he saw one. Thousands of white- and purple-petaled plants glistened in the sun before him. The green, unripened seed capsules containing the oil looked as finely proportioned as beautiful Grecian urns, with their starlike tops that seemed to have an intelligence all their own—he could feel it, as if their heads were nodding at him in secret acknowledgment of their kinship . . . *Papaver somniferum*. Poppies. God's Own Medicine. Divine Repose. A Soldier's Best Friend. Had Carisi been there by himself and had the time, he would have cut the pods lightly with his blade and scraped the sap off for days and days and harvested a knapsack of the stuff, but all he could do was stand there for a few moments and marvel at the beauty and power of those plants and how man had used them since antiquity. He was experiencing exactly what the physicians of the sixteenth century had claimed about the effects and wonders of opium ("It causes Assurance, Ovation of the Spirits, Courage, Contempt of Danger. . . . It prevents, takes away Grief, Fear, Anxieties, Peevishness, Fretfulness. . . . It causes Euphory, or eases undergoing of all Labor, Journeys, etc."). Even when he got wounded, it all seemed perfectly fine—it was as if the shrapnel in his leg were happening to somebody else, and he didn't even feel it as he was running. So content was he, in fact, that he never even needed to get laid, back in Saigon. "Opium was my lover," he declared. "Always was. A lover you don't ever get over."

Ten surreal months of going from the bush directly to his hotel room passed, and then came the day Carisi went home—"It felt like forever when it was happening, and when I was leaving, it was like a second had passed." Had it not been for the big piece of heroin he returned with, Terry Carisi might not have believed it had ever happened at all. The heroin was real enough. It had been so easy to set up the score, easier still to smuggle it in his duffel bag on the military transport. Heroin so pure he could step on it forever. Heroin enough to last for years. Carisi would become one of the biggest heroin dealers in Los Angeles, and like thousands of other vets who put their training to another use and became foot soldiers and pilots and smugglers in the dope trade, his career as a criminal would seem a strange yet natural evolution of his experience in Vietnam.

### III. Of Bloods and Other Statistics

WILLIE JONES DECIDED to become Kimani Jones, Black Panther, on the day his best friend, Otis Nicholson, stepped on a mine while walking point during a sweep in the central highlands. Otis was a basketball player from Cincinnati. He could dribble rings around everyone, and there he was flopping on the ground, screaming, one of his legs blown clear off to the thigh and the other mangled into a bloody mass of shredded meat and bone. The medic did what he could.

As they waited for the dust-off, Jones could feel the fury rising up inside him in a poisonous cloud of red-hot steam. The rage he felt was directed at the enemy, but in this case the enemy wasn't Victor Charlie—it was Mr. Charlie, "the stupid motherfucking peckerwood officers and sergeants who kept putting the brothers out there on point," as Jones described them, "where they would be the first to get shot at or step on booby traps and mines."

All the bloods knew the score. Back in the world, only about one in ten was black. In Vietnam, all you had to do was look around, and you could see that more than one in five were combat troops. "And the casualty rate for us was even higher than that! The army always claimed it was because we were poorly educated, didn't do as well on the tests they gave for specialized training. Well, okay, if that was the truth and the army wasn't racist, then how come we were always passed over for promotions? And how come we were always singled out for the shit jobs?"

Willie Jones personified the increasingly militant attitudes of black draftees after 1968. The war had turned very bitter, and the days of young blacks, or cuffees as they were known, joining up just to escape the ghetto were over. Once in Vietnam, the first thing Jones learned was that whatever racial harmony there was in his unit when they were under fire or in foxholes seemed to vanish as soon as the firing stopped. "Some brothers mixed freely with whites but most tended to hang with their own."

Nineteen sixty-nine was the year of My Lai, the time of Willful Refusal—"say no-no to go-go"—when there was more racist graffiti on the walls of latrines than ever and every incoming bird brought more black troops who had been exposed to the writings of Malcolm X and Eldridge Cleaver, political figures who saw the white man's war as a form of genocide—a way for the Man to conveniently clear a generation of young black radicals away from the restive ghettos. Second-class jobs and second-class treatment but first-class death, that's what they got.

"Black Americans are considered to be the world's biggest fools to go to another country to fight for something they don't have for themselves," Cleaver declared in *Soul on Ice*. Jones's unit was almost 60 percent black. You saw more and more Afros and black power salutes, and it seemed that the bloods out in the swamps and paddies and jungles were angrier, more on edge every day, and the tension only got worse with every black casualty. The more Jones saw of the war, the more he tended to accept Cleaver's analysis. One day they swept through an area that had been napalmed and came across the charred remains of peasants, among them a little girl, and from that day on he couldn't seem to get the stench of burning flesh out of his nostrils. As bad as that had been, it was nothing like the day Otis Nicholson stepped on that land mine. When the patrol came in, Jones saw the Confederate flag on one of the vehicles. Otis had just lost his legs fighting for a country where there were guys proudly flying the Confederate flag, and when the soldier next to the vehicle noticed Jones glowering at the flag and said, "*What're you lookin' at, nigger,*" that was when he snapped.

"It took four or five guys to hold me down. I was going to kill the motherfucker! That night I got down with heroin. I mean, *got down,* man. Right there behind the barracks. Before that it was marijuana all the time and then smoking opium. Reefer and opium were easy to get, but it wasn't so easy getting heroin, but then all of sudden there was more of it around it seemed. Oh, man, once I snorted dope, that was it. It was like I found what I was lookin' for. When bad shit would happen out in the bush, we'd say this thing all the time—'*Don't mean nothin'.*' It meant, like, whatever happened couldn't touch you because it didn't mean shit. No matter how bad it was. Well, heroin was, like, the exact *feeling* of what that saying was all about. Didn't mean nothin'."

Jones had smoked pot a number of times back in the neighborhood and never felt there was anything wrong with it, especially as it became political. Eldridge Cleaver had first gone to prison, in 1954, at the age of eighteen, for being caught with a "shopping bag full of marijuana, a shopping bag full of love" as he related it in *Soul on Ice*: "I had been getting high for four or five years and was convinced, with the zeal of a crusader, that marijuana was superior to lush—yet the rulers of the land seemed all to be lushes." In fact, marijuana was one of the few common-ground experiences left in Vietnam, with dope sometimes being shared and passed between white and black soldiers like a peace pipe.

Heroin was something else. As a boy, Jones had listened to Malcolm X preaching on a Harlem street corner about how black junkies were really trying to "narcotize" themselves against the pain of being a black man in the white man's America and that taking dope was only helping the white man prove that the black man was "nothing." At the time, there were increasing numbers of freshly detoxed, cleanly dressed, newly converted advocates of the Black Muslim program on the streets, the same young men who had been among the first wave in the neighborhood to taste the drug during the 1950s, all of them now strongly indoctrinated by Malcolm's interpretation of the racial pathology of addiction.

While Jones certainly understood the Muslim point of view, it didn't prevent him from using the drug in Vietnam as the winter of 1970 turned to spring. Something had happened; you didn't have to go to Hai Ba Trung Street in Saigon to score anymore; the little plastic vials of almost-pure number 4 heroin were being sold everywhere for two dollars, and every hooch maid at every base camp and every little kid on the side of the road had them. Since the late 1940s, portions of Burma, Laos, and Thailand had formed the major centers of opium cultivation that would become known as the Golden Triangle, but there had never been any facilities in Southeast Asia that could turn raw opium into heroin—a four-part process that chemically binds morphine molecules with acetic acid and then turns the compound into the fluffy-white powder that can be dissolved and injected with a syringe. At the end of 1969, laboratories supervised by master chemists from Hong Kong (until then the main processing site in Asia) became operational in the Golden Triangle for the first time, and within a few weeks of the Cambodian incursion in the spring of 1970, heroin was everywhere. At the same time, the army was cracking down on marijuana, making it harder to get on the bases.

The consequences of almost-pure heroin widely available at dirt-cheap prices to disaffected American soldiers who could no longer easily procure marijuana were both rapid and dire. Back in 1965, you had to go looking for the drug; now the heroin came looking for *you*. Reported deaths from drug overdose in the spring of 1970 were around two a month; by the fall, the figure was two a day. Soon whole platoons were using dope; the Eighty-second Airborne was being called the Jumping Junkies, and Fort Hood, Texas, once home to General George S. Patton, with its large repository of Vietnam returnees, became known as Fort Head. For years, American commanders had denied or minimized the extent of drug use by American troops in Vietnam. By 1971, they would be forced to acknowledge that it was an enemy more formidable than the Vietcong.

"I took my first shot down in Khanh Hoi—you know, they called it Soulsville, the neighborhood in Saigon with all the bars for the brothers," Jones remembered. "They had good music on the jukeboxes and some pretty good ribs down there. I hooked up with this chick named Vanh. Real cute. She was a flatbacker, you know, a prostitute, but I really liked her . . . Anyway, one night I decided to just do it, simple as that. I was gettin' pretty short at that time. Maybe I figured, how much damage could I do in just a couple of months? I just remember layin' on this girl's bed after I did it, a million miles away from everything. Just watchin' her paint her toenails. Oh, man, I could have stayed on that bed forever, the fan goin' round above us. There was nothin' else in the world but the red toenails on those pretty little brown feet and that beautiful black hair comin' down her shoulders . . ."

For those who became addicts in that spring of 1970, the rationalizations were many, but the most fundamental one went like this: Vietnam made me an addict, but when I get back to the world, I'm going to be okay. Of course, black servicemen like Jones had the additional racial justification for addiction above and beyond the war itself as they returned to a world where there were few if any jobs. Jones solved the problem by resolving to join the Panthers as soon as he got home. He would don the boolhipper—"those full-length black leather coats that cats like Huey Newton were always wearing with their black berets and dark shades." The organization, he hoped, would provide structure and political purpose in his life; he wanted to work in the community programs, devote himself body and soul to the Revolution and build the "New City on these ruins" that Cleaver had proclaimed in the last sentence of *Soul on Ice*. "My feeling at that time was that nobody better fuck with me because I was one brother who knew how to use a gun. FREEDOM NOW!"

Came the day, Jones got on the plane, ready to hit the streets of Harlem. "Now I got quite a habit in those final months before leaving. This was right before the urine testing they started later on, so it was no problem to just get on the plane. I didn't take no dope with me, which was a big mistake even though I was afraid of getting busted. I'll never forget that plane ride, just getting sicker and sicker every hour that I got closer to home."

As soon as Jones hit the streets, the first thing he did, even before saying hello to his mother, was go looking for the dope man. "Found this guy around 116th Street. First thing he said was, 'Man, you didn't bring any of that brown dope home with you?' They knew all about it, and he just couldn't believe I didn't smuggle home a piece of it. So I got a bundle from him, and we cook up a couple of bags, and I shoot it. Nothing. Don't feel a damn thing. Cook up a couple more. Still nothing! Then a couple more . . . This dude's lookin' at me, shaking his head like he seen all this before, and that was when I realized what was going on."

In Vietnam, Jones had been using two bags—three at most—of dope that was very pure and powerful—"and this dope in Harlem had an eight cut—meaning it was cut to hell with quinine and mannite—and now I had to shoot a whole bundle, twenty-four bags, just to get straight! It was scary. Where was I gonna get the money for that? First thing comes into my head is, Oh, man, I gotta kick this habit . . . The second thing is, Shit, maybe I should reenlist just so I can go back to Vietnam, just to get the fucking dope!"

Thus began Jones's life as an official government statistic. The large majority of soldiers who had used heroin in Vietnam would eventually be able to stay off dope once they returned to the United States, but the habit that Jones brought home was a ticking time bomb that would drive him into a life of crime. After his first arrest for robbery, that year, he became part of the crime statistics that got Richard Nixon's attention and led to the urine-testing centers at Cam Ranh Bay and Long Binh and in-country detoxification centers. The arrest made Jones part of the statistical jump in heroin addicts, from under 50,000 in 1962 to an estimated 720,000 a decade later, which led to his becoming one of 25,000 Americans on the new methadone maintenance program that year. Jones would be added to other sets of statistics having to do with recidivism, parole, detoxification, veterans benefits, crisis intervention, vocational guidance, individual and group therapy in hospitals, storefronts, residential and clinical facilities. Unemployment and welfare became just as inevitable. Sociologists even invented a new term for him: the career heroin addict. It was an apt description, considering that addiction took up all his time and went on year after year exactly like a career: on dope, off dope, on methadone, off methadone, kick the habit, relapse, go into jail and clean up, come back out and start your next run. The fact that he wasn't included in the statistical tally of overdose victims during those years was nothing short of a miracle.

Kimani Jones was part of a new generation having to reckon with its own historic experience of dope in Harlem—the sons and daughters, younger brothers and sisters, nieces and nephews, of the wave that Claude Brown had chronicled in *Manchild in the Promised Land*. Mobsters like Joey Gallo still controlled the flow of heroin into the community, and the corruption of police was as widespread as ever, but now a number of black gangsters were carving out their own fiefdoms, breaking the trade down into factions at the street level, different pockets of dealers selling at different prices and attracting different clienteles: Hollywood Harold on 118th Street, Fat Jack on 116th Street, Freddie Dino on Eighth Avenue. Each one bought his dope from the mob, but they were their own boss, with their own labels and staff of kids who were runners. Such would be the case until Nicky Barnes came home from prison in 1972 and went about consolidating the neighborhoods by throwing some of these individuals off the rooftops. Dope continued to represent the only means of making money for thousands of unemployed, under-privileged kids, but the game got meaner and harder—hand-to-hand combat, they called it. More kids became familiar with the methods of sifting and cutting the dope, which began to include substances like meat tenderizer along with mannite and quinine. With the Rockefeller drug laws of 1973, penalties became harsher and sentences longer. When drug-enforcement officials decided to crack down on the availability of quinine, they had no idea, or simply didn't care, that the presence of the substance in the dope had been preserving addicts from exposure and illness; soon there were sick junkies freezing to death on rooftops all over Harlem.

Willie Jones joined the Black Panthers, donning the boolhipper, carrying a gun, adopting the Kikuyu name of Kimani—like the Mau Maus of Kenya. After years of police repression, FBI surveillance, and the maneuverings of leftist politics, the organization was on the wane, despite events like the dramatic uprising in the Manhattan detention facility known as the Tombs, in 1972. The impact of dope on the group was equally devastating. Panthers had always been expressly forbidden to use heroin. Weed was perfectly acceptable in private or social situations, but explicit orders had been issued that members could not have narcotics or marijuana in their possession while doing party work. Any member found to be shooting dope was to be expelled. Yet, as Jones recollected, "there were more and more brothers and sisters strung out." Jones spent most of his days ossified on street corners, slumping against walls and receding into a state of mummified oblivion, where there was nothing but spoon and spike and the push that sent the ebb tide of dope flowing out to every filament of his being. Heroin settled over people's lives like a smothering blanket, causing many Panthers to believe that its presence was a government plot to narcotize the Black Revolution and drain it of will and energy. Conspiracy or not, it wasn't hard for Jones to recognize its impact.

"In some ways, dope was more powerful than the FBI or the bullets that cut down guys like Fred Hampton. And it wasn't only the Panthers. I believe that dope slowed down the whole black movement in America."

# 7

## Find the Cost of Freedom

> 66 It was the best of times, it was the worst of times, it was the age of wisdom, it was the age of foolishness, it was the epoch of belief, it was the epoch of incredulity, it was the season of Light, it was the season of Darkness. 99

—Charles Dickens, A *Tale of Two Cities*, 1859

### I. Nobody Lied

"WHAT WAS THE HAIGHT like at its finest? *Nobody lied*," declared Ami Magill, a staff artist for *The San Francisco Oracle* during its twelve-issue run as the world's most noteworthy psychedelic newspaper. "Everything that came out of anybody's mouth was God's truth. We'd have these real slum rats coming out from the Lower East Side of New York, and they would suddenly become very innocent. You could really trust them!"

McGill was sitting in a booth at a large convention of artists and collectors of psychedelia being held in the Hall of Flowers in Golden Gate Park, reflecting on the Haight Ashbury of 1965, when she had first moved into a cavernous old house on Cole Street. Bordered on the north by the verdant strip of the Panhandle, the Hashbury, as it was affectionately called, stretched from Stanyan Street on the eastern edge of Golden Gate Park and ran along Haight Street for twenty blocks, through the Ashbury District, down through the Fillmore District, and on to Market Street, ten blocks away. Most of the buildings had been constructed to house the refugees of the great fire of 1906, and the harmonious style of

Victorian architecture gave the entire district its quaint but run-down charm. For the previous twenty years, it had been an interracial working-class neighborhood. After the campus of San Francisco State College moved from lower Haight Street to the southern end of the city, plenty of students and artists remained, along with pockets of bohemian refugees from North Beach after the police crackdowns at the tail end of the Beat era.

"You could be poor with some dignity in those days, rent a huge place with six bedrooms for maybe forty bucks. Two years before that, it had been a slum, and nobody lived there but pigeons."

Magill was seventeen and pregnant when she graduated from Oakland Technical High in 1958. A tall, striking, dark-haired young woman with exotic interests in peyote and art and a "thing" for poets, she would marry one named George Tsongas and have children all through her Haight Ashbury experience. Not long after moving into the neighborhood, she and her sister opened the store on Haight Street called Headquarters.

"At the time, the only other hip store was the Psychedelic Shop. My sister did this extraordinary facade of all these beautiful monkeys chasing their tails. We found this old costume shop going out of business and bought hundreds and hundreds of these vintage band jackets for a dollar apiece and sold them for three, which showed you what level of retail brilliance we were on. At one point, the entire Haight was running around in these jackets! When Paul McCartney came through, that's what he saw, so that's where *Sgt Peppers* came from."

Magill's impression of the Haight as a place where "nobody lied" typify the recollections of many who experienced the district during the period 1965–67, when the incense and patchouli dreams of a whole psychedelic culture flourished within its forty square blocks and seized the imagination of the nation.

"It was the closest to utopia I'd ever expect to find in my lifetime on this planet," maintained novelist Tom Robbins, who first visited the Haight at the beginning of 1966, when he arrived from Seattle to write a series of front-page articles for the *Post-Intelligencer.* "Things were still very clean and pure, and there was nothing fake about it. You'd walk down the street, and someone would be licking an ice cream, and you'd just happen to glance at it—Gee, that looks good.' 'Here, man, *you* have it!' It was truly blissful." The Haight that Robbins so fondly recalled was a place where complete strangers hugged in the street. "You'd see an attractive girl and smile at her, and she might come over and kiss you, but it wasn't like you were hitting on each other, and it wasn't platonic either. There was no dishonesty, no ulterior motives; it was just the way humans were meant to be in the best of all possible worlds."

David Felton was a reporter for the *Los Angeles Times* when he made his first trip north to the Haight. "There was a flavor on the street that was magical. By and large, you'd walk around and think, Is it possible we could live in a world where we don't have nine-to-five jobs? Is it possible we can just take care of the people who aren't working? *Is it possible to live like a child forever?*"

For Ed Sanders, who came out to the Haight from New York to perform with the Fugs during that exemplary season, the scene evoked a rich collage of cultural elements at play: "It was artistic, literary, political . . . Lust, wild abandon. Love of freedom, love of America, veneration for the Constitution. Affection for Thomas Jefferson and Thomas Paine. Love of Emma Goldman. Delight in the beatniks and the jazz guys. Reverence for Native American culture. The new technical innovations involving light and sound. The rock-and-roll heroes. The protoenvironmentalists had already appeared. There were drugs, of course, and some negative aspects of that, but a lot of positive aspects as well. It's important to celebrate the good things because it's the good things that draw you to it."

To Peter Coyote, the Haight was primarily a place of self-discovery, where you could find out who you were "without props or mediation." Having dropped out of graduate school, Peter (still Cohon) had moved out to San Francisco to join the Mime Troupe. "You could sing, get high, beg, cruise for sex partners, plot the overthrow of the government, sleep, be mad, or do what you would there. It was liberated territory, and it felt like we were creating the world out of a kind of collective imagining. I just remember this sense of wonder, waking up every day and wondering what was going to happen, stumbling over to a friend's house or down to the coffee shop and seeing what walked in the door that day, . . . what kind of surprise, whether it was going out to create an event in the park for forty thousand people or just talking philosophy with smart, interesting people."

LSD was the passkey to this collective imagining. At any given time, a significant portion of the Haight Ashbury's population was likely to be flying on acid, coming down from a trip, or hanging out and contemplating the next one. The combination of the sun and the moisture in the air often created the lighting effect of a giant diffusion filter, casting the eucalyptus-scented streets in the soft magical glow of a movie set at golden hour. The people who strolled about were dressed as if they'd rummaged through the costume department of a major studio. The Haight became many things during that idealistic season of its spring—experiment, ethos, crucible, sanctuary, nirvana, archetype, and myth—a state of mind as much as a place.

"Acid obliterated the ego and put you in the realm of the sensational," Coyote elaborated, "and once you'd seen that—even once—you came back into the world and all you saw were lots and lots of individuals in the Haight expressing themselves. Not just their parents' expectations or their status in capitalistic terms or whether they were good or bad, but the whole mythic history of everything they'd seen or heard or read. It became the center of a national theater, and the street was jammed with every conceivable idea of human identity. People just came down to Haight Street and *acted it out.* I mean, there it *was*—Tonto could go right down the street and mix it up with Sheba!"

## II. The Free Frame of Reference

DURING THE 1960S, a number of groups were committed to living out their psychedelic-inspired ideals of a new culture as uncompromisingly as possible. The Pranksters, the Leary–Alpert–*San Francisco Oracle* axis, the Hog Farm, and the Yippies would all manage to do so with relative degrees of success, but none was more successful than the Diggers. In a place of the most wide-eyes innocence, at a time of the greatest unwariness of heart, the Diggers meant what they said, did what they meant to do, and always played for keeps.

The Diggers had little use for the high-blown psychedelic transcendentalism of the rainbow-colored jasmine-scented *San Francisco Oracle*. To *Oracle* editor Allen Cohen, Timothy Leary and Richard Alpert were important New Age philosophers, but to a Digger like Emmett Grogan, they were "charlatan fools." Spurning the New Leftist politics as just another establishment structure and game, the Diggers were true anarchist revolutionaries, with roots in the San Francisco Mime Troupe, where Coyote, Peter Berg, and others were pushing out the boundaries of the avant-garde theater.

"When I saw plays like *The Brig,* at the Living Theatre in New York, I saw that the key to the radical theater of the Sixties was attacking the fourth wall," Peter Berg reflected, charting the genesis of the group. "That was how you got past the lip of the stage and got the audience directly into the reality of the play, and by that I mean the life, the worldview of the play. We saw people walking down the streets of the Haight in British-army uniforms. Here comes somebody dressed like a Pilgrim; there goes an American Indian—so whether they realized they were acting or not, they were already performing something. All we had to do was shape that performance into some sort of social action."

One of the central concepts of the group came from Berg's reading about Egyptian ritual. "The phrase was 'create the condition you describe,' and it was from the book *Thespis,* about ancient Egyptian theater, and it means that if you're going to do something, by simply doing it, you would bring its intention to life. That became my goal of theatrical exposition." Berg would coin the expression *guerrilla theater* to describe how the radical theater would be extrapolated to the streets. For instance, the Diggers were not afraid to make a point by burning money or butchering a horse at San Quentin as a protest against capital punishment. To Berg and his comrades, it was obvious that this kind of "fourth-wall theater" could be used on the streets to turn participants into a movement—"not through propaganda, not through lecture mode, but by actually getting them to *do* something, in a way that the actual doing of it would make them a different sort of person." Berg would call this "life acting."

The Diggers were artists of the will, anarchists of the deed, existentialists, romantics, theoreticians, performers, activists, and visionaries. The advent of the group can be traced to Billy Murcott, a childhood friend of Emmett Grogan's from New York, whom Coyote remembered as "a strange, hermetic little guy who made wall charts of historical forces and movements." Murcott had come across the name Diggers in a book on utopian anarchism, specifically associated with Gerrard Winstanley and William Everard and the anarchistic group of communal farmers in England who lived on the common parklands around St. George's Hill, in Surrey, in 1649. The farmers wanted the land to be free to all who wanted to use it, a wish that they "created" for themselves by living and farming on it as a protest against high food prices. They provided food for the poor until they were brutally crushed by Oliver Cromwell and his Roundheads. "They were just butchered," Coyote noted, "and they were called the Diggers because every morning they'd be digging graves."

The paradigm worked on many different levels for the Diggers of the Haight, who would apply the condition of "free" to virtually anything, living off the fat and waste of the Great Society as the Diggers of old had tried to live off the public land. Moreover, the fact that the historical group had functioned in the face of a hostile general population and the overwhelming power of the state affirmed the need for total commitment and authenticity in their struggle, for being true "edge dwellers." At the time, the Fillmore District was going up in flames, an event that provided a suitably apocalyptic backdrop to the group's creation. "Billy and Emmett had been on a roof watching the blacks burn the Fillmore during a riot," related Berg. "They thought these were revolutionary times and young white people didn't have a revolutionary purpose. They wanted one but didn't know what it would be. Billy gave me something he had written, called 'The Diggers,' and the next day I was out of the Mime Troupe and with them."

How drugs, particularly psychedelics, would factor into this equation was a multifaceted consideration. "Drugs became the experiment to extend the edges of the envelope to find the limits in the personality, what had been really ground into you by social conditioning before you had the opportunity to really question it," Coyote explained. "Psychedelics did to our perceptions of reality what Einstein did to Newtonian physics. Einstein said it all depends on where you're standing, and that's what we understood. The minute we saw that there was relative reality, we were empowered to change things."

The Diggers practiced a consciously designed social program that was based on practical needs. If you wanted a better world, don't expect the corrupt system to give it to you; rather than fighting it or joining it, *act it out* as boldly as possible; *make it real* for yourself. The Diggers split off from the Mime Troupe because being "free" on a stage just wasn't enough. The Free Store and the fabled Digger stew that was ladled out in the Panhandle every day were examples of this ethic of the deed, but the ideology behind it was also psychedelic. "LSD can be about starting over," Berg allowed. "If you go through the mind bath of heavy psychedelic experience, then what do you start over with? What's important?" The central question for the Diggers was therefore about what to do *after* you deconstruct social forms, and their core belief was that when you no longer had a fixed frame of reference, then you would seek something called the "Free Frame of Reference." This became the name of the Digger Free Store and the thirteen-foot-square wooden frame that Billy Murcott built and Emmett Grogan painted golden orange.

The Free Frame of Reference was both experience and concept. Every day, the orange structure was set up between two large oak trees in the Panhandle at 4:00 p.m. The free Digger stew and home-baked bread were placed on one side of the frame, and the hungry would walk through it to get to the food, "changing their frame of reference" in the process. The people driving by the Panhandle would see "a Renoir of hippies in tie-dyed headdresses, eating out of twenty-five-gallon cans, in a frame," as Berg described it. The Diggers began passing out three-inch wooden Free Frames that people would wear around their necks like medallions and hold up to frame things and look at them from this new vantage point—in effect, to deconstruct social reality exactly as a drug creates an altered state of consciousness. This was an attempt to shake people out of the rut of ordinary perception and catalyze some sort of recognition of the possibility of a better world beyond power and profit, in essence handing them the keys to their own liberation. "Our pitch was 'Everything is free,' " Berg elaborated. "Someone would say, 'What am I supposed to do?' We'd say, 'Put *free* in front of any word that's important to you. Give me a word—*food, water, shelter, police, army, mother, father, love*—just put *free* in front of it, and then just go do it."

The psychedelic consciousness also found its way into various broadsides that were handed out on the streets of the Haight and later collected into *The Digger Papers,* some of them penned by Berg under the pseudonym George Metesky, the name of the Con Edison worker who became the Mad Bomber of New York when denied disability after being blasted in the face with scalding steam. In the "The Ideology of Failure," Berg postulated that to fail in a corrupt society was the only moral thing to do: "We won't, simply won't play the game any longer. We return to the prosperous consumer society and refuse to consume. . . . And we do our thing for nothing. . . . To Show Love is to fail. To love to fail is the Ideology of Failure." In "Trip Without a Ticket," he articulated a philosophy about the meaning of ritual and public events: "Street events are social acid heightening consciousness of what is real on the street. To expand eyeball implications until facts are established through action."

Digger events like "The Death of Money and the Birth of Free" were grand social operas designed to liberate the human spirit. They used the entire community as stage and backdrop, producing their own highs as they blew apart conditioned responses to power, money, class, country, and morality. "There was a lot of acid in the Haight, so a lot of the events we did had acid—Owsley would just give it to us," acknowledged Judy Goldhaft, a dancer who became another core member of the group. The Diggers began creating "planetary" public events in the park to celebrate the winter equinox and the summer solstice. At one of them, huge truckloads of crushed ice were delivered, and people were encouraged to do whatever they wanted with it. As Goldhaft explained, "If you look at this event intellectually—people loaded, playing on this big scaffolding that was put up, throwing snowballs at each other, half of them Hells Angels—this was a potentially dangerous situation, but nobody ever got hurt because something else was going on. People were very protective of each other."

"The brilliance of these events was that people were encouraged to play like children and act out their fantasies," pointed out Lynn "Freeman" House, another core member of the group. "One time, we pulled a flatbed truck through Montgomery Street with these belly dancers on it, encouraging people to take off their clothes. They ended up in the Panhandle, and there was someone who'd made an enormous amount of *majoun,* hashish candy, and people were encouraged to dip their fingers in and feed each other, which created this wonderful voluptuous spectacle." As Berg put it, "We'd really blow out the jams. . . . I tell you, it made it hard to live through the Seventies."

For Lynn House, who adopted Freeman as his nom de Digger (just as Peter Cohon would take Coyote), moving from the Lower East Side to the Haight in the spring of 1967 was like "going from hell to heaven." He joined a group of Diggers living in a beautiful Victorian on Willard—"a gorgeous railroad flat that could sleep seven, with stained glass and beautiful light and bay windows." Every night was an open house with thirty to fifty people coming for dinner, and nobody was ever turned away. At dawn, you might go out with Emmett and the Digger women to hustle the local vendors for produce and meat for the stew, but you always made sure to be at Fisherman's Wharf at noon to lie in the sun and eat fresh crab and drink cold wine for lunch.

"There was a short period of time—it lasted for six months to a year—when it felt inevitable that our kind of life was going to grow until the institutions fell and we would simply be taking care of each other on a block-by-block basis," House reminisced. "I'd walk around from one place to another at night with my mind just completely on fire, racing with possibilities. It animated the whole future course of my life."

While the Diggers practiced anonymity as a group, they tended to be charismatic individuals. Peter Berg was short but pugnacious, with "a running analysis of society that wouldn't quit," as Freeman House described him. In his memoir, *Ringolevio: A Life Played for Keeps,* Emmett Grogan calls Berg "the Hun, because some believed he was his own horde, while others felt he looked like a Mongolian Iago." Coyote was charming and articulate, a smooth operator with the natural instincts of the movie actor he would eventually become, "tall and handsome," as Grogan portrayed him, with "an affinity toward Zen discipline and a scholarly, intelligent mind."

There were many other dynamic and memorable characters at the core or fringe of the group: Lenore Kandel, the belly-dancing poet and author of the controversial erotic work *The Love Book*; her husband, Billy Fritsch, the handsome ex-longshoreman known as Sweet William, a motorcycle gypsy-poet and "free banker" who drove around with hundred-dollar bills in his headband as he mau-maued rock stars and producers and drug dealers to fund events and keep crash pads and communes going. There was a whole crowd of Digger women in addition to Kandel—Natural Suzanne, Phyllis Wilner, Judy Goldhaft, Nina Blasenheim, Cindy Small—all of them every bit as committed and audacious as the men, but nobody, male or female, had the force of Emmett Grogan, the ultimate "life actor" who appeared to have stepped right out of an O'Casey play onto the flower-strewn sidewalks of the Haight Ashbury.

Born Eugene Grogan, the son of a Brooklyn clerk, he grew up wild on the streets of New York, where he played ringolevio, got hooked on junk in high school, and turned to petty theft to support his habit—all games and skills that would serve as groundwork for his singular odyssey through the psychedelic culture and beyond. Discharged from the army as a certified schizophrenic after he deliberately sent himself into an amphetamine-fueled paroxysm of insanity on a bazooka range, Grogan returned to New York and took his first LSD, learning several momentous lessons from the experience—"that there were some things even more important than being alive and one of them was being alive the way you want to be alive, . . . that it was good to be whacked out on acid because it made it difficult to be reasonable, and that way you could see right through things while looking incomprehensible and mad and you could make statements that were frightening and true."

"Emmett was a speed freak, a New York street mick, literally hard as nails, totally fascinated with what was happening out here," recollected Ami Magill, who was cooking her fair share of Digger stew at the time. "He'd see all these lovely little well-bred California girls just there on the sidewalk for his taking, and he couldn't quite believe it himself. Very mysterious—you never knew anything about his private life, where he lived; he came and went like the wind." Grogan's impact on others in the group was powerful. "I'd never met anyone like Emmett," said Freeman House, "the way he could think on his feet, how self-confident he was, the tools he had, the tremendous ambition and vision. Just the most exceptional personality who had been through his own psychotic break and had come out the other side, on his feet and blazing."

### III.  If You Do Not Believe, Wipe Your Eyes and See

THE WEATHER HAD BEEN COLD and rainy that winter, but January 14, 1967, the day chosen by astrologers for the Be-In, dawned so clear and bright that many believed the event had received some divine dispensation. The shops on Haight Street were closed as people made their way through the park, down paths tinkling with wind chimes, to the great, open sunken expanse of the sun-dappled Polo Fields.

"The night of bruited fear of the American eagle-breast-body is over," stated the press release for the event. "Hang your fear at the door and join the future. If you do not believe, wipe your eyes and see"—and as the people came over the crest of the last hill and looked out across the mul-ticolored convocation before them, they had to blink. Words like *biblical* and *army* would henceforth be commonly used to evoke the mass gather-ings of this psychedelic generation, and for very good reason: the swelling hordes looked like nothing so much as the advance guard of an army of happy pilgrims convening to greet a new day. Decked out in denim, Mexican blouses and serapes, desert robes, paisley body stockings and Victorian petticoats, they were carrying flags and drums and cymbals and incense and fruit and flowers, holding children by the hand and greeting one another with smiles. Everywhere the sacrament of LSD was being consumed. The Diggers had made sandwiches out of the turkeys donated by Owsley and generously salted them down with crushed White Light-ning acid and offered a psychedelic repast to anyone who wanted one.

Earlier in the day, Allen Ginsberg and Gary Snyder had led a group of people in the rite of *pradakshina,* or circumambulation, an ancient Hindu ritual of blessing performed by walking clockwise around a sacred spot while chanting prayers, which consecrated the Polo Fields as a *mela,* or pilgrimage festival. Ginsberg was by now every bit as famous and con-troversial as Whitman had been in his time. Since returning from a trip to India in 1965 he had thrown himself body and soul into the birth of the new psychedelic culture, and the word he used to describe the Be-In was *epochal.* Jane Kramer was following Ginsberg for a profile she was writing for *The New Yorker* and noted how the poet had become "a symbol of the profound and often comic incompatibilities between the values of the Establishment and the values of an amalgamated hippie-pacifist-activist-visionary-orgiastic-anarchist-orientalist-psychedelic underground whose various causes and commitments he always managed to espouse." Ginsberg was fully engaged in the public controversy over LSD. Two months earlier, in Boston, in a widely covered speech called "Renaissance or Die" delivered to a group of Unitarian ministers, he had urged that "everybody who hears my voice . . . try the chemical LSD at least once, every man, woman, and child over 14 in good health," declaring that "America's political need is orgies in the parks, on Boston Commons, with naked Bacchantes in the national forests," and that, if necessary, we should "have a mass emotional nervous breakdown in this country once and for all." Ginsberg's prognostication for a national nervous breakdown would come to pass all too soon; within the year, the country would be bitterly polarized by the war and convulsed by assassinations and race riots, but on this exquisite day he stood in black beard and beads and white flowing garments in the same city where the reading of *Howl* had identified the Beat Generation twelve years earlier. "OOOOOMMM," he chanted before the great crowd, his eyes shimmering with joy.

Jack Kerouac's Japhy Ryder in *The Dharma Bums* stood at Ginsberg's side. Gary Snyder, who believed that LSD was the Native American's karmic revenge on the white man, was becoming a key figure in the vanguard of a new environmental movement in the United States. Putting his white conch shell to his lips, Snyder blew a long, rousing blast to summon forth the Great Spirit of the earth and signal the beginning of the event. "The hippies acted out what the Beats wrote about," Gregory Corso was fond of saying, and it certainly seemed true to Ginsberg on that day. "The Be-In was like witnessing the prophecy of *Howl* being fulfilled," Ginsberg commented, "or the rucksack revolution that the Snyder-Japhy character had predicted in *Dharma Bums* materializing in front of my eyes in the form of a new generation of seekers willing to proclaim the holiness of everything and elevate the whole planet with their vibrations." And yet Ginsberg had his doubts. At one point, as he looked out over the awesome spectacle of thirty thousand souls tripping in the golden sun, he turned to Lawrence Ferlinghetti and whispered, "What if we're all wrong?"

"Welcome!" came a voice from the small stage at the east end of the field. "Welcome to the first manifestation of the Brave New World!"

Lenore Kandel, Michael McClure with his autoharp, Ferlinghetti, and Jerry Rubin, who had been bailed out of jail that morning, would all have a brief moment at the microphone, but the speeches and poetry were beside the point. "Speeches were irrelevant," Tim Leary recognized. "The swarming of like-minded souls was the message."

Leary was seated on the stage, playing patty-cake with a succession of little children, clad in white pajamas like a psychedelic superstar of the New Age, flashing his shining and confident smile. He had arrived in town fully prepared with a new show, organization, and slogan. "A Death of the Mind" was a traveling variation of the light show he had been using to evoke the psychedelic experience without the drugs. Recent versions featured dramatic "psychedelic religious celebrations" of the lives of Jesus Christ, Buddha, and other great spiritual figures—primitive by the standards of Bay Area light shows but a suitable promotional tie-in for his latest psychedelic association, the League for Spiritual Discovery. All of it, even the radiant smile chiseled tautly onto his face, was part of a calculated response to his worsening legal problems.

"I was arrested for marijuana while crossing the border at Laredo at the end of 1965—an unfortunate event that changed my whole life, but that was only the beginning," he related. "The police found a small amount of weed on my daughter as we were going into Mexico on a vacation. I told the police that I'd take responsibility for it and then discovered all too soon that I was facing life in prison for ten dollars' worth of marijuana. The sentence was thirty years for me and five for my daughter, and that's when I decided to fight the case all the way to the Supreme Court."

To make matters worse, on the night of April 16, 1966, two dozen Duchess County sheriff's deputies kicked in the front door of the Big House of Millbrook, led by a ferocious assistant DA named G. Gordon Liddy, and rushed up stairs where they found marijuana.

"The time will come when there will be a statue of me erected in Millbrook," said Leary as he was being led away in handcuffs. "I'm afraid the closest you'll come is a burning effigy in the village square," Liddy retorted.

Leary's defense strategy centered on the use of drugs as a form of constitutional religious freedom. The League for Spiritual Discovery was subsequently incorporated as a religion under New York State law, providing the platform from which Leary could urge people to start their own religions based on the sacramental use of marijuana and psychedelics. Leary wanted to put into practice the fifth freedom—the freedom to alter consciousness. The true nature of the conflict facing Leary was becoming obvious. "The vindictiveness in Laredo and in the Liddy raids proved to be a microcosm of the growing nationwide pattern of police harassment," he noted, "which made it clear that rational debate and formal litigation were not the ways this game was going to be played. The battle to license psychedelic drugs and legalize marijuana would have to be fought in the field of public opinion." A conversation with Marshall McLuhan at the Plaza Hotel had only underscored the need for media savvy. "To dispel fear, you must use your public image," McLuhan had counseled Leary. "You are the basic product endorser. Whenever you are photographed, smile. Wave reassuringly. Radiate courage."

After his lunch with McLuhan, Leary began to rack his brains for a slogan that would sum it all up—the perfect aphorism to advertise the fact that he was promoting a product for a "new and improved accelerated brain" and unite it with the youthful demographic of the cultural rebellion. What he wanted was nothing less than the psychedelic revolutionary equivalent of "Give me liberty or give me death." The six fateful words that became one of the most familiar and incendiary catch phrases of the age had come to him in the shower: TURN ON, TUNE IN, DROP OUT. Leary's definition of the expression went as follows: "*Turn On* meant go within to activate your neural and genetic equipment. . . . Drugs were one way to accomplish this end. *Tune In* meant interact harmoniously with the world around you. *Drop Out* suggested an active, selective, graceful process of detachment, . . . self reliance, a discovery of one's singularity, a commitment to mobility, choice and change." Of course, not everyone would perceive it that way. "Unhappily my explanations of this sequence of personal development were often misinterpreted to mean 'get stoned and abandon all constructive activity,' " Leary would later realize but when the moment came to address the Be-In, he chose to recite his new rallying cry and little else. "Turn On, Tune In, Drop Out!" he happily declaimed from the stage. Inevitably, the slogan that Leary presumed would position him as a tireless and optimistic "cheerleader for positive change" would make it even easier for his enemies to paint him as some kind of diabolical mountebank trying to sell the snake oil of LSD to a whole generation of American kids.

The Be-In was a feast for the senses, a repudiation of the past, and a hymn of hope for the future. Bands wailed, and people pranced and twirled like rapturous angels. The Hells Angels were turned into a babysitting organization for the kids who kept getting lost in the crowd. The only police in sight were the two mounted cops off in the distance, who made no attempt to bother anyone. When the cable from the stage to the generator was unhooked and the PA system went dead, it was announced from the stage that the Angels were guarding it. As the afternoon waned, the psychedelic exaltation of the gathering only seemed to soar. Ami Magill, who had come to the event with her friend Hettie McGhee dressed up as manifestations of the goddess Kali, was stunned by the effect of the light as it burnished the vast sea of heads. "It was extraordinary. I kept thinking, Wow, the Chinese are right when they say we have dog-colored hair!—and as I looked out at all those light-colored heads on acid, they were just vibrating like crazy." When Magill saw all of those vivid Tibetan woven designs called god's eyes being held aloft, she felt ensconced in some holy sanctuary of truth and goodness—a true American Shangri-la. "It seemed like even the liars who might be tempted to lie would feel unable to do so in such a place, so they'd better speak the truth, too." So pervasive was this enraptured feeling that when a parachutist came floating down like some paisley apparition during the set by the Grateful Dead, the fantastic rumors flying through the crowd about his identity seemed perfectly plausible: Was it Owsley? the Buddha? a vision of God?

After Gary Snyder delivered another long blast of his conch shell to mark the conclusion of the event, people slowly walked off toward the Pacific Ocean to watch the sunset, but not before Ginsberg led the crowd in a chant of "Om Sri Maitreya" to the Coming Buddha of Love, and the people cleaned up the accumulation of trash on the ground at his request.

In another part of the crowd, Emmett Grogan was having a very different experience. Grogan had cynically watched and listened all afternoon to everyone spouting on in the most fulsome manner about how wonderful it was to see "all that energy in one place at the same time.

Just being. Being together—touching, looking, loving, embracing each other," and when the mantra began and the crowd started chanting, *We are one! We are one!"* he "watched them pretend, wondering how long it was going to take before people stopped kidding themselves."

The Be-In's creators, like Allen Cohen, had wanted to show the world the beauty of what was happening in San Francisco and had correctly calculated that the media would readily cooperate in sending the message. As the *Oracle* editor acknowledged, "We knew we had the tiger by the tail." That spring, Be-Ins cropped up in cities all over the country, and the media discovered the irresistible story of a generation that was rejecting the American Dream for the LSD and crash pads of the Haight. "The big question became how we were going to pull together to survive the onslaught of kids who were going to descend on the Haight that summer. From that moment on, the decline of the Haight began."

"The Be-In was the original mass gathering," Allen Ginsberg reflected. "The early evening came, people went home. And then the police made a sweep down Haight Street, busting everybody with grass and acid. Within two weeks the place was flooded with amphetamine and heroin."

## IV. Serenity, Tranquillity, and Peace

DAWN REYNOLDS christened her arrival in the Haight Ashbury a few days after the Monterey festival by taking a drug called STP at the summer solstice celebration in Golden Gate Park on June 21, 1967. She was staying with friend in a beautiful Victorian on Oak Street and had settled in on an old threadbare couch in the living room in front of a window with beautiful stained-glass panels—not bad accommodations, especially when compared with the average crash pad that summer.

Thousands of people filled the Speedway Meadow that day to officially kick off the Summer of Love. Wearing a pair of pink psychedelic harlequin pants, her face painted in bright Day-Glo swirls, Dawn moved happily through a field full of jugglers and magicians and jubilant people playing flutes and pennywhistles. The Diggers were barbecuing a whole lamb and the Grateful Dead were up on a flatbed truck playing "Beat It on Down the Line." Dawn was certain that she had arrived in the most excellent place in the world. "These little white pills with blue spots came my way," she related. "Someone told me it was STP, which sounded like a motor oil product but was really the new thing—'better than acid.' The letters stood for *Serenity, Tranquillity,* and *Peace.* It was free; everybody was taking it."

So, along with five thousand other people who took it that day in the exultant spirit of the moment, she swallowed one of the pills without knowing anything about its provenance. Had any of them been familiar with the obscure history of the substance, they would have known that it was developed by the noted chemist Alexander Shulgin, then working for Dow Chemical, as DOM (4-methyl-2, 5-dimethoxy-a-methylphenethylamine), a synthetic experimental hallucinogen chemically related to amphetamine and mescaline. The formula had somehow made its way into the hands of Owsley and associates, who produced it in their new Denver lab under the capable supervision of Tim Scully in monster doses of twenty milligrams. The dose was five times more powerful than even the most veteran users of LSD were prepared for—and many took two hits of it. As Grace Slick would remark, "If LSD was like being let out of a cage, STP was like being shot out of a cannon." Richard Alpert took it and felt as if he had "lost something human."

"The rush, I can't describe it . . . like you were a leaf being sucked out of a pipe and pulled hard into a powerful wind tunnel," remembered Dawn. "The sky turned bright orange, but it wasn't pretty, it was scary . . . I thought a nuclear bomb had gone off or something and it was the end of the world. I didn't know what country or century I was in, and my first feeling was *Oh God, help me!*—and that was when I knew I was in trouble. I was shaking all over, like this terrible force of energy was going through my body and was seizing hold of me around the throat and wouldn't let go.

"I started to freak, and I mean *freak.* Some people took me off to the side and tried to talk to me and take care of me. They kept saying, 'Just ride it out, honey, ride it out, you'll be okay,' and they were hugging me, but I just kept going up and up, and I wanted it to stop so badly, and the more I wanted it to stop, of course, the worse it got and the more I'd panic, and I started to vomit, but it wasn't like it was even coming out of me; it sounds strange, but it was like it was coming from another place entirely. I looked at it, and it was, like, *evil*—like everything evil in the world had taken me over and was just being wrenched out of me in these horrible waves of vomit, just vomiting and vomiting until there was nothing left but dry heaving and that horrible bile . . . and that was when I remembered, *Oh, my God, I'm pregnant!*—and I started to freak even worse than before. Why? Well, this was even before all the talk about LSD and chromosome damage, so it couldn't have been that in my mind, but I had read *Rosemary's Baby* not too long before, and maybe that was it, the cause of this deep terror that came over me about this evil thing doing some kind of irreparable harm to the baby I was going to have, and that was when I started to scream, and once I started screaming, it was a nightmare, I just couldn't stop."

Dawn was among the first wave of people who filled the emergency rooms over the next three days, caught in the vise of traumatic bad trips. "I just wanted it to stop; I was so freaked I couldn't breathe, couldn't catch my breath, and they took one look at me and figured, okay, boys, we got a live one here, get out the Thorazine . . . What they didn't know was that the Thorazine just made it *worse*. Oh, they would find out soon enough because as soon as they put that needle in, it just blasted me into an even worse bummer, and then I thought, *How could you do this to me!*—and the paranoia just got worse, and I tried to bolt, and they grabbed me, and that was when I lost control of my body. They held me down, and I screamed and screamed until I had no voice left. I was so weak all I could do was lay there and whimper."

## V. Nebraska Needs You More

THE DIGGERS were trying in vain to warn the city about the influx of kids coming that summer, first predicting fifty thousand, then one hundred thousand, finally as many as two hundred thousand. People in the community would do their best to help out, but resources were limited, especially when it came to shelter. In Ami Magill's basement apartment, "if there was one square foot of space, you put somebody's bedroll on it. That's the way people lived. Especially in the winter when it rained; you just had to take them off the street."

Public services were inadequate. There was the Free Clinic if you were sick and the Switchboard to try to help you find a place to stay, Happening House, but not much more. The Diggers would go out of their way to try to feed and house as many as possible, but all the Digger stew in the Panhandle could not prevent Haight Street from turning into a bad dream.

Mountain Girl experienced the Summer of Love from the steps of 710 Ashbury Street. "The Haight became an open street fair for the mingling and trading of identities. 'Hi, I'm from Detroit!' 'Oh, I'm from Cleveland!' It was a magnet for sixteen-year-old kids, every Saturday morning, a whole new set of them in from somewhere." By March and April, methamphetamine was everywhere. "You'd start seeing these real meth heads hitting on these little girls from Ohio. The criminal element was growing, and it got harder to deal with. The freedom thing was being turned into the freedom to fuck up in public—the freedom to break a bottle, the freedom to hit somebody, the freedom to step on somebody who was sitting on the ground. It became a problem of serious urban overcrowding, but it got really edgy. None of us were Skinnerian psychologists, you know? These powerful elements of destruction had suddenly entered this beautiful street party that had been going on ever since the Be-In."

The grand expectations on the part of the new arrivals were not hard to understand. The radio anthem of the psychedelic spring was, after all, assuring them that they were going to meet "some gentle people" and that summertime would be a "Love-In there." Of course, the fanciful notion that they would somehow be magically taken care of once they got there, that all would be groovy in the Promised Land of the Haight, only made the truth of the life they encountered on the street that much more cruel and disillusioning. Nicholas von Hoffman, a reporter poking around the Haight that summer on assignment for *The Washington Post,* described these defenseless kids as "plankton"—"the simple hippies, the stray teeny-boppers, the runaways, the summer dropouts—the microorganisms without power of locomotion that hung in the heavy water pond of the Haight Ashbury waiting for the more complex creatures to inhale them into their mouths and ingest them into their bellies where they could be food."

The attraction of "the more complex creatures" to the Haight was inevitable. "One of the things that would kill the Haight was the very thing that made it so great—its openness," Tom Robbins pointed out. "All utopias attract thugs, like iron filings to a magnet. The character of the place started changing. People started arriving who couldn't take care of themselves, who couldn't use the drugs and the culture to elevate themselves; and as word got out, the thugs just came in by the caravans, and that's when you got the lying and stealing and violence. In typical fashion, the media was unable to distinguish between that and the original hippie behavior—they just threw it all together."

By April, the transformation of the Haight from Love-In to Hard Truth was described with disturbing clarity in a scathing mimeographed screed passed out on the street by Chester Anderson, called "Uncle Tim's Children": "Pretty little 16-year-old middle class chick comes to the Haight to see what it's all about & gets picked up by a 17-year-old street dealer who spends all day shooting her full of speed again & again, then feeds her 3000 mikes and raffles off her temporarily unemployed body for the biggest Haight Street gang bang since the night before last. The politics & ethics of ecstasy. Rape is as common as bullshit on Haight Street." Anderson blamed just about everyone—the hip merchants, the *Oracle*, "Uncle Tim" Leary—for what he was calling "this summer's Human Shit-In."

From Mountain Girl's vantage point, what was happening to the Haight was like "trampling the meadows in Yosemite. It was getting loved to death. You couldn't find your friends anymore because there were too many people there. The criminal element moved in even bigger. Broken glass became the norm. You'd hear screaming at night. It became a struggle to have a good time; you needed your armor on just to go to the grocery. Then came the tear gas."

The police never had to look very far for reasons to increase their presence in the Haight: street violence, runaways, crash pads cited by the public health department, and the presence of hard drugs became convenient excuses for a steadily escalating campaign of repression and harassment. Ami Magill recalled the conflict growing hotter as soon as Haight Street was made one way to accommodate the buses of tourists coming up from Fisherman's Wharf to see the "crazy hippies."

"They'd be laughing and pointing at us like we were animals in the zoo or something, so we started interacting with them. They were afraid to open the doors of their cars and buses, so we'd put daisies on their windshields, try to hand them sugar cubes with no acid on them just to freak them out, or take these hand mirrors and hold them up, which made the point that if they wanted to see some strange tourist attraction, they should just take at good look at themselves."

When the Diggers started "taking the streets back," as Magill remembered, the game intensified. "The cops got really pissed. They wanted control and started busting more people for smoking pot. As the tour buses would come in, the Diggers would bring out barriers and detours; the cops would move them away, and the Diggers would just put them back. Finally, they just started stacking garbage cans and making barricades."

The Haight became a community under siege. In what became a familiar routine, police in riot gear would mass by the park at the corner of Stanyan in their tactical squads and begin moving up Haight Street, firing off tear-gas canisters into the crowd and riding their motorcycles up on the sidewalks to drive the people in front of them away. The previous Easter, Allen Cohen had pleaded with the police for some time to forestall what looked like a full-scale riot developing. He called the Grateful Dead and begged them to show up ready to play at the Panhandle on a flatbed truck. "I told the police captain what I had done and asked for some time and got up on the roof of a police car with a bullhorn and begged people to go down to the Panhandle—'We don't need any more crucifixions on Easter, we've had our last crucifixion!'—and they just started pouring down there. There were spontaneous events like that almost constantly."

In addition to playing the ballrooms at night, the local bands became an important ingredient that summer in keeping the lid on the social pressure cooker of the Haight. "The Grateful Dead and the other bands decided it was time to reclaim the streets and started doing these block-off-the-street gigs," Mountain Girl explained. "At first, we had permission from the mayor; then it became spontaneous. Everybody started trying really hard to keep the scene together and cool the police out and subvert the bad element that had come into the community. Unfortunately, it didn't work."

The arrival of hard drugs became the perfect excuse for the police to crack down on the Haight. "Their priority was the breakup of the Haight because it was a real center of revolutionary thought and activity, and it wasn't just the local authorities," claimed Allen Cohen. "I think it was the FBI and CIA, too. I've always believed that there was police complicity in the introduction of hard drugs into the community—amphetamines, but especially heroin."

"I was hanging out with this group of girls in that house on Oak Street, and one afternoon it was just *there*," remembered Dawn Reynolds. "It was like one minute we were smoking pot, and then we blinked, and the next minute we were doing heroin." The people doing speed out in the street were also vulnerable; many would find that nothing palliated the jangling crash of a meth jag quite like a good snort or bang of smack.

As the summer wore on, Emmett Grogan's alienated and cynical vision of the Summer of Love was proving to be more accurate than any other. On August 3, an acid dealer named John Kent "Shob" Carter was found dead just a few blocks outside the Haight, stabbed twelve times, his right arm severed cleanly above the elbow. The man who confessed to the murder, another acid dealer, was caught driving a van with the hacked-off arm lying behind the backseat. If that wasn't ghastly enough, on August 6, police found the body of Superspade, a well-known and popular dealer of acid and grass in the Haight, over the cliff at the Point Reyes Lighthouse, with a puncture wound to the chest and a nine-millimeter bullet in the base of his skull.

Charlie Perry, later to compile a definitive social history of the Haight, found the dichotomy between the transcendental vision of the district as a place where "nobody lied" and the reality of what it was becoming to be nothing less than wrenching torture. "Acid dealers killing each other? Was that what the New Age promised? . . . Horror and ecstasy, two sides of the same coin." The painful dilemma facing the residents of the Haight was becoming clear to Perry: "Was it best to stay in the God-fingered neighborhood and ride the drama to wherever it led, or to start anew in the country?"

By the end of the summer, the streets were filled with bad acid, junkie thieves, and physically dangerous, hallucinating speed freaks. When the astute Don McNeil arrived to report on the scene for *The Village Voice,* he found the Haight "mortally wounded. . . . The people I met, many of whom had been here before the Human Be-In and the Summer of Love (some of whom had coined the words) were exhausted and dejected, rather like a bartender counting unbroken glasses after an all-night brawl." The poet Michael McClure was one of those people. "The whole place was charred. It was like someone had come through it with a flame thrower."

The Thelin brothers soon closed the Psychedelic Shop and put a sign in the window: NEBRASKA NEEDS YOU MORE. The shop had been at the center of the psychedelic culture since it opened, in 1965, with seats in the window so that people could enjoy the happy kaleidoscopic cavalcade on Haight Street. If the closing of the Psychedelic Shop wasn't enough of a message that the Summer of Love was over, the Diggers then performed its death rite. The Death of Hippie was a Peter Berg–conceived ceremony designed to ritualize the notion that what had happened to the Haight had been a media-distorted perversion but that the essence of the Digger movement to be FREE was more valid and necessary than ever. The widely covered ceremony began with a Wake for Hippie at All Saints' Church, followed by a funeral procession of veiled mourners down Haight Street, with pallbearers carrying a wooden coffin draped in black and filled with hippie paraphernalia. As the procession passed the now-closed Psychedelic Shop, the screams of someone freaking out on acid in the neighborhood seemed eerily fitting. The coffin was placed atop a pyre and set theatrically aflame; someone played taps, and black-bordered cards of remembrance were handed out that read—

*Once upon a time, a man put on*
*beads and became a hippie—Today*
*the hippie takes off his beads and*

*becomes a man—a freeman!*
*Leaving behind the final remains*
*Of "Hippie—the devoted son of*
*Mass media" and*
*the boundaries are down.*
*San Francisco is free! Now free!*
*The truth is OUT, OUT, OUT!*

## VI. How Peculiar . . .

HUGH ROMNEY and the other Hog Farmers watched the bus come rolling slowly up the road to the top of their mountain. It was the end of 1967. At a time when people couldn't paint the buses they were fixing up with enough color, this one was jet-black. When it came to a stop and everyone piled out, they could see that the man driving it was in his early thirties, with scraggly dark hair and piercing blue eyes. They could also see that the bus was filled with teenage hippie girls and that he was the only man among them.

"There was a guy named Chance who was a member of the Hog Farm, who worked for the phone company, and he took a trip out into the desert with his wife, Shirley, and they met this guy out there named Charlie, who followed them back in this black bus," Wavy Gravy explained, describing how Charlie Manson came to the Hog Farm. "So we welcomed this guy, right? We had a three-day rule. Anybody could stay with us for three days as long as they did their share of chores, and this guy Charlie, there was something about him. He played nice tunes on his guitar and he had an aura—this kind of jailhouse glamour—and spoke in this cool prison patois. He had quite a rap. Very quickly he charmed a number of Hog Farmers."

The extended family known as the Hog Farm had been born shortly after the Watts Acid Test, when the Pranksters were supposed to gather to be photographed for the cover of *Life* Magazine. Ken Babbs had excused himself and made off with the bus called *Furthur* while the shoot was in progress. He, along with a few others, headed down to Mexico, where Ken Kesey was on the lam from his marijuana bust, leaving Romney and

Bonnie Jean Beecher with twenty houseguests crowded into their one-bedroom domicile on Lemon Grove Street.

"We were promptly evicted, but it took no more than two hours for the Universe to conjure up our deliverance in the person of our neighbor, who came by in his battered pickup truck to suggest we move to this place on the mountain in Sunland, in the San Fernando Valley," Wavy continued. "Seems this farmer named Saul had a stroke and needed somebody to slop the breakfast and dinner of his forty hogs, which we agreed to do, of course, in return for living rent free. Bonnie Jean was working occasionally as an actress in television on shows like *Star Trek*, and I was teaching improvisational techniques to brain-damaged kids, as well as contract players at Columbia, where Harrison Ford was one of my students, but all that was a sideshow compared to what was happening up on the mountaintop. Word was spreading about these happenings we were having on Sundays. Each one had its own theme and was designed to turn people on to themselves. There was Kite Sunday, Tiny Tim Sunday, Mud Sunday, and Dress like Kids Sunday. We had croquet parties held in pig-pens and bake-offs and freak shows and the Hog Farm County Fair and Hog Farm Rodeo that featured hippies riding painted pigs down the sides of mountains like wild bucking broncos. Later, when we showed Salvador Dali footage of the event in Paris, he was quite intrigued."

When people found the Hog Farm, they knew they had come upon a very special place, where the new psychedelic culture was able to thrive in an atmosphere that was completely removed from the forces that had turned the Haight Ashbury and the Summer of Love into a cruel sham. People shared everything and helped one another. Instead of their individual concerns, they focused on what Wavy called "the pudding- and sandstone-swept vistas that lay in the light at the end of the tunnel of fun . . . People liked it there, and I guess Charlie Manson was no different, and he might have stayed longer, but as it turned out, he wanted to give me the pink slip for his bus, or any of his wives, as he called them, in exchange for Bonnie Jean. It seems he was rather fixated on my wife—which I could well understand, of course, because she was quite the beauty—but he wanted to make an actual trade! Like they were horses . . . I remember thinking, how *peculiar*, you know?—that he would even *conceive* of such a transaction."

*Peculiar* was certainly one way of describing Charles Milles Manson, though just how peculiar, Hugh Romney and the other Hog Farmers could scarcely have imagined. A few salient details of his life would have quickly disabused them of the notion that he was a typical California hippie migrating down the coast in the jangled aftermath of the Summer of Love. The typical hippie's buttocks were not permanently scarred from beatings with a strap as Manson's had been when, in 1948, at the age of thirteen, he was sentenced to three years at the Indiana School for Boys, where he was assigned to work in the dairy. Manson would claim that he was raped repeatedly by the older boys with the full complicity of a head guard who would "pick up a handful of raw silage from the dairy floor, spit tobacco juice on it and shove it up my ass. I got him lubed,' he'd tell his pets, 'so fuck him if you get the chance.' The tobacco juice and silage burned and I got an infection from it, but the humiliation was worse." The next five months were "unimaginable. . . . At an age when most kids are going to nice schools, living with their parents and learning about all the better things in life, I was cleaning silage and tobacco juice out of my ass, recuperating from the wounds of a leather strap and learning to hate the world and everyone in it."

By the time he was released from Terminal Island on March 21, 1967, Manson had spent over seventeen of his thirty-two years in some form of confinement and was fully schooled in every conceivable kind of jail-house cunning and knowledge. He could play guitar and write songs and quote the Bible at length and had read voraciously in his cell—"the subject that interested me was understanding and knowing my own mind." He had delved into religion, hypnotism, psychiatry, Scientology, magic, astral projection, Masonic lore, subliminal motivation, and had incorporated ideas from Eric Berne's *Transactional Analysis in Psychotherapy* and *Games People Play,* as well as Robert Heinlein's *Stranger in a Strange Land,* whose main character, Valentine Michael Smith, was a telepathic power-hungry alien roaming the land with a harem and a vast sexual appetite and proselytizing for a new religious movement.

The day of his release, when a truck driver who picked him up on the highway casually lit up a joint, Manson saw how much the world had changed. He was flabbergasted by what he encountered in the Haight. "Pretty little girls were running around every place with no panties or bras and asking for love. Grass and hallucinatory drugs were being handed to you on the streets." It was "a convict's dream and after being locked up for seven solid years, I didn't run from it. I joined it and the generation that lived it." One night at the Avalon Ballroom, someone slipped him a tab of acid. The Grateful Dead were playing, and Manson unleashed himself into the frenzy of the music and dancing and lights. The freedom of rebirth he experienced was so overwhelming that he collapsed in the fetal position in the middle of the floor. A new world opened for him: Acid rock. Dope. The politics of free. Peace rallies. Communes. Long hair. Astrology. The occult. Underground newspapers. Crash pads. But to Manson, the most incredible aspect of the new culture by far was its sexual freedom, and it was here that he would develop his adeptness at mind control. He would profess that after his long years in jail, he was an innocent searching for love and happiness—"hey, those kids knew everything and did everything. I was the baby!" But he easily recognized that the very freedom that made this culture such a noble experiment was precisely what made it vulnerable to someone like him. As Ed Sanders pointed out in his epic book on Manson, *The Family,* "the flower movement was like a valley of thousands of plump white rabbits surrounded by wounded coyotes. Sure, the 'leaders' were tough, some of them geniuses and great poets. But the acid-dropping middle-class children from Des Moines were rabbits."

The rabbits came willingly to this coyote—first Mary Brunner, then Lynette "Squeaky" Fromme, soon Patricia Krenwinkel and Susan Atkins—young girls whose names would become forever burned into the consciousness of the age as "the Family." Each one provided Manson with "a fair glimpse of the generation that was so dominant in the 60s," as he recognized it. "While some were running from bad homes and traumatic experiences, others were leaving good homes because of their disenchantment with their parents' code of morality."

As the Summer of Love degenerated, Manson took to the road and came to see himself as the savior of these runaway girls. By all accounts, it was never hard to get them to come along and even easier to get them to stay. "There were about twelve girls," recalled Manson's former cellmate, Phil Kaufman. "Every time Charlie saw a girl he liked, he'd tell someone, 'Get that girl.' And when they brought her back, Charlie would take her out in the woods and talk to her for an hour or two. And she would never leave."

One of the reasons it was so hard to leave was the persuasiveness of his rap. As *Rolling Stone* reporters David Felton and David Dalton would note parenthetically after interviewing Manson during his trial, "Charlie is a super acid rap—symbols, parables, gestures, nothing literal, everything enigmatic, resting nowhere, stopping briefly to overturn an idea, stand it on its head, then exploit the paradox." The other tool that they would identify in Manson becoming "the villain of our time, the symbol of animism and evil," of course was acid. "Lee Harvey Oswald? Sirhan Sirhan? Adolf Eichmann? Misguided souls, sure, but as far as we know they never took LSD or fucked more than one woman at a time."

The exact role that LSD would play in this black transmigration has long been the subject of conjecture and debate. At some point, the phrase *psychedelic satanism* entered the equation. Before leaving the Haight, Manson had encountered a certain "trippy broad, about forty-five years old, who experimented with everything," as he recalled. "When I met her, she was pumped up about devil worship and other satanic activities." Manson maintained that he didn't go to the "places she invited me to" but "often discussed the good and bad sides of different beliefs," and she invited him to visit her home in Los Angeles. That was how Manson and his family came to the old two-story frame house in Topanga Canyon with the "peculiar spiral staircase" that inspired its name.

The Spiral Staircase was a place of "far out, spaced-out, weird people," as Manson described them—a "house of transition" where "mental sickness and mental confusion were the best one could expect." Showing up with a bus full of young girls completely in his sway gave Manson instant cachet; he picked up on the "vibes" quickly enough. "Though I was welcomed to the house by hearty hugs, good music, and passionate kisses, I had bad vibes about being there and staying longer. Yet I stayed. And though I would often leave in weeks to come, I would also return."

As strange as the house was, for Manson it was also "a place to learn. . . . I'm not into sacrificing some animal and drinking its blood to get a better charge out of sex. Nor am I into chaining someone and whipping them to get my kicks like some of those people were. Still, through the drugs and listening to the ways a particular leader or guru maneuvered his people, some of their rap may have become embedded in my subconscious."

On the first day they drove up, the lady of the house welcomed them by passing out LSD, which Manson and his girls took sitting in a circle. "I had in the past felt vibrations of cosmic force and reveled in psychic phenomenon, yet the trip I was about to undergo would give me the deepest penetration into awareness, extra-sensory perception, confrontation with devils, travels in divinity and association with multiple deities I had ever encountered."

A vision of Jesus appeared before him—the same vision he had as a boy of twelve, praying to God and looking out a window at the Gibault Home for Boys. "Now, Charles, these are your loves and you are their need," said the white-robed figure before him. Manson felt himself "suspended in air," looking out "over a sea of faces, faces full of love and trust, looking at me." The vision left, but as Manson returned to the room, he felt a new power. "I realized the image had been nothing but the trippy result of the acid, yet as I looked around the room, all the faces were open books. I could enter their minds or bodies if I chose to."

When Manson concentrated on a particular guy he resented, at the same instant a couple walking by the man overturned an ashtray that put a gash in his head—"I smiled and looked away, feeling very much as though I had delivered the blow." When he felt a twinge of thirst, Lynnette Fromme went right into the kitchen and brought him a glass of water. Manson claimed that he then peered directly into the womb of Mary Brunner, who was carrying his child, actually seeing that the five-month-old fetus was a male. "The experiences and perceptions that seemed to be achieved through the use of acid made it and other mental stimulants a very substantial part of our lives. While being under the influence, certain things became so pronounced and real that I couldn't help but believe in them long after the drug had worn off."

Many would claim that Manson had "Christ vibes" and thought he was Jesus himself. He often spoke of taking acid and having experienced the Stations of the Cross during the crucifixion. His Jesus rap included the very meaning of his name: Charles Manson, the Son of Man. Others claimed that when he gave acid to the girls, he would ask them to imagine him as their father while they were making love and that he liked to dispense acid to the group as the ritual wafer of the sexual psychodramas he orchestrated. One of his favorite questions had become, "Will you give me anything I ask for?" By the time he pulled into the Hog Farm at the end of 1967—a place antithetical to everything that went on at the Spiral Staircase with the exception of people taking LSD—and cast his eyes on Bonnie Jean Beecher, the notion of trading human beings seemed to him the most natural thing in the world.

"Hey, man, I'd like to sleep with your wife," Manson told Romney matter-of-factly. "You can sleep with mine. Anything that's mine is yours—my wives, the bus."

"He said such creepy, contemptible things. I didn't want him to stay," related Jahanara Romney, formerly Bonnie Jean. "That began a hot debate among us. But some people said, 'Why don't you like him, just because he's so unusual?' Then he tried to follow me into the pigeon coop, which was about twenty feet away from the kitchen door. He sat on the steps, and I got this terrible feeling, so I locked the gate behind me. He didn't do anything, but when I ran back out past him and went into the house, he said, 'Boy, you got my number, don't cha?' He had me quaking, and when I started publicly speaking out that I wanted him to leave, there was a family fight about it among the Hog Farmers, and Wavy called a *huna*."

The *huna* was a circle in which the Hog Farmers would all sit together, holding hands and breathing and collectively feeling the energy moving through and around them.

"It was sunset." Jahanara went on. "The black bus was parked nearby, and he and his girls were all inside it. He came out of the bus and gave us a pipe of something. We thought it was marijuana and smoked it, but it wasn't. I have no idea what it was—maybe DMT or something—and suddenly I was stoned—*too* stoned, so stoned I was not comfortable. So we started to hold hands and chant: '*OOMM*' . . . All of a sudden . . . he was swooning, and the girls started making this horrible keening, shrieking sound inside the bus. It was like the sound of us chanting Om was *burning* him or something, and it went through us like a knife—it was terrifying. Then he leapt out of the bus and stood up high in the center of our circle and started chanting and hollering about being the Messiah, and I'm thinking, Oh, my God, I've got to run, but I couldn't move my legs!—it was like I was completely in his power. The best way I can describe the feeling I had was that I knew I was in serious peril and that evil was real. And that was when Wavy got up and confronted him."

Hugh Romney wore a white jumpsuit with a star, the same one worn by the Pranksters for the Acid Test Graduation. On his face was a gentle smile, on his head an old cowboy hat once worn by Tom Mix, star of silent Westerns; sewn inside the hat was a yarmulke that Lenny Bruce had given him. Manson was dressed in black, his face twisted in a paroxysm of rage that made him look like a rabid dog about to leap for Romney's throat.

"I was seized by this colossal energy," Wavy remembered, "and I just rose up and got in his face. I don't know what it was, I'm not especially assertive or brave . . . I told him, 'Get the fuck out of here!' So, amazingly, he got in his bus and left. But not without driving away with the fourteen-year-old daughter of Chance and Shirley."

The Hog Farm would evolve into a resourceful amalgamation of peripatetic artisans, activists, and freaks—"a light show, a rock band, a painting, a poem, a mobile hallucination, a sociological experiment, an army of clowns, an antiwar rally, an anthem for freedom and change," as Wavy called it. Embarking on an odyssey of psychedelic caravans ("Driver, the United States of America, and step on it!" became their driving slogan) that included fifty people, six converted buses, and a four-hundred-pound black-and-white spotted female pig named Pigasus that Hugh Romney would run as a candidate for president of the United States the next year, they zigzagged across the country, from New Mexico to Woodstock, where they achieved fame caring for the acid casualties at the rock festival in 1969 and feeding the hippie multitudes with a new foodstuff called granola. Eventually they journeyed all the way to the Himalayas, delivering medical supplies to the needy and planting the seeds for a foundation called Seva, dedicated to combating preventable blindness by offering cataract operations to hundreds of thousands of people.

Manson and his followers on the black bus soon holed up at the broken-down Spahn's Movie Ranch out in Chatsworth. While Manson tried to make music connections down in Los Angeles, "the Family" began wandering through Inyo County and Death Valley, finding the Goler Wash waterfalls, the Ballart ghost town, Mengel Pass, the Barker and Meyers Ranches, the old mines and shacks and forgotten springs that would become the landmarks of the apocalyptic vision called Helter Skelter.

## VII. The Power to Blow Their Minds

"HERE'S A FACT you may relish," Michael Rossman offered, looking up from his carpentry work in his Berkeley home. "From 1960 to 1969, the number of arrests for marijuana in California doubled every year. One could infer from those statistics that the population of smokers was doubling every year. Why did so many young people start smoking dope at that time? Is it a coincidence that the precise moment when this trend begins, in 1960, is also the precise moment of the birth of the New Left as its historically recorded?"

As one of the leaders of the Free Speech Movement, Rossman was able to chart both the growth and the political significance of marijuana use during the critical fall of 1964, when Leftist politics in the Bay Area erupted into a student movement that signaled the beginning of a politics of confrontation on American campuses. What began as an impromptu demonstration of civil disobedience when UC Berkeley authorities announced that the Bancroft Strip would be completely off-limits to off-campus politics dramatically escalated into a conflict that resulted in the first takeover of a university building by student demonstrators in American history. For thirty hours, one thousand students occupied four floors of Sproul Hall; by the time the building was stormed by police and nine hundred people were arrested, a number of them had smoked marijuana and made love on the roof, acting out their own embryonic version of the new "free" society.

"By the time the FSM erupted, grass and acid had spread significantly in the student population," Rossman observed. "Soon after that time, I had occasion to make some kind of an estimate, and I think three to five thousand of Cal's twenty-five thousand students had smoked marijuana by that fall. On the FSM steering committee, if this is an index, there were three of us who had done acid and five of us who smoked marijuana."

Rossman found the figure highly significant. "To a large extent, we were political people who had grown up with a wariness about radical cultural experimentation like marijuana smoking because of the heritage of paranoia that the New Left had as a consequence of the fate of the Old Left," he explained. "But marijuana smoking started rising the instant we said no to the past, no to political oppression and persecution, yes, we're going to say what we have to say. Ostensibly that was a political cry to the public sphere, and this generation's experience with psychoactive drugs was completely an inward exploration. My thesis has always been that the inward exploration was enabled by the outward expression. In other words, because we said no to 'out there,' we were free to go inside, and with the opening of that, a whole wealth of material—feelings, spirit, sexuality—began to become political, too."

If smoking pot had only been "a kick," it would never have taken hold as it did. In fact, marijuana was arriving at Berkeley and other college campuses when battle lines were being drawn, when stakes were rising and the water was beginning to boil. In 1965, President Johnson was escalating American involvement in Vietnam so fast that it took on a sense of daily apocalypse; Malcolm X was assassinated, and the Watts neighborhood in L.A. went up in flames. At this volatile moment in American history, here was an experience that only crystallized the stark differences between the way you experienced reality in your own nervous system and the official descriptions by the media and government. All you had to do was get high to understand in the most visceral sense that the government was lying about pot; once you saw through that hoax, you started questioning what the authorities were saying about everything else, and at that point, the very inhaling of marijuana became symbolic of engaging in a conspiracy against the state. The next realization was that if you could break the law by smoking pot, well, then, you could do other things equally illegal.

"The Free Speech Movement and the first Vietnam demonstrations in Berkeley had been media orgies, big news all over the country," remembered Jerry Rubin, relaxing in his condominium on Wilshire Boulevard. "And then came the Be-In, with everyone living out their fantasies in this fabulous circus, which sent the word out to kids all across the country that, hey, *this* was the way to have fun! I began to think, Wait a second, what if you juxtaposed that on the news with the casualty reports from Vietnam? What if you could send the message out on the evening news that you could fight the bad guys—and have a really great time doing it? Then you'd have these two strains—kids and serious protesters—organized into one movement, and *boom*!"

By the time he arrived on the East Coast in the fall of 1967 to coordinate the National Mobilization to End the War in Vietnam (the MOBE), Jerry Rubin was transforming himself from someone who smoked pot once in a while to someone who smoked it all the time. He had been one of the last of the Berkeley politicos to smoke pot and take acid, but once the Cincinnati-born sportswriter-turned-Marxist was turned on, he realized that being high certainly made some activities much easier, like appear at the HUAC hearings in Washington in full Revolutionary War regalia, blithely blowing soap bubbles as members of Congress questioned his Communist affiliations. When the HUAC stunt became front-page news, it was clear to Rubin that getting stoned and getting headlines was one of those classic American combinations, like baseball and beer or chocolate and peanut butter.

In New York, Rubin quickly found a collaborator. With his Jewish Afro, impish smile, and clown face, Abbie Hoffman seemed genetically designed to appear in front of television cameras. That the media would play along became obvious on the day Hoffman and Rubin gleefully flung money into the air on the floor of the Stock Exchange, creating mayhem as the traders scrambled for the bills. The message was simple: people in Vietnam were dying, but it was business as usual on Wall Street. As Hoffman recollected, "The TV show that night was fantastic. It went all over the world."

"See, the *real* drug was Walter Cronkite," Rubin allowed. "It's hard to describe how excited we were when we realized how easy it was to get on those sign-off pieces at the end of the evening news broadcasts. At that point, we learned one basic lesson: the more visual and surreal the stunts we could cook up, the easier it would be to get on the news, and the more weird and whimsical and provocative the theater, the better it would play."

And so began the guerrilla media burlesque that would turn Jerry Rubin and Abbie Hoffman into the most famous radicals of the 1960s— the hippie-activist version of *Abbott and Costello.* Phrases like "the power to blow their minds" began to pervade the antiwar movement. Exactly as a drug experience could blow the ballast tanks of the psyche, so certain actions could be designed to blow the political ballast tanks of the government and the nation at large. With young American soldiers returning in body bags at a rate of five hundred a month, the peace movement was reaching a crossroads. Determined to "rescue" the movement from the predictable tactics of the mainstream and Old Left groups, Rubin and Hoffman fixed their sights on the Pentagon.

The Levitation of the Pentagon was designed to "blow minds" in the truest sense of the phrase. Illicit mind-altering substances would be freely consumed to help inspire the group's provocative stratagems and pump up its rhetoric to the heights of preposterousness. When confronted with Hoffman's surreal, overheated bombast—"we will dye the Potomac red, burn the cherry trees, panhandle embassies, attack with water pistols, marbles, bubble gum wrappers, bazookas, girls will run naked and piss on the Pentagon walls, sorcerers, swamis, witches, voodoo, warlocks, medicine men, and speed freaks will hurl their magic at the faded brown walls"—all the government could do was take him at his word and prepare for the worst. On October 21, 1967, when seventy-five thousand souls gathered at the Lincoln Memorial for the first national protest against the war in Vietnam, the Pentagon was surrounded by the stone-faced troops of the Eighty-second Airborne, bayonets at the ready. The media spectacle that followed—protesters smoking pot and screaming antiwar epithets, Ed Sanders and the Fugs conducting an exorcism of the Pentagon ("Out demons, out!") from a flatbed truck, demonstrators planting daisies in the barrels of the guns of young soldiers on the Pentagon steps, groups trying to storm the building and being beaten back in a tense, thirty-hour standoff—would set the tone and style for theatrical hippie activism on a national scale. As Rubin described it in *Do It: Scenarios of the Revolution,* "A new man was born smoking pot while besieging the Pentagon . . . the Marxist acidhead, the psychedelic Bolshevik. . . . A longhaired, beaded, hairy, crazy motherfucker whose life is theater, every moment creating the new society as he destroys the old."

## VIII. Czechago

NOBODY WAS PREPARED for the sheer velocity of the events that preceded the Democratic National Convention, each one raising the temperature and quickening the pulse of the body politic until the sense that life was hurtling out of control began to pervade the national consciousness.

The war rolled pitilessly on: 20,000 Americans dead, 110,000 wounded, countless Vietnamese dead, 2,000 air sorties a week, 1.7 million acres defoliated, nightly scenes of napalmed villages on the evening news, President Johnson continually insisting that there was "light at the end of the tunnel," "we are winning the war in Vietnam"—and then the shock of the January Tet offensive, the gathering momentum of the doves in the Democratic Party, Senator Eugene McCarthy announcing for president and scoring impressively in New Hampshire, Johnson stunning the country on March 31 by announcing that he would not seek re-election.

Four days later, Martin Luther King was shot dead in Memphis and riots exploded in 125 cities, the worst domestic unrest since the Civil War: forty-six dead, twenty-six thousand arrested, the National Guard called in, smoke within blocks of the White House. In April, Columbia University erupted in student revolt: buildings occupied by SDS, pitched battles with police. On hundreds of campuses, there were mass marches, sit-ins, draft card burnings, picket lines, and civil disobedience. By summer, the country was reeling but there was no respite from Black Panthers, black power salutes at the Mexico City Olympic Games, Robert Kennedy dying in a pool of blood, the Democrats fragmenting, the Second Coming of Nixon.

For those like the Yippies who threw LSD into this cyclone, the volume was jacked up to peak distortion. Time was stretched and compressed, images became more surreal and apocalyptic, perceptions changed radically from moment to moment, commitment became more messianic, despair more abysmal, paranoia more acute, and the possibility of a new world seemed ever more limitless and shimmering. The world was on the brink of revolution and it seemed as certain as tomorrow's sunrise.

"The world was going to be one great Be-In!" exclaimed Jerry Rubin, reflecting on the history of the Yippies—the first "national psychedelic political movement" in American history. "I really believed it in my heart. I began to think about organizing young people around the purposes of having fun and overthrowing the government, and marijuana was the critical key to that." The product that Rubin was now going to sell was "the discontentment of post–World War II American youth with lack of purpose and national direction and living on old ideas. The reality already existed—all we had to do was create the myths, and the first myth was called Yippie. A lot of the best ideas of the Sixties were stoned ideas, and what can you say about Yippie except that it was a very stoned idea?"

"Yippie was simply a label to describe a phenomenon that already existed—an organic coalition between psychedelic dropouts and political activists," explained Paul Krassner, the activist-writer, editor of *The Realist,* and the man who coined the term when he smoked some good weed and came up with it at an antiwar movement meeting held in the apartment of Abbie and Anita Hoffman to plan the next big action at the Democratic National Convention in Chicago. The consensus was that while the Democrats would present their tired policies, the demonstrators would present rock bands playing in the park and information booths about drugs and alternatives to the draft, to "counter their Festival of Death with a Festival of Life, "as Krassner put it; the name *YIPPIE,* which stood for the Youth International Party (YIP), also expressed the perfect attitude of exuberance and freedom they wanted to project: "We would *be* a party and we would *have* a party."

After his first acid trip at Millbrook, Krassner thought about putting a big headline about LSD in *The Realist* announcing "It's Very Funny!"— or words to that effect. "I put forth a take-it-or-leave-it kind of attitude at first. But after a while, I became a real psychedelic macho. I would take it and go on *The Tonight Show,* take it in the subway, take it in all these different situations just to enhance the experience and see if I could be in them tripping without other people knowing, kind of like my own private little personal best. I would always take it and go to antiwar rallies. Consequently, many of the major watershed events of the 1960s I experienced under psychedelics, including the Chicago conspiracy trial."

Krassner's use of LSD was emblematic of the complex role that drugs would play in the antiwar movement in the months leading up to the Democratic National Convention in Chicago. Drugs became a rallying point, a magical instrument of subversion, and a political and cultural metaphor. "The escalation of the war so completely dovetails with the introduction of psychedelics that it becomes analytically impossible to separate them," noted Todd Gitlin, former president of SDS and the author of authoritative works on the period like *The Sixties: Years of Hope, Days of Rage.* "Larger and larger amounts of people were having the experience of a different reality, of a different sense of human possibilities, whether in a political or a metaphysical sense. LSD was loaded with a sense of opposition, risk, departure from ordinariness—it was really 'Break on through to the Other Side,' and for many it took a political form."

By 1968, Gitlin had developed an appreciation for marijuana while remaining suspicious of what he called the "hedonist principle" of the new culture. He saw a distinct divide in the movement between those who used drugs and those who did not. "Plenty of people in the movement weren't smoking dope. I remember being at a party at the SDS convention in '67 where I got quite stoned and Tom Hayden gave me this really funny look . . . There was a clash between factions, something of a puritan versus hedonist divide, and it was partly generational. Abbie Hoffman and Jerry Rubin, they were older than me but they were speaking to kids younger than me. Clearly, there was always that tension, and it wasn't strictly over drugs, but drugs were part of the difference in lifestyles."

As a result of this divide between the straight New Leftists and the new stoned politicos, distinctly different political conceptions of the movement began to emerge, giving rise to their own questions. As Gitlin expressed them, "Does one sacrifice for tomorrow, or does one live now? Does one think strategically or act expressively? Does one imagine a new social order or does one imagine disorder? So, even in the counterculture, there was this tension, these divides between the individualist streak and the communitarian, between the people who used drugs and music and hair and style to express the spirit of transgression and those who did not, and it was the same deep divide of civilization that Freud wrote about: the tension between the pleasure principle and the reality principle."

For the Yippies, who believed that their culture *was* their politics, there was no such tension; as far as drugs were concerned, the politics were right there in the very high itself. "LSD was so great because it showed you how fragile reality was," Rubin emphasized. "When you were peaking on acid you were seeing that everything had its purpose. All normal categories disappeared and everything could mean something else. It made you question everything and look at everything differently. There was unlimited political potential in that!"

As an instant political concoction without any grass-roots organization, the Yippies intended Chicago to be the ultimate high and above all were ready to let the chips fall where they may. With the attention of the world media fixed on the city for five straight days in August, their chance had arrived, as Rubin viewed it, to "touch the world's soul." Their mission was to project a new political reality—whether it existed or not was entirely beside the point. At the beginning of 1968, the slogans they disseminated in this media-generated, drug-fueled loop of existence were meant to commandeer the media and create the conditions they described. They would "fuck on the beaches!" and provide "acid for all!" and "yell Yippie! at the moment of orgasm!" The message they sought to project was that millions and millions of kids were ready to materialize in Chicago at their command to make the revolution happen, and that the state was virtually powerless to stop it because it was losing its capacity to govern.

Any understanding of the Battle of Chicago would be incomplete without mention of the hash-oil "honey," introduced by someone variously referred to as the Honeyman aka Jim Morrison, or the Mad Scientist, an American theater artist who went to Paris and returned from the May insurrection with a radicalized sensibility along with suitcases of hashish that he learned how to process into a ruby red liquid of highly concentrated THC extract. This was subsequently turned into cases of honey and distributed by Abbie Hoffman and others to demonstrators in the park, where it would become as much a part of the legend of the event as the brown acid later became at Woodstock.

In the riots that took place virtually every night of the convention, police and demonstrators clashed violently on national television. Amid the madhouse of demonstrators screaming "Pigs eat shit!" and "The whole world is watching!" and mace-spraying cops in gas masks chanting

"Kill, kill, kill!" as they smashed at the heads and limbs and groins of the tear-gassed demonstrators, the hash-oil honey did far more than turn the tanks in the streets into "Creatures from the Smoky Lagoon" and the policemen in gas masks into the "sinister spacemen" and "ghouls in hell" that Rubin described in *Do It!* The strange misty luminescence created by the orange clouds of tear gas and television lights and the blue flashing lights of police cars turned the city into the nightmarish fascist phantasmagoria of "Czechago," the name Rubin and the Yippies would subsequently use for the event. All those who took the substance experienced it as the most potent cannabis product they had ever ingested; even the tiny amount that Ed Sanders took, for example, was powerful enough to turn the grass into "a giant frothing trough of mutant spinach egg noodles." So stoned was Sanders that he had to be helped back to his hotel by the police who were tailing him.

Aside from the hash oil taking many of the Yippie leaders out of the action and decision making, what overall role did drugs play in what had happened in the streets of Chicago? "I've asked myself that question and answered it by saying that I don't know," rejoined Todd Gitlin. "I think it was an element for many people but it's unknowable. It may have made the step into danger, even violence, easier. I don't think it was decisive, but it was an element. The *war*, on the other hand—that was decisive."

"Chicago would have happened the same way with or without drugs," Rubin asserted. "Marijuana was a lure, like music and having a good time was supposed to be a lure, but it would have gone down the same way with or without drugs. I see Chicago as a very positive moment. It was a necessary purge."

But polls indicated that a majority of the public supported the ruthless tactics of the Chicago police—ample proof that despite a youth culture that was making more and more noise, America was seeking deliverance from wild-eyed Yippies, militant Black Panthers, riots, crime, and drugs. The Republican "law and order" candidate, Richard M. Nixon, arguably won the election of 1968 on those nights in Chicago.

Chicago was a decisive turning point for the antiwar movement. In the coming year, the fusion of the movement, drugs, and counterculture picked up even more steam, and there were bitter confrontations at San

Francisco State, Stanford, and Harvard. Black Panther Bobby Hutton had been killed in a shoot-out with police in Oakland; Eldridge Cleaver fled underground; black students with rifles occupied a building at Cornell. When police turned shotguns on the crowds trying to "liberate" People's Park in Berkeley, there were scores of wounded and one shot dead; Governor Ronald Reagan sent in the National Guard to occupy the campus like a vengeful conqueror. Bombings and attempted bombings occurred, as did arson and attempted arson of campus ROTC buildings. The antiwar movement became more paranoid, and the FBI began a concerted program to disrupt the New Left by instigating conflicts and drug arrests (340,000 people were busted for drugs that year). As Nixon's Silent Majority seemed more resentful of the prodrug and antiwar movement and the state seemed ever more punitive, the V sign for peace and the flower that had been the symbols of the peaceful dissent and hope of 1965–67 steadily gave way to the red clenched fist—the radical insignia of revolution that would characterize the period from 1968 to 1970.

"I became aware at some point that the amount of marijuana that my crowd was doing was in some way directly related to the sense of political helplessness and that in some way the grass was a balm for political wounds," reflected Gitlin, who watched SDS fragment, some members organizing into groups like the Weather Underground that were advocating the violent overthrow of the state. "There was a melancholy fatalism with marijuana, a sort of sweet sense of desperation, all part of the gestalt. Certainly, the world looked uglier and uglier. At least one element that was scary for me in drugs was a more intimate connection to that ugliness. Drugs could strip you of defenses, and I didn't want to be stripped. I had few enough defenses to begin with."

If drugs had shaped Yippie behavior before and during the convention, they now helped turn the trial of the Chicago Eight into the most celebrated political circus of the era. Rubin, who was charged with conspiracy to riot along with Abbie Hoffman, Rennie Davis, Tom Hayden, Dave Dellinger, Lee Weiner, John Froines, and Black Panther Bobby Seale, was determined to smoke as much marijuana as possible for the trial despite the dangers of being busted. "I got stoned a lot for the trial because it was such complete theater—a front-row seat to history—and marijuana intensifies every experience. The day Abbie and I came in wearing judges' robes was a stoned idea. It was a turning point in the trial in terms of theatrics, and it just went on from there."

But the Chicago conspiracy trial wasn't all fun and games; Rubin and Hoffman were facing years in jail if convicted. Paul Krassner, ever the psychedelic "macho," showed up to testify with a stash of acid. "I knew if I ingested 300 mikes of LSD after eating a big meal, I was likely to throw up in court. That would be my theatrical statement on the injustice of the trial. Also I wouldn't need to memorize so much information. . . . The prosecutor would ask, 'Now where did this meeting take place?' And I would go, '*Waughhhhhppp!*' "

Hoffman didn't think it was such a great idea; Rubin was all for it. Sure enough, when Krassner was escorted into the courtroom of the diminutive bald-headed Judge Julius J. Hoffman, he was tripping his brains out and the place looked like an other-dimensional Loony Toons cartoon. "Judge Julius Hoffman looked exactly like Elmer Fudd. I expected him to proclaim, 'Let's get them pesky wadicals!' " The prosecuting attorney had metamorphosed into the Big Bad Wolf, and Defense Attorney William Kunstler, the Wise Old Owl. "There was one point where they were asking me where a certain meeting had taken place, and I couldn't think of the word *Chicago*. I'm saying, 'Right *here,* right here, right here in *this* city,' and Abbie is trying to mouth the word *Chicago*—it got a little bizarre. I expected the bailiff to come up there and say, 'No coaching from the audience!' "

Krassner didn't vomit; nor, on the other hand, could he say anything remotely helpful to the defense. Abbie Hoffman was furious. "He thought it was irresponsible, a betrayal. We didn't talk for ten months. I didn't feel there was anything I could do to harm their case, given the way they already acted in court. Abbie was scared. I had never seen him scared before."

On October 15, 1969, millions of people participated in the national antiwar Moratorium; exactly a month later, three-quarters of a million traveled to Washington for the huge Mobilization.

"You started to see more and more people actually high at demonstrations," Rubin acknowledged. "Now everybody got stoned—everywhere you looked, people would be passing the joint, like a peace pipe. Besides opposition to the war, it was the single most important unifying cultural activity."

Jerry Rubin would always claim that from that point on, marijuana sales helped finance the antiwar movement of the 1960s.

"If you do an economic analysis, it was really multilevel marketing, right? A guy sells it, a guy on top of him gets an override, and on and on. It was *classic* multilevel marketing; only the product in our case was marijuana. The movement was always short of money, and a lot of marijuana money was rechanneled among activists and cultural aspects. All those crazy Right Wingers were always saying we were getting our money from Russia, but we were getting it from marijuana smoking. How else could the movement have been financed?"

## IX. The Best of Times, the Worst of Times

ON AUGUST 15, 1969, roughly half a million people gathered in Bethel, New York, for the greatest party of the twentieth century. The Woodstock Festival was the ultimate Be-In of the era.

The impact of acid on the event is incalculable. For three straight days, there were hundreds of thousands of people playing and goofing and freaking in the rain and mud together, in states ranging from infernal discomfort and fatigue to the most primordial ecstasy and transcendent release. Psychedelic drugs not only turned Woodstock into an acid-drenched holy quagmire but also shaped its soundtrack. By Monday morning, when Jimi Hendrix appeared in his fringed white suede shirt and purple headband, there were only about thirty thousand people left, and the field had turned into a garbage-strewn sea of muck that looked like the detritus of a lost civilization. There was haunting stillness in the air as Hendrix's wrenching psychedelic interpretation of "The Star-Spangled Banner" echoed for miles in the far distance. It all seemed to pass through his nervous system and white Stratocaster and come out of the huge towers in monumental glissandos of space-age feedback and distortion, reverberating through the surrounding forests like some ghostly visitation of all that had come before: the ghettos burning and the napalm exploding, the assassinations, the marches, the riots, the flowers, the music, the drugs—all of the wildness and fury and hope coming together in one defining moment. Then he played "Purple Haze," walked offstage, and collapsed from exhaustion.

Woodstock passed quickly into myth and became the ultimate tribal affirmation of the alternative values of a generation—peace, love, freedom, spirituality, sex, drugs, rock and roll—all of which had fused into a single entity called the counterculture. Before long, it was being considered in religious terms—"the people were seekers, the rock stars their prophets and drugs pretty much their staff of life," Barry Farrell wrote in *Life*.

"This is the largest group of people ever assembled in one place," farmer Max Yasgur had tearfully declared from the stage erected on his land on the final day of the festival. "But I think you people have proved something to the world—that half a million kids can get together and have three days of fun and music—and have nothing *but* fun and music!"

The euphoria would be short-lived.

On December 6, 1969, the Rolling Stones played a free concert that was billed as Woodstock West at Altamont Speedway, in Livermore, California, with "security" provided by the Hells Angels in exchange for a truckload of free beer worth five hundred dollars. If Altamont proved anything, it was the power of the delirious stoned-out hubris that reigned in the wake of Woodstock—as if all would just cosmically fall together; everything's cool, man.

Everyone was there, on and around the stage—the legendary bands of the Bay Area, the politicos and countercultural luminaries like Tim Leary, all the players in the psychedelic wave that had been building over the five years since Berkeley and the acid tests, through the blossoming of the Haight and the Summer of Love burnout—surrounded by the most violent motorcycle outlaws in America, with a virtually unlimited supply of the entire rebel pharmacopoeia on hand to feed the party.

As soon as Santana started playing, everyone saw the naked boy in the crowd. It was hard not to notice him, this grotesquely fat Chicano kid tripping his brains out, who took off his clothes and began dancing, flabby breasts and flaccid penis jouncing as he stomped, oblivious to those around him. If the freedom of Woodstock had been personified by the *Newsweek* cover of a beautiful hippie who looked like a sinewy Aztec

warrior in loin cloth, gyrating ecstatically up against a nubile girl, Altamont generated a very different image: this naked fat boy and what happened next. Sick at the sight of him, the Angels waded into the crowd and
began clubbing him viciously with sawed-off pool cues weighted with
lead—apparently their idea of appropriate crowd-control implements.
Eighteen-year-old Meredith Hunter was not the only person to die that
day—there were four fatalities in all, one of them a boy tripping on LSD
who got the bright idea to go sliding down a cement sluice into an irrigation canal, where he drowned—but Hunter was the only one stabbed to
death by the Angels that night, all of it captured by the three cameras of
Albert and David Maysles's documentary crew.

The blame for the debacle was equally apportioned among the Angels, the Rolling Stones, who were onstage when it happened, and the
Dead (the festival organizers, who never played that day). From within
and without the counterculture, the general opinion was that the Sixties
were dead and that Altamont was the nail in the coffin. But it would
never be that simple. Greil Marcus of *Rolling Stone* walked away realizing
that the apocalypse he had witnessed provided an "extraordinary complex
and visceral metaphor for the way things of the Sixties ended. . . . No one
knew how to deal with a spectacle that from the moment it began contra-
dicted every assumption on which it had been based, producing violence
instead of fraternity, selfishness instead of generosity, ugliness instead of
beauty, a bad trip instead of a high."

With the arrest of Charles Manson, the scales had seemed to tip precipitously to the dark side.

The first murders had occurred on August 9, the week before Wood-
stock. From the moment that the bodies of Sharon Tate, Abigail Folger,
Wojciech Frykowski, Jay Sebring, and Steve Parent were found at 10050
Cielo Drive in Benedict Canyon and the story broke in the *Los Angeles
Times,* fear gripped the poolsides of Los Angeles. The following night, the
bodies of Leno and Rosemary LaBianca were discovered on Greenwood
Place in the Los Feliz District of Los Angeles, with the words HEALTER
SKELTER written in blood on the refrigerator door.

The savagery of the murders was unimaginable: 102 stab wounds to
the victims of Cielo Drive. Tate, the beautiful twenty-six-year-old starlet

married to Roman Polanski, was pregnant at the time of her killing. Rosemary LaBianca had been left with a fork sticking out of her abdomen.

"I'm only a mirror," Manson kept repeating again and again after his arrest—an unnerving mantra that would now prompt the counterculture to take a hard look at itself, to see what, if anything, he was reflecting.

For true believers in the psychedelic ethos and the New Age, like the Doors organist Ray Manzarek, the implications of Manson were particularly disquieting. "I could not understand how people who professed to take LSD could actually commit murder. But then you realized that insanity actually exists on the planet. Madness was always glamorized in the artistic community: mad to live, to burn, to create . . . This was a very different kind of madness. When that went down, hippies just looked at each other and said, 'What happened?' "

"It was a horrifying story, America's worst nightmare, not only to the straights but to the hippies," Ed Sanders commented. "It's one of those cases where all the facts will probably never be known, like the Kennedy assassination. Something was violated in that case that really got to me. It went back to the ethic of 'do your own thing.' "

Sanders's book *The Family: The Story of Charles Manson's Dune Buggy Attack Battalion,* was compelling for a multitude of reasons, not the least of which was that it was written by someone of the counterculture about a perversion that had taken root in its own soil. Sanders discovered that speed—the cold, hard drug of the Nazi blitzkreig—and not LSD had been the killers' drug of choice on the night of the murders, but it hardly mattered. From the early 1960s, he'd watched as drugs had become an integral part of the "oodles of freedom" he had perceived in the Constitution. If nothing else, the Manson story was graphic proof to him that the greatest challenge facing those who had entered this uncharted terrain had less to do with the drugs themselves than with the development of a concomitant set of values around their use.

"We have to be willing to make a moral differentiation to find out what we believe and don't believe," he concluded. "With drugs, it can't be some blatant simple thing of, 'Hey, man, let's get high and listen to Miles.' The issue becomes about policing—like an environmentalist policing the bioregion, finding out who's dumping what into the creeks. There have to be values involved. That was the weakness. Mea culpa. We didn't do it enough."

As if Altamont and Manson weren't enough, the Deaths of the Icons further sullied the drug culture. By 1971, Jimi Hendrix, the greatest guitarist in the history of rock, the artist who had symbolized all the creativity and promise of the Psychedelic Age, had kissed the sky. Janis Joplin, whose batty laugh seemed to personify its freedom and fun-loving spirit, had ended on a slab in the morgue with track marks on her arm. Jim Morrison, Wild Child, Lizard King, Erotic Politician, the voice that had urged a generation to dance on fire, had broken on through to the other side. Each one had appeared like an avatar on a special mission to open up the consciousness and soul of the age and then suddenly vanished from the earth as if by some incomprehensibly cruel act of black magic.

"It was horrific to see the blessed falling," Paul Rothchild allowed, "and they were dropping like flies. So many extraordinary, talented people went down because of a lack of understanding of the physiology and chemistry of drugs, but that was only one of the reasons why it was happening."

Rothchild had finally realized his dream of producing Janis Joplin, and she gave him everything she had, blossoming in the studio like a flower. There were eight great songs in the can, five with final vocals, including Kris Kristofferson's "Me and Bobby McGee." When Janis returned to the Landmark Hotel on October 3, 1970, all they needed was to cut her vocal for "Buried Alive in the Blues" and the album would be a wrap. The next morning they found her in her room, naked except for panties, $4.50 in one hand, an unopened pack of cigarettes in the other, and a bruise on her right temple. Rothchild, who would conduct his own investigation into Joplin's death and determine that she had been killed by a hot shot (the trace metallic poisoning from a bad load of heroin), reflected often in the difficult months ahead about Janis and Jim Morrison.

"When I was producing Janis's last album we both had Porsches, and we really liked to race them. One night we were racing down Sunset at one a.m.—Janis is in the oncoming lane going one hundred twenty m.p.h. Cars are lurching out of the way, and she's got her foot to the floor, and she's laughing like crazy, absolute joyous laughter. It was the clearest moment I can remember of seeing that attitude of *Hey, nothing can kill me. Death, I dare you to try it!* She sang with that attitude. She drank with that attitude. She carried on with boys with that attitude. Pedal to the metal. It's what made her so great and what killed her."

Rothchild remembered Morrison's performance at a small club called the London Fog just as the Doors were getting started. "It was one of those four-sets-a-night gigs, and they were playing their last set. There were maybe three people in the audience, two drunken salesmen from Cleveland and Pam, his girlfriend. And Jim was transcendent. Absolutely brilliant. On fire. Beyond greatness. They came down from the stage, and Pamela was so stunned she couldn't say anything in the car. When he finally got her to talk, she said, 'Jim, you just bled onstage. You died for them, and there was nobody there except those drunks and me! Why such an intense performance for virtually nobody?' He said, 'You never know when you're doing your last performance.' See, he knew even then what he was dealing with, and there was that element in everything— that sense of daring, that awareness of death and immortality."

Rothchild wrestled with the issue of why so many people during that time felt the need to walk that edge. "If you're not at the cutting edge, why bother? And of course you can fall off that edge, but that was part of the fascination. To be that high and daring. To tempt death in a thousand ways. But there was something else. It was a feeling like this: Well, I'm not going to make it anyway, this is a short ride, so I'm going to go as far out and blaze as brightly as possible. Add the chemistry of the Sixties to this equation, and it becomes much clearer why so many would go down."

In a sense, the Deaths of the Icons were perfect examples of Sal Paradise's description of people like Dean Moriarty as the ones who "burn, burn, burn, like fabulous yellow roman candles . . ." Indeed, the way of life personified by the passage had seemingly passed directly from the bebop era to the psychedelic age. Kerouac himself had died on October 22, 1969, in St. Petersburg, Florida, after puking blood into a toilet— "hemorrhaging esophageal varices," the classic alcoholic's death—with little use for the hippies who were always claiming him as their inspiration. The same was certainly not true for Neal Cassady. The very heartbeat of the Beat Generation was found comatose in February of 1968 along the railroad tracks between San Miguel de Allende and Celaya, Mexico, where he had dropped from pulque and a handful of Seconals consumed at a wedding party. Cassady had lived and died as Dean Moriarty, Fastestmanalive, burning incandescently to his very last moment of consciousness, counting the railroad ties until he just wore out and dropped, "sixty-four thousand nine hundred and twenty-eight," he said before dying in the nearby hospital.

"It felt so unreal because it happened so far away," related Mountain Girl. "Cassady could feel himself slowing down, and he hadn't built anything for himself in all that craziness—in fact, it just seemed to carry him away from the stuff he cared most about. He was depressed and blamed it on the fact that he was over forty and his nerve impulses were slowing down. He just kind of broke contact with us and went down to Mexico and didn't come back. It was tragic because he was like a family member, like your favorite uncle, the one who could come along and read the situation perfectly and always say the right thing to pop you out of the rut. He was just *gone*—and we never got to say good-bye."

Then she watched Ron "Pigpen" McKernan, the original front man and organist of the Grateful Dead, die of plain, old-fashioned alcoholism in March of 1973 at the age of twenty-seven—the same age, incredibly, as Jimi, Janis, and Jim, as if they were all on the same lethal timetable. "Pig was such a surprise because he had stopped drinking for over a year before he died of alcohol poisoning, but his body just never healed itself. He just slowly disintegrated. It was terrifying."

None of these deaths surprised Grace Slick, any more than it would seem odd that race-car drivers or daredevil athletes would have a higher casualty rate than the average population. "Look, some people stayed in Scotland and raised their herds, others got on the ship and went with Magellan, and those who went on the trip lived with a lot more danger but saw more of the world. It's the same in any culture. If they chose to live on the edge, more will die and die younger than if they don't; more will be damaged than if they don't. Choose it or not, it's your choice— and we, obviously, were choosing it. Paul Kantner once said that because we came out of the 1950s, white and fairly educated and privileged, some people would choose self-destruction not out of a sense of hating oneself or wanting to kill oneself, but out of looking for ways to make our lives more challenging, difficult, authentic. In other words, we needed our own saga. It's an interesting thought."

One would think that hard drugs and the Deaths of the Icons might have provided cautionary tales for an entire generation. In some isolated instances, it did—Marty Balin of the Jefferson Airplane renounced drugs after the death of Janis Joplin—but even as Janis's ashes were being scattered over the coast of California, her myth was gathering force. Her will had provided for a lively wake—"Drinks are on Pearl" read the invitation to the bash at the Lion's Share in San Anselmo. As James Gurley recalled, "Everybody got as drunk and fucked up as they could. I think it was fitting to send her off that way"—and such would always be her legend. People would make the pilgrimage to the Père-Lachaise Cemetery in Paris, where Morrison is buried in the company of Bizet and Baudelaire, among others, to pay homage to his self-immolation as much as to his music or poetry: let's visit Morrison's grave, smoke a joint, toast his beautiful madness, scrawl some graffiti on his headstone. His death had no more of a sobering effect than the death of Bird had had on the bebop generation. If anything, it seemed to stoke the embers.

"I knew that I behaved illogically," Danny Sugarman reflected. "I should have said, 'Gee, you *live* like Jim, you'll *die* like Jim; you better get your shit together or you'll go, too.' But my reaction was to start behaving exactly like him. The idea of going out and throwing the dice, chemically speaking, and playing that sort of roulette, was very attractive to me."

Sugarman was a fourteen-year-old runaway from an affluent Beverly Hills family when he came to work in the Doors office in West Hollywood. Morrison would become his mentor, and Sugarman would become Morrison's first biographer—as well as a heroin addict. After Morrison's death, Pamela Courson confided in Sugarman that Morrison had been using her heroin. Pamela herself would be dead of an overdose within a few years, and Sugarman would spend the next decade wrestling with his addiction. The book that he would write about his journey and finish in rehab, *Wonderland Avenue: Tales of Glamour and Excess,* is a kind of drug addict's coming-of-age version of *Catcher in the Rye.*

"I wanted to tell a story about addiction and rock and roll. I was part of that culture that began with the discovery that music really sounds great when you smoke pot. Then it was, Man, you should hear them on acid!—it's transcendent. It went from that to me trading all my records to buy heroin. The drug worked as a painkiller for many reasons, but I think it was also the story of a lot of our generation, going from drugs that were about opening up and bonding and trusting, about being sensitive and aware, to consciousness-reducing drugs that made you more selfish and closed down."

As Sugarman pointed out, even though Hendrix, Joplin, and Morrison had died, most people hadn't yet known anyone personally who had gotten really fucked up on drugs—"and if they did, the prevailing attitude was—well, they just couldn't handle it. There was a stigma of shame attached to it. Addiction had not yet been defined; the culture had yet to learn those lessons. Me, I lost a whole decade, from the ages of twenty to thirty—gone!—twelve detoxes in those ten years. Blew over two million dollars. When I finally got sober, I was reading Alice Miller, where she was talking about how when adolescents are left by an adult that means a lot to them, they'll incorporate negative aspects of their behavior as a way to punish that adult for leaving. It made perfect sense to me because I knew that in some way what I was doing was keeping Jim alive."

Like the bebop generation before them, the groups and storied artists of the psychedelic era would encompass journeys through the landscape of drugs of every conceivable variety. Of course, what transpired in the community of artists was only replicated on a generation-wide scale—the Deaths of the Icons were merely the most public symbols of the attrition. In the twenty-fifth anniversary edition of *Woodstock,* a section was added to the end of the film to commemorate all those who had passed. The names of Hendrix, Joplin, Morrison, Jerry Garcia, Pigpen, Bob "the Bear" Hite, Tim Hardin, Tim Buckley, Keith Moon—spectacularly gifted individuals who had epitomized the age and died of overdose, flamed out like supernovas, or had been just plain worn out by abuse— were mixed in with the Kennedys, Martin Luther King, and a list of the great causes of the time, all of it scrolling to the song by Crosby, Stills, Nash, and Young—

*Find the cost of freedom, buried in the ground*

## X. The Place Where the Wave Finally Broke
and Rolled Back

"THERE WOULDN'T have been the Sixties without the drugs, at least not the Sixties that we knew," declared Tom Robbins. "There have been so many revisionist histories of that time that talk about the politics and the music but that don't mention the drugs. That music would not have existed without the drugs; the politics wouldn't have existed on that scale without the drugs."

From the publication of *Another Roadside Attraction*, in 1971, in which the mummified body of Jesus Christ turns up at a roadside zoo, Robbins's novels have been embraced by readers as beloved countercultural fables that entertainingly mixed mysticism, whimsy, eroticism, art, politics, romanticism, and humor. "It would have been impossible for me to write as I had without acid, just as it would have been impossible for Hendrix to play as he did—and it wasn't just the riffs; it was the tone, the feedback, the lyrics, the whole palette and package."

By the end of the decade, millions of people had taken LSD like novitiates declaring for some new holy order—and Timothy Leary would be blamed as if he were single-handedly responsible for the creation of a drug culture in America. By 1969, Leary seemed to be everywhere, an elegant psychedelic Brahman prince, with his perpetual Marshall McLuhan smile (detractors like Art Linkletter liked to call him "a grinning caricature of a human being"). That year he got the bright idea of running for governor of California. "We're going to turn on all of California!" he exclaimed grandly, envisioning himself as a psychedelic Harry Truman holding enormous whistlestop campaign rallies featuring the greatest rock bands. One week before filing, he was in prison without bail. When his legal appeal reached the U.S. Supreme Court in May of 1969, the law under which he had been arrested in Texas was ruled unconstitutional. But was subsequently arrested, tried, convicted, and sentenced to ten years in Orange County for two marijuana roaches found in his car. Then federal authorities decided to retry him for his Laredo arrest on another technicality: the result was ten more years, both sentences set consecutively, bail denied. With his eleven Millbrook counts still looming and as the most visible symbol of a general government crackdown on the whole psychedelic culture and radical movement—which included Owsley, the acid manufacturing and distributing network called the Brotherhood of Eternal Love, white radicals like John Sinclair, and the Black Panthers—the High Priest's prospects did not seem good.

Anyone who thinks that a novelist could invent a better thriller than Leary's life need only consider his escape from the California Men's Colony at San Luis Obispo on September 12, 1970, after serving seven months. In an operation aided and abetted by the Weather Underground and financed by the Brotherhood of Eternal Love, Leary shimmied athletically across a wire cable twenty feet high that stretched forty precarious feet from a pole in the prison over a fence to freedom. His escape precipitated one of the greatest manhunts in American history. After a brief and unhappy alliance with the fugitive Eldridge Cleaver in Algeria, Leary sought political asylum in Switzerland and was finally cornered in Kabul. Dragged back to the United States in handcuffs, he was thrown into IV-A in Folsom Prison—"the dread max-max"—celled between Geronimo, the fiercest militant Black Panther in the prison, and a "small man sitting on the floor in lotus position, reading a Bible, smiling benevolently."

"So you finally made it," said Charles Manson. "I've been watching you fall for years, man. I knew you'd end up here!"

The original scholar-politician-philosopher of the first psychedelic movement in American history had landed right next to its greatest nightmare.

The other man who had sat in Timothy Leary's kitchen in November of 1960, weaving the dream that psychedelic drugs could help turn the world into a "universal cosmic network of switched on interconnected minds and exultant souls all spreading peace and love" was living on a farm in Cherry Valley, New York. Ten years later, Allen Ginsberg's prestige and influence were at their peak. The fact that Ginsberg had managed to avoid arrest for possession and use of drugs (despite earlier attempts at entrapment by police and FBI) left him free to pursue travel, writing, activism, and teaching. His use of drugs had become quite moderate compared with the level of his engagement in drug issues. At lectures at Kent State, Wisconsin State, and other universities, the poet now had the opportunity to speak directly to teachers and students about the role that drugs had played in his own life and in the development of his poetics and politics, as well as the lives and literature of the Beat Generation. "All of this would have been unthinkable ten years earlier," he noted. As Ginsberg told his poetry class at Kent State, drugs were just another part of the Vision Quest—"as with American Indians, fasting, going into lonely places, seeking nature-spirit—physically removing yourself from the civilization and going up on a mountain, or into the desert, mountain climbing. Dropping acid or mushrooms or peyote or psilocybin in the company of wise men or Mother Nature. Doing yogas of different kinds, whether chanting or meditating or cross legged sitting."

Allen Ginsberg's journey into visionary and mystical experience was taking him deep into Buddhist study and practice under the guidance of Rinpoche Chogyam Trungpa Tulku. All of it was part of the same spiritual circuit. It was a point of view he would steadfastly maintain for the rest of his life.

Richard Alpert's disillusionment at the realization that acid would not bring lasting enlightenment of any kind had not prevented him from taking along a supply of Owsley's best when he had left for India in the spring of 1967, though in his deepening despair he was not about to take any of it. When Alpert met the man who would become his guru in the foothills of the Himalayas, Neem Karoli Baba, he gave Maharaj-ji, as he was called, fifteen hundred micrograms of LSD, five times the normal dosage. The guru told him that these substances were known in the Kulu Valley long ago, "but all that knowledge is lost now. Then he said, 'It's useful, it's useful, not the true *samadhi*, but it's useful.' " In other words, not the true oneness of mind, not the real, undistracted union of subject and object sought in meditation practice. But if you were "quiet and you're feeling much peace of mind and your mind is turned toward God," he said, "it's useful," but you can't stay there. It allows the visit— the *darshan*—of a higher being, of higher consciousness, but "it would be better to become the saint than to go and have the visit."

"From then on, I took acid about every two years to see what I had forgotten and whether there was still stuff I should learn from it," Ram Dass related. "I'd take it at the ocean, in Bali, in places all over the world, and I kept learning from it, but it became less and less interesting to me.

I realized I knew how to get high, but the game wasn't to get *high,* it was to be *free*—and high wasn't the same as free."

In his transformation into Ram Dass, yoga was only one of the paths to this freedom. There was meditation. And service. By 1971, he'd become one of the foremost spiritual guides and teachers bridging the gap between Western culture and Eastern religion. At the dawn of the new decade, a whole new *sadhana* was rising in the West—a new spiritual way, work, exercise—"another set of cognitive consciousness possibilities," as Ram Dass called it.

Dawn Reynolds became a New Age seeker sometime after the death of Jimi Hendrix. "Something happened to me after Hendrix died," she explained. "I had this little boy now, and I knew somewhere inside of me that I had to change my life, but Hendrix dying was like the symbol for me that whatever started at Monterey when I saw him was now really and truly over. I'd been through the Haight Ashbury and communes, and I just didn't know where to go and what to do, and then I went to a lecture and heard Ram Dass speak, and I realized why I didn't know where to go and what to do. It was because I didn't really know who I was."

After the Summer of Love, Dawn had wandered from scene to scene, drug to drug, man to man, up and down the California coast. Like so many who would join the loose amalgamation called the Human Potential Movement, she found her way to Esalen and took a workshop with William Schutz—and it was there, in the hot sulfur baths overlooking the sea, that she found her own path. "The path was within, and the subject was *me.*"

By 1970, Esalen was recognized as the navel of a whole new movement and lifestyle. Through psychedelic drugs, masses of people had reached some experience or awareness of multidimensional "inner space." LSD was "the direct blow to the solar plexus that woke us up," as Esalen founder Michael Murphy defined it. More and more people were becoming interested in meditation, sensory awareness, expansion of the powers and energies of the mind, body, and spirit. Not only artists and bohemians who were burned out on drugs and searching for something else but middle-class teachers, psychologists, journalists, and businessmen who had taken LSD and smoked grass suddenly found themselves shifting directions in their lives.

"Who came? Everyone from housewives to bricklayers," said Dawn. "Just an amazingly wide range of people interested in seeing who they were and how they could enjoy life more and be more fully present. Some of us were products of experiments in social living, such as communes and new tribal and extended families. There were also activists who had worked so hard for civil rights and world peace and were now looking for inner peace."

For Dawn, it was about learning how to blow the mind without drugs. Immersed in Zen, Vedantism, macrobiotic vegetarianism, reflexology, shiatsu, vitamin therapy, and yoga, she started finding some of the very things she had looked for in acid. "I became a total groupie to self-growth and spirituality."

In the coming years, many epithets would attempt to sum up the substance and cultural ramifications of the Human Potential Movement—Tom Wolfe's "Me Decade," Robert Greenfield's "The Spiritual Supermarket," and Paul Krassner's "The Encounter Culture," to name a few of the more resonant ones. The phenomenon embraced dimensions as varied as biofeedback, est, tantric sex, Sufism, theosophy, flying-saucer cults, Wicca, and the new quantum physics, eventually morphing into still another cultural appellation known as New Age. The psychedelic revolution of the 1960s had catalyzed a profusion of alternative mind styles and spiritual paths that, while having little to do with the use of drugs, would nonetheless alter the cultural landscape in ways that were wholly consistent with the original aims of the psychedelic culture.

Some members of the psychedelic culture turned inward, but others joined the exodus to the country that became known as the back-to-the-land movement. "It was the next logical step in the evolution," observed Allen Cohen. "There was this sense that came out of the psychedelic experience that nature was the great healer for overcrowding and all the other urban problems. Every time you saw a flower when you were high and became one with it, one's inner being identified with nature, so the next phase was to go back to the land. It was like the start of a new pilgrimage, and we were the seedpods."

The Diggers were a perfect example of this new pilgrimage, evolving first into the Free City Collective and then the Free Family. Peter Coyote moved to a three-hundred-acre communal ranch in Olema, at the inland end of Tomales Bay. Exhausted by the sheer intensity of years spent living on the edge, disillusioned by the compromise and repression they encountered while trying to live up to their highest revolutionary ideals, some of the most dynamic members of the group fell headlong into heroin addiction. "Emmett stuck me with a needle twice," Coyote remembered. "The first time, he pierced my ear. 'It'll change ya,' he said . . . The second time was in the living room of a famous Hollywood movie star. This time the needle was a syringe, loaded with heroin. 'It'll change ya,' Emmett said, and it did. It changed a lot." It would take years and a near-fatal bout with hepatitis before Coyote left the China White and Mexican Salt-and-Pepper heroin behind. "At a certain point, I was just not going to die a junkie. And even when I was shooting a lot of dope, I would practice little deceptions to ensure that. I would shoot up in the hands to save the veins on my arms to not collapse them and get terrible tracks, or I would go on bouts of cleaning up and taking very good care of myself."

The man who gave Coyote his first shot would not be so lucky, however. After years of legendary status as an "icon of freedom" courted by rock stars and gang leaders alike, Emmett Grogan would be found dead of an overdose on a New York subway train in 1978. "Emmett got trapped in being Emmett, and the times made a hard shift to the right," Coyote observed. "His persona was no longer appropriate. Get real. Get healthy. Take on the world. We didn't need an underground Robin Hood anymore, and Emmett had invested so heavily that he couldn't get out of it."

These cautionary tales would become obvious only in hindsight. "The failure to curb personal indulgence was a major collective error," Coyote concluded in his incisive memoir, *Sleeping Where I Fall*. "Our journeys down the path along which Verlaine and Rimbaud disordered their senses wasted young lives and often sabotaged what we labored so diligently to construct." At the same time, Coyote recognized that the reckless quest for freedom as represented by people like Grogan was both valid and powerful. "Emmett was a guidon, the emblem carried into battle behind which people rallied their imaginations. He proved with his existence that each of us could act out the life of our highest fantasies."

Peter Berg and Judy Goldhaft began channeling their energy and commitment into environmentalism. The foundation they created,

Planet Drum, became a cutting-edge forum for bioregionalism. "It was no accident that many people in this generation of ecologists were evolving out of the psychedelic culture," Berg maintained. "There was an element of naturism in the Sixties that's hugely ignored and it also involved things like natural childbirth, organic food. From the first time some hippie took some acid on a beautiful day and lay down on his back in Golden Gate Park and, you know, really *got it*—that all of it was alive and that we had a responsibility to preserve it—the ecological movement began to grow in the United States."

Freeman House would also become a committed ecologist. When he moved to Petrolia, California, he dedicated himself to the restoration of wild salmon, work would lead him into the heated politics of the Mattole River watershed as he tried to find common ground among the local ranchers, loggers, and hippies. Freeman found that he could support himself in the work and modestly take care of his family by growing a few marijuana plants on his land. "At the time, very few people were growing marijuana. That would come a few years later and became a big thing because some genius horticulturist kept crossing and crossing strains of marijuana and came up with this fantastic strain called sensimilla."

One of the primary "genius horticulturists" of this nascent culture of marijuana growers was none other than Carolyn "Mountain Girl" Adams Garcia, by that time married to Jerry Garcia of the Grateful Dead. "I started growing great weed when nobody was doing it, right here in my backyard in Marin County, California. We had a wonderful backyard, secluded, with a lot of rosebushes and shrubbery. So I had a secure situation in my backyard where I could really observe the plants and learn from it. Of course, the trick was getting people to keep their hands off the plants long enough to see what the flowers and the seeds looked like."

By 1970, an amazing profusion of different strains of weed was available. "Pot was coming in from Mexico, then Jamaica, Colombia, Hawaii, a lot from Southeast Asia, this tropical weed that was amazingly strong. The Jefferson Airplane had this stuff they called ice bag, which was like being hit over the head with a stick, whereas our thing was Michoacán, from Oaxaca. The first kind I tried to grow was Vietnamese. The first couple of plants I grew were so strong you couldn't smoke it. Two hits and you would turn into the marble Buddha—gone! I had to give it away." By the third year, she found herself with ten pounds, but then people began to rip her off. "You'd come home and half of the plants would be gone. When I realized that there was a potential for unhappiness there, I quit doing it and concentrated on writing a book about how to grow sensimilla."

The book, *Primo Plant,* was the first commercial handbook for home marijuana cultivation written by a woman. "A lot of people who became serious growers started with my book—that's what I meant it to be. By that time, I had a whole circle of friends who were doing it, and I'd go observe the plants in their gardens, this whole group of women growers who started in Mendocino. Before that, it was places like La Jolla that was turning out killer weed, and Santa Barbara would come up with amazing stuff, and wonderful stuff from the Sierras."

The 1970s would become known as the Golden Age of Marijuana, due in no small part to this single garden in Marin County and the love of this one woman for the plant and its culture. But as much as Mountain Girl believed in cannabis as a benign substance with great commercial, spiritual, and medicinal potential, the other drugs that would define the new decade would disquiet and alienate her.

"My whole approach to drugs had been for them to enhance your perception or your feeling of the joy of life, and now they were beginning to change. By 1971, you started to see a lot more cocaine around and Quaaludes. These were mystery drugs to me. I snorted cocaine when it first came around, and it gave me a cold. I'd do a line of coke and listen to music, and all I could hear were mistakes and mediocrity. That was the kicker. Cocaine was nothing, just a bunch of bullshit. It wasn't my thing at all. Unfortunately, it became the thing for everybody else I knew. People were suddenly slipping off to the bathroom. Where's so and so? In the bathroom. But *why?* I isolated myself from the whole Grateful Dead scene at that point because I couldn't stand it. I was very lonely for a number of years. It was the end of that wonderful community of spirit where we shared everything."

There were clear forecasts of the cocaine culture before the Sixties were over. Paul Rothchild saw the implications of the drug very quickly—but his observations would never prevent him from using it. "With pot and psychedelics, it was a society of inclusion—*hey, man, have a hit.* By the late Sixties, one was hard-pressed to find someone who wasn't a dope smoker, even in the sacred antidrug bastions of Texas and the Midwest, and through the pop aristocracy it had crossed all lines—music, film, dance, painting. Cocaine was still the hidden, secret thing, and it was a society of exclusion—*hey, man, let's go to the bathroom, but don't tell anyone.* All of sudden you're cutting off your friends. So what began to happen—rather than drugs drawing people together in this sanctum sanctorum, the drug started blowing them apart, isolating them, and it was because of the nature of the drug itself. One consciousness brought about sharing; the other brought about greed." Rothchild would insist that the seeds of the Greed Decade, which would peak in the Eighties, were firmly planted in the germinal cocaine culture of the early Seventies. "I knew all was lost when I saw what used to be the artists' world of drugs and creative exchange in the hands of lawyers and accountants, and when I saw the lawyers doing blow, I knew that an era had truly ended."

"Most of the San Francisco bands sailed headlong into cocaine," noted Charlie Perry. "You'd walk in, and there would be a little bowl of it next to every chair. There was no longer that feeling during the psychedelic days of the rapport of seeing Janis on the street or of sharing a joint with Jerry Garcia in somebody's bedroom at a party. Rock and roll was becoming a big business. It was the time of big recording contracts and international tours. The Rolling Stones kind of pioneered it in their innocence and arrogance, but for the bands that came after them, cocaine and arrogance were spiritual equivalents."

After Perry had become managing editor of the fledgling *Rolling Stone*, he found himself with less and less time to get high as he was consumed with the effort and responsibility of getting the magazine out. "I concluded at that point that the psychedelic revolution hadn't panned out and that cocaine was just high-powered self-indulgence for those who could afford it. I liked cocaine, which is why I stopped taking it. I realized that if I took cocaine, I wasn't going to think about anything else for the rest of the night except getting more, and I couldn't afford it." Perry wryly acknowledged that perhaps if Jann Wenner, the founder and editor of the magazine, had paid his staff more, "it would have been more of a problem."

For Perry and others, the event that marked the passing of the psyche-delic era as they had known it was *Rolling Stone*'s publication of Hunter S. Thompson's gonzo epic *Fear and Loathing in Las Vegas: A Savage Journey to the Heart of the American Dream,* in November of 1971.

"It knocked us out!—the comic violence and extremism, the lan-guage and humor, and the words just dragged you on. Ben Fong-Torres said it best: for a couple of days after reading it, your life was incredibly dramatic, and you never knew what was going to happen; you expected wolverines to come leaping out at you from alleys!"

In Hunter Thompson's view, the orgy of violence at Altamont merely dramatized a reality that already existed: LSD and high psychedelic ideal-ism had gone out with LBJ; now it was all about getting "stoned, ripped, twisted." From the first infamous sentence—"We were somewhere around Barstow on the edge of the desert when the drugs began to take hold"—the author gobbles psychedelics along with everything else. The itemized list of Thompson's drug consumption in the book is no mere stash—it represents an arsenal, the pharmacological equivalent of nitro-glycerin.

"We had two bags of grass, seventy-five pellets of mescaline, five sheets of high-powered blotter acid, a salt shaker half-full of cocaine, and a whole array of multicolored uppers, downers, screamers, laughers . . . also a quart of tequila, a quart of rum, a case of Budweiser, a pint of raw ether, and two dozen amyls. But the only thing that worried me was the ether. There is nothing in the world more helpless and irresponsible than a man in the depths of an ether binge."

When the piece appeared, readers wrote to the magazine, asking if Hunter Thompson had really taken all those drugs and declaring that not only did they want to *live* like him, they wanted to *be* him. Thompson had intended the piece as "a weird celebration for an era that I thought was ending. . . . I kind of assumed that this was sort of a last fling; that Nixon and Mitchell and all those people would make it very soon impos-sible for anybody to behave that way and get away with it." But it was only the beginning of his myth as gonzo maniac. As Perry put it, "It sounded the death knell for the whole self-conscious, pious Timothy Leary approach to psychedelics, of sitting on a Persian rug and listening to Indian music. There was nothing about taking LSD and seeing God here; it was a matter of survival, dealing with madness, about how some-times you took drugs and you were hopeless, dangerously fucked up—the dark side of psychedelics that people did not want to talk about."

Yet there would always be a bittersweet nostalgia. Thompson marked the passing of the psychedelic era most powerfully in *Fear and Loathing in Las Vegas* when he reflected on what San Francisco had been like in the mid-1960s, when it seemed the energy of the whole generation had come to a head and he was "absolutely certain that no matter which way I went I would come to a place where people were just as high and wild as I was." Beyond even the drugs was "the fantastic universal sense that whatever we were doing was right, that we were winning . . . we were riding the crest of a high beautiful wave. . . .

"So now, less than five years later, you can go up on a steep hill in Las Vegas and look West, and with the right kind of eyes you can almost see the high water mark—that place where the wave finally broke and rolled back."

# 8

# The Golden Age of Marijuana

**❝**Feds estimate they get probably 10% of incoming pot, and they're probably right . . . monster loads that are busted are tip of the iceberg . . . pot so widespread now that enforcement nearly impossible. . . . National Guard was reportedly called in to guard the 25–30 tons busted at Christmastime in Florida, and they reportedly used a Ringling Bros. tent to house it. They burned it as quick as possible to avoid a commando heist that was rumored.**❞**

> — "Flashes," column in the premiere issue of
> *High Times*, Summer 1974

## I. Marijuana as Far as the Eye Can See

GEOFF DUBOIS loved it best when he was squatting in a squalid hut outside Negril before the deal went down and some heavy Rastaman would recite the prayer before lighting the herb.

"Glory be to the Father and to the maker of creation! As it was in the beginning is now and ever shall be! World without end! Jah Rastafari! Eternal God Selassie I!"

Then they would get completely wrecked on the biggest spliffs he'd ever seen, and the higher they got, the more everything would vibrate, and the easier it would become to understand the patois, until they were hanging on every word. The Rasta rap was always the same: ganja was holy herb, wisdom weed, the burning bush of the Bible, the very key to the new understanding of the self, the universe, and God. Man *was* God, but this truth could only come from the use of the herb. To use the herb was to experience yourself *as* God and to have freedom from the culture and laws of BABYLON, which had so brainwashed the people that it was only through smoking the herb that the truth and the true Black Consciousness could be revealed: Haile Selassie was God, and Ethiopia was the true home of the Black People.

It was all hypnotizing enough when you were ripped on that tasty Jamaican Red, but if you didn't believe it, these Rasta dudes had plenty of quotes from the Bible to prove it: "Thou shalt eat the herb of the field" (Genesis 3:18), "Eat every herb of the land" (Exodus 10:12), "He causeth the grass to grow for the cattle, and herb for the service of man" (Psalms 104:14). Of course, the vernacular took some getting used to. *Overstanding* was "understanding," *irie* was something positive, *livication* was used instead of "dedication," and they said *downpression* instead of "oppression"; but the sermons were spellbinding, and the fact that such spirituality was being preached by dreadlocked men with guns in their waistbands who had grown up in Trenchtown and were prepared for just about anything made it all the more compelling. These big Rasta growers were also very close with the reggae musicians, and when Bob Marley and Peter Tosh and Bunny Wailer would come around to smoke some herb, you could feel how powerful it was all becoming. Reggae was beginning to move beyond the fetid back streets of Kingston and go global. Could there have been reggae without marijuana? Impossible! Could there have been reggae without the Rastafari? Also impossible! Rasta *was* reggae, and reggae meant ganja, and the red dope of Jamaica was at the center of a power struggle that would pit the Rastafarians against the police of the government of Michael Manley, the U.S. Justice Department's recently formed Drug Enforcement Administration, and the U.S. State Department's Operation Buccaneer.

There was big trouble in Babylon, but it hadn't started that way. Prime Minister Manley had abolished prison terms for possession of ganja when he first came to power in 1972, but quickly changed his tune when American smugglers began trading U.S.-made weapons for the Jamaican-grown weed. The charismatic socialist had then decided to stabilize the situation by disarming the Jamaican populace, making a deal with the DEA to shut down the ganja trade by attacking everybody, from the farmers in the hills to the dealers in the towns, from the smugglers on the sea to the dope pilots. *Investigation. Interdiction. Eradication.* American technicians set up the first DEA radar station ever on foreign soil, which covered the island like a net and reached far out to sea in every direction. Yachts and sailboats loaded to the gunwales with dope were seized, and giant caches of grass were uncovered in the Trenchtown slums; shootouts erupted between dealers and police. Manley's anticrime, antigun, antidope agenda in the Jamaican parliament was turning the island into a third-world police state, and to the Rastafari there was nothing more Babylonian than that. It was obvious to the Rastafari that indigenous ganja was *good* for the economy and good medicine for the people, and what was happening on the island seemed to them very much like the story of the persecution of the Jews in the time of Pharaoh. The Babylonians were after the Rastafari for the very straws they were using to make their bricks, and the bricks were being made out of holy herb in the beautiful marijuana fields, where there was peace. All you had to do was walk in the fields to recognize this truth—the plants felt *alive,* like a benign intelligence animating the space with energy and goodness, the atmosphere was *charged* with it—

*Legalize it, mon!*

That's what Marley was saying in his songs, but if ganja were ever legalized, then, presumably, there would no longer be much need for smuggling rings like the one Geoff DuBois was a part of, which took advantage of 150 miles of bays and remote beaches, secret docking sites and sneaky little airstrips, to smuggle out the high-quality weed in thousand-pound loads. DuBois was mainly a courier, but he was part of the inner circle, which consisted of boyhood friends from Long Island operating out of Coconut Grove, who drove Ferraris and had huge houses in Putnam County and sprawling apartments in Manhattan, with lots of expensive art on the walls.

"These guys were bringing in tons and raking in millions," DuBois confided. "Basically they were nouveau riche Jewish kids, very neurotic and insecure and insatiable, and if they hadn't attained what they did, they would have been nebbishes, but they had taste and were very smart and clever. They had a ride that lasted about seven or eight solid years, nonstop. God only know how much they brought in over that time!"

Dubois was no smuggler by nature; he was a glamour boy, a sometime male model, bartender, and pool hustler whose girlfriend happened to be one of the top five models in the world at the time. His career with the smugglers began as a driver. The basic routine was "drive to Florida, rent cars, fill up the trunks. You could carry four hundred pounds that way. The biggest available rental car was a Ford LTD—the biggest trunk in the automobile industry at the time—and then it became twenty-six-foot Winnebagos filled to the rafters. Every run I got five thousand dollars. I should have been scared to death, driving it up the coast—we were suspicious-looking characters!—but it was such an elitist feeling, very much about being the hipster outlaw, getting over on the system, and the trappings were always great: the best hotels and restaurants, expense accounts, hookers every night—and Miami had the most beautiful in the world—Dom Pérignon, always an eight ball of cocaine and a big bag of Quaaludes, a lot of flash money to buy huge gold Presidential Rolex watches and handmade Lucchese lizard boots. It was the Seventies high life, and all of it was very addictive, not just the drugs."

Part of the job was dealing with the money. DuBois maintained nine bank accounts in New York. "Days would go by when I would do nothing but drive in the back of a limousine with a huge briefcase of money and go to every single bank account and at each one change five hundred dollars for hundred-dollar bills—if you did more than that, you had to fill out a form—and by the end of the day, I would have changed thirty thousand dollars into hundred-dollar bills. Once I sat in the Presidential Suite of the St. Moritz Hotel and did nothing but count money for three days . . . One deal netted seven million! We were in there with Uzis in case anyone tried to take us off, but the comical thing was that none of us were bad enough to ever use them. These guys were not hardened criminals in any way, shape, or form."

Even though New York was now awash in cocaine, the gang of smugglers DuBois worked for wanted no part of the rapidly increasing coke trade. "Cocaine was bad voodoo, and they wouldn't have anything to do with it even though by that time I knew pilots who had started flying into Cartagena. They used it recreationally but felt the elements they had to deal with were too dangerous, but they also felt that if they were caught, the public and the law would perceive the crime as something much uglier and serious, and they didn't want to be associated with that."

No, the risk of cocaine made absolutely no sense for them, particularly as they were already bringing marijuana into the country by plane- and boatload. The organization rented an eight-hundred-acre farm in South Carolina for its airdrops. Pickup trucks would be waiting with their lights on at the prescribed hour to illuminate the drop zone, and the giant bales would float down out of the night sky and be trucked north, where the organization had set up its distribution points around Woodstock, New York. Guys would mysteriously show up at appointed times to pack their trunks with four-hundred-pound loads and sell them all across the Northeast.

"One Christmas we did nothing but clean pot in one of these warehouses around the clock. They had a giant mound of cocaine to keep us working. We wore masks to protect us from the incredibly strong pollen dust as we broke it down and beat it and mixed it with other pot and shook it down over these giant screens. I have a photo of me lying there with my mask on, in that warehouse, which looked like one of the giant tobacco barns operated by the R.J. Reynolds Tobacco Company or something. Marijuana as far as the eye can see!"

Dubois left the organization after one of the principals was murdered by a childhood friend who went into a jealous rage over how much money he was making. By that time, the organization had moved out to California. "They were doing those big deals of Thai sticks coming into the West Coast during the mid- to late Seventies. Everything came in through San Pedro, San Francisco, and up into Washington. They'd tell me about these big tankers—'You wanna do some offloading?' "

The calls ended in 1977, when the DEA moved on the operation, though the Feds would never catch up with the three surviving masterminds. "They got out of the country and took a lot of their money with them, so they're having a very pleasant exile. Everything was all planned and all downsides taken into account, with a whole battery of legal experts, who had plan A, B, C, and D all ready. That's why they were able to get away—and believe me, there was a real effort to get them."

Before long DuBois's own run with drugs took a hard turn, when he developed a dangerous taste for the top-grade Persian heroin being sold by his next-door neighbor. One night in his New York apartment, he stuck a needle into his arm, and no sooner had he begun jacking the drug into his bloodstream than his legs caved under him and his head went smashing down onto the scalding radiator next to the window where he'd been fixing. It remained there until someone found him and rushed him to the hospital—quickly enough to save his life, but not before burning a deep gash in the side of his head. The scar on his head was one of Dubois's mementos from those years; the photo of him in that Woodstock warehouse was another. It was exactly the kind of photograph that would have appeared in the glossy pages of *High Times*.

## II. We Support America One Hundred Percent, Especially South America

GLENN O'BRIEN just couldn't get good pot when he moved to Chicago to work for *Oui*. He made good money that year, but the extent of his ingestion of substances mostly consisted of hanging out in O'Rourke's every night, getting a little beer belly from all the Guinness. When he came back to New York and became the articles editor of *High Times* in June of 1976, however, the marijuana situation changed dramatically. "I would get pot in the mail from readers all over the world! The best I ever had was sent to me from a guy in the air force in Thailand."

O'Brien arrived at *High Times* with an extensive pharmacological résumé that went all the way back to the paregoric-soaked cigarettes he had dried under a lamp and smoked when he was a teenager in Cleveland— exactly like Gnossos Pappadopoulis, the hero of Richard Fariña's novel, *Been Down So Long It Looks Like Up to Me*. Even though he went to St. Ignatius, an all-boy Jesuit high school, O'Brien knew about Dexamyl and marijuana and jazz and how Robert Mitchum and Gene Krupa had been busted for pot. Along with music, poetry and literature had been the stepping-stones to his drug experimentation—"A lot of kids my age interested in drugs were reading the same books; Rimbaud would lead to Lautreamont and Gérard de Nerval—the Required Reading List, the same shit that Patti Smith and Richard Hell were reading"—but it wasn't until he saw the Velvet Underground play a little club called La Cave that he became intrigued by opiates. "It was so alien but I dug it and went out to get the album that had 'Heroin' and 'Waiting for the Man' on it, and that, plus reading Burroughs, was the beginning of my thinking about heroin . . . It was the first time it was ever dealt with in rock music, and it was ritualistic, the way the Velvets wrote and sang about dope. It really made you want to try it."

It would take him a while to try heroin, until well after he graduated from Georgetown University. O'Brien was a psychedelic hippie during his college years, tripping in Dumbarton Oaks and seeing every band that came through the city at the Ambassador Theater. He had done it all, in fact—gone to Nixon's inauguration on acid and been chased through the teargassed streets by helicopters, gone to Woodstock and skinny-dipped, taken his GREs on acid and "finished a half hour early and scored tremendously well. I wanted to be a writer." Within a month after moving to New York in 1970, he was working for Andy Warhol at the Factory as an editor of the fledgling *Interview* when an unknown singer from England named David Bowie showed up one day to sing a song he had written for Andy, titled, aptly enough, "Andy Warhol." By the time O'Brien left *Interview,* moved to Chicago, and returned to New York, he had lived through every phase of the drug culture and knew as much about dope as anybody in New York.

With a circulation that had jumped from twenty-five thousand to three hundred thousand in its first two years and was rapidly on its way to four million, *High Times* was one of the fastest-growing mass-market publications in the nation, which was hardly surprising considering the twenty-five to thirty million people avidly smoking marijuana in America. In addition to its phenomenal rate of growth, it was undoubtedly the most unusual publication of its time. How many magazines had a publisher who was also an avowed marijuana smuggler? How many employed a staff photographer at sixteen thousand dollars a year plus "all the dope you could smoke, snort or swallow"? Steve Cropper's mission was to photograph the best "merchandise" in the world—"Colombian Cheeba Cheeba, pot that got you so high you felt lonely; specially prepared hash (made with only the first plant rubbings) from the heart of the Bekáa Valley; uncut Peruvian cocaine labbed into rocks the size of canned hams"—

for stunning *Playboy*-like color gatefolds. And how many had backup re-
ceptionists in case the other was too stoned to deal with the job? Such was
the working environment that O'Brien encountered, but it was also
being stirred to maximum turbulence by the magazine's brilliant but
mercurial founder and publisher, Tom Forcade. "I didn't meet Tom until
after I'd been hired. I found him fascinating. He was always the kind of
person who would push you, test you, play with you—very charismatic,
interesting conversationalist, and cultivated an air of mystery because
you knew he was involved in smuggling but never to what level or degree.
But he also wanted you to think that maybe he was some kind of spy. It
was strange; you could never quite pin it down."

Thomas King Forcade, the Hugh Hefner of Dope, who launched the
magazine with twelve thousand dollars from friends and a drug deal, was a
character every bit as singular and emblematic of the drug culture of the
1970s as Augustus Stanley Owsley had been in the 1960s. Born Thomas
Gary Goodson in Phoenix, he was the bright, creative, and unbridled son
of a politically conservative retired officer in the U.S. Army Corps of Engi-
neers who had started his own construction business in Arizona. Forcade
adopted his name (actually that of his maternal grandfather but also an
obvious play on the word *facade*) to spare his family embarrassment. He
was discharged from the air force after convincing his superiors that he
was mentally unbalanced and started *Orpheus,* a radical literary magazine
that he operated out of an old school bus. By that time, he had flown small
planes from Mexico that were filled to the ceiling with grass. In 1969, he
moved to New York and founded the Alternative Press Syndicate, which
provided material for several hundred underground newspapers across the
country. Forcade quickly became embroiled in the spiteful intraparty
feuding that was pulling the Yippies apart, denouncing Abbie Hoffman
and Jerry Rubin as old-hat "sellouts" and "dinosaurs" (Rubin was convinced that Forcade was a police agent). Forcade threw a custard pie in the
face of a congressman while testifying before a congressional commission
on pornography and became the leader of a breakaway faction called the
Zippies ("Put the Zip back into Yip"), which became infamous for their
guerrilla theater and media shock tactics. "The 'movement' was over and I
needed something to keep from killing myself out of boredom," Forcade
later recalled. "And so, aided by many tanks of nitrous oxide, I came up

with *High Times.* . . . It's an all-American magazine with a section on world news. We support America 100 percent, especially South America."

Forcade also considered himself a "social architect," with a vision for his publication as "the Most Dangerous Magazine in America." "It was to be *Playboy's* sexual materialism lampooned in terms of dope materialism," recalled Dean Lattimer, who spent eight years at the magazine. "Pornographic studies of red Leb slabs shot through Vaseline-smeared lenses, dead-serious consumer pieces on state-of-the-art smuggling craft and high-tech head gear. . . . We take the flimsiest muck on the planet—the dope trade—and just glossy it up to hell and gone with super pro printing and page design, and rub Mr. and Mrs. Silent Majority's nose in it. And who knows? Once they get a couple of snorts, they might turn out to *like* it."

From the premiere issue in the summer of 1974, with its cover of a beautiful girl in a white hat holding up a phallic psilocybin mushroom as though she's about to perform fellatio on it, the magazine was a sensation. In fact, no better documentary exists of the month-by-month unfolding of the Great Stoned Age. The Trans-High Market Quotations compiled from the reports of "stringers" around the world and disingenuously described as "intended solely for comparative purposes" and in no way meant as "an inducement to illegal activity, nor as an endorsement to any drug usage or trafficking," immediately became the drug dealer's Dow Jones and its most trusted price index. Each month's advertisements charted the growth and evolution of a billion-dollar paraphernalia industry designed to enhance the conspicuous consumption of a mass culture of illicit drugs by offering such items as Quaalude paperweights, hand-crafted sterling silver accessories for the high connoisseur (only the finest silver clips, silver blades, silver straws), high-tech narc detectors, solar joint lighters, Ohaus triple-beam scales ("No serious dealer should ever be caught without one!"), Rizla rolling machines, pong bongs, Toke-o-Matics, Dealer McDope board games, the very best prices on mannite for the enterprising dealer needing to cut his blow, snowblowers, and Toot-a-Vials.

The editorial content of the publication offered a smorgasbord of material, and it was here that Forcade most clearly understood the basis of his magazine's runaway success. "Dope was a world," observed Albert

Goldman, the former professor of literature at Columbia turned pop critic–biographer and marijuana afficionado. "There were millions of drug users, who had patterned themselves into a vast underground society that had its own myths and folklore, social etiquette and pecking order, songs and language, heroes and humor. There were scores of drugs, each with its special mystique. . . . There was a mountain of undigested botanical, chemical and medical information. There were great stretches of history demanding exploration, underground classics crying for publication and for a whole network of interconnections—between drugs and sex, drugs and health, drugs and religion—about which people were eager to learn.

"Most interesting of all, there was a labyrinthine underground of drug dealers and drug smugglers who journeyed to marvelously exotic places—to the Himalayan countries of Nepal, Bhutan, and Tibet; to the jungles of South America; to the Arab kingdoms of the Middle East; to the war zones of the Far East—to bring back drugs for America. The scams and stratagems of these colorful characters comprised an endless novel of crime, foreign intrigue and high adventure."

Nothing would romanticize smuggling and dealing more than the drug culture journalism of *High Times.* "Highwitness News" kept readers abreast of the latest breaking stories about drugs around the world; interviews detailed the proclivities of outspoken drug-taking celebrities like Hunter Thompson and Richard Pryor; experts like Drs. Michael Aldrich and Andrew Weil illuminated drug history and pharmacology; cultural observers like Goldman and Anthony Haden-Guest reported on the new drug scenes (even reporters from *The New York Times* contributed articles, under pseudonyms). With its rapid success, the magazine moved from a small basement on West 11th Street, with its "satisfying counterculture ambience of pot smoke and rubber cement," as Dean Lattimer recalled, to West Broadway and finally to East 27th Street, where its staff ballooned to a hundred people. As Forcade reminisced, "There were people with pills in one room, grass in another, coke in another room, nitrous in the next room, and so on down the hall."

Tom Forcade swiftly became a strange and shadowy icon of the drug culture. Lattimer depicted him as a "sinister, black-becloaked, slouch-hatted, Fu Manchued caricature of Lee Van Cleef out of a late 60s spaghetti western." Forcade maintained a Greenwich Village safe house called Bobby's as his headquarters that was filled to the ceiling with suitcases of pressed Colombian marijuana. Later he obtained a large loft space at 714 Broadway and turned it into a smoke-easy, where customers came and went like clockwork and never laid eyes on one another, choosing their merchandise from a festively designed menu card: "Thai Stick, $25 per ounce. Indian Hash, $10 a gram. Colombian Gold, $5 a bag, $50 an ounce." Forcade's dope epigrams were legion: "I never met a drug I didn't like," "There are two kinds of dealers: those who need forklifts, and those who don't" (he apparently did), "Most people have a marijuana deficiency," etc. Forcade believed marijuana to be a divine form of medicine, and contributed fifty thousand dollars a year to the National Organization for the Reform of Marijuana Laws (NORML), whose advertisements he ran from the first year of the magazine: "Enough people were arrested for marijuana in 1973 to empty the City of St. Paul, Minnesota. Don't you think it's time it stopped?" As O'Brien put it, "We all believed that the legalization of drugs in America was approaching, that certainly marijuana would be the first one—and that it was inevitable."

In addition to weed, Forcade was a prodigious drug taker, with a particular fondness for the stratospheric effects of nitrous oxide; he transported tanks of the stuff around with him and popped Quaaludes and downs like candy for his depression. He was creative, industrious, self-effacing, and charismatic, but also a megalomaniac and a classic manic-depressive riding the wild seesaw of extreme mood swings. Forcade was also a monumental paranoid who saw CIA and DEA and FBI plots and agents everywhere—including at his magazine, so that he would rage through the office, firing everyone. Sometimes he would just freak out and disappear for long periods of time. Said O'Brien, "Once after he left for a while Andy Kowl offered me the job as editor and I said, 'Andy, you couldn't pay me enough to be the editor of *High Times*,' but he offered me more money than I thought possible, so I took the job. I was so paranoid; there were a lot of things I hadn't been privy to, like where the money came from. I knew there must have been informants there, and I was very suspicious. I didn't know where the Trans-High Quotations came from either, and the relationships with certain advertisers were very suspect."

When O'Brien started going out with Gabrielle Schang, Forcade's beautiful ex-girlfriend and the object of his continuing obsession, their relationship got complicated. "We had all these games going on. Then Gabrielle ended up leaving me and marrying him. I liked Tom, but he scared me. The day before he died, I went over to his house, and Gabrielle was there with her friend . . . Tom was out cold, and I picked him up and put him on a bed. He was in this infantile state, unconscious but kind of smiling and giggling, and we dragged him to his bed and put him in it."

The next day, November 19, 1978, Tom Forcade was dead. He was thirty-three.

"How did he die? He shot himself in the head. He had tried to commit suicide several times. He always had guns—I remember seeing one in his refrigerator!—I used to think he was going to shoot me when I was going out with Gabrielle."

Many of those who knew Forcade surmised that it was the experience of watching the death of his friend Jack Coombs that had propelled the suicide. Both had been on a smuggling run in separate planes, and Forcade had watched his friend's aircraft explode in a ball of flames. The image haunted Forcade to the very end, just as his death would haunt others. His funeral was as surreal as the experience of knowing him.

"When I went to his funeral, I just wanted to touch him," O'Brien related, "to see if it was really Tom in that box. I had this feeling; I really didn't believe he was dead. He was so smart and cool and such a scam artist. It was like rumors about Elvis. If you could ever imagine somebody faking his own death, it would have been Tom Forcade."

In October of 1979, the first ads for freebase kits appeared in the magazine, along with feature articles like "Can You Smoke Cocaine Without Getting Burnt?" "*High Times* got taken over by coke, just like the whole culture got taken over by it," noted O'Brien, who remained with the magazine as a consultant for a while. "I'm sure that if it hadn't been for the mass marketing of cocaine, pot would have been legalized. When we started saying that coke was not harmful and may even be good for you, that's where we blew it and where the magazine lost its editorial legitimacy, as far as I was concerned."

## III. The John L. Lewis of the Marijuana Movement

KEITH STROUP lived right above the offices of the National Organization for the Reform of Marijuana Laws, off DuPont Circle in Washington, D.C., and was working on that Sunday in 1977 when he heard the doorbell ring, opened the door, and was surprised to see an expensive leather attaché case sitting there. When he opened it, he found about twenty thousand dollars in cash and a note saying that it was a contribution to NORML from an organization called the International Association of Marijuana Importers and Dealers.

"Well, *of course*, there was no such goddamned group!" Stroup laughed as he recalled the incident in the office of the Washington, D.C., law firm where he was working. "I didn't know if I was being set up—there was no way for me to know exactly what was happening. I thought it was probably Tom Forcade making a contribution and being cute. So I called the press and had them come over to take pictures of it. I said, 'Look, as far as I know, here's what happened, and there's the money, and as I understand it, I've got a right to deposit it until they tell me to the contrary.' And nobody ever said anything. Today if that happened, the money would be seized without a doubt. Just on the note alone, they would seize it on the basis that it said right where it was from, and I'd be hauled before a grand jury."

By 1977, the dam of marijuana prohibition erected by Harry Anslinger in the 1930s was finally breaking, and it seemed entirely possible that as many as five to ten states would decriminalize within the following year. Oregon had ended criminal penalties for smoking marijuana in 1973, and by the summer of 1975 so had five other states: Ohio, Colorado, Maine, California, and Alaska. Minnesota came along in 1976, to be joined by Mississippi, the first southern state, then New York and North Carolina. It seemed perfectly feasible that the time was not too far off when thirty million American marijuana smokers would be able to possess and use marijuana with relative impunity—a distinct possibility due in no small part to the indefatigable efforts of the thirty-five-year-old founder and head of NORML, Keith Stroup. Each state's decriminalization had taken place through a Herculean reform campaign that had engaged Stroup's formidable lobbying skills, organizational talent, political acumen, and media savvy, as well as selfless dedication. "We were zealots, completely committed, true believers," he reflected. "We cared more about changing marijuana laws than anything. We were willing to do most anything, go anyplace to do it. It took ten years of my life, and I lived in my office about eight of those ten years."

According to Paul Krassner, no less an astute social observer than Lenny Bruce had predicted the coming of someone like Keith Stroup: "Lenny would say, 'Someday marijuana will be legal because of all the law students who are smoking pot.'" Stroup was exactly that: the son of hardworking Southern Baptists, who grew up on a farm in southern Illinois, got caught up in the counterculture of the Sixties, and became a young pot-smoking attorney determined to do something about the nearly six hundred thousand people arrested for marijuana in 1970–71, some of whom happened to be his friends.

"When I started NORML, it wasn't coincidental that certain friends of mine had been busted and I was just getting out of law school and they naturally called me because I was the only lawyer they knew. The first thing I realized was that you weren't going to get very far taking it a case at a time. We therefore decided to take the same approach Ralph Nader took with the Product Safety Commission. Nader demonstrated that if you had access to information and if you know how to work with the media, you can have an enormous impact. So we decided to think about marijuana as a consumer issue, to argue it from the standpoint of those who smoked it. At that time, people debating the issue never thought it was even relevant to ask people who smoke marijuana what they thought. So we followed that model from 1970 to 1979."

Convinced that marijuana enhanced his sex life and was a valuable adjunct to the sexual revolution he promoted in *Playboy,* Hugh Hefner directed the Playboy Foundation to give Stroup the five-thousand-dollar grant that got NORML off and running and began Stroup's crusade as the most effective pot advocate in American history—the "John L. Lewis of the marijuana movement," according to *The New York Times.* Within a few years, Stroup had forged a political movement that was dedicated to debunking the long-held myths about the dangers of the weed. It was a broad-based coalition that included a counterculture wing of wild-eyed Yippies like Aaron Kay and Tom Forcade, entertainers like Willie Nelson, and gonzo journalist Hunter Thompson—but carefully combined with a faction of mainstream politicians, bureaucrats, businessmen, and scientists. As Stroup explained, "I thought we had an obligation to try and present the big tent, but I always thought that the job of NORML was to give a middle-class cover to a movement that had been building for a long, long time, going back to the Beat Generation in this country. It included a lot of Wavy Gravys and Tom Forcades, but for every Forcade there were millions of middle-class dope smokers who weren't raising hell and smuggling dope and setting up a *High Times* magazine. Our job was to minimize the fallout from the people who we knew would culturally turn off Middle America. So when it came to writing testimony or selecting witnesses you didn't see any clowns coming in. It was Harvard and Yale and UCLA professors and psychopharmacologists and eighty-year-old pediatricians who had dealt with kids all their lives and would testify that marijuana was not a big problem."

As good as Stroup was at countering antimarijuana shibboleths like the "stepping-stone theory" and the "amotivational syndrome," as well as the newer charges that marijuana caused immune-system damage and low testosterone levels in males, he realized that the real game was to engage the Carter administration, and it was here that he applied his skills as an infighter, lobbyist, manipulator of opinion, and connoisseur of power.

Even before the Carter administration, the mood in Washington had become more favorable to the decriminalization of marijuana and the liberalization of drug policy. Most people, in fact, assumed that Gerald Ford's son Jack had smoked pot (perhaps even upstairs in the White House?), and First Lady Betty Ford's comment that had someone offered her marijuana, she "probably" would have tried it was a long way from the 1972 presidential campaign, when the Republican Party accused the Democrats of being the party of "acid, amnesty, and abortion." That year, Nixon convened a commission on marijuana, headed by Raymond Shafer, the former Republican governor of Pennsylvania, stacked it with conservatives like Senator Harold Hughes of Iowa, and when the commission infuriated him by recommending that marijuana be decriminalized, he had simply disregarded the results: "I can see no social or moral justification for legalizing marijuana," he pronounced. But with the arrival of the Carter administration in 1976, Stroup was presented with something unprecedented in the history of American politics: a president who as a candidate had actually endorsed the decriminalization of marijuana (and whereas people could only surmise that a hip young guy like Jack Ford might have smoked pot, Jimmy Carter's son Chip openly acknowledged it). Never did the opportunity seem riper for reform. By 1977, Congressman Dan Quayle of Indiana was supporting the decriminalization of marijuana.

"The head of Carter's National Institute on Drug Abuse had come to one of my annual meetings and endorsed marijuana decriminalization," Stroup recalled. "I even drafted a speech for President Carter with his speechwriter, on drug policy." Stroup and the speechwriter, Griffin Smith Jr., had worked together getting the law changed in Texas—and when the job came up, Smith wasted no time contacting Stroup: "You won't believe what I've been assigned."

"We went over to his place and stayed up all night working on the draft. A week later, he called me over and showed me the draft, and next to one of our best lines Carter had commented, 'This almost sounds pro-marijuana.' " Stroup laughed. "Hey, this man understands! So we toned it down a bit, but in essence we were having a great deal of impact."

Among the lines that Stroup had written for the president's 1977 address to Congress on drug abuse that Carter considered too pro-marijuana and was unwilling to deliver were "Marijuana has become an established fact in our society, and the sky has not fallen" and "Research studies indicate it may have beneficial uses in the treatment of certain types of illness." What Carter did say, however, was unparalleled nonetheless. "Penalties against possession of a drug should not be more damaging to an individual than the use of the drug itself, and where they are, they should be changed."

Carter still wanted drug dealers prosecuted, increasing the budget for the Drug Enforcement Administration and initiating the provisions that would lay the basis for what became forfeiture during the 1980s. But he now supported legislation amending federal law "to eliminate all Federal criminal penalties for the possession of up to one ounce of marijuana." A bare six months into his administration, Carter was advocating civil fines for pot smokers, thus delivering just what people like Allen Ginsberg had long dreamed of: the end of the time when people could be sent to prison for small amounts of marijuana, as Neal Cassady had been in 1958.

The architect of this bold and progressive drug policy was Dr. Peter Bourne, an urbane British-born psychiatrist who had helped open the Haight Ashbury Free Clinic before becoming the manager of Georgia's drug-abuse programs when Carter was governor. With more actual experience of drugs and knowledge about their use than anybody who had ever served in the White House, Bourne embraced the liberal Dutch policy of "harm reduction" as his guiding principle, which held that a drug-free society was demonstrably unachievable and that the most effective and realistic role of government should therefore be to reduce the harm that drugs do to individuals and the society. As Carter's midterm drug policy stated, "Drugs cannot be forced out of existence; they will be with us for as long as people find in them the relief or satisfaction they desire." Since Harry Anslinger, in fact, every administration in Washington had demonized drugs, portraying them in moral absolutes of good and evil, and here was a course of action being formulated by someone actually willing to make distinctions between hard and soft drugs, use and abuse. Compared with the rhetoric and policy of Bourne's predecessors, it was as if the perspective of someone like Aldous Huxley were being incorporated into national drug policy.

The story of how the tide of national drug policy turned decisively away from reform for the next quarter century begins, in part, with NORML's annual Christmas party in 1978, the party of the year for the young and the hip of the new Washington Democratic elite. When Peter Bourne, the nation's drug czar, arrived at the NORML headquarters to attend a party where marijuana was being openly smoked, it was clear that a new era had arrived, but then he approached Keith Stroup and asked him if he had any cocaine.

"Now there was a time in the mid- to late Seventies and into the early Eighties where I didn't know very many people who didn't occasionally use cocaine, certainly in my social setting and professional life," Stroup said. "You could go to a dinner party in this town, and they might have after-dinner drinks, and somebody else might pull out a joint and those who didn't smoke would pass, and it didn't offend anybody. Cocaine wasn't that open, but you would notice little pockets of people in the corner, and these weren't people who considered themselves outlaws. I had never done cocaine with Peter Bourne. I knew him well; I had smoked a joint with him a few times. I wasn't surprised that he wanted to do it but a little surprised by the setting—there were four or five hundred people there!"

When Bourne arrived, he was accompanied by the Secret Service. "It was crazy—the Secret Service was essentially running security for us. There was a lot of noise, and the police would stop by and see the Secret Service and go, 'Oh, no problem.' In a sense, we were in the protection of the official system." When a group of a dozen or so of the guests, including two journalists, went upstairs to the private bedroom, Stroup was nevertheless disquieted. "I sort of thought to myself, Jesus Christ, Peter, are you sure about this?" When they got upstairs, some cocaine started going around, and when it got to Bourne, the drug czar sure enough took a little toot. "It certainly wasn't a big deal, wasn't some kind of blowout, but it was the whole concept of that happening at all, I guess. It was a minor little thing that didn't seem nearly as dangerous or as important as it seemed later to other people."

The next day, both journalists called Stroup—"people I knew and worked with for a long time, both sympathetic to our culture, saying, God, can I use this? I said, 'Not from me, come on, this was off the record, a private thing, I don't even think he realized you were a journalist. If you want confirmation from me, you're certainly not going to get it.' "

The story probably would never have seen the light of day had Bourne not gotten himself into serious trouble that summer by writing a Quaalude prescription for one of his assistants. The assistant had been having trouble sleeping after breaking up with her boyfriend and didn't want anyone to know she was taking sleeping pills. Consequently, Bourne wrote the prescription for her under an alias—which was illegal under any circumstances but looked even fishier when the press got hold of it, given the nature of the drug. As Stroup put it, "Quaaludes were used for sex. It was routine, common, that you'd meet a stranger—'hey, got any Ludes?'—and, wham, you're in bed and you forgot who you were with and bumped your head along the way."

As soon as the story broke, Gary Cohn, one of the journalists on Jack Anderson's staff who had been at the party, contacted Stroup to inform him that he was going to print the story of Bourne using cocaine and wanted a quote. Stroup refused, but Cohn called him again later that night at home. Again Stroup refused to go on record. Cohn told him, "We're going with this, how about if I read it to you? I don't want to have an inaccuracy. It's going to be big news."

Stroup said, "Okay, read it to me."

So Cohn did. "Anything inaccurate there?"

"Off the record?"

"Yeah."

"No, there's nothing inaccurate, but I don't think it's smart to run it; there's nothing to gain."

The next morning, *The Washington Post* ran the story and asked Stroup to confirm or deny it. "It didn't name me but referred to a NORML function. Do you either confirm or deny that? I had an easy out; I could have lied for him and should have—and in most cases would have. It's a white lie but the kind that we generally tell to protect our friends or public officials. That was the obvious choice, and I would not have been perceived as helping to bring him down . . . but, well, I was angry with Bourne over paraquat."

The Mexican government's practice of spraying marijuana fields with the herbicide paraquat from helicopters supplied by the United States had been the brainstorm of none other than G. Gordon Liddy at the time of Operation Intercept, in 1969. By 1978, the National Institute on Drug Abuse reported that some five hundred tons—one-fifth of the marijuana smuggled into the United States from Mexico—was contaminated at forty-four thousand times the safe level. NORML wasted no time filing a suit to stop the spraying. Given the model of Nader's consumer-advocate product-safety approach, Stroup felt that his primary responsibility was to protect the health of pot smokers, especially when he started getting reports from NORML members that they were coughing up blood. He had rushed to Bourne's office and demanded that the spraying be stopped—"You cannot do this!"

Bourne blamed the Mexicans for the spraying and was unwilling to make a statement about it. "Keith," he said, by way of justification, "it's *illegal.*"

"Don't give me that shit!" Stroup shot back. "It's illegal to smoke in this country, but if I smoke in my bedroom or living room, you can't tell me that without a search warrant you can come break down my door and shoot me! Essentially, that's what you're saying—that you can use deadly force on these people because they're breaking the law. That is *not* an excuse; you've still got due process, cruel and unusual punishment—all kinds of restrictions on what you can do just because someone breaks the law in a nonviolent way."

Bourne promised that he would look into it, but the spraying did not stop. To Stroup, it was a failure of moral courage on Bourne's part— "he was really selling us out on a life-and-death issue. So when the *Post* called and said, Will you either confirm or deny, I said neither, which is code in Washington for saying of course it happened but I'm not going to admit it."

Jack Anderson broke the story on *Good Morning America* that very morning—drug czar writes illegal scrip for attractive assistant, sniffs cocaine at NORML party—and conservative Republicans like Orrin Hatch were all over it, alleging that Bourne had done "more harm than any official in the history of the government." Bourne denied the story, claiming that he had only been in the room where the cocaine had been sniffed, but the damage was done and his resignation came quickly. "Combined with the Quaalude prescription, I think he still would have had to resign, but it wouldn't have been in such a messy way, and it wouldn't have had the impact that it did on Carter," Stroup commented. "I felt terrible about it and do to this day. I like him a lot and had no intention of hurting him, but I have to concede that I did hurt him and that it was a stupid mistake."

More than passion and anger had influenced Stroup's intemperate response; he also acknowledged the impact of cocaine burnout. "There was no doubt that some of my burnout was attributed to the fact that I was spending too many nights staying up until two, three, four o'clock, and it was hard to get up the next morning, and when you did get up, you still weren't rested because you hadn't had that REM sleep. A lot of the judgments I made about Bourne and the *Post,* if I had taken a week's vacation prior, my guess is that it wouldn't have been difficult to handle at all. But I actually felt like we had gone to war with Bourne and the White House."

Recognizing his political vulnerability, Carter sent a memo to senior staff that expressed his concern over rumors that members of the White House staff were using illegal drugs: "Whether you agree with the law or whether or not others obey the law is totally irrelevant. You will obey it, or you will seek employment elsewhere."

As one official commented, "Drug reform vanished up Peter Bourne's nose," but the Bourne affair was hardly the only reason why NORML would never again have the same kind of impact on government policy. "Anyone who works in major policy making understands that no one little event turns things around—not even one big event," Stroup pointed out. "What really happened, at least in my perception, is that we underestimated the rise of the parents' groups and the importance of that." The groups had already started picketing Stroup's lectures. "I'd see them outside, but we discounted them because the truth is they were reminiscent of a very unsophisticated approach to drug use and policy. They were also focusing on preteen and adolescent drug use, and we had never suggested that school kids should smoke joints—quite the contrary. We were talking about adult use of marijuana in private and assumed that we could keep the eye on our target, but we were totally wrong. Very quickly the major media began doing programs on the problems with young kids and adolescents and drugs, and the parents' groups began to get all the focus."

The parents' movement can be traced back to the Bicentennial summer, when a mother named Marsha Keith Schuchard in suburban Atlanta threw a birthday party for her thirteen-year-old daughter and was horrified to realize that all the glassy-eyed, giggling kids were zonked on pot. Schuchard soon discovered that marijuana was everywhere and easy to get and so was the paraphernalia to use it with (rolling papers were being sold at the 7-Eleven stores!). She was hardly alone in her concern; a whole generation of parents was aghast at the prospect of their teenagers flocking to see Cheech and Chong's *Up in Smoke,* the low-budget smash-hit comedy of 1978 whose advertising slogan was "Don't come straight to this movie!"

Lynn Zimmer, professor of sociology at Queens College and the author of numerous articles and books on drug use, studied the parents' movement. "For the most part, these people came of age during the fairy-tale Fifties, this pure, clean generation of *Father Knows Best,* and they may have watched college students taking drugs during the Sixties, but it didn't touch them; they were in their twenties and thirties and into their lives, not paying attention to these silly hippies until their own children started going to high school in the 1970s. Suddenly, they had children fourteen, fifteen years old, and when they came home and found marijuana after a party, they couldn't imagine what it meant. They basically didn't know anything about it and were scared. So they started getting together as groups, and they'd contact the school, and the school would say, 'Oh, you know, it's not that big of a deal, we know there's some marijuana use.' Then they'd contact NIDA or the state drug-abuse hotline number, and they'd get back something about how we needed to teach people how to be careful with drugs and we have to accept that taking drugs is now part of the American experience. *What?!!* These people were concerned about changes in the culture, and if you look at the antidrug speeches of the late 1970s and early 1980s, they make the clear connection between marijuana use and teen pregnancy and abortion and the ousting of school prayer from the schools."

Schuchard's Nosy Parents Association was only the beginning; before long, she would form a national organization with Thomas J. "Buddy" Gleaton, PRIDE—National Parents' Resource Institute for Drug Education. The parents' movement quickly expanded to four thousand local chapters across the country, and Schuchard became the author of *Parents, Peers, and Pot* (published under her maiden name, Marsha Manatt), an eighty-page NIDA pamphlet that would become the government's official bible on marijuana and teenagers and the most requested publication in the history of the agency. It would claim that marijuana caused gynomastia (breast enlargement) in teenaged boys, as well as sterility, cancer, and scores of other medical maladies, not to mention the negative social and cultural ramifications of teenage marijuana use. The fact that NIDA had allowed an angry parent with no scientific qualifications whatsoever to write a government publication on marijuana was only a harbinger of things to come. As the power and influence of the parents' movement grew, it trained its sights not only on the paraphernalia industry and *High Times* magazine but also on the entire permissive liberal culture that had allowed a mass commercial drug culture to flourish. Presidential candidate Ronald Reagan would wield one of his most effective political cudgels in the election of 1980 when he charged that not only were Democrats soft on crime and Communism, but they were the party of pot, too. For Reagan, it was like preaching to the choir; despite the decriminalization trend, polls had always confirmed that a majority of Americans did not favor the outright legalization of marijuana. As Keith Stroup noted, "Even in the best of years, there was always a strong conservative opposition of southerners and moralists and religious groups who had a problem dealing objectively with marijuana; they couldn't disconnect with fears they had which had nothing to do with the drug." This opposition would join with the parents' movement to form the core constituency of true believers in Reagan's war on drugs.

Yet even as the political winds began to turn unalterably against NORML and drug reform, there was more marijuana on the streets than ever before. Like all other attempts to stamp out the drug trade from the street to the global level, the use of paraquat had led to another unforeseen example of what Ethan Nadelmann, the Princeton sociologist who would later become director of the Drug Policy Alliance, would call the "push-down, pop-up effect": push the trade down here, it will surely pop up over there. After all, it had been Nixon's Operation Intercept at the Mexican border in 1969 that had sent the smugglers to Jamaica, and Operation Buccaneer that had then moved them to Colombia and elsewhere. The DEA was initially thrilled with how the media had fueled the paraquat scare and pushed down the market for Mexican weed, never imagining how within a few years the domestic cultivation of marijuana in northern California would make sensimilla the second or third largest cash crop in America.

## IV. It's Like Free Money . . .

THE WHOLE GARBERVILLE ECONOMY was organizing around marijuana, and a neighbor had come by the previous year to advise Steve Bowser that he would be able to build his house "a lot faster" if only he grew some weed for the market, where it was selling for fifteen hundred dollars a pound. Some guy from Ventura who had serendipitously moved in right down the road from Bowser that winter knew the technique: dig the hole two to three feet in diameter and depth, fill it with fertilizer. And that guy in turn knew some woman who came up and trimmed the buds after the harvest. And when it was all over, it had been a breeze to sell the weed through local contacts.

Six plants, four thousand dollars! That year Bowser became one of some thirty thousand marijuana growers in the northern Californian counties of Humboldt, Mendocino, Sonoma, Lake, Del Norte, Trinity, and Butte taking part in the largest illicit agricultural movement in the history of the United States: an underground society of cannabis farmers. Humboldt County, where Bowser lived, had been sparsely settled for a hundred years. After the Second World War, when sheep and cattle became less profitable, the building boom created great demand for Douglas fir timber. Ranchers made a lot of money throughout the late Forties and Fifties on what they considered useless junk trees cluttering up their grazing lands, but when the trees were all gone, that was the end of their income. That was when they started selling off the land, cutting up the huge ranches of between five thousand and fifteen thousand acres into much smaller parcels, and by the late 1960s those parcels had been subdivided again. By the time Bowser returned from Vietnam and saw the advertisements for "Humboldt County mountain land, 2 percent down payment" in the *San Francisco Chronicle*, the forty-acre parcels of a four-thousand-acre ranch in Honeydew were selling for twelve thousand dollars.

"People would come up in droves on weekends and pitch tents on hillsides, hand the dealer five hundred dollars, and have themselves a parcel of land," Bowser remembered. "A lot of them didn't know squat about what do with it or even how to make the payments. Garberville was a whacked-out little ex–logging town—plywood wooden storefronts, run-down bars, and not much else."

Bowser's status as a Vietnam veteran was typical of the community. "A big part of the back-to-the-land movement, as it turned out, was more about leaving a civilization behind than it was about building an alternative one," observed Freeman House, the ex-Digger turned salmon conservationist, who was also growing a few plants on his land over in Petrolia, along the coast. "It was a way to drop out of the social mainstream."

Freeman's observation certainly applied to Earl Steven Bowser, an ex–air force fighter jock whose experience of the war had been bitterly disillusioning, to say the very least. Born in Columbus, Ohio, Bowser may have looked like an exemplary all-American officer, with his blue eyes and blond crew cut, but he was really an anomaly. Not many pilots had smoked pot and read Kerouac and taken acid and gone off on an exhilarating cross-country railroad-riding adventure before joining the air force. Bowser was completely seduced by jet aviation and found himself flying F-4 Phantoms out of Da Nang in September of 1969. Given the growing antiwar sensibilities that he secretly harbored, he was greatly relieved to be sent back to the States after flying 230 missions; he had only six months to go before being discharged when he was told to pack his bags for Thailand. After a week, he was informed that "the intention was to bomb the shit out of the north," as he put it. The additional 120 missions he flew over North Vietnam in the spring of 1972 horrified him. Just trying to describe what those supersonic minutes over Hanoi were like—the MiGs and antiaircraft fire coming at him, pilots being shot out of the sky all around him by SAMs fired six or eight at a time, some of them coming so close that he would almost shit his pants—made his voice choke up with emotion. By the time he returned to the United States, he wanted to get as far away from civilization as possible.

"Most military pilots go to the airlines when they get out, but not me. I was totally disillusioned with the government. I felt they were completely duplicitous and were perfectly willing to manipulate us like pawns. Vietnam was a direct experience of that—body counts, bomb tonnages—we were blowing up trees and making mud holes in the middle of Laos!—and then the experience of trying to destroy Hanoi, followed by Watergate. I had a genuine fear that the military could lead us into a nuclear conflict. I had known enough really nutty colonels and generals who were willing to play with other people's lives in order to puff their chests out. I wanted to be able to grow food and shoot deer, and I just fell completely in love with the whole region here."

Falling in love with Humboldt County was easy. It was a magical wilderness as far-flung as the moon: golden light, rushing streams clean enough to drink from, dense thickets of thorn and briar and nettle, forests of manzanita, chaparral, black oak, madrone, giant redwood, and rugged coastal mountains with viridescent slopes and blanched hills. The contrasts of the place were dramatic, with mild arid seasons and raging monsoonlike rains, days of pristine cerulean skies and crisp nights luminous with stars. The region was teeming with deer, fox, bobcat, bear, snakes, and salmon. Sometimes, with the white fog rolling in off the ocean, it seemed otherworldly, haunted by the spirits of dead cavalrymen, Indians, and gold prospectors. A more quintessentially American tract of earth would be difficult to find, and the isolation seemed absolute. As one local put it, you could walk out your door stark naked with a joint and go for miles in any direction without ever seeing anyone.

As Ray Raphael, historian of the California backcountry, expressed it in *Cash Crop: An American Dream,* his portrait of the sensimilla culture circa 1984–85, the urban émigrés who arrived in these distant wilds were driven by an abundance of motives, but the underlying impulse was "not to get rich but to get poor." "They wanted to discover for themselves the physical and spiritual fundamentals of a life which seemed concealed by mass culture and urban convenience, . . . to build a new life from the ground up."

Many of these new pioneers smoked marijuana and already regarded themselves as outlaws and anarchists, but now they were faced with the necessity of finding the means to stay on their land and pursue their idealistic goals. It wouldn't take them long to discover that cannabis flourished in this climate, with a six-month growing season. Ray Raphael characterized the phenomenon of sensimilla as a manifestation of the American Dream, not merely a reaction to it: "Even before the marijuana industry blossomed, the seeds to some of these aspects of the American Way had been firmly implanted in the back-to-the-land subculture: the Jeffersonian ideal of independent farmers, the resistance against government interference in private affairs, a compelling belief in personal freedom, and the use of recreational drugs."

Other analogies to American tradition and mythology were equally apt: the California gold rush, the lure of the outlaw frontier, rugged individualism, the tradition of illegal liquor during Prohibition. Add factors that were unique to the time—the decline of the family farm, the newly arrived hippies mixing with rural rednecks to form what Ed Sanders liked to call "hippy-billy" culture, and most important, thirty million Americans smoking marijuana with greater appetites for better weed and deeper pockets to pay for it—and marijuana farming in Humboldt County became what Ray Raphael described as "the perfect embodiment of a people's capitalism. . . . In many respects it's a conservative's delight: no permits required, no zoning regulations, no environmental impact statements to endure. It's free enterprise all the way, with the promise of prosperity for anyone who's willing to work for it."

"For the first couple of years, I treated it like free money, like it was coming right out of the air," Bowser said. "It was magical. The only way people got popped in those days was if they had partners and there was friction between them and one turned in the other. Or people growing it all around their house right next to the road and the sheriff or an assessor came by and discovered it. County officials acted like they didn't know a thing. Way back in 1970, down in the Garberville-Redway area, the sheriff and his deputies had raided somebody's dope garden while he was harvesting, and they shot and killed him, and people were so stunned that somebody had actually been shot for such a minor offense as growing some dope that it encouraged a kind of unspoken consensus: oh, big deal, don't bother them, it's just some crazies growing some pot, and besides, they're buying all those new cars up in Eureka! In those days, there were no overflights yet so you didn't give a damn yet if they could be seen from the sky, so you just put them in a sunny location with plenty of water, where the plants weren't easily observable from the road. I generally had maybe twenty plants in a group, six feet apart, not necessarily in rows, with a chicken-wire fence that kept them from deer. I went into drip irrigation fairly early because it allowed me to work these Forest Service jobs four or five days at a time."

By the end of August, when the plants would begin to sexually differentiate, you'd pull all the males up so that the unfertilized females would be forced to produce the rich, dark-green, THC-laden buds called colas that would make the seedless pot of Humboldt County so sought after. By September, the gorgeous ten- to twelve-foot-tall plants would be swaying in the breeze, their colas so big and dense with resin that they would glisten like gemstones in the sun. At harvest time, the plants would be cut down, taken inside, and hung up to dry . . .

"One of the funnier sights in Garberville in late September was going by the hotels when it would be raining like crazy, and the parking lots would be full. People would rent the rooms and turn the heat up and have whole rooms full of dope drying out, which would go on for weeks. Everyone knew, especially the motel owners, who were very happy to have their rooms rented."

With the buds neatly manicured, the dope would be weighed and bagged. "Finding a buyer was very easy. Everyone knew everyone else who was growing, and word would go out that you were ready to sell, and they'd bring people over. It was real simple, as quaint a system of traditional local agriculture as you're ever likely to see." Bowser sold to a woman who looked like a kindly grandmother; the California Highway Patrol was unlikely ever to suspect that she was trucking fifty-pound loads of Humboldt homegrown down to Marin County on Highway 101. Of course, there was always the possibility that poachers might show up to rip off the plants, but they were few and far between. "The genuinely commercial growers would hire people, or the partners would sit out in the patches during harvest time to prevent that."

Bowser was thrilled to make an extra ten to fifteen thousand dollars a year to supplement his Forest Service income and leave it at that. His biggest windfall year was a twenty-five-pound harvest—about fifty plants, sold for between fourteen hundred and fifteen hundred dollars a pound. "To a certain extent, I liked the outlaw aspect of it, and during the early 1980s, when the first Reagan recession came along, here I was in a cash economy not affected by all this bullshit, people going nuts in the cities and worrying about their decreasing standard of living—hey, mine was actually increasing, and without having to pay taxes! I was especially gleeful about that . . . Did I feel entitled as a Vietnam vet to do this? I've seen that attitude but never felt it myself. The way I justified it in my mind was that marijuana is such a benign drug that what I was doing was not really criminal. I didn't care what the law said—I knew it was not morally objectionable. I also knew it was unlikely that I was introducing schoolchildren to marijuana. The prices were so exorbitant, what kids could afford it?"

The majority of the growers produced at this modest level, particularly the ones like Freeman House, who were involved in other endeavors. "We were looking for just enough money to survive. We grew for three or four years, and our best year was twenty thousand dollars tops, and we managed to make land payments out of that. Also, it financed my ability to do positive things with the ecology." As another local grower put it, "Pot has been like a gift from God that enabled us to do anything we wanted to up here—get the land, live lives of leisure, give money to good causes."

Of course, it wasn't all mom-and-pop hippies down on the marijuana farm working for the New Ectopia. Like all gold rushes, sensimilla also attracted the greedy and the unscrupulous; there were plenty of growers who were anything but good communitarians or ecologists, who were far more interested in buying Harley-Davidson motorcycles and eight balls of cocaine than restoring salmon and reseeding forests that had been clear-cut by loggers. By the late 1970s, there were stories of twenty-acre dope plantations way back in the forests with whole valleys under cannabis cultivation, complete with hired gunmen in camouflage gear and four thousand to six thousand plants in the ground at a time and fifty to sixty trimmers. People began talking about towers with searchlights and machine guns; someone did set off an explosive booby trap, and several people were shot for venturing too close to the fields. These were the incidents that would lead to the sensationalized newspaper articles about terror and intimidation, punji stake pits and bear traps, but all of that wouldn't start in earnest until the Reagan administration. For now, the scene was open and easy. Everyone hung out at the little general store in Honeydew, sipping beers and enjoying the sun, proudly offering one another their merchandise for sampling. As Steve Bowser looked back, it almost didn't seem real.

"We didn't realize that we were living through what would become known as the Golden Age of Marijuana."

## V. We're Here to Bring Humboldt County Back into the United States

Helicopter, helicopter, over my head,
I choose a color, and the color is red.

> —Rope-jumping game played by children in Humboldt County,
> 1985

STEVE BOWSER had moved to the boondocks of northern California to escape what he viewed as a teeming and corrupt American civilization and to put the traumatic legacy of the Vietnam War as far behind him as possible. But all it took to bring it back to him was the invasive *whup-whup-whup* of the DEA's helicopters shattering the quiet of Humboldt County in the fall of 1984.

"My whole time in Da Nang, I never went twenty minutes without hearing that sound, and suddenly there they were, two or three choppers swarming around over the ridge, *Apocalypse Now!*" Bowser exclaimed. "It was eerie, and just like that this whole region changed from being this mellow paradise, a place where you could live out in the woods in this ideal climate with your friends and neighbors in this loose association of people you could trust and make reasonably easy money, into this ugly reality called CAMP."

The strategies of the Campaign Against Marijuana Production seemed oddly familiar to any Vietnam vet—insertion, search and destroy, extraction—only now the body count comprised the number of marijuana plants eradicated. CAMP may have seemed a creepy and paradoxical reprise of Vietnam transplanted to northern California (with the growers now cast in the role of the Vietcong), but it was also the next chapter in a bitter political contest of wills that had begun fifteen years earlier. As Bowser explained, "It was the same battle as when Reagan was governor of California, fighting the radicals of Berkeley—they were the same people who had come up here to do this, and here they were pissing in his face! Of course, he felt that he was absolutely, morally right, and he was going to do this regardless of law or people's rights, and if he couldn't, he would just change the laws. CAMP from the beginning made no observance of any constitutional restrictions on law enforcement."

Reagan arrived in Washington in 1981 convinced that his election gave him the mandate to roll back drug use in the United States right along with the size of the federal government and Soviet expansionism. On June 24, 1982, he stood in the Rose Garden of the White House and declared his War on Drugs. "We're making no excuses for drugs, hard, soft, or otherwise," the president proclaimed. "Drugs are bad, and we're going after them. As I've said before, we're taking down the surrender flag and running up the battle flag. We're going to win the war on drugs."

CAMP was kicked off in the harvest season of 1983. Twenty-seven agencies were involved at the federal, state, and local level, and a federal grand jury was impaneled in Eureka. U-2 planes were used to spot the big fields of the marijuana "plantations," and by the end of that first season the big pot farms were all gone. "Those ridiculously brazen guys who would buy a four-hundred-acre parcel of land, bring in dump trucks with fertilizer and Mexican workers? Those guys disappeared first," Bowser noted. "They just took off and ran!"

CAMP '83 was touted as a great success: at a cost of a mere $1.6 million, 524 raids were made, 128 people were arrested, and 64,579 plants seized with the wholesale estimated cost of $130 million—quite an ROI (return on investment), but according to the DEA's feisty field commander, William Ruzzamenti, the problem in Humboldt County was "so gigantic" that it was only 10 percent of the crop. "Next year, with the resources of the federal government and the state, we will get rid of marijuana in Humboldt County," he predicted. "These people are operating up there in their own little Valhalla wilderness thinking everything is beautiful, knowing they got away with it, but we'll see what happens next year."

The next year, in the harvest season of 1984, CAMP began taking on its true character. That was when one of Bowser's neighbors got busted. "They landed a chopper next to his house, came in, held both guys at gunpoint while they went looking in the garden, and were taunting them, these sheriff's deputies, and one of the things they said was 'We're here to bring Humboldt County back into the United States!'

"These guys were recruits from departments in southern California, young guys who had volunteered to do this for three or four months and were fed a lot of information about armed growers and booby traps," Bowser pointed out. "They were given M-16s to carry on these raids, and it was real scary because they were nervous. They would land on some-body's property and come jumping out, and they wouldn't know if they were going to be cut down or blown to bits or fall on punji sticks or what—and believe me, you wanted to be far away from them."

If that wasn't intimidating enough, the choppers began flying very low, "I don't know if you've ever been dive-bombed by a Huey—it scares the shit out of you," Freeman House related. "They were really buzzing the rooftops, to the point where they were actually scaring cows into abortion. It was like being colonized by some foreign military occupy-ing force." It didn't take long before bumper stickers started appearing: U.S. OUT OF HUMBOLDT COUNTY.

As far as Bill Ruzzamenti was concerned, those who looked the other way in the communities and tolerated marijuana cultivation because they thought that the illicit crop might be good for the local economies were as guilty as the growers. "There were boards of supervisors that thought that way; there were sheriffs that thought that way. Those people are dinosaurs; they're not around anymore. And I think you're going to find that the marijuana grower is a dinosaur. He's not long for the world either."

Second-season tally: 37 sheriffs raiding 398 sites, nabbing 158,493 plants and 218 growers. The cost to taxpayers was $2.3 million, but the cost to the Constitution and the Bill of Rights was beyond measure. The DEA was employing tactics in Humboldt County that were unprece-dented in the history of modern law enforcement: roadblocks set up and families hauled out of cars at gunpoint; homes ransacked without war-rants; surveillance satellites used to spy on American citizens. The tiny village of Denny in Trinity County was virtually occupied "with a small army," as Ruzzamenti called the operation. A troop of DEA deputies marched through town, chanting, *"War on drugs! War on drugs!"*

By the time Steve Bowser was busted, on August 3, 1985, citizens' ob-servation groups had been formed around Garberville, along with civil liberties monitors, who went out into the fields and videotaped the CAMP helicopters as they landed. "They were out there the day my place got raided," he recalled. "This group had their camera pointed at the helicopters, and they were run off by guys with M-16s."

The Omnibus Crime Bill of 1984, signed into law by Reagan that October, would change the whole nature of the campaign by shifting the focus to land seizures. As Ruzzamenti made clear, "Anybody who's growing marijuana on their land, we're going to take their land. It's as simple as that."

It was nasty business. Now the government only had to file a forfeiture action, not against individuals but against their property; the burden of proof was reversed so that individuals had to prove that they weren't involved in marijuana growing on their land or didn't know about it, a difficult and costly undertaking. The DEA had taken pictures of Bowser's garden from an airplane in mid-July and had then flown over in a chopper to gather additional evidence.

"I had just bought this little motel the year before and didn't have it set up to rent yet and was still working these Forest Service jobs, and that morning someone said, 'You better watch out, CAMP is at your house!' "

The CAMP chopper had landed on top of the hill, and twelve guys had come charging down through the woods like a squad of army Rangers attacking a machine-gun nest. "For a half hour, they just tore the house apart, looking for drugs and drug paraphernalia—they found four ounces of dope left over from the year before. I had this *Life* magazine that had an article about dope growing in Humboldt County, and they laid it out on this mess, open to that article. You know, taunting me with these gestures."

The U.S. government had put a lien on Bowser's property at 8:00 a.m. but did not arrive on his land until 9:00 or 10:00 a.m., "so they had seized it before they had any prosecutable evidence in hand," he claimed. "They moved against the property as their means of attack. They made raids on twelve other parcels of land—there was a whole group of us, four or five out in Petrolia, five in Honeydew, some up around Fortuna—and they seized all our property."

Freeman House was growing six plants along with three experimental ones over in Petrolia. "We were growing them over in the brush away from the house, and the water lines were hooked up to our house, which made us culpable. Our neighbors were growing quite a few more plants than we were, but we had just paid off our land six months before and that would happen many times—people paying off their land and *then* they got raided. Our knoll is the best helicopter-landing site on this mountain, visible from the whole valley, so they could really put on a show. They were still using small helicopters during the first or second year, before the Hueys, which could only carry a few people, and they off-loaded twelve people here. Six landings to fly them in, six landings to fly them out—all for six plants."

Freeman would never be prosecuted—"frankly, they were embarrassed," he maintained. "They searched the house so thoroughly that they were able to find things I hadn't been able to—the deed to the property I'd spent six months looking for, peyote buttons which I'd had for fifteen years, which had fallen back into a corner. It was such a feeling of physical violation, watching it all as they walked around with their automatic weapons."

Bowser wouldn't be so lucky; his court date was set for September of 1986, and he would have to go before a federal judge in San Francisco. "I knew that if I pleaded guilty to a felony, I'd lose my pilot's license, which was the worst thing that could have happened to me. So I went for a jury trial on the advice of my lawyer, which meant the federal court up in Eureka. Basically, I claimed no knowledge of how those plants had gotten into my garden." At that point, the prosecutor offered a deal: a ten-thousand-dollar fine, three years of probation, and two thousand hours of community service. Bowser accepted.

"Now you understand, Mr. Bowser, that I don't have to go along with this deal at all," the judge informed him. "I can penalize you any way I want to. Do you have anything to say for yourself regarding this crime against society?"

Bowser's attorney then rose and spoke for fifteen minutes on his behalf. Unbeknownst to Bowser, his attorney had contacted his parents and had them send out all of his war decorations—"stuff I never paid attention to, all these medals that I sent to my parents in case I got killed, shit I'd never even looked at"—which his attorney now displayed before the judge. "Then he mentioned the three hundred combat missions I'd flown and spent maybe ninety seconds on what a sterling character I was in my community of Humboldt County, and the judge turned from this stern, conservative old man into a smiling grandfather before my eyes."

Bowser would always consider it his one tangible benefit from the war; the judge levied the fine and gave him probation but left off the community service. Bowser returned to Honeydew, never to grow weed again. "The whole affair was traumatic. I'd been floating along in this unrealistic cloud. My carelessness about growing the year I was busted was certainly an indication of that." He did manage to retain his pilot's license, however, and as the DEA continued to wage its helicopter war against the community, there were many moments when he wished that he still had his old F-4 Phantom so that he could fly a little "air defense" for his neighbors.

Freeman House's days as a grower were also over. He and his wife, Nina, decided that the stress and paranoia weren't worth it; their daughter, Laurel, was only two years old, and they didn't want her growing up in fear of the sound of the helicopters, so Nina took a job in town. But if people like Bill Ruzzamenti thought that the growers would now disappear like the "dinosaurs," he was sorely mistaken.

"CAMP didn't break the growers; it just changed the nature of the venture," Freeman insisted. "The growers had to become increasingly ingenious, that's all. A lot of people became very adamant about it. The extremes to which they're willing to go in order to pull it off were really quite amazing—packing their own fertilizer for miles, using these inventive water systems that can't be seen from the air. People go way back into the brush, preferably on public land. It's a real job now, and there's a personality type that goes for it. They really enjoy trekking around in the wild, trying to foil the helicopter pilots. But there's still that underlying paranoia."

"Not only is it like having a job every day, it's like having a *serious* job every day," Bowser observed. "There's a whole mystique about beating CAMP. All these minute details and techniques, like hollowing out the top of an oak tree for a single plant—people turn into workaholics, and every plant they grow and harvest becomes a victory for them. To me, they've sort of defeated the purpose of what they came here to do: grow some dope, live a good, easy life, and enjoy it."

Perhaps the greatest impact of CAMP would be the creation of a de facto price-support system. With each year of the campaign, the price of marijuana steadily escalated, creating a market that would allow growers to make more money by growing less and less dope. As the DEA tried to suppress the sensimilla growers of Humboldt County and elsewhere, people began cultivating marijuana indoors, sometimes in large ware-houses—yet another example of the push-down, pop-up effect. Before long, new, incredibly sophisticated hydroponic techniques with grow lights and digitally operated electronic watering systems would allow people to grow dope in basements and closets, forcing the DEA to shift from U-2 surveillance planes and helicopter assaults to the examination of suspiciously high electric bills. The result was that the price of pot soared astronomically at a time when cocaine was becoming purer, cheaper, and more available than ever. People in middle-class and affluent suburbia still managed to buy weed; but in the poor, black inner-city neighborhoods, where jobs were scarce, a new drug called crack began appearing in 1985.

# 9

## Out of the Closets and into the Streets

**❝It's the amyl nitrate. . . . You've confused the amyl nitrate with love.❞**

—John Rechy, *Rushes*, 1979

### I.  Flaunting It in Frisco

"I DON'T USUALLY TELL straight people this, but I came out of the closet in Vietnam, during a rocket attack," confided Dennis Peron, the man who would do more than any one else to bring the issue of medical marijuana into the political and cultural lexicon of the 1990s. "I was stationed at Tan Son Nhut Airport, outside Saigon. There were dozens of rockets and secondary explosions. Everything was dark. I thought I was going to die. There was this guy next to me—I didn't know who he was—but we started rubbing against each other, and before we knew it, we were kissing and then I was blowing him. To this day I don't know who it was. . . . After that I was pretty overt. They didn't know what to do with me. I was a pot-smoking faggot!"

Dennis Peron, perhaps the most notoriously public "pot-smoking faggot" in the history of San Francisco, established a legendary open marijuana market called the Big Top above the Island Restaurant on Castro Street that would represent the closest an American city would ever come to the laissez-faire drug attitudes of Amsterdam. A camera-shop owner named Harvey Milk started hanging out at the Island just as he was getting into politics. Peron and Milk had met in a bathhouse in the early

1970s, forming a relationship that would change their lives, the politics of the city of San Francisco, and the history of drug reform in the city.

Peron's life as an exemplar of alternative culture began early. He knew that he was gay at the age of ten, smoked pot as a senior in Valley Stream High School in New York, and got drafted after dropping out of community college in 1966. He stopped in San Francisco on his way over to Vietnam, and by the time he arrived, he was wearing bells and peace signs—not to mention carrying one hundred hits of acid. His experiences in Southeast Asia— acid trips down Tu Do Street, past the prostitutes and war cripples, becoming a peacenik and leading a moratorium procession in Saigon after the Tet Offensive—were pivotal.

"I turned on a lot of people with the acid. There were a lot of gay guys over there, but I was so damn shy. Half the USO place was gay. I didn't really flaunt it, but I sought out partners for sure. And when they sent me to an air base in Thailand, forget it. Those Thai boys! First night, I went to bed with, like, ten guys. They insisted, and I couldn't decide, so they all came home with me and each took a part of me, and all I remember is being licked."

By the time Peron returned to the States, he was ready to flaunt just about everything in his pursuit of freedom. Arriving on Castro Street as the working-class Irish neighborhood known as Eureka Valley was becoming home to an influx of gay hippies, Peron quickly became a fixture in the community.

"I renounced wealth and power. I wanted to just live in harmony with my brothers and sisters. I was very idealistic. I started a commune, got on food stamps, started dealing pot and going to school. I was going to be a psychiatrist. After a while, my pot-dealing business got so good I thought, Why am I going to school to find out about people's potty training when all they really have to know is to go out and get laid and find themselves? It was another pivotal point in my life. I thought, I'm going to be that psychiatrist anyway; only I'm going to be a pot seller."

As the Castro became the magnet for a new breed of audaciously open gay men whose political interests were very different from what journalist Randy Shilts would identify as the "gentle bourgeois effetism of generations past," San Francisco replaced New York as the center of the gay movement. "The politically conscious men of the Castro did not mince or step delicately down the street, they strutted defiantly," as Shilts observed. "Some called it Mecca, but to most gays it was nothing short of Oz, a place they had never hoped to see in their lifetimes." The Castro became home to twenty-five thousand homosexuals, with a quarter million showing up for events like the Gay Freedom Day Parade. New phrases entered the vernacular: Gay Pride, Gay Power, Gay Consciousness.

At the head of the parade was Harvey Milk. In 1973, Milk became the first openly gay man to run for city supervisor, making his candidacy a symbol of how gays could have an important role in the city leadership; he lost, but collected an impressive seventeen thousand votes. Milk was a charismatic, maverick populist and a brilliant public speaker with a keen wit and sense of humor. "My name is Harvey Milk and I'm here to recruit you," was one of his opening lines—a sardonic allusion to the view that gays wanted to recruit straight people into changing their sexual orientation. Organizing the gay community's businesses into a merchants association called the Castro Valley Association (CVA), Milk envisioned a progressive coalition of liberals, unions, and gays that would exercise its political clout to block the developers from tearing down low-income housing to build expensive high rises; he also wanted to abolish the vice squad that persecuted the gay community with police sweeps, beatings, and arrests. In 1975, he ran for supervisor again and lost, but Mayor George Moscone appointed him to the Board of Permit Appeals, making him the first openly gay city commissioner in the country. At a time when the overwhelming majority of homosexuals still did not live openly, Milk crafted a powerful message of self-reliance and self-empowerment, dedicating his political career to shattering the silence of gays and debunking homophobic myths. "I've got to fight not just for me but also for my lover and his next lover eventually," he declared. "It's got to be better for them than it was for me." The gay community responded in kind. With his next two unsuccessful campaigns for supervisor, Milk began gaining the kind of political credibility and media attention that no gay person ever had, turning out multitudes of "human billboards" along the city's thoroughfares in demonstrations that became, in essence, public declarations of gay pride and freedom.

While Harvey Milk became known as the Mayor of Castro Street—

the personification of the newly liberated spirit of gay identity, activism, and sexuality in San Francisco—Dennis Peron, owner of the restaurant that Milk used as his campaign headquarters, became the district's most prominent pot dealer. Even by the permissive standards of the times and the lively history of counterculture in San Francisco, the marijuana market called the Big Top that he operated on top of the restaurant was one of a kind.

"It was kind of one-stop shopping," Peron explained. "Hostesses. Baskets of pot. No waiting. You would tell them what you wanted and they would give it to you: Colombian, Cambodian, whatever. About two hundred to three hundred people a day came. I treated them with respect and gave them their money's worth. It was like a dream. People loved it."

In his determination to get elected, Milk had given up smoking pot and going to the bathhouses, but everyone else certainly wanted to get stoned; the use of drugs was becoming deeply woven into the new gay lifestyle of cruising, and everyone who went to the Island Restaurant was always given a free joint, courtesy of Dennis Peron.

"Things were getting big. I was grossing twenty thousand dollars a day, making eight thousand dollars, all twenties under the table. I employed two hundred people. I had people just counting, sorting, and stacking it. I was living on Castro Street in a place where I cut the roof out so I had a view of the whole city. I had a lot of lovers during this period. Boys lined up. I was one of the first to have safe sex. Many kids came through my house—America's castaways, gay kids thrown out of their houses; one of them is now a bank president. I gave all my money away, supported a lot of things. I didn't want anything, just to create a whole better way of life for people. I had good karma. Business was going so good that I bought a resort. I was building the coolest New Age place in the world."

If freedom was the defining characteristic of the vision that Milk and Peron shared for the future of San Francisco, they wanted to extend it beyond even sexual choice and political clout to include the freedom to possess and use marijuana. As Milk prepared to make his fourth run for city supervisor, Peron was gathering sixteen thousand signatures for Proposition W, which stated, "We, the people of San Francisco, demand that the

District Attorney, along with the Chief of Police, cease the arrest and prosecution involved in the cultivation, transfer, or possession of marijuana." Not only did Milk avidly support the initiative, but the new mayor, George Moscone, was also a strong supporter of marijuana decriminalization. As a state senator, Moscone had sponsored the Moscone Act of 1976, which reduced the penalty for possession of an ounce or less from a felony to a citable misdemeanor with a fine of a hundred dollars. The act also included a provision that required the destruction of records of any court or public agency pertaining to an arrest or conviction for possession of marijuana after a period of two years—a step toward decriminalization unique in the history of the nation that would infuriate California conservatives. Moscone had won the mayoral election by the slimmest of margins when the political landscape was being redrawn by the increasing power of newly organized neighborhood districts like the Castro over the old Irish-Italian political machine and downtown business interests which had always run the city. In 1977, with the political landscape shifting and district elections replacing citywide elections, Harvey Milk became the first gay person ever to be elected to the board of supervisors of an American city. Moscone now found himself with a new board that included the moderate Diane Feinstein as its president, the newly elected Harvey Milk, and an archconservative ex-paratrooper, fireman, and cop named Dan White, representing the Visitacion Valley.

At a time when the national political scene featured the emergence of an antigay backlash personified by Anita Bryant's "Save Our Children" movement (Byrant advocated a jail sentence of twenty years for anyone caught in a homosexual act), Harvey Milk persuaded the city council to pass a Gay Rights Ordinance that protected gays from being fired from their jobs, which caused Dan White to denounce Milk and resign from the board of supervisors in bitter protest. The hate mail that poured into Milk's office would force him to make a tape recording, with instructions to be read only in the event of his assassination: "If a bullet should enter my brain, let that bullet destroy every closet door."

From Dennis Peron's vantage point, the future never looked more hopeful. The newly emerging gay nation had a noble champion in Harvey Milk, and with the new Carter administration in Washington and George Moscone in San Francisco, the complete decriminalization of marijuana seemed all but inevitable. "And then I was busted running my pot supermarket. Busted *big*."

The day of the big bust at the Big Top began like any other. "People were rolling joints," Peron recalled. "There were about ten people working when I heard a rumbling at the door. I see a gun coming up the stairs, and it was attached to this big black guy in a floppy hat. My first instinct was that these were robbers, and I grabbed the first thing next to me which was a water bottle, and I held it over my head and said, 'Motherfucker, go down the stairs and forget about this, otherwise I'm going to smash you in the head with this fucking bottle!' but I never got to throw it because he immediately shot me in the leg, shattered the femur. Another bullet goes whizzing past my head. Then he put the gun right to my head and I'm saying, 'Take the money,' and another guy comes in and says, 'What's going on?' And he says, 'I'm just putting Mr. Peron under arrest.' "

Peron would be busted sixteen times, but the Big Top bust was certainly the most sensational. The police seized two hundred pounds of pot, three thousand hits of acid, four pounds of mushrooms, a quarter of a million dollars, and arrested a hundred people. "Then, a spectacular trial. We knew the cops hated gay people so we teased them a lot."

The narc who had shot Peron, Paul Macevecis, was a close friend, as it turned out, of Dan White's. "One day outside in the hallway, I said to Paul, 'We love your shoes today. Where'd you get those Guccis?' And he said, 'You motherfucking faggot, I should have killed you so there'd be one less faggot in San Francisco!' He didn't know that there was a whole string of lawyers behind him who heard him say it. They got him back on the stand and then just wore him down."

The defense attorneys asked the policeman to show the exact position he had been in when he shot Peron. Macevecis took out his gun and aimed it right at Peron's chest, and when the lawyers were finished questioning him he just stood there with the gun still aimed at Peron, like he was going to pull the trigger—a chilling moment for all who were present in the courtroom that day, including the jury. Macevecis's testimony was thrown out of court and Peron received a mere six months in the San Bruno jail. "I know people who are still in prison for half the amount I was busted with. I was the media darling: SUPER DEALER'S DAY IN COURT."

Milk told Peron that he was going to appoint him to the city's Commission on Drug and Alcohol Abuse when he got out of jail, but it would never come to pass. The events of November 27, 1978—the day Dan White crawled through a basement window of City Hall to avoid the metal detector, made his way upstairs to shoot George Moscone to death in his office, and then calmly walked to the office of Harvey Milk and fired five shots into his body—would forever haunt San Francisco, but remained uniquely unbearable for Dennis Peron. Many would cite White's rabidly antigay conservatism as the motivating factor for the assassinations; others maintained that White was troubled because he had left the board of supervisors and Moscone had denied his request to return. But as Dennis Peron languished in his San Bruno prison cell and forty thousand mourners silently marched to the City Hall with their flickering candles to sing "Swing Low, Sweet Chariot," there was never any doubt in his mind about what had happened.

"Harvey openly supported drug users. After my bust I was interviewed by the *Chronicle.* They asked if I had any friends, and I said, yes, Harvey Milk is my friend. Then they ran over to Harvey Milk, and he said yes, Dennis Peron is a good man, an upstanding member of the community. So Dan White got up at the board of supervisors and denounced Harvey Milk for supporting a pot dealer. Harvey told him to go blow it out of his ass. And the narcs *hated* me. I'd just finished making fools of them. They planted the seed that killed Harvey Milk." Peron went silent. "I caused Harvey to be killed. Every day of my life since he died I've thought of him, every day it's crossed my mind in one way or another."

The death of Harvey Milk would galvanize more gay people than his election ever had, but the doors of marijuana legalization would remain firmly closed in San Francisco. Proposition W, which passed with 56 percent of the vote, would never be implemented by the administration of Diane Feinstein, and even the coalition that had brought Milk to power would be replaced with the old regime of developers and business interests. But for Dennis Peron and others the dream of making San Francisco the capital of marijuana tolerance—the American Amsterdam—would hardly die. Twelve years later it would reappear in the debate over medical marijuana.

## II. The Smell of a Vanished Era

A TYPICAL NIGHT at the Anvil? Just remembering the night-by-night buffet of drugs and sex that he associated with being gay in the New York of the 1970s was enough to send Lance Loud into a verbal tizzy.

"Okay, here we are, the Anvil. It's 1979. I'm a prostitute, and I'm with Freddie Mercury and a client. The client wanted party favors, and of course I bought them at a very low price—MDA, lots of coke, poppers—and charged him an exorbitant fee, because that's what you do when you're a hustler, right? I encouraged him to go into the back room so I could dump him, and he disappeared into that black pit—I was not into that, I just liked hanging out—and I'd snort coke at the bar until dawn, just watching. Amyl at this point; there was a period when I couldn't have sex without it! There was so *much* in that aroma! It was just *so* wantonly chemical!"

Loud broke off and stared out the café window at the passersby on Santa Monica Boulevard. "It's like revisiting the smell of a vanished era," he said finally.

Although he was famous from being on television, Lance Loud's nights of amyl nitrate were never played out on camera. In 1973, in twelve unscripted installments edited down from three hundred hours of footage shot over seven months, ten million Americans encountered Loud in Alan and Susan Raymond's groundbreaking cinema verité documentary *An American Family*, the forerunner of all "reality-based" television. As a teenager in affluent Santa Barbara, Loud had fallen in love with amphetamines, the drug of choice of the New York underground, hungrily gleaning everything he could from *The Chelsea Girls* and *Screen Test*, dying his hair silver like Warhol's and idolizing Edie Sedgwick and Ondine, dreaming of nights at Max's Kansas City. When he came out in the second episode, Loud became America's first openly gay teenager. Not everyone fell in love with him—Anne Roiphe called him an "evil flower," an "electric eel," a "Goyaesque emotional dwarf," and referred to his "flamboyant leech-like homosexuality" in *The New York Times Magazine*—but there he was, on the cover of *Newsweek* and on *The Dick Cavett Show*. By the time he moved to New York in 1973, to chase a career in rock and roll as well as his romantic visions of the Warholian underground, he had become the kind of cultural icon that only the television age could have produced. "At first, I was shocked when I realized I was being angled as the famous fag son. It was like, my God, this is going to be my title for the rest of my life! I was upset at first, but then I thought, Why not just floor it?"

And so he would.

"Drugs were a means of conforming at that point. You *had* to do it, as opposed to the Sixties, when it was optional, a choice. In the Seventies, being an individual was very out. As a gay man, you had to be part of the group, and part of the group meant that you had to be part of these long, involved sexual-chemical run-ins. Drugs and sex became interlocked. All the time."

It was ironic that Loud became an icon of a culture that he felt out of step with. "I went to the baths and did not like it. I did not like disco; I did not look like one of those tight-T-shirt, blue-jean, work-booted clones. I would take part in the gay sex-drug syndrome with orgies and things like that because I wanted to have sex with guys, but I never really liked it—it all seemed so very boring and plebian. I kept thinking, God, part of the reason I became gay and encouraged this in myself was I liked the idea of being a *pervert*—and here was this whole fucking nation of these middle-class bores on drugs all doing these tired sexual tournaments! So I went along because even though I had that feeling, at the same time I was fighting against the very real need to be a part of something. As a gay man, you *had* to reach out, and drugs were a vital part of that."

Loud was hardly bashful about sharing his impressions of the wide-ranging gay pharmacopoeia. "MDA may have been known as the love drug—for me it was the love-Ex-Lax drug. It gave me diarrhea—I hated it. Coke gave you that fleeting sense of superiority, which lasted about two seconds. I had a season of Quaaludes, but they didn't go with anything in my chemical wardrobe. You'd take a Quaalude, and the coke would invalidate it or a drink would throw you so far over the line you'd either ruin someone's couch barfing or die in your own vomit. We did the Bicentennial thing, all dusted on angel dust. That was fabulous! Do you remember David Lochary, he was in all of John Waters's films and ended up OD'ing on angel dust?—nice way to go, I'm sure. I was with that crowd, and everyone was dusted. It was scary. They'd just get dusted and crawl around on their hands and knees and beg for forgiveness."

And then, of course, there was the great chemical staple, amyl nitrate. "It was like angel dust, one of those impossible things that you'd wonder *how* you ever talked yourself into doing. You could just hear thousands of brain cells jumping to their death with every whiff! I remember being at this producer's apartment at five in the morning, and we lined up these tables, and this amazing drag queen came out and did an Eartha Kitt song, and this producer was *drinking* poppers, and I just thought, This era is going to come to a crashing halt. The rotted normalcy of it—not eloquent or elaborate, just twisted in a gothic, dismally mundane way."

A brief dossier on amyl nitrate. Invented in 1857 for the treatment of angina pectoris. Active only when inhaled. Sold as a clear, yellow volatile liquid in glass ampoules of .2 of a milliliter. Dilates blood vessels and relaxes the smooth (involuntary) muscles (read as *anal sphincter muscles* in the gay world). Quick acting—takes effect within thirty seconds. Lasts only two minutes; side effects may include headache, nausea, flushing of the face, vomiting—all of which was commonly endured by millions of gay men, of course, because of the drug's highly vaunted reputation as a great sex stimulator and orgasm intensifier when popped and inhaled, especially on the precipice of ejaculation. May cause temporary visual disorders, like halos of yellow or blue surrounding dark objects against a light background, that would distort one's visual perception of sex scenes of the most spontaneous, elaborate, and carnally lewd nature imaginable. Sold without prescription in some states.

"Poppers were just one of those accoutrements, one of those side dishes to this increasingly large and cluttered banquet of sexual things. There was a whole status thing with them in the gay culture. There were very good and very bad poppers, and if you were hip and rich and elite, you had the best. A person who had the kind called Locker Room—forget it, nickel-and-dime shit. The good ones were pharmaceutical and came in a tall, thin brown bottle. I could never understand people taking it out and doing hits of it in public—that was not my cup of tequila—but later, when I became a prostitute, it became very important. You'd try to foist it on the guys just to get them really hot and try to get it over with.

Of course, that could backfire. When they'd take too much or weren't used to it, then they'd lose the hard-on, and then it would be *oh, boy.*"

Nobody would document the central role that amyl would come to play in this sexual culture better than John Rechy, author of one of the first classics of the homosexual underground, *City of Night,* as well as *The Sexual Outlaw, Rushes, Numbers,* and *Bodies and Souls.* "I used amyl nitrate a lot back in the Fifties," the author recounted in his apartment in the Los Feliz section of Hollywood. Rechy came of age during the McCarthy hysteria of the 1950s, an era of dark persecution for homosexuals. During the early 1960s, when the hustling scene in downtown Los Angeles centered around Pershing Square, at places like Harry's Bar and Wally's Bar, he went up on the roof of an apartment building on Hope Street and smoked a joint that brought forth the image of freezing angels, which, he claimed, unleashed the poetry that made "The Fabulous Wedding of Miss Destiny" the most famous section of *City of Night.* "It helped me break away from what I thought was my strict chronicling of reality, to find a further reality, which is, of course, the reality of fiction." In the Seventies, after his mother's death, Rechy had a "massive acid bummer," bringing him "to the edge of suicide," after which he began "edging into heroin—not shooting up but snorting it—and it was then that I saw myself in decline. I stopped it all and will not touch it ever again."

By the late Seventies, Rechy had become one of the foremost chroniclers of the gay sexual underground. In *The Sexual Outlaw,* an account of three days and nights in the underground of Los Angeles—"the silently symphonic, intricate, instinctively choreographed beauty of the promiscuous sexhunt"—he put forth his fundamental notion of the promiscuous homosexual as a sexual revolutionary flourishing within the context of his own persecution: "Knowing that each second his freedom may be ripped away arbitrarily, he lives fully at the brink. . . . No stricture— legal, medical, religious—will ever stop him. It will only harden his defiance."

In a world where gays were outcasts, despised by society and murdered by fag bashers for being homosexual, to suck and fuck on the streets was an act of revolution; the "sexhunt" became an art form that, like the priesthood, required "total sacrifice and commitment" but whose meaning would always remain elusive, paradoxical, the object of his continuing exploration. "And what was found?" wonders Jim, one of Rechy's subjects in *The Sexual Outlaw,* after a night of cruising. "How many hands? How many mouths? How many cocks? How many assholes? How many lovers, strangers, men?" As Rechy himself would recognize, "At its best, the gay experience is liberating, adventurous, righteously daring, revolutionary, and beautiful in its sexual abundance. At worst it is a stark vision of hell."

An adjective often used by Rechy to evoke the properties of amyl in this sexual milieu is *afferent:* "bearing inward," conveying impulses toward a nerve center. After the *snap-pop* of the ampoule and the fierce inhalation, the blood would rush, the heart pound so fast that sex would seem to explode, crushing everything—time, reality—into the sexual moment. The "rot-tinged" scent would mix with the aroma of sex; sometimes the odor itself was enough to trigger sex when entering a room.

"I hate the word *gay,*" Rechy declared. "I'm all for calling it *Greek* or *Trojan,* but you can't escape it, and within that sector there was something that was also linked to it, if you're exploring the effects of amyl nitrate—something very terrible, of which I can speak because it was happening to me. There were those who would not even go to those places and participate, it was so entrenched, so woven into the texture of sexuality. I began questioning it very severely, getting obsessed by it, and wrote a book called *Rushes* that I think—and I'm bold enough to say—announces the death of the sexual revolution."

The danger that *Rushes* warned of—"the boundaries being ferociously pushed in the orgy rooms where sex was no longer sex," as the author called it—coexisted with amyl in the gay world. "It was almost as if sex was no longer for pleasure but for bludgeoning. As if you weren't having sex with another person. You had people who no longer went home with anybody. It had to be orgies—orgy rooms were happening in New York, Los Angeles. Nothing was enough. And amyl was central to that. Amyl was the incense."

Rechy based the book on his own forays into the Mineshaft, a well-known "leather-and-Western" bar in New York; he took the very name of the bar and title of the book from a popular brand of amyl called Rush. "It's true that amyl heightens the sexual sensation, but it also turns it very animalistic," he elaborated. "The thing with amyl that I thought was integral, from my experience—it made one sexually mean. If one were going to be sexually mean, it made one meaner; and if one were going to be sexually vulnerable, it made the person more so. If you walked into the Mineshaft, it was like an assault—a phenomenon like nothing else. I recorded it quite accurately in *Rushes*."

It isn't hard to understand why amyl became so integrated into the ritualistic S&M sex of the Mineshaft; or why Rechy, with his Catholic background, would style the book after a mass. "The spectacle was always accompanied by this extraordinary ritual—sexual excess where the boundaries of it were not sex. Inevitably, you would have somebody like an android, with a crushed popper to his nose. I couldn't accept it anymore."

What was happening was becoming very clear to Rechy. In the days of closeted silence, secrecy, and fear in which he had come of age, gay men had been forced to use the abandoned piers of the waterfront for the sexhunt. Now, with liberation, that was no longer necessary, but the leather bars were consciously re-creating that desolate ambience, even importing the debris of darkened warehouses and vanished piers.

"We brought those props in as evidence that we were now celebrating our oppression," Rechy maintained. "Liberation was really reaction. The body was being turned away from, and the costumed body was taking over. You had bars where it had become almost like Puritanism—every inch of the body covered, masks, and gloves. The only antecedent for such a costume is the executioner—I *challenge* anybody else to find a different one for that particular costume! I thought we were at that point moving into an area of ritualizing our own persecution, very much like a mass. In that milieu, again, amyl was the holy incense." But it didn't end there. "The masculine homosexuals had become the new sissy haters, like the bullies who had taunted them as children," Rechy asserted in the book. Sex had become a "soulless reduction." It was a message that not many were willing to accept at the time.

"When I began writing about this, it got me into a lot of trouble and misunderstanding because on the one hand I had been promoting the richness of promiscuity and, on the other, how could I have put down the new frontier? But as I began exploring myself and never disallowing either my fascination or participation, I began wondering, asking, What now? There were great dangers. Where were we going? What's going to happen?"

As AIDS ravaged the gay community during the 1980s, lives became consumed by the most basic questions of survival and the crushing torments of daily death. As for the part that drugs might have played in the contagion, all would agree that they were central to the lifestyle, but very few would agree on the nature and level of their responsibility, particularly as moral indictments began to mount. For John Rechy, who survived, the answer was clear: "AIDS had nothing to do with promiscuity," he insisted. "If it had been an illness like polio that found its way into swimming pools, that would not indict swimming—it just happened there. Legionnaire's disease never became a judgment of reactionary politics! *Drugs* didn't cause AIDS, nor did *promiscuity*—they were merely conduits."

For Lance Loud, who would contract the HIV virus and eventually perish from its complications, the answer was equally obvious: "I think a lot of people don't want to deal with the drug issue because it's very incriminating. All the evidence points to it—that drug use was very important in developing the climate that bred the spreading of the disease. There's a tremendous amount of denial. People just don't want to think about the overall meaning of drugs in the sexual climate of the Seventies—and I don't blame them. We can't deal with it, can't think about it now, because it will drive us insane."

# 10

## The Last Dance

*"There is a lot of wreckage in the fast lane these days."*

—Hunter S. Thompson, "Bad Craziness in Palm Beach:
I Told Her It Was Wrong," 1983

### I. Secret Stash, Heavy Bread

ROLLIE HUGGINS sat in the darkened auditorium. From the opening credits, underscored by the crunching funk of Curtis Mayfield's wah-wah pedal, the movie *Super Fly* was off and running. The fade-in alone—the camera pulling back on Youngblood Priest in bed with the smolderingly sexy black girl as Mayfield sings, *"Can't reason with the pusherman, finance is all that he understands"*—was enough to blow Huggins's mind. He was, after all, watching his own life up on the screen.

It was 1973, and Rollie Huggins was in the auditorium of the medium-security federal prison in Danbury, Connecticut, serving a three-and-a-half-year sentence for exactly the kinds of criminal activities being depicted on the screen. The movie was based on a nonfiction book by Richard Woodley published in 1971 called *Dealer: Portrait of a Cocaine Merchant;* the dealer was "Jimmy," the man who had been Huggins's partner in the cocaine business in New York in the late 1960s. Woodley had spent a lot of time around both men, soaking up the ambience of the Life to tell the story of a man who sold the best stuff in New York—"top-shelf coke, superfly"—who made five thousand dollars a week, carried a small .25 Browning automatic, and wanted to set aside one hundred thousand dollars to "buy a nice house, retire from hustling to run some legitimate business, marry his woman and raise a family."

*Dealer* was as much about the style of the Life as the drug—"a closely studied art, a technique of survival. Flash is in the clothes, the cars, the eyes, the walk, the talk"—and this style had been brought vividly to life by Gordon Parks Jr.'s movie: the New Uptown Flash of the gilded hustlers along Lenox, Seventh, and Eighth Avenues north of Central Park, who drove fifteen-thousand-dollar custom-made two-toned Eldorados and Lincolns with telephones and TVs, special-cut sunroofs, and leopard upholstery. Togged out in their personally tailored velvet suits and high-heeled crocodile shoes, hands dripping with diamond rings, they were usually seen with stunning, fur-clad black women draped on their arms.

The uptown drug game of the previous generation had been largely about heroin and numbers running and the kind of second-story, back-alley crime perpetrated by junkies in need of a fix. It had been a game about horse for losers and punks, with no glamour or power; this was a game about respect and status and having moves, all of it symbolized by the little emerald-and-ivory-encrusted spoons around their necks and the white powder that was known as C, star dust, snow, blow—"a powerful central nervous system stimulant that is the least discussed of the so-called 'hard drugs,' " as Woodley described it, "yet is a staple of the diet of entertainers and the favorite of the drug dealers themselves; the most expensive 'high' of them all; the King." The new aesthetic of cool was about being unashamedly flamboyant, extravagant, and more outrageous than the next guy; funk music provided the soundtrack of the scene, and the all-inclusive adjective used to describe it was *fly*, or *superfly*. One line in the movie seemed to sum it all up: "I'm gonna make a pisspot full of money and I'm gonna live like a fucking Black Prince . . . Yes, this is the *Life*!"

As played by Ron O'Neal, Priest walks a tightrope through a double-crossing world of dirty cops and crooked politicians as he tries to beat the Man at his own game—he's a "a victim of ghetto demands," as one lyric portrays his state of affairs. What he's really about is "having the choice, being able to decide," as Priest puts it, "not to be forced into doing the thing because that's the way it is"—in other words, "it's to be free." In the final, waterfront scene, Priest is surrounded by police and takes a one-and-one snort of blow (a hit up each nostril), kind of like Popeye eating his spinach; then, after kicking ass, he gets into his Eldorado and drives off to the sound of Mayfield's rising track, undaunted, undefeated. *Super Fly* became an instant sensation. It also provided cocaine with a new uptown street mythos ("That's the American dream, nigger") and gave Rollie Huggins a lot to think about as he tossed restlessly in his cell.

Like Youngblood Priest, Rollie Huggins had wanted out of the game. He was increasingly concerned about the possibility of violence that seemed to accompany the growing amounts of money he was handling, and when he was busted for selling a kilo of cocaine to an undercover narc in 1970, there were tickets in his bag for a flight to St. Thomas. At the same time, there was an aspect of destiny about his life as a coke dealer—his whole wild ride in New York had been like one endless matchbook snort of blow. He grew up handsome, popular, and gifted in a small town in western Pennsylvania, the kind of black kid adept at moving in the white world at a time when such social motion was bound to bring him emotional pain. And it did. He was rejected from the college fraternity he pledged because of race, dropped out, joined the air force, and traveled through places like Clarksburg, Mississippi, during that terrible season in 1955 after Emmett Till had been lynched.

Huggins arrived in New York just as the Sixties were beginning to percolate and became part of the elite crowd of young and dynamic black athletes, musicians, and businessmen at the time of Say It Loud, I'm Black and I'm Proud, when the guys all dressed in West African kunte cloth and dashikis and sported extremely belligerent Afros. White girls couldn't seem to get enough of black men; reefer seemed at the center of everything, but cocaine was still only a pantry item in some circles of musicians. Huggins opened up one of the first employment agencies for young black professionals. He drove a red GTO convertible, had a beautiful girlfriend once linked to Miles Davis and Burt Lancaster, was photographed by *Jet* magazine, hung out with the Supremes at Kenneth Gibson's inauguration as the first black mayor of Newark, and planned to retire at forty. It was a glamorous and socially schizophrenic life, in which he was equally at home in the boardroom and on the street, as comfortable among executives, celebrities, and hippies as he was among pimps and hustlers. At some point in the late 1960s, all those characters started to swirl together, and the cocaine scene of New York began to coalesce. Huggins bought his first kilo for eighteen thousand dollars from some Colombians who lived at 106th Street and Central Park West, and from the first deal he loved the adventure. His apartment on 95th Street, with its pulsating strobe lights and water bed, was always open to an ever-growing clientele. It was the sort of place where beautiful girls answered the door naked.

"People were always saying, 'Oh, Rollie, you're a crazy motherfucker,' and that's all I wanted to hear. There was a lot of money starting to flow through the business, but it was all going to my lifestyle. I was dealing to people like a famous bandleader, writers, black intellectuals, well-to-do hippies, the people down on Bleecker and MacDougal, lots of celebrities white and black. Rocks were the big thing, and people were willing to pay premium money if we could deliver them. In a kilo, you would expect two or three hundred grams of rocks. One celebrity told me that instead of paying six hundred to seven hundred dollars for an ounce, he would pay whatever if I could get him an ounce of pure rock."

Huggins had gotten jobs for thousands of young, educated black kids through his business, but he became less and less interested in it and began to withdraw from the world of the Fortune 500. From the outset, it was clear that it was just as easy to get addicted to the life around cocaine as to the drug itself; they became one. He maintained strict standards of behavior and business values, but the ride just kept getting wilder, and the more weight he dealt, the more he worried about having to use the gun he was carrying around, and the more he wanted to do the drug. He was wired all the time and took Valium so often that it virtually stopped working. He experienced states of paranoia, psychosis, depression, and overdose that users would not associate with the drug for another twelve to fifteen years. By the time he made the fateful gesture of authorizing the transfer of a kilo from the trunk of his parked car and was whacked across the face with a pistol by a narc and handcuffed, he was actually relieved that he was being arrested.

"At the West Tenth Street station, I slept for forty-eight straight hours before waking up in the holding tank and seeing the toilet with no seat and realizing I was among a bunch of guys withdrawing horribly from methadone . . . I was glad because I needed to stop and couldn't, but there were no rehabs or detoxes in those days—nothing but Phoenix House, and I couldn't see doing that. This was the only way I could have stopped my obsession with being high every second. It was mental illness in its highest form. When I went into the joint, my appetite came back, and my hand tremor went away."

It was the beginning of the Cocaine Age. In 1970, the year Huggins was busted, seizures of cocaine in the United States exceeded heroin for the first time, at 227 pounds; over the next two years, they went from 408 to 619 pounds—a sevenfold increase since 1969. Though it was still very far from being a phenomenon on the level of grass, acid, or amphetamines (at one thousand dollars an ounce, how could it be?), something was happening to make the demand for the drug surge as never before. Amazingly, it was happening just as the Rockefeller drug laws were going into effect in New York, which made life in prison mandatory for anyone caught with more than two ounces of cocaine. No doubt it had something to do with an article in *Newsweek* in 1973, in which a DEA official observed, "In the last three years the coke traffic has gone through the roof. Right now *anybody* can go down there, turn a kilo for $4,000, and sell it back here for $20,000"—an astronomical profit margin that began to attract a whole new generation of smugglers.

As for Huggins, he would never again be a high-powered dealer, but his own experience with cocaine was far from over. He would maintain his flair for finding thrills and fast money, and everywhere he went for the next fifteen years—the world of heavyweight prizefights, the booming industry of personal computers—the drug would follow.

"When I was released from the prison, the first place I went was the music business and the promotion end of funk music. It was a time when disc jockeys were getting their legs broken and you'd see guys at the Grammy Awards one night getting indicted the next. My job was to get on a train or a plane and get my bag of records airplay on black radio stations around the country. I'd go to the retailers and locations that report to the trades, . . . and I'd get them women and drugs."

The name for it was *drugola,* and while Rollie Huggins would stay straight at the beginning, it was only a matter of time before he dipped back into the bag of blow.

"That was the currency—sex and cocaine. That's what it seemed the Seventies was going to be all about."

## II. Like Flying to Paris for Breakfast

WHEN BOB SABBAG got his contract to write *Snowblind: A Brief Career in the Cocaine Trade,* he knew almost as little about writing books as he did about the history and pharmacology of cocaine. He had kicked around as a newspaper reporter for a number of years before he got the call from an editor at Bobbs-Merrill. The cocaine smuggler Sabbag would call Zachary Swan had been on trial out on Long Island, and the DA had told him that his life would make a "terrific story." The real-life Swan had approached Bobbs-Merrill, publishers of *Raggedy Ann* and *The Joy of Cooking,* and when an editor there realized that writers like Peter Maas and Robin Moore were unavailable to collaborate with the cocaine smuggler, an agent took the opportunity to proffer a completely unknown writer: "Hey, I think *Bob Sabbag* is available!"

"This was as big a scam as Swan ever pulled off right?" Sabbag admitted. "But when the editor, Tom Gervase, told me I could write the book any way I wanted to, it became attractive to me . . . I didn't know anyone personally who was doing cocaine before I met Swan. My relationship to the drug world was with people who were pot smokers and doing hallucinogens, and that was behind me, but what struck me about cocaine as Swan represented it to me was that it was a drug for adults."

Swan was a middle-aged ex–Madison Avenue executive who had discovered marijuana in his early forties and had gone on to have a career as a smuggler, first of marijuana and then of cocaine—"and here he was doing a drug that I only vaguely associated with jazz musicians," Sabbag went on. "I quickly found out that movie stars and athletes were doing it; *The New York Times* had published an article about it in 1974, talking about how it was the drug of the elite, the upper class—the boulevardiers of America—and it was being written about like it was this brand-new discovery. At that time, it was as much about *having* it as *doing* it. The fact that it was seventy-five dollars a gram made it different than any other drug. I described it as like flying to Paris for breakfast—in other words, it was a badge, a statement, and being associated with it and in possession of it was probably even more important than whatever high you got."

The ephemeral nature of the high only added to its reputation as designed for the select few. "It was a very subtle high. You have to come to *cocaine,* cocaine doesn't come to *you.* People would do it and say, 'What is it? I don't feel anything'—it didn't give them the rush they were expecting, like speed. Hunter Thompson called it a 'motor drug' in an interview with *Playboy,* his point being that it was a waste of money, not that powerful, and who would want to spend that kind of money when you could buy something that would *really* fuck you up, like speed or acid? So you had to come to cocaine halfway, and when you first started doing it, in the early stages, that's the kind of relationship you developed, but there's a kind of seduction there that makes it difficult to stay at that level."

Around the time Sabbag started researching his book, Richard Rhodes wrote an article about cocaine for *Playboy* that went a long way toward establishing the myth that the substance was not addictive, that it was "a relatively benign substance no more harmful than marijuana," as Sabbag put it. "Of course, so much of what we heard about drugs up to that point had been bullshit; why not assume that whatever bad rap they might put on cocaine was bullshit, too?"

David Crosby, already deep into his romance with cocaine, would come to know as much about the drug as any man alive, and agreed wholeheartedly with this assessment. "We all knew—because it was common knowledge, accepted knowledge—that cocaine was not addictive. The authorities screwed it up by overdoing it. Remember, they told us that if we took acid, we would burn out our eyes looking at the sun and have bad babies."

Bob Sabbag had no reason to disbelieve that early assessment, given what he was observing about the substance himself. "This notion didn't come from nowhere—it came from anecdotal experience of people who were drug users, including Swan, who was living proof that you could do a line at a time and not become compulsive about it, because he would go off it for months at a time. I was the only guy who knew anybody doing it, and the people I saw would buy a gram for the weekend and share it with six people and have a wonderful time. It wasn't until people started buying it by the quarter ounce and doing megadoses that you started hearing horror stories. In the beginning, my take on cocaine was that Freud had positive things to say about it, the Incas had positive things to say."

By now, there was also a growing body of lore about the drug in the pop culture. Laura Nyro had sung about it as far back as 1966 in "Buy and Sell" ("Cocaine and . . . sweet candy"), and Johnny Cash had a run with the drug in 1969, when he recorded "Cocaine Blues" ("Lay off that whiskey and let that cocaine be"). As Dennis Hopper has pointed out, the drug entered the pharmacological glossary of the youth culture in a big way with *Easy Rider* in 1969. *"It is life,"* declares the Mexican who sells the drug to Hopper and Peter Fonda, who turn around and sell it to the mysterious buyer in the chauffeur-driven Rolls (played by the producer Phil Spector, a classic example of the high-powered music-industry user if ever there was one) to finance their cross-country run. While the duo are perfectly willing to traffic in the drug, they refrain from using it—a clear reflection of the counterculture's distrust of the drug as somehow "bourgeois"—and many would surmise that Fonda's cryptic line that "We blew it" at the end of the film was an allusion to the cocaine. But that image changed soon enough. In 1970, the trademark snort at the fade-in of "Casey Jones" referenced the drug for the ever-growing population of Grateful Dead fans, along with the provocative line about "Sweet Jane" in "Truckin' ": "Livin' on reds, vitamin C, and cocaine, all a friend can say is, 'Ain't it a shame.' " That same year the Rolling Stones dropped a clear mention of it in "Let It Bleed" ("there will always be a space in my parking lot when you need a little coke and sympathy") and the following year etched it vividly as "sweet cousin cocaine" in "Sister Morphine." Then the hit soundtrack of *Super Fly* packaged its glamour for hip, black urban culture in no fewer than four songs. By 1975, the drug was part of the litany of substances Ringo Starr had to give up because he was "tired of waking up on the floor" in "The No No Song."

The drug's presence along the axis of the literary-film world became conspicuous in 1973 with the publication in *Esquire* of "Lady," an installment of Bruce Jay Friedman's novel *About Harry Towns*. Friedman's protagonist was an affluent Manhattan screenwriter who discovers that when he carries his little silver foil packet of Peruvian rock against his thigh, "he felt rich and fortified, almost as though he were carrying a gun." The story was striking for its portrayal of the drug as a sexual tool:

"Lady," the nickname of the drug, "had to do with the fact that ladies, once they took a taste of the drug, instantly became coke lovers and could not get enough of it." Harry Towns has heard that "lovers would receive the world's most erotic sensation by putting dabs of coke on their genitals and then swiping it off." He tries it, of course, only to realize that it's "nothing to write home about. As far as he could see it was a tricky way to get at the coke" (this conclusion, however, would hardly stop other writers of pulp fiction, like Harold Robbins, from turning cocaine-on-genitalia into a cliché). From that point on, the reputation of the drug as an erotic accessory would only increase.

In 1975, the first contemporary book-length study, Richard Ashley's *Cocaine: Its History, Uses, and Effects,* appeared, marking the beginning of serious literature investigating the drug. The paucity of knowledge about the drug was remarkable. "When I started LEMAR in Buffalo in '66, the head of the pharmacology department asked me if I had been aware that there had been a cocaine epidemic in the 1880s," recalled Dr. Michael Aldrich. After writing his dissertation on cannabis and being granted the nation's first "pot PhD" from the botany department of MIT, Aldrich (known as Dr. Dope) had moved to California and become a well-known teacher, activist, writer, and drug historian. "My interest was heavily in the historical and literary side of marijuana, which was a vastly different culture . . . When I arrived in L.A. with my marijuana PhD clutched firmly to my breast, in 1970, the third person I met was a karate expert who ran a record shop—'Have a whiff on me,' he said, and I used cocaine daily for fifteen years after that—and isolated myself from Ginsberg, Leary, and the whole counterculture, except for the fact that I was still advocating the legalization of marijuana. But I was very alone out here—little did I know that Jerry Garcia was starting his coke habit at about the same time." Indeed, all one had to do was to ask Allen Ginsberg for his opinion on cocaine to ascertain why Aldrich had felt so cut off from the traditional counterculture regarding his use of the drug. "I *hate* cocaine," the poet declared. "It's a drag. It struck me from the very beginning as being conducive to psychosis and aggression, completely distinct from pot and LSD." As Tom Robbins put it, "I felt like cocaine put holes in your aura. There's a darkness in it."

Aldrich described his daily use of the drug as a "very sparse, very moderate" exercise in responsible self-control—"four lines a night, two in each nostril, and I'd put it away, and if I did more than one gram a month, I'd cut down"—and then he would work through the night on a history of the Incas and cocaine. As Aldrich delved into its history, he discovered a multicultural lineage that was astonishing. For three thousand years, the Indian *coqueros* had been chewing the leaves of *Erythroxylon coca,* a flowering plant indigenous to the slopes of the Andes from the Strait of Magellan to the Caribbean Sea. The Indians believed it to be a divine gift to help ease their time on earth by providing energy at high altitudes and lifting their spirits; the Spanish conquistadors were convinced that those feats of endurance came directly from a pact with the devil. For the most part, the medical establishment ignored cocaine hydrochloride after it was isolated from coca in 1855, until Freud discovered it as a twenty-eight-year-old neurologist and published "Über Coca" in 1884, in which he detailed its history, surveyed its literature, and reported its effects. Four years later, Sherlock Holmes was using it as a mental stimulant in Sir Arthur Conan Doyle's *Sign of the Four*—"I crave for mental exaltation, Watson!" When newspapers began extolling its virtues, cocaine became increasingly popular among doctors and patent-medicine makers as a local anaesthetic and antidote to low energy and depression; entrepreneurs were soon packaging it for rich and poor and people of all ages, putting it in tea, soda pop, and wine.

In the mid-1880s, Angelo Mariani produced a celebrated coca wine called Vin Mariani that became the favorite infusion of the Prince of Wales, Pope Leo XIII, Jules Verne, and Thomas Edison. It was therefore not surprising that in the "dope-fiend's paradise" that was America before the Harrison Narcotic Act of 1914 outlawed all over-the-counter sales of narcotics, Coca-Cola, which contained a tiny amount of cocaine, was marketed to the American public as the "intellectual beverage." At the same time, however, stories in newspapers and medical journals began associating cocaine with blacks in the South, implicating the drug in violent crime and rape. The "Cocaine Fiend" was a raging black man of superhuman strength and sexual appetite who, the police chief of Asheville, North Carolina, claimed, could take a bullet in the heart and not even be staggered. In the ensuing paranoia, in 1903 Coca-Cola stopped adding the minuscule amount of the substance to its popular beverage.

By the time of the Harrison Narcotic Act, forty-six states had passed laws restricting the use or sale of the drug, but that would hardly stop it. When blacks migrated north to the big cities, an avid subculture of users would follow them. Huddie Ledbetter (Leadbelly) recorded "Honey, Take a Whiff on Me" in 1933; Iceberg Slim documented the use of cocaine in Cleveland and Chicago during the 1940s in his book, *Pimp;* the hustler known as Detroit Red, later to become Malcolm X, used cocaine freely at the same time; and Claude Brown recalled how mobsters like Tony Salerno began marketing a new substance called "horse" (heroin) to the network of users who were already using "girl" (cocaine) in the Harlem of *Manchild in the Promised Land.* Moreover, despite the introduction of amphetamines in the 1930s, cocaine remained very stylish in certain echelons of upper-class society, its presence rendered most notably by the ever-fashionable Cole Porter in his song "I Get a Kick Out of You" ("I get no kick from co-caine"). As Aldrich pointed out, the white cocaine culture was "largely a gay culture, associated with pre-WWII Berlin and French literary salons." Despite a history that reflected diversified usage from upper to lower classes, among hetero- and homosexual, white and black, European and American, so little was known about cocaine that when it began getting at-tention in the mid-1970s, it seemed like some sparkling new invention.

"We were set up for it, by institutional and generational memory loss," Aldrich stressed. "Due to the heavy repressive law-enforcement campaign starting from 1915 and going all the way to the late 1960s, a whole generation's memory of what cocaine was about was so suppressed that by the time it hit big-time in the 1970s, with money, flash, and fan-dango, nobody remembered the dregs of constant cocaine use and what it would do to a person. And because we'd been lied to about marijuana and partly about acid by so many antidrug campaigns that seemed so irrele-vant to our lives, a generation would have to learn again about cocaine."

Bob Sabbag's education about the drug continued in earnest when he persuaded Swan's parole officer to allow him to accompany Swan to Colombia to gather material for the book and Swan began trusting the writer enough to bring him inside his experience as a smuggler just as the cocaine trade was really beginning to escalate. "It was the pre-Medellín cartel Colombia of the American entrepreneur," Sabbag related. "At the time the book was being written, Colombian pot was the best in the world—before Hawaiian or serious domestic cultivation—and American enterprise was being introduced to the Colombians. The people Swan dealt with were half his age, and they were making pretty good bread going down there and buying pot and eventually getting coke and selling it back in the U.S.—not more than a few kilos at a time, five at most. These were not violent people—it was still peace and flowers, guys who had not outgrown the Sixties—and Swan was basically a middle-aged guy who was a gambler and stock investor. He didn't delude himself that he was this romantic piratical buccaneering type—he was a driven personality who'd watched a lot of money change hands, and that's what he knew how to do . . . Yeah, he saw himself as an adventurer, but not like those twenty-year-olds who would become pirates in their DC-3s with one thousand pounds of pot in the back, flying below the radar into Florida while they sucked on a reefer. But what Swan represented was a very transitional moment in the drug culture, and his career was a microcosm of it in the sense that here was a guy who got himself into something that was still relatively innocent."

It wouldn't stay that way for long. Swan's run lasted only a few years, during which time he cleverly smuggled the drug into the United States in schemes that involved hollowing out furniture, among others—and then it started to change. "He almost got killed; his girlfriend got kidnapped; guns started coming out. When a guy comes through your door and rips you off for thirty thousand dollars, it's a lot more serious than three hundred dollars' worth of pot."

When *Snowblind* was published, in 1977, it was reviewed by every publication from *The New Yorker* to the *National Review*. "There weren't any bad reviews," Sabbag recalled. "I had taken what was essentially a very low-down subject and written about it in a very formal way." The following year, *Snowblind* was a big commercial success in paperback. "We did a major publicity tour and were on every morning show across the country, and because it was television, they had to be very careful about getting too excited about the subject or making it look like they were condoning the behavior of this man sitting next to me. And Swan, he wasn't making it easy, saying things like, 'Oh, yeah, it's great, everybody should do it!' He was saying that cocaine was no worse than a couple of cups of coffee, and people were buying it."

Bob Sabbag would wonder how much of the book's success was due to mounting cocaine fever and whether the book itself was responsible for stoking that enthusiasm. "People would come up to me and offer me pharmaceuticals—it seemed like I saw every coke stash in America! Other than *Fear and Loathing,* it was the first best seller about drugs."

*Snowblind* was published at a perfect cultural moment, those pivotal years of 1977–78, when the phenomenon of cocaine was gathering great momentum. Cocaine jokes were beginning to creep into Johnny Carson's monologues on *The Tonight Show.* The new Carter administration in Washington was considering the liberalization of federal drug policy, and the year before, a district court judge named Elwood McKinney in Roxbury, Massachusetts, had actually handed down a decision that declared cocaine "an acceptable recreational drug," ruling, "Cocaine regulation as it now stands is clearly unconstitutional." When Louise Lasser, the popular star of the television show *Mary Hartman, Mary Hartman,* was busted for cocaine, she never missed a show, and the whole affair was treated by sponsors and network executives as much ado about nothing. In New York, a disco opened on West 54th Street where, every night, in a scene right out of Nathanael West's *Day of the Locust,* thousands of frenzied people crowded at the velvet ropes, desperate to gain entry into a debauched fantasyland of the rich and the famous that was symbolized by the colossal coke spoon that swung like a totemic pendulum high above the dance floor, over to the nose of the giant figure of the *Man in the Moon,* where the ingestion of cocaine was portrayed as a magical effervescence of light. On his album *Slowhand,* Eric Clapton released a cover of J. J. Cale's ominously enticing "Cocaine" that would become a rock anthem to the drug: "If you want to hang out, you gotta take her out, Cocaine!" That year's Academy Award winner for Best Picture, Woody Allen's *Annie Hall,* featured a funny scene in which Alvy Singer, the character played by Allen, sneezes just as he is about to try "the latest thing"— and blows God knows how many hundreds of dollars' worth of the drug into the air. The Baby Boomers who had passed through the psychedelic wave were now into their twenties and thirties and had more disposable income than ever. Everywhere they looked in the popular culture, the message was that cocaine was a nonaddictive substance that didn't even promote psychological dependency. It was a subtle, short-lived pleasure that set you apart from the multitudes, "the status symbol of the decade" that ranked "somewhere between mink coats and gold-plated bathroom fixtures," as *High Times* called it—"the modern equivalent of feasting on the tongues of nightingales."

## III. Pagan Rome

**Bob was watching Bianca take poppers and he said to Diana Vreeland, "It really becomes more like pagan Rome every day," and she said, "I should hope *so—isn't that what we're after?*"**

—*The Andy Warhol Diaries*, Monday, March 6, 1978,
at Studio 54

SIMPLY KNOWING that she was going to get in filled Suzie Ryan with a feeling of power, and the few lines of coke she had snorted back in her apartment only augmented the sensation. Just as she had finished putting on her makeup, she had swallowed a Rorer 714 with a healthy gulp of Pouilly-Fuissé. As her cab drove into the floodlighted scene of limousines queuing up along West 54th Street, the Quaalude was kicking in, and she began to feel that familiar tingling of lips, fingers, and tongue.

Stepping out of the cab in Halston sequins, Suzie was instantly caught up in the surging hordes under Studio 54's silver and black Deco marquee. There, amid the bedlam of police and paparazzi and strobes, she spotted Mark Benecke, all-powerful doorman, and then she caught sight of Steve Rubell himself. The new cynosure of New York nightlife had a bent little smile on his face as people desperately screamed his name—Steve, *Steve, STEVE!!* Rubell looked right past the CEOs and rich Saudis and bridge-and-tunnel hopefuls as if they weren't even there, his eyes glazed over with Quaalude bliss, and nodded at her. It was like being anointed. Regarding her with a kind of hushed, envious awe, the crowd parted before her like the Red Sea. She entered the club and began walking down that long, mirrored antechamber of dreams and desires. The closer she got to the entrance, the more the explosive thump of the bass made her heart pound with excitement. The mounting anticipation seemed to kick the methaqualone in her system up to another level, making her feel higher, deliciously loose and lubricious.

Suzie Ryan was a young and very beautiful girl—an ex–Homecoming Queen (as well as a straight-A student) back in her hometown in Virginia, stunning enough to entertain notions of becoming a starlet, with an obsession for exactly the kind of rich and powerful and celebrated men she was certain to find inside. Who would she end up with that night? Egon Von Furstenberg? Vitas Gerulaitis? Warren Beatty? Mick Jagger? Anything was possible in this place. She always felt like Alice in spandex going down the rabbit hole to some glittery gap in space and time, where the only rule was Do What Thou Wilt. Nothing could touch you here, no matter how reckless the gesture. The place swirled in pandemonium as she threaded her way through the three thousand impossibly fabulous people chosen as that night's cast: doyennes and debutantes, leather boys and drag queens, diplomats and models, fashion divas and politicians, most of them stoned out of their skulls. The gigantic sound system pumped out the songs that would forever define those nights for her: George McRae's "Rock Your Baby," Dr. Buzzard's "Cherchez la Femme," Andrea True Connection's "More More More," Chic's "Le Freak," Thelma Houston's "Don't Leave Me This Way," and all of the hits of Donna Summer, the definitive disco goddess.

Studio 54 was the high temple of the Great Stoned Age, a nightly spectacle of wanton debauch fueled by four main ingredients, all of them working toward a common end. The common social drugs were marijuana and alcohol, but the most valued specialty items were Quaaludes and cocaine. The popularity of the nonbarbiturate sedative muscle relaxants had been soaring since the early 1970s; in the halcyon era of Studio, they were still a schedule two substance, and it was relatively easy to get your hands on giant bottles of Rorers, Sopors, Parest, Optimil, Somnafac, Lemmons, and Mandrax. Ludes, as they were universally known, were dispensed by handfuls at Studio 54, sometimes thrown out over the dance floor from the huge balcony like confetti. Quaaludes were famous for producing feelings of quiescence, relaxation, friendliness, paresthesia (the telltale tingling), increased pain threshold, and the impairment of position sense, which produced severe ataxia (lack of coordination)—classic short-term effects that were evident in the slack-jawed, speech-slurred Studio dwellers who were always falling on their asses on the dance floor, tumbling down stairs, and never feeling a blessed thing. But it was the aphrodisiac properties of the drug, combined with vanishing inhibitions, that brought on the flashing of tits and cocks, the women in the stalls of the famous unisexual bathrooms straddling faces with their dresses up above their waists, the fleeting acts of fellatio performed in the many nooks and crannies and corners, and the zipless fucking between total strangers up in the darkened reaches of the balcony. If Margaret Trudeau was doing something wildly inappropriate that night, or Liza Minelli was involved in some sexual intrigue with Scorsese or Baryshnikov, chances are they had popped a couple of Lemmon 714s.

If Quaaludes plus alcohol unleashed the most risqué behavior and produced the juiciest gossip, cocaine made the party never ending. Coke was currency, energy, enticement, power itself; silver packets were placed in the limousines that Steve Rubell and Ian Schrager sent to pick up their guests, and everyone wanted to gain admittance to the sanctum sanctorum of the basement, where the elite tooted up underneath the hissing steam pipes. Nothing enabled the frenetic pace of the nightlife during the late Seventies more than blow, when people went out night after night until late in the morning and then somehow had to show up for jobs the next day.

For Suzie, the whole evening at Studio became a game of connecting the dots from toot to toot. As the night wore on, she would reach the point where a drink or another half of a lude would put her too far over the line into wooziness, and she would then fixate on the need for a hit of blow to blast her back up. Of course, then she would get a bit too wired and have to take the edge off—a hit of a joint, another vodka and cranberry, another half a lude (*half a lude, half a lude, half a lude onward, forward the Lude Brigade!*), like the continual firing of pharmacological boosters and retro-rockets in the synaptic space of her neurochemistry, until the energy built to the point where it would all fuse together: lights, music, people, dancing.

Images come back; it was late in the game, well into the morning, when the air was bathed in a blizzard of glitter and people were leaping from the balcony to clutch on to that giant truss of lights that would slowly descend to the floor, where Calvin Klein was twirling Bianca Jagger. The anthem of this moment of utterly abandoned fabulousness was usually Donna Summer's "Last Dance." The gigantic coke spoon would swing overhead to the Man in the Moon, sending the incandescent coke bubbles up the silver proboscis and making the crowd scream in a way that always made Suzie think of Greek Bacchanalia, Roman orgies, and the worshipping of the golden calf. She had no idea where she was going to get it, but she needed another hit of coke; just one more hit would make it all perfect. She would do anything to get it, so she headed up into the balcony, and that was where she saw Richard for the first time, sitting with his Gucci attaché case that contained every exotic psychoactive substance known to man, surrounded by a gaggle of Wilhelmina models.

With his longish hair and deep George Hamilton tan, Richard Stoltz looked like a Brahman prince who had just stepped off the beach at St.-Tropez. In the social salad that Steve Rubell liked to toss every night at Studio 54, dealers were always part of the mix, and he was definitely one of them, only here, Suzie reckoned, was a dealer with a trust fund.

It didn't take long. Within what seemed like a matter of minutes, they were fucking behind the heavy curtains, Suzie slammed up against the wall with her legs wrapped around him. Their adventures began that morning.

## IV. Adieu, Cocaine

OLIVER STONE moved to Hollywood in 1976 with his newly completed screenplay, *Platoon*. It would take eight years of disappointments and close calls before he would be in any position to get it produced. In the meantime, he turned his attention to establishing his reputation as a writer—and as a freewheeling Hollywood bachelor. Stone incorporated his drug use into both pursuits with the same kind of risk-taking zeal he had brought to riding the subways of New York on acid after returning from Vietnam.

Impressed with the visual and emotional power of his writing, Columbia soon gave Stone the chance to embrace drugs as a subject, offering him the job of adapting *Midnight Express* for the screen. The true story of Billy Hayes was perfect for Stone. Caught with a load of hashish in

Turkey, sentenced to life in a squalid, disease-ridden prison in which he served five brutal years before his dramatic escape, Hayes had lived the nightmare of every American kid traveling abroad during the early Seventies who had ever contemplated smuggling a significant amount of dope back into the United States. By drawing on his own experience of getting busted for marijuana in the weeks after he returned from Vietnam, Stone was able to animate the screenplay emotionally, crafting the story so that violence would erupt with the sudden savagery of a firefight. Directed by Alan Parker, *Midnight Express* was a film of fierce power, suspense, and controversy that won Stone both an Academy Award and a Golden Globe for his screenplay in 1979.

The night of the Golden Globes, Stone got up "stoned out of my head on Quaaludes and coke, and I made this long, obfuscated speech attacking the drug laws. I was saying, 'Don't just look at Turkey, look at America.' " After attacking the television industry for demonizing small-time drug dealers instead of focusing on the "real issues," he was booed and practically dragged off the stage by Chevy Chase and Richard Harris ("like they're models of sobriety"). The incident was a perfect example of Stone's propensity to speak his mind no matter the consequences—one of many to come. After years of marginality, his sudden success as a screenwriter was stunning to him. The next couple of years, during which Stone wore leather pants and had long hair like Jim Morrison and tried unsuccessfully to get films like *Platoon* and *Born on the Fourth of July* made, were like an unrestrained, cocaine-fueled "magic-carpet ride."

"Cocaine was a fever, a rage in Los Angeles," he said. "I never did a lot of it, but I did enough to feel that I should never do it again. About two years' worth. I was never packing my nose like some people I knew. I was always writing, and I always maintained some sort of discipline about taking drugs. It should be a reward, a combination of work and pleasure—that was my attitude."

By 1979, cocaine had engulfed every dimension of the entertainment industry in a white storm that reached from studio executives down to the production assistants.

"It was out of control, everywhere—the agent's offices, the casting director's," related Geoff Dubois, who left New York and the marijuana-smuggling business in 1978 to try to become an actor in Hollywood.

"You'd go in on an audition, and if they knew you, it was, 'Hi, do you want a line?' That's when I first began to get the sense that it was a powerful tool for guys to get girls. That's when the phrase *coke whore* first came into the cultural vernacular. In Hollywood, especially, you already had girls willing to lay down to get a job, and you add coke on top of that, well, it was incredible—it got out of hand. Every guy was holding and every girl wanted it. It was a big joke out there. You didn't say, 'Hi, how are ya?' In the first two minutes of conversation, it was, 'Hi, ya holding?' It was the essential information, the basic means of social currency."

"We quickly found out that cocaine was conducive to sexual excess," David Crosby elaborated. "We just loved the pleasure, and I'm not just talking about the freedom from old restrictions. I'm talking about experimental to the max. You went through stages on cocaine. You started out, it was energy for free, sex for a week, and I'm so intelligent! We called it planning powder, Inca marching powder. Stay up for two or three days and plan everything—you had a plan!—but you never did anything. You started out sharing and talking a lot and having a lot of sex, and then it goes to something else, and if you give it to somebody else, it's usually to manipulate them, particularly women—something very prevalent in coke users that goes on to this day. The coke whore is one of the most tragic figures in all of drug history. It's very often a nice girl who has gotten strung out and is completely opposed to being degraded inside of herself and is helpless, truly a victim, and is being consciously manipulated by the guy . . . I didn't do it viciously, but I did it. The drug was part of the coercive atmosphere of getting what I wanted, which was far-out sex."

"Cocaine was so integrated into our society that after every dinner it seemed the little silver tray and spoon would always be passed around the dinner table," remarked Michelle Phillips, who would never forget her first acid trip but had no idea when she took her first cocaine. "It was supercool. Older people were doing it—everybody was doing it. It was an obsession with everybody I knew, and I prided myself on the fact that I never bought it. But every time I turned around, there was a spoon under my nose, and I inhaled. After a while, I had to recognize the fact that I was doing cocaine even though I said I wasn't. People became coke mean. That's an expression we used to use."

In Hollywood, in a business hard driven by power, ego, money, sex, and glamour, phrases like *coke whore* and *coke mean* would take on special meaning and significance.

"On a surface level, we had fun at first," Stone reflected. "It was a way to drown your deeper thoughts, to drown the realities of life. It's not a drug that sets off deep and abiding friendships or real love affairs between men and women—a terrible sex drug, in my opinion, and a bad-breath drug because it leaves that metallic aftertaste in your mouth. You don't want to get too close to anybody, and you're not even close to yourself—divorced from your true self, really. For anyone to deny the pleasure of cocaine, you can't—but anyone with any brains left realized there was an arc of pleasure that descended disproportionately. They tumbled down much faster at the end than they ever went up. The metaphor was champagne. And Wall Street."

As Oliver Stone tried to maintain a balance between his own use and abuse, he began to feel that his writing was going downhill. "I felt that the product was mechanical rather than felt. I felt like my brain cells were not there." His disenchantment with the drug calls to mind Robert Stone's description of Gordon Walker, the screenwriter-protagonist of his Hollywood novel of the Eighties, *Children of Light:* "He had drugged and drunk too much, watched too many smoky reels of interior montage to command any inner resources." Oliver Stone was still huffing cocaine and had discovered the freebase pipe when the producer Marty Bregman asked him to write a modern version of *Scarface,* the 1932 Howard Hawks gangster classic, and set it in Miami. Like *Midnight Express,* it seemed a perfect vehicle for him; he packed up his bags and his second wife, Elizabeth, and headed to Florida.

Miami in 1980 was a cocaine boomtown of violence and money. The price of a kilo jumped from thirty-four thousand dollars to fifty-one thousand dollars, and the drug was being smuggled in by plane, by cargo container, by speedboat, by human mules coming over on the commercial airlines, by ways and means that have yet to be documented. The DEA would estimate the trade at $7 billion and Customs investigators put the figure of unreported revenue at $3.2 billion. Laundered money was financing a construction boom in South Florida, and the glitzy new clubs of Miami were throbbing to disco music and attracting hard-looking Latin men in white suits with bulges under their arms.

Stone could feel the fever in the air, but there was a chilling undercurrent to it. The rapidly organizing Colombians were vying to take over distribution from the Cuban middlemen they had been supplying. Every year, the number of murders was setting a new record, from 349 in 1979, to 621 in 1981 (the Dade County Medical Examiner's Office even added a refrigerated trailer to handle the surplus of corpses). The weapon of choice was the Miami chopper—the little black Ingram .45-caliber MAC-10, which could riddle a car at the rate of a thousand bullets a minute. Assassinations were carried out in broad daylight; in July of 1979, in a wild shootout on the Dadeland Turnpike, gunmen had turned their weapons on innocent bystanders for the first time, and the national media discovered a new breed of gangster: the cocaine cowboy. These gangsters had names like Conrado Vallencia ("El Loco"), Paco Sepulveda, and Griselda Blanco de Trujillo ("Godmother," "Black Widow"), and they were turning Miami into what one federal prosecutor called Dodge City. A local coroner compared it to the Chicago of Al Capone. Their favorite means of assassination was by machine pistol from the back of a speeding motorcycle. Gunmen cut off body parts as proof of death. Horrible stories abounded, in both Miami and Colombia. Eyes gouged out. Tongues cut off. Castrated corpses with penises stuffed in mouths. Chain saws used to dismember victims while they were still alive.

The deluge of drugs and money and the levels of violence caught law enforcement all but flat-footed. In 1981, the DEA established the Central Tactical Unit (CENTAC), an elite group of DEA agents and New York City and Metro-Dade detectives organized to go after the highest-level traffickers, and the Treasury Department launched Operation Greenback to go after the money launderers. The following year, in response to the pleas of powerful Miami businessmen, President Reagan announced the formation of a cabinet-level task force headed by Vice President George Bush to bring the full force of the federal government to bear on the drug trade in South Florida—a "federal posse" of more than two hundred lawmen, Cobra helicopter gunships, U.S. Navy Hawkeye E2C radar surveillance planes, and navy ships. In fact, the DEA was only starting to hear the names of the men who would organize the trade from top to bottom into true cartels, routinely move multi-ton loads into the United States, and provide cocaine for the masses. Jorge

Ochoa, Pablo Escobar, Carlos Lehder, José Ocampo, José Gonzalo Rodriguez Gacha, and Manuel Garces Gonzalez would make violence and intimidation and corruption the national trademarks of Colombia. Bribing or murdering anyone who opposed them, buying whole islands and banks in the Bahamas, making Manuel Noriega their bagman in Panama, they became important players in the volatile geopolitics of South and Central America through the 1980s.

Stone found himself in a netherworld of dealers, drug agents, CIA-trained Cuban exiles, mercenary pilots, and high-priced drug lawyers. El Salvador and Nicaragua were erupting in revolution, and the new Reagan administration began moving quickly to suppress the spread of Communism in those countries. Somehow, Stone sensed that it was all tied in—drugs, drug money, and the political upheavals that would soak the region in blood—though he could hardly piece it together. The research was absorbing, impenetrable, and dangerous. "I was still doing blow. It got me into a lot of places, that's for sure. I almost got killed one night in Bimini. I was hanging out with some midlevel Colombian guys who were smuggling in cigarette boats to Miami, and we were partying one night in a hotel there, and I dropped a name that was really repugnant to them, of a guy who had put one of them away. In his dim brain, he thought I was there as an undercover cop posing as a screenwriter, and that's when he walked out of the room. I thought he was going to come back in with a gun and blow me away. That night I slept with one eye opened. It was pretty scary, but it gave me insight into the *Scarface* character I would write because these were some stone-cold people that would kill you. The motivation was always cocaine."

It was the taste of this chilling episode that Stone wanted to infuse into his screenplay, but he knew that he would never be able to write quality material and make the kinds of films he wanted to make if he was strung out. "I went cold turkey and went to Paris. I wrote *Scarface* as a kind of homage to cocaine. I had to make it pay me back. I felt, shit, look what it did to my hair, my brain!—it takes you down, that drug."

Stone and his wife holed up in an apartment near the Bois de Boulogne, and he started banging out his tale of Tony Montana, the petty hood who washes up on the shores of Florida in 1980, along with 125,000 other Cuban refugees of the Mariel boatlift. "Cocaine is like a lightning bolt," Stone mused. "It sets off fires. Tony Montana came to this country and was lucky to get a job as a dishwasher, and when he saw cocaine and how a dollar could be made, that became his understanding of capitalism—that you could go right to millionaire status overnight. Moving cocaine in the early Eighties was the way to do that. He did it and got everything he wanted but had nothing really, because cocaine is so insubstantial. That's what he created: a flimsy tissue of dreams. But for a brief time, he had his chariot ride in the sky."

The idea of using cocaine and the Latin immigrant gangsters (as the rackets of the 1930s had been the setting for the original Howard Hawks version) had been Sidney Lumet's, but the director withdrew from the project. Brian De Palma came on board and shot a slimmed-down version of Stone's screenplay. With a histrionic Europop score by Giorgio Moroder and Al Pacino delivering one of his greatest performances as Tony Montana, *Scarface* embraced the notion that cocaine illuminated a moral hypocrisy and dishonesty at all levels of American society—the corruption it engendered went far beyond the machinations of immigrants like Tony Montana using the drug as a vehicle to attain some gaudy and fleeting version of the American Dream.

Critics for the most part hated the film; the charges they leveled at it would typify their critique of many of Stone's films to come—self-indulgent, excessively violent, profane, and manipulative—but the melodramatic brushstrokes that Stone had used to render the city of Miami in 1981 turned out to be the perfect combination of elements. *Scarface* became a commercial success as well as a cult classic, and Stone went on to become one of the most controversial filmmakers working in Hollywood during the 1980s. Themes and images of drugs would continue to appear throughout his work: the heroin-pushing Chinese gangs of *The Year of the Dragon* (a screenplay for Michael Cimino), the pill-popping antics of the journalist Richard Boyle and Dr. Rock in *Salvador,* the heads of *Platoon* and Ron Kovic's excruciating self-obliteration in *Born on the Fourth of July*; Bud Fox's blast of cocaine in the back of a limo in *Wall Street*; Clay Shaw using amyl nitrate in the gay orgy scene of *JFK*; Jim Morrison's psychedelic desert journey in *The Doors.*

If Stone had written *Scarface* as his adieu to cocaine because it had beaten the hell out of him, he had certainly gotten his revenge. Perhaps the most lasting image was Tony Montana falling facedown into a giant mound of blow on his desk as he nears his end.

"I remember writing that image, and that picture for me was very much tied into *Richard III*. My kingdom for a horse!' "

Shakespeare notwithstanding, Oliver Stone had created an enduring image of the moment of overload when cocaine was peaking in America and the drug culture was turning toxic.

## V. A Crazy Glorious Unrestrained Slobbering *Saucier* of Drug-Demented Elation

WHEN JOHN BELUSHI would show up in the middle of the night, all Michael O'Donoghue could do was surrender to the cyclone. There was no use even trying to refuse him. Belushi would torture you until he got what he wanted, and before O'Donoghue was even fully awake, Belushi had put some cocaine up his nose. O'Donoghue knew that there would be no going back to sleep now, and off they went in the limousine, tearing around town to the parties.

O'Donoghue, a cadaverously thin writer for *Saturday Night Live,* looked like a slightly depraved film noir character, in his white suit and dark glasses and rakish Borsalino hat—"Fred MacMurray on drugs" was how he once described himself—and Belushi, well, no matter what he was wearing, he always managed to look like Bluto in *Animal House,* which is what people called him when he showed up at the Grateful Dead concert that night—*"Hey, it's Bluto!"*—where he and O'Donoghue were Jerry Garcia's guests backstage. Mushrooms were duly ingested and chased by weed, weed by more blow, blow by booze, booze by a blast of nitrous . . . and on it went, like ingredients dumped into a caldron, stirred and tasted until it was perfect, and then it would all start to bubble over the edges so they'd have to add still more items. Belushi was like a *saucier,* O'Donoghue thought, as they passed a bottle of Jack Daniel's in the back of the limousine, a crazy glorious unrestrained slobbering *saucier* of drug-demented elation. Suddenly, Belushi pushed the button that opened the roof. "You know what my favorite thing in the whole world is?" he asked, standing up in the driving rain and cackling like an impish child. "*Getting fucked up!*" he screamed up into the rainy night. "*That's what!*"

During his years as one of the primary writers of the flagship comedy show that shaped the humor of the era, O'Donoghue became convinced that comedy was like Zen. "Humor is just icing to make people eat a cake, the cake being ideas," he explained. "Zen teaches you a lot about comedy. On *Saturday Night Live,* you had to come up with ideas very quickly under pressure, and your instinct under pressure is to try harder, whereas Zen will say try half as hard, hardly try at all. And that's how you succeed. It can't be explained; either you achieve it, or you don't. You get satori, or you don't." Another prime ingredient, as he described it, was "that suicide-kamikaze thing that makes for such good comedy. I loved it, and Belushi *lived* that edge."

For O'Donoghue, comic awareness began at the age of five, when he contracted rheumatic fever and had to spend a whole year indoors. "It was a defining event in my life. I learned how to be alone and developed a certain hostility, shall we say, toward the children who played out in the sunshine. Lenny Bruce was a big influence on me. I mean, Lenny wasn't Sid Caesar or Ernie Kovacs! He was the first to work drugs into his routine, way before George Carlin. Then came Lord Buckley, the great hipster . . . Terry Southern was another great influence—very funny and observant, a master of rhythms and dialects. And then the last influence, in terms of dark comedy, was Franz Kafka."

With the exception of Kafka, all were avid drug users, as was O'Donoghue. When he wrote satirical parodies for the *Evergreen Review* during the 1960s, he found that pot helped to release inhibitions and produce ideas by free association; he could stay up forever on amphetamines; psychedelics like mescaline allowed him to play with the clouds in the sky by actually molding them with his hands while he was sitting on a beach—"to this day, I believe I did it—sat on a beach and made them into different objects until I became bored with it." By the time he became one of the original founders of the *National Lampoon* and created *The National Lampoon Radio Hour* (the prototype for *Saturday Night Live*), the pharmacopoeia had rapidly expanded. "There was something called number one in those days," he remembered. "It was resin of marijuana taken down to an oil that came in a little glass bottle with a thing to smoke it with—very expensive, for rock-and-roll stars who were on the road. One hit and you'd be gone. Quite a little substance! And Quaaludes were great. They were called leg spreaders, weren't they?"

Although he never wrote what he would call straight-on drug humor, O'Donoghue would always recognize the potential of humor in the use and culture of drugs—at the time, he created a game in which you would actually take various ups and downs as a means of moving across the game board. It was during his tenure at the *Lampoon,* when he became known as one of the master practitioners of its unique brand of outrageous, merciless satire, that drugs became virtually inseparable from the culture of comedy in both sensibility and content. "We at the *Lampoon* didn't openly advocate legalization because we didn't have any editorial policies whatsoever, but the magazine was on the side of freedom of all sorts—the freedom to use drugs was one of them, and that meant the freedom to kill yourself if that's what you wanted to do. I believe in free will. My attitude was that no one had the right to save you from anything."

At *Saturday Night Live,* John Belushi became the perfect vessel of this "suicide-kamikaze" brand of comedy. From his beginnings with Second City in Chicago, he dove headlong for the comic knife edge of every character, routine, and review, accepting drugs as a central part of the experience of creating and performing. One of his favorite bits of shtick was to die onstage, and the more convulsive and gruesomely spastic his death throes, the funnier it would be. In the show *Lemmings,* he made his name playing a stoned-out doctor in an operating room and introduced something called the All-Star Dead Band and all but stole the show with his brilliant imitation of Joe Cocker, who by that time had become noteworthy for stumbling around on stages, stone drunk, vomiting. It was during *Lemmings* that Belushi tasted his first cocaine, and by the time O'Donoghue and Chevy Chase persuaded the producer Lorne Michaels to hire him for the Not Ready for Prime Time Players of *Saturday Night Live,* cocaine had become his drug of choice, and his reputation as a dazzling but barely controllable maniac was flourishing.

Of course, NBC was duly nervous about Belushi and many other aspects of the new show. When the program debuted, on October 11, 1975, the first thing the television audience saw was O'Donoghue, and then, after a knock on the door, Belushi entered in a shabby greatcoat, playing some kind of Albanian immigrant or something. What followed was an English lesson of sorts. "GOOD EVENING," O'Donoghue said. "*Good eve-eh-ning,*" Belushi repeated in broken English, after which O'Donoghue got him to repeat the following phrase, slowly, carefully enunciating each syllable: "I would like . . . to feed your fingertips . . . *to the wolverines.*" The scene ended with O'Donoghue pitching over on the floor with a massive coronary; Belushi thought about it for a second and then pitched over and died, too. "Live from New York, it's *Saturday Night!*" announced Don Pardo, and virtually from that moment on, the show was on its way to becoming a weekly cultural event with an audience of twenty million.

It was never any kind of big secret that *SNL* was nearly inundated with cocaine from top to bottom; the drug was a perfect fit for the wild, exuberant week-by-week ride as characters and skits emerged that would become legendary and the stars turned into icons of pop culture. "Certain people did cocaine; some didn't," O'Donoghue pointed out. "It wasn't only about drugs, it was about that spirit, that sensibility. Gilda Radner had a certain wild desperation about her. Laraine Newman was pretty out there and could get high with the best of them. Garrett Morris—it's common knowledge that he was a big freebase user; he almost lost his mind. Jane Curtin, to my knowledge, never touched a drug in the world. A lot of people didn't. People want to believe that everyone got into trouble with drugs on the show, but it was really a minuscule number. I mean, you couldn't do a lot of drugs and still do a good show every fucking week!" The staff of the show had only one day off, Sundays, so if you wanted to relax and have fun quickly, drugs were a way of doing that, but you didn't have a three-day weekend where you could do Quaaludes and just float away. Yet people somehow managed to do plenty of drugs anyway. "Getting high was part of the time and place and scene, and we were just part of our culture, not that much more and not that much less. Drugs certainly contributed to the myth of the show, but I think it was probably much more myth than reality. Except, maybe, in the case of John Belushi."

Sudden fame brought money; money, of course, brought more blow; and fame plus money plus more blow equaled hysterical outbursts of show-business egomania and paranoia. As Belushi became a movie star and had his Blues Brothers success with Dan Ackroyd, his cocaine intake became cause for concern, especially to his wife, Judy Jacklin Belushi. When he was persuaded to go in for a checkup in 1976, his substance abuse evaluation was recorded as follows:

> Smokes 3 packs a day.
> Alcohol drinks socially.
> Medications: Valium occasionally.
> Marijuana 4 to 5 times a week.
> Cocaine—snort daily, main habit.
> Mescaline—regularly.
> Acid—10 to 20 trips.
> No heroin.
> Amphetamines— four kinds.
> Barbiturates (Quaalude habit).

Note the "no heroin." Like many of his generation, the fact that Belushi stayed away from junk made it that much easier for him to justify an intake of four grams a day of cocaine as recreational and creative fuel, and he believed that all would be okay as long as he never crossed that line. But unlike most of the people on the show who used cocaine as a pick-me-up or binged out with it at the weekly blowout party after the live broadcast wrapped, Belushi did it pretty much all week long. "John would actually use cocaine on the broadcast," O'Donoghue noted. "When he did that skit of Beethoven snorting cocaine at the piano and then breaking out into a Ray Charles piece, he had a big fat line, and there was that tight shot of him doing it. Lorne was very permissive for the most part, and by that time the network was staying away. Everyone thought it was white powder, but what kind of white powder can you snort like that? Baby laxative?"

The writers were aware that they were putting together a show for a mass audience of viewers who would be staying home and getting high. As O'Donoghue told Susan Wyler for a *High Times* interview in February of 1978, "Lorne has always said that we are counting on at least 80 percent of our viewers to be wrecked—really in Cuckooland." As the king of Cuckooland, Belushi had a lot of fun playing with his image as a stoned-out loon, and the audience always loved it. "I'm not fussy," he said in his Christmas skit with Candice Bergen. "I like candied yams, plum puddings, and roast goose stuffed with drugs." At the fade-in of one show, Lorne Michaels wheeled him out in a chair in a bathrobe, passed out cold. "I can't put this guy on television . . . I mean, he's got to be *awake.*" "I'll be forced to cut him off his drugs," said the doctor, after which Belushi sprang to life—"Live from New York!" In 1978, two weeks after making the cover of *Newsweek,* Belushi did a "Weekend Update" spot about drug policy that began with an earnest talk about decriminalization ("Possession of an ounce is a misdemeanor now. You know how far we've come?") and ended with him pounding on the table in his now-celebrated out-of-control frenzy—*"I want hard drugs!"* Then he pitched over with the now-familiar seizure. Some of Belushi's skits were as haunting and poignant as they were funny. In one of Tom Schiller's films, Belushi appeared at the Not Ready for Prime Time Cemetery in Brooklyn. "They all thought I'd be the first to go," he said, pointing out the graves: Gilda, Laraine, Jane, Garrett ("He died of a heroin overdose"), Chevy ("He died right after his first movie with Goldie Hawn"), Danny Ackroyd. "Now they're all gone and I miss every one of them. Why *me?* Why'd *I* live so long? I'll tell you why. 'Cause I'm a *dancer,*" and he began his funny little jig over the graves . . .

"He *was* a dancer," O'Donoghue emphasized. "How dangerous was the dance he was doing? Well, here's the thing. You couldn't drown John. He would find a way to save things. That's why he was sent onstage for some very bad sketches—because you knew he'd always save it! He hated to go under. Taking it to the edge—that's how he lived his whole life. It was that crazed death-oriented gusto that put the edge on his performance, which gave him the edge and put him *over* the edge. One time in the main writer's room he lay on the ground and took these pink and white Necco wafers that looked like huge pills and scattered them around him—it looked just like he OD'd. It made me laugh so hard because you sensed that *was* what was going to happen to him. He *knew* it, and he had this humor which confronted it and was honest about it, which is the core of every good joke."

The dance ended in Bungalow 3 of the Chateau Marmont on the morning of March 5, 1982—death by overdose, reportedly from the injection of speedballs—heroin mixed with cocaine. "The horrible thing is that he'd only done heroin a few times in his life, and this time it appeared that he just got caught off base. People had been doing it for fifty years, and here John does it a few times and overdoses, and immediately everyone starts saying he was a junkie. But that wasn't really the case at all. He was just screwing around a little bit. He just got *unlucky.* It's a great disservice to misinterpret his relationship to heroin because John Belushi wasn't a junkie. He was also capable of cleaning up, too. For long periods of time, he was clean, did exercise. He had some discipline."

Belushi's death did not stop O'Donoghue from taking heroin himself on the dreadful day of the funeral at Martha's Vineyard. "I just thought, They're going to take this and turn this into some cautionary tale for us, and I just felt like, well, fuck you all! So I took drugs and went, because that's exactly how he would have done it."

And then came the insufferable indignity of *Wired: The Short Life and Fast Times of John Belushi* by Bob Woodward. O'Donoghue and others had been very suspicious of the circumstances surrounding the death, especially after learning about Cathy Smith, the dealer whom John had been hanging around with before and on the night he died. O'Donoghue cooperated with the Watergate reporter for the book because Judy Belushi had encouraged him to do so, hoping that with all of his clout and credibility as an investigative journalist, Woodward might shed some light on what had happened.

"Judy told me that the book would be a 'tribute' to John, and we thought he was going for a specific story—that the LAPD hated John Belushi," O'Donoghue explained. "It was well-known that they hated him. I always thought there was a damn good chance they may have killed him, and Danny Ackroyd was thinking the same thing at the time. We heard things that made us very suspicious—that the brother of a very-high-up official in the LAPD may have been a high-level dealer himself and was tight with Cathy Smith—and began to think that John may have been slipped a hot shot. Oh, the LAPD has an incredible history of blackmail, murders, and things . . . *That's* the story we thought Woodward was going for. I always thought that either he couldn't get the story or backed off so he just went on and wrote an entertainment industry drug exposé. As it turned out talking to him was like letting the fox into the henhouse. Bill Murray was the only one who had the good sense not to cooperate with him."

It wasn't so much what Woodward wrote that embittered people, although O'Donoghue would insist that the book was factually inaccurate as well—"so inaccurate that upon reading it, Penny Marshall said, 'It makes you think that Richard Nixon may have been innocent.' It's that shocking." Rather, it was what was left *out* that was so hard to abide. "Not being a wild and crazy guy himself, Woodward just didn't *get* it. How wonderful John was. How talented. The generosity of John. How life making he was. Just a gypsy king. You don't get that from the book at all."

Bob Sabbag, who had been Belushi's guest on *SNL* and at his Blues Bar, felt the same way. "One of the things that people don't know about Belushi, was that he was a gentleman. He *was* that character—crazy—but underneath he was a gentleman, a happily married man who had a very close relationship with his wife, a nice, down-to-earth guy who was victimized by his celebrity, drawn into this career that was larger than him. Everywhere he went people wanted to give him cocaine, and he had a hard time saying no." Sabbag believed that Belushi's death was "like getting hit by a train. If he had gone left instead of right, it wouldn't have happened. He died in the midst of a binge that was not characteristic of him; the lifestyle that represented his last two weeks was not the lifestyle he lived in New York. Woodward's take on his story was that John Belushi's death was a logical extension of his life, and I really don't think that's true."

Whatever one's opinion, Woodward's book was a best-selling sensation. Far more than a cautionary tale about an individual life, the book would stand as an indictment of an entire generation's self-indulgent fast-lane lifestyle. Woodward's straightforward approach meant that unlike other biographies of legendary self-destructive characters of immense appetite who lived out their own myths, like Bird, Neal Cassady, or Jim Morrison, Belushi's story was largely stripped of in-depth analysis of artistic context, cultural interpretation, or character analysis. (It isn't surprising that *Time* would see Belushi as little more than "a volatile combination of Lou Costello and Vlad the Impaler" in its review of the book.) At a time when the entertainment industry was awash in cocaine, Woodward essentially did what he knew how to do best—followed the trail of the drugs and reported the Watergate of Belushi's abuse. It was a trail that led from the green room of *Saturday Night Live* to Studio 54, out to Hollywood, onto movie sets, into offices and studios and Jack Nicholson's home on Mulholland Drive, where Woodward was able to report that Jack kept two kinds of cocaine: the downstairs coke for the guests and the exceptional upstairs stash for the special friends. There was nothing mythic or romantic about John Belushi's manic dance as portrayed by Bob Woodward; it looked wasteful, stupid, shockingly ugly, a perfect allegory for a drug culture that seemed to be spiraling out of control.

The death sent shock waves to every corner of the entertainment industry. Robert De Niro, who had partied with Belushi on the night of his death, was called to testify before a grand jury; Robin Williams, who had also been around Belushi on that last run, was so distressed that he gave up the drug and moved out of Los Angeles. "You could see the curve coming," Sabbag observed. "Everyone in Hollywood started backing away; nobody wanted to be associated with it anymore."

If cocaine had entered the culture as the drug of the entertainment elite— the "boulevardiers of America," as Sabbag had called them—it was clear that it had now peaked and turned bad. The cocaine phenomenon seemed perfectly book-ended by the publication of Sabbag's *Snowblind* in 1977 and Woodward's *Wired* in 1984, which more or less coincided with the burnout of its first wave of users. Belushi's death marked the beginning of an antidrug tide in the industry that would eventually require studios to administer urinalysis tests to actors in order to get production insurance. The sea change that followed would be the product of many factors, but as antidrug opinion and attitude gathered momentum and poisoned the whole atmosphere surrounding drug use, Michael O'Donoghue and many others who had known and loved John Belushi would always regret that his other qualities would be obscured by the handy symbolism of his death.

"They were very elusive qualities to get. It's like the stones you bring back from the ocean. They're very pretty, but when you get home and look at them, they're just some dopey fucking stones, and you throw them away. But in seawater and in certain light, they were very beautiful."

## VI.  Park Avenue Nosebleed

SUZIE RYAN had been right. Richard Stoltz had a trust fund. At the age of twenty-one, he had gained access to the five hundred thousand dollars his grandfather had left him, but by that time it was almost beside the point. It was the trust funds of others that Stoltz would invest and make millions on during the 1980s, getting his investors high with his blow and luring them into his schemes with Suzie, the perfect party hostess and trophy girl.

By the late 1970s, there was a kid like Richard in every suburban high school: the rich man's son with the killer stereo and great clothes, who smoked bones of primo weed on the way to school in the morning in a sports car his father had bought for him, a car he was very likely to wreck. Stoltz was a quintessential Reagan-era kid, and what distinguished this generation from that of its predecessors was that it started getting high at a much younger age. Having missed out on Woodstock, they felt robbed, as if the party had passed them by, and so they had a lot of catching up to do. Hippies, happenings, and great causes had vanished like the great buffalo herds; what was bequeathed them were the drugs. Stoltz had been a daily marijuana user since he was thirteen. Stoners—that's what they were now called—with huge glass bongs filled with Hawaiian buds, who bought one thousand Quaaludes at a time and acted out the Teenage Wasteland that Pete Townshend was singing about in "Baba O'Reilly."

By the time he was fifteen, cocaine was just another drug to Stoltz, though it was infinitely more interesting to him because he was a born thrill seeker and the life around it evoked the same rush he had gotten from selling illicit fireworks or burglarizing a house or betting at the track with the wise guys. He knew more about cocaine than anyone—flake, pink, pearl, oiled, cocaine that smelled like bubble gum, cocaine that smelled like dirty socks. The weighing and cutting and splitting of it had always been like a high in itself. While still in high school, he was copping from a guy in Jackson Heights who lived right off the Long Island Expressway in an apartment with four women and a machine gun, a Colombian who called him "the Keed." Selling quarters and half ounces to older people (mostly women), Richard was known to lay out long extravagant lines in snaking concentric patterns that looked like mandalas. People would begin on the outside and snort their way around and around until they got to the middle (sometimes that could take a couple of days). By the time he went to Wall Street, Richard Stoltz could touch a bit of coke to the tip of his tongue and know the exact cut.

The other operating principle in Stoltz's life was money, which he knew even better than cocaine because it was in his blood. His father was a venture capitalist, and Richard had learned at his father's knee. He started making serious money even before turning twenty-one, trading on the markets and investing and reading every prospectus he could get his hands on. Aggressive, self-confident, great with numbers, he developed a polished rap, got his broker's license, and learned to leverage the new issue markets, becoming the number-one producer at his firm but always working fewer hours than his staid colleagues with their MBAs from Wharton and Harvard. Everyone knew this kid was something special. He had an entourage that included a private butler, a chauffeur, a secretary, and a computer consultant. This kid did things like buy a Maserati and a Mercedes on the same day. It was the dawning of the age of merger mania, leveraged buyouts, and municipal bonds, and Richard Stoltz was right at the center of it. Money was like oxygen to him, and he made it as naturally as other people breathed.

"Blow was just perfect for that power liquid environment," Stoltz commented in his high-rise condo on Manhattan's West Side. "People did it in bathrooms, in offices, on conference tables. Wall Street is a tense environment, and to be good at selling, you needed to impart a sense of urgency, and cocaine multiplied that urgency. People would be on those phones just wired! Wall Street was powering that whole fuck-'em-up-the-ass economic boom of the Eighties, and cocaine was powering Wall Street. The administration was saying Just Say No to drugs, but at that time drugs *were* capitalism."

In Stoltz's mind, cocaine and the financial markets were both street games about turf that required being smart and fast and being willing to bend the rules. Money and power and cocaine were interchangeable, acquired tastes that only whetted the appetite for more. By the time he left the Street to become what he called a "maverick entrepreneurial pioneer," these parallel worlds had become one in his life, giving entirely new meaning to the phrase *high finance.* Cocaine was a perfect fit with this aggressive acquisitiveness, feeding Stoltz's sense of invincibility and generating monumental hubris. After building a penthouse, he and Suzie began traveling the world. They were regulars at Petrossian, Café des Artistes, the Russian Tea Room, 21, and came to know the players in New York, Palm Beach, Los Angeles, Aspen, and Monte Carlo. They moved easily between enclaves of Texas oil barons, Park Avenue arbitrageurs, Pebble Beach blue bloods, and Palm Beach dowagers. Like the new generation of whiz kids working the programs at Lehman Brothers or Smith Barney during the Eighties, they were young, but they certainly weren't conservative, and that's what made them so different on this circuit—they were excessively wild.

Beautiful women were a prized commodity, no different from stock portfolios, property, antiques, and art, and Suzie Ryan was an asset that never depreciated. She had quit her job at a Madison Avenue boutique to live and travel with Richard, and the immaculately manicured fingernail on her right pinky was always kept at a length perfect for dipping into bags of cocaine and getting a large hit. Everywhere Richard went, Suzie was on his arm; everywhere Suzie went, men wanted to get into her pants. Richard knew it. Suzie knew it. "I suppose we loved each other in our own way," Suzie would later say. "But it was also just one more game that Richard could engage in to play the players." Suzie would go along to help him, just so long as she would never have to do anything that she didn't really want to do. Once when he asked her to do something he knew she wasn't up for, she got herself good and loaded and readily complied. The next day there were flowers, a bottle of Dom, and a box with the most exquisite pearl choker she had ever seen in her life.

It all worked like clockwork; one deal netted enough money to live on for five years. When Oliver Stone's movie *Wall Street* opened, Richard and Suzie hurried to see it. There were obvious differences between Richard Stoltz and Gordon Gekko, the ruthless corporate raider played by Michael Douglas, but the film accurately portrayed the moral ambience of their lives. Gekko believed that the entire world was fundamentally divided between the shepherds and the sheared, and so did Stoltz. Gekko obviously made more money but never did drugs the way Stoltz did. "I'd have them FedExed to us all over the world, expensing it so that I could write it off—something that was commonly done by more companies than you would care to think."

Eventually the bubble would burst, of course. But even when the saga was all over, Richard Stoltz was still liquid—after twenty-eight days of rehab, he still looked like he'd just stepped off the beach at St.-Tropez. Neither Richard nor Suzie ever bargained on addiction and the kind of human frailties on which it preys, but it was precisely because they were so comfortably insulated from life's insecurities that they would need the most graphic evidence possible of principles violated, damage done, lives unraveling.

In the summer of 1986, they were at a dinner party in Manhattan. Richard needed to raise a quick couple of million dollars and was trolling the room for investors. Suzie was sitting with a cocktail in her hand, chatting up the wife of a diplomat. There is never any warning of a nosebleed, and this one was like a pipe that had suddenly burst in her head. Before anyone could make a move to stanch it, the couch of beautiful white woven silk upholstery was spattered with blood. People gasped and rushed to help her to the bathroom.

Suzie would reflect on that nosebleed often in the years to come. She would remember the shock on the face of the diplomat's wife, the red blood soaking the white couch, and the embarrassment she felt. But mostly she would remember having one overriding thought, one requirement that superseded all others.

How am I going to snort the next line?

# 11

## Hangin' Bangin' and Slangin'

**Never trust a drug that's named after a part of your ass.**

— Street saying

**Life is fresh, crack is whack.**

— Another street saying

### I. Gangstress

SYLVIA NUNN ran her fingers across each group of bullet holes in the front of her family's house. "Drive-by, drive-by, drive-by. All of these came from people after me and my brother."

The holes in the siding were from a .38; the ones in the door came from a 12-gauge shotgun blast; those around the window from a shotgun and a semiautomatic rifle.

"These right here, I was sitting in that chair right there, caught a couple of buckshot from that—that was cool, though, because they just, like, *popped out* after a while. Did I know the guys? I knew the semiautomatic and the .38s. One of them is still alive, one of them is not, and one is paralyzed."

The sun was just setting, burnishing the neighborhood in soft yellow light.

"One come in daylight, the rest come just this time of the evening. *This* is drive-by time right here, when it's just getting dark."

As a car passed slowly in front of the house and the sun went down, you could feel the level of peril rising palpably in the neighborhood. One of the most surreal aspects of the Compton neighborhood of Los Angeles, for an easterner, is how normal, even nice-looking it can appear, with its neat and orderly houses on blocks of sun-dappled streets—very different from the drab inner-city blight of Bed Stuy or the South Bronx.

"When you look at these homes over here, you are not gonna believe that the top of the line coldhearted killers come from families like this," Sylvia pointed out. "If I never knew, it would be hard for me to drive down a street like this and say, Yeah, the guy that killed those seven people and them three little kids lives in that house—and that couldn't be his mom out there waterin' her garden! Understand what I'm sayin'?"

Night was the killing time, and Sylvia Nunn was most definitely a potential target. The knowledge that you could die at any moment, just standing here with her like this, was bloodcurdling.

"I ain't ever done a fuckin drive-by, 'cause that's how innocent people get killed, and kids. I do a fuckin' *walk-up*. If a motherfucka want me, I want him to come and knock on this door and say, 'Hey, Mrs. Nunn, is Sylvia here?' And when I step out, take my black ass out and don't be shootin' my motherfuckin' momma or my niece tryin' to get to me. Have enough heart to come get *me*! 'Cause if I want you, that's definitely what I'm gonna do. Just knock on yo' door, ask for you, and let you have it."

They called her Rambo because she was a gangstress and a shooter, a storied thirty-year-old Blood who had been gangbanging since the very beginning of the scene—*OG*, as they called it, Original Gangster. The most remarkable thing about Sylvia, besides being a woman in a world of violent men and the utter miracle of her survival, was how characteristic she was of what had happened in Compton. As she put it, "I can outshoot any nigga in this neighborhood. You think I'm gonna live here in this life and *not* shoot anybody? Yeah, I got a few 187s on my rap. What was the drive-bys over? *Revenge.* I mean, we done so much shit, and they'd come and shoot at our house. Just like, oh, what did you do last night? But we didn't receive no mo' than we dished out. Matter of fact, we were overblessed, very much overblessed."

Sylvia remembered her childhood as a world vastly different from this life of 187s, the police code for homicide. Life for kids was about going to Lueders Park, church, Ping-Pong, swimming pools, sock hops, and a program called the Get High on Life Summer Club—it seemed inconceivably, heartbreakingly innocent compared with what it had become. Her mother was the head of the household because her father had been sent to the penitentiary—"first time for sales of drugs and the robberies. He was makin' a livin', for ends to meet; he was always back and forth."

At Regina Caeli High, Sylvia was Miss Sophomore, Miss Junior, Homecoming Queen, and honor roll. "I had education, never wanted for nothin'. I've always had everything I wanted—but in between everything, I always gangbanged." She learned how to shoot from her father when he was out on one of his paroles; when she became Homecoming Queen, her mother gave her flowers and her father presented her with a sawed-off pump shotgun. In her progression into gang life, certain moments stand out as milestones. She was only "six goin' on seven" when her older brother, Marcus "China Dog" Nunn, one of the original Bloods, was trying to break into a gas station but couldn't fit through the window, "so they got me and put me up through the window, and I opened up the door. 'Oh, look, Sylvia did it!' 'You a *homegirl* now!' 'You gonna be with us *forever!*' "

And so she would be. In the beginning, Sylvia never even labeled herself as a gang member—"I would say '*organization*' "—and hanging out with her homeys was as natural to her as getting high. From Sylvia's earliest awareness, there had always been a street ethos to being in the gang; more than anything, being OG was about the fiercest kind of loyalty and self-respect. "Bein' OG, we got seniority; it's like we own the company. The OGs, they my heart, a do-or-die thing. They became like my brothers. We ate out of the same bowl, wore the same clothes, shot the same guns, and cried over the same caskets—you know what I'm sayin'? I'm *OG*. I don't change for nothin' or nobody. I'm good as gold. I give you everything I got—*if* I got it to give to you and I *want* to give it to you. But you can't *make* me give you shit, and you ain't gonna *take* shit from me."

Such was the essential philosophy of gang life. In the beginning, it was fun, but somewhere along the line it became about shooting people, and the greatest tragedy of all was how that part of it got to be so natural. "It's just like they say—once you chop down a tree, it becomes easy to chop down the tree. You know? And that's how it is with shootin' a gun. And that's how it is with 187s, to be honest with you. Once you take somebody's life and you make it through—you know what I'm sayin'?—

without a nervous breakdown, then it ain't hard to do it no mo'. It's like it becomes a habit, like."

The habit of killing would be reinforced by the brutal truths of gang warfare. "In this day and time, if somebody fuck with me, I'm not gonna shoot nobody and leave 'em livin' to come back at me or my family, so the only thing to do is just go on ahead and kill them. That's sad to say because there is another side of me, because we was brought up in a church. I got a good heart; I'm good people; I know God for myself. I know that I didn't give life, and life ain't mine to take away . . . But yet, it's still like that other part of me come out. It's like, *fuck it.*"

Drugs were only one of many privations that turned the inner cities of America into a special form of hell during the 1980s, all of them interconnected. Joblessness, racism, poverty, violence, disease, and hopelessness took their toll, but the role that crack—or rock cocaine, as it was known here—had played in reinforcing that fundamental street attitude—*fuck it*—was nothing less than commanding.

## II. The Most Addictive Drug Known to Man

THEY CALLED JIM GALIPEAU Kojak and Mr. Clean down here. He was tall, hulking, fearless, and bald-headed, but it was his heart that had made him a legend in the neighborhoods of South Central Los Angeles. Throughout his long career as a probation officer with the Metropolitan Specialized Gang Unit, Galipeau always went the extra mile to help people and bring peace to streets that had been ravaged by violence and drugs. As a result, he was perhaps the only white man who could go into any of the projects at any time of the day or night. Even so, he carried two guns, a .45 and a 9-millimeter, one in his belt and the other in his bag.

"People have shot at me, but it's just random shots. If people want to shoot me, I'll stand right up to them. They don't have to chase me—they know where I live . . . Last time I actually used a gun was in Vietnam. But being prepared to use one makes it so you don't have to."

There was a certain comfort factor in riding with Galipeau. When touring a war zone, it always helps to be with a guide who is less likely to be a target.

"This is one of the main north-south streets of the ghetto," he pointed out, turning onto Figueroa Street. "This is called the West Coast. Over there is the Harbor Freeway—that's the East Coast. This is Hoover Crip territory here; right across the freeway is East Coast Crip. Anybody from East Coast who came over here was a dead man. Any Hoover who crossed over there would be killed on sight."

Every street was the turf of a different set of Crips or Bloods, each one with its own history and legends, and Galipeau knew all of them.

"On the other side of this are the Denver Lane Bloods, who are surrounded by Crips, as Bloods always are . . . Over here on the left is Empire Market, where Soon Ja Du blew away Latasha Harlins. She was a badass street urchin who was stealing from them, but nothing justifies shooting a fourteen-year-old kid. It was a million-dollar business."

Now the Empire was nothing but a charred shell, a reminder that Galipeau's career had been book-ended by two climactic ghetto uprisings: the riots of '65 and '92. During all of that time, the most destructive influence on the gang culture he had observed was rock cocaine, but rarely in ways that had been accurately portrayed by the media.

"One of the biggest frauds that the press and police perpetrate on society is that there is money being made in these neighborhoods with drugs," he maintained. "There isn't. The only people who make money are the big-time guys who bring it in—the rest of it is chickenfeed. The guy with the Colombian connections is the dope man—that's the multimillionaire living in Encino or Beverly Hills who comes down here and buys everybody, buys a whole army of gang members. I've got twenty thousand gangbangers on my hands, and I can count on one hand the number of guys who can actually support themselves with a wife and kid in a seven-hundred-dollar-a-month apartment from drugs. It's a big myth. All this stuff about these kids rising from the streets and becoming drug lords is the bullshit of Hollywood and the media."

He broke off for a moment and pondered the landscape passing by. "I'll tell you what drugs are. *Misery,* and that's all."

The evidence of the misery was everywhere. Guys on the street corners had bodies like Mike Tyson, but were so wasted you could walk up and slap the shit out of them and they couldn't do a damn thing. And there were the young girls who had become base-head hookers—"they call them strawberries, and by the time they're twenty-two, if they ain't dead, they'll just sit there and turn tricks all day long, go buy a rock, turn another trick, go buy a rock. They get older and they gotta turn more tricks, give more head. You see these beautiful young girls getting into an ugly old truck to go down on some stinking, greasy, unshaven sixty-year-old guy for five dollars—just to get the next rock! It's so tragic, and yet it's an everyday occurrence."

Galipeau turned into Nickerson Gardens, home of the gang of Bloods called the Nickerson Gardens Bounty Hunters. "This is the projects. All that's supposed to be here is females and dependent children. No male is supposed to be here, and look what you see. Nothing but men. These guys take the fucking welfare checks on the first and fifteenth, give the women a couple of bags of cocaine, and they're gone until the first, when the checks come again. And fuck 'em—the kids got nothing."

He sighed as if he were carrying the full weight of it on his chest. "This is the main street in Nickerson Gardens—it's called *Success Avenue,*" he said with a sorrowing laugh. "Isn't that something? It's always cracked me up."

Many users and observers of cocaine had apprehended the potential dangers of a cheap, smokable form of the drug from its first appearance on the streets of America in 1985. Having wrestled with his own addiction, the film director Paul Schrader recalled reading a small article in the back of *The New York Times* that reported that police had become aware of a low-priced synthesized form of coke being sold on the streets. "The rich and powerful always figure out a way to take care of themselves—they had parents, they could go to hospitals," Schrader observed in his office. "But when they figured out how to market cocaine for the poor and the uneducated, that was something else . . . I just turned to my wife and said, 'This is a nightmare.' "

Bob Sabbag had been no less concerned, especially at a time when the Reagan administration was cutting back so much federal funding for urban programs. "A lot of people who got lost on cocaine up to that point had education, jobs, families, experiences—a life. The tragedy of what would happen with crack in the inner cities is that these resources never existed for these people. A lot of them were products of family abuse, a total breakdown of what we would consider a real life. They had nothing to reach for, nothing to look forward to even if they could come out of it."

In 1978, Sabbag had portrayed cocaine as a nonaddictive substance in his book *Snowblind;* by February of 1985, with more than twenty-two million Americans acknowledging that they had tried the drug at least once, *Newsweek* was calling it the "Evil Empire" in a cover story. One year earlier, on July 4, 1984, Nancy Reagan visited the fourth grade of the Longfellow Elementary School in Oakland and reduced the entire national crusade against drugs to three words: *Just Say No.* In ruling after ruling, the Supreme Court paved the way for the drug war by allowing "good faith" exceptions to the exclusionary rule of the Fourth Amendment. The Omnibus Crime Act of 1984 boosted maximum sentences and allowed prosecutors to confiscate anyone's assets and any property *believed* to have been purchased with drug money (with a special "poetic justice" provision that allowed the assets to be distributed among the law-enforcement agencies involved in the case). The drug lords who were smuggling cocaine into the United States never looked more malevolent, especially after the torture-murder of DEA agent Enrique "Kiki" Camarena in Mexico. By that time, drug-related kidnappings, assassinations, and bombings were commonplace in Colombia, and the first American helicopter crews were arriving to carry local police on raids against cocaine laboratories deep in the jungle.

Crack began as a marketing ploy due to a cocaine glut. Most people in the inner cities had never been able to afford cocaine, but with marijuana scarce and the price soaring in response to the DEA's three-year-old war on sensimilla, cocaine was not only cheaper but also more available than ever before. What appeared as rock in Los Angeles, growl in Miami, and crack in the South Bronx, was vastly different from freebase in that it was cocaine cooked with water and baking soda instead of ether, which not only made it inexpensive but meant that any twelve-year-old could now concoct his own batch and sell it in amounts as small as a single-hit rock for a few dollars.

If ever a nation was ready to perceive a new drug as an epidemic, plague, or scourge, it was America in that hot, troubled summer of 1986. *Newsweek* was the first to get a real whiff of the crack story. In a cover story called "Kids and Cocaine" in March of 1986, Arnold Washton of the 1-800 COCAINE hotline declared that the new drug was "instantly addictive," "the most addictive drug known to man right now," but the problem didn't stop there; the drug was "rapidly spreading to the suburbs." In a front-page report on March 20, *The New York Times* followed the drug into the wealthiest suburbs of Westchester. On May 23, Tom Brokaw reported on the *NBC Nightly News* that crack was "flooding America and that it had become America's drug of choice." On June 16, in a full-page editorial entitled "The Plague Among Us," *Newsweek* likened it to "the plagues of medieval times" and "the Japanese attack on Pearl Harbor." These kinds of extreme analogies—comparing a drug that had just appeared on the streets with the Black Plague, which wiped out one-third of the population of Europe—would now begin to echo throughout the media. In July, *U.S. News & World Report* pronounced illicit drug use "the No. 1 problem we face." And so it would go, in a veritable stampede of coverage that with time and perspective would provide graphic evidence that the media had become as addicted to crack stories as any crackhead had to the substance itself. Worsening economic and social conditions and the scarcity of affordable marijuana were no doubt important factors in the deep hold that crack would take in the inner cities, but the level and hysteria of the coverage would become paramount, both in the swift proliferation of the drug and in the political response to it.

"When the crack scare began, there were no reports of crack outside of three cities, New York, Miami, and Los Angeles," noted Craig Reinarman, professor of sociology at the University of California, Santa Cruz. Along with Harry G. Levine, a fellow professor of sociology at Queens College in New York City, Reinarman would carefully chart the role of the mass media in the spread of crack, as well as edit the definitive anthology on the phenomenon so far, *Crack in America.* "This was not something that you found on your average street in even a medium-sized city; in fact, it was only known in certain circles within certain neighborhoods of those three cities. In the summer of 1986, there had been several network shows on crack, and by the time they were done, there wasn't a farm kid in Idaho who didn't know what it was. If you really look at the casual arrow between stories and use, the stories preceded the mass use of crack." Reinarman's argument was simple and compelling: "The media did more to market crack than a team of a thousand dealers could ever do with an ad budget of one hundred million dollars."

In June of 1986, the death of Len Bias, the University of Maryland basketball star drafted by the Boston Celtics and fatally poisoned by cocaine right after his signing ceremony, presented the leading public example of the menace of the drug. Bias had consumed between three and five grams of cocaine that had been shaken up in an eight-ounce soda—a fact discovered by the autopsy that was all but completely overlooked by the public. After Bias's death, the media made less and less distinction between smokable crack and intranasal cocaine, and people began to think for the first time that *one line of cocaine* could be lethal.

But of all of the mounting public fears about the horrors of cocaine, nothing compared with "crack babies." The first wave of stories began in 1985, with the appearance of an article in *The New England Journal of Medicine* by Dr. Ira Chasnoff, who had conducted a study of twenty-three women and reported that cocaine appeared to be associated with miscarriage, prematurity, and "depression of interactive behavior" in their newborns. The Chicago-based doctor had been careful to point out that his study represented only a tiny and imperfect sampling and suggested that further study of the issue was necessary. After the *CBS Evening News* picked up the story on September 11, 1985, however, and showed a newborn screaming and trembling piteously, caught in the throes of cocaine "withdrawal" ("If you are pregnant and use cocaine, *stop,*" admonished the correspondent Susan Spencer), the mad dash to document the phenomenon of crack babies began in earnest. By 1986, a picture was emerging of low-birth-weight, learning-disabled babies who lacked "normal human feelings," cried inconsolably, suffered from "Alzheimer's-like symptoms," and perhaps most tragic of all, were incapable of love. Before long, the U.S. Department of Health and Human Services was predicting that there would be 100,000 crack babies born a year at an annual cost to society of twenty billion dollars; the figure most commonly bandied about in the media was 375,000 crack babies a year.

Time and perspective would prove the occurrence of "crack babies" to be a myth—"like Max Headroom and reincarnations of Elvis, a media creation," as Lynn Zimmer and Dr. John P. Morgan described it in their analysis of the phenomenon. Nobody would ever be foolish enough to assert that the ingestion of cocaine in any form or amount could be a positive thing for a pregnant women or her fetus, but in fact the kind of physical "withdrawal" being portrayed in news stories about babies born addicted to cocaine was a biological impossibility. Yes, cocaine would prove itself to be powerfully "reinforcing"; people were capable enough of becoming psychologically compulsive about using it in the worst ways, and the substance could certainly be physically harmful if ingested in large quantities over a period of time, but the kind of physical craving involved in heroin addiction simply did not exist. Claire Coles had been studying the effects of fetal alcohol syndrome for five years at Emory University when Chasnoff's article appeared and CBS aired its story. Coles noted that all the women in Chasnoff's study also drank alcohol and smoked pot and cigarettes; when TV news crews sought her out, she pointed out to reporters that those babies had been born to mothers with many other risk factors— poor nutrition, poor prenatal care, violence, heavy drinking, other drugs— and asserted that as a result, you couldn't accurately call them "cocaine babies." At that point, the news crews simply stopped calling her and started interviewing nurses and even nonmedical employees at the hospital about "cocaine babies." Babies suffering from heroin withdrawal were in fact filmed as examples of "cocaine withdrawal." In a society where police, media, and politicians frequently referred to cocaine as a "narcotic" (rather than the stimulant that it is), such distinctions would become less and less meaningful. As for the figure of 375,000 crack babies a year being predicted by the media, Chasnoff had reported that 11 percent of the mothers he surveyed were exposed to the full range of illegal drugs, marijuana included. The media had reported instead that 11 percent of all babies would be exposed to cocaine. The figure was so universally accepted as fact that dire warnings of a lost generation in the making were sounded—a "biologic underclass whose biological inferiority is stamped at birth," as columnist Charles Krauthammer called it.

And so here it was: a substance that seemed to fit the drug warriors' most apocalyptic predictions of a demon drug contagion: instantly addictive, spreading to the middle class, threatening every neighborhood in America, killing our most promising young athletes, poisoning innocents in the womb, turning them into tiny addicts, and condemning them to a hellish life as tragically defective human beings.

That summer and fall of 1986, the networks aired no fewer than seventy-four news stories about crack and cocaine, among them the highly rated, hour-long CBS special *48 Hours on Crack Street* in September and NBC's *Cocaine Country*. It was in this national atmosphere—with clips of Senator Alfonse D'Amato and U.S. Attorney for the Southern District of New York Rudolph Giuliani buying crack undercover on a street in Washington Heights along with news footage of doors being kicked in by police on drug raids being shown continuously—that Congress raced to introduce tougher antidrug legislation. The critics who counseled restraint were few, and those who did speak out were attacked, ridiculed, or ignored. "Bills were tossed into legislative hoppers all over the country as if they were sandbags heaved onto dikes hastily erected to control a rampaging flood," recalled Arnold Trebach, the author, professor, and founder of American University's Institute on Drugs, Crime, and Justice. A veteran of the civil rights movement, Trebach had dealt with the likes of Bull Connor in Birmingham and was not about to be intimidated; if there was a "national epidemic," he damn well wanted to see the hard proof. He called NIDA and the DEA, only to find out that they had no data on the new drug and what little they knew had come from the media. Moreover, for a drug that was supposed to be so lethal, Trebach saw no indication of any kind of significant increase in the number of cocaine deaths from the Drug Abuse Warning Network (DAWN). At the end of the summer, the DEA issued its special report, "The Crack Situation in the United States," which seemed remarkably balanced and levelheaded compared with the press coverage. It noted that the media storm had created a "distortion of . . . the extent of crack use compared to other drugs." But that would have no impact at all on the mounting national uproar. As Trebach saw it, "Measures were proposed on both ends of Pennsylvania Avenue in Washington to demand mass urine tests of government officials, to deploy the military to control drug trafficking, to impose the death penalty for certain homicides connected with drug sales. . . . It was a scary time to sit here . . . and sense my own government coming apart, losing its guts, blowing its cool, prostituting itself."

On August 9, President Reagan and Vice President Bush and scores of White House staffers showed their support for the new drug war by taking "voluntary" urine tests—only the symbolic beginning of a pursuit of drug users in the workplace that would turn urine testing into a one-hundred-million-dollar industry. On Sunday night, September 14, the president and First Lady Nancy Reagan appeared on television together to make an appeal for a national crusade against drugs, comparing it with the Second World War, and urging Americans to adopt an attitude of "outspoken intolerance." If crack meant high ratings for the media and one of the biggest stories since Watergate and Vietnam, it was also a safe issue in a congressional-election year, allowing Republicans to lead the charge in the war on drugs and Democrats to show that they were tough as well and try to win back some of those Reagan Democrats. Drugs were now "a threat worse than any nuclear warfare or any chemical warfare waged on any battlefield," pronounced Representative Thomas Hartnett, Republican of South Carolina. The result was the two-billion-dollar Drug-Free America Act of 1986—a watershed in American history that established new mandatory-sentencing guidelines, taking the power to sentence defendants away from judges. The punishments for crack would be particularly stringent. Distribution of five grams or more, worth about $125 on the street, now resulted in a five-year mandatory sentence—no matter that it would require five hundred grams of cocaine powder worth roughly fifty thousand dollars to trigger the same sentence. This made one gram of crack the legal equivalent of one hundred grams of powder. The United States would soon have the greatest incarceration rate in the world, with vast racial discrepancies in its prison population. While blacks represented only 15 percent of all illegal drug users, they would constitute 41 percent of all those arrested on cocaine or heroin charges, giving the appearance of a drug war that was being concentrated largely on the low-level street dealing going on in the inner cities.

But for all the hysterical media coverage, the subsequent political demagoguery, and the racist implications of the drug prosecutions, there was also no denying the pernicious impact of crack on lives and communities. After all, people on the street didn't call smoking a crack pipe "sucking on the Devil's dick" for nothing.

"I looked down on crack addicts" said Vic Graziello, a junkie for almost twenty-five years on the Lower East Side of Manhattan who had used every conceivable drug in the pharmacopoeia before picking up the crack pipe. "I never freebased cocaine but I snorted and shot it. When crack came out, I kept running into people I had used all kinds of drugs with during the Sixties, and they kept saying, 'This crack—watch out, Vic; it's a different ballgame, stay away from it.' So I started up with this Spanish girl who lived in Williamsburg, and she would smoke it, and I wanted to keep away from it, but one day I picked up her pipe and she lit it for me. One hit and I was gone. She kept saying, *All right, all right, go easy!*'

"What was there about the high that was so addictive? It was so instant, so instant! When that pipe would get red hot, I knew it would have to cool off, but I could never wait and would always burn my hands. Even though my heart was going so fast and felt like it was going to explode, I couldn't get enough and had to hit it." Once, in a fit of despair during his junkie days, Gaziello had plunged a butcher knife into his chest in an attempt to end his own misery, but he made clear that his three-month run on crack was far worse than anything he had ever done or experienced in his most strung-out days as a hope-to-die dope fiend. "Within a few days, I had ripped off somebody at knifepoint and beat people. There were times I was using five hundred dollars a day. I pulled a knife on my uncle to get money—an old man. And then when my father died, I said to my mother, 'Your wedding ring, let me have it. Pop is dead; you don't need it anymore—give me that fucking ring!' She just looked at me in complete horror."

Graziello had known the agony of kicking numerous heroin habits and even methadone but had never experienced anything like the severe dysphoria and psychological cravings of trying to kick his addiction to crack. In his case at least, addiction had certainly been instantaneous.

By the late 1980s, such anecdotes were common, and the rooms of recovery fellowships were filled with people telling stories about how the drug was like an express train to the bottom. If one couldn't become physically addicted to crack, it was clear enough that it could indeed become the worst kind of mental obsession. The running observation was that if a person was telling their personal story and crack came into the picture, you could rest assured they'd be in detox or rehab or jail shortly thereafter.

In the gang culture of South Central, rock cocaine would take on a destructive power that was unparalleled in any other city. Jim Galipeau remembered when heroin had entered the neighborhoods and the effect it had on the Hispanic gangs of East Los Angeles and elsewhere, but that was child's play compared with what would happen with rock.

### III. A Whole New Class of Hero Coming Up

When did the gang killing in L.A. begin? Different people remember different incidents, all with identically lethal results. Galipeau says that the first fatality that actually made the news was over a leather jacket taken off a boy at the Palladium all the way back in '70; others say, no, what started it was the satin jacket of a gang member that a girl had been wearing at Horace Mann Junior High in '79. Either way, somebody died, and it was the taking of revenge that had made reputations.

And then rock appeared. Before, heroin dealers in the ghetto aspired to become heavies like Tootie Reese, but Tootie was a quaint relic compared with the high rollers and ballers of the 1980s, like Wayne Day, Michael "Harry O" Harris, and Freeway Ricky Ross—"the New Gang Godfathers," as local news stations began calling them when they picked up on this latest story of "the most violent gangs in America" and this "new game" being molded by drugs and big money, beepers and gold.

The New Gang Godfathers became neighborhood folk heroes easily enough by bankrolling huge street parties, paying for funerals, giving money to poor families, and establishing neighborhood parks. So rapid was the emergence and rise of the elusive Ricky Ross that they called him Freeway. Ross did his business on the run and used the Seventy-Four Hoovers as his enforcers, operating his rock houses like fast-food chains. The word on the street was that he always carried a briefcase that contained a million dollars in large bills, and when he was cornered by police he would just hand it to them and let them take what they wanted. The money generated by rock would only increase the already significant potential for police corruption. As Galipeau put it, "These guys in their mid-twenties who suddenly see a million dollars lying in a backyard, knowing they can die any day doing their twenty-five-thousand-dollar-a-year jobs—it's no mystery why they do it." The only reason the drug dealers couldn't get to Galipeau was that "by the time they started offering me money, I was well along the way to retirement."

The media portrayed the new kingpins as South Central's versions of the great gangsters of the Twenties and Thirties, rising from the mean streets to become multimillionaires, insulated from the law by power and money and their attorneys. In the case of Michael Harris, at least, the stereotype was completely accurate. At the age of twenty-six, Harris built an organization that began in the ghetto and expanded to distribute cocaine clear across the country. In a two-month period in 1986, he made eighteen million dollars and purchased beautiful houses in Encino and Tarzana, as well as an auto-leasing company in Beverly Hills.

The most fearsome of the new kingpins was Wayne Day. When a secretly shot video was broadcast showing Day addressing some five hundred Crips in the bleachers of the Compton Stadium about how to properly execute drive-bys, the city of Los Angeles was suitably unnerved. When a DEA task force went after him and Day had to lie low, an upcoming opportunist tried to take advantage by contacting Day's connection; the message Day sent was clear enough. "They found the guy nude," Galipeau remembered, "with his balls and his dick cut off and stuffed in his mouth and a great big cucumber sticking out of his ass, and that just terrorized everybody. From then on, nobody challenged him."

By the late 1980s, all the New Gang Godfathers had been taken down, but for every kingpin there were now thousands of young wannabes on the streets, including a young member of the Rolling Twenties Crips named Calvin Broadus, who would become known as Snoop Doggy Dogg when he started rapping. By the time Snoop was selling rock on the streets, it had become almost a rite of passage, a matter of survival. As he wrote in *The Doggfather,* his 1999 autobiography, "There was a whole new class of hero coming up—the pimp and the outlaw, the thug and the gangster—and if you wanted to stay alive on the streets of Long Beach or Watts or Compton and anywhere else where the American Dream was falling apart and fading away, you better get with the program. It was the only game in town."

Snoop had attended the Trinity Baptist Church, and sold candy on the streets of Compton as a boy; for this new game, all he needed was somebody to watch his back and three ounces of decent-quality rock, worth about eighteen hundred dollars an ounce, that would be fronted to him by the Insanes, a Crip gang. It was a volume business, a seller's market, "any nigger with a third grade education" could do it, and you could sure make better money than "flipping fishwiches at McD's." As was not the case with selling candy, Snoop didn't have to go looking for customers—they came to him, "twenty-four seven, three hundred and sixty-five, with those big bills clenched in their sweaty hands and their eyes all beady and bright and that rasp in their voice that's about halfway between a whisper and a scream."

The economics went like this: twenty little rocks to a vial, called a dub rock or a twenty piece, sold for twenty-five dollars. A good count could produce a hundred dub-rock packages from an ounce; each ounce might turn a seven-hundred-dollar profit. Dealing dub was about keeping risk down to a minimum and letting everybody know what they were getting. For Snoop Dogg, it was an education.

"That's where I learned the true nature of black and white, rich and poor, self-esteem and self-destruction. Selling rock is the best way I know to get a good look at human nature on the flip side, down and desperate, with none of the fake bullshit that's supposed to make us civilized. A white man in a Mercedes and a two-thousand-dollar suit is no different than a nigger in a Hyundai and three-day-old sweats when it comes to getting high. They're both ready to do what it takes, pay what it costs, and take any risk just to draw down on that rock one more time."

In the world that Snoop and his homeboys would call *gangsta* and *thug life,* the word *dope* itself would become an adjective synonymous with *cool* or *phat.* The arrival of rock cocaine signaled a new way of life in the ghetto—*hangin' bangin' and slangin':* hanging out with the homeboys in the hood, gang banging, and selling drugs. The money that gang members made on drugs was never enough to escape the ghetto, of course, but certainly sufficient for buying fancy wheels for their cars and big-link gold chain necklaces, called Turkish ropes, and—most ominously—better weapons: Uzis, MAC-10s, AK-47s, shotguns, and a large array of heavy-caliber handguns, along with hollow-point ammo. And that's when the slaughter began in earnest. A whole new word, *drive-bys,* would enter the popular glossary to describe the payback killings done from passing automobiles by groups of young men in their corn-rowed braids,

G'ed up in their low-slung baggy shorts and Nikes, two-toned ball caps, and do-rags, all of them strapped down with their gats purchased with drug money. It was outright warfare: Crips versus Bloods, Crips versus Crips, gangs versus cops. South Central became like Beirut, a nightmare world of police helicopters with searchlights chasing young men with mad-dog stares through the night, young men who cared little about dying and even less about killing someone else. The phrases associated with murder became terrifyingly mundane on the streets—

*I'll bust a cap in yo' ass, bitch.*

*Motherfucka, killin' don't mean nothin' to me.*

*I'll smoke you and yo' whole family, nigga.*

If you happened to miss and shoot an innocent bystander, *yo, that's how it happens sometimes.* The word most commonly used for the kind of behavior that went over the line for even the most hard-core gangbangers was *scandalous,* as when a baby would get shot in the head by a stray bullet. One's home address and the wearing of gang colors—red for the Bloods, blue for the Crips—were reason enough to die. But nobody outside the communities seemed to care too much. In fact, the more yellow homicide tape appeared in South Central, the more the nation seemed to want to turn its head away. After all, this place where dogs outlived kids—it wasn't really America, was it? No, these weren't kids; these were bloodthirsty animals gone wild in some insane concrete wilderness of poverty, rage, and drugs—and then, on April 29, 1992, in the aftermath of the Rodney King verdict, it all exploded at the corner of Florence and Normandie. As Sanyika Shakur (aka Monster Kody Scott) of the Crips so eloquently put it, "The scar of over twenty years that had been tucked out of sight and passed off as 'just another ghetto problem' burst its suture and spewed blood all over the belly of America."

Perhaps the greatest shock of that night was how quickly the LAPD was routed, how fast the police abandoned the place to complete anarchy as cars were pelted with rocks, people were pulled from vehicles and beaten, and Los Angeles went up in flames. Statements were issued about staffing and strategy, but the bottom line was that the police knew full well that there were now twenty thousand armed gang members prowling the streets, God knows how many of them "cluckheads" buzzed out of their minds—and if they wanted to burn down their own neighborhoods, well, let 'em.

As Galipeau saw it, even the all-important loyalty that had been the very basis of the gangs started to go out the window. "I used to see cops knocking the living shit out of fourteen- and fifteen-year-old kids at the police station, beating them so bad that it made the Rodney King thing look like a bitch slapping, and they wouldn't give up their homeboy—they would rather die from a beating! Now guys would roll over on a homeboy just to get back out to their dope."

Eventually, tired of the risks and arrests, Snoop Dogg would leave the business altogether—"The whole fucking game was a scam. Big cheese, free pussy, gats and gangsta style—and then they put you away for the duration." Another game would draw him in, one that would consume him body and soul and shape his destiny. Retreating to an old toolshed filled with busted mowers, he would go from sunup to sundown finding the rhymes in time and sound that would become his essence, the "vicious lazy drawl" that would become known as the Snoop Sound and make him one of the foremost rappers of his generation, one of the first superstars of hip-hop music. "It was like I'd had an itch way down deep on the inside someplace that I'd never been able to scratch."

At the same time that rock was ravaging a community, it was also giving rise to the form of folk expression that would most authentically document it. When Snoop hooked up with Dr. Dre at Death Row Records for albums like *The Chronic* and songs like " 'Nuthin' but a G-Thang,' " the hard-core truths of the ghetto that he would convey—"about conditions on the street, what homies' lives were really like and how gangs and drugs and violence had become part of our everyday routine of survival"—would find their way to a mass white audience. Conservatives like William Bennett and Lynne Cheney would excoriate the rappers for their lyrics: "America's cities are about to be victimized by a paradigm-shattering wave of ultra-violent, morally vacuous young people some call 'superpredators,' " Bennett warned in a book called *Body Count.* Yet by the mid-'90s, hip-hop was the dominant youth culture of the land. As

Snoop put it, "We were telling it like it was, not like it should be or even could be, but the actual stone-cold facts, straight from the 'hood and into the suburban living rooms of America."

There was never any confusion in Snoop's mind about the purpose of his rapping—to increase the peace, to spread the music, to elevate and educate—just as there was never any uncertainty about the "stone-cold facts": "Cocaine is poison, straight up, and if you're looking for what brought life in the ghetto down to a dog-eat-dog level, then you've sure enough got your culprit."

The remedies, however, would be far more elusive.

"We've got to stop killing each other. We've got to turn our rage and righteous anger on the target where it belongs—the system that keeps us oppressed and down and addicted to crack and attacking in the dead of night like wild animals tearing at each other's throats."

## IV.  Crumb Sack

A BOY PASSED by in a car, and Sylvia whistled at him—a very loud two-finger whistle, the kind that could have hailed a cab in New York from blocks away.

"I know damn near everybody that drives down this street . . . He's lookin' for some stuff, he wants to get him some goods, but I ain't sellin' no mo'. I ain't fuckin' with it, and I want to quit usin'. Drugs ain't nothin' but an excuse, a lack of facin' life on life's terms, usin' a crutch instead of dealin' with reality."

Few people were more honest or clear about how bad rock was for the people of her community than Sylvia—"What kills me about them that smoke cocaine is that they won't eat, won't comb their hair, won't change their clothes, won't take a bath, and won't brush their teeth"—and her mother had put her in numerous rehabs and recovery homes, but she'd always gone back to using. "Golly, I can't honestly say that I'm not addicted *right now*. I've done everything for drugs. I ain't no prostitute, but I'll get right out there and jack me a motherfucka. I'd shoot me a motherfucka before I'd suck his dick. Suck *what*?"

For Sylvia, the use of rock had gotten far more complex than money, much deeper than gang affiliation or even a question of straight-out addiction. It was obvious from neighbors that she was a beloved figure in the 'hood—the very personification of "heart" as it had come to be defined in the ghetto. There was a homeless boy living in her car whom she was feeding and clothing with what little money she had. "I have gifts from God. There's nothing in the house I can't fix, no type of person I can meet that I can't communicate with, no type of person I can't get along with."

These things had hardly served to insulate her from the pain of her life and surroundings, however. A few years back, she had been shot six inches above her heart in a confrontation with her Crip boyfriend—"It was like somebody took a torch and went *whoosh!* straight through me, like a red hot arrow"—and had spent six months on a respirator. She had tried to commit suicide at least four times. "Why? Self-pity. Feelin' like if I wasn't around, wouldn't nobody have to deal with the asshole that I was. The last two times doctors walked away, certain I was dead."

But nothing was as bad as the death of her brother, Bobby Ulysses Nunn Jr., on July 23, 1991. The boy they called Bopete had never even gangbanged—"he was the sweet one, so harmless he wouldn't fight"—but he did get high and was on his way to meet a girl and wanted some stuff when he ran into two guys from the 'hood who were twinkin'—searching for dope—when they came across some homeboy's twenty-dollar crumb sack. "A 'crumb sack' mean that after you cut up all your dope, you got some crumbs left," Sylvia explained, "and you give your crumbs to your workers—it ain't really shit." Bopete had a lighter; they gave him some crumbs and used the rest. When the homeboy came looking for his stuff and drew down on the guys who took it, they fingered Bopete. That was how Bopete died, lying with a bullet in the back of his head not far from the Theodore Roosevelt Elementary School. Life had become cheaper than a crumb sack worth twenty dollars.

"My brother in the penitentiary is like my best friend and my crimey, but Bopete, he was my heart, my shadow. My mother said that if they'd called her and said, Mrs. Nunn, we got China Dog down here at the morgue with a bullet in the back of his head or we got Sylvia down here, she would have understood it, but she couldn't understand this . . . There has not been a day, evenin', mornin', that has passed that I have not looked for my brother. On the inside, I died. I get loaded out here because ain't nowhere I can go in this house, ain't nowhere I can go in this community, that I don't see my brother. So if I stay loaded, if I stay under the influence, then my mind can't think about it."

The guy who pulled the trigger was doing time up in Wayside, and one of the guys who had accused Bopete of taking the dope had already been found, shot twenty-eight times, with a pipe stuck in his mouth. Which left one guy still around, unfinished business—and as Sylvia put it, "It ain't over till it's over." The impulse to take revenge, inbred by a lifetime of gangbanging, was visceral; Sylvia was very graphic about what she would like to do to the guy.

"I wanna start out by maybe shootin' the motherfucka in the ear with a .22, then shoot him in his nuts, then take the motherfuckin' nose of a .45 and, excuse me, stick it up the head of his penis, and shoot him. See, I wanna do that kind of shit, cut around his heart—you know what I'm sayin'?—'cause he couldn't have no heart to do what he done. Then shoot him between the eyes. Then the last place I wanna shoot him is right where he shot my brother. Then I wanna spit on him or somethin' . . . "

Sylvia got quiet for a moment and gazed off down the street. "And then another part of me want to ask him if he repented, because I constantly ask God for forgiveness. I'm constantly repenting because I done so much wrong. All the time, I ask for forgiveness. Even if I'm hittin' the pipe, I'll go out in the middle of the street and praise God. I don't care where I'm at or who around or what's goin' on, and every dope house around here knows it, every dope dealer knows it. My brother would say, 'She outta her mind!' "

In Ed Bullins's one-act play *Salaam, Huey Newton, Salaam,* a character calls crack "the last weapon in the Devil's arsenal for the Black Nation. . . . We come out of slavery, we can come outta this. . . . When we overcome this, he'll never be able to come at us again, in this world or the next." It was clear to Sylvia that she had reached a precipice, the kind of crossroads with crack that Bullins had described.

"This is my bottom, right here and now. I hurt more than ever in my life. I don't like it here; I hate every day I have to wake up and still be here. Sometimes I'd rather be dead—this ain't nothin' but death no way. I tell you, if Hell is anything like this here, as God is my witness, I sho' don't wanna go. I mean, if it's even a *taste* of something like this here."

On the day her mother told her that Bopete was dead, Sylvia was overwhelmed by the urge to go right over to the house of the mother of the man who shot her brother, knock on the door, and shoot the woman right between the eyes. She was armed and on her way when she fell down on her knees right on her own porch and prayed.

"I said, 'Lord, I don't know what's happenin' because I'm trying to leave you alone right now; I'm on my way to do this mission. But if it's somethin' you tryin' to say, you better speak—not now but *right now.*' And my mind said, Sylvia, just think about the many lives you have taken, think about the lives yo' brothers has taken, and think about someone knockin' on the door and killin' yo' mother. It's the same thing. And I just started crying. And all I could say was 'Lord, have mercy, Lord, have mercy' . . . "

Such were the moments of Sylvia Nunn's life, and they were being played out in a hundred different variations everywhere you looked—Avalon Gardens, Nickerson Gardens, Grape Street, Piru Street, Lime, Holly, Oleander Avenue, Leuders Park, east side, west side, in black inner-city neighborhoods all across the United States —choices constantly being made that meant life or death, ruin or redemption. In this world of Crips and Bloods, OGs and baby gangsters, where a person could be killed for the contents of a crumb sack, every right choice, no matter how small, had become nothing less than a miracle, nothing less than transcendence in the face of total despair, nothing less than reclamation of the soul.

# 12

## Spiritus Contra Spiritum

66Abandon yourself to God as you understand God. Admit your faults to Him and your fellows. Clear away the wreckage of your past. Give freely of what you find and join us. We shall be with you in the Fellowship of the Spirit, and you will surely meet some of us as you trudge the Road of Happy Destiny.99

> —"A Vision for You," *Alcoholics Anonymous,*
>    The Big Book, 1939

### I. That's Why They Call It Recovery

DAVID CROSBY STRUMMED a chord on his guitar, and the rich sound filled the living room of his Encino home. "I was in full flower in '85," he said of his addiction. "There were a tremendous number of freebasers by then. We thought we were the Dark Side. We thought we were going to buck the trend. But that's about when the turning point came, when it hit the streets as crack."

Crosby hit another chord.

"I was a stone-cold junkie. Sores all over my body. Numerous car wrecks from having grand mal seizures while driving. Multiple seizures from toxic saturation. I'd tried several times to straighten out, six times in hospitals and at least four times on my own, all utter, miserable failures, each of which made me less able to try it the next time. I was dead but still walking around. Stole drugs. Dealt drugs. Pleaded, begged, borrowed, and told any lie to get drugs. The only thing left was my wife, Jan, and we would lie down on our bare mattress on our bare floor, throw a blanket over ourselves, and just hold on to each other."

Freebase is produced by mixing cocaine hydrochloride powder with ether and water to switch the drug's pH back from acid to alkaline, reducing the substance to its base so that it can be smoked. As Crosby noted, "All basers are obsessed with it. They all think they know everything about it. Basers imagine they're chemists, scientists, doctors, and pharmacists, and everybody has a slightly different theory about how to make it right." Scads of accoutrements were required: little pieces of glass, tubes, bottles, stoppers, screens, pipes, and pieces of rubber, scrapers, containers for liquids and powders, pH papers, water, ammonia, baking soda. And the all-important torch, of course. The problem with basing was that ether was highly flammable—and the higher you were, the easier it was to start fires, as Richard Pryor discovered on that night in 1980 when he ran screaming down the streets of the San Fernando Valley, engulfed in flames. The second problem was the two-minute high, which the filmmaker Paul Schrader described as "falling down a dark elevator shaft." The ascent was so fast and so intense that it made the descent that much more severe and the desire to get high again that much more compulsive. This made freebasers frighteningly greedy—"like starving Dobermans waiting for red meat," as Michael O'Dongohue characterized them. The final problem was paying for the damn stuff. An ounce a day was common on a really bad jag, which would cost twenty-four hundred dollars. David Crosby's habit eventually consumed a personal fortune of about seven million dollars.

"I sold that piano. I sold these guitars. I got them back, but there's a story about them."

The guitar that Crosby was holding was a gorgeous vintage twelve-string Martin conversion, purchased with some of the first money he'd ever earned as a performer, at clubs like Mother Blues. Crosby played the guitar in the Byrds during those years when he was living in Laurel Canyon, cultivating the sybaritic lifestyle of his wildest fantasies—he was Lawrence of Laurel Canyon, as one of his friends called him, one of the princes of the new psychedelic spring. He later used the guitar to write such classics as "Long Time Gone," "Guinevere," and "Wooden Ships" for Crosby, Stills, and Nash. At the nadir of his addiction, Crosby had taken his guitars along to a hospital in Altoona, Pennsylvania, called Cold Forge.

"It was one of the places I tried to get straight, and when eight thousand forty-nine minutes later I got up and split—and believe me I counted every one of them!—there was a guy there who had befriended me and my wife who said, 'Don't worry, I'll send you your stuff COD,' and he went right out and sold my guitars. It was like losing your best friend! I tried everything; the guy was gone, the guitars were gone, the trail was cold."

Over the next few years, Crosby served time in a Texas penitentiary and became one the most public recovering drug addicts in America. Then he completed an autobiography (*Long Time Gone,* written with Carl Gottlieb) that would stand as one of the most powerful documents ever published on the era of Sex, Drugs, and Rock and Roll. Over the course of his dramatic recovery, much of what Crosby had lost along the way was restored to him: career, self-esteem, and friends. He purchased a beautiful house in Encino and fathered a boy named Django, but like a metaphor of his addiction, his guitar was lost—a continuing reminder, perhaps, that notwithstanding all the wonders of his new clean and sober life, some things might never be recovered. Once, outside a concert hall in Pennsylvania that he was playing with Graham Nash, his wife, Jan, saw a boy go by who she was certain was wearing a shirt of hers that had disappeared from the hospital along with the guitars. They brought the guy backstage, and it turned out that he was engaged to a girl whose father had both guitars—an Armenian fellow who had never taken them out of the cases the whole time he'd had them. The promoters then called and tried to convince him to sell the guitars back to Crosby; everyone from the CS&N camp, in fact, called at one time or another, but the response was always the same: "Fuck you, I paid for them." Then, with Crosby's fiftieth birthday approaching, his wife decided to make one final attempt and asked Graham Nash, the diplomat of the group, to handle it. Nash came back downcast. "It's hopeless, David. We will not get those guitars back."

At the party, where two hundred of Crosby's friends gathered to celebrate his birthday and the miracle of his life, Glenn Close and Woody

Harrelson came up to him. "David," Close said, "you know Woody is a guitar player, too, and he would really love it if you would show him how to play one of your songs."

Harrelson then said, "Come on, I've got my guitar right over here."

When Crosby opened the case, there was his darling Martin conversion.

"They set me up good!" Crosby exclaimed. "My heart stopped, and my eyes filled with tears."

He went silent for a moment. "You gotta be *real* bad to leave something like this behind."

The costs of David Crosby's addiction were not over. Within two years, he would almost die of liver failure and struggle back yet again from the brink of death after a transplant. After that, he would find the long-lost son he'd fathered out of wedlock back in the Sixties and play in a band with him. And so it would go with him: things lost, things regained with new meaning.

"I've had a lot of wonderful things happen to me in sobriety. Anybody who tells you they got their life back isn't lying. That's why they call it *recovery.*"


## II. Then Came the Bugs

CRACK WAS THE DRUG of the underclass. It produced headaches and body aches. The hangovers were terrible and you could never be sure what was in it. The freebase that Suzie Ryan and Richard Stoltz smoked was refined and smelled sweetly medicinal. Richard hired a Colombian chef who cooked their cocaine as well as their food. After long days of smoking, she would make them a special stew called Back to Life—and that's what it was, nourishment that would bring you back from the dead.

Because Richard always paid, he went first all the time, smoking huge rocks out of a bent diet Coke can with holes in the side. People's eyes would go wide at his gargantuan three-gram hits. Sometimes he and Suzie would smoke for four days in a row. Once when they ran out and he had to go to a meeting, they hired a limo and copped down on the Lower

East Side, and Richard cooked it up in back. They must have gone around the park forty times smoking before the driver started getting uptight. Just keep driving no matter what, Richard told him. I'll buy you a car.

Maybe it was the time that Richard stepped on a glass and cut his foot badly and couldn't get to the hospital for days because he couldn't stop smoking for fifteen minutes that should have alerted Suzie to how bad things were. There were many such episodes during that nightmarish eighteen-month jag; the vignettes and images that later resonated as the most obvious warning signs of their descent failed to sound alarm bells as they occurred. Like the time they had sex on the living room floor of one of Richard's potential investors just so that he and his guests could watch. It was a line Suzie had told herself she would never cross—and yet she did it without so much as a thought. Maybe it was the time they were flying to Florida and Richard cooked up half an ounce and insisted that she store it in her vagina during the trip so they wouldn't get busted.

Hallucinations became common—"the bush people," as David Crosby would call them—but the worst was the police paranoia. Richard became certain that they were under constant surveillance and hired a security guard and stationed him in the stairwell because he was certain that a SWAT team was lurking there, ready to bust down the door. When they checked into a hotel, he would pile all the furniture in front of the door, leaving one piece in the middle of the room that he intended to use to break the windows so that he could throw the drugs out should the police succeed in smashing their way in with a battering ram.

I can't stop this so I *must* be a drug addict, Suzie would tell herself sometimes as she looked in the mirror—never a good idea during a freebase jag. No, she would then think, I *can't* be a drug addict, I was a *Homecoming Queen!*—and she would try to conjure up that beautiful autumn day, but it always seemed as if it had happened to another person in another lifetime.

Other times she knew exactly what was happening. Good, she would think. It's working; I'm going to die.

Then came the bugs. She might have kept going had it not been for the bugs crawling under her scalp. There was actually a medical word for it: *formication,* the hallucination of bugs crawling around, over, or under the skin. It was one of the symptoms of cocaine psychosis, but she was never more certain of anything in her life than the fact that they were absolutely real, nesting, multiplying, swarming. John Phillips experienced them as maggots when he was shooting cocaine. He was so determined to prove to other people that they were real that he would wrap his whole body in cellophane so that he would be able to trap them when they crawled out of his skin. But Suzie's would never crawl out, so she had to dig them out with sharp objects: paper clips, metal nail files, letter openers, the smallest blade of a Swiss Army knife.

There were deep, open festering sores on her head, and her skin was putrescent from vodka and cranberry. It was as if every toxin, every chemical, was coming out of her pores at once, but the smell wouldn't go away, no matter that she stood in the shower and scrubbed her skin until it was raw. Later, when she smoked, she was hearing voices and had no feeling in her hands. Her arms felt like they weighed hundreds of pounds as she crawled around on the rug to pick up some rocks, and when she righted herself in front of the mirror and looked, that's when it happened.

She had the eyes of a rabid animal. She looked into those eyes and knew that she was stark raving mad. There was death in them; she could touch it, feel it enveloping her like a shroud. When she saw Richard in the mirror lighting the pipe and realized that in spite of all that she was seeing and knowing she still wanted it more than anything else in the world, something broke loose inside of her. It was like a veil suddenly being pulled back to reveal that most basic human desire to survive, but combined with it was the acknowledgment of how much help she would need. The words she cried out to the image being reflected at her were simple but came from the depths of her soul.

"Please, God, help me!"

It was the prayer of a frightened child calling out into the dark, of a scared soldier in an isolated foxhole. She would always liken it to the prayer of George Bailey, the character played by Jimmy Stewart in Frank Capra's classic, *It's a Wonderful Life,* when he stands on the bridge on that snowy Christmas Eve and begs God to give him back his life, to put things back the way they were.

### III. The Only Real Revolution

THE SEX, Drugs, and Rock and Roll Generation gave up getting high very reluctantly at first. One at a time, those who were in trouble with drugs came to their reckonings like missing kids straggling in from a bash that had been out of hand since the Sixties. The reasons for turning away from drugs were varied. As Grace Slick emphasized, "It was not *my* idea to stop using drugs. It was the *highway patrol's*. They said, 'If you don't do this, you'll lose your car keys,' and I was more addicted to cars than I am to drugs."

In Slick's case, despite the many illicit substances she may have consumed, alcohol had become her drug of choice during those turbulent years of the Jefferson Starship, the successor to the Jefferson Airplane. Along the way there were three DUIs, though they were hardly of the ordinary variety. One time she was driving 125 m.p.h. at about three in the morning. The light was out on the oil gauge, so she couldn't have known that she had no oil, but that explained why flames were shooting out from under the hood. She pulled the car over; the highway patrolman said, "All right, what's going on here?" Whereupon Grace looked at him levelly and said, "What's going on here is that it's three in the morning and I'm a woman out here alone and my car is in *flames,* you fucking idiot"—or words to that effect, and off she went to the Marin County Jail. Another time she was parked up on a mountain in Mill Valley, sitting on the ground, reading a book, and drinking wine. "I'm arresting you for being drunk in public," said the policeman who asked her what she was doing there. "What kind of public," she sputtered; "there's nothing up here but *squirrels and trees,* you moron!"—or words to that effect, and off she went to the Marin County Jail. "This was Public Intoxication." Slick admitted. "These were not Moving Violations; these were Drunken Mouth violations."

In addition to her impudent lip, Slick's other major problems with alcohol were the horrific hangovers and blackouts. "I don't mind radical things, but I do mind not remembering. I never felt jerky about anything I'd done until around 1976. Most people had started cutting down on their drug use, and it wasn't really fashionable to be this raving idiot except if you were a punk in Great Britain." Slick, however, was a thirty-six-year-old mother of a little girl. Increasingly aware that she had a problem with drinking, she was becoming interested in controlling it, if not stopping it entirely; she wasn't quite sure what she wanted to do. The fellowship of Alcoholics Anonymous was roughly forty years old by the time Slick was sentenced to six months of meetings in 1977. Among her peers, nobody was going to A.A.

"I was sort of out there on a limb by myself. There would be twenty people in the room, none of them rock-and-roll people. They were all accountants and waitresses and housewives from Belvedere, and the only place I would ever come into contact with these kinds of people would be in the grocery store."

Slick found herself fascinated by A.A. "A shoe salesman would get up and talk, and I'd realize how isolated I'd been. It was like watching a live soap opera. Saying the wrong thing, falling down, vomiting—these kinds of things were *very* embarrassing for these people—and they would just talk about their personal lives, and I was very impressed by that. These people were not performers, and it was very cathartic for them. But I'd be thinking, Gee, I've had worse things said about me in *newsprint* than anything they ever did in their actual lives! They'd talk about having an affair with a friend of their husband and he didn't know, and I'd be going, Well, aren't we risqué?"

Slick also found that she liked the cultural and political structure of A.A.. "See, I always hated the Catholic Church, and in A.A. there was no pope, no president, no fancy outfits or fancy rooms. These meetings were all in hideous rooms in civic centers and churches or something, and everybody was equal, it was a true democracy—the best structure of an organization I've ever seen. That's why it works as well as it does; that and the fact that the desire to kick drugs and have a better life can be real powerful."

Over the years, Slick would come and go with A.A., but what kept her coming back was that beyond the focus on alcohol there was a learning curve about life in the program that provided valuable information, and she was conscious of its potential value for others. Most people who used drugs and alcohol were not caught in the throes of serious problems. Antidrug rhetoric aside, it's a statistically irrefutable fact that the vast majority of people who had smoked marijuana and used psychedelic drugs and later tried and used cocaine were capable of controlling their drug use. At one time or another, those people had used drugs for the same wide variety of reasons: recreation, relaxation, sexual and social adjunct, creative instrument, intellectual stimulation, cultural identity, peak and mystical experience, hobby, avenue of hipness and romanticism, tool of rebellion, rite of passage, lifestyle, ideology, object of connoisseurship, and conspicuous consumption. Most had been moderate social users who would continue to control their use or simply outgrow drugs and move on with their lives.

But there were those who used drugs for very different reasons: as anaesthesia, coping mechanism, escape from life, self-obliteration, or outright death trip. For myriad reasons having to do with self-will, genetic disposition, psychological and emotional makeup, aspects of environment and conditioning, or the substances themselves, those people had gotten stuck in patterns of serious abuse and addiction. By the mid-1980s, with the rise of the mass cocaine culture, more of them were in trouble with drugs than ever before, and many were going to need help.

"Once you go into A.A. and start hearing about all of this and you reflect on your own actions and how you got there, then you start thinking about your friends," said Slick. "I knew that it was an experience that would have to come to a lot of people whether they liked it or not. But I didn't realize how big A.A. would get."

Ronnie Cutrone was coming to the same realization. Cutrone had been one of the first painters to move into Tribeca—into a big two-thousand-square-foot loft on Vestry Street—and it was there that he fell into the vise of heroin addiction.

"I was shaking and withdrawing, trying to work at the Factory and start up the Mudd Club," he recalled. "I was fighting with my wife, Gigi, nonstop. We'd get violent. I was always in blackouts. Sometimes when I came to the next day, there would be blood on the floor and I didn't know whose it was, mine or Gigi's or somebody else's. Then she left me and I was alone, sweating on heroin."

Cutrone would wake up on Sunday and watch the Tarzan movies and just start crying—Tarzan and Jane represented some kind of primordial purity to him that seemed to bring home the pain and pathos of his addiction. "There was a hole in my heart that nothing could fill except heroin. I've always been, at best, an agnostic, never really believing in anything, but for some reason at that point I asked God to help me."

His moment of clarity was dramatic—"this peace just came over me that I can't describe, and everything became crystal clear and calm." Cutrone flushed his drugs down the toilet and went dancing at the Mudd Club; the next day, January 21, 1980, he walked into the meeting of a 12-step recovery fellowship, where he would stay, clean and sober, as practically everybody else he knew went off on a cocaine binge that lasted for years.

"I remember being sober and sitting in my chair and thinking, God, this is lonely. I know it's the right thing to do, but it's lonely. And then I thought, Well, maybe if I sit here long enough, the people I know out there will either die or they will come in to receive help. And sure enough, they started pouring in about three years later."

For Cutrone, the benefits of recovery were beyond measure. "My art got a hundred times better, and I was able to keep the money I made from it; I was able to have love affairs and be a hundred percent present for them. Whatever I do, I own it, good or bad, so I can learn from the mistakes; I own all my emotions, my behavior, and my art. I know who's doing it—it's not the marijuana or cocaine or heroin or speed. It's really *my* life now."

The decades of the 1980s and 1990s would mark the greatest growth of recovery fellowships like Alcoholics Anonymous, but the impact of this expansion would extend far beyond the lives of alcoholics or addicts. "In my opinion, the only real revolution is recovery," said Cutrone. "I've lived through so many would-be revolutions since the Sixties in America—in drugs, art, politics, culture—and the only one I know of is a quiet, personal revolution where a lot of people know the same thing about themselves and are able to help others with that knowledge and pass it on. You can't change anything except yourself; and once you've done that, you've already changed something important and powerful; and then another person can change, and another . . . And what you have is more people being honest and seeking spirituality—not in some pseudo religious way, but in a way that can really have an impact on your life and the others around you. It's truly the only revolution."

In 1993, the American Society of Addiction Medicine stated that "alcoholism is a *primary,* chronic *disease* with genetic, psychological and environmental factors influencing its development and manifestations. The disease is often *progressive* and *fatal.* It is characterized by continuous or periodic *impaired control* over drinking, preoccupation with the drug alcohol, use of alcohol despite adverse circumstances, and distortion in thinking, most notably *denial.*" The society also emphasized that the disease represented an "involuntary disability."

Through the steady lobbying and public education efforts of the National Council on Alcoholism, the disease model was gradually accepted as the primary definition of alcoholism and addiction in the United States. Perhaps the most dramatic result was that the slow but steady removal of the social stigmas attached to these conditions made it progressively easier for individuals and families to seek help rather than be inhibited by shame and hopelessness. At the same time, the disease model has generated momentum and support for treatment by marshaling the resources of medicine, mental health, nursing, social work, and other communities that had not been officially mandated to treat the affliction.

Alcoholics Anonymous, along with Narcotics Anonymous, with their 12 steps and emphasis on the "disease model" of alcoholism and addiction, would become the paradigm for other fellowships dealing with substance abuse and addiction, like Cocaine Anonymous and Marijuana Anonymous. The A.A. program would provide the spiritual philosophy, mode of healing, and way of life for millions of people, but the paradigm of the program would be extended to a wide variety of compulsive behaviors dealing with sex, gambling, debting, and overeating. Al-Anon, the sister fellowship of A.A. that was founded to address the emotional problems of the families and friends of addicts and alcoholics, and ACOA (Adult Children of Alcoholics), established to deal with the personality problems developed as a consequence of growing up in an alcoholic home, would provide the inspiration and model for still other recovery fellowships dealing with "co-dependency"—and on it would go. During the 1980s, recovery would become a mass movement with a "hugs not drugs" sensibility exemplified by best-selling authors like John Bradshaw, Melodie Beattie, Marianne Williamson, and Louise Hay, each with their own tapes and videos, seminars, and workshops. Oprah Winfrey would provide the most far-reaching forum for the movement with her phenomenally popular daytime talk show. Before long, phrases like *powerlessness, toxic shame, inner child, dysfunctional family, healthy boundaries, letting go, enabling, enmeshment,* and *unconditional love* would become a part of the cultural lingo. From 1969 to 1989, there was a 300 percent increase in the number of officially listed A.A. groups. In 1990, *Newsweek* reported that the number of other 12-step offshoots had quadrupled in the previous ten years and estimated that some fifteen million Americans were attending some form of 12-step group. With groups that ran the gamut from Obsessive-Compulsives Anonymous to Workaholics Anonymous, it isn't hard to understand why sociologist Craig Reinarman, studying the proliferation of the 12-step movement, would call addiction and the loss of control "the reigning metaphor—or meta-metaphor—for all human troubles in *fin de millénium* America."

The recovery culture would produce its lampooners, like *Saturday Night Live* regular Al Franken, whose Stuart Smalley character would gaze into the mirror and deliver his smarmy self-affirmations: "I'm *smart* enough, I'm *good* enough," he would lisp, "and doggonnit, *people like me!*" It would also produce its critics and cynics. "I'd like to take your inner child and kick its little ass," sneered Don Henley in his song "Get Over It." But whatever one's experience and opinions of the value of recovery, one thing was clear: exactly as drugs had shaped American civilization and produced addicts and alcoholics in the process, not taking drugs had become one of the next significant chapters in the story of its drug culture. Sobriety was nothing less than a new vogue. More and more people at parties were turning down joints and cocktails in favor of club soda and cranberry juice.

"No once-wild 'party' in Hollywood or Aspen or even Greenwich Village is complete, these days, without the overweening presence of super wealthy, hard-hitting ex-addicts, 'recovering alcoholics,' beady-eyed fat women who never let you forget that they 'used to hang out' with doomed friends and dead monsters like Janis, Jim Morrison, The Stones, John Belushi, or even me," Hunter Thompson observed contemptuously in his 1989 piece "I Knew the Bride When She Used to Rock and Roll." "They roam the chic anterooms of movies and music and publishing like vengeful *golems* from some lost and broken Peter Pan world of Sex Drugs and Rock and Roll, and other unspeakable tragedies that crippled the lives and crazed the souls of . . . *so many.*"

By the mid-1980s, the treatment of alcoholism and addiction had become a national industry, shaping corporate health insurance policies as well as the criminal-justice system. Courts began directing felons with chronic substance abuse problems into treatment programs and mandating that people arrested for Driving Under the Influence and Public Intoxication attend A.A. groups. By the 1990s, *Larry King Live* and a whole assortment of daytime talk shows were filled with celebrities fresh out of the Betty Ford Center discussing their recoveries and describing the 12-step program as the best—if not the only—way of recovering from alcoholism and addiction, and the way to deal with the drug problem in the United States. David Crosby, for example, firmly believed that there was nobody better equipped to talk to kids about drugs than recovering alcoholics and addicts. "It's hard for anybody who's straight or a normie or a psychiatrist or a teacher or a lecturer or a cop to do that. It takes a junkie. It takes an alcoholic. They ought to take the circuit speakers of A.A. and put them in every high school in America—those Irish drunks from Boston with twenty-five years of sobriety who will blow your mind and make you stand up and cheer. Now we have a whole generation of great communicators who can talk about the experience from the inside, from their hearts, from bitterly paid-for experience."

With most rehabs basing their programs on the 12 steps and recovering addicts and alcoholics all over TV, with judges sending people to A.A. meetings and people in the recovery community publicly advocating treatment as a policy, to some critics it looked like Alcoholics Anonymous was evangelizing, hijacking the national discourse on drug treatment policy and rehabilitation.

"Those people who hurt themselves with their private drug use, who took so much acid that they were spaced out for years or did so much cocaine that they couldn't function or smoked dope every day all day long, if getting into a 12-step program or whatever worked for them, I'm actually delighted," commented Keith Stroup. "I'm pleased they got their life back together. What I object to is relying on the person who had the biggest failure. As if, boy, you really fucked your life up, lost your wife, lost your kid, lost your business . . . Now tell us, what should our drug policy be?"

Criticism of the disease concept and the recovery movement, while relatively small and mostly academic, has been strident. Some have quibbled with the frameworks and models for viewing addiction as disease; other objections have come from within the treatment community itself, from those concerned that if addiction is defined as disease, only a doctor will be qualified to treat it, or that a disease would imply the possibility of a cure (an important precept of the disease model as viewed by A.A. is that alcoholism is incurable but treatable by abstinence practiced one day at a time, a "daily reprieve" contingent upon one's spiritual condition). Conservative social critics, on the other hand, have pointed to how the classification of addiction as disease has allowed it to be used as a excuse for moral failing, leading to abnegation of personal responsibility and excusing behaviors for which people must be held accountable.

The most far-reaching critique of the disease model has come from Stanton Peele, a psychologist and health-care researcher who debunked the addiction-as-disease model and the "myths" of the recovery movement as a "strange amalgamation of religion and pseudoscience" founded on "simpleminded supposition" and "glib rationalizations." Peele's thesis is simple: "What has been presented as straightforward data about alcoholism and addiction is in fact an implausible mélange of scientific, cultural and historical prejudices." Peele backs up his argument with a considerable amount of statistical and analytical data, along with a wealth of anecdotal observation, but as good as he is at stating his case—in books like *Diseasing of America: How We Allowed Recovery Zealots and the Treatment Industry to Convince Us We Are Out of Control* and *The Truth About Addiction and Recovery*—that the disease model as propagated by A.A. is fundamentally a travesty and the treatment industry a sham, it is just as easy to rip gaping holes in many of his arguments. To say that many addicts and alcoholics recovering in 12-step programs find his point of view unhelpful would be grossly understating their antipathy. As they see it, Peele's ideas represent a dangerous, potentially lethal heresy.

## IV.  Trudging the Road of Happy Destiny

SUZIE RYAN would find the most accurate and useful description of her addiction in a book called *Staying Sober: A Guide for Relapse Prevention* by Terence T. Gorski and Merlene Miller. "Addiction is distinguished from drug use by the lack of freedom of choice: using a mood-altering substance is a choice. Addiction is a condition that robs a person of choice and dictates the frequency, the quantity, and the nature of use. All addiction begins with use, but all use does not lead to addiction."

That was the essence of what had happened to her: she'd lost the *choice*—she'd *had* to use drugs. She came across the passage long after leaving Hazelden, a rehab facility situated on a bucolic lakeside in the middle of Minnesota, where Richard Stoltz had sent her to recover and where she had come to understand that if he didn't seek help and stop using drugs himself, she would have to leave him. By that time, she was one of an estimated five to six million regular users of cocaine in the United States out of some twenty-one million people who had tried the drug at least once. When she arrived, she could barely talk, let alone read. She was kept in the medical unit for a long time—the sores on her head were only one of the problems. They called people like her low bottoms, *mocus* being the characteristic condition (mind out of focus). Her nervous system was completely shot. She had spatial problems and was unable to think straight. She stammered as thoughts misfired in her brain. After a seizure, she became terrified that she would die.

Eventually, an "addictionologist" on staff would explain to her the neurochemical effect of great quantities of freebase cocaine on the brain, how in essence it prolonged the action of neurotransmitters and led to dopamine hyperstimulation of postsynaptic neurons. It sounded like gobbledygook, but she was able to grasp at least the gist of the explanation: the drug had caused her brain to lie to her and tell her that she was experiencing pleasure when she wasn't. Her condition was seriously compounded by prolonged alcohol abuse and the steady consumption of Valium, Xanax, and Ativan—cross-addiction, it was called. The detoxification was brutal, with extreme mood swings, depression, and sleeplessness that lasted for what seemed like three months.

As gentle as her counselors were, however, Suzie could only curse at them. But she did whatever they told her to do because that's how much she wanted to get better, and they promised her that she would. With the emphasis on becoming educated about the disease, the initial focus was on the first three steps—

1. We admitted we were powerless over alcohol—that our lives had become unmanageable.

2. Came to believe that a Power greater than ourselves could restore us to sanity.

3. Made a decision to turn our will and our lives over to the care of God *as we understood Him.*

All she had to do was include the word *drugs* with *alcohol* to realize that she had certainly been powerless—the cocaine had controlled her completely. Unmanageable? All she had to do was think about where it had taken her—to having sex in front of Richard's clients and to places where cocaine-dealing practitioners of Santeria were sacrificing chickens—and well, that seemed unmanageable enough. The next two steps were much trickier, however. She knew she had been insane during that last run and recognized the ongoing component of insanity in her recovery, but she had no distinct notion of a Higher Power. There were aspects of the God she had been given in the Lutheran Church that she retained but others that she did not accept at all, such as the notion of hell. She could embrace the idea that her recovery might be the divinely inspired answer to her prayers. She chose to see this Higher Power as a benevolent, loving force. It was about spirituality and not religion (there was a saying in the program that she liked: religion is for people who are afraid of going to hell; spirituality is for people who have already been there). Beyond that, she knew nothing. She was told, however, that there might very well come a time when there would be nothing between her and that drink or drug but her Higher Power, and that if she took that drink or drug, it would trigger the "obsession." The words used to describe the disease were *cunning, baffling,* and *powerful.*

Such a moment came only five months later. Suzie was living in a halfway house in a Minneapolis suburb, working in an Arby's—up at six, make the bed, go to the job at the mall, come back, sit in a group, go to bed. A sobriety job, it was called. Getting humble. Learning to keep it simple and live life, on life's terms, a day at a time. But this day, flipping those burgers and frying potatoes really got to her. She felt devastated, ashamed of where she had come to since Studio 54 and the highflying life she had led with Richard Stoltz. After all, for the previous ten years, she had bought her clothes in the salons of Paris, and here she was, dressed in her little Arby's hat and polyester outfit with her nurse's shoes and her hair in a bun.

The good news is you're going to have feelings, Suzie was told; the bad news is you're going to have feelings. It would be hard to find the words to express the level of self-loathing and shame she felt as she left the job that day: the insecurity, the darkness and doubt, the blind rage at how things had turned out. Worst of all was the fear. Is *this* what my life is going to be like? Who am I? Where will I go? What will I become? How will I live? She was least of all prepared for the fear. At that moment, nothing seemed more terrifying on earth than the prospect of life on life's terms. It was all like some horrible cacophony inside her head that she couldn't stop. The more she wanted relief from it and the more she wanted to change what she was feeling, the more she thought of getting high until she wanted it so badly that her very cells seemed to cry out.

The few times she had spoken to Richard had been difficult; she knew he was still using drugs, and she had been instructed to avoid the "people, places, and things" around which her drug use had revolved. Richard was certainly the epitome of that. She knew that all she had to do was call him, and he would be on a plane. She could be high in a matter of hours and stay high for as long as she wanted.

So there she was, at a phone booth. She could feel the pipe in her hands and the smoke filling her lungs as it made her head blast off, actually taste the drink going down her throat and feel it warming and centering her, and that was when she uttered the same foxhole prayer.

"Please, God. Help me!"

It was at Town's Hospital in New York, on December 11, 1934, that A.A. founder Bill Wilson (Bill W), at the very end of his long and destructive years of drinking, looked into the abyss of madness and death.

"If there be a God, let Him show himself!" he cried out—and his room had suddenly "blazed with an indescribably white light. I was seized with an ecstasy beyond description. Every joy I had known was pale by comparison. The light, the ecstasy—I was conscious of nothing else for a time."

Wilson saw a beautiful mountain: "I stood upon its summit, where a great wind blew. A wind, not of air, but of spirit. In great, clean strength, it blew right through me. Then came the blazing thought, 'You are a free man.' I know not at all how long I remained in this state. . . . As I became more quiet, a great peace stole over me, and this was accompanied by a sensation that was difficult to describe. I became acutely conscious of a Presence which seemed like a veritable sea of living spirit. I lay on the shores of this world. 'This,' I thought, 'must be the great reality. 'The God of the preachers.' "

Wilson's experience had been a remarkable confirmation of what William James, in his seminal work *The Varieties of Religious Experience,* had written about the pathology of alcoholism: "The sway of alcohol over mankind is unquestionably due to its power to stimulate the mystical faculties of human nature, usually crushed to earth by the cold facts and dry criticisms of the sober hour. Sobriety diminishes, discriminates, and says no; drunkenness expands, unites, and says yes. . . . Not through mere perversity do men run after it." The drunken consciousness was but "one bit of the mystic consciousness," James believed, "and our total opinion of it must find its place in our opinion of that larger whole."

The great Swiss psychiatrist Carl Jung had also postulated that the spiritual awakening was the most effective antidote to addiction. Mere belief in God was not enough, Jung had claimed after attempting to treat the alcoholic known as Rowland H, who seemed beyond hope. Something was required that would transform the entire spiritual landscape of the alcoholic-addict. Rowland's craving for alcohol was "the equivalent on a low level of the spiritual thirst of our being for wholeness," as Jung described it in a letter to Bill Wilson; "expressed in medieval language: the union with God." As Jung noted, alcohol in Latin is *spiritus,* "and you could use the same word for the highest religious experience as well as the most depraving poison. The helpful formula therefore is *spiritus contra spiritum.*"

Bill Wilson was thirty-nine when he had his white-light experience in Town's Hospital, and he never took another drink. Suzie Ryan was thirty-two as she clutched her fragile sobriety and walked tremblingly into the first meeting she could find. She had never been to this particular meeting before, but she knew exactly where it was and headed there as soon as she finished her prayer—having smart feet, it was called. A very respectable-looking middle-aged woman came up to her as soon as she walked into the room. Suzy explained that she was looking for a meeting because she wanted to get high very badly and the woman nodded. At that moment Suzie was struck by something in the woman's eyes as she smiled. There was a certain quality of light. A serenity. All Suzie had to do was see it to know that she didn't have it and she desperately wanted it. She cried softly at first, then a little harder, and then it all started pouring out of her, and when the woman said, "Honey, you're in the right place," it was as if someone had reached inside her and flipped a switch—"you never have to be alone with this again," and that was when she started to weep. They were the most comforting words she had ever heard in her life precisely because they were the words she longed most to hear. She sat there and cried for what seemed like a very long time. The woman held her in her arms and rocked her like a baby. At that moment, she experienced a much deeper surrender, a much more heightened understanding that the miracle of her recovery was not one day at a time but really one minute at a time. She now realized what they were talking about when they referred to alcoholism in sobriety as "*dis*-ease." At some point, she looked up at the 12 steps on the wall and realized that her craving for the drug was completely gone and that she had taken the third step. Her experience of that day and the spiritual awakening of gratitude and faith it evoked would animate the entire future course of her life.

If every addict's story is an epic of self-destruction, each recovery is a series of milestones passed along a long and winding trail, "trudging the road of happy destiny." First, the senses are reborn. The sound of birds, the feeling of warm sun on the face, the scent of spring in the air, the laughter of little children in the park—all became vehicles of this rebirth for Suzie Ryan, avenues of the most extravagant pleasure. At the same time, she experienced the scary and disorienting feeling of having to do things without drugs for the first time, like having sex without being high. She began to accept that it was going to take time for the circuitry to be rewired. After moving back to New York, where she began to attend various A.A. groups, her isolation and loneliness began to melt away.

As Suzie connected with more people and began going into jails and hospitals to tell her story, she began to realize that she had something very important to share. She started working with crackheads and found that everything she had been through had significance, had in some way enriched her ability to help others. In her work over the years, she would see miracles: the lowest-bottom street drunks, dope fiends, and crackheads reclaiming their lives and families, becoming productive members of their communities.

But the journey was far from smooth and graceful. Like all recovering addicts and alcoholics, with the passing of time, she would run headlong into the thorny truths of herself and become increasingly aware of the engines that drove her addiction. Everything gradually surfaced: her aching emptiness, self-centered fears, resentments, grandiosity, narcissism, and her reluctance to grow up and take responsibility for herself. These were the "defects of character" described in the fourth step ("Made a searching and fearless moral inventory of ourselves"), and she would have to face all of them: her willingness to stay in an abusive relationship with Richard for so many years, in which she had been emotionally and financially dependent, her anxieties at being abandoned by him, how she had been sexually controlled by him. In the end, she would have to admit to herself that she had turned into the classic coke whore. All of it would come out in the wash of her sobriety. You can't heal what you can't feel was the operative philosophy of the program: no pain, no gain. As expressed in the tenth step, "Pain is the touchstone of all spiritual progress."

Perhaps the hardest thing for Suzie to deal with was her seemingly innate desire to avoid feeling all of it by reflexively substituting behaviors and attitudes. It was called symptom substitution. As a result, she would gain weight and lose weight, act out sexually and become celibate, become a spendthrift and turn into a tightwad, get depressed and go on medication, go off medication and become overwhelmed with stress, learn how to meditate and go into psychotherapy, become enraged at her family, and ultimately, learn how to let go and forgive them. Getting clean, she would realize, while nothing short of a miracle, was only the tip of the iceberg. Recovery was about real growth, which was perhaps the hardest thing in the world. Meetings were temples of resurrected souls. The 12 steps were an ingenious codification of the wisdom of the ages— a form of spiritual orthodontia. Like braces on teeth, the steps were uncomfortable, painful, downright unsightly, and then one day the braces would come off, and Suzie would realize that something that had been painfully awry for so long had moved beautifully into a new alignment. It was a program of change and action. In the end, recovery for her was about service, being present, honesty, balance, wholeness, goodness, inner peace, acceptance of self and others. It was nothing less than a yes to life and a no to death, one day at a time. That was the A.A. message that she tried her best to live and carry, joining hands with her recovering brothers and sisters at the end of every meeting to say the Serenity Prayer—

*God grant me the serenity to accept the things I cannot change, courage to change the things I can, and wisdom to know the difference.*

As the Great Stoned Age turned into the Age of Recovery, one of the most powerful ironies was how so many people would find in recovery the very freedom they had sought in drugs. Of course, there would always be questions. Would they have gotten to that place had they never done the drugs? Was the price they paid worth it? Why does one person become an addict and another not? And why does one addict get the gift of recovery and another die?

There are many who purport to have insights into these issues, but for Suzie Ryan the questions were pointless intellectual exercises. Some things were inexplicable. If addiction had been a low-level search for God, then recovery was *spiritus contra spiritum.* It was God's will.

# 13

## Nouveau Psychedelia

**"Every generation finds the drug it needs. "**

—P. J. O'Rourke, "Tune In. Turn On. Go to the Office Late
on Monday," *Rolling Stone*, 1985

**"Before long I was feeling better than I'd ever felt in my life
(and I've had some pretty good times). "**

—Timothy Leary, "MDMA: The Drug of the 1980s,"
*Chaos and Cyber Culture*, 1994

### I. A Strange and Wondrous Atmosphere of Collective Intimacy

IMAGES AROSE and dissolved in rapid-fire succession. The face
of an ancient patriarch morphed into pulsing amoebic cells,
which were followed by a pointillist excursion of rainbow cumulus clouds. A ginger sunburst turned into praying hands, the North Star, the face of a beautiful Asian girl, and a field of pink roses that stretched to infinity. On the floor, the dancers were illuminated by a digital riot of lasers, data flashes, and visual-feedback loops: blue daisy wheels, crimson seas of phosphorescent silicon chips, solar flares, soft white lotus blossoms that floated ethereally on the ceiling. When the lights went down, leaving only a pale yellow radiance cutting through the darkness, the dancers with their arms raised aloft looked like a sinuous sea of innocent little children at play, moving through hyperspace together, greeting a new dawn.

It was December 1992, and A Rave Called Sharon was being held in a large industrial-warehouse space in San Francisco. The crowd was multiracial and multicultural. There were people of all ages, but most were young: skater kids in baggy T-shirts down to their knees, twirling black girls with platinum-pink hair and green glow sticks, lots of college undergrads with clunky shoes and turned-around caps—children of the Gulf War and the first Bush recession, very different from the Reagan-era kids of boom and cocaine. If the Baby Boomers were the first generation to be weaned on television, this was the first one raised on computers. They were clearly searching for something beyond the self-interest and gross materialism of the Eighties; what they were finding was unmistakable in their exuberant grins and love-flushed faces, instantly recognizable in the way they would openly hug each other.

"You look *great*!"

"God, I *love* you, dude, I really do!"

The music being played, called house music, was electronica that featured bass like you'd never heard before, produced at 120 beats per minute—the frequency of the fetal heart rate, the very same beat used by the shamans of South American cultures to transport their tribes into states of pure transcendence. In fact, there was much talk of technoshamanism and neotribalism during that season of raves, along with subjects like quantum physics and fractals, Gaia consciousness and the Oversoul. The cutting edge of digital technology was being integrated into the environment of these events, and a new generation was obviously seeking its own values and trying to write its own story. But the real news here was MDMA: Ecstasy, E, Ex, XTC.

A quarter of a century after the acid tests and seminal psychedelic happenings like the Trips Festival, the generation that was supposed to Just Say No to drugs was clearly Just Saying Yes. After all, this was a generation that had come of age with phrases like *zero tolerance, user accountability,* and *just deserts,* when the federal government was spending twenty billion dollars a year on its drug war. In addition, these kids had been exposed to more than four hundred print and television ads designed to "de-glamorize" and "de-normalize" drug use which were created by the Partnership for a Drug-Free America. Running in all the media from March 1987 through the end of 1993, the total broadcast time and print space for the ads was valued at over $1.7 billion. How many times had they seen that signature television ad with the frying pan ("This is your brain") and the egg being cracked into it, followed by that loud sizzle ("This is your brain on drugs")? And yet here they were, another generation tinkering with the psychedelic experience. As easy as it was to recognize the influence of the counterculture of the Sixties on this emerging rave culture ("The Nineties are really the Sixties turned upside down," Wavy Gravy remarked), it was just as apparent that this was a generation gestating its unique identity. LSD, also making a comeback at the time, was a "mind" drug, an intense roller-coaster ride of the psyche; E, as everyone was quick to tell you, was a "heart-opening" drug. The semi-synthetic phenethylamine MDMA (methylenedioxymethamphetamine), chemically related to the amphetamines but first cousin to mescaline, was more easily controllable and more predictable and quiescent than acid—in fact, a chemical relative of the antidepressant Prozac as well. What exactly was a "psychedelic amphetamine?" Analyses would abound in years to come. As Simon Reynolds, certainly one of the more astute journalists to cover the rave scene, would later describe it, MDMA was "a remarkable chemical, combining the sensory intensification and auditory enhancement of marijuana and low-dose LSD, the sleep-defying energy-boosting effects of speed, and the uninhibited conviviality of alcohol. If that wasn't enough, MDMA offers unique effects of empathy and insight."

These "unique effects" were precisely what had caused therapists to label the drug an "empathogen" (creating an empathetic state) or an "entactogen" (creating a touching within) before MDMA was made illegal in the mid-Eighties. By that time, its reputation had been well established in certain therapeutic circles, and it was being described evocatively as "penicillin for the soul" and "psychic pain reliever." MDMA was "medicine for a new millennium," wrote Dr. Julie Holland in her introduction to *Ecstasy: The Complete Guide*, which could produce "a fortified self-image, a sense of enhanced capacity and strength. Taking that a step further, it becomes euphoria, intense self-love and self-acceptance. This is why MDMA can be so curative. . . . MDMA increases the ratio of love to fear. The capacity to love yourself and others triumphs over the anxiety of doing just that."

The value of any drug that increased the "ratio of love to fear" as a tool for self-discovery or an adjunct to therapy designed to promote bonding between couples or the healing of post-traumatic stress disorder had been only one of the story lines of MDMA; what happened when the substance was adopted by the youth culture of the 1990s was something else. As Reynolds observed, "When large numbers of people took Ecstasy together, the drug catalyzed a strange and wondrous atmosphere of *collective intimacy,* an electric sense of connection between complete strangers. Even more significantly, MDMA turned out to have a uniquely synergistic/synesthetic interaction with music, especially up tempo, repetitive electronic dance music."

Then it became the "we drug," the "flow drug," with masses of kids flocking to raves like this one to take the drug together and dance. At A Rave Called Sharon, you could feel all the kids coming on to it together. At 2:00 a.m., something palpable happened on the dance floor. It was like someone hit a toggle switch and sent a cohesive jolt of electricity through the place, after which the kids seemed to hit a plateau. They danced on for the next six straight hours, lost in movement and music and the bombardment of lights and images, stopping only to hydrate or take a break in one of the "chill-out" rooms. What was going on was clearly beyond a party, beyond a high. Kids were coming to raves and taking Ecstasy and leaving as changed people; the events were becoming equal parts therapy, mass catharsis, and primordial tribal bonding. As inhibitions toppled and egos dissolved completely away to Group Mind, thousands of tranced-out kids began screaming ecstatically. Even when the doors opened and the morning light came streaming in, many of the ravers would just keep going, moving on to after-hours clubs like DNA at Eleventh and Folsom, where they would dance until midday.

Within a matter of a few years, rave would grow from an underground subculture to a global cultural movement with a philosophy defined by the tenets of Peace, Love, Unity, and Respect, a cohesive culture that engendered its own visual art, fashions, music, technologies, commerce, and sensibilities regarding politics and sexuality. It was metaprogramming; Ecstasy had become the vehicle for a generation's attempt to set itself apart from the world and find its own place where it could Let Love Rule.

Within a ten-month span in 2000 alone, U.S. Customs would seize a record number of eight million hits of Ecstasy at airports and ports of entry. At a club-drug conference in July of 2000, the DEA estimated that 750,000 hits were being sold in New York and along the Jersey shore every weekend, with two million tablets coming into the country every week. Every weekend around the world, nearly a million people were taking the drug; how many doses had been consumed in the previous ten years was anybody's guess.

## II. The Quaint Little Laboratory on the Sloping Hill

THE WORLD OF SASHA SHULGIN was far removed from the raves going on across the bay in San Francisco. The path that led to the lab on his property in Lafayette was surrounded by ivy, live oak, Chinese elm, myrtle, and laurel. "I own right up to the edge, where it becomes city parkland," he pointed out. "This is a sort of meditation spot, away from the jingle and jangle of the telephones. It's very pleasant."

Shulgin picked a bay leaf off a bush and proffered it. "Here, try this. Rub it on your finger, and tell me if you like the smell." As he opened the door to his lab, he seemed utterly intoxicated by the scent of the fresh geraniums and rosemary—a scientist who relished the world of the senses every bit as much as the mysteries of chemical structures. Shulgin built the lab after leaving the Dow Chemical Company, in what had been the basement of his parents' home here on this sloping hill. "This is my hideaway. It's a little bit different from your average lab. I had a compliance visit from the DEA about a year and a half ago."

Classical music automatically went on as soon as we entered. "Chemistry is an art. You've got to have all the artistic accoutrements: isotope transfer line, vacuum distillation, vacuum pump, stills, rotary, evaporator systems, aspirator systems, steam lab, top-loading balances. Everything that's needed for truly sophisticated work is right here."

Outside, birds were singing; inside, within this lab and storage room—"one of those late-night-movie laboratories in which a mad scientist with wild hair and blazing eyes attempts to wrest from the gods that which no mortal can be allowed to discover, et cetera," as Shulgin jocularly described it—was the potential to produce every conceivable psychoactive drug known to man, and the license to possess, identify, and analyze it.

There it was, right up there on the door: "Controlled Substances Registration Certificate, United States Department of Justice, Drug Enforcement Administration, Registration No. P50061616." It was truly one of the great ironies that Alexander T. "Sasha" Shulgin, PhD, this courteous, scholarly man with his elegant mane of white hair and beard, who had done more than anyone else to bring MDMA to the attention of the world, was a DEA-certified chemist allowed to work with drugs in each of the five schedules as a result of serving as an analyst and expert witness. In the process, Shulgin had become the most prolific psychedelic chemist and pharmacologist of his time, a figurehead of the MDMA movement and a folk hero to the worldwide psychedelic community.

"The DEA have a strange way of visiting" he noted. "They came through and made all kinds of suggestions. I said, thank you, I really do appreciate your input, these are useful suggestions. And they went away—no humor, of course, but that's one of their traits—but when they filed their report, I was really wondering what they said, and I happen to have a mole in intelligence there, and I found out that they used a word I never would have conceived of. They said my laboratory was *quaint*."

*Quaint* was a curious description of the lab. Shulgin had synthesized no fewer than two hundred never-before-known chemical psychedelic structures in it over the past thirty years, all of which he'd taken and evaluated himself, along with his therapist wife, Ann, and a dedicated group of close friends. The book that Sasha and Ann had recently published, *PIHKAL* (an acronym for Phenethylamines I Have Known and Loved), subtitled *A Chemical Love Story,* is unique in the annals of literature. The first 434 pages contain the stories of their psychedelic explorations—a kind of Huxleyan journey of experimentation combined with their own love story in the form of a fictionalized "autobiographical novel"—but the next 474 pages are the actual transcriptions of Shulgin's laboratory notebooks, "an almost encyclopedic compendium of synthetic methods, dosages, durations of action, and commentaries for 179 different chemical materials," as David E. Nichols, PhD, noted in his foreword. "Someday in the future, when it may again be acceptable to use chemical tools to study the mind, this book will be a treasure-house, a sort of sorcerer's book of spells, to delight and enchant the psychiatrist/shaman of tomorrow."

Of course, the publication of Shulgin's formulas meant that you didn't necessarily have to be a "psychiatrist/shaman of tomorrow" to avail yourself of the material—indeed, any underground chemist could now concoct the analogues. That only compounded the irony because not only had Shulgin developed the substances legally as a result of the license, but when the DEA obtained these samples of the drugs he'd invented, Shulgin would be the very one to analyze them. His reason for publishing this remarkable collection of how-to recipes was twofold. The first explanation was philosophical. "Every drug, legal or illegal, provides some reward," he wrote. "Every drug presents some risk. And every drug can be abused. Ultimately, in my opinion, it is up to each of us to measure the reward against the risk and decide which outweighs the other. . . . My philosophy can be distilled into four words: be informed, then choose." The other reason had to do with his passionate belief in the freedom of information. As he explained it, "You know where all of Wilhelm Reich's notes and his manuscripts and writings went after he died? The FDA burned them. I felt the same thing could have happened to my work, which is why I wanted to get the stuff scattered as widely as I could."

Perhaps more than anything, it was the unhappy fate of MDMA that had motivated him.

Born in 1925, Sasha Shulgin grew up in nearby Berkeley, the brilliant son of a Russian émigré professor. While serving on a destroyer escort during the Second World War, he became fascinated with pharmacology after he suffered a painful infection of the thumb and was treated with morphine. His degree in biochemistry from UC Berkeley led him to Dow Chemical, where he became one of their most promising young researchers, but the day he took four hundred milligrams of mescaline sulfate in 1960 "will remain blazingly vivid in my memory, and . . . unquestionably confirmed the direction of my life." The colors, the details, and the wonders of being able to experience the world again as a child—all of it brought about by "a fraction of a gram of a white solid"—presented the young researcher with his true "learning path." Fascinated by substances that resembled mescaline, Shulgin began working with "the magnificent essential oils that are the smells of the spice cabinet; the oils of nutmeg, clove, parsley, dill, and apiole. And on and on. This little studied collection of chemicals proved to be an unending source of ideas in the psychedelic area."

MDMA, first synthesized in 1912 by Merck Pharmaceutical in Germany in an attempt to develop a new styptic medication, was a relative of MDA derived from nutmeg. Unlike MDA, however, which was patented by SmithKline and tested as an appetite suppressant and abandoned because of its psychoactive properties, there was no use mentioned for MDMA in Merck's patent application and little mention of it in the scientific literature before 1953, when the U.S. Army tested it for its potential as a "brainwashing" agent. Of course, MDA had been a known commodity in the Haight Ashbury and became a popular part of the illicit pharmacopoeia of the Seventies as the "love drug," but MDMA was all but forgotten until Sasha Shulgin, having parted company with Dow Chemical because of the controversial direction of his interests, first synthesized it from myristicin in 1976. He and his friend and colleague David Nichols described it as "an easily controlled altered state of consciousness with emotional and sensual overtones." As Shulgin expressed it in *PIHKAL,* "It did not have the bells and whistles, the drama of mescaline, but was considerably more benign. It was (I thought at the time) my first truly new discovery, and I moved very carefully with it into my small group of colleagues."

And so began the quiet and cautious dissemination of the substance, known as Adam, among a network of progressive therapists on the West Coast. Prominent among them was the Chilean psychiatrist Claudio Naranjo, an old friend of Shulgin's who had studied the effects of MDA as a budding gestalt therapist and published a groundbreaking book in 1969 called *The Healing Journey.* Naranjo called MDA a "feeling optimizer" and believed that "much of our learning to live right—the 'gate to happiness,' we might say—lies in finding another attitude toward pain, another way of being face to face with pain." MDMA, he found, was a nontoxic alternative to MDA of shorter duration; the most important quality of the substance was "a sense of what I call 'the eternal now.' " Another noteworthy figure was Ralph Metzner, one of Leary's and Alpert's former colleagues at Harvard and Millbrook who had played a key role with them in formulating the bedrock tenets of "set and setting" in psychedelic theory—it was Metzner, in fact, who had coined the term *empathogen* for the substance, helping the therapist Sophia Adamson compile and edit the influential first book about the substance, *Through the Gateway of the Heart: Accounts of Experiences with MDMA and Other Empathogenic Substances.* By the early Eighties, a whole New Age, therapeutic-spiritual cult coalesced around MDMA. It included therapists like Leo Zeff and highly respected authorities on consciousness-altering substances like Dr. Andrew Weil, author of *The Natural Mind.* "I thought it had a unique effect and recommended it to a lot of people," recalled Weil. "It seemed to me one of the more useful substances I'd ever seen for communication, interpersonal exploration, human potentials."

Another fervent proponent was Rick Doblin, who formed a group called Earth Metabolic Design Laboratories and helped coordinate the first meeting on MDMA at an Esalen ARUPA (Association for the Responsible Use of Psychoactive Agents) conference in 1985. Much like the researchers of the early Sixties contemplating the possible applications of LSD, these people viewed the drug's potential as vast. Addiction, emotional trauma and incest, couples therapy, post-traumatic stress disorder, and terminal illness and dying were only some of the areas being considered for study. For the most part, the researchers found the substance remarkably safe, reliable, and effective when carefully controlled and applied with intelligence and sensitivity. The last thing they wanted to see was the kind of public hysteria that had caused LSD to be declared illegal in 1966. When Rick Doblin funded a study to determine the safety of the substance, he did so as silently as possible, for fear that the DEA might get wind of what was going on; sympathetic journalists were discouraged from writing stories (and nothing about MDMA would appear in the major media until a story ran in June of '84 in the *San Francisco Chronicle*). For a brief time, then, it was largely a growing word-of-mouth association of friends and colleagues quietly initiating other people.

"I was working with a guy who was dealing it, and I didn't even know what it was," remembered Marsha Rosenbaum, author of *Pursuit of*

*Ecstasy: The MDMA Experience,* and the pioneering study *Women on Heroin.* "What is Ecstasy? This was '84, summer of '85. Already it was all over *Newsweek* and *Time.* It came with these flight instructions distributed by the therapeutic community. 'This is not a drug to be done alone.' 'Make sure you are with people you are comfortable with, in comfortable surroundings, preferably in nature.' 'Take it in the middle of the day on an empty stomach.' Every detail, and being the controlled, organized person that I am, I followed everything to the letter. I thought I was going on an acid trip. I kept calling my friend who had FedExed it to me. 'Now listen,' she said, 'would you just shut up and take it? All you need is a comfortable chair!' So we did it, at the beach, with the kids squared away and comfortable chairs and plenty of water, at the right time of day, on an empty stomach . . . It was probably the most wonderful drug experience I ever had—a warm feeling of acceptance and tolerance and peace. It was hard to believe that you had the capacity to feel that good."

The degree to which the story of MDMA repeated the paradigm of LSD, legally and socially, was astonishing. The whole tale would have been very different had MDMA remained a tool used quietly by therapists and researchers and New Age seekers, but as Andy Weil noted, "It seemed inevitable that it was going to become illegal at some point, inevitable that it was going to be a party drug on college campuses; otherwise I think they would have continued to ignore us."

As surely as LSD had become acid, the transformation of MDMA into Ecstasy (the name given to it by an anonymous dealer, reportedly for "marketing purposes") guaranteed a public firestorm. Most of its manufacturers and distributors were discreet and conscientious, except for a group in Texas that began producing it in small brown bottles under the name Sassafras, the name of one of the essential oils in the drug. Ecstasy, as it was now commonly called, swept through the club scene of Dallas and Fort Worth as a new party dance drug and was soon available through a toll-free number, where it could be ordered with an American Express card. The initial users of the drug were frat boys and yuppies and "real middle-class girls in their twenties," according to Marsha Rosenbaum, "people who came from the straightest background." Before long, Senator Lloyd Bentsen heard about what was happening and brought the drug to the attention of the DEA. At that point, the "Texas group" (playing the role of Owsley in this case) began producing it in large amounts, possibly as many as two millions hits.

When the DEA made known its intention to declare MDMA a schedule one drug, which prohibits a substance from any application and recognizes no medical use whatsoever, a group of doctors and psychiatrists led by Dr. Lester Grinspoon of Harvard requested a hearing within the thirty-day period allotted by law. DEA administrator Francis Mullen granted the request, and hearings were scheduled for Los Angeles, Kansas City, and Washington, D.C., but with politicians falling all over themselves to get tough on drugs, the DEA, declaring that the drug was already being "abused" in twenty-eight states, was in no mood to wait. Moving to schedule the drug on an emergency basis while the hearings were completed, the DEA banned MDMA on July 1, 1985.

In the hearings that followed, the government presented its case that Lewis Seiden's MDMA caused "brain damage," which it based on MDA animal studies at the University of Chicago. Seiden had injected large amounts of MDA into rodents and observed changes in their axon terminals. Notwithstanding the facts that MDA and MDMA have different effects and durations and that MDMA is taken orally and not by injection, the DEA was able to establish the basis for a case that the drug caused neurotoxicity in humans. Subsequently, the agency sought to confirm this conclusion with the NIDA-funded research of George Ricautte, a neurologist at Johns Hopkins University, who gave large doses of MDMA to laboratory animals. The Grinspoon group sought to demonstrate that the substance was a valuable tool in the therapeutic process, enhancing insight and communication, but in the absence of the double-blind, placebo-controlled clinical studies normally used to establish a drug's value, its evidence was anecdotal. Nevertheless, on May 22, 1986, Judge Francis Young recommended to the DEA that the drug be placed in schedule three, which would allow research to continue and would permit doctors to prescribe it. But the new DEA administrator, John C. Lawn, ignored the recommendation. Despite another appeal by Grinspoon, MDMA's fate was sealed on March 23, 1988, when it was permanently placed in schedule one.

But as the DEA fastened its legal handcuffs, the popular mythology and sociocultural uses of MDMA were also being established. By now, the drug was all over the media and being subjected to the same kind of sensational and superficial reporting that typically accompanies any new drug fad in America—a tradition going back to Reefer Madness. In the case of MDMA, the media would spread its reputation as a "miracle medicine party drug," and at the same time portray it as a killer drug that caused irreversible brain damage, drained your spinal fluid, and put holes in your brain—claims that would never be scientifically substantiated. As with the LSD stories of chromosome breakage and retinal damage, people believed many of these rumors; for example, one claimed that MDMA caused Parkinson's disease. This distortion derived from a misreported story about heroin users in northern California who had injected themselves with a bad synthetic opiate called MPTP. In the end, none of these scare stories was enough to stop the drug from spreading like wildfire from club scenes across the United States, to college campuses, and to other countries, most notably the United Kingdom.

"Texas was the demise of E," reflected Marsha Rosenbaum, who would undertake the first significant sociological study of MDMA populations, with Jerome Beck. "We interviewed people from Dead heads to physicians to Dallas yuppies. These folks were highly educated, middle and upper class—a lot were very affluent. Some had psychedelic backgrounds, some didn't; some were ex-hippie types who'd gone through a lot of countercultural drug experience and came at Ecstasy recreationally and not through the therapeutic avenue. The great lesson for me was that no matter what world they came from, whether they used it as a therapeutic adjunct or just wanted to go dancing or sit on a beach and hold hands with a friend, they all said the exact same things: that it gave them a sense of acceptance, that they were being accepted in a global sense, not just by the people around them, that they were more tolerant and were being looked at more tolerantly, and that it was a loving and connected kind of experience. It was the absolute antithesis of the cocaine culture."

"I looked at it with great sadness," Sasha Shulgin remarked about the fate of MDMA. "But the commitment had been made that it was a dangerous evil by people in power—and since they were in power, their statements had to be correct, of course, and they just set out to document it. All the money that's been put out by the government to study it ever since, from the mid-Eighties to the early Nineties, had been awarded to affirm and describe and show the extent of this evil danger. If you want a grant to study MDMA, all you have to do is demonstrate some interaction that might serve as an explanation for its neurotoxicity. The question hasn't been Gee, I wonder how MDMA might be used in therapy to overcome some personal trauma? No one wants that kind of answer. They want to know why it's dangerous and why they were correct in portraying it so and why all these schedule-one drugs have to stay that way."

Dr. Andrew Weil was equally distressed. "I think MDMA is going to continue to be one of the most popular drugs in the world. We've lost a tremendous amount by disallowing research on the psychedelics. These drugs are some of the most useful and least harmful drugs known; they have incredible potential, not just in psychiatric medicine but also in physical medicine and personal development. By denying and excluding that from legitimate research, we've maximized the negative potential of these substances and denied ourselves something vitally useful as a culture."

There were those like Rick Doblin who simply refused to let the issue die. Forming the nonprofit MAPS (Multidisciplinary Association for Psychedelic Studies), Doblin has been indefatigable in his efforts to get the government to reconsider its position on allowing research on MDMA and the terminally ill and sufferers of post-traumatic stress disorder. It was therefore no small victory for Doblin and others when the FDA gave approval in July of 1992 for Dr. Charles Grob at UCLA to perform clinical research and give MDMA to human subjects. Meanwhile, the DEA trained its sights on the illicit underground use of the drug, along with LSD, that old villain of the Sixties counterculture, when it began resurging in popularity.

"The DEA hosted a meeting on LSD in San Francisco due to increased interest in it on the part of young people—'The New Problem,'" Shulgin related. "They invited law-enforcement people in to bring out the facts because 'there's a problem with our schoolchildren.' I was invited to give the background, but I allowed myself to be disinvited—I didn't want to hurt anybody or have anybody get egg on his or her face for inviting me there. Here were a few examples of the facts they presented: LSD is a drug so potent that just taking it once will leave residual molecules in the body, stored in the frontal lobes of the brain, and they may be there for twenty years, until some trauma brings them out in flashback and drives a person psychotic—one of the greatest myths about it, but presented as fact in front of the law-enforcement community. They pointed to the homeless people here in San Francisco, the mentally ill on the streets, as being the products of this molecule lingering in their frontal lobes for twenty years, from the Summer of Love. This went on for two days. Two days! And they don't need any statistics because these are accepted facts and presented as such, and the academic community was stone quiet."

The growing popularity of LSD along with Ecstasy was particularly notable, for to make LSD in the America of 1992 was a breathtakingly dangerous thing to do. Since the Anti–Drug Abuse Act of 1986, the amount of prison time a person convicted of an LSD offense would serve depended entirely on the weight of the material used to carry the drug, not the potency of the drug itself. Therefore, five milligrams of pure LSD might net you a year in jail, but one gelatin cap of 225 milligrams would put you away for two to three years; blotter paper weighing 1.4 grams would get you five to six; and sugar cubes—well, don't even ask. LSD offenses were being punished much more severely than cocaine or heroin arrests. Michael Rossman, the former activist and leader of the Free Speech Movement, was blunt about the impact of this war on psychedelics. "Those fuckers won. The forces of constraint won this Pyrrhic victory of suppressing the use of these drugs, shifting uses to other drugs like cocaine in the process, brutalizing the whole front of exploration of inner consciousness for an entire generation."

In this atmosphere, Shulgin went quietly on, teaching his class in toxicology at Berkeley and working in his lab, but it was obvious that he and Ann would have to self-publish *PIHKAL*. "Publishers were interested, but they didn't have the nerve. They were chicken." With *PIHKAL*, Shulgin, in his own courageous (and some would say foolhardy) way, made his unique statement about the continuing value of psychedelics and the existence of a community that would always be enthralled by them. "I hope this is the raw seed for others who want to discover things for themselves. This was one of the purposes for writing the second half in the way that I did."

Shulgin readily acknowledged an international psychedelic community that was thriving in the Nineties. "Oh, yes, it's alive and well today—a small, self-contained, quiet, loose reticulum of people with many motives. It's a social movement—not just this country, not just California—it's in the labs and basements of health-food stores in Austria. When I go to a meeting, there are the general audience and press, and you'll suddenly discover that there are thirty more people who are absolutely intrigued by this area. Things are being quietly, continuously discovered and distributed, though not in the way of flagrant taunting or actions that might trigger a response from people who are invested in enforcing that aspect of the law."

In fact, after publishing his voluminous catalog of phenethylamines, Shulgin embarked on a sister project—"on the use of the tryptamines, the other half of the psychedelic world: DMT, mushrooms, psilocybin, LSD." He was going to call the book *TIHKAL* (Triptamines I Have Known and Loved).

In September of 1994, two years after the publication of *PIHKAL,* the DEA showed up with a warrant to make an unannounced inspection of Shulgin's lab. Finding anonymous samples of substances that people had sent to Shulgin for analysis, the agent in charge claimed that Shulgin's license no longer authorized him to do that kind of work. Shulgin had assumed—perhaps naively—that since his license had to be renewed each year, the DEA would have notified him of any changes in regulations and rules. Each infraction would now subject him to a fine of up to twenty-five thousand dollars.

"And this vial with something called N-hydroxy-MDMA from someone called Charles; who is Charles?" The agent in charge wanted to know.

"I can't remember," Shulgin replied, assuming that he had the legal right to analyze these substances without having to identify the sources and believing that to do so would be "a complete betrayal of trust, and an unforgivable act of cowardice."

One morning after the Shulgins returned from a trip to Spain, no fewer than eight vehicles appeared at the lab, headed by a decontamination unit of the state Environmental Protection Agency, complete with men in silvery moon suits with helmets and a chemist who was one of the most highly placed administrators of the DEA. During the strange and difficult hours that followed, Sasha Shulgin was asked questions about

*PIHKAL* while state EPA people searched the soil for the pollution that they hoped would allow them to tear down his lab (they would find a fraction too much mercury in one soil sample). Shulgin managed to maintain his poise until an agent informed him that they were going to have to destroy his peyote cactuses. No one had been able to definitively analyze the trace alkaloids of peyote, and Shulgin had been growing the specimens for years just for that purpose. When he insisted that his license gave him the legal right to possess them, the agent threatened to handcuff him and read him his rights. All he could do was watch helplessly—"they'd gotten to him," as Ann Shulgin observed. "He was the one they wanted to punish. . . . The peyote were his darlings, his treasures . . . full of mysteries called alkaloids, mysteries called Time and Space and Pattern and Meaning; it had taken ten years for the baby peyotes to grow to the modest size they were now, and before our eyes they were being ripped out of their pots and trampled under boots."

It could have been worse; nothing was planted on them, and no soil samples were doctored, though the DEA bad-mouthed Shulgin to a lab and two chemical supply companies that were connected to his research. The bottom line, as one agent told Shulgin, was that "Washington wants your license." The Shulgins now understood that the real issue was the book they'd published; someone in Washington wanted Sasha's hide for it. As the court battle to retain the DEA license would have cost more than they could have afforded, Shulgin had no choice but to relinquish it and pay the fine of twenty-five thousand dollars.

The "magical lab" of Alexander T. Shulgin remained standing but never again would he be allowed to work with the same absolute freedom. As Ann Shulgin expressed it, "The authorities intended to frighten him and perhaps they even hoped to silence him, but that is not and will not be possible, while we are alive and able to speak and write."

*TIHKAL* was published in 1997.

## III. Déjà Vu All Over Again

"I HAD A REAL PROBLEM when A Rave Called Sharon started happening," said the girl called Sharon over a cup of cappuccino in the

Haight. "People wanting to meet me and know who I was— *'Oh, my God, you're Sharon!'* It was bizarre. It's not about that. It's about coming here and dancing and feeling good and important *yourself.* Everybody's saying the same thing: raves are about the music and the dancing, but they're also about caring for each other—what you're doing, where you're going, what's happening, people wanting to be involved in each other's lives. That's how the rave scene has changed; people are realizing that it has values beyond the party that are about wanting to be honest and truthful with each other."

In many ways, this twenty-five-year-old woman from Birmingham, England, embodied the rave phenomenon. Like rock and roll, the popular use of MDMA was born in the U.S.A., traveled to Britain, and then came back in the form of a British Invasion; Sharon was part of the first generation of British ravers to migrate to San Francisco, where they were catalyzing its next wave.

MDMA first made its way to Britain from the United States via the Mediterranean isle of Ibiza, a popular summer resort for English youth. There, in the climactic summer of 1987—dubbed the Summer of Love by rave enthusiasts—the use of Ecstasy combusted with the three distinctive genres of electronic dance music of the time: Detroit techno, deep house–garage of Chicago and New York, and acid house. After an untamed summer of all-night, MDMA-fueled dance parties, a core group of promoters and DJs returned to the United Kingdom, where "house parties" began cropping up at London venues like Project Club, Shoom, the Trip, R.I.P., the Spectrum, Confusion, Rage, Babylon, Enter the Dragon, and Elysium. Then the parties began moving to large warehouses for one-shot events that were completely outside the rules and restricted hours of the licensed clubs.

From the beginning, rave had its own distinctive fashion style—"a weird mix of Mediterranean beach bum, hippy, and soccer hooligan— baggy trousers and T-shirts, paisley bandannas, dungarees, ponchos, Converse All Star sneakers—loose-fitting, because the Ecstasy and non-stop trance dancing made you sweat buckets," as Simon Reynolds described it. Being "cool" was out and so was alcohol (ravers, in fact, would became famous for preferring water and glucose-rich soft drinks). From the outset, the scene was infused with an idealism and set of values about spirituality, social consciousness and unity that seemed a complete departure from the sex-driven solipsism of the disco-cocaine-alcohol club culture and the cold self-aggrandizing materialism of the Thatcherite Eighties. The audience was the star, the whole point of the experience; over the next two years, raves became massive outdoor marathons in aircraft hangars and open fields, with tens of thousands of people dancing in MDMA-inspired delirium. The power of the chemical was obvious enough in how it seemed to take those well-known British character traits of emotional reserve and inhibition and wash them away in the course of an hour, not to mention how it could seize the most boorish drunken football hooligans and turn them into cuddly teddy bears who wanted to do nothing but dance and hug. What's more, the new music sounded especially great on E. As Reynolds noted, "House and techno sounded especially fabulous. The music's emphasis on texture and timbre enhances the drug's mildly synesthetic effects so that sounds seem to caress the listener's skin . . . sound becomes a fluid medium in which you're immersed."

Of course, growing popularity and the prospect of a whole nation of "E'ed up" teenagers brought increased scrutiny and condemnation by press and politicians. Like all drugs, the potential for abuse of MDMA was there at the start. The typical side effects included dry mouth, speedy jitteriness, nausea, and the kind of jaw tension that could lead to excessive grinding of the teeth (bruxism), but the most unpleasant repercussion by far was the "comedown." Users in the aftermath of an E excursion could feel listless, emotionally burned out, irritable, and melancholic, and for those who really abused the drug on the weekends, the midweek crash could be particularly wicked. Perhaps the greatest danger was "emotional addiction," the sense that any kind of normal consciousness paled in comparison to the energized, blissed-out state of the Ecstasy high. There were other risks, of course—bad drugs, the mixing of the drug with amphetamine and other chemicals and alcohol—but the real problem with using MDMA excessively was a dynamic that Simon Reynolds would identify as its "diminishing-returns syndrome to form a vicious cycle, a negative synergy. The individual's experience of Ecstasy is degraded; on the collective level, Ecstasy scenes lose their idyllic luster and become a soul-destroying grind. . . . This shift from paradise regained to pleasure prison is a recurring narrative experienced by successive Ecstasy Generations across the world. For seemingly programmed into the chemical structure of MDMA is the instruction *use me, don't abuse me.*"

Perhaps the most substantial danger of the raves themselves were the effects of overexertion and dehydration leading to heatstroke, which ravers countered by drinking lots of fluids and taking regular breaks in the "chill-out rooms," but with the first reported death from MDMA in June of 1988—twenty-one-year-old Ian Larcombe, who was alleged to have taken eighteen hits—came the predictable Fleet Street hysterics, politicians passing decrees against raves to save civilization, and the police crackdown. In response, rave organizers became exceedingly wily, using lookouts armed with cell phones and walkie-talkies to monitor police-band frequencies and passing out flyers that directed ravers to secret locations. By the end of 1989, the events had spread throughout northern England and the Midlands, where Manchester had become the center of the vortex, and where people like Sharon had encountered the phenomenon.

"House music is the beginning of the future of modern music, and all these kids dancing their pants off to it are the future of humankind," declared Sharon. "Now, more so than ever, it's important to nurture an open mind, and that's what this scene does—it nurtures freedom, an open mind, and questions. Thinking about things, not just accepting them. I personally think we're coming to the end of history. Morality, religion, politics—it's all going to have to change if we're going to evolve further as a race of people."

Such weighty declarations were common among ravers, though few were as articulate or as emblematic of the sensibility as Sharon. With her Jamaican father and Irish mother ("she was a mad Irish Catholic woman who tried to impose all this religion on me"), she grew up beautiful, talented, and mulatto in the bleak, depressed city of Birmingham, learning from an early age to transcend any aspect of her background or environment that might limit her in any conceivable way, studying art and dance and traveling the world before arriving in San Francisco. The great lesson of her travels and readings and experiences was "that people all over the world are the same. Some of them base their choices on love and caring, on what really matters; some of them base their choices on their history, and that's where problems occur."

When Sharon arrived in the Bay Area, she found Ecstasy. "I'd experienced euphoria through my art, but this was different. When you're dancing on Ecstasy, a lot of historical boundaries in society just dissolve, and you can dance yourself into a frenzy, into a trance—just like the Sufis, the whirling dervishes. That's why when people experience this scene, it's more about the dancing than the drugs, but Ecstasy was quick access—a wonderful, quick way of getting to that beautiful place. I remember my boyfriend at the time said, 'There should be a day when everybody takes a hit of E!'

"Now that I've been there through drugs, I know I can get there in other ways. I like taking them, but I don't need to do it. Soon people start to realize that it isn't just the drugs—it's something else, the state of mind that drugs put you in. They stop taking drugs, and they still feel as euphoric. I'm speaking for myself now, but I've talked about it with so many people, why they are into this scene. It gives them a freedom they've never had and a feeling of unity that's lacking everywhere else."

Sharon's boyfriend, Preston Lytton, had left Kansas City as a teenager and had become one of the key promoters of the burgeoning rave scene in San Francisco. Sharon had been in town only a few months and was dancing at Mr. Floppy's in Oakland, at one of the first big house parties in the summer of 1991, when the idea to name a rave after her was born. "They were unique, these parties, all weird, strange people just doing their thing, and I'd become famous as this lunatic who just ran around dancing. I was on Ecstasy, dancing on a stage, and it felt like there were sparks coming out of my hair and out of my womb and out of my mouth! I don't know what it was—just a good feeling, like a positive energy, and I was just shaking it out over the people, sharing it, spreading it all over, and he said, 'Let's have a party, and let's call it Sharon!' It was just a joke, but eventually they did just that, and it stuck."

In November of 1990, Lytton had produced the first house music parties at the Tower, the influential warehouse events called Toon Town that shaped the whole San Francisco rave scene. "Toon Town was revolutionary because so many people who became creative in the rave scene got their inspiration on the dance floor there," Lytton explained. "A lot of the party icons were born there—the smart bar, the deejays, the music—feelings and intentions coming together. At that point, word got out to a lot of people. There were two front-page articles here, a big article in *Rolling Stone* on the smart drugs, a ten-page article in *Tempo*. A lot of people came in and started getting passionate. Then there was the cyberpunk aspect and the whole influence of Silicon Valley here, and it created a union."

Bryan Hughes, a digital whiz kid from Omaha, was starting the Renaissance Foundation and experimenting with virtual reality when Lytton and the other promoters of Toon Town asked him to bring his computer to a warehouse party at One Federal. "It was the first underground party I'd ever been to—I'd only gone out to bars and had never heard house music or anything like that. It got shut down at four a.m. but to me it was completely amazing, to be out there with that music and those lights. I had done Ecstasy, and I was beside myself. I almost can't describe it. Oh, my God!"

When Toon Town moved to 650 Howard and became a weekly event, Hughes became a partner. "We developed a following at this small venue, a core group of three hundred fifty to five hundred people who came every Saturday and stayed to eight a.m., and this whole culture started developing. They were sharing this intense experience though the drugs and the music and the lights together. If we saw each other out on the street, you'd stop and hug like a long-lost relative. You knew this person was not part of your everyday life but part of your church. When the rest of the world started seeing these club kids dressing really wild, having the most amazing time of their lives because they were letting themselves be completely free, people from the whole Bay Area started coming."

On New Year's Eve of 1991, Toon Town took over the eighty thousand square feet and four floors of the Fashion Center. As Hughes recalled it, "Eight thousand people showed up; by three a.m., there were sixty-five hundred people dancing together. We had to close the doors! There was a line to get in until five in the morning. A lot of money was made."

Ecstasy had always been plentiful as the scene coalesced; several of the largest underground labs happened to be located on the West Coast. "Actually that's how we started Toon Town, how we funded it—by selling Ecstasy," Lytton admitted. "At first, we only had two or three hundred dollars to produce a party, but with selling E, it was no problem; my partner was selling it, and the reason was that to her it was basically a public service. Exactly the same way Owsley might have sold acid in the San Francisco of the Sixties."

It was, as Yogi Berra had once put it, déjà vu all over again: a new boundary-dissolving psychedelic wonder drug, a small enclave of devotees, a few defining events and messianic personalities, media coverage, money to be made, a fresh generation seeking meaning on the cusp of a new era and . . . voilà.

"There was always a psychedelic culture out here, big-time; it just went really underground," Lytton pointed out. "These people started building computers and designing programs instead of making tie-dyed shirts. Psychedelics and computers—that was the combination."

## IV. The Future Has Imploded onto the Present

"THIS GENERATION absolutely swallowed computers whole, just like dope," Stewart Brand observed back in 1984. Theodore Roszak underscored this remark in his slim 1986 volume, *From Satori to Silicon Valley.* As Roszak made clear, the psychedelic counterculture had always embraced the "technophiliac utopians" like Buckminster Fuller and Marshall McLuhan. By the early Nineties, this natural kinship between the Sixties counterculture, the new information technologies, and the neopsychedelic rave culture was efflorescing into a novel digital milieu called cyberdelic.

"Our computer networks give us the best clue to the nature of our latest increase in dimensional thinking as well as to the reason why MDMA, in particular, became the drug of choice among the newly 'networked,' " wrote Douglas Rushkoff, author of *Cyberia* and *Playing the Future.* Rushkoff cited "fractional dimensionality," or fractals, as one example of how mathematicians had used the paradigm and experience of psychedelics to comprehend unfathomable systems. The point was simple: if a fractal was a shape whose details resemble the whole (as a mountain range is a kind of fractal, since if you look at an outcropping of rock, it looks like a small mountain), the connection between fractals and certain acid visions that deconstructed images and textures was obvious enough.

Rushkoff also pointed to the new holographic techniques, which could represent the passage of time as well as depth, as another significant development. "It seemed that those who had experience navigating the hallucinatory realm of an LSD trip were most comfortable learning the languages and confronting the yet uninvented worlds of cyberspace. As fledgling Silicon Valley firms became dependent on Grateful Deadheads as programmers, cyber culture became known as a 'cyberdelic' movement." As articulated by William Gibson, author of the seminal novel *Neuromancer* and the man who literally invented the term *cyberpunk,* cyberspace was "a consensual hallucination that these people have created daily by billions of legitimate operators, in every nation. . . . A graphic representation of data abstracted from the banks of every computer in the human system. Unthinkable complexity. Lines of light ranged in the nonspace of the mind. Clusters and constellations of data."

A number of the Brits who'd come to San Francisco had been influenced by cyberdelic ideologues like Fraser Clark, the founder of *Evolution Magazine,* and Psychic TV's Genesis P-Orridge. In the Bay Area, they hooked up with a whole new crowd pursuing the same interests.

"I think Rudy Rucker, in our first issue, coined a cyberpunk slogan when he said, 'How fast are you, how dense?' " reflected *Mondo 2000* editor RU Sirius. "Dense meaning complex, of course, not stupid. The speed and density of input, the amount of stuff that you can take in, and being able to find patterns in that, which is what happens in the computer world, is precisely reflected in psychedelic experience. Also, the whole hacker ethic is about getting as much out of a particular system any way you can do it; whether you're breaking the rules or not is beside the point. You have a piece of software, a piece of hardware, and a social situation; you have your brain and your nervous system, and you try to get as much as possible out of it. That ethic emerges and comes together between the people who use drugs for visionary experience or personal enhancement or whatever, and the hacker attitude toward external technology."

At the time, the *Mondo* crowd was very fond of prankish cyberpunk pseudonyms like Queen Mu and Michael Synergy. RU Sirius was really Ken Goffman, an ex-Yippie activist and writer from New York who had started an "irreverent neopsychedelic" magazine in 1984 called *High*

*Frontiers* that blended science, technology, culture, and modern art. His interests inevitably led him to the psychedelic community that included Bruce Eisner, Peter Stafford, Timothy Leary, Terence McKenna, and others. "There was this strange subculture, these stoned scholars and these crazed chemists," Sirius continued. "It was a fascinating world—people who had spent their lives debating whether Gordon Wasson was right and psilocybin really was the soma of the gods. Sixty percent of the people at these parties or a Terence McKenna lecture were major people at Apple or IBM or Hewlett-Packard—the top software programmers. I was very impressed that these figures like Leary and McKenna were so sophisticated about technology and where it was driving the future of humanity."

*Mondo 2000* quickly emerged as the most popular and slickly produced journal of the New Edge–futurist–posthuman–cyberpunk sensibility—the very nexus of Silicon Valley and the nouveau psychedelia. You could read the latest information about the action of MDMA on dopamine and other neurotransmitters, but you could also get the most up-to-date data on artificial intelligence, brain implants, designer aphrodisiacs, DNA engineering, digital-imaging techniques, hacker pranks, electronic telepathy, freedom of information issues relating to the Internet, postindustrial house music, rave wear, fiber optics, hypertext, robotics, cryonics, multimedia, nanotechnology, personal computing, smart drugs, transrealism, technoerotic paganism, and virtual reality. Everything in *Mondo* was culturally theorized, presented from the point of view of an emerging cyberpunk worldview. Another *Mondo* contributor, Gareth Branwyn, summarized the fundamental precepts and "related attitudes" of the sensibility as follows:

A. The future has imploded onto the present. There was no Nuclear Armageddon. There's too much real estate to lose. The new battlefield is people's minds.
B. The megacorps *are* the new governments.
C. The U.S. is a big bully with lackluster economic power.
D. The world is splintering into a trillion subcultures and designer cults with their own languages, codes and lifestyles.
E. Computer-generated info-domains are the next frontiers.
F. There *is* better living through chemistry.

In this cultural configuration, freedom of information and unlimited access to computers were the imperatives; cyberpunks should always Mistrust Authority, Promote Decentralization, Do It Yourself, Fight the Power, Feed the Noise Back into the System, and Surf the Edges. As far as drugs were concerned, the *idea* of drugs and what they represented were every bit as significant as the drugs themselves. "I enjoy READING about people taking psychedelics, and I like to THINK ABOUT the effects they have, but I don't like to TAKE them, nor would I wholeheartedly recommend them to others," stated Rudy Rucker, one of *Mondo*'s primary writers. "To me the political point of being pro-psychedelic is that this means being AGAINST consensus reality, which I very strongly am. Psychedelics are a kind of objective correlative for being weird and different."

Sirius, who'd made a career out of being "weird and different" with *Mondo,* recognized several landmark theorists on the subject of drugs and technology who were shaping the cyberpunk worldview. Unique among them was Terence McKenna, although technology was only one aspect of his visionary philosophy. "Terence McKenna is a very, very amazing brain. Back in 1984, he was uttering things to me like 'We're moving toward the interiorization of the body and the exteriorization of the soul.' I thought, What the fuck is this guy talking about? And then, slowly, as we built cyberspace, as we build virtual reality, I began to see . . . Terence McKenna just nails it on the head so often."

The man everybody was talking about—author, shamanologist, ethnobotanical philosopher, and scholar—was sitting cross-legged on his living room floor in Occidental, California, casually pulling on a thick joint.

"In the last two or three years, this acid-house rave culture has practically made me a star," McKenna related. "Bands now sample my voice and put me on their CDs! When I go to England, no one in my audience is over twenty-five. It's an ocean of black leather, not eggheads, academics, or old hippies. As of three years ago, that house scene in England was an Ecstasy scene, and now the hard core has all gone toward psychedelics and plants. To my mind, that means we've crossed a certain frontier. The basic assumption of the acid revolution of the Sixties was that acid was icing on the cake of the Better Living through Chemistry revolution:

penicillin, polio vaccine, Valium, LSD. It took the experience of the Seventies, Eighties, and Nineties to say that this isn't something that came out of the genius laboratories of Swiss pharmaceutical chemists; this is what people have been doing for thousands and thousands of years. It's all about getting in touch with what has been suppressed by history. The Shaman is now emerging as the central ideal figure: sexually ambiguous, healing, connected to the earth and nature. And as it's ultimately understood, *psychedelic*."

McKenna paused to take a hit.

"Shamanism without psychedelics is like wife beating without alcohol—it just doesn't happen."

It was one of those classic McKenna lines, and there were multitudes of them. Born in the largely fundamentalist Christian western Colorado town of Paonia "fourteen months after Hiroshima in a place downwind of the atomic tests," McKenna was in school at UC Berkeley in 1966 when someone boosted a fifty-five-gallon drum of pure crystal DMT at Stanford that was headed for the army arsenal at Edgewood, Maryland, and released it into the dope-dealing machinery of the university. Four or five grams of the rare, explosively potent substance came into his circle.

"I was told it only lasted five minutes. I said, Hey, no big deal, bring it on, let's smoke some." The usual method of ingestion was simply to soak parsley in the substance, let it dry, smoke it, and fifteen to thirty seconds later—to use the popular onomatopoeia of comic books—*KABAM!* "I had *no idea*. It was so fast, powerful, and so reality obliterating, so filled with alien content that it seemed to me it was going to create a cultural crisis—just as if a flying saucer were to land on the South Lawn of the White House."

That single experience began McKenna's lifelong fascination with psychoactive mushrooms. DMT (N,N-dimethyltryptamine) is a semi-synthetic fast-acting psychedelic chemical similar in structure to psilocin, the substance into which psilocybin, the active ingredient in psilocybin mushrooms, is converted in the body (it was also the active ingredient in the hallucinogenic plants of the Amazon basin *Piptadenia peregrina* and *Banisteriopsis caapi*, known as yage or ayahuasca). Since the 1970s, McKenna had been busy formulating an entire history of human evolution based on plants and drugs—the subject of his 1992 book, *Food of the Gods: The Search for the Original Tree of Knowledge*. At doses of more than five dried grams that he would characterize as "committed" or "heroic," psilocybin would literally "speak" to him, in ways that combined with the visions, creating "three dimensional colored modalities that have linguistic content." These "entelechies" seemed to be drawn from an alien intelligence and not from the personal history of the individual or even collective human experience: "Are we dealing with an aspect, an autonomous psychic entity, as the Jungians would style it—a subself that has slipped away from the control of the ego? Or are we dealing with something like a species Overmind—a kind of collective entelechy?"

McKenna began calling this interior voice the Logos, using the Greek word: "The Logos spoke the truth—an incontrovertible Truth. Socrates had what he called his *daemon*—his informing Other." He had visions of "enormous machines in orbit on distant planets and strange creatures and vast biomechanistic landscapes." As if these "elfclowns of hyperspace" weren't fantastic enough, the Logos was revealing truths of human history that concerned the very fate of the species. The bottom line as McKenna was experiencing it through psychedelics was that history, as we know it, was coming to an end. The portents of extinction were everywhere: the toxification of the oceans, the disappearing atmosphere. The cause as he saw it was plain and simple: "the untrammeled expression of ego," which over the centuries had constructed a culture of governments and corporations that were destroying the planet. The choices were equally stark: "Extinction or the reengineering of human psychology and society. We have to change our behavior, and that means pharmacology."

To sum it up, all primate forms of organization clear down to the squirrel monkeys had been male-dominance hierarchies, but sometime in evolutionary history (the last million years or so) and ending only fifteen thousand years ago, these male-dominated hierarchies were suppressed by the introduction of psilocybin into the diet, which promoted a lifestyle of psychedelic intoxication and orgiastic sexuality in a religious context. McKenna would call this period the Archaic—actually the

Upper Paleolithic period of seven to ten thousand years ago, immediately before the invention and dissemination of agriculture, "a time of nomadic pastoralism and partnership, a culture based on cattle-raising, shamanism, and Goddess worship."

According to McKenna's theory, about ten thousand years ago, when the mushrooms became less available in large population areas and the psychedelic lifestyle disappeared, old male-dominated behavior patterns that gave rise to the evolution of Western culture as we know it emerged: the marking off of territory, the invention of agriculture, the end of nomadism, anxiety between the haves and the have-nots, the rise of classes, kings, standing armies—in other words, "the whole gamut of cultural furniture, that has made us so pathological." In essence, the species had been "wrenched out of a fairly workable dynamic balance and flung into history, and history is the story of one wretched, miserable group going up against another, just creating more misery and negotiating some standoff. And we have now pushed ourselves to the brink of extinction."

The key elements of McKenna's solution, which he called the Archaic Revival, were "the re-empowerment of ritual, the rediscovery of shamanism, the re-cognition of psychedelics, and the importance of the Goddess." Goddess meant the Gaia of the Upper Paleolithic period—the Great Goddess, mistress of the animals. Shamanism, of course, was the worldwide tradition of natural magic of that time; McKenna embraced Mircea Eliade's definition of it as "the archaic techniques of ecstasy," and viewed ecstasy mainly as the "contemplation of wholeness."

As the Amazon forest people would take ayahuasca and enter into that place of Group Mind where they would make decisions for the tribe, the psychedelic shamanic acts that McKenna was promulgating would involve the experience of ecstasy and the contemplation of wholeness. There was an Oversoul of all life on earth, he believed, a guiding Mind that psychedelics could put you in touch with, which was vegetable, Gaian; only through this plant-based view would a return to a perspective on self and ego that places mankind within the larger context of planetary life and evolution become possible. Drugs, computers, and people were all becoming extensions of one another, moving the human race toward transition to some higher cybernetic dimension of existence. The chaos of the age was thus nothing unusual but rather "the normal situation when a species prepares to leave the planet." As the species comes to realize more and more that its aspirations are increasingly alien to the ecology of the planet, it will become obvious that "it and the planet must part. The transformation of humanity into a space-faring, time-faring race is on a biological scale, the great goal of history."

Properly used, psychedelics were nothing less than windows on the future, "the last best hope for dissolving the steep walls of cultural inflexibility that appear to be channeling us toward true ruin," and to legally proscribe their use was more than folly—it was suicide because they were the essential Darwinian tool. Nevertheless, McKenna was anything but a populist promoter like Timothy Leary, who demanded psychedelics for the masses in the Sixties. On the contrary, he was advocating a kind of "deputized minority—a shamanic professional class, if you will—whose job it is to bring ideas out of the deep, black water and show them off to the rest of us," a "shamanic guild" that would need to be strengthened rather than broadened. Until such time as the use of psychedelics might become decriminalized, he advocated great caution.

"The way to put something over on a government is by moving so slowly that they don't notice that the landscape is changing. If you suddenly jump up with ten million hits of a drug, they go berserk. A strategy of stealth is much better. I've been doing this since 1983 pretty heavily, and I think the government understands that as long as they don't call attention to me, this stuff will never surface. It's very hard to imagine how society has been able not to look at this. But I intend to keep talking about it until somebody snuffs me or we get some action, because I have taken a complete inventory of world civilization, and DMT is definitely the most interesting thing on this planet."

McKenna had been largely dismissive of MDMA because it was synthetic, and he believed that the Gaian Mind could best be accessed through the natural psychedelics; he'd always felt that Ecstasy was not really connected to the larger issues of ecology because it was narcissistic, all about you, your lover, your parents, your feelings. But ironically, by the time of his death—from brain cancer in 2000—the intensely odd, brilliant, and spellbinding McKenna had become a kind of Joseph Campbell figure to the rave generation. After all, it was MDMA that was the psychedelic of the Nineties—and as McKenna said, shamanism without psychedelics was like wife beating without alcohol.

## V. The World's Oldest Cyberpunk

THE LOS ANGELES TIMES had called Terence McKenna "the Tim Leary of the 90s." McKenna had even used his own playful variation of Leary's infamous catchphrase of the Sixties: "Log on, tune in, and drop out." Even Tim Leary called McKenna "the Tim Leary of the Nineties," but that did nothing to diminish Leary's stature in the story of the psychedelic culture. Cyberpunk had more than vindicated Leary. By the winter of 1993, his smiling countenance was being widely featured in a print campaign for the Gap. Twenty years later, the same man who had once been labeled the most dangerous man in America by a federal judge in California was selling blue jeans and T-shirts to a whole new generation as Timothy Leary, Philosopher. Leary had successfully surfed his way right onto the cybercultural cutting edge. He had become what *Mondo 2000* was calling a "cyber-delic guru. . . . The MVP (Most Valuable Philosopher) of the 20th Century." "The 90s are here," declared William Gibson, the cyberpunk novelist, "and the Doctor is in!"

As he looked back and totaled the assets and subtracted the costs of the use of drugs in America since the 1960s, Leary blamed many of his "mistakes" on simple naïveté. "For example, I made the classic mistake that we all make. It was wonderful for thin intellectuals like Aldous Huxley and me to get high and suddenly enjoy the pleasures of the body and aesthetics and sensuality and music: My *God,* this is *wonderful*! What I didn't realize is that eighty percent of the people out there are *not* motivated, and if they smoked marijuana, no question it could take away what little motivation they might have had. Tragically, in the cases of many younger people I observed, I didn't realize that there *is* a real problem with marijuana and young people who would smoke pot in the morning and not go to school—what's the difference, put on another Grateful Dead record! You know, the last thing I ever had in mind was to create a whole subculture of adolescent *haschischines*! I cite this as one of my many mistakes of omission and naïveté, and I blame it on the tendency of every philosopher—of every human, in fact—to believe that everyone's like *you,* when of course they're *not!*—"

He laughed, one of those Timothy Leary laughs, bittersweet and full of irony, self-deprecating honesty, and Irish blarney, more about the cosmic joke of the human condition than anything else.

"Oh, yes, we were well meaning good natured primitives back at Harvard. We didn't know anything about computers, nor did we realize anything about the implications of quantum physics, chaos theory, and fractals. We did know that when you had a visionary experience with a psychedelic drug, you were exposed to what we now call chaos. BOOM! You were experiencing a thousand times more information in a minute than in normal life. But we knew we needed to have a new language to describe it. We didn't have the language of technology back then, and now we do."

And so had Dr. Timothy Leary become America's oldest cyberpunk, a "neurologician" who portrayed the brain as "a galactic network of a hundred billion neurons," each one "an information system as complex as a mainframe computer." "The PC is the LSD of the Nineties," Leary declared in no uncertain terms, now speaking the language of fractals, digital information algorithms, virtual reality, and quantum electronic engineering as fluently as he had once spoken the language of transactional psychology and psychedelic transcendentalism. Lately he'd constructed a new philosophical platform based on the legend of the ronin (translated as "wave people"), a metaphor derived from the Japanese word for the samurai who had left the service of their feudal lords to become warriors without masters. It was the cyberpunks who were now the "pilots of the species," as Leary observed, the clear and creative thinkers who used "quantum-electronic appliances and brain know-how," the "strong, stubborn, creative individual who explores some future-frontier, collects and brings back new information, and offers to guide the gene pool to the next stage."

Cyberpunks were "mavericks, ronin, free-lancers, independents, self-starters, non-conformists, odd-balls, trouble-makers, kooks, visionaries, iconoclasts, insurgents, blue-sky thinkers, loners, smart alecks"—in other words, exactly like Leary. He was certain that the policies of Ronald

Reagan had not been what caused the Soviet Union to topple; rather, it had been the yearning on the part of Soviet-bloc youth for the very freedoms represented by the Beatles, Bob Dylan, the Rolling Stones, blue jeans, computers, and—yes—LSD. In Leary's mind, the whole Reagan-conservative counterreaction to the Sixties that had demonized the psychedelic movement as misguided and immoral hedonism run amok was to have been expected.

"It happened after the Italian Renaissance, too, when they came in and busted all the naked statues and took down all the Venuses from the museum walls! Quite predictable, and I must say that every time we move it ahead—and by 'we' I mean the humanists, those who believe in the human spirit and potential and believe you have to question authority—every time we move it ahead, it's thrown back. But the base camp has been made, and the next wave will come and find your wreckage, and they'll be encouraged to go beyond that."

Of course, there were those in America who viewed any kind of "base camp" that Leary and his constituency might establish on the American cultural landscape as a kind of malignant plant that should be uprooted and eradicated—just like the marijuana plants of Humboldt County. Those people were hardly downhearted by the news of Leary's prostate cancer in the next few years, any more than Leary was saddened by the demise of J. Edgar Hoover. As the media learned that Timothy Leary was dying and that he planned to have himself cryogenically frozen and "re-animated," journalists began a pilgrimage to his home in Los Angeles, where, for a fee of one thousand dollars, they could take their measure of the man in his final days. Most, of course, were unable to get past the most hackneyed sobriquets—"High Priest of LSD," "Acid Guru," "Drug King of the Sixties Generation," and so on—and asked questions like "Do you have any regrets about all the LSD you took, all the drugs that were taken in your name?" As for Leary's response to them, it was usually similar to the words he proclaimed so emphatically that day in his backyard—

"I still honor botanical substances that activate the brain. I *honor* cannabis; I *honor* lysergic acid, mescaline, psilocybin mushrooms! I honor at least a hundred new botanical brain drugs which aren't even *discovered* yet, for all the receptor sites in the brain! I honor the ancient tradition of using the gifts of the vegetable kingdom—or queendom! I *do* believe that the brain needs them; the brain *loves* electrons and psychoactive chemicals!—"

He was smiling again.

"Hey, the receptor sites are *there*! Just like you have lungs—well, they must want *air*! You got a belly, the body must want *food*! You got these receptor sites in your brain, it's *obvious*! Most human beings *love* to get high, *love* to alter their consciousness with *vegetables*! That's why you have *taboos*! That's why you have these *prohibitions*! That's why you have the *war on drugs*! Because people *love* it! The inevitable complication here is that the people in *control,* the top management, always make the idea of altering consciousness or changing your own brain something immoral, illegal, or unethical! Only *God* can do that, right?—particularly if it's *enjoyable*! Well, *naturally,* it's enjoyable! Brains *love* electrons!! Brains *love* to be strobed by *colors* and *images*!! But you're not *supposed* to enjoy it, right?—"

Timothy Leary laughed again, delighted by his own rant, forever tweaking the authorities, the theologians, the conservatives—the ronin on the white horse, without masters, unrepentant, unbowed. He died on May 31, 1996, with the words *"Why not?"* on his lips. Having abandoned the plans to have himself cryogenically frozen, Leary nevertheless managed to have his ashes shot into space in a capsule. It was, as his official Web site readily pointed out, his Final Trip.

# 14

## Just Say Know

*"What we believe is that the war on drugs constitutes a fundamental evil, in American society and in global society at large."*

—Ethan Nadelmann, speech to NORML, November 12, 1998

### I. The Second Smallest Political Movement in the World

IS IT BETTER to have more kids using drugs responsibly or fewer kids using drugs harmfully?

Such were the questions being raised in the conference room of the law firm of Dewey Ballantine, where the Princeton Working Group on the Future of Drug Use and Alternatives to Drug Prohibition was meeting on May 23, 1994. A war on drugs that included the stated goal of a "drug-free" America to be reached by 1995 was now the law of the land, but this group's central thesis was that most of America's drug problems were in fact the result of the failed policies of drug prohibition. The other think tanks and government agencies that were formulating policy recommendations were trying to figure out more effective ways of prosecuting the drug war, which made the Princeton Group all the more exceptional. Most of its members were academics who'd had positive experiences with drugs and believed that such a thing as "controlled, responsible drug use" was possible, a notion that was antithetical to the federal drug war. All of them believed that "harm reduction" should be the ultimate goal of drug-policy reform but recognized that they would never be able to make their prescriptions for policy change until they somehow dealt with the long-standing fear that any change in policy would automatically shove the nation down some "slippery slope" and inevitably lead to a civilization riddled with drug addiction. As Craig Reinarman put it, "You can't avoid that slippery slope. What we have to do is make it *less slippery.*"

No easy task, but was it even possible? Ethan Nadelmann thought so. In 1988, Nadelmann's articles in *Foreign Policy* and *The Public Interest* had attracted a great deal of attention by criticizing the drug war during its most dramatic escalation; the grant he'd received from the Smart Family Foundation had allowed him to assemble this group for three weekends and a series of smaller meetings between September of '90 and December of '91. As the study of drugs was so uniquely multidisciplinary, the group included eighteen scholars in a dozen different fields. There were sociologists like Reinarman of the University of California at Santa Cruz, Lynn Zimmer and Harry Levine of Queens College, and Marsha Rosenbaum; medical doctors with expertise in pharmacology and drug issues like John P. Morgan of the City University of New York, Lester Grinspoon of Harvard, and Andrew Weil; well-known writers on drug history like Dr. Michael Aldrich; addiction researchers like Robin Room and Stanton Peele; and chemist-psychopharmacologist Alexander T. Shulgin.

"We were trying to think through how not only to change things in the short term à la Europe, but in the long term," Nadelmann explained. "What if we had a regulatory regime and what would it look like and how would you do it? And that gets you into a whole other area of questions that aren't being asked anymore . . . What about the positive uses of drugs? In a world where the whole pharmacopoeia would be available to adult citizens at a reasonable price, how would competition among the makers of psychoactive drug substances affect which ones were more popular? Would drugs, like cigarettes, fall by the wayside to other substances, which might be equally as addictive but not nearly so harmful? Would alcohol use or abuse diminish if marijuana were legalized? Would crack have much of a market? That's the kind of model I'm playing with, and it's a revolutionary type model."

Nadelmann found several analogies useful to this endeavor. As early as 1942, the War Department began envisioning what the world might look like if the United States won the war and occupied Japan and Germany. The other paradigm was the crumbling of Communism. "The socialist dictatorships of Eastern Europe were the devil they knew, which was a corrupt and inefficient system that worked to some degree because it provided some degree of security based upon the assumption that human beings did not know how to operate in their own best interests and had to be told what to do by the state," Nadelmann pointed out. "It relied very heavily on intensive surveillance and an informant system. Drug prohibition makes the same assumptions."

For a brief time, the Princeton Group was the most dynamic de facto drug-reform think tank in the United States. "Everybody was learning from each other at such a rate, it was marvelous—almost like a spiritual experience," noted Dr. John P. Morgan. "The dilemma is that it's a little hard to know where to go from here." The Clinton administration was brand-new, and the group was hopeful that it would be ripe for some kind of drug reform. "We'd all like to be some part of that, but I'm not quite clear about what the future holds for us . . . Here's the line. Marsha Rosenbaum's husband is a very well-known criminologist named John Irwin. Marsha was talking about the movement, and John said, 'What movement?' 'The *drug legalization movement.'* He said, 'It's the second smallest political movement in the world, the only smaller one being the *Man Boy Love Association!'* "

It was a line that William Bennett probably would have appreciated.

## II. Psychopharmacological McCarthyism

FOR THOSE LIKE Keith Stroup who had worked so hard to reform the drug laws in the Seventies, the war on drugs was particularly bitter. After leaving NORML, Stroup worked as a defense attorney specializing in drug cases. "I had a woman, a lovely lady as a client down in South Carolina," he recalled. "We represented her boyfriend and got him a light sentence for something in Virginia, but while he was in, she picked up his business and got popped on one of the earliest mandatory minimums back when the feds didn't have them but some of the states did. She was looking at thirty years. After weeks and weeks of pretrial motions, I worked out a deal. She was going to have to serve a year, which she said was fine and I thought was fine. I flew off to Detroit to go to another hearing and was supposed to come back in two days. She hung herself that night."

Stroup lost heart and eventually left his practice to go back into political work. "There's no doubt that part of what the Reagan revolution was about was trying to reverse a lot of the things they didn't like about the Sixties and Seventies, but I think it was driven even more strongly by the fact that it was a cheap way to get reelected. If you could paint your opponent as soft on crime, soft on drugs, you could beat them—it was that simple. It became an easy way to tar people, destroy their careers and lives, and it had nothing to do with whether or not there was a real need for government. It didn't matter if you were a middle-class person who held a respectable job and went home once a week and smoked a joint or you were a heroin addict on the street corner; we were all lumped together. It was Lester Grinspoon of Harvard who began calling it psychopharmacological McCarthyism."

Ed Sanders fell prey to this psychopharmacological McCarthyism in 1989, when he ran for the county legislature from Woodstock, where he had moved in the early Seventies with his wife, Miriam, seeking a sane and quiet place to raise their daughter. Sanders had made his commitment to preserving the ecology of the area the centerpiece of his campaign and might have won had his conservative opponent not managed to dig up some incriminating old tidbits about his colorful past. "I believe you shouldn't allow yourself to be marginalized, so I ran for public office. If the Right Wing doesn't like your overall thrust, they'll look for some hook to trash you with. They found me in one of those encyclopedias of American writers, and in looking me up, they saw under my heading that I'd helped found something called the Committee to Help Legalize Marijuana, and they found my magazine, *Fuck You: A Magazine of the Arts*."

Sanders's opponent wasted no time plastering the information on windshields all over town—which meant losing the election, of course. It was a classic example of what Sanders called the "I-fucked-a-chicken-in-the-Sixties" syndrome, which he also likened to McCarthyism. It had been a common tactic during the Sixties to use the issue of drugs to discredit the counterculture and the antiwar movement; now it was possible to make the Sixties itself the issue by simply hoisting up the values and alternative lifestyles for political target practice—and drugs had become the fattest mark of them all.

In the case of Judge Douglas Ginsburg, just having smoked marijuana once as a student during the Sixties and a few times during the Seventies was more than enough for President Reagan to withdraw his nomination to the Supreme Court in 1987, despite Ginsburg's being a conservative jurist who would probably have been acceptable to Democrats on the Senate Judiciary Committee. It was a time when Dr. Carlton Turner, Reagan's drug czar, told *Newsweek* that pot could make you gay. William von Raab, head of the Customs Service, instituted a policy he called "zero tolerance" and encouraged the State Department to revoke the passport of any U.S. citizen caught with a single joint. Attorney General Ed Meese hired the public relations firm of Hill and Knowlton to burnish the image of the drug war and sent a memo to U.S. attorneys exhorting them to go after "middle- and upper-class" drug users—"to send the message that there is no such thing as 'recreational' drug use." First Lady Nancy Reagan went further at a White House drug conference, calling such casual drug users "accomplices to murder."

Everywhere the policies of the drug war were taking firm hold. The mandatory minimum sentences enacted by the Anti–Drug Abuse Act of 1986 went into effect, taking power and discretion away from judges and giving it to prosecutors. Sentences were automatically triggered solely by the quantity of drugs involved in the case; factors like a defendant's remorse, criminal history, level of involvement, and extent of cooperation with police and whether the defendant was armed and violent or not no longer mattered. With urban murders rising after the appearance of crack, Senator Jesse Helms of North Carolina called for a mandatory minimum for the drug: five grams, five years. As jail cells filled up, new prisons had to be built. Having already sanctioned anonymous tips, the Supreme Court ruled, "The government's regulatory interest can, in appropriate circumstances, outweigh an individual's liberty interest." "Drug-courier profiles" were now being routinely applied by law enforcement and forfeitures accelerated (federal seizures had increased twenty-fold in the previous four years). A new law of "civil" fines enacted by Congress allowed penalties of ten thousand dollars to be imposed by the attorney general, reviewable by a judge but only at the expense of the defendant. Ninety-five percent of the value of those seizures went directly into the treasure chests of law-enforcement organizations, turning forfeiture money into a bonanza for police and raising the incentive to pursue drug cases and take them federal. That made the drug war more profitable than ever, turning it into "the goose that laid the golden egg," as one North Carolina law-enforcement official put it, transforming police departments into bounty hunters whose discretionary budgets had become as dependent on the drug war as any addict was on a drug supply. Drug offenders and their families were liable to be thrown out of public housing; first-time offenders for possession could lose all benefits, contracts, student loans, mortgages, and licenses. In only a few years, America had become a place where it was perfectly legal to seize a person's car if a single marijuana seed was found in the ashtray.

With the election of George Bush and the appointment of William Bennett as head of the Office of National Drug Control Policy in 1989, the war on drugs would reach an ideological zenith. Harry Anslinger must have been smiling in his grave on the day Bennett took office as drug czar, calling for a massive wave of arrests in the nation's capital. As an archconservative ideologue, Bennett had become the bane of the "liberal elite," but as a drug czar he had the makings of a real Torquemada. Pugnacious, uncompromising, hectoring, holier than thou—he was "Pat Buchanan with a Harvard degree," as one moderate Republican called him. Of course, that's just the way Bennett liked it. Having grown up as a bookish Catholic boy in Flatbush, he had seemed on his way to becoming just another typical college kid swept up in the Sixties. He played in a band called Plato and the Guardians, briefly toyed with the idea of joining SDS, and once even had a date with Janis Joplin, when he was studying philosophy at the University of Texas ("we just drank a couple of beers"). By the time he went to Harvard Law School, however, Bennett was thoroughly disgusted by the Left Wing, the counterculture, and everything he thought they represented: promiscuity run amok, unbridled pornography, the condemnation of America implicit in the antiwar movement, and especially the drugs.

As drug czar, Bennett would advocate the same fundamentalist conservative philosophy of personal responsibility that he had promoted as secretary of education: enough of the tired liberal pablum of multiculturalism; enough of moral relativism; no more blaming drugs on chronic problems of the social environment like poverty or racism. The drug problem, as he saw it, was always one of "character" and "morality" and "values." Before, the government had tried to persuade people not to do drugs because they were bad for *you;* under Bennett, the policy would reflect his belief that the immorality of drugs stemmed from their illegality itself: "The simple fact is that drug use is wrong. And the moral argument, in the end, is the most compelling." Drugs were inherently *bad,* and so were the people who did them; American society therefore needed to stigmatize all drug users; anyone who did them deserved everything they got. Bennett's *National Drug Control Strategy* would include a budget that more than doubled drug-enforcement spending and increased spending for new federal prisons by 130 percent, but the most significant thrust of the program was "user accountability."

As a first step, Bennett would turn up the heat on crack users in the inner cities, but it was the "casual" white users that he really wanted to go after: those middle-class and professional folks who paid taxes, maintained careers, took care of families, but thumbed their nose at authority by their use of drugs. These were the real villains to him because they sent the worst message possible: that it was possible to use drugs and still be a decent citizen. "And he is thus much more willing and able to proselytize his drug use—by action or example—among his remaining non-user peers, friends, and acquaintances. A non-addict's drug use, in other words, is *highly* contagious." In effect, Bennett wanted to target the very same crowd he had come to abhor at Harvard. For the first-time or occasional recreational users, he wanted to suspend their driver's licenses, take their cars, hold them in detention, notify their employers, and publish their names in newspapers. And if he could not enact those new forms of pillory for drug users, he was at least going to make them pee in a cup. By 1990, he would turn drug testing into a three-hundred-million-dollar industry.

Bennett's approach quickly provoked the outrage of some liberals, like Lewis H. Lapham. In a *Harper's Magazine* article called "Political Opiate—The War on Drugs Is a Folly and a Menace," Lapham characterized Bennett's proposals as an attempt to impose "de facto martial law on citizenry it chooses to imagine as a dangerous rabble." His criticism of the new drug czar would typify the alarm of an entire segment of American society that would now feel itself under siege: "Bennett's voice is the voice of an intolerant scold, narrow and shrill and mean-spirited, the voice of a man afraid of liberty and mistrustful of freedom. He believes that it is the government's duty to impose on people a puritanical code of behavior best exemplified by the discipline in place at an unheated boarding school."

On September 5, 1989, George Bush, in his first televised address to the nation from the Oval Office, called the drug crisis the "moral equivalent of war" and the "gravest threat to our national well-being."

"This—this is crack cocaine," said Bush, dramatically holding up a plastic bag filled with white rocks that was marked EVIDENCE, "seized a few days ago by Drug Enforcement agents in a park just across the street from the White House. It could easily have been heroin or PCP."

Crack babies, hypodermic needles in playground sandboxes, and drug dealers so brazen as to sell crack right across the street from the residence of the president of the United States—given the severity of the crisis, any use of law enforcement to get "much tougher than we are now" was surely warranted: the death penalty for drug kingpins, "appropriate" use of the armed forces to stop drug smugglers.

Seventeen days later, when *The Washington Post* broke the story that the DEA had lured an eighteen-year-old dealer named Keith Jackson from his neighborhood to Lafayette Park to set up the buy for the crack Bush had displayed, the revelation that the president had obtained his sample by entrapment provoked remarkably little indignation. Jackson hadn't even known where the park was and had to be given written instructions to get there, but hardly anyone seemed to care. Bush's speech was a watershed moment; opinion polls indeed showed that a large majority of the public saw the "drug crisis" as the greatest threat facing America. It isn't hard to understand why so many people now viewed the drug crisis as far more severe than a soaring national deficit and an economy reeling from the loss of jobs, decaying public infrastructures, the problems of inner cities, hunger, poverty, AIDS, the depletion of the ozone layer, guns in the hands of schoolchildren, racism, political gridlock, the possibilities of terrorism, nuclear accident, or war. In six weeks alone, between August 1 and September 13, there were 347 reports about crack and cocaine produced by *The New York Times, The Washington Post,* and the three major networks. In one *ABC News* piece about crack, Peter Jennings told his audience, "Using it even once can make a person crave cocaine for as long as they live."

In fact, in July of 1989, NIDA was actually reporting significant reductions in drug use since 1985 in every category except those who used cocaine on a daily basis. The fact that whatever "drug crisis" existed was abating before William Bennett even took office went unnoticed; it was the increasingly shrill voices of the drug warriors that were heard on television and in the halls of Congress. Senator Phil Gramm and Congressman Newt Gingrich wanted to round up masses of drug users, herd them onto military bases that would be converted into prisons, and make them pay the court costs. Not to be outdone, Congressman Richard Ray, a Georgia Democrat, proposed the Pacific islands of Wake and Midway for the same purpose. Police Chief Daryl Gates of Los Angeles declared that casual drug users should be "taken out and shot" because they were guilty of "treason." The Delaware State Legislature debated bringing back the whipping post for drug users, a punishment that may very well have been too mild for William Bennett, who at the time told Larry King that the beheading of drug dealers was "morally plausible."

Those who had the audacity to point out that the goal of "drug-free" America was a fantasy—indeed, that the millions of arrests, the billions of dollars spent, and the transformation of the country into a place where citizens were encouraged to inform on one another was far more destructive than helpful—now faced a dauntingly vindictive national atmosphere.

## III.  Ethnography and Other Heresies

WHEN ETHAN NADELMANN started smoking pot as an eighteen-year-old freshman at McGill University, he quickly realized the kind of trouble he could get into if ever he was caught with it at the border. But his sense that there was something fundamentally wrong with the drug laws truly began to resonate when he read John Stuart Mill's *On Liberty* the following year. The great libertarian thinker believed that the only justifiable reason for restricting human liberty was to prevent harm to others. When applied to drug use, this concept would form the very philosophical underpinnings of the harm reduction movement. As Nadelmann expressed it, "There has to be something wrong with a law that says that what you do in the privacy of your own home, by yourself or with friends or loved ones—that the cops have a right to arrest you irrespective of whatever harm you've done to anybody else."

As the son of a prominent Reconstructionist rabbi in Scarsdale, Nadelmann considered himself to be a moral person. The graphic lessons of Jewish history had taught him that the darkest and most dangerous times for Jews were when the majority had felt the need to impose its morality and religion on them. Nadelmann was struck by the argument made by Thomas Szasz in *Ceremonial Chemistry* that there was a logical continuum between the persecution of witches and that of Jews and homosexuals and drug users. He also believed that the drug issue provoked the same kind of hysteria during the 1980s that the fear of Communism had unleashed in the America of the 1950s.

"What you had with McCarthyism was a legitimate threat from abroad, from the Soviet Union and world Communism. Yes, there *were* domestic spies and Communist infiltration, but there weren't Communists under every bed and around every corner, and yet some leaders could persuade America, for all sorts of reasons, that they had everything to fear, and that all sorts of persecutions were justified by it. It's the same thing with drugs. There *are* drugs and drugs *are* a problem, but it's not the world's biggest problem. We have a problem with drug addiction, but we're not the most addicted country, and we don't have the worst drug-abuse problems, and yet people can be persuaded that this is the worst thing that's ever happened to America. Why is that happening?"

It was similar to the fear of homosexuals. Nadelmann noted how people's view of homosexuals could often change when they came to know them. "An incredible amount of Americans have known drug users, but they don't *know* they are drug users, right? In this country, you have sixty to seventy million people who have used illicit drugs, twenty-five million who have used cocaine, five to ten million who have used hallucinogens; these people are known and respected by tens of millions of other Americans if not a hundred million, and yet they don't know it.

There's tremendous fear based on ignorance. If you were to run a yes-or-no fact test that had questions like, Is marijuana the least toxic substance known in human history? Is it less toxic than aspirin? What are the consequences of pure heroin on the human body? What is the addiction rate to cocaine among the middle class? You would get ninety percent wrong by the majority of Americans. It's stunning."

The reasons for such misapprehension about drugs on the part of so many Americans were obvious to Nadelmann.

"Drugs are infinitely interesting and infinitely complex—they tap into everything: history, sociology, anthropology, politics, the arts, humanities, chemistry, biology, medicine. So they're not easy to understand to begin with, but there's also another reason why accurate information is not put forth and marketed: it's clear that it doesn't sell newspapers. Then, you take these substances that are strange and alter people's states of consciousness, and nothing scares people more than the notion of people's minds being altered, especially if they're your children! That's the scariest thing in the world—that your children are doing it. Also, drugs have always been associated with ethnic minorities and with people being out of control."

Nadelmann had initially chosen Middle East politics as his field of study at Harvard, before he became interested in U.S. international drug control policy. It was 1983, and Reagan's drug war was just getting under way. Nadelmann got a security clearance and worked as a consultant to the State Department's Bureau of International Narcotics and Law Enforcement Affairs, and wrote the first classified report on U.S. anti–money-laundering efforts. He traveled to nineteen countries, interviewed hundreds of DEA and foreign drug-enforcement agents, customs agents, the CIA, and prosecutors to find out how the United States was enforcing the drug laws overseas. He found himself in secret-police headquarters observing the interrogations of prisoners (in Santiago, Chile, several traffickers under DEA surveillance were taken to police headquarters and tortured, though Nadelmann was not in the room when that occurred). With the publication of his doctoral dissertation, *Cops Across Borders: The Internationalization of U.S. Criminal Law Enforcement,* he turned his attention to the issue of the harms created by drug prohibition. "Nobody was doing this when I got into it—nothing policy oriented."

Nadelmann's approach had been shaped by several key people, among them Dr. Andrew Weil. "His influence on a lot of academics like myself has been profound because in his writing, there have been key insights into the nature of the drug experience."

Weil's study of drugs was both far-reaching and wide-ranging. As a Harvard undergrad fascinated by psychedelics, he had covered the Leary-Alpert controversy for *The Harvard Crimson* and wrote the exposé for *Look* that led to their dismissal. After receiving his degree from Harvard Medical School, he helped initiate the first serious objective study of the effects of marijuana since the La Guardia Commission Report of 1944, then moved to San Francisco in 1968 and interned at a hospital that observed and treated users and addicts. His growing interest led him up the Amazon River to explore the uses of psychedelic substances by native cultures. In 1972, he published *The Natural Mind: A New Way of Looking at Drugs and the Higher Consciousness,* one of the signature works on the uses of drugs and the issues surrounding them. It was his year spent with the National Institute of Mental Health, however, that convinced him beyond any doubt that all conventional policies and ways of looking at drugs were disastrous and had to be abandoned.

"It is my belief that the desire to alter consciousness periodically is an innate, normal drive analogous to hunger or the sexual drive," Weil wrote. He asserted that the use of drugs "is nothing more than a logical continuation of a developmental sequence going back to early childhood. It cannot be isolated as a unique phenomenon of adolescence, of contemporary America, of cities, or of any particular social or economic class." Weil concluded, "Drugs are here to stay. Fight them and they will grow ever more destructive. Accept them and they can be turned into nonharmful, even beneficial forces." The best way to accomplish this goal, he believed, was to give kids straight and reliable information about drugs and their use, the more honest the better. Everything about this stance was anathema, of course, to the very concepts of prohibition, the drug war, and a "drug-free" America. In 1983, when Weil published such a compendium of information, called *Chocolate to Morphine: Understanding Mind-Active Drugs,* Senator Paula Hawkins, Republican of Florida, denounced it.

The seminal figure of this tradition of nonconforming academics and the first prominent scholar to challenge American thinking on drug policy was Alfred E. Lindesmith, a sociologist at the University of Indiana whose books on heroin addiction in America—*Opiate Addiction* (1947) and *The Addict and the Law*—refuted virtually everything that the Federal Bureau of Narcotics had been saying about the subject for decades. Lindy, as he was called, had been a student of Bingham Dai at the University of Chicago. Dai was a central figure in what became known as the Chicago school of social research. In 1937, Dai published the first drug ethnography in American history, *Opium Addiction in Chicago*—the first time a sociologist had ever actually asked drug users what their lives were really like instead of just going to the narcotics police or, worse, the media.

The very idea of applying ethnography—the study of a population from the perspective of its members, as Margaret Mead had so famously done in *Coming of Age in Samoa*—to drug users rather than blindly accepting the line of the Federal Bureau of Narcotics, was tantamont to subversion. It was an approach that would lead other sociologists, like Everett Hughes and Charles Winick, to study "careers" and "lifestyles" of drug users (occupational ethnography), studies which, in turn, would produce all sorts of heretical revelations about drug addicts, such as how many of them seemed to "mature out" of drugs as they entered their forties. This idea alone was a direct negation of such accepted notions as "once an addict always an addict," and that the only way an addict could ever stop using drugs was through some form of forced abstinence. In "On Becoming a Marijuana User," a single chapter of his 1963 book, *Outsiders,* Howard S. Becker shattered every single claim that Harry Anslinger had ever made during the 1930s about marijuana causing violence, insanity, crime, and death. Small wonder that Anslinger, a notoriously autocratic bully, had tried to ruin Lindy and have him fired (unsuccessfully, as it turned out; it was Lindesmith's drug files, the most extensive anywhere in America, that Allen Ginsberg had studied for a whole summer in the professor's basement).

When objective techniques of ethnographic research were applied to drug-using populations, it was hard to avoid the conclusion that many of the government's statements about drugs seemed skewed, grossly oversimplified, and exaggerated, if not fabricated out of thin air—"the routinization of caricature," as Craig Reinarman would call it: "worst cases framed as typical cases, the episode rhetorically recrafted into the epidemic." Moreover, whatever material on drugs that the government disagreed with could be suppressed, at least in the sector of public education. A year into the Reagan administration, NIDA circulated a letter to school libraries stating that "all" of the government information about drugs put out in the late Seventies was false and should be removed from the shelves. From that point on, the ethnographers and liberal drug-policy experts would become more and more marginalized. By the time of Bush and Bennett, the government's portrayal of the experience of illicit drugs in America was so far removed from the truths and patterns as observed by the sociologists studying them in the lives of users that it seemed like a radically different universe—a disconnect of reality itself. Undoubtedly the most daunting challenge facing the would-be critics of the drug war was the disturbing evidence that this disconnect of reality had become so great that the very facts themselves no longer seemed to matter.

When George Bush held up that bag of crack to the television camera and told America that it was purchased "in a park right across the street from the White House," the fact that the whole thing had been completely manipulated was, to the drug warriors, entirely beside the point: crack was bad, out of control, and drastic measures were needed. The nation, after all, was at *war,* and in times of war truth is often "the first casualty," along with the curtailment of rights.

To Ethan Nadelmann, the tactic represented the worst kind of prevarication. It was a clear-cut symbol of everything he felt was wrong with the war on drugs: policies founded on myths, fears, exaggeration, and lies.

## IV. Saying the Unsayable

THERE WAS NOTHING ORIGINAL about Ethan Nadelmann's ideas in 1987–88, but in the bellicose atmosphere of an escalating drug war, his cogently presented observations and proposals nevertheless seemed shockingly radical.

In "U.S. Drug Policy: A Bad Export," published in *Foreign Policy* in the spring of 1988, Nadelmann attempted to put the "drug crisis" in some rational perspective. At a time when drugs were being portrayed as the gravest threat facing the nation, his most effective point was by far the most obvious one: that in a society where the total cost of alcohol abuse was estimated at one hundred billion dollars annually and included 80,000 to 100,000 direct deaths a year as a result, *only 3,562 people* were known to have died in 1985 from all illegal drugs combined.

In 1987, the nation spent a whopping eight billion dollars on the drug war. But worse than the expenditure was the diversion of resources in terms of judges and prosecutors and law-enforcement agents. The policies accomplished little and clogged the courts and prisons with non-violent offenders arrested for possession. There was also ample proof that the vastly increased spending for interdiction had been woefully ineffective: the purity of cocaine had risen from 12 to 60 percent, smoking crack was just as widespread, and high-potency black-tar heroin from Mexico had appeared on the streets.

The "most unfortunate" victims, in Nadelmann's view, were the law-abiding citizens of the ghettos being terrorized by drug dealers who owed their very existence to the fact that drugs were illegal, but there were others. In New York City, intravenous drug users accounted for more than 50 percent of all deaths reported from the AIDS pandemic from 1981 to 1986, and the government had simply refused to acknowledge and accept that free needle-exchange programs would have formed an easy-to-implement, cheap, and highly effective bulwark against the spread of the disease. Marijuana was being denied for "legitimate" medical purposes, such as reducing the nausea of chemotherapy patients and palliating the "wasting syndrome" of AIDS victims.

Nadelmann took his arguments for legalization and harm reduction even further in "Drug Prohibition in the United States: Costs, Consequences, and Alternatives," published in *Science* in September of '89. "Between reduced government expenditures on enforcing drug laws and new tax revenue from legal drug production and sale, public treasuries would enjoy a net benefit of at least $10 billion per year and possibly much more; thus billions in new revenues would be available, and ideally targeted, for funding much-needed drug treatment programs as well as the types of social and educational programs that often prove most effective in creating incentives for children not to abuse drugs. The quality of urban life would rise significantly."

With repeal of the drug laws, Nadelmann predicted the fall of homicide rates and crime, devastating setbacks to organized crime, and ghetto residents turning their backs on criminal careers. "And the health and quality of life of many drug users and even drug abusers would improve significantly. Internationally, U.S. foreign policymakers would get on with more important and realistic objectives, and foreign governments would reclaim the authority that they have lost to the drug traffickers."

Nadelmann then trained his sights on the "cocaine epidemic": "Clearly, many tens of thousands of Americans have suffered severely from their abuse of cocaine and a tiny fraction have died. But there is overwhelming evidence that most users of cocaine do not get into trouble with the drug. So much of the media attention has focused on the relatively small percentage of cocaine users who become addicted that the popular perception of how most people use cocaine has been badly distorted." As the rise in heroin use during the Sixties leveled off "for reasons having little to do with law enforcement, so we can expect, if it has not already occurred, a leveling off of the number of people smoking crack."

Nadelmann would never endorse the blanket legalization of all drugs as an "all or nothing alternative to current policies"; on the contrary, he believed the shift should be gradual, "with ample opportunity to halt, reevaluate, and redirect drug policies that begin to prove too costly or counterproductive." State and local governments should take the initiative in implementing their own programs and policies. "The first steps are relatively risk free: legalization of marijuana, easier availability of illegal and strictly controlled drugs for the treatment of pain and other medical purposes, tougher tobacco and alcohol control policies, and broader and more available array of drug treatment programs."

There would always be the risk that legalization might lead to increased numbers of people who used or abused drugs, but even that was by no means a certainty, Nadelmann argued. Present policies had failed miserably, and the newly proposed ones only promised to be "more costly and more repressive." Worst of all was that you could no longer even evaluate the drug issue openly. "Unless we are willing to honestly evaluate all our options, including various legalization strategies, there is a good chance that we will never identify the best solutions for our drug problems." To begin this process, Nadelmann proposed something along the lines of the Wickersham Commission that President Herbert Hoover had appointed to evaluate the repeal of alcohol prohibition during the 1920s—"precisely the same sorts of efforts are required today."

Nadelmann's proposal for such a commission was sure to fall on deaf ears in the government, but within a matter of weeks after his article appeared, *The Economist* endorsed his views in an editorial. His article in *Science* would have even more impact. Word started getting around that George Shultz, Reagan's cautious and respected former secretary of state, was going to come out for legalization; the drug warriors couldn't believe it, but it was true. "Whoa, he's been out on the West Coast too long, hasn't he?" was the derisive comment of Bush's press secretary, Marlin Fitzwater. As Shultz explained to the *Los Angeles Times,* "We're not really going to get anywhere until we can take the criminality out of the drug business and the incentives for criminality out of it."

Social conservatives were flummoxed, but none more offended than William Bennett: "This may explain why we weren't putting as much pressure as we should have on some of those [drug-producing] nations," he observed caustically. On December 11, Bennett delivered a speech at Harvard targeted at the "legalizers," called "Drug Policy and the Intellectuals." These "whole cadres of social scientists, abetted by whole armies of social workers" were "stupid," Bennett charged, and the arguments they were advancing were "morally scandalous," "a series of superficial and even disingenuous ideas that more sober minds recognize as a recipe for a public policy disaster." After heaping scorn on these "academic cynics," Bennett invited them to "get with the program." The real enemies of the drug war were "timidity, petulance, false expectation," and its greatest foes were "surrender, despair and neglect."

On Wednesday, December 13, 1989, only days later, a surprising headline appeared in *The New York Times*: "Federal Judge Urges Legalization of Crack, Heroin and Other Drugs." Robert W. Sweet, a sixty-seven-year-old judge of the federal district court, had called the drug war "bankrupt." "If our society can learn to stop using butter, it should be able to cut down on cocaine," Sweet told the *Times*. "If it cannot, no prohibition can be effective." Then, in mid-April 1990, Kurt Schmoke, the new mayor of Baltimore, addressed the U.S. Conference of Mayors in Washington, D.C., and called drug prohibition a failure. Schmoke, a former chief prosecutor, was disturbed by what he observed happening in the courts and police force in his city, by the spread of the HIV virus among IV drug users and the ban on needle exchange. The few voices for legalization so far had come from a small cabal of mostly conservative intellectuals who supported the issue on libertarian principles, among them the economists Milton Friedman and Gary Becker, the criminologist Ernest van den Haag, and the author–editor–television commentator William F. Buckley. None of them had the impact of a black mayor of a major American city repudiating prohibition on C-SPAN at a defining moment in the drug war. By early June, there was a *Time* cover story, "Should Drugs Be Legal?"

Before long, the DEA would feel the need to create a pamphlet designed to advise agents on how to counter the arguments of the legalizers, and Congress would pass a resolution calling legalization an "unconscionable surrender" in the national crusade to make America a "drug-free" nation.

By 1990, William Bennett was claiming significant victories in the war on drugs: "We are starting to win," he told *Newsweek* in March. The legalization story would continue playing out in the media through the spring of '90—and then, as Nadelmann related, "people burn out on the drug issue. The sixty-five percent of Americans saying that drugs are the most serious issue facing the country, which breaks the record of all time in American opinion polls, goes down to ten percent within twelve months, which just shows in a way that it was essentially a media-political hype, because there was very little substantive change in anything during that time. That's what was so amazing."

Of course, the Gulf War had a lot to do with this change of focus, but the drug crisis seemed to be the kind of issue that could easily be switched to the back burner and kept on a slow simmer. At that point, both William Bennett and Ethan Nadelmann found themselves moving toward similar kinds of projects in the private sector. Bennett resigned as drug czar and, with Jack Kemp, formed the organization Empower America to pursue his conservative social and economic agenda. Nadelmann received a grant from Ray Smart and put together the Princeton Group. "Then one day out of the blue in the summer of '92, I got a call inviting me to lunch with George Soros. We hit it off, and at the end he said, 'Look, we basically agree on the core issues. Now I'm a very busy man, but I have substantial resources, and what I want to do is empower you to accomplish our common objectives.' I sort of laughed—and gave him a proposal."

"Substantial resources" in the case of the Hungarian-born Soros was a net worth estimated at the time at seven billion dollars. When Soros created the Open Society Institute, Nadelmann was invited to set up his own interdisciplinary center for drug policy, with a promise of having "full intellectual freedom." Nadelmann left Princeton, and on June 1, 1994, opened the Lindesmith Center in New York, named in honor of the maverick scholar who had once stood up to Harry Anslinger and the Federal Bureau of Narcotics.

## V. Inhale to the Chief

THE PRESIDENTIAL ELECTION of 1992 featured the drug issue in all of its cultural paradoxes, contradictions, hypocrisies, and sanctimonies.

Candidate Ross Perot favored the cordoning off of American inner cities and conducting house-to-house searches and, when apprised of Bill Clinton's economic plan, remarked with characteristic Texan folksiness, "Well, raising taxes now would be like giving cocaine to someone in a detox!"

Of course, William Jefferson Clinton admitted that he'd tried marijuana as a college student during the Sixties but "didn't inhale." Few comments in the history of American politics would provoke more conjecture, bewilderment, disbelief, derision, and censure. The comment would prove to be quintessentially Clintonian. If nothing else, you had to admire Clinton's sheer gall. If he *was* dissembling and really *had* inhaled the marijuana smoke, it was a brilliant parsing of the truth because it allowed him to walk down the middle road on a delicate issue, sending the message to Baby Boomers and the MTV Generation that on the one hand he was hip and one of them because he'd at least been inclined to try it; on the other, showing that he was responsible enough not to have actually inhaled the stuff. At the same time, Clinton was also making himself more palatable to swing-vote parents concerned about drugs and covering his ass against the attacks of those Right Wingers howling for his hide for being a draft dodger and a womanizer and anything else they could think of. And if it actually was true and Clinton *hadn't* inhaled—well, that gave rise to a whole other set of questions about him: how lame could this guy be, that he would actually try marijuana and *not inhale*? Of course there were those who would have preferred a much different kind of response. As comedian Dennis Miller so vividly expressed it on *The David Letterman Show,* "I need Bill Clinton to look America in the face, and say, 'Yeah, not only did I inhale, but I *drank the bong water*—now *what are you gonna do about it?!*' "

As for the Republicans, it was business as usual. Marilyn Quayle stood at the podium of the Republican National Convention on Family Values Night and proudly proclaimed, "I didn't rebel; I didn't smoke pot in the Sixties!"—a classic effort to paint the other side as the party of drug permissiveness, even though the Democrats had all but marched in lockstep with them in the war on drugs. Likewise, former president Reagan got off one of his best lines when he remarked, "When we see all that rhetorical smoke billowing out from the Democrats—well, in the words of their candidate, *don't inhale,*" provoking cheers from the delegates eager to portray Clinton and the Democrats as a bunch of irresponsible potheads who would no doubt lead the country to ruin. What Reagan very conveniently omitted, of course, was that his own daughter Patti Davis had not only managed to inhale very effectively for years but had used amphetamines addictively, dropped acid, snorted cocaine, and had even grown pot in the backyard of her Topanga Canyon home, according to her 1992 autobiography, *As I See It.* Davis also described what she viewed as her mother's "addiction" to prescription tranquilizers and surmised that Nancy Reagan's Just Say No antidrug campaign may have been a subconscious plea for help and a form of "denial." By no means was Reagan the first president ever to have a family member who had used illicit drugs; the use of these substances had also permeated the lives of various Kennedys, Fords, and Carters. In any case, the First Daughter's revelations provided scant consolation for millions of beleaguered pot smokers looking for any way at all to point out the hypocrisy of the antidrug zealots who wanted to throw people in jail for smoking marijuana while countenancing their own legal use of prescription drugs, alcohol, and tobacco. By this time, according to the FBI, there were more people arrested for violating marijuana laws than at any time in the nation's history: 535,000 arrests for possession, sale, or manufacture of marijuana in 1992 alone, with one out of every six inmates in the federal prison system incarcerated for a marijuana offense.

Whatever interest Clinton may have maintained during the first six months of his administration in tempering the drug war evaporated with the mauling he suffered at the hands of conservatives over the issues of gays in the military and health care. There seemed little public support for drug reform, and if nothing else Bill Clinton was a creature of the polls, especially after the Republicans took back control of the House in 1994. Clinton would eventually propose that teenagers pass a drug test in order to get a driver's license. Meanwhile, the drug war dragged on, with ever-increasing budgets for the DEA and new prisons, "three strikes and you're out" life sentencing, and new intensive rounds of the Campaign Against Marijuana Production in northern California. When Surgeon General Joycelyn Elders gave a speech to the National Press Club in 1993 and admitted that "I do feel that we would markedly reduce our crime rate if drugs were legalized," acknowledging that "we don't know all the ramifications of this" and suggesting "some studies," conservatives screamed for her head, and Clinton wasted no time repudiating her through his press secretary. Elders wouldn't be around for very long; she resigned after another ill-advised and culturally "radical" remark, this time about how "masturbation is normal." As it turned out, Elders would soon enough gain firsthand knowledge of just how severe the sentencing laws had become, when her son found himself facing ten years without parole for possession of two grams of cocaine.

General Barry McCaffrey, on the other hand, was a shrewd choice for drug czar—a decorated soldier who seemed willing to moderate the harsh rhetoric of the drug war but not the policies themselves and therefore could get away with orchestrating the single major change in drug policy during the Clinton years: a measurable shift in support for treatment over incarceration for nonviolent drug offenders. The bulk of the government's drug-fighting budget, which would jump to $20 billion by 2001 from $13.5 billion in 1996, would go to interdiction and enforcement, but financing for treatment and prevention programs would increase by 55 percent. But treating addicts surely did not mean further liberalization of drug policy. Under McCaffrey, the White House would reject all recommendations by the U.S. Sentencing Commission for the equalization of penalties for crack and powder cocaine. After belatedly agreeing to support needle exchange, Health and Human Services Secretary Donna Shalala dropped federal funding support for the programs after the conservative Family Research Council persuaded McCaffrey that it was "sending the wrong message"—despite the fact that the president's AIDS Advisory Commission recommended the initiative. Most disappointing of all was the administration's stubborn refusal to support any of the public initiatives for medical marijuana. Not only was this the single issue for drug reform that actually showed public support, but that support was growing. By the mid-1990s, medical marijuana was becoming an issue with so much traction that it looked as if it might turn out to be the one stone that the David of the drug policy reform movement might actually be able to sling at the Goliath of the drug war.

## VI. Woe to the World If They Succeed

UNLIKE SO MANY OTHERS in the gay community of San Francisco, Dennis Peron had no interest at all in cocaine during the 1980s. The few times he did the drug, his reaction was as follows: "This stuff is doing nothing but shriveling my dick and making me paranoid!"

Marijuana and magic mushrooms were another story. During the Eighties, said Peron, "I lived my dream of being an architect and remodeling houses. I also sold pot; I'm adored by a lot of people in this city who smoke pot, so it wasn't really hard to crank it up again." His life was relatively quiet compared to the days of the Big Top and Harvey Milk, but when the police broke down his door at midnight on January 27, 1990—

"on a tip that I was selling marijuana"—everything changed. When Peron was charged with possession of marijuana for sale, it was the behavior of the drug-warrior cops that galvanized him into action. "They found this picture of me and Harvey Milk hugging, and one of the narcs that had been the bodyguard of George Moscone said how much he hated him—twelve years later! And I'm thinking, what is this?"

Peron's best friend, Jonathan West, was downstairs at the time, dying of AIDS. "He was using the marijuana as his medicine. He was eighty-seven pounds, and they took him out of his room and threw him on the floor. Those cops would have made the Nazis blush." West got up on the stand, covered in lesions, and testified that the marijuana had been his; Peron was let off, and West died shortly thereafter. "It was in his memory that we collected signatures to put marijuana as medicine on the ballot."

It wouldn't take long for Peron to spark a movement in California that would bring the medical-marijuana issue directly into the political vocabulary of America. As Proposition P, the Medical Marijuana Initiative stated, "Licensed physicians shall not be penalized for or restricted from prescribing hemp preparations for medical purposes to any patient." Peron's initial campaign vehicle was quite ingenious: a sweet little gray-haired seventy-year-old woman named "Brownie Mary" Rathbun, who'd come to California to "chase men" and had worked as a waitress for fifty years, smoking pot the whole time. Brownie Mary, who looked like a kindly grandmother, had baked her legendary brownies for profit at first, running a business out of her house until she was first busted, in 1981; her customers had been largely gay, and when the AIDS epidemic slammed into the city, she began giving the brownies to her "kids." Nothing seemed to help the wasting syndrome more than the ingestion of marijuana, and the same seemed to be the case for cancer patients. Half a brownie before chemotherapy, she found, and "within an hour he'll be eating a huge lunch instead of being consumed with nausea." People began donating marijuana to her, and for the next nine years she baked thirty-five or forty dozen brownies every three or four months and distributed them free of charge to thousands of people suffering from the diseases. She also believed that marijuana was legitimate medicine for stress and scores of other ailments.

On July 21, 1992, Mary Rathbun was busted at a friend's home in

Sonoma. Gene Tunney, the Sonoma County DA, determined that Brownie Mary would be treated like any other marijuana dealer, but it was soon clear that this was no ordinary case, especially after Peron became her adviser. For one thing, she was facing five years in prison but refused to make a deal. "I'm going to push them to a jury trial, and I'm going to be vindicated by the State of California. . . . I'm that adamant. I know it sounds stupid and arrogant, but I will be damned if I'll give in to their bullshit." Before long, she was on *Good Morning America* saying that the federal government should be paying her to make the brownies. The San Francisco supervisors designated August 25 Brownie Mary Day and called her San Francisco's Mother Teresa; the more publicity she received, the more the DA's office started wishing the case would just go away. "They can't drop the charges without saying I haven't done anything wrong. And if they do that, I'm going to ask for my marijuana back." Peron's strategy was simple but effective: collect signatures, get the issue on the ballot, spend money where it would do the most good, carefully pick your places to make a stand, and publicize as much as possible. "We want to let them know that this is going to cost them tons of money. No more deals, jury trials for everybody, and we're going to let the chips fall where they may."

The thirteen "cannabis clubs" that cropped up in California in the name of "compassionate use" were created as a Gandhian form of civil disobedience that would inevitably set in motion a confrontation with the federal government. The initial idea was to offer six "marijuana sprouts" to those who could document medical need and let them grow their own medicine. The battle lines began forming in 1996 with Proposition 215, the Compassionate Use Act. Although Peron and other activists in California had drafted the initiative, it was Ethan Nadelmann who recruited a political professional, Bill Zimmerman, to manage the effort and put together the key funding, which included Soros's money. The resounding victory that followed was "a real eye opener" for Nadelmann.

"It transformed the image of the marijuana smoker. Before the medical-marijuana issue emerged in a major way, inevitably the image of a kid in a tie-dyed T-shirt with long hair smoking a joint was every parent's worst nightmare. After Prop 215, the image became somebody dealing with AIDS and wasting syndrome smoking it as medicine. Also, when the government claimed that it was sending the wrong message, that claim became almost ludicrous on its face. I think Prop 215 showed that we had emerged as real political players. We won one in the real world of American politics. And then we won it again and again—"

Since 1996 eight states in addition to California—Alaska, Arizona, Colorado, Maine, Nevada, Oregon, Hawaii, Maryland, as well as Washington, D.C.—enacted their own laws allowing marijuana reform in some instances, but the federal government only dug in its heels. When the initiative passed in Arizona, General McCaffrey's comment was that the voters in that state "must have been asleep at the switch"; he warned that doctors who prescribed marijuana could be disqualified from federal health programs, have their prescribing privileges revoked, and even face federal prosecution. When the initiative was put on the ballot in Washington, D.C., Representative Bob Barr, Republican of Georgia, passed a resolution denying federal funds even to have the votes counted. But the support of the public seemed only to grow. As Nadelmann pointed out, "The federal government has been so obstinate, so underhanded and venal in the way it has handled this issue that I think there's been a little bit of backlash against that."

When the U.S. Court of Appeals for the Ninth Circuit ruled that the Oakland Cannabis Buyers' Cooperative could raise a medical-necessity defense against the federal government's attempt to shut it down and prevent it from distributing marijuana to those with doctors' prescriptions, the issue made its way to the Supreme Court. The club in Oakland, impeccably run by Jeff Jones, had been set up with the blessing of the city government and the police department. Completely ignoring the position of the California Medical Association, the court ruled eight to zero with Justice Clarence Thomas arguing that the federal court had "misread" federal law in its ruling. Thomas affirmed in effect that Congress could put any drug it wants into schedule one, irrespective of scientific or medical evidence. The decision was a political one; while it may have dealt a setback to the movement, it could not, however, challenge the validity of the initiative, only the federal court's response to the government's request for an injunction. The fight would rage on.

As Nadelmann understood it, there was now a large majority of reasonable citizens who believed in people's access to "proper medicine," but the drug warriors fully grasped that "Americans are nervous about distribution, about control. . . . People don't like the words *legalize* or even *decriminalize* marijuana. What they like are the words *tax, control, regulate,* and *educate.*" Whether or not the success of the initiatives might translate into any broader consensus for decriminalization remained to be seen. "Part of the initiative's value is that it's one of the ways in which a majority of Americans can see the ways in which the drug war has gone too far. . . . Notice how McCaffrey was never willing to go out in public and debate a doctor face-to-face, nor were any of those other people. Against their demonization campaign, it's our humanization campaign."

The success of the initiatives alerted the DEA to the potential inroads being made among the electorate by those seeking to make a case for drug-law reform. The advancement of the reform agenda also aroused the sleeping giant of the parents' movement, which had long held that the direct support of Ronald and Nancy Reagan and the Just Say No campaign for groups like National Families in Action (NFIA), National Parents' Resource Institute for Drug Education (PRIDE), and the National Family Partnership (NFP) had led to a 50 percent drop in illicit drug use, as documented by the Substance Abuse and Mental Health Services Act (SAMHSA). Compared with the rampant permissiveness of the late 1970s, when SAMHSA's National Household Survey and the Monitoring the Future Survey reported that 10.7 percent of high-school seniors were using marijuana daily, the parents' movement believed that what it had accomplished was nothing short of a reversal of Armageddon. The coalition had expanded over the years to include groups like Drug Awareness Resistance Education (DARE), Partnership for a Drug-Free America, and the Drug Free America Foundation, Inc. The parents' groups weren't about to stand idly by and see the initiative in the debate over drug policy pass to the reformers.

A report by the Miami Field Division of the DEA, published as a booklet in December of 1998, typified the gathering counterattack. The "loosely worded" Proposition 215, it claimed, "does not make provisions for protecting children or consumers. There is no mention of age limits of users, potency or content of marijuana, nor does it require Food and Drug Administration (FDA) approval of the so-called medicine, which would then require a registered physician's prescription." The cannabis clubs were dispensing marijuana "for illnesses such as foot pain, headaches, and premenstrual syndrome, with 'caregiver's' recommendations written on such items as notepads and napkins."

Moreover, it was a scientifically proven "fact" that marijuana was *bad* for AIDS patients. The DEA cited a report by Janet Dundee Lapey, MD, of Drug Watch International, stating that marijuana contained over four hundred chemicals and pollutants (hydrogen cyanide, ammonia, carbon monoxide, acetone) and carcinogens (benzopyrene, benzanthracene, and benzene), had four times the amount of carbon and tar as tobacco smoke, increased fungal and bacterial pneumonias (which suppressed the immune system and could hardly be beneficial to AIDS patients), and inflamed the lungs and surrounding areas, causing acute and chronic bronchitis and airway injury. It also impaired the ability of white blood cells to kill bacteria and tumor cells and raised the heartbeat and blood pressure among the elderly. "Many users suffer from hallucinations, memory impairment, paranoia, depression and panic attacks and withdrawal symptoms."

Such claims about the health risks of marijuana, combined with the perennial charge that today's marijuana was so much more potent than the weed of decades ago and the permanent conviction that it was a gateway to more dangerous drugs, formed the basis of the prohibitionists' offensive. As much as the drug warriors targeted cocaine, crack, heroin, underground amphetamine, or the psychedelics, the national crusade against marijuana remained the DEA's *casus belli*—the leading justification for drug testing in the workplace, the target of antidrug efforts in the schools and the media, and the main focus of drug warriors in and out of government.

In this ongoing war waged against the substance in the name of science and health, every claim would produce a counterclaim, but this battle of the scientists was a losing game for the reformers because the burden always fell on them to disprove the government's findings. Whether it was the debate about potency or how marijuana purportedly causes breast enlargement or lowered testosterone levels in adolescent males, the government was the side funding the studies and publicizing the latest findings. "Right now if you're the head of a department of medicine at some major university, you've got to be very careful about what you're going to say about drug policy because if it's perceived as too radical, you're not going to get tenure, and you may even find yourself not wanted at that university," Keith Stroup commented; "the battle of the experts has caused science to become a tool for people with nothing but a political agenda." Because of this chilling effect, it was usually left to a few renegade academics like Dr. John P. Morgan to point out that the research had consisted of rhesus monkeys with electrodes in their heads being given giant doses of THC, and that to insist that the studies had not been definitely proved was the worst kind of sham science. With the issue of medical marijuana, the claims that the substance's damaging effects on the immune system far outweighed any possible benefits of increased appetite in AIDS patients became still another widely circulated argument of the prohibitionist canon.

"Regardless of how it is couched, what Soros and friends want to do is legalize drugs for personal use," stated Wayne Roques of Drug Watch International, pointing to the "seasoned out of state signature gatherers" who were used to carry petitions and how the campaigns targeted college campuses and the elderly, duplicitously packaging their initiatives as "compassion" and "medical necessity." "Disingenuous ads were used to convince the public that marijuana, a drug that destroys families, wreaks havoc on the immune system, impairs memory and motor skills, causes premature deaths of sperm cells, is associated with head and neck cancer in young users, and through pre-natal use can lead to a tenfold increase in childhood leukemia, should be made legal for anyone with a physical ailment, validates the axiom that whoever controls the media controls the mind of the public." The initiatives were about the personal right to use psychoactive and addictive substances. "That, not compassion for the sick, is what this is all about. Woe to the world if they succeed."

To make certain the "legalizers" would not succeed in duping Americans into accepting marijuana as legitimate medicine, the Drug Free America Foundation sponsored a two-day conference, on May 3–4, 2000, in Lansing, Michigan, called "Training the Trainer: Putting the Brakes on the Drug Legalization Movement." With a medical-marijuana initiative looming in the state, the focus was on "the drug problems that threaten the health and safety of our communities: the deception of 'harm reduction,' school education programs encouraging drug experimentation, needle giveaways and heroin maintenance programs promoting addiction, the medical excuse marijuana scam, and more."

For a fee of one hundred dollars, the conference attendees heard Dr. David Gross of the International Scientific and Medical Forum of Drug Abuse refute the efficacy of marijuana as medicine, and Jack Hook, chief of the Demand Reduction Section of the DEA, state unequivocally that one joint was the carcinogenic equivalent of fifteen to twenty cigarettes. "Remember, they don't use the *L* word," emphasized Calvina Fay, executive director of the Drug Free America Foundation, in her presentation called "Drug Legalization in the New Millennium," noting that "in the Sixties we fought hippies" but that "now they look and act mainstream." The legalizers were "brainwashing our children to think they can use safely" and "attacking an employer's right to maintain a drug-free workplace."

The conference ended with a strategy for "putting the brakes on": "Hold the Media Accountable" and "fight fire with fire"; "Fund Raise Fast and Furious" by "tying into" the business community and "playing on" business losses from drug use such as absenteeism, lower quality of work, and loss of productivity; "Establish a Strong Grassroots Organization" that includes the business and medical communities, as well as recovering addicts; and "Choose Your Campaign Spokesperson Carefully", who ideally should be a "medical person" and not a law-enforcement officer because "they'll use that against you."

George W. Bush may have campaigned as a "compassionate conservative," but it was clear from his appointment of John Walters, one of Bill Bennett's lieutenants, as drug czar, that his compassion did not extend to those seeking marijuana as medicine.

The Los Angeles Cannabis Resource Center, the leading club in southern California, was hit by the DEA only weeks after the events of September 11, 2001. The club was dissolved, and its directors were forced to plead guilty to federal felonies. This action was followed by raids on the Aiko Club of Santa Rosa, and on the Wo/Men's Alliance for Medical Marijuana in Santa Cruz, which led to the arrests of Valerie and

Mike Corral, who were growing marijuana plants for the Santa Cruz club. On September 17, 2002, Mayor Christopher Krohn of Santa Cruz and two of the city's former mayors gathered in front of City Hall to witness a marijuana giveaway as a protest. "We are not California whackos," the mayor told *The New York Times*. "We are trailblazers. We are normal. This is not an attempt to embarrass the DEA but rather a compassionate gathering in support of sick people who need their medicine." After their arrests, Valerie and Mike Corral were made deputies by a vote of the Santa Cruz City Council.

California Attorney General Bill Lockyer, a strong proponent of Proposition 215, sent a scathing letter to Attorney General John Ashcroft criticizing the "punitive raids." By that time, San Francisco was debating whether it would go into the marijuana-growing business in order to supply patients; Nevada was deciding whether to allow adults twenty-one and older to possess as much as three ounces of marijuana whether they were sick or not with no threat of criminal penalty; and Arizona, Ohio, and Michigan all had initiatives on the ballot that would reduce penalties for possession.


## VII.  One Big Child-Protection Act

IN THE WAKE of September 11, 2001, Ethan Nadelmann recognized that "there are going to be powerful reasons to reduce as much as possible the anonymity of people walking around in the U.S., and that's going to lead to the emergence of all sorts of surveillance systems that are going to transform this country in potentially historical ways, and not for the better. All in the hope that it will protect us a little more against terrorism, yet we know we can never be perfectly safe." He was also concerned about "this absurd war on drugs, which appeals to people's worst fears, where people are willing to go to any lengths. Take my freedoms! Search me! The expansion of prisons and drug testing. The total disconnect between the policies themselves and any connection with economic self-interest or public-health-driven concerns."

When Nadelmann considered the people in power—Bush, Attorney General Ashcroft, drug czar John Walters, Majority Leader Tom DeLay,

Antonin Scalia and Clarence Thomas on the Supreme Court—he saw that all three branches of government were being controlled by people who came from "the radical reactionary Right Wing who are not only more antagonistic to more liberal, progressive values but also to Right Wing libertarian values. I look at Scalia and I think that if this man were born in another age and time, he would be sitting on the Inquisition."

What made Nadelmann truly queasy was the growing sophistication of the new surveillance technologies. "Take the GPS devices that will make it possible to have a little device implanted in the skin or wired on the body to keep track of everybody . . . And then to find out what's going on with drug testing, where more and more it's not just going to be about drug testing; it might be implants—and not just passive ones to detect what drugs you've taken but active ones, so that if you take a drug, it will make you sick, like an Antabuse-type drug." Maybe they would give you a choice between going to prison or having the implant—"this sort of next step of the coerced drug-treatment model." When Nadelmann looked at the rational fears of the war on terrorism coming together with the irrational fears fueling the war on drugs, with "profoundly reactionary people" dominating significant parts of federal policy, all merging with the new surveillance capacities, it made him very uneasy. But he retained a sense of optimism.

"The intense pessimism that I feel, it's similar to periods of pessimism that my predecessors had in the 1950s. There have been other bleak periods in history that have led to their own counterreaction, and I think that there's a chance here that this, in turn, in ways that we can't quite predict, may lead to a new countermovement against where the government is headed today. It's starting to break down some of the barriers to left and right. It's already an interesting issue where some of our best allies in the drug-policy reform movement are some of the people on the libertarian right, like Governor Gary Johnson of New Mexico."

At the Shadow Convention, organized by Arianna Huffington during the national political conventions in 2000 as a forum to propose alternative approaches to major issues like the war on drugs, Nadelmann compared the state of the drug-reform movement to the gay rights movement during the 1960s, the civil rights movement during the 1940s, the women's rights movement in the 1890s, and the movement to abolish the slave trade in the first half of the nineteenth century. His point was clear enough: at those junctures, each movement had a significant distance to go in order to attain its goals, but had laid critical groundwork. In the previous eight years, Nadelmann had witnessed the emergence of a real drug-policy-reform movement in the United States. After a number of years spent developing the Lindesmith Center as "an activist think tank," he merged his organization with the Drug Policy Foundation in Washington, D.C., in July of 2000 to form the Drug Policy Alliance, with headquarters in New York and offices in Oakland, New Mexico, and Sacramento. The drug-reform movement was no longer "the second smallest political movement in America." As Craig Reinarman and Harry Levine wrote, "At the level of ideas, floodgates have been opened that moral fundamentalists and other prohibitionists will probably not be able to close again."

"People come to this from all levels," Nadelmann observed. "Some are concerned about issues of social justice and the racial discrimination of the war on drugs. Some are concerned about issues of public health policy; they're worried about HIV-AIDS or treatment. Other people are concerned about what we're doing in Latin America or concerned about the environment. And others come because for them it's really an issue of personal freedom and autonomy. At its core, and also in terms of the long-term vision, it boils down to the notion that people should not be punished for what they put into their bodies. Hold people responsible for their actions, but don't punish them for what they put into their bodies."

With its theme of "America's Failed War on Drugs," the Shadow Convention carefully laid out the movement's most up-to-date case for reform. That year, forty billion dollars in taxpayer money was spent trying to make America "drug free," and almost half a million people were locked up on drug charges, some serving fifteen years to life as first offenders, with people peripherally involved in nonviolent drug offenses routinely sentenced to harsher sentences than those involved in rapes and second-degree murder. Despite equal rates of drug use, black men were being sent to state prison at far greater rates than white men in some states. A marijuana smoker was being arrested every fifty-two seconds, yet after two decades of "zero tolerance," 90 percent of high-school seniors were reporting that marijuana was easier to buy than alcohol. If interdiction had been working at all, there would be fewer drugs with less purity at higher cost—in fact, the opposite had happened. After seventeen years of DARE, numerous scientific studies showed no difference in drug-usage rates between those with exposure to the most prevalent youth drug-prevention curriculum and those without. That year, more than half of the graduating class of high-school seniors nationwide had tried illicit drugs despite the drug war. Syringe sharing among intravenous drug users was associated with 250,000 HIV infections in the United States; 157 syringe-exchange programs in thirty-eight states had been initiated to deal with it, all started by individuals without the help of one federal dime.

Of all the speakers, it was Gary Johnson, the Republican governor of New Mexico, who created the most buzz. It was always big news when a Republican joined the cause. The Right Wing, with its base of sixty million Christian conservatives, seemed no more willing or able to relinquish its tight grasp on the reins of drug prohibition than liberals had wanted to abandon the welfare state. Most conservatives weren't the slightest bit interested in doing an analysis of whether the drug war was really working or not—all they cared about was that the policy was consistent with their ideology, just as doctrinaire liberals hadn't been interested in evaluating whether the policies of welfare were working. Both were willing to just keep throwing money at the problem—perhaps the ultimate form of political denial. Gary Johnson, on the other hand, was a pragmatic conservative Republican whose conversion was based on the kind of traditional cost-benefit analysis that he claimed any fiscal conservative would make. Ignoring all criticism, he had boldly undertaken a relentless campaign to liberalize drug-possession laws, make rehabilitation available rather than prison terms, allow pharmacies to provide syringes to addicts, and generally treat drug abuse as a public health issue rather than a criminal-justice matter.

To a large degree, Johnson's pragmatism was an example of something Ethan Nadelmann had been saying for a long time: that the drug-reform movement would never really get anywhere until conservatives, police, and parents began to see the efficacy of change—and in ways that were consistent with their own values and social vision. This transformation would require getting people to look honestly at the negative consequences of both drug use and prohibitionist policies. People would need to see that the violence, the crime, and the corruption were the results of prohibition and not the drugs themselves. The prohibitionists tended to view all problems regarding drugs in society as being about the drugs—what Craig Reinarman called "pharmacological determimism"—and if there was one thing that the academic reformers who had gathered around Nadelmann strongly believed, it was that when drugs entered society, they combusted with a complex set of social factors in a particular setting—the drug "set and setting" that had been codified by Norman Zinberg of Harvard in his book, *Drug, Set, and Setting: The Basis for Controlled Drug Use*. But it was going to be a long, slow, difficult process.

"Until the basic thinking of harm reduction and commonsense drug policy begins to be more mainstream," Nadelmann told a NORML audience, "until we get to a point where we start to evaluate the success or failure of drug policy based not upon the drug war criteria like how many people broke the drug laws last year but by harm reduction criteria like how many people were harmed by the drug war last year, until we shift that playing ground, we engage in a debate where we can be spoofed and parodied and where people edging their way toward us will be pushed away again."

Before that could happen, the reformers would to have to address the ideology of abstinence itself—"pharmacological Calvinism," as Dr. John P. Morgan liked to call it —and this was perhaps the biggest challenge of reform because it was so deeply embedded in the culture of the prohibitionists, with its long history of temperance. It was this ideology more than anything else that disinclined the drug warriors to accept the basic evidence of drug use in America as the reformers had both experienced and documented it—that "the vast majority of American illegal drug users do so responsibly," as Nadelmann emphasized. "The vast majority of marijuana smokers don't have any problems—you know that, I know that. Vast amounts of kids who use marijuana never go on to use hard drugs and never go on to have marijuana problems or become regular marijuana users."

The phrase that Nadelmann liked to use as the guiding principle for his vision of reform and harm reduction was the adoption of "mensch-like" policies. The demonizing of fellow citizens would clearly not be an example of a mensch-like policy. The basic components of the vision he promulgated were threefold: individual freedom, individual responsibility, and social responsibility based on some element of compassion.

"What you and I know is that telling the truth about drugs, that having a decent and compassionate drug policy, should not be based on ignorance and fear and prejudice and profit but upon common sense, science, public health, and human rights, plus a dose of compassion. That, ultimately, is the drug policy that's going to protect our kids and lead to a better world for our kids."

In the end, it was all about kids, and it was here that the issue was most laden with emotion and ideology—this was the true "third rail" of the drug-reform movement and something that the other side had always understood and played on. "People are scared about drugs; we all want to put our children in a bubble and are worried that somehow drugs will pierce that bubble. . . . In some respects, America's drug war is justified as one big child-protection act."

The drug policy reform movement continued to make significant progress on several fronts. In 2000, California passed Proposition 36, mandating one hundred and twenty million dollars annually to pay for providing treatment services for first- and second-time nonviolent drug possession offenders as an alternative to incarceration—a measure that passed by sixty-one percent of the vote despite opposition from the entire law-enforcement establishment and much of the political establishment. In addition, the California state PTA endorsed Marsha Rosenbaum's seventeen-page booklet, *Safety First: A Reality-Based Approach to Teens, Drugs and Drug Education,* which offered honest, science-based information meant to inform parents about drugs, rather than scare them. Following the lead of progressive sexual education, the Drug Policy Alliance launched the Safety First program to promote abstinence while focusing on safety and providing parents with the tools needed to evaluate and discuss strategies for realistically protecting their teens from drug abuse. It had taken twenty years since the parents' movement took control of the direction of public drug education with publications like Marsha Manatt's *Parents, Peers, and Pot* for a state PTA to sanction any harm reduction–based drug education strategies and distribute such a publication to all of its statewide chapters.

It was an important victory. As Ethan Nadelmann saw it, in the end it was a simple equation. "If we win the battle over kids and drugs, we win drug-policy reform."

# 15

## The Temple of Accumulated Error

**"** Every generation searches for an experience it can pass on to the next. **"**

> —Amy Wu, nineteen-year-old college student covering
> Woodstock '94 for *People* magazine

### I. By the Time I Got to Woodstock

EARLY ON THE MORNING of the first day, I came across a group of kids in the woods. One boy looked about eighteen and was bare chested with shoulder-length brown hair and a beaded headband, his face painted in colorful streaks like a Native American brave. As soon as he opened his eyes, I knew that he was tripping his brains out. We had startled him by walking up with the camera as he was lying peacefully on his back, no doubt watching the movie of his subconscious mind exploding behind his eyelids. *"Whoa, dude,"* was all he could say, his astonished blue eyes growing enormous, like two satellite dishes.

I gazed into those eyes. What was he seeing as he hurtled through time and space? Was he contemplating what Aldous Huxley had once called "the unfathomable mystery of pure being"? In *The Doors of Perception,* Huxley had written that the function of the brain was eliminative and not productive and that each person at every moment was capable of remembering "all that has ever happened to him and of perceiving everything that is happening everywhere in the universe." According to that theory, to take a psychedelic drug was like opening up the valve that normally kept this awareness to a manageable trickle and flooding one's being with a kind of superconsciousness. But Huxley had written *The Doors of Perception* in 1954, and this was exactly forty years later, August 12, 1994. It was the Age of Beavis and Butt-head. America was supposedly in the throes of an "acid flashback," and the media were full of tales of caution and horror about a new generation of kids taking LSD. Was it possible that this kid even knew Huxley's name?

I realized I was still gawking at him and felt embarrassed. He was obviously having a powerful psychedelic experience, and here I was stalking him with a sixteen-millimeter movie camera like he was some exotic species of wildlife, but still I couldn't stop staring. Then, in a breathless instant, I realized what it was—I saw myself in his face exactly as I was at eighteen and felt the weight of my years and the freedom of his youth and innocence—and for a moment, I had to struggle to keep myself together. All I could do was stand there, overcome with emotion, bantering inanely with him, and when I asked him if this was really Woodstock or just some poor facsimile, he and his friends just stared back at me.

"Of course this is *Woodstock*," a girl said, as if I had asked the most obvious question in the world. "This is *our* Woodstock!"

"Take care," I said, "be careful, have a great time," and moved off with my crew. By that time, the festival had built into the hundreds of thousands, and more were still pouring into Winston Farm, the 840-acre spread in Saugerties, New York, where the silver-anniversary celebration was being held. For someone who had grown up in the 1960s, it was an astonishing sight, as if some great ragtag guerrilla army had materialized from the mists of time and bivouacked overnight. Moving off the field, we went down a path, and the deeper we proceeded into the woods, the more it was like walking into some fantastical time warp. Naked kids sat about like fairies and elves, frolicking and romping and loping through the woods and campsites. I had to blink. I saw visions of be-ins and love-ins and festivals and tribal gatherings that had existed in a thousand different places and had then vanished like fading sunlight.

My job at the festival was to record everything I saw that I felt would be of any significance for a documentary feature of the event. "This film is really going to be a document of where the culture has come to in the last twenty five years," explained the two-time Academy Award–winning filmmaker Barbara Kopple before hiring me as a field producer.

With the sun setting over the green hills, the smell of the weed drifted across the meadow in a dense resinous cloud of skunk bud that seemed to turn the very air psychoactive, declaring in a single whiff that a whole new generation had embarked on its own maiden voyage through the landscape of illicit drugs. The familiar and potent bouquet was enough to stop me dead in my tracks. It was the fifth year of my sobriety—a long time since I had smelled that much pot. I quickly learned that there were two kinds of blotter acid going around in the massive crowd, each stamped with a different figure: Felix the Cat and Skeleton. My mind began overheating, conjecturing the possibilities of how these tiny pieces of paper soaked with lysergic acid diethylamide, concocted by some outlaw chemist in an underground lab who had managed to get his hands on some ergotamine tartrate, might engineer the collective and individual experience of what might transpire here. But as much as I may have understood and even empathized with the desire to take some acid, I experienced a powerful maelstrom of conflicting emotions about it, a deep ambivalence born of concern.

But concern for what? For the people taking the acid? For what the world had become in the past twenty-five years? For how it made me feel about myself, my own experiences, my own generation? If these kids had come here in search of some great mythos of the 1960s that they associated with the *idea* of Woodstock and what it represented (something that they could only have seen in a twenty-five-year-old movie or heard about from their parents), or if they had come looking to create their own thing, it really didn't matter. What was quite apparent was that the use of illicit drugs had been passed on to a whole new generation as a part of some kind of cultural search for identity and rite of passage. Society would be forced officially to condemn it as the transmission of some bad viral infection, but here it was, plain as day, and the real question was, Had we managed in the course of twenty-five years to *learn* anything about drugs beyond mere rhetoric and polemics? Was this new generation destined to make all the same mistakes with drugs that we had?

Heading up the backstage road toward the artists' compound, I ran into Wavy Gravy, who had stood in front of the first festival twenty-five years ago, smiling toothlessly as he uttered the immortal words, "There's a little bit of heaven in every disaster area . . . *We must be in heaven, man!*"

Now in his late fifties, Wavy looked like an aging, overweight leprechaun with his twinkling blue eyes and puckish smile. Over the years, he'd become a clown, a world-class environmentalist, and a Ben and Jerry's ice-cream flavor. He devoted himself fully to the Seva Foundation and ran Camp Winnarainbow, a performing-arts camp in northern California where homeless and refugee kids went on scholarships to experience what it was like to run away and join the circus. Wavy still served as the emcee of countless benefit shows. "Hello, I'm Wavy Gravy, activist clown, frozen dessert flavor, and *Temple of Accumulated Error*!" That last phrase bore witness to the considerable wisdom and folly and grace that had built up over the course of his very colorful life, a unique body of experience that was always being processed, evaluated, and reevaluated.

"Wavy, what's going to happen if these kids get too dosed on the acid?" I wondered. "Is there anything that can be done to help them?"

Back in 1969, of course, it was the Hog Farm that had helped set the spirit of the whole event and had taken on the responsibility of caring for the acid casualties at the festival.

"I guess the same thing we did in 1969," he said. "I start with the name . . . 'Okay, what's your name?' "

"Martin."

" 'Okay, that's very good. That's a good name that you've got there, Martin, and you obviously *remember* it, so you therefore know you must be here on *Planet Earth,* right?' That's a very good start! Now, once they know that, the next thing I say is, 'Hey, Martin, you've taken *a little pill* called LSD. And guess what? The good news is it's just a drug; it's going to wear off in a while, I promise you're going to come down, and if you're having a bad time, you can sit right here by my side, and I'll keep you company; I'll even hold you and keep you warm and try to make you laugh, and when you come down, the beautiful thing is, Martin, then *you* can help some other kid who might come in here with those Lost Hotels coming out of *his* eyes too, feeling exactly like you did' . . . That's the best way I know, and if that doesn't work—well, then, there's always the Thorazine!"

Just as Joe Cocker finished his set, it began to drizzle. By the time Henry Rollins hit the massive north stage, the rain was slashing down in torrents. Rollins refused to be daunted by the storm. Ripping off his shirt, he stood there, completely drenched, bulging pectorals and rippling arms festooned with tattoos. He shook his fist at the heavens and went after the crowd with a single-minded ferocity, throwing himself into his set like a deranged punk shaman. Responding to his call, large groups of kids began pushing down to the mosh pit at the front of the stage. They were covered in mud from head to toe, and many of them were tripping. All you could see were their eyes, the whites of their eyes. They looked feral, these Mud People, crazed, like the wigged-out natives at the end of *Apocalypse Now,* like a tribe of peyotized aboriginals observing their most sacred and primordial rite. The hundreds quickly became thousands, and the whole front of the stage erupted, bodies squirming and jackknifing and catapulting wildly through the air, being caught and passed over the heads of the crowd like offerings of human sacrifice. In the deepest sense, it was like watching the triggering of some great collective psychedelic orgasm, the ceremonial retrieval of the ecstatic but humbling knowledge buried deep in the cells that as much as man had succeeded in pulling himself out of the muck and mire of evolution over the millennia, as far as he had traveled to erect his great skyscrapers and satellite dishes, he was never really far away from the mud and could return at any time. The festival seemed to begin at that very moment. It was Woodstock for the Slacker Generation.

It continued to rain heavily off and on during Saturday night, and by Sunday morning, when Allen Ginsberg appeared in the artists' compound, Woodstock looked like the Russian front after the great spring thaw.

"Marijuana should be treated as just another part of life," Ginsberg pronounced when I asked him if his feelings about it had changed any in the bitter climate of the war on drugs. He was now sixty-eight, a thin, goateed, ascetic-looking figure whose face showed traces of Bells palsy but whose spirit radiated with gentle Buddhist illumination. "Everybody should try it at least one time. Marijuana can be a very useful educational tool. It's as much a natural part of life as getting laid, having a homosexual experience, or going to Europe!"

Such comments were Ginsberg trademarks, and he had now been making them for forty years.

"I'm astounded at how many kids are doing acid on the campuses of the Midwest," Ginsberg went on. "Of course, it's not on the same scale of the Sixties when LSD became a deconditioning agent for an entire generation of middle-class American kids. It's much quieter these days. People don't freak out as much now; there seems to be a lot more granny wisdom about doing it. The interesting place to look is in Eastern Europe, where acid and rock and roll and blue jeans have helped to overturn the Communist system, just like drugs during the Sixties liberated kids from the kind of narrow-minded mom-and-pop American chauvinism of the Vietnam War."

Marijuana was very much in vogue at the time of the festival, and not just on the college campuses but in the ghetto. Cypress Hill, one of three rap groups at the festival, was known for outspoken dope-tap songs like "Light Another," "Stoned Is the Way of the Walk," and "Something for the Blunted." To them, marijuana represented a benign counter to the use of drugs like crack and PCP, drugs that had decimated their Los Angeles neighborhoods. They performed with a big model of black fingers holding a giant joint, and to make his point, lead rapper B-Real fired up a blunt in front of the cameras and several hundred thousand people and announced, "I'm taking a hit for every one of y'all!" Later, in interviews, the group called for the legalization of marijuana, only they were careful to call it hemp. Marijuana, after all, was the name the Man had given the weed when he had banned it in 1937, but hemp was natural, the most industrially useful plant on earth. The hemp movement had made it to the ghetto; the cannabis leaf was now a part of hip-hop chic.

Just as there were the nouveau pothead and psychedelic bands, there were also the junkies, past and present. If you believed the media, the country was in danger of another heroin "epidemic." There was an unprecedented plethora of heroin around, from Afghanistan, Africa, South America, Mexico, and of course the good old Golden Triangle. It was cheaper and purer. Being smoked at chic parties. Skin-popped. Jacked into a new generation of veins. No matter that heroin couldn't possibly be making a "comeback" because it had never really gone away. No matter that the media and law- and drug-enforcement communities had been talking about a new heroin "epidemic" for the past quarter of a century, when in fact the number of heroin users had remained remarkably stable for all of that time. But the new generation already had its dead-junkie tragedies, its doomed and beautiful losers to romanticize, like River Phoenix and Kurt Cobain. The grunge-rock scene of Seattle had certainly proved fertile ground for heroin. Fashionably cadaverous and dissipated-looking models like Kate Moss were appearing on billboards, testifying to the strange appeal of a style being labeled the New Heroin Chic, originally made famous by such legendary emaciated Sixties wastrels as Edie Sedgwick and Keith Richards. Going all the way back to Charlie Parker and Billie Holiday, nothing had provided more heavy artillery for the cause of drug prohibition than heroin. Here you could feel its presence mostly in the endless references to those it had claimed, from Lenny Bruce to Johnny Thunders, but you could sense its haunted history easily enough behind Gregg Allman's dark glasses. All you had to do was look at Perry Farrell of Porno for Pyros, and there it was.

Finally, there were the clean and sober rock stars, a phenomenon that did not even exist twenty-five years earlier.

"David, there's a tent at the back of the north field holding continuous N.A. and A.A. meetings," I told David Crosby. "What do you think about that?"

"That's great," Crosby said. "It certainly shows how times have changed."

"What do you think of the prospect of a whole new generation of kids coming into the experience of drugs?"

"What I have to say about that is this. We were right about a lot of things twenty-five years ago. We were right about the war. We were right about the environment. We were right about civil rights and women's issues. But we were *wrong* about the drugs."

The mud seemed only to make Carlos Santana happy. On Sunday afternoon, the guitarist was walking around the artists' compound before his set, wearing a yellow bandanna around his head and a flaming red Jimi Hendrix T-shirt. Santana felt that the mud only brought people together. "You need a strong spirit to deal with the mud," he said, telling me that he could feel the spirits of John Coltrane and Jimi Hendrix hovering over this event—these were the great musical spirits that guided him.

"Carlos, do you think people are taking psychedelics here in that same spirit as twenty-five years ago?"

"Yeah, I think that the young people are realizing that you need to shed your skin sometimes, which is really what it is; that's what's really going on here. You know, the young people need to know the difference between drugs and medicine. Man makes drugs, in a laboratory. But medicine grows from the ground naturally. So there's a big difference between medicine and drugs. Watch out for the drugs. As for the medicine, just pace yourself. I always tell people when they ask about drugs—I say, there's a difference between self-*expansion* and self-*deception*. You know? Whether it's Coca-Cola or cocaine—that's self-deception. But if you take something that makes you into a better human being and you start thinking about the highest good of all people, that's medicine. If you're only thinking, What's in it for *me,* that's drugs—"

Of course, the whole notion of viewing consciousness-altering substances like psychedelics as natural "medicine" as opposed to the "self-deception" of "drugs" reflected a point of view not commonly espoused in a society that steadfastly refused to make even the most basic legal distinction between marijuana and heroin—yet somehow Santana had managed to get right to the core of the eternal dilemma of drugs: the question of use versus abuse.

The skies finally began to clear late that afternoon, and by the time Bob Dylan took the stage, the sun was beginning to set. Dylan had still never acknowledged his drug experiences in public; he'd always continued to deny that images like "take me for a trip upon your magic swirling ship" had anything at all to do with drugs, but We Who Had Closely Listened knew better. The troubadour laureate of his generation had avoided the first Woodstock, but now here he was, twenty-five years later, singing "Rainy Day Women #12 & 35" to a whole new generation: *"Everybody must get stoned . . ."*

As Dylan sang, the sky turned into a fiery covering of color. After the dark skies and all the rain, it looked as if a video special-effects artist working in the pay-per-view truck had flipped a cosmic chroma-key switch on cue, saturating the heavens with brilliant filaments of orange and vermilion. The population of souls that by now had grown to the size of the city of Syracuse watched, hushed and awestruck. Even the moshing diminished. A sunset of such profound beauty could only mean one thing: their Woodstock was no mirage. They would carry it away and wear it inside of them for the rest of their lives.

I wondered how many of them were tripping at that very moment, and the boy I had found in the woods two days earlier filled my thoughts. Once again, I was breathless at the thought of him. I could only wish him a safe and happy shedding of his skin. "Drugs are a bet with the mind," Jim Morrison had once said, and who can ever really know if Skeleton would turn out to be bad or Felix the Cat good.

I could only wish this whole generation self-expansion and not self-deception. The story of my own generation's journey through drugs had already been written. The story of this one had yet to be lived.

## II. Huxley's Question

IN 1934, twenty years before taking the mescaline that led him to write *The Doors of Perception,* Aldous Huxley published a newspaper feature called "A Treatise on Drugs," one of his earliest writings on the subject. Huxley had come across "a ponderous work by a German pharmacologist" on the dusty shelves of a local used bookshop, a nearly unreadable encyclopedia of drugs, and yet he had read it "from cover to cover with a passionate and growing interest."

Huxley had been astonished to learn that "our ancestors left almost no natural stimulant, or hallucinant, or stupefacient, undiscovered," and the article he wrote displayed his remarkable ability to foresee the psychosocial implications of mind-altering substances, as well as their problems.

"The story of drug taking constitutes one of the most curious and also, it seems to me, one of the most significant chapters of human beings," he wrote. "Everywhere and at all times, men and women have sought, and duly found, the means of taking a holiday from the reality of their generally dull and often acutely unpleasant existence. A holiday out of space, out of time, in the eternity of sleep or ecstasy, in the heaven or limbo of visionary phantasy . . ."

But Huxley also recognized that for those unfortunates who would abuse the substances, drugs could be "treacherous and harmful. The heaven into which they usher their victims soon turns into a hell of sickness and moral degradation. They kill, first the soul, then, in a few years, the body."

Huxley then posed a simple question: "What is the remedy?"

A daunting question, but it is one we must ask ourselves in setting our policies and laws about drugs. The prohibitionists certainly think they know the answer to it, and so do the reformers. I have my opinions as well—about decriminalization, medicalization, the rescheduling of certain drugs, other issues of reform. But it wasn't Huxley's question that framed the whole journey of this book but rather my father's when he asked in that conversation before he passed away, "Go ahead, you tell me how it all happened and what it all meant . . . In the end, what did any of it really mean?"—the question of how, in effect, the American Century had turned into the Great Stoned Age.

During the years since Woodstock '94, the use of illicit drugs, new and old, has continued unabated, popping up in new scenes and contexts. Rohypnol, a sedative manufactured by Hoffmann-LaRoche in Switzerland, swept through the clubs of Texas and Florida as "roofies" to become "the date-rape drug of the Nineties" before it was criminalized by the DEA. After the "comeback" of LSD, words like *plague* and *epidemic* were once again bruited about to describe the rage of methamphetamine use sweeping the nation as "crank" and "ice." A whole subculture of opiate addicts coalesced around the painkiller OxyContin. Ketamine, or "Special K," enjoyed a moment as the new club drug of choice, and Ecstasy continued to ascend in popularity.

That the Great American Drug War is a failure in our time becomes increasingly evident, but as still another generation embarks on its transit through the experience of illicit drugs, the time has come to ask some hard questions: Why hasn't the war on drugs worked? Is it because we've held back from waging the struggle with our full national might, because to do so would somehow demolish the very precepts of the free and open society we so cherish? Why, after all, do people use drugs? Does drug use really represent a crisis of national values and will, or should it more accurately be understood as individual prerogative? Is it simply inherent in the human condition to want to alter consciousness and "get high"? Are the problems we face today merely the modern manifestation of the fact that mind-altering drugs have been around since the beginning of human experience? Is our drug policy therefore realistic? And will it ever be reasonable to expect people to abstain from illegal drugs when the legal ones—alcohol and tobacco and prescription drugs—are accepted despite the fact that they harm people in far greater numbers?

Of several things I am certain. Illicit drugs have long since become part of a deeply personal and complicated prism of American national life. We have used them, waged holy war against them, and indulged in great public outcries, hysterias, and confessions, obsessively making policies and shaping whole ideologies around them. From politics to the arts, drugs have shaped the American cultural landscape in profound ways. Like it or not, drugs have entered the mainstream of American social experience.

The idea of a "drug-free" America, then, is a chimera, and not simply because such a society has never existed in history. What makes it an even more extravagant fantasy is the reality that during the twentieth century, America had become something wholly unprecedented: a mass-consumption culture that has mixed and matched the most ancient and natural psychotropic substances with the full panoply of modern synthetic drugs, produced by the most affluent, technologically advanced consumer society on the face of the earth: Cannabis of Sinaloa and Panama and Jamaica, Colombia and Hawaii, Humboldt County and a hundred other places: Hashish from Morocco, Lebanon, Afghanistan, and Tangier. The peyote cactus of Laredo and northern Sonora. The opium of Turkey, Afghanistan, and Southeast Asia, processed into illegal heroin, smuggled and distributed by criminal syndicates but also marketed as legal narcotics throughout the world under the names Darvon, Demerol, Dilaudid, morphine, Pantopon, codeine. The coca plant of the Andes and its refined product of cocaine hydrochloride. The psilocybin mushrooms growing naturally in the damp pastures of America and Mexico. The synthetic psychedelics like mescaline and psilocybin and LSD. Tryptamines like DMT and DET. Exotica like the ayahuasca vine of the Amazon basin. Morning-glory seeds with names like Heaven Sent and Pearly Blue. Nutmeg derivatives related to the amphetamines like MDA and the whole family of phenethylamines, Ecstasy and otherwise. The cobalt-blue liquid solution of methedrine and amphetamine pills marketed in the billions by the American pharmaceutical giants like Eli Lilly, Bristol-Myers Squibb, and GlaxoSmithKline—a never-ending array that includes the likes of Biphetamine, Desbutal, Dexedrine, Benzedrine, Desoxyn, Dexamyl, Daprisal, Preludin, Ritalin. Barbiturate pills of every conceivable shape and color and variety, among them Amytal, Tuinal, Nembutal, Seconal, Luminal, and chloral hydrate. Entire generations of tranquilizers like Compazine, Librium, Thorazine, Miltown. A whole new generation of antidepressants. Deliriants like nitrous oxide. Quaaludes and other nonbarbiturate sedatives. Inhalants like amyl nitrate, model-airplane glue.

Of course, the existence of such an immense pharmaceutical cornucopia in a nation where the Protestant parent culture had always sought to emphasize temperance and rectitude as bedrock values has set up one the great paradoxes of the modern American experience. From the very beginning of prohibitionism, with the Harrison Narcotic Act of 1914, and continuing right up to George Bush's 1989 pronouncement that the drug crisis called for nothing less than "the moral equivalent of war," there has always been a fundamental clash between those who would seek to punish users of illicit drugs and those who would condone and indulge their use. The cultural, social, and political agenda behind the prohibition of drugs has often been driven by a fear of the minorities using them, whether it was the ethnic immigrants of the Twenties, the Mexicans of the Thirties, the jazz musicians of the Thirties and Forties, the beatniks of the Fifties, the hippies and student radicals of the Sixties, or the crack-smoking inner-city gangs of the Eighties. What began as a basic conflict between a dominant alcohol culture and a minority culture that used these illicit substances has, over the last half century or so, developed into a gaping cultural divide. At the same time, the crusade against drugs has always been portrayed as a life-and-death struggle for the hearts and minds of America's children. At stake is nothing less than their innocence, their future—the lifeblood of the nation, the destiny of the civilization. It is only in the light of this historical perspective that the harshness and distortions and passions surrounding the use of illicit drugs become comprehensible.

I am certain of several other things, too. We live in a society where a drug culture was never supposed to have developed in the first place, and to say otherwise in a public arena has become tantamount to heresy. Because of this denial, an enormous amount of knowledge, accrued over several generations, is being only minimally accessed. The public discourse is defined by the simpleminded rhetoric and posturing of politicians, the always-questionable statistics of policy makers, the self-aggrandizing alarmism of the drug-enforcement community, and the sensationalized superficiality of the mass media. Yes, we get plenty of ide-ology and moralization, but what was actually lived and learned—the whole Temple of Accumulated Error—rarely seems to get passed on, pro-ducing a cultural amnesia about drugs that has become so pervasive that we scarcely even notice it, let alone discuss it. For over half a century now, this amnesia has consigned us to dealing with one of our most vital issues from the shadows of ignorance, fear, and denial. And the more this great Temple of Accumulated Error is ignored, the more successive generations will go off to make the same mistakes with drugs over and over again. For this reason, it becomes more important than ever to speak the truth about drugs. As Wavy Gravy recognized, "Talking about it is one thing; living it is another. So many people have come to grips with these partic-ular demons, and these people can become the signposts. How wonder-ful it would be if we would all admit the truth of our experiences, the good *and* the bad, in an obvious and clear way."

Again, my thoughts turn to that boy at Woodstock. No doubt he felt that he could "handle" the drugs he was taking and that real problems with drugs happened only to other people, never to people like him; everything would be fine because he was fearless, immune, and ready for all—exactly as I thought I had been. Of course, some of those young peo-ple may very well have been serious substance abusers in the making. Somewhere along the line, some of them might lose the ability (if they ever had it in the first place) to tell the difference between what Carlos Santana had called "self-expansion" and "self-deception." Some of them might one day come to hold a crack pipe, become alcoholics, or even pop a needle in the main line. When I think of that boy at Woodstock, I would like to save him from what Huxley called the "hell of sickness" of drug abuse and addiction—something that I had experienced firsthand. But had I been given the opportunity to talk to him, I would have shared *all* of my experiences with him, from the heavens of transcendent self-expansion to the hells of the most dreadful self-deception and moral squalor. When I look back, I know that being told in simplistic terms that smoking marijuana would lead to ruin and hard drugs had only set me up to take more and more license once my own experiential evidence proved otherwise. As a Temple of Accumulated Error myself, I know that for the vast majority of people the truth of drugs will always lie somewhere between the extremes, neither as destructive as we have feared nor as harmless as we would like to believe, and that the best thing we can possibly do is to demystify them. We should do everything possible to denude them of all of the distorted and supercharged manifestations of identity that they represent, whether as forbidden, romantic, mystical, rebellious, dysfunctional, tormented, creative, beautiful, or doomed. What drugs do to us is a function of who we are and where and when and how we take them. To say anything else, and to impute innate qualities of good or evil to them, is simply not to tell the truth.

However, while neither inherently good nor evil, drugs are nevertheless profoundly and uniquely powerful. They can alter what we see and how we see it, what we do and how we do it, what we feel and how we integrate it into our lives. As William Blake put it, "The eye altering alters all." If there is one fundamental truth about the experience of drugs, it's that they *change things*, if only for as long as we're affected by them. Drugs thus contain nothing less than the power to change who we are. A part of that transformation can always include a dimension of the unknown. But there is much that we know as well. In retrospect, I realize that the best drug education I could possibly have received would have been the inculcation of a humble respect for their powers, the means to recognize how those powers can distort and deceive in ways that can damage us, and the responsibility and self-esteem to take the actions necessary to prevent that from happening. Call it harm reduction, progressive drug education—it hardly matters. I call it telling the truth about drugs and learning how to tell the truth about ourselves. There will always be those among us who will stop playing with fire only after we get burned, and there will always be parents, like my father, who will look into their children's eyes and worry. But until we start telling the truth about drugs to ourselves and to each other, the best answers to Huxley's basic question—"What is the remedy?"—will continue to elude us, and the same problems with drugs that so bedeviled America in the twentieth century will only be carried into the new millennium.

## III. Once Known, Never Forgotten

MY JOB is to pick up an old, homeless, alcoholic junkie named Wilbur who's being released from a detox ward in a Staten Island hospital, bring him back into Manhattan, and put him on a train at Grand Central to an upstate retreat called Graymoor. We have to be at the hospital by 5:00 a.m. so why even bother going to sleep? A light snow is beginning to fall as I meet Jimmy K at the corner of Broadway and 79th Street at 3:30 a.m., and we hop on the number 1/9 subway train heading downtown to the Staten Island ferry terminal.

Maybe it's those kids who get on the train at Times Square obviously coming from or going to a rave, or maybe it's just staying up all night like this that brings back those wild nights on drugs for me, when time was meaningless and all that mattered was the sensation of the moment. As we come up out of the subway at the ferry terminal, I flash back to a certain mescaline morning in the summer of 1970, when something about the Day-Glo sunrise possessed me to get in my Volkswagen and drive into the city to visit my sister. I'd never driven into the city by myself. She was living on Staten Island at the time, and as soon as I got out of the Midtown Tunnel and headed downtown, I got hopelessly lost. By the time I parked the car at the Fulton Fish Market to ask somebody for directions, I was peaking on the drug, and it was like I'd wandered onto some phantasmagoric stage set specially designed by Salvador Dali to fuck with my mind. I was certain that the fish were not dead but alive, that every fish eye in every stall in the market was staring at me—and that was before they started to talk.

You're not supposed to do these 12-step assignments alone, and that's why Jimmy K is along with me—a tough Boston Irish kid who was always in trouble with the law, on his way to the penitentiary when a judge gave him the chance to get clean. He went away to a rehab, and it turned his life around; now he's in New York trying to be an actor, working in a restaurant, going to meetings. He wants to try to get a little sleep on the way, so I leave him curled up on one of the benches on the ferry and go outside, onto the wide bow, and stand there in the dark and let the wind and snow lash me in the face as I watch the Statue of Liberty go by.

It was a stupid thing to do, driving into the city like that for my first time alone on mescaline, but hadn't Dock Ellis once pitched a no-hitter on LSD? I could have easily smacked up the car or hit some pedestrians, and yet we took drugs like that all the time, so many of us, as if it were the most natural thing in the world. I'm filled with gratitude that I didn't end up maimed or dead or brain-dead or in jail like so many others from all my years of doing drugs, but how ironic to have ended here. My father had told me long ago that I would become a drug addict if I smoked marijuana, and though I never stuck a needle in my arm, had you told that seventeen-year-old boy that one day twenty-five years later he would find himself standing on the bow of the Staten Island ferry on an icy morning, going across the harbor to pick up an old, homeless, alcoholic junkie, it would have seemed just as remote a possibility. In some strange way had my father's prophecy come true? The marijuana hadn't led me to heroin, but it had certainly been a gateway to being here.

By the time we trudge up to the hospital, it's still dark, and the deserted streets are filled with snow, silent and spectral. A security guard lets us in, and we take the elevator up to the detox ward, where an orderly meets us and escorts us down the hall, past sad, gray figures in hospital gowns and slippers, shuffling slowly along with lifeless eyes, down to the room where our charge awaits.

Wilbur is in his late sixties, hands gnarled and cracked from exposure, the insides of his arms crisscrossed with scars like a road map of his addiction—it's like the whole story of heroin in Harlem since the 1950s is right there on the arms of this one man. We hand him the clean clothes we've brought along, and he puts them on. As many times as he's been through this routine, he still can't quite believe that a couple of strange white boys would just show up for him on a snowy morning like this, and his smile makes me remember why I do these things.

On the way back, the ferry is crowded with rush-hour commuters, and we find ourselves packed in with businessmen and secretaries on the benches. I get Wilbur a buttered roll and a tea and pick up the paper. There's a story about two guys getting busted after stowing away with a large load of cocaine in the propeller shaft of a ship coming from Colombia, and I'm struck as always by the uninterrupted levels of madness and danger and greed that drive the drug trade and how unstoppable it seems. But what comes back, too, is another morning, this one in 1976. Cocaine was brand-new and something like the Medellín cartel and mutilated bodies washing up at the mouths of Colombian rivers was unimaginable to us. Dawn was just breaking over Hudson Street as my friends and I went spilling out of an after-hours club after one of those nights of mad dancing and drugging, parading boisterously through the streets as the city came to life, all of us filled with the indescribable delectation of feeling somehow separate from humdrum human existence, above the rat race of jobs and mortgages and taxes—not just the rapture and risk of being alive but so high that it felt as if we would live forever, that's what it was really about, that's what the drugs gave us. Now the question is how to reconcile those experiences with my present life and this man sitting next to me.

Between bites of his buttered roll, Wilbur tells us a little about his life. He served a serious stretch of time for manslaughter after shooting a man on Lenox Avenue as a teenager back in the late 1950s. If nothing else, the story is another example of how drugs have changed this country—a boy shooting someone over drugs on the very block where he'd grown up, only doors away from the building where his mother had rocked him in her arms—and how he would spend the rest of his life shooting dope, living on the streets. But it's only one piece in the vast mosaic of drugs in this country, just as those middle-class rave kids on the subway who use Ecstasy to access some form of divinity are another—worlds apart, yet equally criminal in the eyes of the law: Wilbur and Ecstasy and the smuggling of cocaine from Colombia—emblematic parts of a day in the life of drugs in America—heaven and hell and everything in between.

At Grand Central, we find the right train in the morning crush and rush to get Wilbur aboard—he squeezes our hands tightly before we leave him, and for a moment he looks like a little boy about to cry. It breaks my heart because Wilbur won't make it; he's been in dozens of detoxes, and his chances of staying clean are slim to none. The odds are overwhelming that he'll return to the streets, and I know there's nothing I can do about it and that this is the real meaning of the word *powerlessness*. But in some sense it doesn't really matter whether he makes it or not. I'm not trying to be some saint or savior by doing these things. I do them selfishly. The real reason is beyond my own desire not to do drugs, because that was lifted long ago. In the beginning, drugs opened me up in new and wonderful ways, but over time they closed me down, froze me up inside, distorted my perception of who I really was. Something always happens when I do these things, and now as we watch the train pull out of the station, it happens again: I can feel the glacier inside me, left over from twenty-plus years of drugs and alcohol, melt just a little more, feel something spiritual move that makes my own continued healing and growth more possible. Some might call the dark wind that blows inside my soul melancholia or depression, others the disease of addiction. Whatever it may be, I've learned that the only true antidote for it is the sunlight of the spirit. I had to leave drugs behind to find out who I really am, and who I am is a person who must spend the rest of his life learning to speak the language of the heart. I'm quite certain that I would never have discovered this truth had I not embarked on the journey that began with those openings made possible by drugs, and quite certain I could never have come to this realization without looking into the abyss of myself when it all turned desperate and I hit bottom. So, paradoxically, I found exactly what I was looking for when I picked up that first joint. What I always feel in the deepest sense from doing this work with people like Wilbur is that, after all this time, I've found my way home.

I say good-bye to Jimmy K in the terminal, and we go our separate ways. I head out the exit ramp with the rush-hour throngs—not separate anymore but a part of these people. I relish the blast of frigid air on my face and go plunging into the honk and bustle and awesome onslaught of the city morning.

Maybe Blake had it right when he wrote that the path of excess leads to the temple of wisdom. The rub is that there will always be those who won't live to tell about it.

I'm fifty years old now, in the fifteenth year of my sobriety, married with a child, and I have never been happier. Sometimes I still get the urge to smoke a little pot and listen to some Hendrix or Coltrane, or to nibble a magic mushroom and go for a walk in the woods, but I always make the choice to let it pass. Maybe it's because somewhere inside myself I know that you have to give something to get something in this life, and this is what I choose to give up. And maybe it's because even after all this time, I'm still worried that I might like it a little too much. After all, as Herbert Huncke told me when I began this journey so long ago, Once known, never forgotten.

# ACKNOWLEDGMENTS

The following people sat for interviews for this book: Dr. Michael Aldrich, James Allen, Al Aronowitz, Peter Berg, Steve Bowser, Stewart Brand, Bernard Brightman, Ed Bullins, Marcelle Clements, Allen Cohen, Peter Coyote, David Crosby, Stanley Crouch, Ronnie Cutrone, Vincent Cyrus, Diane Di Prima, Gretchen Douglas, David Felton, James Fogel, Jim Galipeau, Carolyn "Mountain Girl" Adams Garcia, Gary Giddins, Ira Gitler, Todd Gitlin, Judy Goldhaft, Wavy Gravy, Steve Hagar, Steven Halpern, Ansley Hamid, Billy Hayes, Richard Hell, Jack Herer, John Holmstrom, Michael Horowitz, Lynn "Freeman" House, Bryan Hughes, Joyce Johnson, Denise Kaufmann, Orrin Keepnews, Paul Krassner, Michael Lang, Preston Lytton, Ami Magill, Gerard Malanga, Ray Manzarek, Ginna Marston, Michael McClure, Jackie McLean, Taylor Mead, Lewis Merenstein, Dr. John P. Morgan, Michael Musto, Eileen Myles, Ethan Nadelmann, Sylvia Nunn, Glenn O'Brien, Cynthia Palmer, Sudi Pebbles Trippet, Edie Kerouac Parker, Dennis Peron, Charles Perry, Michelle Phillips, Ram Dass, John Rechy, Ishmael Reed, Craig Reinarman, Jeffrey Robbins, Tom Robbins, Jahanara Romney, Marsha Rosenbaum, Michael Rossman, Bob Sabbag, Ed Sanders, Paul Schrader, Hubert Selby Jr., Sharon, Bernard Sherman, John Shirley, Sasha and Ann Shulgin, RU Sirius, Grace Slick, Oliver Stone, Robert Stone, Keith Stroup, Danny Sugarman, Bob Timmons, Arnold Trebach, Ann Waldman, Dr. Andrew Weil, Mary Woronov, Sonny Wright, and Lynn Zimmer.

A number of people who provided vital interviews and invaluable assistance over the years have passed away during the writing of this book. I shall always be indebted to Claude Brown, Allen Ginsberg, Herbert Huncke, Ken Kesey, Timothy Leary, Rose Leone, Lance Loud, Terence McKenna, Michael O'Donoghue, David Rattray, Larry Rivers, Paul Rothchild, Jerry Rubin, and Terry Southern.

Thanks to Jann Wenner, Jeff Levenson, Jeffrey Daneman, Michael Horowitz, Steven Saporta, and Ethan Nadelmann for making key suggestions, introducing me to people, and opening doors. John Holmstrom was very helpful in allowing me to rifle through the files and back issues of *High Times.* I am particularly grateful to Michael Horowitz for helping me obtain so many important but hard-to-find books and reference materials and to Lisa Cahn for all of her transcribing. Ed Sanders allowed me access to materials in his personal files about LEMAR and sent me a copy of his book *Fame and Love in New York;* Larry Sloman was kind enough to provide a copy of his excellent history of marijuana, *Reefer Madness.*

Many thanks to all the friends who sat down and helped me remember those times good and bad: Robert Alexander, Ben Davidson, Brian Delate, Ralph Desefano, Michael Dobbs, Neil Hallenborg, Arthur Hechtman, Larry Joshua, Brian Keane, Andy Kent, Jim King, Michael Loeb, Vic Losick, Judy Orbach, and John Ryder.

This book could never have been written without the following individuals, friends and family, who provided a sympathetic ear and every conceivable kind of support—emotional, spiritual, material, and editorial—along the way. You all know who you are and how you've helped me over these long years—God bless all of you: Carole Ash, Jesse Ash, Matthew Ash, Richard Benedek, Julia Cameron, Ben Davidson, Michelle Esrick, Eileen Garrish, Wavy Gravy, Joe Jingoli, Larry Joshua, Lewis Merenstein, Ron Orbach, Doug Richardson, Brian Rosenberg, Elaine Rosenberg, Barnaby Spring, Smith Stanley, and Bess Torgoff. A special note of thanks must go to my bookish and beautiful wife, Laura Last, who scrutinized every word of this work with the sharp literary eye of an E. B. White. The ways she helped this project these last few years are too numerous to mention; by the time the book was completed she lived every line of it with me. *Grazie amore mio, la Principessa di Piccadente.*

A wonderful chap named Jim Moser signed this book up eons ago at Grove Press, and publisher Morgan Entrekin was gracious enough to let it have a life somewhere else; thank you both for being such an important part of its journey.

Heartfelt thanks to my agent and friend, Russell Galen—unwavering, savvy, tough, funny, and kind, a true lover of words and books—how truly fortunate I am to have him on my side. And, finally, very special thanks to Bob Bender, my editor at Simon & Schuster, for being so encouraging, patient, firm, and so generous with his time and attention.

# NOTES

## 1  Fearless, Immune and Ready for All

### I. A Real Pack of Idiots

6  *Charles Robert Manian* is a pseudonym, as are David Benjamin and Larry Insdorf.

### II. One of the Greatest Myths of the Age

14  *Katrina* is a pseudonym.

## 2  Bop Apocalypse

### I. Ready to Introduce New Worlds with a Shrug

18  *"People have moralized":* Herbert Huncke to MT.
18  *"a little late for the hard-core old junkies":* Ibid.
19  *"smugglers and Chinese junks":* Huncke, *Guilty of Everything,* p. 26.
19  *"hennaed hair a fire engine red":* Ibid., p. 29.
19  *"They used to sell it in decks":* Ibid., p. 31.
20  *" 'Get a load of this degenerate bastard' ":* Ibid., pp. 32–33.
20  *"At that time in my life":* Allen Ginsberg to MT.
21  *"I'm sort of a legend here":* Herbert Huncke to MT.
21  *"like hearing Charlie Parker playing 'Lover Man' ":* Ibid.
22  *"It's all right there in Junkie ":* Ibid.
22  *"We were living in this apartment":* Ibid.

### II. Lover Man and the Ultimate Truth

23  *prodigious amounts of drugs and alcohol:* Recounted by Teddy Blume in Reisner, *Bird,* pp. 56–57.
24  *an addict for a solid decade:* in Davis, *Miles,* p. 90; also in Gillespie, *To Be or Not to Bop,* p. 250.
25  *his entire existence:* in Davis, *Miles,* p. 89.
25  *"He was always up":* Howard McGhee quoted in Gitler, *Swing to Bop,* pp. 172–74.
25  *"That's why I went to Ross":* McGhee quoted ibid., p. 173.
25  *the horrible symptoms of heroin withdrawal:* Recounted by Howard McGhee in Reisner, *Bird,* p. 145.
26  *"a shot of dope at the hospital":* McGhee quoted in Gitler, *Swing to Bop,* p. 173.
27  *"amoral, anarchistic, gentle":* Reisner, *Bird,* p. 25.

27  *"Music is your own experience"*: Bird's statement originally appeared in *Downbeat*; quoted ibid., p. 27.

28  *"When I came early one night"*: Hampton Hawes quoted in Chambers, *Milestones*, p. 139.


III.  Eye Altering Alters All

28  *"Oscar Wild types"*: Huncke, *Guilty of Everything*, p. 73.
29  *"There was really no place"*: Allen Ginsberg to MT.
29  *"a red letter day in my life"*: Ginsberg's first marijuana experience recounted in Sloman. *Reefer Madness*, p. 174; also MT conversations with Ginsberg.
30  *"This great plate of white ice cream"*: Allen Ginsberg quoted in Sloman, *Reefer Madness*, p. 174.
30  *"It all just seemed so perfectly joyful"*: Ibid., p. 175.
30  *"I was studying art at the time"*: Ibid., pp. 174–75.
31  *"Remember, there was always the association"*: Ibid., pp. 176–77.
31  *"the trouble we could get into"*: Allen Ginsberg to MT.
31  *The Times Square night*: Nicosia, *Memory Babe*, pp. 157–58; see also Ginsberg's prose sketch of the time, "The Great Molecular Comedown," in Knight and Knight, *Beat Vision*.
32  *"the New Vision"*: in Schumacher, *Dharma Lion*, pp. 33–34.
33  *"From the beginning"*: Allen Ginsberg to MT.
34  *"Benny has made me see a lot"*: Kerouac, *Selected Letters*, p. 100.


IV.  Looking for Bird

34  *Jackie McLean begged his stepfather*: Related by Jackie McLean to MT.
35  *"So many people"*: Jackie McLean to MT.
36  *"I went out there with my friend Jelly"*: Ibid.
37  *"I would got to a party"*: Ibid.
37  *a Sunday-afternoon cocktail sip*: Related by Jackie McLean to MT.
38  *"I ran down there"*: Jackie McLean to MT.
38  *"That was our badge"*: Red Rodney quoted in Gitler, *Swing to Bop*, p. 282.
40  *"two bars on every street"*: Max Roach quoted in Gillespie, *To Be or Not to Bop*, p. 397.
40  *how heroin had come to flood the neighborhoods of Harlem*: McCoy, *The Politics of Heroin*, pp. 38–40; Sterling, *Octopus*, pp. 95–101; Newsday editors, *Heroin Trail*, p. 199; Moscow, *Merchants of Heroin*, p. xiv; also MT interview with Claude Brown.


V.  The Season of Wild Form

42  *"a huge Dostoyevskyan novel"*: Kerouac, *Selected Letters*, p. 371
42  *"from moment to moment"*: Nicosia, *Memory Babe*, p. 279.
42  *"a young Gene Autry"*: Kerouac, *On the Road*, p. 2.
44  *to elitch*: Nicosia, *Memory Babe*, p. 322.
45  *a series of letters to Neal Cassady*: Kerouac, *Selected Letters*, pp. 267–315; also Nicosia, *Memory Babe*, pp. 336–37.
45  *to simply sit down and write a book*: Story of the writing of *On the Road* in Nicosia, p. 343; also in Kerouac, *Selected Letters*, p. 315.
49  *"a jazz poet blowing a long blues"*: Jack Kerouac, Foreword to *Mexico City Blues*.

### VI. An Awareness of His Most Human Pain

50  *"The last time I saw him"*: Frank Sanderford quoted in Reisner, *Bird*, p. 206.
50  *"In attempting to escape the role"*: Ellison, *Shadow and Act*, p. 227
50  *One night at Birdland in 1955:* Incident recounted in Gillspie, *To Be or Not to Bop*, p. 393.
51  *"He knew I loved him so much"*: Jackie McLean to MT.
51  *"She didn't know anything about drugs"*: Ibid.
52  *"He always wanted me not to use"*: Ibid.
52  *hanging out with Bird at the Open Door:* Related by Jackie McLean to MT.
53  *his next gig at the Open Door:* Ibid.
53  *McLean read about the death of Charlie Parker:* Ibid.
54  *Almost immediately, the legend began appearing:* Graffiti story in Ronald Sukenick, *Down and In*, p. 86.
55  *Jackie McLean would continue recording fine jazz for Prestige:* Details of McLean's life after the death of Bird related by Jackie McLean to MT.

### VII. Angel in Moloch

57  *"That first line of* 'Howl' *that could never have been written"*: Allen Ginsberg to MT.
57  *"the sound of an iron jail-cell door"*: Ibid.
58  *Ginsberg had taken peyote:* Related by Allen Ginsberg to MT.
59  "Moloch! Moloch!": Ibid.
59  *"What I had heard about peyote"*: Allen Ginsberg to MT.
60  *peyote cults:* History in High Times, *Encyclopedia of Recreational Drugs*, pp. 203–8.
60  *"The legend of peyote"*: Allen Ginsberg to MT.
61  *Artaud had taken the substance:* Artaud, *Peyote Dance*, p. 78.
61  *"people started chopping them up"*: Terry Southern to MT.

### VII. A Conspiracy to Overthrow Civilization

62  *"a mystery about drugs"*: McClure, *Scratching the Beat Surface*, p. 5.
62  *"Six poets at the Six Gallery"*: Quoted in Schumacher, *Dharma Lion*, p. 214.
62  *"It was a mad night"*: Sketch of Six Gallery reading in Kerouac, *Dharma Bums*, pp. 13–14.
63  *"standing in wonder"*: McClure, *Scratching the Beat Surface*, p. 15.
63  *"I greet you"*: Lawrence Ferlinghetti quoted in Schumacher, *Dharma Lion*, p. 216.
63  *"the pleasure of a 'teahead joyride' "*: Allen Ginsberg to MT.
64  *the most important poem published in America since the Second World War:* Lawrence Ferlinghetti's analysis of *Howl* in Schumacher, *Dharma Lion*, p. 253
64  *Judge Clayton W. Horn had released his twelve-point opinion:* Ibid., p. 264.
65  *"Virtually from that moment on"*: Allen Ginsberg to MT.
67  *"To me, Neal's arrest was graphic proof"*: Ibid.

# 3  Psychedelic Spring

### I. The Buzz Begins

68  *"What was it like in the beginning?"*: Timothy Leary to MT.
69  *"Nile palaces"*: Leary, *High Priest*, p. 25.

69 *"Like almost everyone"*: Leary, *Flashbacks*, p. 33.
69 *"one drop in an ocean of intelligence"*: Ibid., p. 33.
69 *"It's axiomatic in psychology"*: Related by Timothy Leary to MT.
70 *"I shook out a few of the pills"*: Leary, *Flashbacks*, p. 43.
70 *"First I read my William James"*: Timothy Leary to MT.
70 *"Huxley was actually in town"*: Ibid.
71 *"That first year"*: Ibid.

## II. I've Come Down to Preach Love to the World!

72 *"I remember lots of people coming"*: Susan Leary quoted in Leary, *High Priest*, pp. 84–85.
72 *"a secret priestly class"*: Leary, *Flashbacks*, p. 46.
72 *"a rootless city-dweller"*: Leary, *High Priest*, p. 4.
73 *"Tote dropped out"*: Leary, *Flashbacks*, p. 40.
73 *Coventry was a watershed experience*: Ibid., pp. 103–7.
74 *His whole being was pervaded by an awareness*: Related by Allen Ginsberg to MT.
74 *"I'm the Messiah!"*: Related by Allen Ginsberg to MT; also Leary, *Flashbacks*, p. 48.
75 *"narrow social conditioning"*: Leary, *Flashbacks*, p. 49.
75 *"respectable and notable people"*: Allen Ginsberg to MT.
76 *"blueprint to turn on the world"*: Leary, *Flashbacks*, p. 60.

## III. It All Started in California

76 *jagged waves of frost*: Related by Robert Stone to MT; Stone also discussed this experience in Perry, *On the Bus*, p. 28.
76 *the French attack on Port Said*: Related by Stone in *Paris Review* interview, 1986.
78 *"death and transfiguration and rebirth"*: Related by Stone ibid.
78 *"It all started in California"*: Kesey, *Demon Box*, p. 72.

## IV. Here We Go, Dick

78 *"Tim was way ahead of me"*: Ram Dass to MT.
79 *"But who's minding the store?"*: In Alpert (Ram Dass) *Be Here Now*, pp. 6–7.
79 *"The next morning"*: Ram Dass to MT.
79 *"a Sundance–Butch Cassidy alliance"*: Leary, *Flashbacks*, p. 77.
80 *"Suddenly, all of the mystical literature"*: Ram Dass to MT.
80 *"exploring this inner realm"*: Ibid.

## V. Harvard Eats the Holy Mushroom

82 *"Cultural stability is maintained"*: Leary, "How to Change Behavior" (Address presented to the XIV Congress of Applied Psychology, Copenhagen, 1961).
82 *"Drug-induced satori"*: Ibid.
82 *"shape and change all our lives"*: Ram Dass to MT.
83 *the hardened cons of Concord State Prison*: Related by Ram Dass to MT; also in Leary, *Flashbacks*, pp. 88–89.
83 *a bitter debate within the Social Relations Department*: In Stevens, *Storming Heaven*, pp. 162–63.
84 *"Harvard would provide neither setting nor drugs"*: Ram Dass to MT.

84 *Good Friday 1962:* Description of Miracle of Marsh Chapel related by Ram Dass to MT; also in Leary, *Flashbacks,* p. 108.
85 *"they had to organize against the results":* Ram Dass to MT.

## VI. Breaking Free and Running for Open Country

86 *"Innocence is a funny thing":* Robert Stone to MT.
87 *"lit by whiskey and anarchism":* Ken Kesey quoted in profile of Robert Stone in *New York Times Magazine,* January 10, 1992.
87 *"stand in the broken glass":* Ibid.
88 *"the weird kid":* Ken Kesey quoted in Whitmer, *Aquarius Revisited,* p. 199.
88 *"a bunch of people that we had always been looking for":* Robert Stone to MT.
89 *"We kept them in stock":* Ibid.
89 *"around the time we first started calling it acid":* Ibid.
89 *"marching across the Stanford Golf Course":* Ibid.
90 *"They gave me mine":* Kesey, *Garage Sale,* p. 221.
91 *"double-aught capsule of pure mescaline":* Ibid, p. 12.
91 *"not just shock not just invention":* Ibid., p. 14.
91 *"When we first took those drugs in the hospital":* Ken Kesey quoted in Whitmer, *Aquarius Revisited,* p. 202.
92 *"I saw the looks":* Ken Kesey quoted ibid., p. 202.
93 *"American society as a loony bin":* Gurney Norman quoted in Perry, *On the Bus,* p. 22.
94 *"Ken was far from your average fellow":* Robert Stone to MT.

## VII. The Beginning of the Great Happening

95 *"with his bony Irish face":* Kesey, *Demon Box,* p. 82.
95 *"dealing with the end of time":* Ken Kesey quoted in Whitmer, *Aquarius Revisited,* p. 204.
96 *"A lot of it changed when Cassady showed up":* Robert Stone to MT.
97 *"there was the structured session of the research approach":* Stewart Brand to MT.
97 *"The attraction of being part of it":* Ibid.
98 *"trying to make it out of there":* Robert Stone to MT.
98 *"a full-time job":* Ibid.
98 *"much less realistic":* Ibid.
99 *"those early days with Kesey":* Ibid.
99 *"Everyone went their separate ways":* Ibid.
99 *"this party I had gone to in 1963":* Ibid.

## VIII. Our Assignment Is to Topple This Prudish, Judgmental Civilization

100 *six sublime weeks of psychedelic summer camp:* The events of the summer and fall of 1962 in Leary, *Flashbacks,* pp. 140–43; also in Stevens, *Storming Heaven,* pp. 197–99.
100 *"That was the year the shit really hit the fan":* Ram Dass to MT.
101 *"stern-eyed business-suited WASPS":* Leary, *Flashbacks,* p. 178.
101 *"We were trying to control it":* Ram Dass to MT.
102 *"the very definition of pathology":* Ibid.
102 *"The university was right to fire me":* Ibid.

102  *"almost all intellectual breakthroughs"*: Timothy Leary to MT.

102  *"We went to the isle of Dominica"*: Ram Dass to MT.

103  *the baroque sixty-four room, four-story mansion:* The Big House of Millbrook in Kleps, *Millbrook,* pp. 17–18; Leary, *Flashbacks,* pp. 189–90, pp. 21–29; Stevens, *Storming Heaven,* pp. 208–12.

104  *"like a ship on the high seas"*: Ram Dass to MT.

104  *"Our precise surgical target"*: Timothy Leary to MT.

## 4  Everybody Must Get Stoned

### I.  Vikings in Your Oatmeal

105  *"crazed with this strange sense of release"*: Sanders, "Total Assault Cantina," in *Tales of Beatnik Glory,* pp. 26–27.

106  *"The timidity of 1950s American culture"*: Ibid., pp. ii–iv.

106  *"like the tornado that had uprooted the cherry tree"*: Sanders, "A Book of Verse," in *Tales of Beatnik Glory,* p. 269.

107  *"controlled wildness"*: Sanders, "Mindscape," in *Tales of Beatnik Glory,* p. 90.

107  *"it was the best of times"*: Sanders, "Wild Women of East Tenth," in *Tales of Beatnik Glory,* p. 365.

107  *"There was already plenty of pot around"*: Ed Sanders to MT.

107  *"a mom-and-pop operation"*: Ibid.

107  *"There was the paradigm from* Howl*"*: Ibid.

108  *"people like Julian Beck"*: Ibid.

108  *"The gestalt provided the high"*: Ibid.

108  *"On the Lower East Side, it was grass"*: Ishmael Reed to MT.

109  *"You had to be* extremely *careful"*: Wavy Gravy to MT.

109  *"food tasted better"*: Ibid.

109  *"It was a period that only lasted in its pure state"*: Ibid.

109  *"Oh, yes, there was Mexican shit"*: Ibid.

111  *"white people felt completely trumped"*: Peter Coyote to MT.

112  *"I had dropped out of graduate school"*: Ed Sanders to MT.

112  "Federal Narcotics Agent": LEMAR release from the files of Ed Sanders.

112  *"Around the first of that year"*: Ed Sanders to MT.

### II.  A Gang of Innocents Playing with Fire

113  *the painted bus called* Furthur*:* Related by Carolyn "Mountain Girl" Adams Garcia to MT, hereinafter referred to as Mountain Girl in notes as well as in text.

113  *Neal Cassady suddenly appeared:* Ibid.

113  *"About a week later they had a party"*: Ibid.

114  *"a smile that lit up one's gizzard"*: Wolfe, *Electric Kool-Aid,* p. 117.

114  *"The forest was turned on!"*: Mountain Girl to MT.

114  *"He was the center"*: Ibid.

115  *What happened to the Merry Band:* Bus trip in Wolfe, *Electric Kool-Aid,* pp. 60–110.

115  *"To me, the real significance of Kesey's bus trip"*: Allen Ginsberg to MT.

116  *"I never got to see it"*: Mountain Girl to MT.

117  *"When we left the Angel hangout"*: Hunter Thompson quoted in Perry, *On the Bus,* p. 131.

117 *"they were a cross between the lost boys and the pirates"*: Mountain Girl to MT.
118 *The party wailed on:* Hells Angels bash with the Pranksters chronicled in Wolfe, *Electric Kool-Aid*, pp. 150–61; Perry, *On the Bus*, pp. 113–14, 129–35.

### III. Enough Acid to Blow the World Apart

118 *"the* epoch *of the psychedelic style"*: Wolfe, *Electric Kool-Aid*, p. 202.
119 *"Everybody's eyes turn on like headlights"*: Ibid., p. 212.
119 *"They were attempts to engage people in their senses"*: Ram Dass quoted in Perry, *On the Bus*, p. 151.
119 *"thousands of people, all helplessly stoned"*: Jerry Garcia quoted in Gans and Simon, *Playing in the Band*, p. 45.
120 *"If the Acid Tests hadn't happened"*: Jerry Garcia quoted ibid., p. 45.
120 *"dragon music"*: Harrison, *Dead Book*, p. 138.
121 *"messing around with ancient wisdom"*: Stanley Owsley quoted in Gans, *Conversations with the Dead*, pp. 307–8.
121 *"sort of like a crash course"*: Stanley Owsley quoted ibid., p. 308.
121 *"better to take a known substance in a known quantity"*: Stanley Owsley quoted ibid., p. 309.
121 *"But Owsley could surprise the hell out of you"*: Charlie Perry to MT.
122 *"devastatingly strong"*: Recounted by Charlie Perry in "Owsley and Me," *Rolling Stone*, November 25, 1982.
122 *a wizard alchemist with a messianic philosophy:* Portraits of Stanley Owsley in Lee and Shlain, *Acid Dreams*, pp. 146–47; Stevens, *Storming Heaven*, pp. 311–17; also MT interview with Charlie Perry.
123 *"When he started making acid"*: Charlie Perry to MT.
123 *"Bear came with a price"*: Mountain Girl to MT.
123 *"enough acid to blow the world apart"*: Jerry Garcia quoted in Greenfield, *Dark Star*, p. 82

### IV. How I Passed the Acid Test

124 *"like a really crack terrorist group"*: Ken Kesey quoted in Greenfield, *Dark Star*, p. 78.
124 *"They were really going to sock it to him"*: Mountain Girl to MT.
124 *"If ever I wanted to draw a crowd"*: Ken Kesey quoted in Graham and Greenfield, *Bill Graham Presents*, p. 138.
124 *"For the acid heads themselves"*: Wolfe, *Electric Kool-Aid*, p. 234.
125 *"When LSD exploded inside a body"*: Bill Graham quoted in Graham and Greenfield, *Bill Graham Presents*, p. 136.
125 *"There were a lot of people"*: Bill Graham quoted ibid.
126 *"If society wants me to be an outlaw"*: Ken Kesey quoted in Wolfe, *Electric Kool-Aid*, p. 235.
126 *"So I Ken Kesey"*: Ken Kesey quoted ibid., p. 236.
126 *"Everyone had been through so much together"*: Mountain Girl to MT.
127 *"We used these little six-ounce cups"*: Ibid.
127 *a woman became seriously unhinged:* Related by Wavy Gravy to MT.
128 *"in a condition of planetary emergency"*: Ibid.
128 *"At that moment some deep instinct took over"*: Ibid.
129 *"with no* anaesthetico*"*: Mountain Girl to MT.
130 *"Guys would be walking down the street"*: Ibid.

## V. This Was Not "My Boy Lollipop"

130 *a single candle where the band was set up:* Related by Paul Rothchild to MT.

131 *"the most intelligent piece of music I'd ever heard":* Paul Rothchid to MT.

132 *"From the very first joint":* Ibid.

133 *"The marijuana seemed to catalyze and enhance everything":* Ibid.

134 *"We became groupies":* Ibid.

134 *"an experience I might never have allowed myself":* Ibid.

134 *"that we were brothers":* Ibid.

135 *"From that moment on":* Ibid.

135 *"It was a magical night of camaraderie":* Ibid.

136 *"Bebop had featured a small community of musicians":* Ibid.

137 *"It was all a ruse":* Ibid.

137 *"I went to the control room":* Ibid.

## VI. A Snide Piece of Writing If Ever There Was One

137 *"a snide piece of writing if ever there was one":* Grace Slick to MT.

138 *"When I said, 'Feed your head' ":* Ibid.

138 *"Grace had such attitude":* Charlie Perry to MT.

138 *"tremendously outspoken person":* Mountain Girl to MT.

139 *"a crocheted top":* Grace Slick to MT.

139 *"You could hang out":* Ibid.

139 *"it didn't do for me":* Ibid.

139 *"but walls didn't breathe":* Ibid.

140 *"Time would be so different!":* Ibid.

141 *"Fifteen minutes into the performance":* Ibid.

141 *"It wasn't a goal-oriented process":* Grace Slick quoted in Rowes, *Grace Slick,* p. 95.

## VII. A Darkened Dance Floor Full of Astonished, Conspiratorial Glee

141 *"Who knew how many people":* Charlie Perry to MT.

142 *"it hurt my eyes":* Related by Charlie Perry to MT.

142 *"like everyone was going to a costume party":* Gleason, *Jefferson Airplane,* pp. 6–7.

143 *"as many vibrating colors":* Victor Moscoso quoted in Henke and Puterbaugh, *I Want to Take You Higher,* p. 99.

144 *"You walked onto a darkened dance floor":* Essay by Charles Perry, in Henke and Puterbaugh, *I Want to Take You Higher,* pp. 95–96.

144 *"LSD raised questions":* Charlie Perry to MT.

145 *"We never locked the door":* Mountain Girl to MT.

145 *"Back then, Garcia was an early riser":* Ibid.

146 *"Blow my mind to see a bunch of wiggly lines":* Janis Joplin quoted in Selvin, *Summer of Love,* p. 102.

146 *"Janis Joplin's talent":* Bill Graham quoted in Greenfield, *Bill Graham Presents,* p. 204.

## VIII. Acid Angel

147 *Dawn Reynolds* is a pseudonym. Some of the details of her story have been altered.

148 *"the most powerful aphrodisiac ever discovered by man":* Timothy Leary, "The Playboy Interview," *Playboy,* September 1966.

## IX. Monterey Purple

150 *"The entire place was getting off"*: Paul Rothchild to MT.
150 *"All of a sudden, the nation"*: Ibid.
152 *"Now there was an album"*: Phillips, *Papa John,* p. 173.
152 *"It just galvanized me"*: Paul Rothchild to MT.
152 *"Even the stalls selling food"*: Slick, *Somebody to Love?* p. 132.

# 5 White Light, White Heat

## I. Babylon in Flames

156 *The band was always dressed in black:* Velvet Underground and Exploding Plastic Inevitable described in Bockris and Malanga, *Uptight,* pp. 29–37; Bockris, *Transformer,* pp. 120–25; Bockris, *Life and Death,* pp. 186–88; Warhol and Hackett, *Popism,* pp. 162–63; also MT interviews with Mary Woronov, Gerard Malanga, and Ronnie Cutrone.
157 *"Concerning the Rumor That Red China Has Cornered the Methedrine Market"*: Title by Lou Reed with Angus MacLise, quoted in Bockris, *Transformer,* pp. 91–92.
157 *"You could do any drug you wanted"*: Ronnie Cutrone to MT.
158 *"People thought it was a needle"*: Gerard Malanga to MT.
158 *"Oh, it was all very prodrug"*: Mary Woronov to MT.
158 *"The flowers of evil are in bloom"*: Bockris, *Transformer,* p. 126.
158 *"We spoke two completely different languages"*: Mary Woronov to MT.

## II. The Perfect Time to Think Silver

160 *"It must have been the amphetamine"*: Warhol and Hackett, *Popism,* pp. 64–65.
160 *"Amphetamines were unique"*: Grinspoon and Hedblom, *Speed Culture,* p. 13.
161 *"This was all amphetamine busy work"*: Warhol and Hackett, *Popism,* p. 65.
161 *"a Pop temple"*: Bourdon, *Warhol,* p. 205.
162 *"It represented the true cracking"*: Mary Woronov to MT.
162 *"He didn't know that people were shooting up"*: Billy Linich quoted in Bockris, *Life and Death,* p. 146.
162 *"Oh, you were like God"*: Mary Woronov to MT.
163 *"I think I suffered from insecurity"*: Ibid.
164 *"It was so much fun"*: Ibid.
165 *"Paranoia was really our drug of choice"*: Ronnie Cutrone to MT.
165 *"Amphetamine doesn't give you peace of mind"*: Warhol and Hackett, *Popism,* p. 63.
165 *"sing until you choke, dance until you drop"*: Ibid., p. 64.

## III. Our Godless Civilization Approaching the Zero Point

166 *"This giant hypodermic needle"*: Ronnie Cutrone to MT.
166 *"the constant stretching of time"*: Gerard Malanga to MT.
167 *"People took us seriously"*: Ibid.
167 *The most spectacular was Freddie Herko:* The death of Freddie Herko in Bourdon, *Warhol,* p. 191; Warhol and Hackett, *Popism,* pp. 83–85; Bockris, *Life and Death,* p. 157; also MT interview with Diane di Prima.

168 *"Why didn't he tell me he was going to do it?"*: Bockris, *Life and Death*, p. 157.

168 *"Edie wasn't happy"*: Billy Linich quoted in McNeil and McCain, *Please Kill Me*, p. 13.

168 *"the nearly incommunicable torrents of speed"*: Edie Sedgwick, tapes of *Ciao! Manhattan*, quoted in Stein, *Edie*, p. 266.

168 *"turn on the whole world just for one moment"*: Ibid., p. 323.

169 *"Their lives became part of my movies"*: Warhol and Hackett, *Popism*, p. 180.

170 *Others might have stopped the camera*: Related by Gerard Malanga to MT.

170 *"The terror and desperation of Chelsea Girls "*: Bourdon, *Warhol*, p. 248.

171 *how he was trying to curtail his use of the drug*: Warhol and Hackett, *Popism*, p. 259.

171 *"deeper into the drug culture"*: Mary Woronov to MT.

171 *"locked in my apartment"*: Ronnie Cutrone to MT.

171 *"I think it was partly due to amphetamine"*: Gerard Malanga to MT.

172 *"Debbie Dropout, she's about sixteen here"*: Ibid.

172 *"The drugs were fuel and inspiration"*: Mary Woronov to MT.

173 *"Do I miss those years?"*: Ibid.

## 6 Next Stop Is Vietnam

### I. The Worm Has Definitely Turned for You, Man

175 *"In the Twenty-fifth Infantry"*: Oliver Stone to MT.

175 *"They were great parents but not always consistent"*: Ibid.

176 *"I wanted to see what I was made of"*: Oliver Stone quoted in Riordan, *Stone*, p. 40.

176 *" 'shotgunning' it into Chris' lungs"*: Scene in Stone, "Platoon," in Stone and Boyle, *Original Screenplays*, pp. 46–47.

177 *"On the one hand, the lifers"*: Stone, foreword to "Platoon," in Stone and Boyle, *Original Screenplays*, p. 9.

177 *"you'd feel it right down to your balls"*: Ibid., p. 9.

177 *"dashingly handsome"*: Ibid., p. 8.

178 *"I had never heard Motown before"*: Oliver Stone quoted in Riordan, *Stone*, p. 46.

178 *"The times in the field deadened me"*: Oliver Stone quoted ibid., p. 46.

178 *"as long as I could get it"*: Oliver Stone to MT.

178 *"The grass over there was whacko"*: Ibid.

178 *"What made it worse"*: Oliver Stone quoted in Riordan, *Stone*, p. 48.

178 *The pitched battle*: VC attack on Firebase Burt in Riordan, *Stone*, pp. 48–50.

179 *"There was this feeling in the air"*: Oliver Stone to MT.

179 *"I was with a wonderful girl"*: Ibid.

180 *"How did marijuana change me"*: Ibid.

180 *"A lot of people who were smoking"*: Ibid.

180 *"I took major acid in the Santa Cruz area"*: Ibid.

181 *"I was back and a criminal"*: Ibid.

181 *"The good news is I'm back"*: Ibid.

181 *"He thought that we were doing the right thing"*: Ibid.

181 *"I gave him a heavy dose"*: Ibid.

181 *"my first time on my own"*: Ibid.

182 *"solitary and wide-eyed youth"*: Stone, foreword to "Platoon," in Stone and Boyle, *Original Screenplays*, p. 5.

182 *"Conventional memory and narrative"*: Oliver Stone to MT.

## II. A Soldier's Best Friend

182 *Terry Carisi* is a pseudonym. Some of the details of his story have been altered.

188 *"It causes Assurance, Ovation of the Spirits":* Dr. John Jones, *The Mysteries of Opium Revealed* (1700), *High Times Encyclopedia*, p. 215.

## III. Of Bloods and Other Statistics

189 *Kimani Jones* is a pseudonym. Some of the details of his story have been altered.

190 *"Black Americans are considered to be the world's biggest fools":* Eldridge Cleaver, *Soul on Ice*, p. 120.

191 *"a shopping bag full of love":* Eldridge Cleaver, *Soul on Ice*, p. 18.

191 *little plastic vials of almost pure number 4 heroin:* The arrival of heroin in the spring of 1970 described in Spector, *After Tet*, pp. 276–77, and in McCoy, *Politics of Heroin*, pp. 222–23; also MT interview with Robert Stone.

192 *Reported deaths from drug overdose in the spring of 1970:* Spector, *After Tet*, pp. 276–77.

192 *whole platoons were using dope:* Westin and Shaffer, *Heroes and Heroin*, p. 48.

194 *the statistical jump in heroin addicts:* From 1963, when the McClellan Committee made the estimate of fewer than 50,000 heroin addicts for 1962, no official figures were kept in the United States until 1979—and the accuracy of those would always be suspect (different departments would have different statistics). The figure of 720,000 for 1972, cited by Sterling in *Octopus* (see p. 339), was given to him in 1989 by a spokesman for the U.S. State Department's Bureau of International Narcotics Matters—most likely an inflated estimate. In any event, the figure would eventually stabilize at just less than half a million, where it would remain and fluctuate by 100,000 to 200,000 over the years.

194 *its own historic experience of dope in Harlem:* Portrait of the heroin street trade related to MT by Vincent Cyrus of the Addicts Rehabilitation Center in Harlem.

195 *the organization was on the wane:* State of Black Panther movement and dope in Marine, *Black Panthers*, pp. 45–46.

# 7 Find the Cost of Freedom

## I. Nobody Lied

196 *"What was the Haight like?":* Ami Magill to MT.

197 *"You could be poor":* Ibid.

197 *"At the time, the only other hip store":* Ibid.

197 *"It was the closest to utopia I'd ever expect to find":* Tom Robbins to MT.

198 *"There was a flavor on the street":* David Felton to MT.

198 *"It was artistic, literary, political":* Ed Sanders to MT.

198 *"You could sing, get high":* Peter Coyote to MT.

199 *"Acid obliterated the ego":* Ibid.

## II. The Free Frame of Reference

200 *"When I saw plays like* The Brig*":* Peter Berg to MT.

200 *"The phrase was 'create the condition you describe' ":* Ibid.

200  *"not through propaganda"*: Ibid.

200  *The advent of the group:* Related by Peter Coyote to MT; also in Coyote, *Sleeping Where I Fall*, pp. 68–69.

201  *"Billy and Emmett had been on a roof"*: Peter Berg quoted in Sloman, *Steal This Dream*, p. 67.

201  *"Drugs became the experiment"*: Peter Coyote to MT.

202  *"LSD can be about starting over"*: Peter Berg to MT.

202  *"a Renoir of hippies in tie-dyed headdresses"*: Ibid.

202  *"Our pitch was 'Everything is free' "*: Ibid.

203  *"We won't, simply won't play"*: "The Ideology of Failure," *Berkeley Barb*, November 18, 1966.

203  *"Street events are social acid"*: "Trip Without a Ticket," *Digger Papers*, reprinted in *Realist*, August 1968.

203  *"There was a lot of acid in the Haight"*: Judy Goldhaft to MT.

203  *"If you look at this event intellectually"*: Ibid.

203  *"The brilliance of these events"*: Freeman House to MT.

204  *"We'd really blow out the jams"*: Peter Berg to MT.

204  *"a gorgeous railroad flat"*: Freeman House to MT.

204  *"There was a short period of time"*: Ibid.

205  *"that there were some things even more important"*: Grogan, *Ringolevio*, p. 220.

205  *"Emmett was a speed freak"*: Ami Magill to MT.

206  *"I'd never met anyone like Emmett"*: Freeman House to MT.

## III.  If You Do Not Believe, Wipe Your Eyes and See

206  *"a symbol of the profound and often comic incompatibilities"*: Kramer, *Allen Ginsberg in America*, p. 13.

207  *"everybody who hears my voice"*: Allen Ginsberg quoted in Lee and Shlain, *Acid Dreams*, p. 161.

207  *"The Be-In was like witnessing the prophecy of* Howl*"*: Allen Ginsberg to MT.

207  *"What if we're all wrong?"*: In Stevens, *Storming Heaven*, p. 331.

208  *"Speeches were irrelevant"*: Leary, *Flashbacks*, p. 259.

208  *"I was arrested for marijuana"*: Timothy Leary to MT.

208  *"The time will come"*: in Stevens, p. 271.

209  *"The vindictiveness in Laredo"*: Ibid.

209  TURN ON. TUNE IN. DROP OUT: Leary, *Flashbacks*, p. 253.

210  *"all those light-colored heads on acid"*: Ami Magill to MT.

210  *Grogan had cynically watched and listened:* Grogan, *Ringolevio*, p. 275.

211  *"we had the tiger by the tail"*: Allen Cohen to MT.

211  *"The Be-In was the original mass gathering"*: Allen Ginsberg quoted in Sloman, *Steal This Dream*, p. 58.

## IV.  Serenity, Tranquillity, and Peace

212  *developed by the noted chemist Alexander Shulgin:* In Shulgin and Shulgin, *PIHKAL*, pp. 53–56.

212  *"STP was like being shot out of a cannon"*: Grace Slick to MT.

212  *"lost something human"*: Stevens, *Storming Heaven*, p. 343.

## V. Nebraska Needs You More

214  *"if there was one square foot of space":* Ami Magill to MT.

214  *"The Haight became an open street fair":* Mountain Girl to MT.

214  *"the simple hippies, the stray teeny-boppers":* Von Hoffman, *We Are the People,* p. 175.

215  *"All utopias attract thugs":* Tom Robbins to MT.

215  *"rape is as common as bullshit on Haight Street":* Chester Anderson, "Uncle Tim's Children," quoted in Lee and Shlain, *Acid Dreams,* p. 186.

215  *"trampling the meadows in Yosemite":* Mountain Girl to MT.

216  *"They'd be laughing and pointing":* Ami Magill to MT.

216  *"taking the streets back":* Ibid.

216  *"I told the police captain":* Allen Cohen to MT.

216  *"The Grateful Dead and the other bands":* Mountain Girl to MT.

217  *"Their priority was the breakup of the Haight":* Allen Cohen to MT.

217  *"Acid dealers killing each other?":* Perry, *Haight-Ashbury,* p. 227.

218  *"mortally wounded":* McNeil, *Moving Through Here,* p. 137.

218  *"The whole place was charred":* Michael McClure to MT.

218  *The Death of Hippie:* Perry, *Haight-Ashbury,* p. 244; also MT interviews with Peter Berg and Peter Coyote.

## VI. How Peculiar . . .

219  *"There was a guy named Chance":* Wavy Gravy to MT.

220  *"We were promptly evicted":* Ibid.

220  *"People liked it there":* Ibid.

221  *"pick up a handful of raw silage":* Manson, *His Own Words,* pp. 42–45.

221  *"the subject that interested me":* Ibid., p. 69.

221  *magic, astral projection, Masonic lore:* These additional interests, including Eric Berne and Robert Heinlein, which are more indicative of the occult and mind-control techniques that Manson would become infamous for, were not mentioned by Manson in his book but are catalogued by Sanders in *Family,* pp. 28–30.

221  *The day of his release:* Manson, *His Own Words,* p. 79.

221  *"Pretty little girls":* Ibid., p. 81.

222  *One night at the Avalon Ballroom:* Acid trip described ibid., p. 82; also in Sanders, *Family,* p. 35.

222  *"hey, those kids knew everything":* Manson, *His Own Words,* p. 81.

222  *"the flower movement":* Sanders, *Family,* p. 37.

222  *"While some were running":* Manson, *His Own Words,* p. 97.

222  *"There were about twelve girls":* Phil Kaufman quoted in Felton, *Mindfuckers,* pp. 74–75.

223  *"Charlie is a super acid rap":* Felton, *Mind Fuckers,* p. 53.

223  *"Lee Harvey Oswald?":* Ibid., p. 26.

223  *"When I met her":* Manson, *His Own Words,* p. 122.

223  *The Spiral Staircase:* Ibid., pp. 122–23.

224  *The lady of the house welcomed them:* Detailed ibid., pp. 124–26.

225  *"Hey, man, I'd like to sleep with your wife":* Wavy Gravy to MT.

225  *"He said such creepy, contemptible things":* Jahanara Romney to MT.

225  *"It was sunset":* Ibid.

226  *"I was seized by this colossal energy":* Wavy Gravy to MT.

## VII.  The Power to Blow Their Minds

227  *"Here's a fact you may relish"*: Michael Rossman to MT.

227  *"By the time the FSM erupted"*: Ibid.

228  *"To a large extent, we were political people"*: Ibid.

228  *"The Free Speech Movement and the first Vietnam demonstrations"*: Jerry Rubin to MT.

229  *"The TV show that night was fantastic"*: Hoffman, *Best of*, p. 21.

229  *"See, the real drug was Walter Cronkite"*: Jerry Rubin to MT.

230  *"the power to blow their minds"*: Phrase first coined by the Free Speech Movement leader Mario Savio at Berkeley in 1964.

230  *"we will dye the Potomac red"*: Hoffman, *Best of*, pp. 26–27.

230  *October 21, 1967*: Accounts of Levitation in Rubin, *Do It!* pp. 75–78; Mailer, *Armies of the Night*, pp. 139–43; Sloman, *Steal This Dream*, pp. 99–100.

230  *"the Marxist acidhead"*: Rubin, *Do It!* p. 82.

## VIII.  Czechago

232  *"The world was going to be one great Be-In!"*: Jerry Rubin to MT.

232  *"the discontentment of post–World War II American youth"*: Ibid.

232  *"Yippie was simply a label"*: Krassner, *Confessions*, p. 157

232  *"We would be a party"*: Ibid., p. 157

232  *"I put forth a take-it-or-leave-it kind of attitude"*: Paul Krassner to MT.

233  *"The escalation of the war"*: Todd Gitlin to MT.

233  *"Plenty of people in the movement"*: Ibid.

233  *"Does one sacrifice for tomorrow"*: Ibid.

234  *"LSD was so great"*: Jerry Rubin to MT.

234  *the hash-oil "honey"*: Related in Krassner, *Confessions*, p.161, and in Sloman, *Steal This Dream*, pp. 143–148.

235  *"a giant frothing trough of mutant spinach egg noodles"*: Krassner, *Confessions*, p. 161.

235  *"I've asked myself that question"*: Todd Gitlin to MT.

235  *"Chicago would have happened the same way"*: Jerry Rubin to MT.

236  *"There was a melancholy fatalism with marijuana"*: Todd Gitlin to MT.

236  *"I got stoned a lot for the trial"*: Jerry Rubin to MT.

237  *"I knew if I ingested 300 mikes"*: Krassner, *Confessions*, p. 177.

237  *"Judge Julius Hoffman looked exactly like Elmer Fudd"*: Ibid., p. 177.

237  *"There was one point"*: Paul Krassner to MT.

237  *"He thought it was irresponsible"*: Ibid.

237  *"You started to see more and more people"*: Jerry Rubin to MT.

238  *"If you do an economic analysis"*: Ibid.

## IX.  The Best of Times, the Worst of Times

240  *"extraordinary complex and visceral metaphor"*: Greil Marcus, "The Apocalypse at Altamont," in *Sixties*, p. 308.

241  *"I could not understand"*: Ray Manzarek to MT.

241  *"It was a horrifying story"*: Ed Sanders to MT.

241  *"We have to be willing to make a moral differentiation"*: Ibid.

242  *"It was horrific to see the blessed falling"*: Paul Rothchild to MT.

242  *"When I was producing Janis's last album"*: Ibid.

243  *"It was one of those four-sets-a-night gigs"*: Ibid.

243  *"If you're not at that cutting edge":* Ibid.
244  *"It felt so unreal":* Mountain Girl to MT.
244  *"Pig was such a surprise":* Ibid.
244  *"Look, some people stayed in Scotland":* Grace Slick to MT.
245  *"Everybody got as drunk and fucked up as they could":* James Gurley quoted in Amburn, *Pearl,* p. 308.
245  *"I knew that I behaved illogically":* Danny Sugarman to MT.
245  *"I wanted to tell a story about addiction":* Ibid.
246  *"and if they did, the prevailing attitude":* Ibid.


### X.  The Place Where the Wave Finally Broke and Rolled Back

247  *"There wouldn't have been the Sixties":* Tom Robbins to MT.
247  *"It would have been impossible to write":* Ibid.
248  *"So you finally made it":* Related in Leary, *Flashbacks,* p. 337.
249  *"All of this would have been unthinkable":* Allen Ginsberg to MT.
249  *"as with American Indians":* Ginsberg, "Lounge Talks," (Kent State University, Kent, Ohio, April 15, 1971), in *Allen Verbatim,* p. 117.
249  *"but all that knowledge is lost now":* Related in Alpert, *Only Dance,* p. 112.
249  *"From then on":* Ram Dass to MT.
250  *"the direct blow to the solar plexus":* Michael Murphy quoted in Gustaitis, *Turning On,* p. 86.
251  *"It was the next logical step in the evolution":* Allen Cohen to MT.
252  *"Emmett stuck me with a needle twice":* Coyote, *Sleeping Where I Fall,* p. 73.
252  *"At a certain point, I was just not going to die a junkie":* Peter Coyote to MT.
252  *"Emmett got trapped in being Emmett":* Ibid.
252  *"The failure to curb personal indulgence":* Coyote, *Sleeping Where I Fall,* p. 350.
252  *"Emmett was a guidon":* Ibid., p. 326.
253  *"There was an element of naturism":* Peter Berg to MT.
253  *"At the time, very few people were growing marijuana":* Freeman House to MT.
253  *"I started growing great weed":* Mountain Girl to MT.
253  *"Pot was coming in from Mexico":* Ibid.
254  *"A lot of people became serious growers":* Ibid.
254  *"My whole approach to drugs":* Ibid.
254  *"With pot and psychedelics":* Paul Rothchild to MT.
255  *"I knew all was lost":* Ibid.
255  *"Most of the San Francisco bands":* Charlie Perry to MT.
255  *"I concluded at that point":* Ibid.
256  *"It knocked us out!":* Ibid.
256  *"We had two bags of grass":* Thompson, *Fear and Loathing,* p. 4.
256  *"a weird celebration for an era":* Hunter S. Thompson in *High Times* interview, September 1977.
256  *"It sounded the death knell":* Charlie Perry to MT.
257  *"absolutely certain that no matter which way I went":* Thompson, *Fear and Loathing,* p. 68.

## 8 The Golden Age of Marijuana

### I. Marijuana as Far as the Eye Can See

258 *Geoff DuBois* is a pseudonym. Some of the details of his story have been altered.

259 *There was big trouble in Babylon:* Portrait of Jamaican ganja trade and politics in Goldman, *Grassroots*, pp. 100–108; also in "Talk Rasta, Smoke Rasta," *High Times*, September 1976.

### II. We Support America One Hundred Percent, Especially South America

263 *"I would get pot in the mail":* Glenn O'Brien to MT.

263 *"A lot of kids my age interested in drugs":* Ibid.

264 *"all the dope you could smoke":* "From the Secret Scrapbooks of Steve Cropper, Dope Photographer," *High Times*, May 1984.

265 *"I didn't meet Tom until after":* Glenn O'Brien to MT.

265 *"The 'movement' was over":* Tom Forcade quoted in "The Gospel According to Tom," *High Times*, June 1984.

266 *"It was to be* Playboy's *sexual materialism":* Dean Lattimer, "Sex, Drugs and Tom Forcade," *High Times*, June 1982.

266 *"Dope was a world":* Albert Goldman, "Thomas King Forcade: Living and Dying the Great Adventure," *High Times*, January 1983.

267 *"There were people with pills in one room":* Tom Forcade quoted in "The Gospel According to Tom."

267 *"sinister, black-becloaked":* Lattimer, "Sex, Drugs, and Tom Forcade."

268 *a Greenwich Village safe house called Bobby's:* In Bob Lemmo, "Another Side of Tom Forcade," *High Times*, June 1982; also in Goldman, "Thomas King Forade."

268 *"We all believed":* Glenn O'Brien to MT.

268 *"Once after he left for a while":* Ibid.

269 *"We had all these games going on":* Ibid.

269 *"How did he die?":* Ibid.

269 *Forcade had watched his friend's aircraft explode:* Goldman, "Thomas King Forcade."

269 *"When I went to his funeral":* Glenn O'Brien to MT.

269 *"*High Times *got taken over by coke":* Ibid.

### III. The John L. Lewis of the Marijuana Movement

270 *"there was no such goddamned group":* Keith Stroup to MT.

271 *"We were zealots":* Ibid.

271 *"Lenny would say":* Paul Krassner to MT.

271 *"When I started NORML":* Keith Stroup to MT.

272 *"I thought we had an obligation":* Ibid.

273 *"The head of Carter's National Institute on Drug Abuse":* Ibid.

273 *"We went over to his place":* Ibid.

274 *The story of how the tide of national drug policy turned:* MT interview with Keith Stroup; also in Anderson, *High in America*, pp. 17–24, and Baum, *Smoke and Mirrors*, pp. 104–5, 113–14.

274 *"Now there was a time":* Keith Stroup to MT.

275   "It was crazy": Ibid.
275   "people I knew": Ibid.
275   "Quaaludes were used for sex": Ibid.
275   As soon as the story broke: The Bourne affair related by Keith Stroup to MT; also in Anderson, *High in America,* pp. 275–81, and Baum, *Smoke and Mirrors,* pp. 113–15.
276   *The Mexican government's practice:* The paraquat issue related by Keith Stroup to MT; also in Anderson, *High in America,* pp. 203, 206, 216–17, 228–29, 249–52, 265–67, 269–75, and Baum, *Smoke and Mirrors,* 106–9, 126–27.
277   "he was really selling us out": Keith Stroup to MT.
277   "Combined with the Quaalude prescription": Ibid.
277   "There was no doubt": Ibid.
278   "Anyone who works in major policy making": Ibid.
278   "these people came of age during the fairy-tale Fifties": Lynn Zimmer to MT.
280   "Even in the best of years": Keith Stroup to MT.
280   "push-down, pop-up effect": Many have made this basic observation about the drug trade, but Nadelmann was the first to use this phrase, when he was teaching and writing articles at the Woodrow Wilson School of Public and International Affairs at Princeton University, Princeton, N.J.
280   the second or third largest cash crop in America: According to NORML estimate in 1983, it was third—behind corn and soybeans, just ahead of wheat.


IV. It's Like Free Money . . .

281   "People would come up in droves": Steve Bowser to MT.
281   "A big part of the back-to-the-land movement": Freeman House to MT.
282   "Most military pilots": Steve Bowser to MT.
283   "not to get rich but to get poor": Raphael, *Cash Crop,* p. 25.
283   "Even before the marijuana industry blossomed": Ibid., p. 173.
284   "the perfect embodiment of a people's capitalism": Ibid., p. 171.
284   "For the first couple of years": Steve Bowser to MT.
284   "One of the funnier sights in Garberville": Ibid.
285   "Finding a buyer was very easy": Ibid.
285   "To a certain extent, I liked the outlaw aspect of it": Ibid.
285   "We were looking for just enough money": Freeman House to MT.
286   "Pot has been like a gift": Quoted in Raphael, *Cash Crop,* p. 146.
286   "We didn't realize": Steve Bowser to MT.


V. We're Here to Bring Humboldt County Back into the United States

287   "Helicopter, helicopter, over my head": In Raphael, *Cash Crop,* p. 133.
287   "My whole time in Da Nang": Steve Bowser to MT.
287   "It was the same battle": Ibid.
288   "Those ridiculously brazen guys": Ibid.
288   CAMP '83: Figures cited in Trebach, *Great Drug War,* p. 154.
288   "Next year, with the resources of the federal government": William Ruzzamenti quoted ibid., pp. 154–55.
288   "They landed a chopper": Steve Bowser to MT.
288   "These guys were recruits": Ibid.
289   "I don't know if you've ever been dive-bombed by a Huey": Freeman House to MT.

289  *"There were boards of supervisors":* William Ruzzamenti quoted in Raphael, *Cash Crop,* p. 106.

289  *Second-season tally:* Figures cited in Trebach, *Great Drug War,* p. 155.

289  *"They were out there the day my place got raided":* Steve Bowser to MT.

290  *"Anybody who's growing marijuana on their land":* William Ruzzamenti quoted in Raphael, *Cash Crop,* p. 105.

290  *"I had just bought this little motel":* Steve Bowser to MT.

290  *"For a half hour, they just tore the house apart":* Ibid.

290  *"so they had seized it":* Ibid.

290  *"We were growing them over in the brush":* Freeman House to MT.

291  *"frankly, they were embarrassed":* Ibid.

291  *"I knew that if I pleaded guilty":* Steve Bowser to MT.

291  *"stuff I never paid attention to":* Ibid.

291  *"Then he mentioned the three hundred combat missions":* Ibid.

292  *"The whole affair was traumatic":* Ibid.

292  *"CAMP didn't break the growers":* Freeman House to MT.

292  *"Not only is it like having a job":* Steve Bowser to MT.

## 9  Out of the Closets and into the Streets

### I.  Flaunting It in Frisco

294  *"I don't usually tell straight people this":* Dennis Peron to MT.

295  *"I turned on a lot of people":* Ibid.

295  *"I renounced wealth and power":* Ibid.

295  *"The politically conscious men of the Castro":* Shilts, *Mayor of Castro Street,* p. 175.

296  *"I've got to fight not just for me":* Harvey Milk quoted ibid., p. 72.

297  *"It was kind of one-stop shopping":* Dennis Peron to MT.

297  *"Things were getting big":* Ibid.

299  *"And then I was busted":* Ibid.

299  *"People were rolling joints":* Ibid.

299  *"Then, a spectacular trial":* Ibid.

299  *"One day outside in the hallway":* Ibid.

299  *"I know people who are still in prison":* Ibid.

300  *White's rabidly antigay conservatism:* In the trial that followed, White's so-called "Twinkie Defense"—that junk food had exacerbated his already severe depression—resulted in an outrageously light sentence of five years with parole, handed down by a jury in which anyone even remotely pro-gay was barred, which detonated rioting in the Castro. As for Dan White, he committed suicide after serving five years and being paroled.

300  *"Harvey openly supported drug users":* Ibid.

300  *"I caused Harvey to be killed":* Ibid.

### II.  The Smell of a Vanished Era

301  *"Okay, here we are, the Anvil":* Lance Loud to MT.

302  *"At first, I was shocked":* Ibid.

302  *"Drugs were a means of conforming":* Ibid.

302  *"I went to the baths":* Ibid.

302   *"MDA may have been known"*: Ibid.
303   *"It was like angel dust"*: Ibid.
303   *A brief dossier on amyl nitrate:* In Lingeman, *Drugs from A to Z,* pp. 11–12.
303   *"Poppers were just one of those accoutrements"*: Lance Loud to MT.
304   *"I used amyl nitrate a lot back in the Fifties"*: John Rechy to MT.
304   *"It helped me break away"*: Ibid.
304   *"edging into heroin"*: Ibid.
304   *"the silently symphonic, intricate"*: Rechy, *Sexual Outlaw,* p. 196.
304   *"Knowing that each second"*: Ibid., p. 31.
305   *"And what was found?"*: Ibid., p. 107.
305   *"At its best, the gay experience"*: Ibid., p. 242.
305   *"I hate the word* gay": John Rechy to MT.
305   *"It was almost as if sex"*: Ibid.
305   *"It's true that amyl heightens the sexual sensation"*: Ibid.
306   *"The spectacle"*: Ibid.
306   *"We brought those props in"*: Ibid.
306   *"When I began writing"*: Ibid.
307   *"AIDS had nothing to do with promiscuity"*: Ibid.
307   *"I think a lot of people don't want to deal with the drug issue"*: Lance Loud to MT.

# 10  The Last Dance

## I.  Secret Stash, Heavy Bread

308   *Rollie Huggins* is a pseudonym. Some of the details of his story have been altered.
309   *"a closely studied art, a technique of survival"*: Woodley, *Dealer,* p. 2.
309   *"a powerful central nervous system stimulant"*: Ibid., p. 12.
312   *a sevenfold increase since 1969:* Cited in Ashley, *Cocaine,* p. 125.
312   *"In the last three years the coke traffic"*: "The VOS Caper," *Newsweek,* December 17, 1973.

## II.  Like Flying to Paris for Breakfast

313   *"This was as big a scam as Swan ever pulled off"*: Bob Sabbag to MT.
313   *"and here he was doing a drug"*: Ibid.
314   *"It was a very subtle high"*: Ibid.
314   *"a relatively benign substance"*: Ibid.
314   *"We all knew"*: David Crosby to MT.
314   *"This notion didn't come from nowhere"*: Bob Sabbag to MT.
316   *"When I started LEMAR in Buffalo"*: Michael Aldrich to MT.
316   *"My interest"*: Ibid.
316   *"I hate cocaine"*: Allen Ginsberg to MT.
316   *"I felt like cocaine"*: Tom Robbins to MT.
317   *"four lines a night"*: Michael Aldrich to MT.
318   *"We were set up for it"*: Ibid.
318   *"It was the pre-Medellín cartel"*: Bob Sabbag to MT.
319   *"He almost got killed"*: Ibid.
319   *"There weren't any bad reviews"*: Ibid.

319  *"We did a major publicity tour"*: Ibid.
320  *"People would come up to me"*: Ibid.
320  *"an acceptable recreational drug"*: Ruling quoted in *High Times,* April 1977.
321  *"the modern equivalent"*: High Times, *Encyclopedia of Recreational Drugs,* p. 176.


## III.  Pagan Rome

321  *Suzie Ryan* is a pseudonym. Some of the details of her story have been altered.
324  *Richard Stoltz* is a pseudonym. Some of the details of his story have been altered.


## IV.  Adieu, Cocaine

325  *"stoned out of my head on Quaaludes and coke"*: Oliver Stone quoted in James Riordan, *Stone,* p. 109.
325  *"Cocaine was a fever"*: Oliver Stone to MT.
326  *"We quickly found out"*: David Crosby to MT.
326  *"Cocaine was so integrated"*: Michelle Phillips to MT.
327  *"On a surface level"*: Oliver Stone to MT.
327  *"I felt that the product was mechanical"*: Ibid.
327  *a cocaine boomtown of violence and money:* Gugliotta and Leen, *Kings of Cocaine,* pp. 6–7.
328  *The deluge of drugs and money:* Ibid., pp. 14–15, 106–7.
328  *the formation of a cabinet-level task force:* Ibid., pp. 110–11.
329  *"I was still doing blow"*: Oliver Stone to MT.
329  *"I went cold turkey"*: Ibid.
329  *"Cocaine is like a lightning bolt"*: Ibid.
331  *"I remember writing that image"*: Ibid.


## V.  A Crazy Glorious Unrestrained Slobbering *Saucier* of Drug-Demented Elation

332  *"Humor is just icing"*: Michael O'Donoghue to MT.
332  *"It was a defining event"*: Ibid.
332  *"It was resin of marijuana"*: Ibid.
333  *"We at the* Lampoon*"*: Ibid.
334  *"Certain people did cocaine"*: Ibid.
335  *his substance abuse evaluation:* Quoted in Woodward, *Wired,* p. 111.
335  *"John would actually use cocaine on the broadcast"*: Michael O'Donoghue to MT.
336  *"He was a dancer"*: Ibid.
337  *"The horrible thing"*: Ibid.
337  *"I just thought, They're going to take this"*: Ibid.
337  *"Judy told me that the book would be a 'tribute' "*: Ibid.
338  *"so inaccurate"*: Ibid.
338  *"One of the things that people don't know about Belushi"*: Bob Sabbag to MT.
339  *"You could see the curve coming"*: Ibid.
339  *"They were elusive qualities to get"*: Michael O'Donoghue to MT.

# 11 Hangin' Bangin' and Slangin'

## I. Gangstress

344  *"Drive-by, drive-by, drive-by":* Sylvia Nunn to MT.
344  *"These right here":* Ibid.
344  *"One come in daylight":* Ibid.
345  *"When you look at these homes":* Ibid.
345  *"I ain't ever done a fuckin' drive-by":* Ibid.
345  *"I can outshoot any nigga in this neighborhood":* Ibid.
346  *"so they got me and put me up through the window":* Ibid.
346  *"Bein' OG, we got seniority":* Ibid.
346  *"It's just like they say":* Ibid.
347  *"In this day and time":* Ibid.

## II. The Most Addictive Drug Known to Man

347  *"People have shot at me":* Jim Galipeau to MT.
348  *"This is one of the main north-south streets":* Ibid.
348  *"On the other side":* Ibid.
348  *"One of the biggest frauds":* Ibid.
348  *"I'll tell you what drugs are":* Ibid.
348  *"they call them strawberries":* Ibid.
349  *"This is the projects":* Ibid.
349  *"This is the main street in Nickerson Gardens":* Ibid.
349  *"The rich and powerful":* Paul Schrader to MT.
349  *"A lot of the people who got lost":* Bob Sabbag to MT.
350  *The Omnibus Crime Act of 1984:* Baum, *Smoke and Mirrors,* p. 203; also in Joseph E. DiGenova and Constance L. Belfiore, "An Overview of the Comprehensive Crime Control Act of 1984—The Prosecutor's Perspective," *American Criminal Law Review* 22 (1985).
350  *Crack began as a marketing ploy:* "The Men Who Created Crack," *U.S. News and World Report,* August 19, 1991; also related to MT by Ansley Hamid of the John Jay College of Criminal Justice, City University of New York.
350  *Newsweek was the first to get a real whiff of the crack story:* The explosion of media hysteria over crack in Reinarman and Levine, "Crack in Context," in *Crack in America,* pp. 3–5; also in Reinarman and Levine, "The Crack Attack: Politics and Media in the Crack Scare," in *Crack in America,* pp. 20–22, 28–32.
351  *"When the crack scare began":* Craig Reinarman to MT.
352  *the death of Len Bias:* In "The Mystery of a Star's Death," *Newsweek,* June 30, 1986; also, the evaluation of its impact from MT interviews with Marsha Rosenbaum and Lynn Zimmer.
352  *"crack babies":* Origins of story, media coverage, and political ramifications in Baum, *Smoke and Mirrors,* pp. 218–19, 267–72; Loren Siegel, "The Pregnancy Police Fight the War on Drugs," in Reinarman and Levine, *Crack in America;* and John P. Morgan and Lynn Zimmer, "The Social Pharmacology of Smokeable Cocaine: Not All It's Cracked Up to Be," ibid.; also MT interviews with John P. Morgan, Lynn Zimmer, and Craig Reinarman.
352  *low-birth-weight, learning-disabled babies:* Siegel, "The Pregnancy Police," p. 255; *New York Times* editorial, August 19, 1990.

352 *"like Max Headroom and reincarnations of Elvis":* Morgan and Zimmer, "The Social Pharmacology of Smokeable Cocaine," p. 152.

353 *Claire Coles:* In Baum, *Smoke and Mirrors,* pp. 217–218, 338.

353 *"biologic underclass":* Joanne Jacobs, "To Help the Child, Help the Man," *San Jose Mercury News,* July 2, 1991.

354 *the highly rated, hour-long CBS special* 48 Hours on Crack Street*:* In Trebach, *Great Drug War,* p. 13. Crack meant big money for the networks. According to the Nielsen ratings, this was the highest rated of any news documentary for any network in five and a half years, watched by fifteen million people.

354 *"Bills were tossed into legislative hoppers":* Trebach, *Great Drug War,* pp. 7–8.

354 *"Measures were proposed":* Ibid.

355 *"outspoken intolerance":* Ronald Reagan and Nancy Reagan, National Address on Drug-Abuse Prevention, Office of White House Press Secretary, September 14, 1986.

355 *Drug-Free America Act of 1986:* U. S. Sentencing Commission, *Special Report to the Congress: Mandatory Minimum Penalties in the Federal Criminal Justice System* Appendix A, August 1991.

355 *the greatest incarceration rate in the world:* In Ira Glasser and Loren Siegel, "When Constitutional Seem Too Extravagant to Endure: The Crack Scare's Impact on Civil Liberties," in Reinarman and Levine, *Crack in America,* pp. 229–43; also in Marc Mauer, *Americans Behind Bars: A Comparison of International Rates of Incarceration* (Washington, D. C.: Sentencing Project, 1991).

355 *41 percent of all those arrested on cocaine or heroin charges:* Lusanne, *Pipe Dream Blues,* p. 45; Jack Kelley and Sam Vincent Meddis, "Critics Say Bias Spurs Police Focus on Blacks," *USA Today,* December 20, 1990.

355 *Vic Graziello* is a pseudonym. All experiences rendered and quotations attributed herein come directly from this individual.

## III. A Whole New Class of Hero Coming Up

357 *"These guys in their mid-twenties":* Jim Galipeau to MT.

358 *"They found the guy nude":* Ibid.

358 *"There was a whole new class of hero":* Snoop Dogg, *Doggfather,* p. 41.

359 *a volume business:* Ibid., p. 92–94.

359 *"twenty-four seven":* Ibid., p. 59.

359 *"That's where I learned the true nature of black and white":* Ibid., p. 60.

360 *"The scar of over twenty years":* Shakur, *Monster,* p. xiii.

361 *"I used to see cops":* Jim Galipeau to MT.

361 *"The whole fucking game was a scam":* Snoop Dogg, *Dogg father,* p. 149.

361 *"It was like I'd had an itch":* Ibid., p. 129.

361 *"about conditions on the street":* Ibid., pp. 158–59.

362 *"We were telling it like it was":* Ibid., p. 173.

362 *"Cocaine is poison":* Ibid., p. 93.

362 *"We've got to stop killing each other":* Ibid., p. 210.

## IV. Crumb Sack

362 *"I know damn near everybody":* Sylvia Nunn to MT.

362 *"What kills me about them":* Ibid.

362 *"Golly, I can't honestly say that I'm not addicted":* Ibid.

363  *"I have gifts from God"*: Ibid.
363  *"It was like somebody took a torch"*: Ibid.
363  *"he was the sweet one"*: Ibid.
363  *"A 'crumb sack'"*: Ibid.
363  *"My brother in the penitentiary"*: Ibid.
364  *"It ain't over till it's over"*: Ibid.
364  *"I wanna start out"*: Ibid.
364  *"And then another part of me want to ask him"*: Ibid.
364  *"the last weapon in the Devil's arsenal"*: Ed Bullins, "Salaam, Huey Newton, Salaam,"
       in Stein and Young, *Short Plays,* p. 10.
364  *"This is my bottom"*: Sylvia Nunn to MT.
365  *"I said, 'Lord, I don't know what's happenin'"*: Ibid.

## 12  Spiritus Contra Spiritum

### I. That's Why They Call It Recovery

366  *"I was in full flower in '85"*: David Crosby to MT.
366  *"I was a stone-cold junkie"*: Ibid.
367  *"All basers are obsessed with it"*: Crosby, *Long Time Gone,* p. 294.
367  *"falling down a dark elevator shaft"*: Paul Schrader to MT.
367  *"like starving Dobermans waiting for red meat"*: Michael O'Donoghue to MT.
367  *"I sold that piano"*: David Crosby to MT.
368  *"It was one of the places I tried to get straight"*: Ibid.
368  *At the party:* Related by David Crosby to MT.
369  *"They set me up good!"*: David Crosby to MT.
369  *"You gotta be real bad"*: Ibid.
369  *"I've had a lot of wonderful things happen"*: Ibid.

### II. Then Came the Bugs

371  *John Phillips experienced them as maggots:* Phillips, *Papa John,* p. 338.

### III. The Only Real Revolution

372  *"It was not my idea to stop using drugs"*: Grace Slick to MT.
372  *Along the way, there were three DUIs:* Ibid.
372  *"This was Public Intoxication"*: Ibid.
372  *"I don't mind radical things"*: Ibid.
373  *"I was sort of out there on a limb by myself"*: Ibid.
373  *"A shoe salesman would get up"*: Ibid.
373  *"See, I always hated the Catholic Church"*: Ibid.
373  *Most people who used drugs:* The generally accepted figures are as follows: some thirty
       million smoked pot, twenty million tried cocaine, and ten million took psyche-
       delics. The rationale for this statement is simple: at any given time, there were never
       more than roughly five hundred thousand heroin addicts or five million daily users
       of cocaine. Therefore, the overwhelming majority of those who tried or used
       illicit drugs clearly did not become addicts.

374 *"Once you go into A.A.":* Grace Slick to MT.

374 *"I was shaking and withdrawing":* Ronnie Cutrone to MT.

375 *"There was a hole in my heart":* Ibid.

375 *"this peace just came over me":* Ibid.

375 *"I remember being sober":* Ibid.

375 *"My art got a hundred times better":* Ibid.

375 *"In my opinion, the only real revolution is recovery":* Ibid.

377 *a 300 percent increase in the number of officially listed A.A. groups:* A.A. World Services, *Analysis of the 1989 Survey of the Membership of A.A.*

377 *some fifteen million Americans were attending some form of 12-step group:* "Afflicted? Addicted? Support Groups Are the Answer for 15 Million Americans," *Newsweek,* February 5, 1990.

377 *"the reigning metaphor":* Craig Reinarman, "The Twelve Step Movement and Advanced Capitalist Culture: Notes on the Politics of Self-Control in Postmodernity," in Darnovsky, Epstein, and Flacks, *Contemporary Social Movements and Cultural Politics,* p. 97.

377 *"No once-wild 'party' in Hollywood or Aspen":* Hunter S. Thompson, "I Knew the Bride When She Used to Rock and Roll," in *Songs of the Doomed,* pp. 270–71.

378 *"It's hard for anybody who's straight":* David Crosby to MT.

378 *"Those people who hurt themselves with their private drug use":* Keith Stroup to MT.

379 *"What has been presented as straightforward data":* Peele, *Diseasing of America,* p. vii.

## IV. Trudging the Road of Happy Destiny

380 *"Addiction is distinguished from drug use":* Gorski and Miller, *Staying Sober,* p. 39.

381 *"We admitted we were powerless over alcohol":* Twelve steps in Alcoholics Anonymous, *How It Works,* p. 59.

383 *"If there be a God":* Bill Wilson quoted in A.A. World Services, *Pass It On,* p. 121.

383 *"I stood upon its summit":* Bill Wilson quoted ibid., p. 121.

383 *"The sway of alcohol over mankind":* James, *Varieties of Religious Experience,* p. 387.

383 *"the equivalent on a low level of the spiritual thirst":* Carl Jung letter to Bill Wilson cited in A.A. World Services, *Pass It On,* p. 384.

385 *"Pain is the touchstone of all spiritual progress":* A.A. World Services, *Twelve Steps and Twelve Traditions,* pp. 93–94.

# 13  Nouveau Psychedelia

## I.  A Strange and Wondrous Atmosphere of Collective Intimacy

388 *exposed to more than four hundred print and television ads:* Figures from Partnership for a Drug-Free America, 1995 Fact Sheet.

389 *"a remarkable chemical":* Reynolds, *Generation Ecstasy,* p. 81.

389 *"medicine for a new millennium":* Holland, *Ecstasy,* p. 9.

390 *"When large numbers of people took Ecstasy":* Reynolds, *Generation Ecstasy,* p. 83.

391 *a record number of eight million hits:* Cited in Holland, *Ecstasy,* p. 1.

391 *a club-drug conference in July of 2000:* Ibid., p. 395.

391 *Every weekend around the world:* Ibid., p. 1.

## II. The Quaint Little Laboratory on the Sloping Hill

391  *"I own right up to the edge"*: Sasha Shulgin to MT.

391  *"Here, try this"*: Ibid.

391  *"This is my hideaway"*: Ibid.

391  *"Chemistry is an art"*: Ibid.

392  *"one of those late-night-movie laboratories"*: Shulgin and Shulgin, *PIHKAL*, p. 57.

392  *"The DEA have a strange way of visiting"*: Sasha Shulgin to MT.

392  *"an almost encyclopedic compendium of synthetic methods"*: Nichols, foreword to Shulgin and Shulgin, *PIHKAL*, p. x.

393  *"Every drug, legal or illegal"*: Ibid., pp. xiv–xv.

393  *"You know where all of Wilhelm Reich's notes"*: Sasha Shulgin to MT.

394  *"the magnificent essential oils"*: Ibid.

394  *MDMA:* Early history in Eisner, *Ecstasy,* pp. 1–3; also in Holland, *Ecstasy,* pp. 11–12.

394  *"It did not have the bells and whistles"*: Shulgin and Shulgin, *PIHKAL*, p. 34.

394  *the quiet and cautious dissemination of the substance:* In Holland, *Ecstasy,* p. 12; Eisner, *Ecstasy,* pp. 4–5; and Beck and Rosenbaum, *Pursuit of Ecstasy,* pp. 13–15; also, MT interviews with Marsha Rosenbaum, Sasha Shulgin, and Andrew Weil.

394  *"feeling optimizer"*: Claudio Naranjo, M.D., "Experience with the Interpersonal Psychedelies," in Holland, p. 210.

395  *"I thought it had a unique effect"*: Andrew Weil to MT.

395  *"I was working with a guy"*: Marsha Rosenbaum to MT.

396  *"It seemed inevitable"*: Andrew Weil to MT.

396  *the transformation of MDMA into Ecstasy:* Holland, *Ecstasy,* pp. 13–14; Eisner, *Ecstasy,* pp. 4–15; Beck and Rosenbaum, *Pursuit of Ecstasy,* pp. 16–19; also, MT interviews with Sasha Shulgin, Andrew Weil, and Marsha Rosenbaum.

396  *"real middle-class girls in their twenties"*: Marsha Rosenbaum to MT.

397  *to declare MDMA a schedule one drug:* Criminalization and hearings in Holland, *Ecstasy,* pp. 14–16; Eisner, *Ecstasy,* pp. 18–27; and Beck and Rosenbaum, *Pursuit of Ecstasy,* pp. 19–25.

398  *"Texas was the demise of E"*: Marsha Rosenbaum to MT.

398  *"I looked at it with great sadness"*: Sasha Shulgin to MT.

399  *"I think MDMA is going to continue"*: Andrew Weil to MT.

399  *"The DEA hosted a meeting"*: Sasha Shulgin to MT.

400  *"Those fuckers won"*: Michael Rossman to MT.

400  *"Publishers were interested"*: Sasha Shulgin to MT.

400  *"I hope this is the new seed"*: Ibid.

401  *"Oh, yes, it's alive and well today"*: Ibid.

401  *"on the use of the tryptamines"*: Ibid.

401  *the DEA showed up with a warrant:* Entire story related in Shulgin and Shulgin, *TIHKAL*, pp. 17–37.

402  *"He was the one they wanted to punish"*: Ibid., p. 32.

402  *"The authorities intended to frighten him"*: Ibid., p. 37.

## III. Déjà Vu All Over Again

402  *"I had a real problem"*: Sharon (declined to provide last name at the time) to MT.

403  *MDMA was born in the USA, traveled to Britain:* Rave scene in the United Kingdom in Holland, *Ecstasy,* pp. 17–18; Beck and Rosenbaum, *Pursuit of Ecstasy,* p. 53; and Reynolds, *Generation Ecstasy,* pp. 57–79.

403 *"a weird mix of Mediterranean beach bum"*: Reynolds, *Generation Ecstasy*, pp. 58–59.

404 *"House and techno sounded especially fabulous"*: Ibid., p. 84.

404 *"diminishing-returns syndrome"*: Ibid., pp. 89–90.

405 *"House music is the beginning"*: Sharon to MT.

405 *"that people all over the world are the same"*: Ibid.

406 *"I'd experienced euphoria through my art"*: Ibid.

406 *"Now that I've been through drugs"*: Ibid.

406 *"They were unique, these parties"*: Ibid.

406 *"Toon Town was revolutionary"*: Preston Lytton to MT.

407 *"It was the first underground party"*: Bryan Hughes to MT.

407 *"We developed a following at this small venue"*: Ibid.

407 *"Eight thousand people showed up"*: Ibid.

407 *"Actually that's how we started Toon Town"*: Preston Lytton to MT.

408 *"There was always a psychedelic culture out here"*: Ibid.

## IV. The Future Has Imploded onto the Present

408 *"This generation absolutely swallowed computers"*: Stewart Brand to MT.

408 *"Our computer networks give us the best clue"*: Douglas Rushkoff, "Ecstasy: Prescription for Cultural Renaissance," in Holland, *Ecstasy,* p. 352.

409 *"It seemed that those who had experience"*: Ibid., p. 352.

409 *"a consensual hallucination"*: William Gibson, *Neuromancer,* p. 3.

409 *"I think Rudy Rucker, in our first issue, coined a cyberpunk slogan"*: RU Sirius to MT.

410 *"There was this strange subculture, these stoned scholars"*: Ibid.

410 *The future has imploded onto the present:* In Rucker, Sirius, and Mu, *Mondo 2000,* p. 64.

411 *Mistrust Authority:* Ibid., p. 66.

411 *"I enjoy READING about people taking psychedelics"*: Rudy Rucker, "On the Edge of the Pacific," ibid., p. 11.

411 *"Terence McKenna is a very, very amazing brain"*: RU Sirius to MT.

411 *"In the last two or three years"*: Terence McKenna to MT.

412 *"Shamanism without psychedelics"*: Ibid.

412 *"I was told it only lasted five minutes"*: Ibid.

413 *"Are we dealing with an aspect"*: McKenna, *Archaic Revival,* p. 28.

413 *"The Logos spoke the truth"*: Ibid., p. 241.

413 *"Extinction or the reengineering of human psychology"*: Terence McKenna to MT.

414 *"a time of nomadic pastoralism"*: Ibid.

414 *"the whole gamut of cultural furniture"*: Ibid.

414 *"the re-empowerment of ritual"*: McKenna, *Archaic Revival,* p. 248.

414 *"the archaic techniques of ecstasy"*: Ibid., p. 13.

415 *"it and the planet must part"*: Ibid., p. 61.

415 *"the last best hope"*: Terence McKenna to MT.

415 *"deputized minority—a shamanic professional class"*: Ibid.

415 *"The way to put something over on a government"*: Ibid.

## V. The World's Oldest Cyberpunk

416 *"For example, I made the classic mistake"*: Timothy Leary to MT.

417 *"Oh, yes, we were well meaning good-natured primitives"*: Ibid.

417 *"a galactic network of a hundred billion neurons"*: Ibid.

417 *"The PC is the LSD of the Nineties"*: Ibid.

417 *"pilots of the species"*: Leary, "The Cyberpunk: The Individual as Reality Pilot," in *Chaos and Cyber Culture*, pp. 62–69.

417 *"Mavericks, ronin, free-lancers"*: Ibid., p. 63.

418 *"It happened after the Italian Renaissance"*: Timothy Leary to MT.

418 *"I still honor botanical substances"*: Ibid.

419 *"Hey, the receptor sites are there!"*: Ibid.

## 14 Just Say Know

### I. The Second Smallest Political Movement in the World

421 *"You can't avoid that slippery slope"*: Reinarman's comment made to a meeting of the Princeton Working Group, May 23, 1994.

421 *"We were trying to think through"*: Ethan Nadelmann to MT. (This interview took place on October 11, 1992, when Nadelmann was still at the Woodrow Wilson School of Public and International Affairs of Princeton University.)

422 *"The socialist dictatorships of Eastern Europe"*: Ibid.

422 *"Everybody was learning from each other"*: John P. Morgan to MT.

422 *"We'd all like to be some part of that"*: Ibid.

### II. Psychopharmacological McCarthyism

422 *"I had a women, a lovely lady"*: Keith Stroup to MT.

423 *"There's no doubt that part of what the Reagan revolution was about"*: Ibid.

423 *"I believe you shouldn't allow yourself to be marginalized"*: Ed Sanders to MT.

424 *the case of Judge Douglas Ginsburg*: Baum, *Smoke and Mirrors*, p. 247; "Pot and Politics," *Newsweek*, November 16, 1987.

424 *pot could make you gay*: "The Great Drug Debate: Reagan Aide Takes Issue with *Newsweek* Story," *Washington Post*, October 22, 1986.

424 *"zero tolerance"*: Baum, *Smoke and Mirrors*, p. 244.

424 *to burnish the image of the drug war*: Ibid., p. 253; Aaron Epstein, "Meese Seeks Positive PR on Drug War," *Atlanta Constitution-Journal*, May 14, 1988.

424 *"no such thing as 'recreational' drug use"*: Baum, *Smoke and Mirrors*, p. 253; Steven Wisotsky, "A Society of Suspects: The War on Drugs and Civil Liberties," *Cato Policy Analysis* (October 2, 1992), p. 21.

424 *"accomplices to murder"*: Baum, *Smoke and Mirrors*, p. 253.

424 *mandatory minimum sentences*: Ibid., pp. 246–47; Trebach, *Great Drug War*, p. 153; U.S. Sentencing Commission, *Special Report to the Congress: Mandatory Minimum Penalties in the Federal Criminal Justice System*, August 1991.

424 *new prisons*: Doubling of U.S. prison budgets in U.S. Department of Justice, *Sourcebook of Criminal Justice Statistics, 1993*, p. 19.

424 *"The government's regulatory interest"*: U.S. v. Salerno, 481 U.S. 739 (1987).

424 *"Drug-courier profiles"*: U.S. v. Sokolow, 109 S. Ct. 490 (1989).

424 *forfeitures accelerated*: Baum, *Smoke and Mirrors*, pp. 282–83; *Federal Forfeiture of the Instruments and Proceeds of Crime: The Program in a Nutshell*, Executive Office of Asset Forfeiture, U.S. Department of Justice, 1990.

425 *another typical college kid swept up in the Sixties*: Bennett's background in Jacob Sullum, "Bill Bennett's Blinders," *Reason*, March 1990; Michael Isikoff, "Sharp

Tongued Intellectual Faces a Different Problem," *Washington Post,* January 13, 1989; and Frank Deford, "The Fabulous Bennett Boys," *Vanity Fair,* August 1994.

425 *the same fundamentalist conservative philosophy of personal responsibility:* Bennett's views on drugs and drug policy in Baum, *Smoke and Mirrors,* pp. 262–67; Lusane, *Pipe Dream Blues,* p. 70; "Bennett's Big Battle," *Time,* March 13, 1989; Bennett, *De-Valuing of America;* and MT interviews with Ethan Nadelmann, Lynn Zimmer, and Craig Reinarman.

426 *"user accountability":* Office of National Drug Control Policy, (Washington, D.C.: U.S. Government Printing Office, 1989).

426 *"highly contagious":* Ibid.

426 *"a three-hundred-million-dollar industry":* Lynn Zimmer and James B. Jacobs, "The Business of Drug Testing: Technological Innovations and Social Control," *Contemporary Drug Problems* (Spring 1992), and Cindy Skrzycki, "Drug Testing Industry Shows Its Wares," *Washington Post,* October 17, 1990.

426 *"de facto martial law":* Lewis H. Lapham, "Political Opiate—The War on Drugs Is a Folly and a Menace," *Harper's Magazine,* December 1989.

427 *"This—this is crack cocaine":* George Bush, Address by the President on National Drug Policy, Office of White House Press Secretary, September 5, 1989.

427 *the DEA had lured an eighteen-year-old dealer:* Michael Isikoff, "Drug Buy Set Up for Bush Speech; DEA Lured Seller to Lafayette Park," *Washington Post,* September 22, 1989; Tracy Thompson, "Drug Purchase for Bush like Keystone Cops," *Washington Post,* December 15, 1989; Jefferson Morley, "The Kid Who Sold Crack to the President," (Baltimore) *City Paper,* December 15, 1989.

427 *the greatest threat facing America:* Richard Morin, "Many in Poll Say Bush Plan Is Not Stringent Enough," *Washington Post,* September 8, 1989.

427 *347 reports about crack and cocaine:* Cited in Lapham, "Political Opiate."

428 *reporting significant reductions in drug use since 1985:* Bush admitted as much himself in his speech of September 5, citing the Substance Abuse and Mental Health Services Administration, National Household Survey on Drug Abuse, in stating that "almost nine million fewer Americans are casual drug users."

428 *herd them onto military bases:* Michael Isikoff, "Penal Colonies for Drug Criminals?" *Washington Post,* September 19, 1989.

428 *the Pacific islands of Wake and Midway:* National Drug and Crime Emergency Act HR 4079, sponsored by Phil Gramm and Newt Gingrich, 1990.

428 *"taken out and shot":* "Casual Drug Users Should Be Shot, Gates Says," *Los Angeles Times,* September 6, 1989.

428 *the beheading of drug dealers:* William Bennett made the comment on Larry King's radio show; quoted in "Crackmire," *New Republic,* September 11, 1989.


III. Ethnography and Other Heresies

429 *"There has to be something wrong with a law":* Ethan Nadelmann to MT. (All of Nadelmann's quotations in this section are from MT interview of October 1992.)

431 *"It is my belief that the desire to alter consciousness":* Weil, *Natural Mind,* p. 19.

431 *"nothing more than a logical continuation":* Ibid., p. 24.

431 *"Drugs are here to stay":* Ibid., p. 200.

431 *this tradition of nonconforming academics:* Harry W. Feldman and Michael R. Aldrich, "The Role of Ethnography in Substance Abuse," in *Research and Public Policy: Historical Precedents and Future Prospects, from the Collection and Interpretation of Hidden Populations,* NIDA Research Monograph 98 (Rockville, Md.: National In-

stitute of Drug Abuse, 1990), pp. 18–22; also, MT interviews with Michael Aldrich, Ethan Nadelmann, Marsha Rosenbaum, Craig Reinarman, Lynn Zimmer, and Allen Ginsberg.

433 *"the routinization of caricature":* Reinarman and Levine, "The Crack Attack: Politics and Media in the Crack Scare," in *Crack in America,* p. 24.


## IV. Saying the Unsayable

434 only 3,562 people: Ethan A. Nadelmann, "U.S. Drug Policy: A Bad Export," *Foreign Policy* 20 (Spring 1988), p. 92. Nadelmann cited a figure released by the American Council on Alcoholism reported by Tom Wicker, "Drug and Alcohol," *New York Times,* May 13, 1987.

434 *"Between reduced government expenditures":* Ethan A. Nadelmann, "Drug Prohibition in the United States: Costs, Consequences, and Alternatives," *Science* 245 (September 1989), p. 943.

435 *"And the health and quality of life":* Ibid., p. 943.

435 *"Clearly, many tens of thousands of Americans":* Ibid., p. 945.

435 *"The first steps are relatively risk free":* Ibid., p. 945.

436 *"Unless we are willing to honestly evaluate":* Ibid., p. 946.

436 *"Whoa, he's been out on the West Coast too long":* Marlin Fitzwater quoted in Stanley Meisler, "Drug Legalization: Interest Rises in Prestigious Circles," *Los Angeles Times,* November 20, 1989.

436 *"We're not really going to get anywhere":* George Shultz quoted ibid.

436 *"This may explain why":* William Bennett quoted ibid.

436 *"whole cadres of social scientists":* William Bennett, "Drug Policy and the Intellectuals" (speech delivered to the Kennedy School of Government, Harvard University, December 11, 1989), reprinted in Trebach and Zeese, *Drug Prohibition,* pp. 14–20.

437 *"If our society can learn to stop using butter":* Robert W. Sweet quoted in "Federal Judge Urges Legalization of Crack, Heroin and Other Drugs," *New York Times,* December 13, 1989.

437 how to counter the arguments of the legalizers: Drug Enforcement Administration, *How to Hold Your Own in a Drug Legalization Debate,* 1994.

437 *"people burn out on the drug issue":* Ethan Nadelmann to MT (July 2002).

438 *"Then one day out of the blue":* Ibid.


## V. Inhale to the Chief

438 *"Inhale to the Chief":* Slogan on a button being sold on the streets of Washington, D.C., at the inauguration of Bill Clinton, January 1993.

439 *What Reagan very conveniently omitted:* Details of Patti Davis's drug use in Patti Davis, *The Way I See It,* pps. 158–159, p. 162 pps: 197–197, p. 212.

440 *more people arrested for violating marijuana laws:* U.S. Department of Justice, FBI Crime Statistics, 1992.


## VI. Woe to the World If They Succeed

441 *"This stuff is doing nothing":* Dennis Peron to MT.

441 *"I lived my dream of being an architect":* Ibid.

442 *"They found this picture of me and Harvey Milk":* Ibid.

442 *"He was using the marijuana as his medicine":* Ibid.

442 *"Licensed physicians shall not be penalized"*: Proposition B, in *High Times,* June 1992.

442 *"Brownie Mary" Rathbun:* Background in Peter Gormon, "Brownie Mary Rathbun," *High Times,* January 1993.

442 *"within an hour he'll be eating a huge lunch"*: Ibid.

443 *"I'm going to push them to a jury trial"*: Ibid.

443 *"We want to let them know"*: Dennis Peron to MT.

443 *"It transformed the image of the marijuana smoker"*: Ethan Nadelmann to MT, July 2002.

444 *"The federal government has been so obstinate"*: Ibid.

444 *the issue made its way to the Supreme Court:* Linda Greenhouse, "Justice's Bar Medical Defense for Distribution of Marijuana," *New York Times,* May 15, 2001.

445 *"Americans are nervous about distribution"*: Ethan Nadelmann, speech delivered to NORML, November 12, 1998.

445 *"Part of the initiative's value"*: Ibid.

445 *A report by the Miami Field Division of the DEA:* Drug Enforcement Administration, Miami Field Division, *DEA Survey of the Marijuana Situation in the Miami Field Division,* December 1998.

446 *a report by Janet Dundee Lapey, MD"*: "Medical Consequences of Marijuana Use," ibid.

446 *this ongoing war:* For a point-by-point scientific rebuttal of every major claim made against marijuana over the years, see Zimmer and Morgan, *Marijuana Myths, Marijuana Facts.*

447 *"if you're the head of a department of medicine"*: Keith Sroup to MT.

447 *"Regardless of how it is couched"*: Wayne Roques quoted in *Sacramento News and Review,* July 12, 2002.

447 *"Training the Trainer: Putting the Brakes on the Drug Legalization Movement"*: Description of this event obtained through the Drug Policy Alliance.

449 *"We are not California whackos"*: Christopher Krohn quoted in Charles LeDuff and Adam Liptak, "Defiant California City Hands Out Marijuana," *New York Times,* September 18, 2002.

## VII.  One Big Child-Protection Act

449 *"there are going to be powerful reasons"*: Ethan Nadelmann to MT (July 2002).

449 *"this absurd war on drugs"*: Ibid.

450 *"the radical reactionary Right Wing"*: Ibid.

450 *"Take the GPS devices"*: Ibid.

450 *"this sort of next step"*: Ibid.

450 *"The intense pessimism that I feel"*: Ibid.

451 *"At the level of ideas"*: Reinarman and Levine, "Real Opposition, Real Alternatives," in *Crack in America,* p. 346.

451 *"People come to this from all levels"*: Ethan Nadelmann to MT.

451 *"America's Failed War on Drugs"*: All statistics presented at the Shadow Convention, released on a tape of the event by the Drug Policy Alliance.

452 *a relentless campaign to liberalize drug-possession laws:* Michael Janofsky, "Governor's Drug Efforts Show Fruit in Santa Fe," *New York Times,* February 14, 2001.

453 *"pharmacological determinism"*: Reinarman and Levine, "Crack in Context: America's Latest Demon Drug," in *Crack America,* p. 8.

453 *"Until the basic thinking of harm reduction"*: Ethan Nadelmann, speech delivered to NORML, November 12, 1998.

453   *"pharmacological Calvinism"*: Reinarman and Levine, "Real Opposition, Real Alter-natives." p. 347.

453   *"the vast majority of American illegal drug users"*: Ethan Nadelmann, "Urban Drug Problems, Solutions" (speech delivered to the Hoover Institution, November 6, 1997).

454   *"menschlike policies"*: Ibid.

454   *"What you and I know"*: Nadelmann, speech delivered to NORML, November 12, 1998.

454   *"People are scared about drugs"*: Ibid.

455   *"If we win the battle over kids"*: Ibid.

## 15  The Temple of Accumulated Error

### I.  By the Time I Got to Woodstock

456   All comments in this chapter were made to me either in conversation with the indi-viduals at the event or in interviews done for a documentary on the festival.

### II.  Huxley's Question

464   *"A Treatise on Drugs"*: Aldous Huxley, reprinted in the Albert Hoffman Foundation *Newsletter* 2, no. 2/3 (spring–summer 1991).

# BIBLIOGRAPHY

A.A. World Services. *Pass It On: The Story of Bill Wilson and How the A.A. Message Reached the World.* New York: A.A. World Services, 1984.

———. *Twelve Steps and Twelve Traditions.* New York: A.A. World Services, 1996.

Aaronson, Bernard, and Humphrey Osmond, eds. *Psychedelics: The Uses and Implications of Hallucinogenic Drugs.* Garden City, N.Y.: Anchor Books, 1970.

Adamson, Sophie, ed. *Through the Gateway of the Heart: Accounts of Experiences with MDMA and Other Empathogenic Substances.* Foreword by Ralph Metzner. San Francisco: Four Trees Publications, 1985.

Algren, Nelson. *The Man with the Golden Arm.* New York: Four Walls Eight Windows, 1990.

Alpert, Richard [Ram Dass]. *Be Here Now.* San Cristobal, N.M.: Lama Foundation, 1971.

———. *The Only Dance There Is.* Garden City, N.Y.: Anchor Books, 1974.

Alpert, Richard, Sidney Cohen, and Lawrence Schiller. *LSD.* New York: New American Library, 1966.

Amburn, Ellis. *Pearl: The Obsessions and Passions of James Joplin.* New York: Warner Brothers, 1992.

Amram, David. *Vibrations: The Adventures and Musical Times of David Amram.* New York: Macmillan, 1968.

Anderson, Patrick. *High in America: The True Story Behind NORML and the Politics of Marijuana.* New York: Viking Press, 1981.

Andrews, George, and Simon Vinkenoog, eds. *The Book of Grass: An Anthology of Indian Hemp.* New York: Grove Press, 1967.

Anson, Robert Sam. *Gone Crazy and Back Again: The Rise and Fall of the Rolling Stone Generation.* Garden City, N.Y.: Doubleday, 1981.

Anthony, Gene. *The Summer of Love: Haight Ashbury at Its Highest.* Millbrae, Calif.: Celestial Arts, 1980.

Artaud, Antonin. *The Peyote Dance.* New York: Farrar, Straus and Giroux, 1976.

Ashley, Richard. *Cocaine: Its History, Uses, and Effects.* New York: St. Martin's Press, 1975.

Bakalar, James, B., and Lester, Grinspoon. *Drug Control in a Free Society.* Cambridge: Cambridge University Press, 1984.

Bangs, Lester. *Psychotic Reaction and Carburetor Dung.* New York: Alfred A. Knopf, 1987.

Baum, Dan. *Smoke and Mirrors: The War on Drugs and the Politics of Failure.* Boston: Little, Brown, 1996.

Beaulieu, Victor-Lévy. *Jack Kerouac: A Chicken Essay.* Toronto: Coach House Press, 1975.

Beck, Jerome, and Marsha Rosenbaum. *Pursuit of Ecstasy: The MDMA Experience.* Albany: State University of New York Press, 1994.

Becker, Howard. *Outsiders: Studies in the Sociology of Deviance.* New York: Free Press, 1963.

Bedford, Sybille. *Aldous Huxley, A Biography.* 2 vols. New York: Alfred A. Knopf, 1975.

Bennett, William. *The De-Valuing of America: The Fight for Our Culture and Our Children.* New York: Touchstone Books, 1994.

Bing, Leon. *Do or Die.* New York: HarperCollins, 1991.

Biskind, Peter. *Easy Riders, Raging Bulls: How the Sex–Drugs–and–Rock 'N' Roll Generation Saved Hollywood.* New York: Simon & Schuster, 1998.

Bockris, Victor. *The Life and Death of Andy Warhol.* New York: Bantam Books, 1989.

————. *Transformer: The Lou Reed Story.* New York: Simon & Schuster, 1994.

————. *With William Burroughs: A Report from the Bunker.* New York: Seaver Books, 1981.

Bockris, Victor, and Gerard Malanga. *Uptight: The Velvet Underground Story.* New York: Omnious Press, 1983.

Bonnie, Richard J., and Charles H. Whitebread II. *The Marijuana Conviction: A History of Marijuana Prohibition in the United States.* Charlottesville: University of Virginia Press, 1974.

Boon, Marcus. *The Road to Excess: A History of Writers on Drugs.* Cambridge, Mass.: Harvard University Press, 2002.

Booth, Stanley. *Dance with the Devil: The Rolling Stones and Their Times.* New York: Random House, 1984.

Bourdon, David. *Warhol.* New York: Abradale Press, 1989.

Boyle, T. Coraghessan. *Budding Prospects: A Pastoral.* New York: Penguin Books, 1984.

Braden, William. *The Private Sea: LSD and the Search for God.* New York: Bantam Books, 1968.

*The Essential Whole Earth Catalog.* Introduction by Stewart Brand. Garden City, N.Y.: Doubleday, 1986.

Brecher, Edward M., and the editors of Consumer Reports. *Licit and Illicit Drugs.* Boston: Little, Brown, 1972.

Brown, Claude. *Manchild in the Promised Land.* New York: Signet / New American Library, 1965.

Brown, Peter, and Steven Gaines. *The Love You Make: An Insider's Story of the Beatles.* New York: Signet Brooks, 1984.

Burnham, David. *The Rise of the Computer State.* New York: Random House, 1983.

Burns, Glen. *Great Poets Howl: A Study of Allen Ginsberg's Poetry, 1943–1955.* New York: Peter Lang, 1983.

Burroughs, William S. *The Burroughs File.* San Francisco: City Lights Books, 1984.

————. *Exterminator!* New York: Viking Press, 1973.

————. *Interzone.* New York: Viking Press, 1989.

————. *The Job: Interviews with William S. Burroughs.* With Daniel Odier. New York: Grove Press, 1972.

————. *Junkie.* New York: Ace Books, 1953.

————. *The Letters of William S. Burroughs, 1945–1959.* Edited by Oliver Harris. New York: Viking Press, 1993.

————. *Letters to Allen Ginsberg, 1953–1957.* New York: Full Court Press, 1981.

————. *Naked Lunch.* New York: Grove Press, 1959.

————. *Queer.* New York: Viking Press, 1985.

————. *Roosevelt After Inauguration.* San Francisco: City Lights Books, 1979.

Caldwell, W. V. *LSD Psychotherapy: An Exploration of Psychedelic and Psycholitic Therapy.* New York: Grove Press, 1968.

Carr, Ian. *Miles Davis: A Biography.* New York: William Morrow, 1982.

Carroll, Jim. *The Basketball Diaries.* New York: Penguin Books, 1978.

Cassady, Carolyn. *Heart Beat: My Life with Jack and Neal.* Berkeley, Calif., Creative Arts, 1976.

Cassady, Neal. *The First Third.* San Francisco: City Lights Books, 1971; rev. ed., 1981.

Castañeda, Carlos. *The Teachings of Don Juan: A Yaqui Way of Knowledge; A Separate Reality: Further Conversations with Don Juan; Journey to Ixtlan; Tales of Power.* 4 vols. New York: Simon & Schuster, 1970–75.

Chambers, Jack. *Milestones,* vol. 1, *The Music and Times of Miles Davis to 1960.* New York: Beech Tree Books, 1983.

Chapple, Steve. *Outlaws in Babylon: Shocking True Adventures on the Marijuana Frontier.* New York: Pocket Books, 1984.

Charters, Ann. *Beats and Company: Portrait of a Literary Generation.* Garden City, N.Y.: Doubleday, 1986.

Clark, Walter Houston. *Chemical Ecstasy Psychedelic Drugs and Religion.* New York, Sheed and Ward, 1969.

Clarke, Arthur C. *Childhood's End.* New York: Ballantine Books, 1971.

Clarke, Donald. *Wishing On the Moon: The Life and Times of Billie Holiday.* New York: Viking Press, 1994.

Cleaver, Eldridge. *Soul on Ice.* New York: Delta, 1992.

Clements, Marcelle. *The Dog Is Us and Other Observations.* New York: Penguin Books: 1987.

Cohen, John, ed. *The Essential Lenny Bruce.* New York: Random House, 1967.

Cohen, Sidney. *The Beyond Within: The LSD Story.* New York: Atheneum, 1965.

Colacello, Bob. *Holy Terror: Andy Warhol Close Up.* New York: HarperCollins, 1990.

Collin, Matthew. *Altered State: The Story of Ecstasy Culture and Acid House.* With John Godfrey. London: Serpent's Tail, 1997.

Connolly, Cyril. *Enemies of Promise.* New York: Persea Books, 1983.

Cook, Bruce. *The Beat Generation.* New York: Charles Scribner's Sons, 1971.

Corso, Gregory, *Elegiac Feelings American.* New York: New Directions, 1970.

———. *Gasoline.* San Francisco: City Lights Books, 1958.

Courtwright, David. *Dark Paradise: Opiate Addiction in America Before 1940.* Cambridge, Mass.: Harvard University Press, 1982.

Coyote, Peter. *Sleeping Where I Fall.* Washington, D.C.: Counterpoint, 1998.

Crosby, David. *Long Time Gone: The Autobiography of David Crosby.* With Car Gottlieb. Garden City, N.Y.: Doubleday, 1988.

Crowley, Aleister. *Diary of a Drug Fiend.* London: Sphere Books, 1972.

Darnovsky, Marcy, Barbara Epstein, and Richard Flacks, eds. *Cultural Politics and Social Movements.* Philadelphia: Temple University Press, 1995.

Davenport-Hines, Richard. *The Pursuit of Oblivion: A Global History of Narcotics.* New York: W. W. Norton, 2002.

Davis, Miles. *Miles: The Autobiography of Miles Davis.* With Quincy Troupe. New York: Touchstone Books, 1989.

Davis, Patti. *The Way I See It: An Autobiography.* New York: Jone Books, 1993.

Denisoff, R. Serge. *Great Day Coming. Folk Music and the American Left.* Urbana: University of Illinois Press, 1971.

Densmore, John. *Riders on the Storm: My Life with Jim Morrison and the Doors.* New York: Delta, 1990.

de Ropp, Robert S. *Drugs and the Mind.* New York: Grove Press, 1961.

Dery, Mark. *Escape Velocity: Cyberculture at the End of the Century.* New York: Grove Press, 1996.

Dickstein, Morris. *Gates of Eden: American Culture in the Sixties.* New York: Basic Books, 1977.

Didion, Joan. *Slouching Toward Bethlehem.* New York: Simon & Schuster, 1979.

Di Prima, Diane. *Revolutionary Letters.* San Francisco: City Lights Books, 1971.

Drake, William H. *The Connoisseur's Handbook of Marijuana.* San Francisco: Straight Arrow, Books, 1971.

———. *The Cultivator's Handbook of Marijuana.* Berkeley, Calif.: Book People, 1970.

Drug Abuse Council. *The Facts About "Drug Abuse."* New York: Free Press, 1980.

Duke, Steven B., and Albert C. Gross. *America's Longest War: Rethinking Our Tragic Crusade Against Drugs.* New York: G. P. Putnam's Sons, 1993.

Duster, Troy. *The Legislation of Morality: Law, Drugs, and Moral Judgment.* New York: Free Press, 1970.

Dylan, Bob. *Tarantula.* New York: Macmillan, 1966.

Ebin, David, ed. *The Drug Experience: First-Person Accounts of Writers, Scientists, and Others.* New York: Grove Press, 1961.

Eisner, Bruce. *Ecstasy: The MDMA Story.* Berkeley, Calif.: Ronin, 1989.

Ellis, Brett Easton. *Less Than Zero.* New York: Simon & Schuster, 1985.

Ellison, Ralph. *Shadow and Act.* Vintage Books, 1995.

Eszterhas, Joe. *Nark.* San Francisco: Straight Arrow Books, 1974.

Fariña, Richard. *Been Down So Long It Looks Like Up to Me.* New York: Penguin Books, 1966.

Feather, Leonard. *Encyclopedia of Jazz,* rev. ed. New York: Bonanza Books, 1960.

———. *Encyclopedia of Jazz in the Sixties.* New York: Bonanza Books, 1966.

———. *From Satchmo to Miles.* London: Quartet, 1974.

Feather, Leonard, and Ira Gitler. *Encyclopedia of Jazz in the Seventies.* New York: Horizon Press, 1976.

Felton, David. *Mindfuckers: A Source Book on the Rise of Acid Fascism in America.* San Francisco: Straight Arrow Books, 1972.

Finlator, John. *The Drugged Nation: A Narc's Story.* New York: Simon & Schuster, 1973.

Fisher, Carrie. *Postcards from the Edge.* New York: Pocket Books, 1988.

Flynn, John C. *Cocaine: An In-Depth Look at the Facts, Science, History and Future of the World's Most Addictive Drug.* New York: Birch Lane Press, 1991.

Foley, James. *Drugstore Cowboy.* New York: Delacorte Press, 1990.

Frank, Mel, and Ed Rosenthal. *The Indoor Outdoor Highest Quality Marijuana Grower's Guide.* Berkeley, Calif.: And/Or Press, 1974.

Frazier, Jack. *The Marijuana Farmers: Hemp Cults and Cultures.* New Orleans: Solar Age Press, 1974.

French, Scott. *Complete Guide to the Street Drug Game.* New York: Lyle Stuart, 1976.

Freud, Sigmund. *Cocaine Papers.* Edited by Robert Byck. New York: Stonehill, 1975.

Furst, Peter. *Flesh of the Gods: The Ritual Use of Hallucinations.* New York: Praeger, 1972.

Gahlinger Paul. *Illegal Drugs: A Complete Guide to Their History, Chemistry, Use, and Abuse.* Las Vegas, Nev.: Sagebrush Press, 2001.

Gaines, Steven. *Simply Halston: The Untold Story.* New York: G. P. Putnam's Sons, 1991.

Gans, David. *Conversations with the Dead: The Grateful Dead Interview Book.* New York: Citadel, 1991.

Gans, David, and Peter Simon. *Playing in the Band: An Oral and Visual Portrait of the Grateful Dead.* New York: St. Martin's Press, 1985.

Gaskin, Stephen. *Amazing Dope Tales and Haight Street Flashbacks.* Summertown, Tenn.: Book Publishing, 1980.

Gibson, William. *Neuromancer.* New York: Ace Books, 1984.

Gidal, Peter. *Andy Warhol: Films and Painting.* London: Studio Vista, 1971.

Gifford, Barry. *Kerouac's Town.* Berkeley, Calif.: Creative Arts, 1977.

Gifford, Barry, and Lawrence Lee. *Jack's Book: An Oral Biography of Jack Kerouac.* New York: St. Martin's Press, 1978.

Gillespie, Dizzy. *To Be or Not to Bop.* With Al Fraser. New York: Doubleday, 1979.

Ginsberg, Allen. *Allen Verbatim: Lectures on Poetry, Politics, Consciousness.* Edited by Gordon Ball. New York: McGraw-Hill, 1975.

————. *Howl and Other Poems.* San Francisco: City Lights Books, 1956.

————. *Howl: Original Draft Facsimile, Transcript, and Variant Versions.* Edited by Barry Miles. New York: Harper and Row, 1986.

————. *The Yage Letters.* With William Burroughs. San Francisco: City Lights Books, 1956.

Gitler, Ira. *Swing to Bop: An Oral History of the Transition in Jazz in the 1940s.* New York: Oxford University Press, 1985.

Gitlin, Todd. *The Sixties: Years of Hope, Days of Rage.* New York: Bantam Books, 1987.

————. *The Whole World Is Watching: Mass Media in the Making and Unmaking of the New Left.* Berkeley: University of California Press, 1980.

Gleason, Ralph J. *Celebrating the Duke . . . and Other Heroes.* Boston: Little, Brown, 1975.

————. *The Jefferson Airplane and the San Francisco Sound.* New York: Ballantine Books, 1969.

Gold, Mark. *800-COCAINE.* New York: Bantam Books, 1984.

Goldberg, Joe. *Jazz Masters of the Fifties.* New York: Macmillan, 1956.

Goldman, Albert. *Grass Roots: Marijuana in America Today.* New York: Harper and Row, 1979.

Goodman, Paul. *Growing Up Absurd: Problems of Youth in the Organized System.* New York: Random House, 1960.

Gorski, Terence T., and Merlene Miller. *Staying Sober: A Guide for Relapse Prevention.* Independence, Mo.: Herald Publishing House, 1986.

Gottlieb, Adam. *Sex, Drugs, and Aphrodisiacs.* New York: High Times / Level Press, 1974.

Graham, Bill, and Robert Greenfield. *Bill Graham Presents: My Life Inside Rock and Out.* Garden City, N.Y.: Doubleday, 1992.

Gravy, Wavy. *Something Good for a Change: Random Notes on Peace thru Living.* New York: St. Martin's Press, 1992.

Gray, Mike, ed. *Busted: Stone Cowboys, Narco-Lords, and Washington's War on Drugs.* New York: Thunder's Mouth Press / Nation Books, 2002.

————. *Drug Crazy: How We Got into This Mess and How We Can Get Out of It.* New York: Routledge, 2000.

Greenfield, Robert. *Dark Star: An Oral Biography of Jerry Garcia.* New York: William Morrow, 1996.

Grinspoon, Lester, and James B. Bakalar. *Cocaine: A Drug and Its Social Evolution.* New York: Basic Books, 1985.

————. *Marijuana: The Forbidden Medicine.* New Haven, Conn.: Yale University Press, 1993.

————. *Psychedelic Drugs Revisited.* New York: Basic Books, 1979.

————, eds. *Psychedelic Reflections.* New York: Human Sciences Press, 1983.

Grinspoon, Lester, and Peter Hedblom. *The Speed Culture: Amphetamine Use and Abuse in America.* Cambridge, Mass.: Harvard University Press, 1975.

Grof, Stanislav. *LSD Psychotherapy.* Pomona: Calif.: Hunter House, 1980.

————. *Realms of Human Consciousness.* San Francisco: Esalen Books, 1975.

Grogan, Emmett. *Ringolevio: A Life Played for Keeps,* New York: Avon, 1972.

Gugliotta, Guy, and Jeff Leen. *Kings of Cocaine: An Astonishing True Story of Murder, Money, and Corruption.* New York: Harper and Row, 1989.

Gustaitis, Rasa. *Turning On: One Woman's Trip Beyond LSD Through Awareness Expansion Without the Use of Drugs,* New York: Macmillan, 1972.

Haden-Guest, Anthony. *The Last Party: Studio 54, Disco, and the Culture of the Night.* New York: William Morrow, 1997.

Hafner, Katie, and John Markoff. *Cyberpunk: Outlaws and Hackers on the Computer Frontier.* New York: Simon & Schuster, 1991.

Harrison, Hank. *The Dead Book,* Millbrae, Calif.: Celestial Arts, 1980.

Hawes, Hampton. *Raise Up off Me: A Portrait of Hampton Hawes,* New York: Coward, McCann, with Don Asher and Geoghegan, 1974.

Hayes, Billy. *Midnight Express.* With William Hoffer. London: Sphere Books, 1978.

Heather, Nick, Alex Wodak, Ethan Nadelmann, and Pat O'Hare, eds. *Psychoactive Drugs and Harm Reduction: From Faith to Science.* London: Whurr, 1991.

Heinlein, Robert A. *Stranger in a Strange Land.* New York: Avon Books, 1967.

Heirich, Max. *The Beginning: Berkeley, 1964.* New York: Columbia University Press, 1970.

Helmer, John. *Drugs and Minority Oppression* New York: Seabury Press, 1975.

Henderson, David. *'Scuse Me While I Kiss the Sky: The Life of Jimi Hendrix.* New York: Bantam Books, 1981.

Henke, James, and Parke Puterbaugh, eds. *I Want to Take You Higher: The Psychedelic Era, 1965–1969.* Presented by the Rock and Roll Hall of Fame and Museum: With essays by Charles Perry and Barry Miles. San Francisco: Chronicle Books, 1997.

Hentoff, Nat. *Jazz Is.* New York: Random House, 1976.

Herer, Jack. *The Emperor Wears No Clothes.* Seattle: Queen of Clubs, 1985.

Herr, Michael. *Dispatches.* New York: Avon Books, 1978.

Hesse, Hermann. *The Journey to the East.* Translated by Hilda Rosner. New York: Noonday, 1965.

———. *The Glass Bead Game.* Translated by M. Savill. Picador, 2002.

———. *Steppenwolf.* International Thomas, 1963.

Heylin, Clinton. *From the Velvets to the Voidoids: A Pre-Punk History for a Post-Punk World.* New York: Penguin Books, 1991.

High Times. *Encyclopedia of Recreational Drugs.* New York: Stonehill, 1978.

Hodgson, Godfrey. *America in Our Time.* New York: Doubleday, 1976.

Hoffman, Abbie, *The Best of Abbie Hoffman: Selections from "Revolution for the Hell of It," "Woodstock Nation," "Steal This Book," and New Writings.* Ed. with Daniel Simon. New York: Four Walls Eight Windows, 1989.

———. *Soon to Be a Major Motion Picture.* New York: G. P. Putnam's Sons / Perigee Books, 1980.

———. *Steal This Urine Test: Fighting Drug Hysteria in America.* With Jonathan Silvers. New York: Viking Press, 1987.

Hofmann, Albert. *LSD, My Problem Child: Reflections on Sacred Drugs, Mysticism, and Science.* Los Angeles: J. P. Tarcher, 1983.

Holiday, Billie. *Lady Sings the Blues.* With William Dufty, Garden City, N.Y.: Doubleday Books, 1956.

Holland, Julie, ed. *Ecstasy: The Complete Guide. A Comprehensive Look at the Risks and Benefits of MDMA.* Rochester, Vt.: Park Street Press, 2001.

Hollingshead, Michael. *The Man Who Turned on the World.* London: Blond and Briggs, 1973.

Holmes, John Clellon. *The Horn.* New York: Random House, 1958.

———. *Visitor: Jack Kerouac in Old Saybrook,* California, Penn.: *The Unspeakable Visions of the Individual.* 1981.

Hopkins, Jerry, and Danny Sugarman. *No One Here Gets Out Alive.* New York: Warner Books, 1981.

Horowitz, H. H., ed. *Drugs: For and Against.* New York: Hart, 1970.

Horowitz, Michael and Palmer, Cynthia, eds. *Shaman Woman, Mainline Lady: Women's Writings on the Drug Experience.* New York: Quill, 1982.

Huncke, Herbert. *The Evening Sun Turned Crimson.* Cherry Valley, N.Y.: Cherry Valley Editions, 1980.

———. *Guilty of Everything: The Autobiography of Herbert Huncke.* New York: Paragon House, 1990.

———. *Huncke's Journal.* New York: Poet's Press, 1965.

Huxley, Aldous. *The Doors of Perception and Heaven and Hell.* London: Penguin Books, 1961.

———. *Island.* New York: Perennial Classic, 1972.

———. *Letters of Aldous Huxley.* Edited by Grover Smith. New York: Harper and Row, 1969.

———. *Moksha: Writings on Psychedelics and the Visionary Experience.* Los Angeles: J. P. Tarcher, 1982.

———. *The Perennial Philosophy.* New York: Harper Colophon, 1970.

Huxley, Laura Archera. *This Timeless Moment: A Personal View of Aldous Huxley.* New York: Farrar, Straus and Giroux, 1968.

Inciardi, James A. *The War on Drugs: Heroin, Cocaine, Crime and Public Policy.* Palo Alto, Calif.: Mayfield, 1986.

James, William. *The Varieties of Religious Experience.* New York: New American Library.

Johns, Christina Jacqueline. *Power, Ideology, and the War on Drugs: Nothing Succeeds Like Failure.* New York: Praeger, 1992.

Johnson, Bruce D., Paul J. Goldstein, Edward Preble, James Schmeidler, Douglas S. Lipton, Barry Spunt, and Thomas Miller. *Taking Care of Business: The Economics of Crime by Heroin Abusers.* Lexington, Mass.: D. C. Heath, 1985.

Johnson, Joyce. *Minor Characters: A Beat Memoir.* Boston: Houghton Mifflin, 1983.

Johnston, Lloyd D., Patrick, M. O'Malley, and Jerald G. Bachman. *National Survey Results on Drug Use from the Monitoring the Future Study, 1975–2002.* Washington, D.C.: U.S. Department of Health and Human Services, Public Health Service, 2002.

Jones, Hettie. *How I Became Hettie Jones.* New York: E. P. Dutton, 1990.

Jones, Landon Y. *Great Expectations: America and the Baby Boom Generation.* New York: Ballantine Books, 1981.

Jones, LeRoi. *Blues People: Negro Music in White America.* New York: Quill, 1963.

Jonnes, Jill. *Hep-Cats, Narcs, and Pipe Dreams: A History of America's Romance with Illegal Drugs.* Baltimore: Johns Hopkins University Press, 1999.

Kaminer, Wendy. *I'm Dysfunctional, You're Dysfunctional: The Recovery Movement and Other Self-Help Fashions.* New York: Addison-Wesley, 1992.

Kamstra, Jerry. *Weed: Adventures of a Dope Smuggler.* New York: Bantam Books, 1974.

Kaplan, John. *Marijuana: The New Prohibition.* New York: World, 1970.

Kerouac, Jack. *A Bibliography of Work by Jack Kerouac.* Compiled by Ann Charters. New York: Phoenix Bookshop, 1967.

———. *Big Sur.* New York: Farrar, Straus and Cudahy, 1962.

———. *Book of Dreams.* San Francisco: City Lights Books, 1961.

———. *Desolation Angels.* New York: Coward-McCann, 1965.

———. *The Dharma Bums.* New York: Viking Press, 1958.

———. *Dr. Sax.* New York: Grove Press, 1959.

———. *Jack Kerouac: Selected Letters, 1940–1956.* Edited by Ann Charters. New York: Viking Press, 1995.

———. *Mexico City Blues.* New York: Grove Press, 1959.

———. *On the Road.* New York: Viking Press, 1957.

———. *Pull My Daisy.* New York: Grove Press, 1961.

———. *The Subterraneans.* New York: Grove Press, 1958.

———. *The Town and the City.* New York: Harcourt, Brace, 1950.

———. *Visions of Cody.* New York: McGraw-Hill, 1972.

Kesey, Ken. *Demon Box.* New York: Viking Press, 1986.

———. *The Further Inquiry.* New York: Viking Press, 1990.

———. *Kesey, Ken. Kesey.* Edited by Michael Strelow, Eugene, Ore.: Northwest Review Books, 1977.

———. *Kesey's Garage Sale.* New York: Viking Press, 1973.

———. *One Flew Over the Cuckoo's Nest.* New York: Viking Press, 1962.

———. *Sometimes a Great Notion.* New York: Penguin Books, 1998.

Kleiman, Mark. *Against Excess: Drug Policy in Moderation.* New York: Basic Books, 1992.

Kleps, Art. *Millbrook: The Story of the Early Years of the Psychedelic Revolution.* Oakland, Calif.: Bench Press, 1975.

Knapp, Bettina, L. *Antonin Artaud: Man of Vision.* New York: Discus Books, 1971.

Knight, Arthur, and Kit Knight, eds. *The Beat Vision.* New York: Paragon House, 1987.

Koch, Stephen. *Stargazer: Andy Warhol's World and His Films.* New York: Praeger, 1973.

Kramer, Jane. *Allen Ginsberg in America.* New York: Random House, 1969.

Krassner, Paul. *Confessions of a Raving Unconfined Nut: Misadventures in the Counter-Culture.* New York: Simon & Schuster, 1993.

———. *How a Satirical Editor Became a Yippie Conspirator in Ten Easy Years.* New York: G. P. Putnam's Sons, 1971.

Krim, Seymour, ed. *The Beats.* Greenwich, Conn.: Fawcett, 1960.

———. *What's This Cat's Story?* New York: Paragon House, 1991.

Kuhn, Cynthia, Scott, Swartzwelder, and Wilkie Wilson. *Buzzed: The Straight Facts About the Most Used and Abused Drugs from Alcohol to Ecstasy.* 2nd ed. New York: W. W. Norton, 2003.

Lande, Nathaniel. *Mindstyles, Lifestyles: A Comprehensive Overview of Today's Life-Changing Philosophies.* Los Angeles: Price, Stern, Sloan, 1976.

Leamer, Laurence. *The Paper Revolutionaries: The Rise of the Underground Press.* New York: Simon & Schuster, 1972.

Leary, Timothy. *An Annotated Bibliography of Timothy Leary.* Compiled by Michael Horowitz, Karen Walls, and Billy Smith. Hamden, Conn.: Shoe String Press, 1988.

———. *Changing My Mind, Among Others.* Englewood Cliffs, N.J.: Prentice Hall, 1982.

———. *Chaos and Cyber Culture.* Berkeley, Calif.: Ronin, 1994.

———. *Flashbacks: An Autobiography.* Los Angeles: J. P. Tarcher, 1983.

———. *Greatest Hits,* vol. 1, *Monographs 1980–1990.* Studio City, Calif.: KnoWare, 1990.

———. *High Priest.* Cleveland: World, 1968.

———. *Jail Notes.* New York: Grove Press, 1970.

———. *Neuropolitique.* New Falcon, 1988.

———. *The Politics of Ecstasy.* London: Granada, 1973.

Leary, Timothy, Ralph Metzner, and Richard Albert. *The Psychedelic Experience: A Manual Based on the Tibetan Book of the Dead.* New York: Citadel, 1964.

Lee, Martin A., and Bruce Shlain. *Acid Dreams: The CIA, LSD, and the Sixties Rebellion.* New York: Grove Press, 1986.

Levine, Mark L., George C. McNamee, and Daniel Greenberg, eds. *The Tales of Hoffman.* New York: Bantam Books, 1970.

Levy, Steven. *Hackers: Heroes of the Computer Revolution.* New York: Dell, 1984.

Lewin, Louis. *Phantastica, Narcotic and Stimulating Drugs.* New York: E. P. Dutton, 1931.

Lindesmith, Alfred R. *The Addict and the Law*. Bloomington: Indiana University Press, 1965.

———. *Opiate Addiction*. Bloomington, Ind.: Principia Press, 1947.

Lindner, Robert. *Must You Conform?* New York: Grove Press, 1961.

Lingeman, Richard R. *Drugs from A to Z: A Dictionary*. New York: McGraw-Hill, 1969.

Louria, Donald. *The Drug Scene*. New York: Bantam Books, 1970.

Lukas, J. Anthony. *Don't Shoot—We Are Your Children!* New York: Random House, 1971.

Lusane, Clarence. *Pipe Dream Blues: Racism and the War on Drugs*. Boston: South End Press, 1991.

Mailer, Norman. *The Armies of the Night: History as a Novel*. New York: New American Library, 1968.

———. *Miami and the Siege of Chicago*. New York: New American Library, 1968.

———. *The White Negro*. San Francisco: City Lights Books, 1958.

Mairowitz, David Zane. *The Radical Soap Opera: Roots of Failure in the American Left*. New York: Avon, 1976.

Makower, Joel. *Woodstock: The Oral History*. New York: Tilden Press, 1989.

Malcolm X: *The Autobiography of Malcolm X*. With the assistance of Alex Haley. New York: Grove Press, 1964.

Manatt, Marsha. *Parents, Peers, and Pot*. Rockville, Md.: National Institute on Drug Abuse, 1979.

Mandlebrot, Benoit B. *The Fractal Geometry of Nature*. San Francisco: W. H. Freeman, 1983.

Mann, Peggy. *Marijuana Alert*. New York: McGraw-Hill, 1985.

Manson, Charles. *Manson in His Own Words*. As told to Nuel Emmons. New York: Grove Weidenfeld, 1986.

Manzarek, Ray. *Light My Fire: My Life with the Doors*. New York: G. P. Putnam's Sons, 1998.

Marcus, Greil. *Lipstick Traces: A Secret History of the 20th Century*. Cambridge, Mass.: Harvard University Press, 1989.

Margolis, Jack S., and Richard Clorfene. *A Child's Garden of Grass*. New York: Pocket Books, 1970.

Marine, Gene. *The Black Panthers*. New York: Signet Books, 1969.

Masters, Robert, and Jean Houston. *The Varieties of Psychedelic Experience*. New York: Holt, Rinehart and Winston, 1966.

McClure, Michael. *Scratching the Beat Surface*. San Francisco: North Point Press, 1982.

———. *Selected Poems*. New York: New Directions, 1986.

McCoy, Alfred W. *The Politics of Heroin: CIA Complicity in the Global Drug Trade*. Chicago: Lawrence Hill Books, 1991.

McDarrah, Fred W., and Timothy S. McDarrah, eds. *Kerouac and Friends: A Beat Generation Album*. New York: William Morrow, 1985.

McInerny, Jay. *Bright Lights, Big City*. New York: Vintage Books, 1984.

McKenna, Terence. *The Archaic Revival: Speculations on Psychedelic Mushrooms, the Amazon, Virtual Reality, UFOs, Evolution, Shamanism, the Rebirth of the Goddess, and the End of History*. San Francisco: HarperSanFrancisco, 1991.

———. *Food of the Gods: The Search for the Original Tree of Knowledge: A Radical History of Plants, Drugs, and Human Evolution*. New York: Bantam Books: 1992.

———. *True Hallucinations: Being an Account of the Author's Extraordinary Adventures in the Devil's Paradise*. San Francisco: HarperSanFrancisco, 1993.

McLuhan, Marshall. *Understanding Media: The Extensions of Man*. New York: McGraw-Hill, 1964.

McNally, Dennis. *Desolate Angel: Jack Kerouac, the Beat Generation, and America.* New York: McGraw-Hill, 1980.

———. *A Long Strange Trip: The Inside History of the Grateful Dead.* New York: Broadway Books, 2002.

McNeil, Don. *Moving Through Here.* New York: Lancer Books, 1970.

McNeil, Legs, and Gillian McCain. *Please Kill Me: The Uncensored Oral History of Punk.* New York: Grove Press, 1996.

Meltzer, David, ed. *The San Francisco Poets.* New York: Ballantine Books, 1971.

Metzner, Ralph, ed. *The Ecstatic Adventure: Reports of Chemical Explorations of the Inner World.* New York: Macmillan, 1968.

———. *Opening to Inner Light: The Transformation of Human Nature and Consciousness.* Los Angeles: J. P. Tarcher, 1982.

Mezzrow, Mezz, and Bernard Wolfe. *Really the Blues:* New York: Random House, 1946.

Mikuriya, Tod H., ed. *Marijuana Medical Papers, 1839–1972.* Oakland, Calif.: MediComp Press, 1973.

Miles, Barry. *Ginsberg: A Biography.* New York: Simon & Schuster, 1989.

———. *William Burroughs: El Hombre Invisible: A Portrait.* New York: Hyperion, 1993.

Miller, Michael V., and Susan Gilmore, eds. *Revolution at Berkeley: The Crisis in American Education.* New York: Dell, 1965.

Mills, James. *Panic in Needle Park.* New York: Farrar, Straus and Giroux, 1965.

Mingus, Charles. *Beneath the Underdog: His World as Composed by Mingus.* New York: Alfred A. Knopf, 1971.

Morgan, Bill, and Bob Rosenthal, eds. *Best Minds: A Tribute to Allen Ginsberg.* New York: Lospecchio Press, 1986.

Morgan, Ted. *Literary Outlaw: The Life and Times of William S. Burroughs.* New York: Henry Holt, 1988.

Morrison, Jim.: *The Lost Writings of Jim Morrison: The Poems and Diaries of a Rock 'N' Roll Legend,* vol. 1, *Wilderness.* New York: Vintage Books, 1989.

Moscow, Alvin. *Merchants of Heroin: An In-Depth Portrayal of Business in the Underworld.* New York: Dial Press, 1968.

Mottram, Eric. *Allen Ginsberg in the Sixties.* Seattle and Brighton, U.K.: Unicorn Bookshop, 1972.

Mulligan, Gerry. Liner notes for *The Complete Birth of the Cool.* Capitol M-11026. 1971.

Musto, David. *The American Disease: Origins of Narcotic Control.* New Haven, Conn.: Yale University Press, 1973.

———, ed. *Drugs in America: A Documentary History.* New York: New York University Press, 2002.

Nadelmann, Ethan A. *Cops Across Borders: The Internationalization of U.S. Criminal Law Enforcement.* University Park, Pa.: Penn State University Press, 1993.

Naranjo, Claudio. *The Healing Journey: New Approaches to Consciousness.* New York: Pantheon Books, 1973.

National Commission on Marijuana and Drug Abuse. *Marijuana: A Signal of Misunderstanding.* Washington, D.C.: U.S. Government Printing Office, 1972.

Newsday editors. *The Heroin Trail.* New York: Signet Books, 1973.

Nicholl, Charles. *The Fruit Palace: An Odyssey Through Colombia's Cocaine Underworld.* New York: St. Martin's Press, 1985.

Nicosia, Gerald. *Memory Babe: A Critical Biography of Jack Kerouac.* New York: Grove Press, 1983.

Nisenson, Eric. *Ascension: John Coltrane and His Quest.* New York: St. Martin's Press, 1993.

Norman, Philip. *Shout! The Beatles in Their Own Generation.* New York: Warner Books, 1982.

——. *Symphony for the Devil: The Rolling Stones Story.* New York: Linden Press / Simon & Schuster, 1984.

Nuttall, Jeff. *Bomb Culture.* New York: Dell, 1968.

Nyswander, Marie. *The Drug Addict as Patient.* New York: Grune and Stratton, 1956.

O'Day, Anita. *High Times, Hard Times.* With George Eels. New York: G. P. Putnam's Sons, 1981.

Obst, Lynda R., ed. *The Sixties: The Decade Remembered Now, by the People Who Lived It Then.* New York: Rolling Stone Press, 1976.

Oss, O. T., and O. N. Oeric [Terence McKenna and Dennis McKenna]. *Psilocybin: Magic Mushroom Grower's Guide.* Foreword by Terence McKenna. Berkeley, Calif.: Ronin, 1976.

Page, Tim, and John Pimlott, eds. *Nam: The Vietnam Experience, 1965–75.* New York: Barnes and Noble, 1995.

Parsons, Edward E., *Humboldt Homegrown: The Golden Age.* Eureka, Calif.: Egret, 1985.

Peck, Abe. *Uncovering the Sixties: The Life and Times of the Underground Press.* New York: Pantheon Books, 1985.

Peele, Stanton, *Diseasing of America: How We Allowed Recovery Zealots and the Treatment Industry to Convince Us We Are Out of Control.* Boston: Houghton Mifflin, 1989.

Peele, Stanton, and Archie Brodsky. *The Truth About Addiction and Recovery.* New York: Fireside Books, 1992.

Pepper, Art, and Laurie Pepper. *Straight Life: The Story of Art Pepper.* New York: Schirmer, 1979.

Perry, Charles. *The Haight-Ashbury: A History.* New York: Rolling Stone Press, 1984.

Perry, Helen Swick. *The Human Be-In.* New York: Basic Books, 1970.

Perry, Paul. *On the Bus: The Complete Guide to the Legendary Trip of Ken Kesey and the Merry Pranksters and the Birth of the Counterculture.* Edited by Michael Schwartz and Neil Orienberg. Introduction by Ken Babbs. New York: Thunder's Mouth Press, 1990.

Phillips, John. *Papa John: An Autobiography.* With Jim Jerome. Garden City, N.Y.: Dolphin Books, 1986.

Phillips, Julia. *You'll Never East Lunch in This Town Again.* New York: Signet Books, 1992.

Phillips, Michelle. *California Dreamin': The True Story of the Mamas and the Papas.* New York: Warner Books, 1986.

Plummer, William. *The Holy Goof: A Biography of Neal Cassady.* Englewood Cliffs, N.J.: Prentice Hall, 1981.

Podhoretz, Norman. *Making It.* New York: Random House, 1967.

Point Foundation staff. *The Essential Whole Earth Catalog.* Introduction by Stewart Brand. Garden City, N. Y.: Doubleday, 1986.

Ram Dass. See Alpert, Richard.

Raphael, Ray. *Cash Crop: An American Dream.* Mendocino, Calif.: Ridge Times Press, 1985.

Rechy, John. *City of Night.* New York: Grove Press, 1963.

——. *Numbers.* New York: Grove Weidenfeld, 1990.

——. *Rushes.* New York: Grove Press, 1979.

——. *The Sexual Outlaw: A Documentary.* New York: Grove Weidenfeld, 1977.

Reinarman, Craig, and Harry G. Levine, eds. *Crack in America: Demon Drugs and Social Justice.* Berkeley: University of California Press, 1997

Reisner, Robert, ed. *Bird: The Legend of Charlie Parker.* New York: Citadel, 1962.

Reynolds, Frank. *Freewheelin Frank: Secretary of the Angels.* As told to Michael McLure. New York: Grove Press, 1968.

Reynolds, Simon. *Generation Ecstasy: Into the World of Techno and Rave Culture.* London: Little, Brown, 1998.

Richards, Eugene. *Cocaine True Cocaine Blue.* New York: Aperture, 1994.

Richardson, Jim. *Sinsemilla: Marijuana Flowers.* Berkeley, Calif.: And/Or Press, 1976.

Riordan, James. *Stone: The Controversies, Excesses, and Exploits of a Radical Filmmaker.* New York: Hyperion, 1995.

Riordan, James, and Jerry Prochnicky. *Break on Through: The Life and Death of Jim Morrison.* New York: Quill, 1992.

Rogin, Michael Paul. *Ronald Reagan, the Movie: and Other Episodes in Political Demonology.* Berkeley: University of California Press, 1987.

Rosenbaum, Marsha. *Women on Heroin.* New Brunswick, N.J.: Rutgers University Press, 1981.

Rosenthal, David H. *Hard Bop: Jazz and Black Music, 1955–1965.* New York: Oxford University Press, 1992.

Rossman, Michael. *The Wedding Within the War.* Garden City, N.Y.: Doubleday, 1971.

Roszak, Theodore. *The Cult of Information: The Folklore of Computers and the True Art of Thinking.* New York: Pantheon, 1986.

———. *From Satori to Silicon Valley: San Francisco and the American Counterculture.* San Francisco: Lexikos, 1986.

———. *The Making of a Counter Culture.* Garden City, N.Y.: Anchor Books, 1970.

Rowes, Barbara. *Grace Slick: The Biography.* Garden City, N.Y.: Doubleday, 1980.

Rubin, Jerry. *Do It! Scenarios of the Revolution.* New York: Ballantine Books. 1970.

———. *Growing (Up) at 37.* New York: Warner Books, 1976.

Rucker, Rudy, RU Sirius, and Queen Mu. *Mondo 2000: A User's Guide to the New Edge.* New York: HarperCollins, 1992.

Rudgley, Richard. *Essential Substances: A Cultural History of Intoxicants in Society.* New York: Kodansha International, 1995.

Rushkoff, Douglas. *Cyberia: Life in the Trenches of Hyperspace.* New York: HarperCollins, 1994.

Russell, Ross. *Bird Lives! The High Life and Hard Times of Charlie (Yardbird) Parker.* New York: Charterhouse, 1973.

Sabbag, Robert. *Snowblind: A Brief Career in the Cocaine Trade.* New York: Bobbs-Merrill, 1976.

Sale, Kirkpatrick. *SDS.* New York: Vintage Books, 1973.

*The San Francisco Oracle.* San Francisco, 1966–68.

Sanders, Ed. *Fame and Love in New York.* Berkeley: Turtle Island Foundation, 1980.

Sanders, Ed. *The Family: The True Story of Charles Manson's Dune Buggy Attack Battalion.* New York: E. P. Dutton, 1971.

———. *Tales of Beatnik Glory.* New York: Stonehill, 1975.

Santelli, Robert. *Aquarius Rising: The Rock Festival Years.* New York: Delta, 1980.

Saunders, Nicholas. *Ecstasy and the Dance Culture.* London: Nicholas Saunders, 1995.

———. *Ecstasy Reconsidered.* London: Nicholas Saunders, 1997.

———. *E for Ecstasy.* London: Nicholas Saunders, 1993.

Schultes, Richard Evans and Albert Hoffman. *The Botany and Chemistry of Hallucinogens.* Springfield, Ill.: Charles, C. Thomas, 1973.

Schumacher, Michael. *Dharma Lion: A Critical Biography of Allen Ginsberg.* New York: St. Martin's Press, 1992.

Scott, Peter Dale, and Jonathan Marshall. *Cocaine Politics—Drugs, Armies, and the CIA in Central America*. Berkeley: University of California Press, 1991.

Seaver, Richard, Terry Southern, and Alexander Trocchi, eds. *Writers in Revolt: An Anthology*. New York: Frederick Fell, 1963.

Selvin, Joel. *Summer of Love: The Inside Story of LSD, Rock and Roll, Free Love, and High Times in the Wild West*. New York: E. P. Dutton, 1994.

Shakur, Sanyika, aka Monster Kody Scott. *Monster: The Autobiography of an L.A. Gang Member*. New York: Penguin Books, 1993.

Shales, Tom, and James Andrew Miller. *Live from New York: An Uncensored History of "Saturday Night Live."* Boston: Little, Brown, 2002.

Shapiro, Harry. *Waiting for the Man: The Story of Drugs and Popular Music*. New York: William Morrow, 1990.

Shapiro, Nat, and Nat Hentoff. *Hear Me Talkin' to Ya*. Mineola, N.Y.: Dover, 1955.

Sharpe, Elaine B. *The Dilemma of Drug Policy in the United States*. New York: HarperCollins, 1994.

Shaw, Arnold. *The Street That Never Slept: New York's Fabled 52nd Street*. New York: Coward, McCann and Geoghegan, 1971.

Shelton, Robert. *No Direction Home: The Life and Music of Bob Dylan*. New York: William Morrow, 1986.

Shilts, Randy. *The Mayor of Castro Street: The Life and Times of Harvey Milk*. New York: St. Martin's Press, 1982.

Shulgin, Alexander T. *Controlled Substances: Chemical and Legal Guide to Federal Drug Laws*. Berkeley, Calif.: Ronin, 1992.

Shulgin, Alexander, and Ann Shulgin. *PIHKAL: A Chemical Love Story*. Foreword by David E. Nichols. Berkeley, Calif.: Transform Press, 1991.

———. *TIHKAL: The Continuation*. Berkeley, Calif.: Transform Press, 1997.

Siegel, Ronald. *Intoxication: Life in Pursuit of Artificial Paradise*. New York: E. P. Dutton, 1989.

Slack, Charles W. *Timothy Leary, The Madness of the Sixties, and Me*. New York: Peter H. Wyden, 1974.

Slick, Grace. *Somebody to Love?* With Andrea Cagan. New York: Warner Books, 1998.

Sloman, Larry. *Reefer Madness: The History of Marijuana in America*. New York: Bobbs-Merrill, 1979.

———. *Steal This Dream: Abbie Hoffman and the Countercultural Revolution in America*. Garden City, N.Y.: Doubleday, 1998.

Smith, David E., and John Luce. *Love Needs Care: A History of San Francisco's Haight-Ashbury Free Medical Clinic and Its Pioneer Role in Treating Drug-Abuse Problems*. Boston: Little, Brown, 1970.

Snoop Dogg. With Davin Seay. *The Doggfather: The Times, Trials, and Hardcore Truths of Snoop Dogg*. New York: William Morrow, 1999.

Snyder, Gary. *Myths and Texts*. New York: Totem Press / Corinth Books, 1960.

Solomon, David. *LSD: The Consciousness-Expanding Drug*. New York: Berkeley Medallion, 1966.

———, ed. *The Marijuana Papers*. New York: Bobbs-Merrill, 1966.

Southern, Terry. *Red-Dirt Marijuana and Other Tastes*. New York: New American Library, 1967.

Spector, Ronald H. *After Tet: The Bloodiest Year in Vietnam*. New York: Vintage Books, 1994.

Spellman, A. B. *Black Music: Four Lives*. New York: Schocken, 1970. Reprint of *Four Lives in the Bebop Business* (1966).

Spitz, Robert Steven. *Barefoot in Babylon: The Creation of the Woodstock Music Festival, 1969.* New York: Viking Press, 1979.

Stafford, Peter. *Psychedelic Baby Reaches Puberty.* New York: Praeger, 1971.

————. *Psychedelics Encyclopedia.* Los Angeles: J. P. Tarcher, 1983.

Stafford, Peter, and Bonnie H. Golightly. *LSD: The Problem-Solving Psychedelic.* New York: Award Books, 1967.

Starks, Michael. *Cocaine Fiends and Reefer Madness: An Illustrated History of Drugs in the Movies.* London: Cornwall Books, 1982.

Stein, Howard, and Glenn Young. *The Best American Short Plays 1990.* New York: Applause Theatre and Cinema Books, 1991.

Stein, Jean, *Edie: An American Biography.* Edited by George Plimpton. New York: Alfred A. Knopf, 1982.

Sterling, Claire. *Octopus: How the Long Reach of the Sicilian Mafia Controls the Global Narcotics Trade.* New York: Touchstone Books, 1991.

Stevens, Jay. *Storming Heaven: LSD and the American Dream.* New York: Perennial Library, 1988.

Stone, Oliver, and Richard Boyle. *"Platoon" and "Salvador": The Original Screenplays.* New York: Vintage Books, 1987.

Stone, Robert. *Children of Light.* New York: Alfred A. Knopf, 1986.

————. *Dog Soldiers.* New York: Ballantine Books, 1975.

————. *A Hall of Mirrors.* Boston: Houghton Mifflin, 1966.

Strausbaugh, John, and Donald Blaise, eds. *The Drug User: Documents, 1840–1960.* New York: Blast Books, 1990.

Sugarman, Danny. *Wonderland Avenue: Tales of Glamour and Excess.* New York: New American Library, 1989.

Sukenick, Ronald. *Down and In: Life in the Underground.* New York: Collier Books, 1987.

Szasz, Thomas. *Ceremonial Chemistry: The Ritual Persecution of Drugs, Addicts, and Pushers.* Garden City, N.Y.: Anchor Press, 1974.

Taylor, Derek. *It Was Twenty Years Ago Today.* New York: Fireside, 1987.

Thomas, J. C. *Chasin' the Trane:* The Music and Mystique of John Coltrane. Garden City, N.Y.: Doubleday, 1974.

Thompson, Hunter S. *Fear and Loathing in Las Vegas.* New York: Random House, 1971.

————. *The Great Shark Hunt.* New York: Rolling Stone Press / Summit Books, 1979.

————. *Hells Angels.* New York: Ballantine, 1966.

————. *Songs of the Doomed: More Notes on the Death of the American Dream.* New York: Pocket Books, 1990.

Thomson Corporation. *Physicians' Desk Reference.* Montvale, N.J.: Thomson. Published annually.

Trebach, Arnold S. *The Great Drug War.* New York: Macmillan, 1987.

————. *The Heroin Solution.* New Haven, Conn.: Yale University Press, 1982.

Trebach, Arnold S., and Kevin B. Zeese. *Drug Prohibition and the Conscience of Nations.* Washington D.C.: Drug Policy Foundation, 1990.

————, eds. *Strategies for Change: New Directions in Drug Policy.* Washington, D.C.: Drug Policy Foundation, 1990.

Trocchi, Alexander. *Cain's Book.* New York: Grove Press, 1960.

Tytell, John. *Naked Angels: The Lives and Literature of the Beat Generation.* New York: McGraw-Hill, 1976.

Ullmann, Michael. *Jazz Lives.* Washington, D.C.: New Republic Books, 1980.

Ultra Violet [Isabelle Dufresne]. *Famous for Fifteen Minutes: My Years with Andy Warhol.* San Diego, Calif.: Harcourt Brace Jovanovich, 1988.

Viorst, Milton. *Fire in the Streets: America in the 1960s.* New York: Simon & Schuster, 1979.

Viva, *Superstar.* New York: G. P. Putnam's Sons, 1970.

von Hoffman, Nicholas. *We Are the People Our Parents Warned Us Against.* New York: Quadrangle, 1968.

Waldorf, Dan, Craig Reinarman, and Murphy, Sheigla B. *Cocaine Changes: The Experience of Using and Quitting.* Philadelphia: Temple University Press, 1991.

Warhol, Andy. *a: A Novel.* New York: Grove Press, 1968.

———. *The Andy Warhol Diaries.* Edited by Pat Hackett. New York: Warner Books, 1989.

———. *Andy Warhol's Exposures.* With Bob Colacello. New York: Andy Warhol Books / Grosset and Dunlap, 1979.

———. *The Philosophy of Andy Warhol: From A to B and Back Again.* New York: Harcourt Brace Jovanovich, 1975.

Warhol, Andy, and Pat Hackett. *Popism: The Warhol 60s.* New York: Harcourt Brace Jovanovich, 1983.

Warhol, Andy, and Gerard Malanga. *Screen Tests: A Diary.* New York: Kulchur Press, 1967.

Wasson, R. Gordon. *Soma: Divine Mushroom of Immortality.* New York: Harcourt Brace Jovanovich, 1968.

Watts, Alan. *In My Own Way.* New York: Vintage, 1973.

———. *The Joyous Cosmology: Adventures in the Chemistry of Consciousness.* New York: Vintage, 1962.

Weil, Andrew. *The Natural Mind.* Boston: Houghton Mifflin, 1972.

Weil, Andrew. and Winnifred Rosen. *Chocolate to Morphine: Understanding Mind-Active Drugs.* Boston: Houghton Mifflin, 1983.

Wells, Tim, and William Triplett. *Drug Wars: An Oral History from the Trenches.* New York: William Morrow, 1992.

Westin, Av, and Stephanie Shaffer. *Heroes and Heroin.* New York: Pocket Books, 1972.

White, John Warren. *Frontiers of Consciousness.* New York: Avon Books, 1974.

Whitmer, Peter O. *Aquarius Revisited: Seven Who Created the Sixties Counterculture That Changed America.* With Bruce Van Wyngarden. New York: Citadel, 1991.

———. *When the Going Gets Weird: The Twisted Life and Times of Hunter S. Thompson: A Very Unauthorized Biography.* New York: Hyperion, 1993.

Williams, Terry. *The Cocaine Kids: The Inside Story of a Teenage Drug Ring.* Reading, Mass.: Addison-Wesley, 1989.

Wilson, Robert Anton. *Cosmic Trigger.* New York: Pocket Books, 1977.

———. *Sex and Drugs.* Chicago: Playboy Press, 1973.

Wistosky, Steven *Beyond the War on Drugs.* Buffalo, N.Y.: Prometheus Books, 1990.

Wolf, Leonard, ed. *Voices from the Love Generation.* With Deborah Wolf. Boston: Little, Brown, 1968.

Wolfe, Tom. *The Electric Kool-Aid Acid Test.* New York: Bantam Books, 1981.

Woodlawn, Holly. *A Low Life in High Heels: The Holly Woodlawn Story.* With Jeff Copeland. New York: St. Martin's Press, 1991.

Woodley, Richard A. *Dealer: Portrait of a Cocaine Merchant.* New York: Holt, Rinehart and Winston, 1971.

Woodward, Bob. *Wired: The Short Life and Fast Times of John Belushi.* New York: Pocket Books, 1984.

Yablonsky, Lewis. *The Hippie Trip.* New York: Pegasus, 1968.

York, Phyllis, David York, and Ted Wachtel. *Toughlove.* Garden City, N.Y.: Doubleday, 1982.

Zimmer, Lynn. *Operation Pressure Point and the Disruption of Street-Level Trafficking.* New York: New York University Law School Center for Crime and Justice, 1987.

Zimmer, Lynn, and John Morgan. *Marijuana Myths, Marijuana Facts: A Review of the Scientific Evidence.* New York: Lindesmith Center, 1997.

Zinberg, Norman E. *Drug, Set, and Setting: The Basis for Controlled Drug Use.* New Haven, Conn.: Yale University Press, 1984.

Zinberg, Norman E, and John A. Robertson. *Drugs and the Public.* New York: Simon & Schuster, 1972.

# INDEX